George Peele

The University Wits
Series Editor: Robert A. Logan

George Peele

Edited by

David Bevington

University of Chicago, USA

ASHGATE

Wherever possible, these reprints are made from a copy of the original printing, but these can themselves be of very variable quality. Whilst the publisher has made every effort to ensure the quality of the reprint, some variability may inevitably remain.

Published by
Ashgate Publishing Limited
Wey Court East
Union Road
Farnham
Surrey GU9 7PT
England

Ashgate Publishing Company
Suite 420
101 Cherry Street
Burlington
VT 05401-4405
USA

www.ashgate.com

British Library Cataloguing in Publication Data
George Peele. – (The university wits)
 1. Peele, George, 1556-1596–Criticism and interpretation.
 2. Authors, English–Early modern, 1500-1700.
 I. Series II. Bevington, David M.
 828.3'09-dc22

Library of Congress Control Number: 2010931590

ISBN 9780754628569

MIX
Paper from responsible sources
FSC
www.fsc.org
FSC® C013056

Printed and bound in Great Britain by
TJ International Ltd, Padstow, Cornwall.

Contents

Acknowledgements

The editor and publishers wish to thank the following for permission to use copyright material.

Berghahn Books for the essay: Mary Ellen Lamb (2002), 'Old Wives' Tales, George Peele, and Narrative Abjection', *Critical Survey*, **14**, pp. 28–43.

Cahiers Élizabéthans for the essay: R. Headlam Wells (1983), 'Elizabethan Epideictic Drama: Praise and Blame in the Plays of Peele and Lyly', *Cahiers Élizabéthans*, **23**, pp. 15–33.

Cambridge University Press for the essay: David Bradley (1992), '*Alcazar*: The Text and the Sources', *From Text to Performance in the Elizabethan Theatre: Preparing the Play for the Stage*, Cambridge: Cambridge University Press, pp. 127–74; 255–7. Copyright © 1992 Cambridge University Press.

Cengage publishing for the essays: A.R. Braunmuller (1983), 'Entertainments for Court and City', *George Peele*, Boston: Twayne Publishers, pp. 11–29; 135–8. Copyright © 1983 Gale, a part of Cengare Learning; A.R. Braunmuller (1983), '*Edward I*: In Peace Triumphant, Fortunate in Wars', *George Peele*, Boston: Twayne Publishers, pp. 87–106. Copyright © 1983 Gale, a part of Cengage Learning.

Early Modern Literary Studies for the essay: Annaliese Connolly (2007), 'Peele's *David and Bethsabe*: Reconsidering Biblical Drama of the Long 1590s', *Early Modern Literary Studies*, **16**, pp. 355–76.

Johns Hopkins University Press for the essay: Louis Adrian Montrose (1980), 'Gifts and Reasons: The Contexts of Peele's *The Araygnement of Paris*', *English Literary History*, **47**, pp. 433–61.

Harvard University Press for the excerpt: Hallett Smith (1952), 'Pastoral Poetry: The Vitality and Versatility of a Convention', *Elizabethan Poetry: A Study in Conventions, Meaning and Expressions*, Cambridge, MA: Harvard University Press, pp. 1–11.

Manchester University Press for the essay: Philip Edwards (1986), '"Seeing is believing": Action and Narration in *The Old Wives Tale* and *The Winter's Tale*', in E.A.J. Honigmann (ed.), *Shakespeare and His Contemporaries*, Manchester: Manchester University Press, pp. 79–93. Copyright © 1986 Philip Edwards.

Medieval and Renaissance Drama in England for the essay: Frank Ardolino (2005), 'The Protestant Context of George Peele's "Pleasant Conceited" *Old Wives Tale*', *Medieval and Renaissance Drama in England*, **18**, pp. 146–65. Copyright © 2005 Frank Ardolino.

Northwestern University Press for the essays: Andrew von Hendy (1968), 'The Triumph of Chastity: Form and Meaning in *The Arraignment of Paris*', *Renaissance Drama*, **1**, pp. 87–101; Joan C. Marx (1981), '"Soft, Who Have We Here?": The Dramatic Technique of *The Old Wives Tale*', *Renaissance Drama*, **12**, pp. 117–13; Inga-Stina Ewbank (1965), 'The House of David in Renaissance Drama: A Comparative Study', *Renaissance Drama*, **8**, pp. 3–40.

Oxford University Press for the essays: Hugh Gazzard (2006), '"Many a *Herdsman* More Disposde to Morne": Peele, Campion, and the Portugal Expedition', *Review of English Studies*, **57**, pp. 16–42; Eldred Jones (1965), 'The Battle of Alcazar', *Othello's Countrymen: The African in English Renaissance Drama*, London: Oxford University Press, pp. 40–49; 136–8. Copyright © 1965 Eldred Jones; Brian Boyd (2004), 'Mutius: An Obstacle Removed in *Titus Andronicus*', *The Review of English Studies*, **55**, pp. 196–209.

Palgrave Macmillan for the essay: Inga-Stina Ewbank (1975), '"What words, what looks, what wonders?": Language and Spectacle in the Theatre of George Peele', in George Hibbard (ed.), *Elizabethan Theatre V*, Archon: Macmillan of Canada, pp. 124–54.

Parergon for the essay: Peter Hyland (1999), 'Moors, Villainy and *The Battle of Alcazar*', *Parergon*, **16**, pp. 85–99. Copyright © 1999 Peter Hyland.

SEL Studies in English Literature for the essay: Susan T. Viguers (1981), 'The Hearth and the Cell: Art in *The Old Wives Tale*', *Studies in English Literature*, **21**, pp. 208–21.

University of Texas Press for the essay: John D. Cox (1978), 'Homely Matter and Multiple Plots in Peele's *Old Wives Tale*', *Texas Studies in Literature and Language*, **20**, pp. 330–46.

Every effort has been made to trace all the copyright holders, but if any have been inadvertently overlooked the publishers will be pleased to make the necessary arrangement at the first opportunity.

Series Preface

In 1887, the literary historian and critic, George Saintsbury, coined the term "University Wits" to apply to six, university-trained Renaissance writers: John Lyly (1554–1606), Thomas Lodge (1558–1625), and George Peele (1558–1597), all graduates of Oxford, and Robert Greene (1558–1592), Christopher Marlowe (1564–1593), and Thomas Nashe (1567–1601), Cambridge graduates. Although Marlowe has acquired a reputation among scholars and critics as the most prominent of the group, this series seeks to give equal attention to all six writers, making clear how they were responsible for major improvements in the course of English drama and how their works provided Shakespeare with a context of theatrical possibilities that helped spur him to success. Although the details are sparse, there is clear evidence that these writers either knew or knew of one another, even if they never formally acknowledged themselves as a group of educated elite.

To be sure, there are similarities in the University Wits that have had a lasting impact – for example, their heightened awareness of style and form, a likely stimulus for Shakespeare's imaginative handling of stylistics. Moreover, in writing plays, the Wits learned to abide by the established aesthetic requirements and commercial demands of popular theater even as they sought to make changes that would permanently affect both conditions.

The volume editors evince a healthy skepticism toward attempts to isolate these six figures from their early modern context, and yet, concomitantly, manifest a desire to draw most of them from the shadows where they have remained for far too long. Thus, the volumes attempt to illuminate the distinctive characteristics of each writer through selections of the most perceptive, wide-ranging scholarship and criticism written about them. The reprinted pieces in each volume are preceded by generous introductions that not only offer fresh perspectives on the biography and literary output of the writers but also give a sense of what has been achieved by scholars over time and, in some cases, what needs still to be done.

These six volumes raise questions that bring into focus with fresh insight both familiar and new issues. For example: What do we know of the friendships among the six members of the University Wits and of the influence their bonds with one another, as well as their writings, may have had on each other's works? What impact did the University Wits have on the rapidly developing course of English drama? To what extent did the Wits' need to earn a living, along with the evolving standards and pressures of commercialism, determine the content and style of their compositions? How aware were the Wits of their status as university graduates? What were the personal and professional ramifications of Greene and Nashe's unabashed snobbishness; was it the result of their status as university graduates? Are we able to detect the specific consequences of the Wits' education in the substance and manner of what they write? What might Shakespeare have found in the behavior and plays of the University Wits to influence the mix of commercialism and aesthetics in his dramas? Are we able to detect any influence from the Wits on Shakespeare's poetry? What longstanding myths about the University Wits do these volumes denounce? What patterns do we see in the criticism and scholarship on the University Wits? This six-volume series will provide answers to these questions and many others of interest to students, teachers, and scholars eager to contextualize the work of writers in the late sixteenth and early seventeenth centuries.

A substantial portion of the leading scholarship on the University Wits has been published in scholarly journals and volumes of collected essays. The editors of the six volumes have winnowed these pieces, organizing them coherently into successive sections that, taken as a whole, present an up-to-date view of where the scholarship and criticism have brought us. Portions of book-length studies have sometimes been included. When it was impossible to include texts because of their length, editors have nevertheless directed readers to them, indicating what they are likely to find of value. In addition, the editors have provided their volumes with extensive bibliographies. Students, teachers, and scholars will find the series invaluable for both research and pedagogy. All the editors have carefully reviewed the expanse of articles and monographs written about their authors in order to make manifest the most advanced thinking about them and, thereby, to provide a resource of enduring value. Highly accessible and authoritative, these volumes represent the most important work done to date on the University Wits.

ROBERT A. LOGAN
Series Editor
University of Hartford, USA

Introduction

The life of George Peele reads in many ways like those of his fellow University Wits and fellow dramatists. He was born in 1556, two years before Queen Elizabeth came to the throne. He was two years younger than John Lyly (b. 1554), a year older than Thomas Kyd (b. ?1557, not a university graduate), two years older than Thomas Lodge (b. ?1558), four years older than Robert Greene (b. ?1560), eight years older than Christopher Marlowe (b. 1564) and Shakespeare (b. 1564, not a university graduate), and eleven years older than Thomas Nashe (b. 1567). Peele's father, James, was the author of a book on 'advanced' accounting methods who earned his livelihood as a bookkeeper, as a contributor to annual Lord Mayor's pageants, and, in 1562 and afterwards, as Clerk of Christ's Hospital in London. Though a tradesman, James entertained literary ambitions for himself and for his son, whose education proceeded accordingly at the grammar school of Christ's Hospital, at Broadgates Hall, Oxford, beginning in 1571, and then at Christ Church, Oxford, from 1574 to 1577. George Peele was awarded the MA in 1579, to which he was entitled without further academic work, two years after the awarding of the BA.

By the time he finished his undergraduate study, Peele had translated a play, now lost, on Iphigenia – perhaps Euripides' tragedy on that subject. Lyly and Lodge were his fellow Oxfordians, though whether he knew them personally during his undergraduate days cannot be determined. He appears to have stayed on at Oxford for a time, marrying Ann Christian, the daughter of an Oxford merchant, in 1580 and writing *A Tale of Troy* in 500 verses evidently at about the same time. It treats its well-visited classical subject with suitable scholarly archaic spirit but also with a chauvinistic delight in warfare that was to be a hallmark of Peele's writing throughout his career. He published it in 1589 with his *Congratulatory Poem of Farewell* to Sir Francis Drake and Sir John Norris on the eve of their setting forth on an ill-fated expedition to vanquish the Spaniards once more in the wake of the defeat of the Spanish Armada in 1588.

By this time Peele had been in London for the best part of the decade of the 1580s. Having moved there in 1581, he soon took to writing entertainments for the court and city, in the vein of his father's work as a sometime writer for Lord Mayor's pageants. Peele may have contributed his first such pageant soon after he arrived in the city.

What Peele had discovered by this time, if he did not know it already from his father's experiences and from worried talk about future employment among his fellow undergraduates at Oxford, was that he and his peers were about to enter a work force substantially over-supplied with college-educated young men in search of intellectually satisfying careers. The sons of gentry generally had no such worry; they had connections enabling them to move comfortably in a world of privilege that made room for the younger generation of the upper class. Oxford graduates willing or eager to serve as clergy in the Reformation Anglican church could count on finding a clerical position of sorts, though doing so generally required the endorsement of a well-to-do patron and might be wretchedly paid. Others, like Peele and Marlowe and the rest of the 'University Wits', found themselves rather brutally thrown on their own resources.

The social backgrounds of the University Wits were not identical, to be sure, and accordingly their options might have seemed more varied, though in fact they all ended up having to live by their skill as writers. John Lyly's grandfather, William Lilly (?1488–1522), was an Oxford-educated scholar who had become high-master of St Paul's School in London and whose Latin grammar was widely known. Assisted by such a family reputation, Lyly managed to become the master and playwright for boys' acting companies at the Chapel Royal and Blackfriars; yet even he must have squirmed under the necessity of depending for patronage on the loutish seventeenth Earl of Oxford. Thomas Lodge, whose father Sir Thomas Lodge was Lord Mayor of London and knighted in 1562, was educated at the Merchant Taylors' School in London and Trinity College at Oxford, after which he studied law in Lincoln's Inn but soon abandoned the law for a career as a writer. Thomas Nashe's family were sufficiently well-to-do that he embarked on the obligatory European tour after college. Following his return to London, Nashe endeavoured to secure the patronage of the Earls of Southampton and Derby, though his lack of continued success in these attempts meant that he too became a professional writer.

Christopher Marlowe, on the other hand, came from a social environment closer to that of Shakespeare (the son of a Stratford glove manufacturer and trader in agricultural produce) or Kyd (whose father was a scrivener) or Ben Jonson (the stepson of a bricklayer) or John Webster (son of a London tailor), along with others like Anthony Munday and Thomas Dekker, many of whom did not receive university educations. Marlowe, the son of a Canterbury shoemaker, was endowed with enormous gifts that led to academic advancement through church scholarship, at King's School, Canterbury, and then Corpus Christi College at Cambridge. Of the University Wits, he was the most successful as poet and dramatist until his notorious death by murder at the age of twenty-nine ended a truly promising career.

Peele's life story is in some ways like that of Robert Greene, who did manage to earn the BA (St John's) and MA at Cambridge, but, once in London, found no way of supporting a Bohemian life-style other than to turn to pamphleteering and playwriting in vast and poorly remunerated swatches. Greene died in 1592, at the age of thirty-two or so, in a wretched state, having come to his untimely end, according to one contemporary (though not necessarily reliable) account, by a surfeit of pickled herring and Rhenish wine. Peele died in 1596, at the age of forty, in poverty. Like Dekker and Webster, he was never far from the threat of debtors' prison. After his wife Ann died, perhaps in 1587, Peele seems to have married again in about 1591, to a woman named Mary Yates. Whether his life was as dissolute as is sometimes alleged seems unlikely and certainly not proved by any documentary evidence, but he did become the subject of a scurrilous book called *The Merry Conceited Jests of George Peele*, published in 1607. The swindles it chronicles cannot be reliably ascribed to Peele. What it demonstrates nevertheless is that he was remembered, in some quarters at least, as the quintessential debauched London scribbler of the 1580s and 1590s. Legends of this sort tend to gather around writers and theatre folk, then as now. What we can perceive is that Peele, like Greene and Marlowe, was caricatured in his immediate afterlife as the embodiment of a popular and thriving literary culture in London of the late sixteenth century: a world that was competitive and relentlessly unforgiving in its economic pressures, but also colourful, adventuresome, and vital.

Another resemblance to Greene, perhaps – and to other University Wits to some degree – is Peele's opportunistic way of writing on subjects of immediate popular appeal, especially in matters of patriotic national defence and flattery of England's Queen in an era of military crisis and greatness. England's naval heroes had managed in 1588 to defeat the Spanish Armada of Philip II of Spain, with the timely assistance of stormy weather off the west coast of Ireland that had brought many of Philip's ships to grief. That this intervention of the weather was universally interpreted in England as divine deliverance did not lessen the worshipful gratitude with which the English people celebrated the achievements of their military leaders and Queen. Here was a an opportunity ripe for exploitation by an ambitious Oxford graduate, newly come to London, in need of recognition and of financial support.

One of Peele's first achievements in these terms was to receive a handsome payment of £20 from his college, Christ Church, in May of 1583, after his move to London, for his involvement in devising 'plays and entertainment' for the visit to Oxford of Albert Alasco, the Count Palatine of Siradia in Poland. The Queen was present on this festive occasion, along with other foreign dignitaries. By 1584 Peele had written *The Arraignment of Paris*, for performance before Queen Elizabeth at court, and with the Queen herself included in the flattering spectacle. We will return to this first major play of his in a moment. The point here is that Peele's ambition to achieve recognition as a writer seems to have begun with notable successes at Oxford and at court.

Lord Mayor's Pageants, Court Entertainments, Occasional Poems

Meantime, Peele began writing for the bourgeois trade guilds of London, and for the officers of those guilds who advanced through the system to become aldermen and lord mayors. Here was another obvious opportunity for him. His father had written pageantry of this sort, as we have seen, and Peele himself had established some degree of literary expertise with the Iphigenia play he had written while at Oxford. Seemingly, he wrote his first Lord Mayor's pageant in 1581, shortly after having moved to London (these pageants were ceremonial celebrations for the annual installation of the city's Lord Mayor). Others by Peele seem to have followed in 1585, 1586, 1587, and 1588, by which time he had established himself as a provider of scripts for these civic occasions.

'The Device of the Pageant Borne before Wolstan Dixi, Lord Mayor of the City of London' (1585), is the first of his civic texts to survive. In it, a Presenter 'appareled like a moor' and various 'children of the pageant,' – to wit, London, Magnanimity, Loyalty, and The Country, The Thames, The Soldier, the Sailor, and so forth – all lay down their tributes in honour of Dixi as mayor of 'New Troy' or 'Lud', after which London was thought to have been named. Peele was named City Poet again in 1588, when he authored 'the device of the pageant borne before the Right Honorable Martin Calthrop, Lord Mayor'.

The most sophisticated of Peele's civic pageants is his *Descensus Astraeae* (*The Descent of the Goddess Astraea*), 'the device of a pageant borne before M. William Web, Lord Mayor of the City' in 1591. Like other Lord Mayor's pageants, this one involved an elaborate procession from the city to Westminster, where the new mayor would be presented to the monarch or to the royal justices for royal approval, according to a tradition laid down in the reign of King John in the thirteenth century. Since 1422 the procession had moved by many barges on the Thames, stopping off (since 1540) at the Guildhall for a show on a pageant stage. Here it was that Peele's show would have been produced. Its central conceit was that of the return of the Goddess Astraea, personating Justice, to earth, where she had sojourned in the Golden Age but had long since been recalled to heaven by Jove because human society had deteriorated in the Iron Age into warfare and corruption. Now, under enlightened mayoral governance in London and under the royal beneficence of Queen Elizabeth, Astraea could once more take her place among her chosen people. Since the myth of Astraea, as portrayed in Ovid's *Metamorphoses* and in Virgil's Eclogue IV, was widely interpreted as an allegory of the Christian incarnation, Elizabeth could be celebrated as a saviour in every sense of the term.

As A.R. Braunmuller observes in the first of the essays in this present volume (Chapter 1), Peele's *Descensus Astraeae* offers celebratory praise not only for the London civic hierarchy but for the court and the Queen. Classical figures like Caesar, Pompey, Alexander, and Hector all contribute their noblest qualities to the composite portrait of Elizabeth as Defender of the Faith. Protestant allies abroad in the Netherlands and in France are appealed to for support in the great causes of reform and peace. The enemies in this pageant represent the forces of reaction threatening the stability of Elizabeth's reign; with names such as 'Superstition, a Friar' and 'Ignorance, a Priest', they are manifestly images of Catholicism and Philip II of Spain. Arrayed on the side of virtue and justice are the Three Graces and the three theological virtues of Faith, Hope, and Charity, along with Honour and Champion. A Presenter greets the Mayor, 'A worthy governor for London's good', as underbearing, 'under his Sovereign's sway, / Unpartial Justice'. Her Majesty the Queen is attended in her throne, the Presenter tells us, by Honour, Virtue, and Steadfastness, while her Champion 'Sits at her feet to chastise Malcontents / That threat Her Honor's wrack'. Elizabeth is not only Astraea but also fair Pandora and 'Sweet Cynthia's darling, beauteous Cyprias' (that is, Venus). These are like the flattering comparisons that, as we shall see, are central to Peele's celebration of Elizabeth in *The Arraignment of Paris.* Peele's final speech in *Descensus Astraeae* is delivered by Time 'on the water', 'in the morning at my Lord Mayor's going to Westminster'. Throughout, the glory of 'Troynovant' is linked to that of the Thames, the 'silver stream' lying in the heart of that great city.

Peele's courtly entertainments, written concurrently with his civic pageants, stress similar themes of celebrating Elizabeth as the embodiment of both classical and Christian virtues. At the same time, these entertainments are aimed directly at royal patrons in the hope of attracting their support: not only Elizabeth's, but also that of Robert Devereux, the second Earl of Essex, and members of his circle. An especially inviting target for Peele's aspirations was the annual Accession Day celebrations commemorating Queen Elizabeth's attaining the English throne on 17 November 1558. This was the day chosen in subsequent years to honour England's deliverance from her Catholic enemies. Because these celebratory events featured tilts or jousts, the various 'champions' who put themselves forward in the competitive display of martial valour could use the occasion to dramatize themselves as chief among the Queen's followers. Writers like Peele could be recruited to spin a tale of glory on behalf of Essex or some rival lord. The more lavish the expenditure on the devising of such courtly entertainments, the more the ambitious courtier – aided by his script writer – could call attention to his importance in the scheme of courtly politics.

Peele's *Polyhymnia*, written for the Accession Day tilt of 1590, is a vivid illustration of how such an entertainment might be devised. Its central purpose, as Braunmuller notes, was to honour the retirement of Sir Henry Lee, who had been Queen's Champion since 1559, and to give special prominence to the display of Essex, 'all in sable sad,' in a 'stately chariot' drawn in by 'coal-black steeds of lusty hue', all of it presented in mournful remembrance of the death of Sir Philip Sidney, that 'well-lettered warrior', in 1586. Suits of armour, emblematic accoutrements, the hierarchical ordering of the participants – all take on political valence in an event intended to impress upon the Queen the crucial importance of Essex as, in his view, her chief counsellor.

Polyhymnia thus invokes, or at least idealizes, a court and English nation united under Elizabeth in the years after the tremendous success of the Spanish Armada defeat in 1588. As Braunmuller argues, however, Peele's *Anglorum Feriae* (*England's Festival Day*), celebrating the Accession Day tilt of 1595, reflects a much-changed mood at court. By this time, Essex had made such intemperate efforts to advance himself and his entourage that the court had become a place of unceasing factionalism. Moroever, Catholic attempts at subversion, from abroad and from within, had fostered an atmosphere close to that of hysteria. Radical Protestantism of a Puritan stripe threatened from the opposite extreme of the religious-political spectrum. Accordingly, Peele's championing of Essex in *Anglorum Feriae* takes on a defensive tone. Essex had by this time experienced two frustrations in his hopes for personal glory and prestige; his candidacy of Sir Francis Bacon to be Attorney General and then Solicitor General had both gone down in defeat to the favoured candidacies of Sir Edward Coke and Sir Thomas Fleming. Thus, a bare year before he was to die, Peele betrays in this outwardly celebratory pageant an uneasiness about England's political and religious future.

Gone, then, or at least diminished, are the patriotic optimism and fervent admiration for Essex that Peele had shown shortly after the Armada defeat of 1588. The ebullient mood of that earlier era can be seen in two occasional poems written in 1589 by Peele: his *A Farewell to the most famous generals of our English forces by land and sea, Sir John Norris and Sir Francis Drake, knights as they were about to set sail on an expedition to drive the Spanish from Portugal*, and *An Eclogue Gratulatory* written to laud Essex on 'his welcome into England from Portugal' later that same year. Hugh Gazzard's essay in Part I of the present volume (Chapter 2) recounts the extraordinary circumstances. Norris and Drake's intent was to recover Portugal from Catholic Spain's annexation of that country in 1580 by installing the Portuguese pretender, Don Antonio, as a native Portuguese ruler. The cause was popular in Protestant England, but similar support failed to materialize in Portugal when the expeditionary force arrived. Essex had by this time joined the enterprise, much to the displeasure of Queen Elizabeth. The loss of life was appalling. Peele's enthusiasm is vibrantly evident in *A Farewell*, but by the time he wrote *An Eclogue Gratulatory*, argues Gazzard, the encomiastic praise for Essex is muted. Essex was in some disgrace. People knew that he had gone on the expedition without the Queen's leave, and had greatly exacerbated that insubordination by purloining one of the Queen's ships for his own purposes. She was understandably furious, leaving Peele in a delicate spot in his presumed hopes of lauding Essex without losing royal favour.

The story of Peele's espousal of Essex's cause continues in the Accession Day pageants of 1590 and 1595 described above. Perhaps he became aware, ultimately, that he had hitched his fortunes not to a rising star but to a dangerously unstable supernova. As in the case of John Lyly also, it seems, the pursuit of successful patronage in the court of Queen Elizabeth proved more and more frustrating and unrewarding in her final years.

The Arraignment of Paris

The Arraignment of Paris, written in the euphoric years of the early 1580s, was Peele's first professional play. It was also to be his one and only drama presented at court, in the presence of, and with the participation of, the Queen. In it, Peele makes far more successful use of the hugely familiar story of the Trojan War than he had managed to deploy in the effusion of his Oxford days, *A Tale of Troy*. Queen Elizabeth is presented in the play's finale, in a deliberately outrageous rewriting of legendary history, as the reincarnation of the three goddesses among whom Paris had had to choose in 'the Judgement of Paris', but without any of their shortcomings and with none of the factionalism of that portentous event.

As Peele tells the story, Paris, son of King Priam of Troy and now living as a 'shepherd swain' on nearby Mount Ida, is enjoined to award the goddess Ate's outwardly beautiful apple of discord to 'the fairest' among the three Olympian goddesses, Juno, Pallas Athene, and Venus. They vie for the prize by offering Paris their own special gifts of majesty (Juno), 'the beauty of the mind' (Pallas Athene), and amorous love and physical beauty (Venus). Paris, by choosing Venus's gift of amorous beauty in the person of Helen, wife of Menelaus of Sparta, sets in motion 'the tragedy of Troy', since the rape of Helen will become the *casus belli* in the great war between Greece and Troy celebrated by Homer and by countless subsequent tellers of the tale. Now, in Peele's play, Eliza (Queen Elizabeth) trumps history and legend by embodying in herself the majesty, mind, and physical beauty of the three classical goddesses, thereby quelling all strife. Troynovant, the 'new Troy' signifying London and England, is Peele's revisionary modern substitute for an ancient world of strife and tragedy. As in the title of Peele's later *Descensus Astraeae* (1591), the goddess of Justice has returned to earth once more in the person of Elizabeth. The Golden Age is born again.

Peele surrounds his fanciful account of the Judgement of Paris with the sorts of allegorical fancy that suit well with a work of hyperbolical courtly flattery. Taking his cue from the mythological tradition that Paris, though a prince of the royal family of Troy, was somehow a shepherd swain enamored of the shepherdess Oenone on Mount Ida, Peele introduces a pastoral world peopled by Pan (a shepherd), Faunus (a hunter), and Silvanus (a woodman), attendant on the country gods, along with Flora, Pomona, and a choir of Muses. Shepherds are present as well, bearing names like Colin, Hobbinol, Diggon, and Thenot, that had become thoroughly familiar in the many pastoral fictions produced in the 1580s and 1590s, including Spenser's *The Shepherds Calendar*. These fictions, indebted to Virgil, Sannazaro, and other pastoral writers, had become a staple of the literary landscape. The pantheon of Olympian gods is enlarged to include not only the three contending goddesses but also Jupiter, Bacchus, Mars, Mercury, Neptune, Pluto, Saturn, and Vulcan with his Cyclopes. By adding the Three Fates (Clotho, Lachesis, and Atropos), along with various masques and dumb shows of Nine Knights, Helen and the Four Cupids, and Thestilis and a Foul Crooked Churl, among others, Peele armed himself with as much mythological apparatus as a flattering court poet could wish.

Many of these elements had appeared in earlier pastoral entertainments designed for court festivities and weddings, as for instance at the wedding of Prince Arthur to Katharine of Aragon in 1501. John Lyly's *Campaspe* and *Sappho and Phao*, produced more or less at the same time as *The Arraignment* (1580–84), offer further models. Lyly's plays were acted by Oxford's boys; *The Arraignment* was performed, also by boys, at the Chapel at court. A Prologue by Ate, come from 'lowest hell', sets the mood of Senecan revenge tragedy that was to be used also by Kyd in the opening chorus of his *The Spanish Tragedy*. In *The Arraignment*, to be sure, the foreboding Senecan Prologue is a deliberately misleading move on Peele's part, since the play will end, surprisingly, in the triumph of Eliza and Troynovant.

The play is richly masque-like in its visual and verbal ornamentation. The three contending goddesses are identifiable by the colours and flowers they wear – Juno in yellow gold oxlips, Pallas Athene in martial red July-flowers, Venus in blue violets. In addition, Juno has her peacocks, Pallas Athene her tigers, Venus her sparrows. The songs are gracefully lyrical. Each goddess contends for the prize with an elaborate visual display: Juno's tree of gold, Pallas Athene's nine knights in armour, and Venus's four Cupids, 'each having his fan in his hand to fan fresh air in her face'. Oenone manifests her sorrow at having been deserted by Paris 'with a wreath of poplar on her head' and sings a mournful complaint. When Paris is arraigned before Jupiter (hence the play's title) of partiality in his judging the case of the three goddesses, he defends himself to the council of the gods by arguing that he was dazzled by Venus's beauty.

Louis Montrose, in a seminal New Historicist essay on *The Arraignment* (included in Part II as Chapter 3), sets the play in the cultural and political environment that we have seen as the background of Peele's Lord Mayor's pageants, courtly entertainments, and occasional poems. *The Arraignment* has secured a worthy place in recent study of Renaissance dramatic texts, in Montrose's view, because 'it is so characteristic and compendious a production of Elizabethan court culture'(433). The very fact that critics have seen the play as both a hyperbolic royal entertainment and a pastoral celebration of humble retirement – and hence either a glorification of political power or a quiet repudiation of worldly striving – bespeaks the play's complex relation to the Elizabethan culture from which it has emerged and to which it has made its own fascinating contribution. Citing Hallett Smith essay on *The Arraignment* (included here as Chapter 5), Montrose sees Paris's choice as one of action vs. contemplation, worldly achievement vs. the pursuit of knowledge, *negotium* vs. *otium*. This binary opposition structures the play even as it also reflects a profound ambivalence in the Elizabethan world of political competition and of spiritual idealism. The opposition may also reflect some part of Peele himself, torn as he was between his eagerness to succeed and his self-idealization as a serious thinker and writer.

Peele's chief object of analysis and flattery, in Montrose's interpretation, is Queen Elizabeth, who prized both her political mastery and her maidenhood. Elizabeth's Catholic and older sister, Mary Tudor, and her subversively Catholic Scottish cousin, Mary Stuart, were, for the Queen, equally negative models of foolish and self-destructive romantic infatuation. That is why the cult of royal virginity at Elizabeth's court was so emphatically promulgated in the early 1580s, when *The Arraignment* was written and produced. Royal virginity was now the Queen's source of magical power, acquired by her giving up all hopes of marriage in the wake of the failure of the marital negotiations with the French Duc D'Alençon. What she asked in return for her self-sacrifice was that her court and her subjects bestow on her the gift of adulation. In practice, says Montrose, courtly politics were gritty, competitive, corrupt, inequitable, and above all self-serving, but Elizabeth's myth of harmony demanded that the court dance to the tune of royal celebration. In place of the buying and selling of offices that was so dismayingly common, Elizabeth insisted on acts of giving, to her, as the expression of a loving devotion. The New Year gifts that came into the royal coffers were accordingly far from negligible in value. The symbolic custom quickly took on aspects of gift-giving so astutely analysed by Marcel Mauss in his epic study of *Le Don* (*The Gift*).

In these terms, *The Arraignment* is Peele's gift to the Queen. It has the double-edged characteristic of such gifts, as one that is freely and lovingly offered by a donor whose hope notwithstanding is for personal advancement. Peele's gift ultimately did not succeed, in Montrose's estimate, any more than did the plays of that same decade by John Lyly. This was to be Peele's only play presented to the Queen in her own person, at court. In that heady moment, nonetheless, Peele must have thought he had achieved what he had dreamed about. The Queen herself took part in the finale, graciously receiving gifts from the three classical goddesses. Venus contentedly resigned her qualities of loveliness to Eliza, Pallas Athene bequeathed her titles to a queen both 'beautiful and wise', and Juno, the 'queen of heaven', yielded her dynastic title to a greater successor. The three Fates similarly bestowed their control of human destiny on a 'fair queen of rare renown / Whom heaven and earth beloves amid thy train'. In a finale that, as Montrose shows, lessened the boundary between reality and dramatic fiction, Peele's *Arraignment* became the symbolic re-enactment and embodiment of England's celebratory gift of devotion to her virgin queen.

In Chapter 4, Andrew von Hendy adds to Montrose's depiction of *The Arraignment* in its cultural context by seeing the play as a celebration of the triumph of chastity. The apparently trivial nature of the play that is deplored by some earlier critics disappears when we recognize in Peele's text many characteristics of courtly masques and entertainments. Like the opulent masques of the Elizabethan and later the Jacobean court, *The Arraignment* culminates by absorbing its audience into its own imaginary world. The performance becomes what celebratory drama of this sort usually becomes, a cultural event in which the realities of jostling for position at court are transmuted into a cultural fantasy of enactment of the rituals of power. Accordingly, the play takes on qualities of dreamlike fulfilment resembling those features of romance noted by Northrop Frye (1957, 1965). The very remoteness of the pastoral and mythological setting in time and place underscores the ways in which seemingly fanciful and even absurd actions take on serious political and cultural meaning.

For Headlam Wells, these qualities of *The Arraignment* point to its nature and genre as epideictic drama, the function of which (as in Spenser's *Faerie Queene*, for instance) is to offer instructive models to princes by reproving what is erroneous, arousing what is indolent, and commending what is worthy of praise. Peele's play is thus, in Wells's view (see Chapter 6), highly didactic, inheriting its rhetorical models from Aristotle (who distinguishes praise from mere flattery) and other great rhetoricians. The model is often abused, of course, in writers who fail to resist the blandishments of promised good fortune, and Peele is not exempt from temptations of this sort. Even so, the literary critic today can obtain a more incisive view of a play like *The Arraignment* by seeing that its genre invites the use of royal pageantry and of rhetorical debate. Peele's play makes extensive use of both, most of all when it incorporates Queen Elizabeth into its harmonious ending, thereby resolving both royal pageantry and debate into a unified tribute to England's great queen.

The Old Wives Tale

Peele's *The Old Wives Tale*, written seemingly in the late 1580s or early 1590s, more or less a decade after *The Arraignment*, is a play for the popular stage in London and the provinces. It was part of the repertory of the Queen's Men, a politically powerful troupe that was assembled in 1583, by the Queen's ministers and doubtless with her blessing, to further the cause of Protestantism. Their mission was to entertain audiences with lively plays while also impressing upon those audiences the vital importance of England's new reformed and nationalistic ideology. To Anglican authorities, such indoctrination was urgently needed, especially in those parts of the country that were remote from London and were, in many locales, not yet fully comfortable with the new Anglican faith. The company's roster of plays included Robert Wilson's *The Three Lords and Three Ladies of London*, the anonymous *The Chronicle History of King Leir* (a precursor to Shakespeare's tragedy), Robert Greene's *Friar Bacon and Friar Bungay*, and the anonymous *The Famous Victories of Henry the Fifth*. The Queen's Men toured the provinces, since that was their mandate, though they also turned up occasionally at court. Peele's *The Old Wives Tale*, as we shall see below, seems also to have been put to the task of promoting the new Protestant gospel. In the 1590s, as Scott McMillin and Sally-Beth MacLean have shown in their study *The Queen's Men and Their Plays* (1987), the company lost out to new and enterprising acting companies who had discovered how to woo London audiences with a large repertory of freshly written plays staged in fixed theatrical locations, while the Queen's Men continued to rely on the few plays it needed for provincial touring.

The Old Wives Tale has attracted more attention, both critical and admiring, than Peele's other plays. In the early twentieth century, folklorists were understandably attracted to its medley of folk motifs, including the tales of the Grateful Dead, the Poison Maiden, the Ransomed Woman, the Well for the Water of Life, the Well of the World's End, and Jack the Giant Killer (see, for example, Lewis and Clapp, 1926), but these same scholars tended to disparage the play artistically as a hodge-podge of heterogeneous materials. F.W. Gummere, editing the play for C.M. Gayley's anthology of *Representative English Comedies* (1903), found the chief value of Peele's play in the way its framing plot might be seen as anticipating Francis Beaumont's *The Knight of the Burning Pestle* (*c.* 1607). Critical debate has posed the question as to whether Peele's play is a satire of old-fashioned romance or a sentimental remembrance of endearingly childlike folk stories.

Whether told naively or from a sophisticated and ironic viewpoint, *The Old Wives Tale* is indeed a medley of narratives. Peele calls attention to its being 'an old wives winter's tale', anticipating, as Philip Edwards observes in Chapter 9, a theme similar to that of Shakespeare's *The Winter's Tale*. The recurring phrase 'a merry winter's tale', or 'an old wives winter tale', is the way that old Madge and her listeners, in the play's choric frame induction, characterize the yarn that she is about to spin for three benighted wanderers who have lost their way in a dark wood and have sought shelter beside Madge's hearth. A Smith named Clunch conducts the three wanderers to the hospitality of his 'cottage', where Madge can provide them with a piece of cheese and a pudding of her own making, along with a story to while away the hours of darkness. Dogs are heard to bark. Songs enliven the atmosphere of homely camaraderie. 'Once upon a time there was a king, or a lord, or a duke, that had a fair daughter, the fairest the ever was', Madge begins, cueing the audience on stage and in the theatre to expect traditional romantic fare. Madge's promise that the king's fair daughter will be stolen away by a conjurer who turns himself into a great dragon and carries her off to his stone castle, that her two brothers will seek her out, that a 'proper young man' will be turned by the sorcerer into a bear by night though a man by day while he dwells by 'a cross that parts three several ways', and that the lady will be made to run mad, adds further guarantees of a deliciously improbable tale of magic and transformation.

No sooner has Madge laid out for her listeners a bill of fare for her magical story than the two brothers she has mentioned enter in search of their sister Delia. They immediately encounter the old man who dwells by the cross, to whom they charitably offer alms and receive in return riddling advice about their quest. After they have set off on their mission, the old man recalls in soliloquy that he lived a happy and honourable life until Sacrapant, 'that cursed sorcerer', lusting after the old man's beauteous wife, turned the old man into a bear and put a curse of madness on the lady, Venelia, who indeed flits on stage and off again to show us how mad she truly is. The story that Madge has undertaken to tell the three young wanderers now takes on theatrical concreteness. The tale is to be enacted before our eyes and those of the onstage audience. Madge and her 'listeners' will remain on stage throughout, silent until the very last moment, by which time dawn is about to break and old Madge needs to be awakened from her slumbers. Having made an end of her tale, she offers the young men a breakfast of bread and cheese before they go.

How was this avowedly claptrap narrative, ingeniously presented as a play within a frame, to be staged for Peele's original audiences, presumably on tour and in London? Susan Viguers, in her essay 'The Hearth and the Cell' (Chapter 12), offers an intriguing stage plan and interpretation, based on her own experience in directing an informal production of *The Old Wives Tale* at the Philadelphia College of Art some time in the late 1970s. The plan is admittedly speculative, since indications of staging in the original text are sparse, but it brings order to the play's multiple actions. For Viguers, the two central figures of the play are Madge and Sacrapant. They represent two fundamentally opposite views of dramatic art. Both are creators of illusion, but of contrasting methods and intents. Madge's imaginative world is vibrant, vital, charitable, and hospitable; Sacrapant's world is secret, malign, perverted, lustful, and enslaving. Madge presides at a welcoming cottage hearth and warming fire; Sacrapant's flame is a sinister light hidden under a turf that must be extinguished before his magical power is finally quelled. Madge delights with shows and stories of fruition and of life as a restorative journey; Sacrapant frightens, frustrates, and denies. Madge's art is realized in time; Sacrapant's art is undone by time.

Given this polarity, Viguers proposes that Madge's hearth is to be located downstage and to one side, near the audience and placed so that her function as presenter and interpreter is made visually clear; the theatre audience sees the acted-out story over her shoulder, as it were. At the diametrically opposite side and upstage, away from the audience and hidden in shadows, is Sacrapant's cell. Correspondingly, Viguers groups the other acting areas in thematic opposition, with the restorative Well of Life on Madge's side and the sinister Light under the Hillock near Sacrapant's cell. At centre stage is the cross where dwells the hero, Erastus, who has been transformed by Sacrapant into an old man by day and a bear by night. Whether the original staging would actually have looked like this is hard to say, but the thematic oppositions offer a meaningful insight into the play's structure.

John Cox's essay on multiple plots (Chapter 8) lends itself to a similar interpretation. Making good use of Richard Levin's *The Multiple Plot in English Renaissance Drama* (1971), Cox elucidates how the various elements of Madge's story are interwoven in such a way that, for example, the beleaguered and mad Venelia, wife of the old man, is needed to extinguish Sacrapant's black-magical lamp and thereby bring a happy resolution to the romantic plot of Eumenides, the play's wandering knight, and his lady-love Delia. Even when a plot element does not directly impinge on the other stories, Cox argues for the conscious artistry of a 'direct contrast plot.' A good example is the charmingly ludicrous story of Huanebango and Booby. Huanebango, a blustering braggart soldier type, having been deafened by Sacrapant's magic, can marry the attractive but shrewish Zantippe without having to listen to her scolding rant, while the clownish Booby, having lost his sight to the malevolent power of the magician, can couple amicably with the mild-tempered but hideously ugly Celanta, sister of Zantippe. The polarity of this account thematically reinforces the polarities that Viguers outlines in her staging of the play.

In Chapter 11, Joan Marx's analysis of dramatic technique in *The Old Wives Tale* finds similar oppositions, between enchantment and parody, ingenuous comic spirit and sauciness. As Marx sees the play, each plot element is presented 'straight' and is then upended or juxtaposed, with a daring that is perfectly suited to the play's defiance of conventional generic boundaries. The play is naive romance offered to a knowledgeable audience that knows how to read its unexpected and surprising shifts in tone.

Mary Ellen Lamb's essay (Chapter 10) turns these oppositions to good use in a feminist reading of *The Old Wives Tale*. Noting that the all-too-familiar antagonism toward older women in the early modern period lends itself to a defamatory contrast between literate male culture and oral female culture, Lamb explains how women are thus associated with the spoken word, with superstitious tales, and with bedtime stories told by 'mumping beldames' who are characterized as toothless and bent with age. Men, conversely, inhabit a world of literate but often pretentious learning, as parodied in Huanebango's spouting of Latin nonsense. In *The Old Wives Tale*, as Lamb sees it, this dialectical opposition works paradoxically to the advantage of the female oral tradition. Although Madge is presented on stage as an old crone, apt to fall asleep in the corner of her hearth, her stories offer what Lamb calls an alternative space of resistance, a place of childhood memories and of oral legends marked by the soothingly familiar 'Once upon a time'. The play thus opposes classical learning with folk tradition. Virtue ultimately resides with those who practise narrative art. The sinister power of Sacrapant, so reliant on the book learning that also ensnares Marlowe's Doctor Faustus, is ultimately defeated by the world of generosity and imagination.

Lamb notes (29) that the phrase 'old wives' tales' was often used in Protestant England to defame Catholicism for its allegedly superstitious ways. Frank Ardolino takes up this hint in his discussion of 'The Protestant Context' of Peele's *The Old Wives Tale* (Chapter 7). The proposition that the play is polemically anti-Catholic is inherently plausible, since, as we have seen, the acting company known as the Queen's Men, who performed Peele's play, were assembled in the 1580s and early 1590s to proselytize on behalf of the Anglican reformed faith throughout England. Ardolino argues that Sacrapant is Peele's defamatory representation of Catholicism. Sacrapant's nefarious machinations hint at imperialism, simony, and the Catholic Eucharist. Similarly, the braggardly Huanebango is, for Ardolino, a lampoon of Catholic bluster and aggression; Huanebango refuses to give alms to the old man, whereas his virtuously blind and mild-mannered counterpart, Booby, is generous. Catholic religious practice was often lampooned by the Protestant reformers as obsessively devoted to the spectacular and visual and to the performance of the Mass, whereas Anglicans preferred the sermon with its emphasis on the spoken word and the verbal text of the Scriptures.

On the side of Protestant virtue, then, in Ardolino's reading, we find the innocent Booby, blind to outward appearances and charitable. Also unassailably virtuous, in Protestant terms, are Jack (whose actions recall those of St George and Spenser's Redcross knight), the old man

Erestus, Eumenides, Delia, and Venelia: all those, in other words, who suffer at the hands of the priestlike Sacrapant, with his dragon and his obscene conjurations, but who ultimately prevail because they are protected by divine Providence – or at least, in this play, by the spirit of comic romance. To the extent that magic is associated throughout with Catholicism, the play thus lends itself in an informal way to an allegory of the Reformation. The motif of the bear, as part of the old man's saga, recalls for Ardolino (and may have done so for Peele's audience) the family badge of Robert Dudley, Earl of Leicester, Elizabeth's Protestant champion in the Netherlands until his death in 1588 and a powerful supporter of the Queen's Men. Ardolino's thesis is thus very suggestive, even if it pushes some details a bit too far (Booby the clown, for instance, seems hardly dignified enough to represent Protestantism). In any case, the opposition of oral vs. visual cultures that Ardolino posits is nicely complementary to the structural and thematic analyses of Viguers, Cox, Marx, and Lamb.

The Battle of Alcazar

Recent critical interpretations of Peele's *The Battle of Alcazar* centre on the events of 1588–1589, when the play was written and produced, and especially on England's worrisome involvement (or meddling, one might say) in the affairs of Portugal and Spain. All three essays in Part IV of this present collection take up the consequences of this military and diplomatic tangle. As we saw, Peele celebrated in his poem *A Farewell to ... Sir John Norris and Sir Francis Drake* the departure of Sir John Norris and Sir Francis Drake on their feckless attempt in 1589 to inflict another defeat (after the Armada victory of 1588) on the Spanish and install the Portuguese Pretender, Don Antonio, on the Portuguese throne, which had been seized by Philip of Spain in 1580. The failure of Drake and Norris's undertaking had resulted in the temporary disgrace of the Earl of Essex for taking part without the Queen's permission. Peele did what he could to proclaim the virtues of his hero, Essex, while trying, in his more muted poem *Eclogue Gratulatory*, to greet the homecoming warriors without incurring royal disfavour for having sided with insubordination.

Peter Hyland's 'Moors, Villainy and *The Battle of Alcazar*' (Chapter 14), along with the other two essays in Part IV (Chapter 13 by David Bradley and Chapter 15 by Eldred Jones), deftly lays out the issues of 1588–1589 for England and for Peele. The Spanish takeover of Portugal in 1580 was galling to the English because Philip II of Spain represented such a huge threat to Protestant England throughout the latter part of the sixteenth century. Don Antonio, the Pretender to the Portuguese throne, represented for England an opportunity to intervene on behalf of an anti-Spanish and purportedly legitimate dynastic claim to Portugal. The English knew that Philip of Spain had been able to seize power in Portugal in 1580 because of the defeat and death two years before of the Portuguese King Sebastian at the Battle of Alcazar. Sebastian having died without a male heir, Philip, as his first cousin, was in a position to seize Spain's neighbouring kingdom.

The Battle of Alcazar in 1578 was, for this reason, a key to English-Portuguese politics in 1588–1589. Hyland explains what had happened. Sebastian of Portugal, arrogating for himself the role of championing the Christian faith against Islam (only recently expelled from the south of Spain after a prolonged presence there), had intervened, in 1580, in a dynastic struggle for the throne of Morrocan Fez, on the side of Mohammed el-Mesloukh (represented in Peele's play by Muly Mahamet) against Mohammed's uncle, the reigning Abd-el-Malek.

Sebastian clearly hoped that Fez would eventually become his by this intervention, but the campaign ended in the slaughter at the Battle of Alcazar of Sebastian's army, of Sebastian himself, and of Abd el-Malek and his rebellious nephew. Philip II of Spain, having failed beforehand to dissuade Sebastian from such a foolhardy venture, had reluctantly seemed to offer his support while secretly forming an alliance with Abd el-Malek.

Elizabeth's government sided with Abd el-Malek, but the dynastic situation was fraught with difficulties. Earlier, in 1557, Abd el-Malek's royal father had established the succession on his eldest son Abdallah and thereafter on the next son, the eldest of Abdallah's brothers. When Abdallah came to power in 1557, he attempted to settle the succession on his own eldest son rather than on a younger brother, and accordingly ordered the murder of both of his brothers. One of these, Abd el-Malek, had escaped and had then retaliated by deposing the uncle, Abdallah's son Mohammed el-Mesloukh, who, in Abd el-Malek's view, had usurped what was Abd el-Malek's by the terms of the 1557 settlement. The English supported this state of affairs, albeit with some discomfort that the cherished principle of patrilineal succession had been abused.

This sensational story was sure to recommend itself to George Peele, in Hyland's view, for its political relevance to England's hostility toward Catholic Spain and that country's takeover of Portugal in 1580. The story also offered Peele an opportunity to introduce into the saga Captain Thomas Stukeley, a swashbuckling adventurer of Catholic persuasion who had fled after the arrest of his master, the Duke of Somerset, in 1551, to France where he became a favourite of King Henry II. Stukeley then returned to England and revealed French plans for the capture of Calais and invasion of England, a scheme he may have helped originate. Imprisoned in the Tower of London for some months, he found himself penniless and obliged to turn soldier of fortune once more. Having made his way into the favour of Queen Mary Tudor, he then managed to accommodate himself to the new Protestant regime of Queen Elizabeth. Briefly allowed to engage in piracy on behalf of England, he was then disowned by Elizabeth in the cause of international diplomacy. His next attempted adventure, to Ireland, was frustrated by Elizabeth's government on the ostensible grounds that he sympathized with the Irish nationalists there, though mainly because the profits that accrued were not munificent enough. On the pretext of sailing for England, he headed instead for the court of Philip of Spain at the Escorial, where he was made much of until Philip dropped him as a token of acquiescence in peace negotiations with England. Turning now to Rome, where he was handsomely received by Pope Pius V, Stukeley offered to free Ireland from Protestant English rule, and, after he had proved his military prowess against the Turks at the Battle of Lepanto in 1571, was dispatched by the militantly inclined Gregory XIII to Ireland. Accompanied by a meagre force, Stukeley stopped off first at Lisbon, where he was recruited by King Sebastian of Portugal to assist in the campaign of Alcazar; there he died bravely in the fighting. This story was of such legendary dimensions that it led to Stukeley's becoming a folk hero in England, despite his Catholic loyalties, and hence of compelling interest to Peele in writing *The Battle of Alcazar*. (For further details, see Joseph Candido's 1987 article on Captain Thomas Stukeley.)

Peele thus found himself with two larger-than-life-size figures for his play: Stukeley, and the Moroccan king's rebellious nephew, Mohammed el-Mesloukh, whose name Peele simplifies to Muly Mahamet. Despite Stukeley's fascinating biography, Muly Mahamet takes precedence as the central villain of *The Battle of Alcazar*. Edward Alleyn, lead player for the Admiral's company (who was later to star, in 1596, as Stukeley in the Admiral's *Captain*

Stukeley), assumed the part of Muly Mahamet in Peele's play. Muly is a charismatic over-achiever in the style of Marlowe's Tamburlaine (1587–88): ruthless, unlimited in his ambition for power, superbly self-confident – just the part for Alleyn to tear a cat in. Muly resembles the Vice of the late medieval morality play in his chortling treachery. Onto this compelling figure, argues Hyland, Peele displaces English anxieties about Catholic duplicity. Conversely, Abdelmelec, Peele's name for the uncle and reigning monarch whom Muly is challenging, is presented as a virtuous and heroic defender of the right. As such, in Hyland's view, he is analogously a stand-in for all Protestant champions of the true faith. Peele's play has two major Moorish figures, one evil and one good. The fact that Philip of Spain, though not in the play in person, stands behind Muly makes plain to Peele's Elizabethan audiences that *The Battle of Alcazar* could be interpreted as a salvo in the wars of religion.

Edward I

Edward I, written in the early 1590s not long after *The Battle of Alcazar*, is of a similarly patriotic and Protestant stamp, this time dealing directly with English history. The seeming difficulty of making a proto-Protestant hero out of a king who ruled from 1272 to 1307, well over two centuries before the English Reformation, poses no difficulty for Peele. Edward Longshanks is presented as a model ruler, as indeed he was popularly regarded by Elizabethans. Peele rewrites history to fashion Edward as the undisputed victor in Wales and Scotland, unlike Henry IV, for example, who faced continual resistance in those outlying regions of Great Britain. Peele's Edward I is a ruler of all the British people. He is associated in the play with the legends of Robin Hood and Lluellen of Wales. He has just returned from a holy crusade against pagan Muslims in the Holy Land. As A.R. Braunmuller argues in Part V of the present collection (Chapter 16), Edward is contrasted throughout with friends and enemies in such a way as to glorify his kingship. He is an able diplomat and builder of consensus. He is sensitive to regional loyalties and customs to such an extent that he travels with his wife to Wales in order that their son, the future Edward II, will be born a native Welshman and thereby fulfill Welsh demands for a native prince. Thus is born the now-customary title for the heir to the throne as Prince of Wales. Edward is the moulder of English tradition at its best.

Peele rewrites the history of Edward's marriage with a cheerfully blithe disregard for facts. As Braunmuller shows, the point is to celebrate Edward's English customs and mores as incomparably superior to those of Catholic Spain. Elinor of Castile is a caricature of all that Protestant Londoners seem to have felt about queens imported from Spain for marriage into the Tudor royal line. The most important of these, of course, had been Katharine of Aragon, the widow of Henry VII's son Arthur who then in 1509 became the spouse of Henry VIII, with far-reaching consequences for the Reformation. Katharine, a loyal Catholic whose marriage to Henry was defended as lawful by the papacy and by Philip of Spain, was divorced in 1533 in order that Henry might marry Anne Boleyn. Anne's daughter Elizabeth became the Protestant ruler of England in 1558, after Katharine's Catholic daughter Mary, older half-sister of Elizabeth, had ruled from 1553 to 1558 in a vain but bloody attempt to recover England to the Catholic fold. Protestant Londoners could hardly be expected to greet with shouts of welcome an arrogant royal bride from Castile, especially after the Spanish had attempted to invade their country with Philip II's great Armada in 1588. Yet, as Marie Axton points out in

The Queen's Two Bodies (1977), one group of writers in the 1590s actually put forward the name of the Spanish Infanta, Isabella, as potential successor to the English throne.

Elinor of Castile, in Peele's play, lives up to her lurid billing. She insists that her son, young Edward, be dressed in expensive finery and fed nectar and ambrosia, in defiance of her husband's protestations that 'This Spanish pride 'grees not with England's prince'. When the King attempts to soothe her fury by promising to grant anything that she chooses to ask, Elinor has the audacity to demand that all Englishmen shave their beards and all English woman cut off their right breasts. Edward's resourceful response is to offer his own beard to the barber's shears and to tell his wife, 'Here must the law begin, sweet Elinor, at thy breast'. His riposte wittily makes the point that enlightened rulers, in the best of English traditions, must lead by example rather than tyrannously inflicting arbitrary punishments on their subjects. Elinor is, however, incorrigible. Having murdered the Mayoress of London by means of a poison serpent at the poor woman's breast, doubtless to the horror of all Londoners in the audience, Elinor swears a solemn oath that she is guiltless of that crime, declaring, 'Gape earth and swallow me and let my soul / Sink down to hell if I were author of / That woman's tragedy'. Forthwith the earth at Charing Green obligingly does what she has bid it do, and the Queen disappears into the ground, to be coughed up some time later at Potter's Hive (that is, Pottershithe).

Having confessed to committing incest with Edward's brother Edmond and to having begotten her daughter Joan of Acon in an adulterous relationship with a friar, Queen Elinor dies a divinely ordained death. Little does she realize that the supposed friars who have heard her confession are none other than the King and his philandering brother in disguise! Edmond attempts to deny his guilt, but the truth is too plain. Joan of Acon, confronted with the painful reality of her parentage, falls grovelling to the ground and perishes as well. Edward, now freed of all Spanish family contamination, grievingly orders that his dead wife and daughter are to be given honourable burial and that his troops are to continue the fight against the invading Scots. Edward is thus a champion against Catholic perfidy, much as Shakespeare's Henry V (1599) manages to be a true son of the church even while upholding the traditions of English patriotism and independence from continental meddling.

Historically, Elinor (or Eleanor) of Castile appears to have been a devoted and almost inseparable companion of her husband, supporting him during the Second Barons' War of the 1260s and accompanying him on several crusades, including the eighth crusade in 1270–71. She was not popular in England because of her foreign birth and her aggressive acquisition of lands, but she patronized writers and artists, handsomely supported the Dominican order of friars, and was sumptuously buried by her grieving husband in Westminster Abbey. (Her viscera were separately interred in Lincoln Cathedral beneath a replica of the Westminster monument.) Stone crosses, known subsequently as Eleanor crosses, were erected to mark the stopping-places of her funeral cortege, from Harby in Leicestershire, where she had died in 1290, to Westminster Abbey, the last of these being Charing Cross, where, in Peele's play, Elinor had disappeared into the ground. She did famously give birth to a son, Edward, at half-built Caernarfon Castle in Wales in 1284, accompanying her husband, as she so regularly did, on his military campaigns in Wales. Peele's wholesale disregard of history is part and parcel of his appeal to anti-Catholic and anti-foreign sentiment in the early 1590s. (See Vickers, 2004.)

David and Bathsheba

David and Bathsheba, or *Bethsabe* as Peele spells her name, is his one play based on biblical narrative. Yet it is not the only biblical play of the 1590s. As Annaliese Connolly explains in her essay in Part VI (Chapter 17), biblical drama became a kind of fad in that decade, in part because it offered a practical way for London's acting companies to recycle Marlovian themes of ambition and lust and thus keep up with their audiences' seemingly unquenchable appetite for Tamburlaine-like stories of aspiration and daring. This strategy enabled the acting companies to balance their revivals of Marlowe's plays and others of the same fascinating largeness with new plays on similar themes.

Philip Henslowe's *Diary* documents the currency of biblical plays in the repertory, even if few have survived. For the Admiral's Men's at the Rose and later at the Fortune, these plays provided juicy roles for Edward Alleyn. Along with King David and his adulterous affair with Bathsheba, Old and New Testament narrative highlighted, among many others, such troubled or villainous protagonists as Nebuchadnezzar, Judas Iscariot, Pontius Pilate, Samson, Jephthah (who vowed that if he obtained victory over the Ammonites he would sacrifice to God whatever came to him first out of his house on his return home, only to have his daughter and only child be the one whom came first). Plays on all these subjects, and still more, are recorded by Henslowe. Connolly's essay is somewhat technical, but it gives a significant account of London drama during the last years of Peele's life.

David and Bethsheba offers a clear example of what proved so successful with London audiences. Its multiple account of intemperate lust, voyeurism, adultery, incest, murder, civil conflict, rebellion, usurpation, and penance is lurid enough in outline at least to invite comparison with the horrors depicted in ancient classical drama by Aeschylus, Sophocles, or Seneca. As told in 2 Samuel 11–18, David, King of all Israel, happens one evening upon the beauteous Bathsheba as she is at her bath and conceives a lustful desire for her that can be satiated only by David's ordering that her husband, Uriah the Hittite, be set 'in the forefront of the hottest battle' and left there unprotected in order 'that he may be smitten and die'. Once Bethsheba has finished mourning for her dead husband, she becomes David's wife and bears him a son; however, as the narrator of the biblical account observes, 'The thing that David had done displeased the Lord'. David's remorse is deepened when he is told that his son must die as a consequence of his sin, but is then comforted by the birth of another son, Solomon, to Bathsheba. Yet tragedy strikes again when David's son Amnon deceptively and forcefully rapes his sister Tamar. This crime in turn prompts their brother Absalom to hate Amnon and order his servants to kill the guilty brother. Absalom then flees to a neighbouring kingdom, much to David's dismay. Despite a seeming reconciliation achieved with great difficulty over a period of time, Absalom rises up in rebellion against his father, winning many Israelites to his cause by means of his great physical beauty, and David is obliged to flee for safety. Absalom, not heeding the counsel of Ahithophel (who thereupon hangs himself), goes down to defeat before the army of his father and is slain in the fighting, leaving David to lament, 'O my son Absalom, my son, my son Absalom! Would God I had died for thee, O Absalom, my son, my son!'

The biblical account, as summarized above, makes no attempt to find a causal link between David's troubled story and that of his children. Peele's *David and Bathsheba*, according to Inga-Stina Ewbank's compelling essay on 'The House of David in Renaissance Drama' (Chapter 18), attempts to do just that. Peele's play is not organized by traditional 'rules' of dramatic construction, but it does succeed as a drama by means of its imaginative shape and thematic unity. Renaissance audiences, argues Ewbank, would have been familiar with two responses to the saga of King David. On the one hand, his story was one of the triumph of love over adversity, as in the well-known legends of Alexander (a great commander who learned to control his own amorous passions), Pyramus and Thisbe, and Hero and Leander. Conversely, David had become identified in medieval and Renaissance iconography with the inveterate sinfulness that had been the lot of the human race ever since the Fall in the Garden of Eden. Bathsheba, both victimized and sensuously beautiful, could be seen a figure simultaneously of Eve and of the goddess Venus. Bathsheba was thus both a person of great innocence and a cautionary model of woman as temptress. The story became a natural meeting ground for a fusion of Christian and classical pagan imagery. It embodied the biblical resonance of the Song of Songs together with the eroticism of Ovidian love poetry. The penitential psalms of the Old Testament stood in fruitful tension with the image of Cupid firing his love dart at a naked, golden-haired young woman. David, in this dual interpretation, was both the mighty King of Israel and a penitent sinner. He was an adulterer and murderer who was also forgiven and loved by God. Hans Sachs, among other Renaissance writers, saw David's story as one of sin, penitence, forgiveness, and eventual triumph.

Peele connects the story of David in *David and Bathsheba* to that of the King's own children, in Ewbank's interpretation, by suggesting that David's lechery and the consequent disordering of his royal house reap their grim reward in Amnon's rape of his sister, Absalom's retaliation against his brother Amnon for this outrage, and Absalom's subsequent rebellion against his father and attempted usurpation of the throne. Amnon's crime of incestuous rape is implicitly a re-enactment of the homicidal lust of his father. Peele finds in this family saga a recurrent image of the Fall of Princes through individual failures to live in accord with the dictates of God. By giving the story a neo-Senecan twist, Peele reminds his audience of the great classical heritage of passion, incest, revenge, and fratricide that is so starkly the substance of Seneca's tragedies, and, before Seneca, of the tragedies of Aeschylus, Sophocles, and Euripides. David's revolt against his best self in his lust for Bathsheba engenders a pattern of personal guilt and civil disorder in his own royal family and in his nation. Through his abuse of royal power, argues Ewbank, David even becomes, however briefly, a type of Antichrist.

Yet all is not lost. David's son Solomon, begotten on Bathsheba with the Lord's blessing, will go on to become the mighty king that David imperfectly adumbrates. God works His will in mysterious ways, according to this providential reading of history. The turbulent personal tragedies of David's family are ultimately the historical grounds out of which Solomon will arise to become the true leader of his people. Solomon is thus like the Earl of Richmond in Shakespeare's *Richard III*: a triumphant figure of virtue who mysteriously emerges out of the imperfections and missteps of human experience.

Ewbank's second essay, Chapter 19 on 'Language and Spectacle in the Theatre of George Peele', takes a theatrical approach to the success of Peele's play. A dominant theme in *David and Bathsheba* is wonder – a wonder that appeals to both the eye and the ear. The opening scene of Peele's play, with its spectacle of David's spying of Bathsheba at her bath, is also a feast for the ear with her lovely song asking her Nurse to help shade her fair skin from the burning sun. The song is as sensuous as the Song of Songs; it also betokens her innocence as David '*sits above, viewing her*'. Renaissance drama at its best, in Ewbank's view, is an emblematic art, one in which the values of sexual concupiscence and ravishing female beauty can be held in fruitful balance with considerations of moral restraint. Peele's play is, in these terms, a banquet of the senses that celebrates wonder through its visual and aural appeal. Drama, in Peele's practice, is a vehicle for poetry. It offers the perfect blend of picture and language. *David and Bathsheba* is itself both a poem and a play.

Peele and *Titus Andronicus*

Many critics and scholars today maintain that *Titus Andronicus*, written in the early 1590s, is the product of a collaboration by Shakespeare and Peele. Shakespeare is generally given credit for the overall conception and some big scenes, but Peele is thought by many to have been the author of the opening scene, act 2 scenes 1 and 2 (introducing Aaron the Moor and Tamora's two vicious sons, Chiron and Demetrius), and act 4 scene 1 (in which the ravished and tongueless Tamora is instructed to spell out the names of her assailants in the sand by guiding a staff with her feet and mouth). Much of the innovative scholarship by MacD.P. Jackson (1996), Brian Vickers (2002), and others is rather more technically complex than can easily be digested in a volume of the present sort, but Brian Boyd's essay on the character Mutius in Part VII (Chapter 20) is usefully up to date and clear in its summary of the argument.

Boyd allows, as do others, that the structure of the play as a whole must have been Shakespeare's. Yet traces of Peele's vocabulary, word patterns, and the like are visible in those parts of the play generally thought to be his. Act 1, according to Vickers's investigations, owes much to Peele's Latin education and his knowledgeability about obscure episodes of Roman history, with the result that we find in act 1, as Vickers characterizes it, an 'overambitious display of imperfectly remembered classical learning' (2002). The plural form 'brethren', favoured elsewhere by Peele, turns up eight times more frequently in the parts of the play purportedly by him than 'brothers', the form preferred by Shakespeare and found in his purported assignment. The wording of the stage direction '*and others as many as can be*' is seemingly a mannerism of Peele here and in *Edward I*. The word 'palliament' is apparently an invention of Peele's, occurring here and in his *The Honour of the Garter*, but nowhere else in Renaissance writings. Such are the kinds of evidence amassed to demonstrate the thesis of divided authorship. Jonathan Bate, editor of *Titus* in the new Arden Shakespeare third series (1995), is entirely unpersuaded, but the consensus now favours collaboration. The argument is of genuine interest because collaboration also emerges as a phenomenon in Shakespeare's late career.

Boyd's contribution to the debate is to argue that the killing by Titus of his son Mutius in the play's opening scene is just the sort of thing Shakespeare might well have avoided if he had written the entire play itself. The killing may have satisfied Peele's penchant for symmetry and for the sacrifice of one's children, but it is inconsistent, in Boyd's view, with the character of Titus overall. Later in the play Titus begs mercy for two of his sons even though they appear to be guilty of murder. The slaying of Mutius, on the other hand, is an abrupt and unconsidered response to something far less offensive than murder. Whether or not one finds Boyd's particular argument convincing (since, after all, Titus changes greatly in the course of this tragedy), the essay is a useful illustration of ways in which current scholarship pursues the technically difficult question of sorting out writing assignments in plays of purportedly divided authorship.

Peele's apparent collaboration with Shakespeare in the writing of *Titus Andronicus* makes sense when we consider what Shakespeare may well have learned from this writer for the popular stage who was some eight years his senior. Apart from *Titus*, Shakespeare's early work is devoted to English history plays and romantic comedies. From Peele's *Edward I*, Shakespeare might have seen ways in which he too could combine chronicle history of the late medieval period with unhistorical anecdotes of monarchs designed to present them as frail and human, like Prince Hal in his fondness for Falstaff's roguish company. King Edward's verbal fencing with his queen is a bit like that of Henry V with Katharine of France. *The Battle of Alcazar* offered Shakespeare patterns for sieges and battles and for flamboyant rhetoric in addressing the troops. *The Old Wives' Tale* could suggest ways of interweaving multiple plots in a romantic comedy quite unlike anything that neoclassical comedy had to offer. *David and Bathsheba* showed how a dramatist could transform a tale of adultery and murder into a tragicomic saga of contrition and forgiveness, as in *Cymbeline* and *The Winter's Tale*. *The Arraignment of Paris* showed how history and legend could be put to work in celebrating England's greatness under Queen Elizabeth, as Shakespeare was to do in *Richard III* and *Henry VIII*. Other playwrights of the 1580s like Lyly, Nashe, Lodge, Greene, and of course Marlowe have left their mark on Shakespeare's dramaturgy as well, but Peele deserves to be counted among the host of talents. Shakespeare learned a lot from the University Wits, of whom none was more witty than Peele.

References

Axton, M. (1977), *The Queen's Two Bodies: Drama and the Elizabethan Succession*, London: Royal Historical Society.

Bate, J. (ed.) (1995), *Titus Andronicus*, The Arden Shakespeare, third series, London: Cengage Learning.

Candido, J. (1987), 'Captain Thomas Stukeley: The Man, the Theatrical Record, and the Origins of Tudor "Biographical" Drama', *Anglia*, **105**, pp. 50–68.

Frye, N. (1957), *Anatomy of Criticism: Four Essays*, Princeton NJ: Princeton University Press.

Frye, N. (1965), *A Natural Perspective: The Development of Shakespearean Comedy and Romance*, New York: Columbia University Press.

Gayley, C.M. (ed.) (1903), *Representative English Comedies: From the Beginnings to Shakespeare*, vol. 1 of 4 vols, London: Macmillan.

Jackson, MacD.P. (1996), 'Stage Directions and Speech Headings in Act 1 of *Titus Andronicus* Q (1594): Shakespeare or Peele?', *Studies in Bibliography*, **49**, pp. 134–48.

Levin, R. (1971), *The Multiple Plot in English Renaissance Drama*, Chicago and London: University of Chicago Press.

Lewis, S. and Clapp, C. (1926), 'Peele's Use of Folk-Lore in *The Old Wives' Tale*', *University of Texas Studies in English*, **6**, pp. 146–56.

Mauss, M. (1990). *The Gift: The Form and Reason for Exchange in Archaic Societies*, trans. W.D. Halls, New York: W.W. Norton.

McMillin, S and MacLean, S.-B. (1987), *The Queen's Men and Their Plays*, Cambridge: Cambridge University Press.

Vickers, B. (2002), *Shakespeare, Co-Author: A historical Study of Five Collaborative Plays*, Oxford: Oxford University Press.

Vickers, B. (2004), '*The Troublesome Raigne*, George Peele, and the Date of *King John*', *Words That Count: Essays on Early Modern Authorship in Honor of MacDonald P. Jackson*, ed. Brian Boyd, Newark: University of Delaware Press; Cranbury NJ: Associated University Presses, 2004, 78–116.

Part I
Lord Mayor's Pageants, Court Entertainments, Occasional Poems

[1]

Entertainments for Court and City

A.R. Braunmuller

Public ceremony, festival, show, the drama of street and hall, village green and innyard, permeated Elizabethan life. Many of these events were deliberately, if subtly, political. Ruled and ruling classes expressed their loyalty, their power, and their sense of community in ways generally foreign to modern nation states, especially those states which emphasize the individual rather than a group as the fundamental social unit. A modern citizen's allegiance may still employ public totems—the eagle, lion, or bear, for example—but the emblems have neither a vital connection with a single individual leader nor the power to evoke unified and delimited ideas, attitudes, and meanings. In Elizabethan society—a society divided over religion, the distribution of political authority, and indeed the state's very definition—images of power and ceremonies of mutual responsibility asserted, and even seemed to "prove," the existence of a splendidly reassuring universal order.[1] Court drama, city pageant, and the renewal or invention of medieval and pseudo-medieval public ceremonies all worked to announce and exploit the public values essential for public harmony. Thus, a great deal of what today appears to have been independently conceived "literature" or "art" served also, perhaps even primarily, as propaganda.

Elizabethan patrons might not have stipulated the philosophical and political programs of their artistic employees with quite the tenacity or rigor of Italian princes, but they could trust the power of convention and the purse to "guide" and shape that artistic product. Moreover, the hired artist (like Peele or Lyly) and the amateur one (like Sidney) almost certainly shared the patrons' values and ambitions, at least in general.[2] Consequently, a substantial body of literary and subliterary works promoted various public myths, national self-conceptions, and the half-begged, half-demanded de-

sires of many different social groups. Courtly recreation became not
only a recognized way to affirm larger social, political, and religious
values, but also a means to promote specific policies and to advance
specific individuals.[3] Eager, ambitious, and poor, Peele attempted
to supply what his society seemed to want. At the start of his
professional career, he offered *The Araygnement of Paris* to the court
and sometime later contrived *The Old Wives Tale,* possibly for a
similar audience. He also sold his talents to others, individual and
corporate. Like his father before him, he tapped an important mid-
dle-class and mercantile vein by writing pageants for the annual
installation of London's Lord Mayor, and he exploited some of Elizabeth's most successful minglings of honor and publicity, the elab-
orately revitalized Knights of the Garter and the annual tournaments
celebrating her accession to the throne. This chapter examines Peele's
works deliberately tailored to specific courtly and civic occasions,
the Accession Day tilts, the Lord Mayor's pageants, and the Garter
installation ceremony. These occasional poems provide an excellent
context for two of Peele's finest dramatic works, *The Araygnement of
Paris* and *The Old Wives Tale,* the subjects of the next chapters.

Accession Day Poems

The tilts, or jousts, which marked the anniversary of Elizabeth's
accession, 17 November, were the most spectacular regular public
events of the period. Shortly after the day had been established as
the year's most significant secular holiday, that is, from the early
or mid-1570s, the annual events became elaborate and costly ex-
travaganzas. Roy Strong describes them as "a marriage of the arts
in the service of Elizabethan state-craft," a phrase which describes
virtually every major form of court revel.[4] Like other entertainments,
the Tiltyard shows served as coded exchanges between subjects and
sovereign. Through his choice of armor, supporting cast, and allegorical decoration—for example, the riddling visual motifs painted
on his shield—a nobleman could protest, palliate, request, or advocate some royal action or reaction. Other tilters might amplify,
or challenge, that "speech" to the queen, and she, in turn, might
respond very bluntly or join in the allusive symbolic conversation.
Polyhymnia (1590) and *Anglorum Feriae* (1595) record two Accession Day tilts and introduce very clearly some of the "conversational
formulae" exchanged by court and monarch. A pastoral and chivalric

ambience, for example, or repeated contests requiring the queen to act as an arbiter appear and reappear in the tilts, in the country-house entertainments which Elizabeth saw on her frequent progresses, and *mutatis mutandis* in *The Araygnement of Paris* and many other works of court literature. Just as the country-house entertainments became individually and collectively "a . . . serial . . . in which courtiers cast themselves in whatever rôle suited the moment and their plea,"[5] so too, the tilts apparently develop a slightly disjointed continuous story. This continuity of material and political design appears in all forms of court entertainment and literature. Thus, the "pastoral preoccupation" of the country-house revels and the Tiltyard pageants passes—in demonstrably textual ways—into literature as diverse as *The Arcadia,* the lyric poetry of the 1580s, John Lyly's plays, and *The Araygnement of Paris.*[6]

Peele himself first appears as a recorder, rather than inventor, of court festivities in *Polyhymnia,* his account of the 1590 Accession Day tilt. *Polyhymnia* has the chief advantages of an Elizabethan occasional poem—immediacy, a kind of breathless vivacity—and the main disadvantage—a dreary duty to include every event and every participant. Consequently, Peele divides his poem into sections recording (often in no very specific detail) the combats of thirteen pairs of eminent Elizabethans. Sometimes this journalistic determination makes for a "then-and-then-and-then" structure with hardly any individual features to distinguish the parts. Nonetheless, verbal archaisms do catch the "gothick" quality of Elizabethan nobles pretending to be medieval knights:

> Wherefore it fares as whilom and of yore,
> In armour bright and sheene, faire Englands knights
> In honour of their peerelesse Soveraigne:
> . . . .
> Make to the Tylt amaine. . . . (12–14, 16)

This same early passage underlines the tilt's official and very political purpose: honoring Elizabeth (see also lines 78–79, 90–93, and 172). While every Accession Day tilt made a uniform political statement, they permitted many eccentric individual performances and could simultaneously, as in 1590, seem to create an overall theme.

The unofficial and unannounced theme in 1590 might be called "change and continuity." Peele's chief poetic problem was welding thirteen different but virtually indistinguishable pseudomedieval pseudocombats into some sort of coherence. He took his clue from the 1590 tilt's most prominent event, the retirement of Sir Henry Lee as Queen's Champion, and from the tilt's most extravagant individual display, the earl of Essex's appearance, "all in Sable sad" (98), mourning Sir Philip Sidney's death. Using Cumberland's succession to Lee and Essex's replacement (matrimonial and political) of Sidney, Peele refers the changes within unchanging patterns to the queen herself, *semper eadem,* always the same. To distinguish one pair of combatants from another, Peele chose to emphasize the contrasting colors of their armor and the variety of heraldic detail each combatant bore on his shield.

This emphasis upon appearance—the colors, emblematic details, the order and number of participants—makes *Polyhymnia* a fascinating record of Elizabethan society amid its serious pastimes and reminds us that the slightest detail in such events almost certainly had a significance. Thus, even when Peele cannot explain something, he assumes it has an interpretation: ". . . gentle Gerrarde, all in white and greene, / Collours (belike) best serving his conceit" (56–57).[7] More often, of course, the details of appearance could be explained. Lee's "Caparison charg'd with Crownes, / Oreshadowed with a withered running Vine" (22–23) represents the aged Champion's retirement, and "the golden Eagle" Lord Ferdinando Strange bore was the "Stanleyes olde Crest and honourable badge" (40–41). The choice and use of some costly and often enigmatic emblem or more elaborate decorative scheme pleasantly puzzles the spectators and compliments the sovereign; thus, Peele found William Knowles, "in his plumes, his colours and device, / Expressing Warriors wit and Courtiers grace" (179–80).

Peele's determination to record the tilt's visual aspects produces detailed accounts of the knights' ceremonial entries. Some tilters simply rode into the yard, saluted the queen, and approached the barriers to fight. More costly and elaborate equipment would include a "pageant," or horse-drawn wagon, carrying the tilter and his symbolically clad servants, the tilting horses and armor (usually painted or adorned with emblematic designs), and finally a "Trounchman" (47), or interpreter, to explain the symbolism and present the knight, who then "Dismountes him from his pageant" (50). The "shows" and "devices" often seem like vivified illustrations from contemporary emblem books.[8] Robert Cary entered with a common emblem, a heart surrounded by flames, probably painted on his shield or a scroll (lines 154–58), and Anthony Cooke offers other images familiar from emblem books (lines 189–93). If allegorical interpretations were easy, so were classical and mythological analogies: Robert Knowles appears "with golden boughes" (probably his lances, or perhaps some image on shield or armor), "Entring the listes like Tytan, arm'd with fire, / When in the queachy plot Python he slew" (211–13) and Thomas Sidney "So well behav'd himselfe . . . As Paris had to great Achilles Launce / Applied his tender fingers and his force" (242–44).

The most extravagant "show" of the tilt belonged to the earl of Essex and commemorated the friend, Philip Sidney, whose widow Essex had married and whose political and "mythological" heir he hoped to be.[9] Peele carefully surrounds the central event with details of other tilters' bright, contrasting colors—red and green for Lord Burgh and Edward Denny, Lord Strange's gold, "Or and Azure" and "Orenge-tawnie" for Sir Charles Blunt and Thomas Vavasor. The color contrast and a long grammatical suspension which refuses to name the subject intensify the entry's surprise:

> Then proudly shocks amid the Martiall throng,
> Of lustie Lancieres, all in Sable sad,
> Drawen on with cole-blacke Steeds of duskie hue,
> In stately Chariot full of deepe device,
> Where gloomie Time sat whipping on the teame,
> Just backe to backe with this great Champion;
> Yoong Essex, that thrice honorable Earle,
> Yclad in mightie Armes of mourners hue,
> And plume as blacke as is the Ravens wing,
> That from his armour borrowed such a light,
> As bowes of Vu [Yew] receives from shady streame,
> His staves were such, or of such hue at least,
> As are those banner staves that mourners beare,
> And all his companie in funerall blacke,
> As if he mourn'd to thinke of him he mist,
> Sweete Sydney, fairest shepheard of our greene,
> Well lettred Warriour, whose successor he
> In love and Armes had ever vowed to be. (97–114)

Peele's affection for Sidney, mentioned in lines 225–26, and his profound admiration for Essex give this passage an unusual density and attractiveness.[10] Varying hues of black and the pageant's funereal purpose allow two nicely judged similes: the black colors reflect one another as a stream's dark waters reflect the symbolically mournful yew tree, while the banners Essex's servants carry remind Peele of the banners carried in Sidney's own funeral procession. Time hastens us all toward death: first Sidney and now his dear friend making this ceremonial and memorial entry.

Essex's magnificent "device" echoes throughout the poem. Thomas Knollys, a "friend and follower" of Essex, also appears "In mourning Sable dight by simpathie" (201), and Cooke of course portrayed "Life and Death . . . in his show" (189). Despite time's destruction and sorrow's shows, Peele ends his description of the tilt by promising renewal and perpetuation because 17 November is "that golden time . . . the byrth-day of our happinesse, / The blooming time, the spring of Englands peace" (262–64).

After the tilt comes a coda describing Sir Henry Lee's resignation. The elderly knight tells the Queen

> He would betake him to his Oraysons:
> And spend the remnant of his waining age,
> (Unfit for warres and Martiall exploites)
> In praiers for her endlesse happines. (296–99)

Lee then advances Cumberland as his replacement, and Elizabeth (now employing couplets) "seem'd to say,"

> Good Woodman, though thy greene be turn'd to gray,
> Thy age past Aprils prime, and pleasant May:
> Have thy request, we take him [Cumberland] at thy praise,
> May he succeed the honour of thy daies. (301–4)[11]

Age, retirement, and death are not conclusions, but the springs of renewal: "many Champions such may England live to have / And daies and yeares as many such, as she in heart can crave" (308–9). The suddenly longer lines in poulter's measure mimic the extension of Elizabeth's reign "beyond" iambic pentameter, just as the couplet and the ceremony serve to conclude the poem. Change—Sidney's death or Lee's retirement—takes place within a secure frame—the tilt, England's peace, Elizabeth's immutable nature—which provides continuity.

Peele's poem celebrating the tilt of 1595, *Anglorum Feriae,* survives only in an autograph manuscript dedicated to Katherine, countess of Huntingdon.[12] Peele may have chosen the countess because she was Northumberland's daughter and therefore a potential source of reward as her father had been for *The Honour of the Garter* (1593). Given the poem's character, however, a political explanation is also possible. The countess's husband, Henry Hastings, third earl, was Lord President of the North until his death on 14 December 1595 and a strong Puritan and noted priest-hunter.[13] Intense patriotism and Protestant sympathies would be appropriate in the dedicatee because the poem is more topical than *Polyhymnia* and much less detailed in its description of the tilt's events. In fact, the tilt is first mentioned at line 163, almost halfway through the poem. The opening sections hardly prepare the reader for the second half. Instead, a series of blank-verse paragraphs, each ending in a couplet, reviews Queen Elizabeth's career and defines her place in English society and English hearts.

Behind the extravagant praise of Elizabeth and equally extravagant condemnation of England's foes, one senses how radically Peele's poetic program has changed since he wrote *Polyhymnia.* That change arises from the social, political, and religious crises which had forced themselves on public attention in the five years since *Polyhymnia.* In 1590, the queen, the court, and the people were still united in the aftermath of the Armada. Or if they were not entirely in accord, they could nonetheless be portrayed that way, as Peele does in *A Farewell . . . to . . . Norris and . . . Drake* (1589). Essex might mourn Sidney, and the spectators sympathize, but there was little reason to doubt—again, publicly—that the future would be any different from or any worse than the past. Without straining the facts unacceptably, *Polyhymnia* could envision an almost immutable aristocratic and royal future, effortlessly resisting foreign and native threats. The period between 1590 and 1595 had, however, made that vision much less certain. Essex's own efforts to advance himself and his friends, his intemperance, and his glamour had all begun to disturb the courtly and political balance which the older generation of Elizabethan politicians and aristocrats had forged. Many of the great names were gone: Leicester, Walsingham, Hatton. In their place appeared men not less able, but less adept at cloaking self-interest in public duty.

If the court began to seem a less secure place, so too did other areas of society. The festering problem of religious schism—the challenge to central authority posed by both radical Protestantism and clandestine Roman Catholicism—now produced serious and very public threats. These difficulties had surfaced before, in the Babington conspiracy to free Mary Queen of Scots, for example, and earlier in the revolt of various Roman Catholic nobles, but religious issues now found a twin focus: the problem of Elizabeth's successor and Parliament's outspoken desire for religious reform. Whispers and more than whispers of Spanish-sponsored plots against Elizabeth's life reached the government. On slender evidence and perhaps chiefly to feed Essex's *amour propre,* the queen's physician, Roderigo Lopez, was executed for conspiring to poison her. Other plots and other conspirators, some madcap and some deadly, were uncovered.[14] Exiled English Roman Catholics bombarded their co-religionists with propaganda from various Continental towns and seminaries and sent many priests into England secretly. The poet-priest Robert Southwell, for example, was arrested, tortured, and executed in February 1595, and another Jesuit, Robert Parsons, helped to write the seditious *Conference about the next Succession,* arguing the Spanish claim on the English throne. The book began to circulate in England around September of 1595.[15]

Religious belief and political activity went hand in hand among the more radical Protestants, too. Peter Wentworth repeatedly (and loyally) raised troublesome issues of Parliament's independence, of the Church's organization, and of the need to determine Elizabeth's successor before her death. Wentworth and a number of like-minded men went to the Tower for their pains, and Parliament was obliged to pass the last and in some ways most stringent religious legislation of the period, the "Act to retain the Queen Majesty's subjects in their due obedience" (1593).[16]

All these upheavals and more define the context of *Anglorum Feriae.* Doubtless each separate problem had appeared in the past, often decades in the past, but in 1595 it was certainly possible to feel—as Peele apparently did—that many single troubles had begun to unite into battalions. Such a conviction makes the poem's tone and structure explicable. Before reaching his nominal subject, the tilt, Peele invokes the muse of history, Clio, "sagest of these sisters nine," and invites her to "Elizaes Coort, Astraeas earthlie heaven" (6, 8). The verbal repetition which marks the poem's first half soon appears: "Write write you Croniclers of Tyme and Fame, / Elizabeth by miracles preserved" (17–18). The next three verse paragraphs record Elizabeth's life before the coronation (55–74), her anointed accession to "hir kingly Fathers seate" (75–93), and London's special love, the "holy tunes and sacrifize of thankes, / Englandes Metropolis as incense sendes" (94–113). Loyal and well-written as each paragraph is, the poem becomes almost a guide to the tilt's propagandistic, metaphorical, and political meanings. *Anglorum Feriae* analyzes values.

The gaudy trappings which fill *Polyhymnia* are not entirely forgotten, of course. Clio and her sisters (or perhaps all Englishwomen) must become emblematic Tudors: "weare Eglantine / And wreathes of Roses red and white" (39–40). Despite the rustic touches— "Lovely Shepherdes" dance "alonge the chaulkie clyffes of Albion" (43–44)—the day's true tenor cannot be long ignored: "Clio recorde howe shee hathe bin preserved / Even in the gates of deathe and from hir youthe, / to govern Englande in the waies of Truthe" (56– 58). Religious allusions emphasize the special Providence which guards England and equally stress Elizabeth's personal importance to her people's faith.[17] Mention of religious schism naturally prompts thoughts of Henry VIII, who founded the national church, and of foreign religious enemies. Peele lightly omits Edward VI and Mary in order to place Henry's "massie scepter and that swoorde / that awed the worlde" (78–79) directly in his younger daughter's hand. These instruments have driven "the daringe foe / back to his Den . . . weried with wars by lande and wrack by sea" (81–83); thus England's escape from the Armada and her more equivocal military successes in France and the Low Countries are made to confirm the nation's faith and Elizabeth's right to rule.

Peele meets the twin issues of religion and succession more openly in the paragraph following the personification of "Londons Shepherde Gardian." Abstract loyalty becomes concrete: "in sympathie and sweete accorde / all loyall subjects joine" (114–15). More specifically yet, Elizabeth's subjects give thanks for

> . . . That day whereon this Queen
> inaugured was and hollyly installd
> anointed of the highest kinge of kinges
> in hir hereditarie royall righte
> successively to sit enthronized. . . . (120–24)

The passage sounds like a contribution to the pamphlet warfare over the succession. Such phrases as "hollyly installd" and "hereditarie royall righte" are not complimentary small coins, but the language of political controversy and crisis. Polemic surges through the personification of "pale Envie" which flees England "to murmur that abroade / hee durst not openly disgorge at home" (130–31). "Envy" of course is that body of English Roman Catholics who undertook to minister to the spiritual needs of their fellows in England and in so doing "revolt from their allegeance" (140). Freed of their duty to Elizabeth by the papal bull which excommunicated her, these men are "condemned amonge the Turkes and infidells" (142). Invited by Catholic propaganda to overthrow the English government, they become "false Architects of . . . bloodie stratagems" (143, 145) and "cruell seige they laie unto hir life" (146).

The near hysteria and lurid language contrast markedly with Peele's usual poise and often rather pallid diction. However uncharacteristic, this violent outburst forms the poem's logical hinge. Now, at last, we reach the tilters who are introduced as a "troupe of Loyall English knightes . . . reddy to do their Duties . . . against the mightiest enemie shee [Elizabeth] hathe" (159, 164, 165). After renegade traitors, a representative band of true knights and true Englishmen appears. Their leader, of course, is the earl of Cumberland, the man who replaced Sir Henry Lee as "Knighte of the crowne" (173), and Peele alludes gracefully to the family seat, Pendragon Castle: "his Holde / Kept by a Dragon laden with faire spoiles" (175–76). Although Peele just manages to include the names of all twenty participants, *Anglorum Feriae* gives much less detail of the tilt than *Polyhymnia*. There remain obligatory references to classical myth and heroes (e.g., "K[ing] Priams Valeant sonnes" in line 266), but romance references predominate. *Polyhymnia* described the sons of Francis Knollys as "Horatii" or the sons of "olde Duke Aymon," an allusion to *Les Quatre Fils Aymon,* a French romance. *Anglorum Feriae* exploits medieval legend and romance more frequently. Peele makes a typical romance pun on Sir James Skidmore's name, just as Spenser seems to do: "Le Scu d'Amour: The armes of Loialtie / lodgd Skydmore in his harte" (319–20).[18] Shakespeare's patron, the earl of Southampton, recalls an earlier hero: "South Hampton ran / as Bevis of South Hampton that good knighte" (227–28). More British legend appears with Knollys's three sons: "they showed as were K[ing] Arthures knightes / he whilom usd to feast at Camilot" (264–65). Although the tilt's pseudomedievalism may domesticate these allusions, the contemporary threat of foreign aggression makes native hero-worship more apt in 1595 than it would have been in 1590. Even more than *Polyhymnia*, *Anglorum Feriae* stresses tradition, England's ancient peace, and the monarchy's long history.

Five years have not changed Essex's character, and once again he has the grandest show. Renowned for both "wisdome in his younger yeares / and Love to armes" (192–93), Essex enters apparelled in appropriate Tudor colors, "white and faire carnacion" (191). A contemporary observer wrote that Essex's device was "much commended," as well it might be since Francis Bacon apparently wrote most of it.[19] Having entered the Tiltyard, Essex met three representative figures: a hermit, a Secretary (or politician), and a Soldier. An interpreter's speech explained that each figure "sollicited diversly" (196) the earl, urging their respective careers. Although Peele politely comments that any choice Essex makes "shall his nobilitie become" (205), the knowledgeable spectator could hardly miss the hint that Essex was uncertain about how to direct his energies. Given his past military escapades and his intense efforts to become politically indispensable to Elizabeth, the show might also hold the threat of independent, rebellious action or (equally disobedient) a refusal to participate in public life if his desires were unsatisfied. The queen and many courtiers would know, moreover, that Essex had recently suffered two notable defeats in his attempts to win Bacon high legal office: first Coke became Attorney General and then, only twelve days before the tilt, Fleming gained the Solicitor General's post. Essex had supported Bacon's candidacy for both.[20] Thus, the public ceremony which expressed so many royal attitudes and values once again served to expound a personal crisis as well. Essex's little psychomachia had a happy ending. At the banquet following the tilt, a page delivered a speech declaring that Elizabeth's service surpassed and combined the alternatives Essex had faced in the Tiltyard. According to Rowland Whyte, the queen was bored that evening, but others—especially Essex's colleagues on the Privy Council—must have been relieved that this ambitious and unpredictable nobleman professed fidelity, at least for now.

After the intensely anxious tone of the first half, *Anglorum Feriae* settles into a more documentary mode. Only Essex's show implicitly reminds us of political maneuver and ambition. The festival itself reassures the poet, just as it aimed to reassure the spectators. Ceremonial order, loyal jousting, the queen's life-giving powers—all these qualities balance and overcome the fears of assassination, of foreign attack, and of religious discord which fill the poem's opening. At the very end, however, Peele's obligatory prayer for perpetual happiness once more edges from hyperbole into near hysteria:

> Longe may they run in honor of the Day
> Longe may shee live to do them honors right
> to grace their sportes and them as shee hath donne
> Englands Astraea Albions shininge Sunne.
> and may shee shine in beautie freshe and sheene
> Hundreds of yeares our thrice renowmed queen. (328–33)

To hope that the sixty-three-year-old Elizabeth might reign for "Hundreds of yeares" is unnecessarily fatuous. Even a poem tied to the rules of flattery could avoid such inelegant excess, just as it could avoid the triple repetition of "write." Once again, contemporary dangers frighten the poet, and he retreats into formula, almost incantation. Within the grand display itself, a spectator might find Essex's device a troubling hint of instability. In 1601, two of the day's tilters would die as rebels against their queen. *Anglorum Feriae* is probably Peele's last surviving work, and like his other writings it mirrors his increasingly apprehensive and fragmented society.

Lord Mayor's Pageants

The two poems on the Accession Day tilts have both literary and historical value. *Anglorum Feriae* especially is a fine occasional poem; and together the poems are also the fullest surviving accounts of these important events. Peele's scripts, or scenarios, for pageants marking the annual installations of London's Lord Mayors have some remarkable parallels with the tilt poems. "The Device of the Pageant Borne before Wolstan Dixi" (1585) is the first complete surviving text for such an occasion, and *Descensus Astraeae* (1591) is the first to have its own title and therefore to claim a place as an independent creative work rather than as a piece of civic public relations.[21] The parallels extend beyond coincidence. The Dixi pageant is a simple praise of London and Elizabeth and their mutual loyalty and affection. In it, Peele describes a relation between citizen and queen very like the relation between noble and queen in *Polyhymnia,* and the pageant's emotive moments resurface in the fervent passage devoted to London in *Anglorum Feriae.* With *Descensus Astraeae,* however, he approaches the more ambiguous atmosphere of *Anglorum Feriae's* overt political and social commentary. These similarities arise from Peele's own preoccupations and from the fact that the Lord Mayor's pageants were the civic equivalent of various court entertainments.[22] Consequently, both forms often employ similar tactics to praise and admonish the spectators or to debate contemporary issues.

London's Lord Mayors were selected from the members of her twelve great livery companies, or guilds, and the inauguree's company spent large sums of money on the public procession which welcomed their member on the day of his installation, 29 October. Great care and energy went into selecting the men to write the script (or "device") and to construct the actual pageant itself, carried by porters in the procession.[23] Each company naturally wanted to advertise itself as well as the new Lord Mayor, so the pageants often included references to the company and to the mayor's name. Wolstan Dixi was a member of the Skinners' Company, whose emblem was a lynx or "lucerne." Thus, in the 1585 pageant, the "Presenter" (an interpreter similar to the "Trounch-man" who preceded some knights into the Tiltyard) appears riding on "a Luzarne," probably made of plaster and lath. The procession also typically included "wildmen," legendary giants, devils, and other exotic personages: in 1585, the Presenter was *apparelled like a Moore.*[24] The Presenter calls the allegorical figures on the pageant "This Emblem" (8) and provides a brief synopsis of their meaning. He emphasizes the "Service of Honour and of Loyaltie" London owes the sovereign and then describes the various figures—a franklin, a farmer, a soldier, and a sailor, for example, along with a "reverend honorable Dame, / Science [Knowledge] the sap of every common wealth" (29–30)— who contribute to London's prosperity and safety. The opening speech advises the new mayor: "This now remaines right honourable Lord, / That carefully you doo attend and Keep, / This lovely Lady [London] rich and beautifull" (43–45).

Now it is the turn of the children seated on the pageant to speak their various pieces. London herself is represented along with "The Thames," "The Cuntry" (that is, London's economic hinterland), "Magnanimity," and "Loyaltie." To distinguish these speeches from the Presenter's blank verse, Peele gives the children varied prosodic

forms, usually six-line iambic-pentameter stanzas rhyming *a b a b c c.*
The pageant ends with four nymphs, each bearing a lighted torch
and praying for Elizabeth's honor and continued happiness. The
script does little more than mouth the expected platitudes of con-
gratulation, loyalty, and social interdependence, and it has no "plot"
or structure other than a simple honoring of Queen, Lord Mayor,
and City.

   The same cannot be said for *Descensus Astraeae.* The passage of six
years, growing social and political difficulties, and Peele's evident
attempt to make the pageant a work of art as well as publicity
produce the most sophisticated of the Elizabethan Lord Mayor's
pageants. Peele introduces a rudimentary plot concerning the social
and political forces arrayed against Queen Elizabeth, and to the
morality-abstractions of the Dixi pageant he now adds several figures
from classical mythology. Principally, he draws upon the classical
myth of "Astraea daughter of the immortall Jove" (14), a shepherdess, according to Peele, who lived on earth during the Golden Age,
but when "yron age had kindled cruel warres . . . the thundring
Jove, / raught hence this gracious nymph" (67, 70–71) and took
her up to heaven. As the title indicates, this pageant will show the
return of Astraea to earth, signaling the return of the Golden Age
itself. Naturally, there can be no question of Astraea's identity:
"heere she sits in beautie fresh and sheene, / Shadowing the person
of a peerelesse Queene" (74–75). In short, Elizabeth is Astraea, or
as *Anglorum Feriae* puts it: "Englands Astraea Albions shininge
Sunne." The primary literary source for the Astraea myth and its
pastoral accoutrements is Vergil's Eclogue IV, which many Christian
readers interpreted as a prediction of the coming of the Savior.

   As the Accession Day tilts and Peele's own *Araygnement of Paris*
show, the search for pagan and mythological figures to describe
Queen Elizabeth was a general literary preoccupation. That Astraea
should appear in a civic pageant, carefully explained for a public
which lacked classical training, gives the myth much more than a
courtly or purely complimentary value.[25] *Anglorum Feriae* clearly
indicates that the 1590s were a period of great anxiety. Worries
over the succession, religious controversy, increasing economic difficulties exacerbated by foreign wars and bad harvests, the loss of
an older, reassuring generation of senior politicians—all these factors
had begun to seep into public ceremonies and festivals. In short,
London and England needed the image of Elizabeth-Astraea as much

as the court for its own propagandistic and sycophantic purposes also needed that image.

Political and religious issues are at the heart of *Descensus Astraeae.* As the Presenter ends his speech with a catalog of popular leaders— Caesar, Pompey, Alexander, Hector—each of whom contributes some quality to the paragon Elizabeth, he explicitly mentions foreign Protestant friends (at this time, the Dutch and French) who need assistance: "Strengthen thy neighbours, propagate thine owne" (49). Astraea *"with hir sheephook"* (alluding to both the pastoral and Christian meanings of her myth) addresses the London-folk, urging them to "Pay to immortall Jove immortall thankes" (57) for peace and prosperity. The pageant then alternates between the forces of disruption and the allegorical figures who support Elizabeth's reign. Sitting by a fountain on the pageant's platform, *"Superstition. A Friar"* and *"Ignorance. A Priest"* attempt to poison the commonwealth's life-giving well, but Astraea-Elizabeth's glorious chastity holds them rapt and ineffective: "It is in vaine hir eye keepes me in awe" (62). A carefully selected group of pagan, Christian, and chivalric figures now hymns Elizabeth's praises: first the three Graces, then the three theological virtues (Charity, Hope, and Faith), and finally Honor and "Champion." This last figure, perhaps alluding to the Queen's Champion (as in the tilts) or to the giants who often accompanied the pageant, vows to "Breath terror to the proud aspiring foe" (102) and assures Elizabeth she will suffer no harm from the last threatening persons, two "Malecontents." These native enemies admit that they "faint and quaile, / For mightie is the truth and will prevaile" (112–13).[26]

True to her celestial origin, Astraea-Elizabeth surpasses the mundane disputes and protectors we have seen. All nature, time, and fortune concur to "Produce hir yeares to make them numberlesse" (34). Astraea descends to inaugurate a period of happiness and peace in the midst of England's troubles. Peele's show takes a number of contemporary difficulties and blends them into a reassuring pageant. More overtly than most civic pageants, *Descensus Astraeae* uses the materials and expresses the contemporary concerns which also appear in court entertainments.

Occasional Court Poems

Peele's intense patriotism and his political awareness appear throughout the civic pageants, the Accession Day poems, and even the minor poems written to celebrate the departure of Drake and Norris for Portugal or for Essex's return from that ill-starred adventure. Political sympathy, love of nation, and professional ambition all mingle inextricably. Peele offered what his clients wanted, and he wanted what they wanted. In these matters his finest occasional poem, *The Honour of the Garter* (1593), is no different, but Peele now responds to a major political and social event more personally. Although Edward III founded the Order of the Garter about 1344, its ceremonies and especially the crowd-pleasing procession of the knights were revived and developed under the Tudors. Elizabeth made "deliberate use of the Garter to create another Day in honour" of herself and her knights.[27]

The gorgeous ceremonial show of 26 June 1593 obviously intrigued the poet, and he provides a virtual guidebook not only to that particular installation of five men as Knights of the Garter, but to the order's entire history. At the same time, he seeks to honor one man specifically, Henry Percy, ninth earl of Northumberland, who paid him £3 for the poem commemorating his own installation.[28] Northumberland befriended many "artizans and schollers," and his own reputation as a student of "Mathematique skill" and "of Trismegistus and Pythagoras" (Prologue, 6, 8, and 14) earned him the contemporary nickname of "the Wizard Earl." The happy economic fortune of a commission also allowed Peele to frame his poem with a prologue and epilogue speaking directly to Northumberland, the "Muses love, Patrone, and favoret" (Prol., 5), about contemporary poetry. Poetry is in a sorry state. Her patrons, "liberall Sidney, famous for the love / He bare to learning and to Chivalrie; / And vertuous Walsingham" (Prol., 36–38), are dead, and Peele wonders why all the other poets he names have not fled a "world, / That favours Pan and Phoebus both alike" (Prol., 52–53).[29] Only Northumberland remains, a "Heroycall" spirit in "these unhappy times," to support "learning . . . with glorious hands" (Prol., 23–25).

Biased though Peele may be, it is still quite extraordinary to regard literary patronage as the distinguishing mark of "Heroycall spirites." Peele makes a political statement as well as an economic plea or professional observation when he singles out three men eminent for their radicalism—Sidney, Walsingham, and the suspiciously learned and occult-leaning Northumberland. Alongside the prologue's compliments and its age-old cry for more support, there runs a more subtle argument which connects political failings with the collapse of patronage. The only hope for poets left behind in this "Center, barren of repast" is that "Augusta," Queen Elizabeth herself, "will restore, / The wrongs that learning beares of covetousnes / And Courts disdaine, the enemie to Arte" (Prol., 65–68). "Covetousness" and "disdain" are synonyms, in this context, for "envy," a word threaded through the poem itself, and each term applies equally to vilified art and political chicanery. Just as the poem honoring the Garter sees Elizabeth as a new Edward III restoring the Order, so, too, perhaps will come a new age of patronage, a restoration of learning.

By addressing Northumberland directly and naming contemporary poets and their misfortunes, Peele gives the poem a highly personal cast. This quality continues in the form—a dream-vision—he chooses to celebrate "The Honour of the Honourable Order of the Garter." Peele imagines a massive, almost eternal Garter procession, stretching from the Order's founding to the present day. As the dream-procession passes through the sky, making its way to Windsor Castle, seat of the Order of the Garter, Peele recalls the romantic anecdote of the garter's origin (lines 112–31). Later, "Fame" shows the dreamer "a golden Booke," a "Register . . . Consecrate to S. Georges chosen Knights" (173, 181–82). This register allows Peele to identify the famous knights who follow Edward III in the heavenly concourse; he lists them all, "the first / Created of that order by the King" (232–33). Even here, contemporary Elizabethan matters are not far away. In order to insinuate a comment on the Elizabethan earl of Southampton, Peele makes his ancestor (incorrectly)[30] one of the original Knights of the Garter (lines 210–18). As he did in describing the Accession Day tilts, Peele has understood completely the contemporary political value of revived medieval ceremony. Delight as they may in the spectacle, neither the poet nor the more thoughtful of his readers can miss the implied connections: Edward III and Elizabeth I; ancient loyalty and modern duty; ancestral heroism and contemporary courage. Placing a fictitious earl of Southampton among Edward's train is, in fact, the literary equivalent of dressing modern political issues in fancy armor or, more humbly, in the allegorical personifications of the Lord Mayor's pageant.

As witness and recorder, Peele can shape the poem to link the Order of the Garter with the status of poetry. Honor, fame, glorious accomplishment, *and* poetry suffer the same detraction: "Yet in the house of Fame and Courtes of Kings, / Envy will bite, or snarle and barke" (340–41). In Peele's imagination, Edward must assure his knights that their names will remain registered "Out of Oblivions reach, or Envies shot" (411). With the brief Epilogue, the strategy becomes clear. The poem compliments Northumberland and honors the Garter, but it redirects that honor toward the poet's social role and station:

> And then thought I: were it as once it was,
> But long agoe, when learning was in price,
> And Poesie with Princes gracious:
> I would adventure to set downe my dreame,
> In honour of these newe advaunced Lords
> S. Georges Knights. I was encouraged
> And did as I have doone. . . . (Epilogue, 2–8)

The Elizabethan revival of the Order of the Garter is unquestionably part of the period's politics as well as part of its hankering after romantic chivalry. Peele seized these facts as an opportunity to make poetry and political life parallel. Patronage *is* heroical. Just as a self-conscious and mildly *ersatz* medievalism may assist modern political propaganda (or truth, as Peele probably believed), so too the poet may employ the same tactic to restore a long-lost respect for his art.

Conclusion

In these courtly and civic poems, Peele is more than a hack journalist or Grub Street penny-a-word man. The earl of Northumberland's three pounds, or the money paid by the Salters' or Skinners' Company, were vital, no doubt. At the same time, Peele shared the social, religious, and political anxieties of his particularly anxious time, and these concerns appear again and again in his poems. Sometimes, as in *Anglorum Feriae*, they even seem to unbalance the poem; on the other occasions, as in *Descensus Astraeae*, the full design may have escaped its principal audience. Throughout all these poems, it is nonetheless possible to trace a professional poet's attempt to earn a living, to give value for money, and to express his culture's abiding interests. He certainly understood the way in which public ceremony has a social function, and he was no less adept when inventing fictions for the court, as *The Araygnement of Paris* and *The Old Wives Tale* show.

Notes

1. For the general argument and many illustrative details, see, respectively: E. W. Talbert, *The Problem of Order* (Chapel Hill: University of North Carolina Press, 1962); Stephen Orgel, *The Illusion of Power: Political Theater in the English Renaissance* (Berkeley and Los Angeles: University of California Press, 1975); Marie Axton, "The Tudor Mask and Elizabethan Court Drama" in Marie Axton and Raymond Williams, eds., *English Drama: Forms and Development* (Cambridge: Cambridge University Press, 1977), pp. 24–47.

2. See Hunter, *John Lyly,* and Daniel Javitch, *Poetry and Courtliness in Renaissance England* (Princeton: Princeton University Press, 1978).

3. A famous example is Elizabeth's response to an entertainment allegorically urging her marriage: "This is all aimed at me" (see Martin Hume, ed., *Calendar of Letters and State Papers . . . preserved in . . . Simancas, 1558–1567* [London: H. M. Stationery Office, 1892], pp. 404–5). Marie Axton analyzes many politically oriented entertainments, especially those at the Inns of Court, in *The Queen's Two Bodies: Drama and the Elizabethan Succession* (London, 1977).

4. Roy Strong, *The Cult of Elizabeth: Elizabethan Portraiture and Pageantry* (London, 1977), p. 129; see Chapter 4. For the celebration's origin, see John Neale, *Essays in Elizabethan History* (New York, 1958), pp. 45–58.

5. M. C. Bradbrook, *The Rise of the Common Player* (London: Chatto and Windus, 1962), p. 251, commenting on the Kenilworth entertain-

ment (1575), but the argument could be extended to connect that entertainment with the one at Woodstock (1592) and Ben Jonson's *Mask of Owls* (1624). See also Axton, "The Tudor Mask," p. 25, and, for tilts, Strong, *The Cult of Elizabeth,* pp. 139–40.

6. The quoted phrase comes from Strong, *The Cult of Elizabeth,* p. 149; see also Bradbrook, *Rise of the Common Player,* p. 247; J. H. Hanford and S. R. Watson, "Personal Allegory in the *Arcadia:* Philisides and Lelius," *Modern Philology* 32 (1934):1–10; Frances Yates, *Astraea: The Imperial Theme in the Sixteenth Century* (London, 1975), pp. 29–111.

7. Gerrarde intends to compliment Elizabeth (green and white were Tudor colors), and his choice recalls a tournament-challenge claiming green and white were not the best colors in Thomas Blenerhasset's *A Revelation of the True Minerva* (1582), a poem filled with allusions to Elizabethan court festivals.

8. The influence may sometimes have gone from tilt-devices into emblem books; see Strong, *The Cult of Elizabeth,* pp. 144–45.

9. Strong believes a portrait of Essex as he appeared at the 1590 Tilt survives (see *Cult of Elizabeth,* illus. 39); more persuasively, Strong argues that Essex's show attempted to palliate Elizabeth's anger at his recent marriage (ibid., p. 152).

10. Peele's nearly contemporary poem *An Eglogue Gratulatorie* (1589) welcomes Essex home from that year's abortive Portuguese expedition. Peele describes him in adulatory pastoral terms as "a great Herdgroome . . . but no swaine, / Save hers that is the Flowre of Phaebes plaine" (48–49). The dialogue devotes three stanzas to the fact that Essex was "Fellow in Armes . . . With that great Shepherd good Philisides" (i.e., Sidney) and finds that in Essex "all his [Sidney's] Vertues sweet reviven bee" (61–62, 74).

11. These lines were originally printed in italics to indicate semiquotation. The phrase "Good Woodman" probably refers to Lee's status as Lieutenant of the Manor of Woodstock, a royal appointment which included the titles "Ranger of the Park and Master of the Game"; see Edmund K. Chambers, *Sir Henry Lee: An Elizabethan Portrait* (Oxford: Clarendon Press, 1936), p. 81. Lee's mention of "his Oraysons" is part of a pattern begun in his 1575 entertainment for Elizabeth and continued in the entertainment of 1592, where he is explicitly called an "owlde Knight, nowe a newe religious Hermite." See A. W. Pollard, ed., *The Queen's Majesty's Entertainment at Woodstock in 1575* (Oxford: n.p., 1903, 1910) and Chambers, *Sir Henry Lee,* pp. 276–97.

12. The manuscript is British Library Additional MS. 21432 (see Frontispiece). Some sections are now illegible; for these portions, the only source is W. S. Fitch's unreliable transcript (printed in Ipswich, ca. 1831). The Yale edition brackets lines deriving from Fitch's transcript, but I have

omitted the brackets. The Yale edition also silently expands abbreviations and does not note Peele's own corrections and changes; I have silently corrected a few errors in the edition.

13. Hastings "leaped for joy," we are told, when Father Henry Walpole broke under interrogation and led his captors to some cached documents; see Mary A. E. Green, ed., *Calendar of State Papers, Domestic Series . . . 1591–1594* (London: H. M. Stationery Office, 1867), p. 417. Since Peele's dedication does not mention Hastings, it probably postdates his death; the countess was a member of the Sidney family, perhaps another reason for Peele's admiration.

14. For a general survey of these episodes, see Martin Hume, *Treason and Plot: Struggles for Catholic Supremacy in the Last Years of Queen Elizabeth* (London: Nisbet, 1901), Chapters 4 and 5.

15. See Arthur Collins, comp., *Letters and Memorials of State,* 2 vols. (London: Osborne, 1746), 1:350.

16. For Wentworth's troubles and the debate over the Act of 1593, see John E. Neale, *Elizabeth I and Her Parliaments 1584–1601* (London: Cape, 1957), pp. 251–66 and 180–97.

17. The coronation entry of 1559 bluntly acknowledges the queen's personal involvement in England's spiritual health; in one pageant she seems indeed to be Time's daughter, Truth. That coronation followed the terrible Marian persecutions, and Peele may be worried, here and elsewhere, that the country now faces similar troubles. See John Nichols, *The Progresses and Public Processions of Queen Elizabeth,* 2d ed., 3 vols. (London: Nichols and Son, 1823), 1:38–60, and Sydney Anglo, *Spectacle, Pageantry, and Early Tudor Policy* (Oxford: Clarendon Press, 1969), pp. 257–58.

18. The pun turns on *écu* and *écusson* ("coat of arms"), cognate with "escutcheon"; cf. *Faerie Queene,* IV:x, and William Higford, *Institution of a Gentleman* (London: W. Lee, 1660), pp. 69–70, which describes this James Skidmore's appearances in the Tiltyard. For the tilts' "neo-medievalism," see Yates, *Astraea,* pp. 108–10, and Strong, *The Cult of Elizabeth,* pp. 161–62.

19. See Rowland Whyte's letter of 22 November 1595 in Collins, *Letters and Memorials,* 1:362; for Bacon's contribution, see James Spedding, Robert Ellis, and Douglas Heath, eds., *The Works of Francis Bacon,* 14 vols. (London: Longman, Green, 1857–74), 8:374–86, and Strong, *The Cult of Elizabeth,* p. 209.

20. For the general outlines of this episode, see John E. Neale, *Queen Elizabeth I* (1934; rev., London: Cape, 1967), pp. 334–36.

21. Some of the printed texts seemed to have been intended as souvenirs of and/or guides to the pageants. Many basic documents and facts are collected in Robertson and Gordon, "A Calendar of Dramatic Records." Peele also wrote a pageant in 1588 (now lost) and probably wrote the

138   GEORGE PEELE

1595 pageant; he may have written those for 1581, 1584, 1586, and 1587; see pp. xxxiv and 56. A standard modern discussion of the shows is David M. Bergeron, *English Civic Pageantry 1558–1642* (London, 1971).

22. Glynne Wickham makes this point about later civic pageants in *Early English Stages, 1300–1660,* vol. 2, part 1 (London: Routledge, Kegan Paul, 1963), p. 237.

23. The word "pageant" signifies both the portable or fixed scaffolding on which various characters sat and from which they delivered their speeches and the entire exhibition itself; "device" refers to the characters and speeches. Thus the title of the Dixi-pageant precisely identifies Peele's contribution as "The Device of the Pageant." See Yale ed., 1:157, and Robertson and Gordon, "A Calendar of Dramatic Records," p. xxii n3.

24. The pageants fascinated foreign visitors. Samuel Kiechel wrote a description of Peele's 1585 effort; he thought the lynx was a camel. See Jean Robertson, ed., "A Calendar of Dramatic Records of the London Clothworkers' Company," *Malone Society Collections* 5 (1960 for 1959):6 n2, and K. D. Haszler, ed., *Die Reisen des Samuel Kiechel,* Bibliothek des litterarischen Vereins in Stuttgart, 86 (1867):26–27.

25. For an account of contemporary Astraea mythology, see Yates, *Astraea,* pp. 29–87.

26. Although the sentiment is a commonplace, it may recall—as does the fountain Superstition and Ignorance wish to poison—Elizabeth's 1559 coronation entry. See above, note 17.

27. Strong, *The Cult of Elizabeth,* p. 173; for the Elizabethan revival, see pp. 165 and 172.

28. Yale ed., 1:96. Since the payment predates the ceremony by three days, Peele may have relied on earlier installations for his description, which lacks any specific details from 1593.

29. The complaint is common; both George Chapman in several early poems and Marlowe himself in *Hero and Leander* (also published in 1593) make similar remarks. D. H. Horne makes the important point that "All five living poets and two of the three contemporary dead ones [mentioned in the prologue] were court writers inclining toward the classical . . . ." (Yale ed., 1:96).

30. D. H. Horne comments, in Yale ed., 1:280, "a curious mistake for Salisbury (William Montacute, the second Earl)," but I believe the substitution is deliberate.

[2]

'MANY A *HERDSMAN* MORE DISPOSDE TO MORNE': PEELE, CAMPION, AND THE PORTUGAL EXPEDITION OF 1589

BY HUGH GAZZARD

This article examines one Latin and two English poems occasioned by the English military expedition to Portugal of 1589: George Peel's *A Farewell* and *An Eglogue. Gratulatorie*, and Thomas Campion's 'Ad Daphnin', a dedicatory poem prefacing his collection of Latin verse, *Poemata* (1595). Through close analysis of the formal and stylistic aspects of the poems, reading them also alongside their literary sources and analogues, and through contextualization of the poems with the troubled events and aftermath of the expedition, the article seeks to show that these works—which have been given little scholarly and critical attention—are unexpectedly complex and nuanced. Attention is paid to the poems' encomiastic elements, and they are positioned in the careers of their authors. These analyses have implications for our understanding of early modern interactions between the text and the event; the motives for and modes of public, occasional poetry; and the possibilities of reading closely the Anglo-Latin poetry of the Renaissance

The events of a few tumultuous weeks in the summer of 1588 still have a talismanic power in English, and British, narratives of national history, and of course they had a far stronger talismanic power for those who lived through them: 'Triumph (*O English people*) leap for ioy', James Aske exhorted in that fateful year.[1] Less memorialized, both now and at the time—with good reason—was England's Counter-Armada of the following year, the expedition to Portugal under the command of Sir Francis Drake and Sir John Norris. But the expedition's hopeful outset, and its far from triumphant return, were marked in two poems by George Peele, poems by turns heroic and ambivalent, and in a short Latin poem (published later) by Thomas Campion. In this article I shall closely examine these poems both in their character as public, occasional verse, and in the contexts of the events and the poets' wider careers.

---

1 James Aske, *Elizabetha Triumphans* (London, 1588), A4^b. Surveys of the English literary response, and attempts (variably successful) at reconstructing the Armada as context, include J. J. McAleer, 'Ballads on the Spanish Armada', *Texas Studies in Literature and Language*, 4 (1962), 602–12; A. Esler, 'Robert Greene and the Spanish Armada', *English Literary History*, 32 (1965), 314–32; J. Shapiro, 'Revisiting *Tamburlaine: Henry V* as Shakespeare's Belated Armada Play', *Criticism*, 31 (1989), 351–66; F. Ardolino, *Apocalypse and Armada in Kyd's Spanish Tragedy*, Sixteenth-Century Essays and Studies (Kirksville, Mo., 1995), and 'The Effect of the Defeat of the Spanish Armada on Spenser's *Complaints*', *Spenser Studies*, 16 (2002), 55–75. See also B. T. Whitehead, *Brags and Boasts: Propaganda in the Year of the Armada* (Stroud, 1995).

The explicitly public character and public frame of reference of so much early modern literary production is an aspect of that culture which can hardly be emphasized too strongly, and which indeed is far from unacknowledged in today's critique of that culture. Yet an adequate and exhaustive poetics of that public character—and more especially a poetics of topical, *occasional* verse—is a major desideratum of early modern literary studies. This public scope of the literary was the inevitable outcome of the grounding of so much early modern literary production in networks of individual and institutional patronage—in the more or less direct link between that literary production and the court, the aristocracy and gentry, the academic institutions. Since much literary production was to a large degree sustained by these networks of patronage, it was equally inevitable that in turn it should have held a mirror up to that rarefied world.

It hardly needs restating that much of, say, Elizabethan and Jacobean poetic output—in English and in Latin, in print and in manuscript—is marked by or explicitly marks the emergent public occasion. Hence the proliferation of the public kinds of poetry: the funerary genres, the epithalamia, the panegyric and encomiastic genres, the 'anniversaries' of various kinds, the coronation odes. Hence, in print, the verse miscellanies sponsored by the universities, for example; hence, in manuscript, the burgeoning body of verse written, circulated, and read by and for courtiers and those around the court, however ostensibly 'private' some of its concerns might have been. All this was entirely consonant with the early modern sense of the centrality of what was termed the *epideictic*, in the Aristotelian schematization of rhetoric, to literary production—and to rhetoric as an important constituent of civil society generally. The 'epideictic' (in Aristotle's rhetorical theory, and in much of the literary and rhetorical practice of early modernity) describes the public language of praise, exhortation, and dispraise applied to the public individual and the public event.

Here I shall attempt to show how a sufficiently rigorous examination of the relation of a work to the bounded context of its historical occasion, combined with an interrogation of its more strictly formal and technical components, and an interrogation of the network of literary borrowing and allusion sustaining it (or of, more broadly, its intertextuality), can reveal an unexpected richness in ostensibly slight and ephemeral writing. In the case of Campion's Latin poetry, I shall try to demonstrate something of the potential for fruitful reading afforded by the hitherto largely neglected field of neo-Latin literature of the English Renaissance. This is promising territory, which the scholarship of James Binns has just begun (in effect, single-handedly) to prepare for sustained critical cultivation.[2] Additionally, since the poems considered are all written in praise of various participants in the Portuguese venture, I shall have something to say about the interaction between their topical and encomiastic aspects.

2 See in particular J. W. Binns, *Intellectual Culture in Elizabethan and Jacobean England: The Latin Writings of the Age*, ARCA: Classical and Medieval Texts, Papers and Monographs 24 (Leeds, 1990) for an overview of the corpus of neo-Latin literature.

The expedition to Portugal of 1589, commanded by Sir John Norris and Sir Francis Drake, was intended to be a punitive reply to the Spanish Armada.[3] It is notable as the most substantial concerted offensive action mounted by England during the intensification of the conflict with Spain in the late 1580s. Its generals were issued with instructions reflecting the multiple objectives of the mission: to drive Spain from Portugal (Spain had annexed Portugal in 1580) and install the Portuguese pretender, Dom António, as king—on condition that there was suffi-cient popular support upon António's arrival there; to attack Spain's shipping along its coast; and to attempt to take a redoubt in the Azores, preparatory to intercepting the Spanish fleet bearing bullion from Spain's colonial possessions in the Americas.

However clearly stated these aims might have been, from the very earliest stages of its preparation the venture was beset by controversy and difficulties. There were arguments over the financing and supply of the expedition and over the joint commanders' remit, and there was uncertainty about the queen's willingness even to countenance the venture. After all this, with the fleet ready at Plymouth, bad weather delayed its departure for several weeks, and the com-manders faced problems with indiscipline and, once again, lack of supplies. Controversy was intensified just at the point of departure, when the latest courtly favourite of the queen, Robert Devereux, second earl of Essex, joined the fleet without the queen's authority.

Once under way there were yet more problems. The fleet was scattered by a storm, and the commanders missed the opportunity of attacking Spanish ship-ping at Santander, but did disembark to mount a brief and inconclusive siege at Coruña. Thence they sailed to the river Tejo in Portugal, and landed the army at Peniche to march on Lisbon. Popular Portuguese support for Dom António failed to materialize, and desertion, disease, and the heat of the Iberian summer depleted the English forces. The invading army camped out before Lisbon for three days but did not assault the city nor engage the Spanish army in any decisive action. The army retreated and re-embarked, but storms struck again and pre-vented the fleet from reaching the Azores. The forces returned to England by 2 July. The return was some way short of triumphal. As early as mid-May the queen had been heard to complain that the generals had failed to attack Spanish ship-ping. Soon after that, she wrote to them reprimanding them for disregarding their instructions. When the expedition returned, its commanders were immedi-ately involved in disputes with the Privy Council over such spoils as it had brought back. Controversy over this, and over payments to those who had backed and taken part in the venture, rumbled on until the following summer.

3 The best guide to the planning, execution, and aftermath of the expedition, from which my summary account is derived, is *The Expedition of Sir John Norris and Sir Francis Drake to Spain and Portugal, 1589*, ed. R. B. Wernham, Publications of the Navy Records Society 127 (Aldershot, 1988), which collects primary documents and has (pp. xi–lxvi) a commentary on the expedition. See also R. B. Wernham, *After the Armada: Elizabethan England and the Struggle for Western Europe, 1588–1595* (Oxford, 1984), 1–21 and 48–130, and W. T. MacCaffrey, *Elizabeth I: War and Politics, 1588–1603* (Princeton, 1992), 73–96.

In the autumn of 1589 the Privy Council was examining in detail the generals' actions and omissions. Contemporary observers were critical. The expedition failed financially and tactically, and exacted a terrible human cost: probably somewhere between 4,500 and 11,000 men died, out of the force's total of 13,500.

George Peele's patriotic and morale-boosting *A Farewell*, chiefly remembered now as the source for the title of Hemingway's novel *A Farewell to Arms*, was published in anticipation of the expedition's departure. *A Farewell* was dedicated ('Entituled', says its title page) to the designated generals, Sir John Norris and Sir Francis Drake, 'and all theyr braue and resolute followers'. The poem was entered in the Stationers' Register on 23 February 1589: not, as Peele's modern editor states, the date of the generals' commissions, but of a detailed (though apparently not final) draft of their instructions.[4] Presumably the printed poem was in circulation at the same time as troops were mustering and embarking at Plymouth, through March and early April.

It is with a call to quick embarkation that Peele's memorably fluent piece of blank verse begins. The whole book is dedicated to the generals and their followers; the dedicatory epistle, by the prevailing standards of these things, employs relatively simple and unobsequious formulas of address and subscription; the poem itself is subscribed, familiarly, 'Yours. *G.P.*'; and the poem sets itself up as a direct and familiar address to all the soldiery, as though from a comrade-in-arms—they are '*my harts . . . my boyes . . . my fellow Souldiers . . . my Mates*'.[5] This should be set alongside Peele's claim, in his dedicatory epistle—a not inherently implausible claim— that he is '*a man not vnknowne to many of your braue and forwarde followers, Captaynes and Souldiers*'.[6] In the poem, the everyday armoury of early modern warfare ('*Rests and Muskets*') is matched with the '*Helme and Targe*' of the heroic word-hoard.

The *Farewell* relies for much of its vivid impact upon the impression of direct address, with Peele artfully disposing the dramatic monologue in a heightened form as though the poem were a speech of farewell delivered to the fleet at the quayside:

> *In Gods name venture on, and let me say*
> *To you my Mates, as Cæsar sayd to his*
> *Striuing with Neptunes hils: You beare quoth he,*
> *Cæsar and Cæsars fortune in your ships.*[7]

4 Text from George Peele, *A Farewell Entituled to the Famous and Fortunate Generalls of Our English Forces* (London, 1589; STC 19537). On the date of the SR entry see *The Life and Works of George Peele*, ed. C. T. Prouty, 3 vols. (New Haven and London, 1952–70), i. 161; MacCaffrey, *Elizabeth I*, 85.

5 Peele, *A Farewell*, A3ᵃ, A3ᵇ.

6 See *Life and Works of Peele*, ed. Prouty, i. 100, for the probability that Peele served in some capacity under Sir Robert Carey during the earl of Essex's Normandy expedition of 1591—as did a number of the 1580s–1590s literati. The definite evidence for Peele's service there, apparently first unearthed by W. B. Austin, has, to the best of my knowledge, still not been published.

7 Peele, *A Farewell*, A3ᵃ.

The poem's peal of imperatives, culminating in the clarion refrain '*to Armes, to Armes, to glorious Armes*', '*to Armes, to Armes, to honourable Armes*', adds to the immediacy and urgency of address. Peele rehearses the names of the possible destinations of the expedition with a Marlovian rhetorical relish, with 'the Marlovian music of polysyllabic place names', as a commentator puts it.[8] The enterprise is represented in heroic, chivalric, and militantly Protestant terms: it might even head for

> *the Gulfe that leades to loftie Rome,*
> *There to deface the pryde of Antechrist,*
> *And pull his Paper walles and popery downe:*[9]

The favourite myth of the Britons' Trojan origins heightens the poem's nationalistic rhetoric: London is figured as '*statelie Troynouant*'. And in fact Peele appended his *A Tale of Troy*, a digest of the Trojan war, in couplets, to the *Farewell*. (So it is styled on the title page; its half-title is 'The beginning, accidents and *ende of the warre of Troy*'.) He describes the *Tale* in his book's dedicatory epistle as a '*pleasaunt dyscourse, fitly serving to recreate, by the reading the chiualrie of* England', and recommending its record of exemplary heroism as a prompt to his contemporaries to compare '*in equipage of honour and Armes, wyth theyr glorious and renowned predicessors the* Troyans'. It is likely that he originally composed the *Tale* towards the end of his time at Oxford, probably *c.*1579–81; it shows some traces of influence in diction from Spenser's *Shepheardes Calender*, but it takes its material chiefly from Caxton's *Recuyell of the Historyes of Troye*.[10] Peele's editors from Dyce onwards have noted that the *Tale* must have been included principally on order to fill out an otherwise very thin pamphlet: the *Farewell* proper occupies only three pages. It is entirely possible, too, that Nashe was gibing at this in his reference, in the preface to Newman's edition of *Astrophel and Stella*, to 'Others' who

are so hardly bested for loading that they are faine to retaile the cinders of *Troy*, and the shiuers of broken trunchions, to fill vp their boate that else should goe empty: and if they haue but a pound weight of good Merchandise, it shall be placed at the poope, or pluckt in a thousande peeces to credit their carriage.[11]

Peele renders the soldiery's cavalier, bonnet-vailing valediction to '*freends*' and '*Dames*' '*at home*', coupled with one to

> *Theaters and proude Tragædians,*
> *Bid* Mahomets Poo, *and mightie* Tamburlaine,

8 L. R. N. Ashley, *George Peele* (New York, 1970), 175.

9 Peele, *A Farewell*, A3[b].

10 On the *Tale*, and on the record of a lost edition of it printed in 1604 which was a bibliographical curio (its format was apparently 48mo: quadragintimo-octavo), see *Life and Works of Peele*, ed. Prouty, i. 149–53.

11 *The Works of Thomas Nashe*, ed. R. B. McKerrow, rev. F. P. Wilson, 5 vols. (repr. Oxford, 1966), iii. 332. The likelihood of a swipe at the *Farewell* is surely increased—Nashe's encomium of Peele in his preface to Greene's *Menaphon* notwithstanding—by this passage's nautical imagery.

> King Charlemaine, Tom Stukeley *and the rest*
> *Adiewe:*[12]

Here the implication is that the men of action are to emulate, just as they have watched, the heroics on the Elizabethan stage. The lines are made all the more pointed by the near-certainty that Peele's own play on Portuguese and Spanish affairs, *The Battle of Alcazar*, was composed and staged around this time, and that it is this play which is implied by his reference to 'Tom Stukeley'.[13] Peele is advertising his own play, and deftly making a bridge between the world of letters which he certainly knew and the military milieu which his verse is courting.

There are in fact plentiful parallels in diction between *A Farewell* and *Alcazar*, not detailed by previous commentators, which both serve conclusively to confirm Peele's authorship of the play, and show him striving insistently for heroic effect in his style at this time.[14] *A Farewell* has '*aborde amaine, | With stretching sayles to plowe the swelling waues*' (ll. 1–2); *Alcazar* has 'now prepares amaine | With sailes and oares to crosse the swelling seas' (ll. 739–40).[15] In *A Farewell* the soldiers are to

> *bid statelie Troynouant adiewe,*
> *Where pleasant Thames from Isis siluer head*
> *Begins her quiet glide, and runnes along,*
> *To that braue Bridge the barre that thwarts her course*
> (ll. 4–7)

while in *Alcazar* Stukeley himself relates how

> In Englands London Lordings was I borne,
> On that brave Bridge, the barre that thwarts the Thames.
> (ll. 1328–9)

A Farewell has '*God Mars his consort*' of instruments (l. 12); *Alcazar* 'God Mars his drum' (l. 1360). Both have 'propagate' in the transitive sense of 'to cause to increase' (*A Farewell*, l. 26; *Alcazar*, ll. 765, 766, 872)[16]—and, where *A Farewell*

---

12 Peele, *A Farewell*, A3[a].

13 I cannot see why D. H. Horne should conclude that the reference is 'more probably' to the anonymous play *Captain Thomas Stukeley*, which is of uncertain date, rather than to Peele's own, and definitely contemporary, *Alcazar*. Horne identifies the other plays glanced at by Peele as Greene's *Alphonsus*, 'perhaps' the anonymous *Charlemagne or the Distracted Emperor*, and of course *Tamburlaine*. *Life and Works of Peele*, ed. Prouty, i. 277. On the date of *Alcazar* see J. Yoklavich, ibid. ii. 221–6, where it is dated to between July 1588 and the entry of the *Farewell* in the Stationers' Register in February 1589.

14 H. M. Dowling, 'The Date and Order of Peele's Plays', *Notes and Queries*, 164 (1933), 167, says that 'Peele used material from this play in his "Farewell" ', and notes the 'liberal sprinkling in the "Farewell" of some of the more notable lines of the play'—but he does not itemize them. In his edition of *The Battle of Alcazar*, in vol. ii of *Life and Works of Peele*, ed. Prouty, Yoklavich notices Dowling's assertion of links between the two works, but does not adduce any evidence (pp. 224–5).

15 Text and line-numbering are as in Yoklavich's edition of the play.

16 These are antedatings of *OED* 'propagate' v. 2a, as are the occurrences of the verb in a similar sense in Edward Hall, *The Vnion of the Two Noble and Illustre Famelies of Lancastre [and] Yorke* (London, 1548; STC 12722), 3B6[a], and in *An Almond for a Parrat* [London? 1589? STC 534], E1[a].

has 'To propagate religious pietie' (l. 26), *Alcazar* has the comparable collocations, 'To propagate the fame of Portugall, | And plant religious truth in Affrica', and 'Thereby to propagate religious truth, | And plant his springing praise in Affrica' (ll. 766–7, 872–3). *A Farewell* has 'And henœ a passage with your conquering swordes' (l. 27); *Alcazar*, 'make a passage with my conquering sword' (l. 1080). *A Farewell* has 'What euer course your matchles vertue shapes' (l. 43); *Alcazar*, 'Tom Stukley shapes his course' (l. 736).[17] And both have '*Auernus cragges*' (l. 46; l. 38).

Indeed, *Alcazar*—an unwieldy imitation of the horrors and grandeur of *Tamburlaine*—makes most sense when seen as a play exploiting the topicality in 1588–9 of Spanish and Portuguese affairs, albeit in unexpected ways. The play dramatizes the attempt by the Portuguese sovereign Sebastian, portrayed in an unflattering light, to lend aid (seeking it also from Philip of Spain) to a usurping villain determined to wrest power from its rightful possessor, the Moor Abdelmelec—whose situation comes closer than anyone else's in the play to resembling the real Dom António's. Yet in respect of the play's insistence upon the villain Muly's *reclaiming* of power, with Sebastian's aid, it was this strand of the drama which was most likely to look topical, given the attempts under way to aid António's quest to claim power in Portugal. We should not overlook the sub-plot concerning Sir Thomas Stukley and the English adventurers, very much cast in the spirit of the gentlemen volunteers who went on the Portuguese expedition, and which demonstrably drew on the English version of Dom António's *apologia* then in print.[18]

The whole poem, then, presents an address to the soldiery as above all others its prime implied audience and readership. It is cast as a dramatic monologue, its speaker urging on the forces as they embark. And it is cast in blank verse which is very much in the heroic manner of much of Peele's own quasi-Marlovian *Alcazar*, with which it is roughly contemporary. It might almost stand as a martial oration excerpted from some notionally typical play of the late 1580s, full of high-astounding bombast and nationalistic fervour. This slight, small, ephemeral pamphlet production speaks volumes about Peele's positioning of himself in the literary marketplace as a kind of self-crowned, *soi-disant* popular and populist laureate, one who appropriates the dialect of the stage for a poetry of the public occasion and of public acclamation, a poetry disseminated in self-evidently cheap and accessible pamphlet form—not so many steps removed in fact from the printed poetic broadside. It is as though the declamatory public and occasional broadsides of, say, Thomas Churchyard—typically done in cumbrous fourteeners—were suddenly reinvigorated with the charge of the rhetoric just then resounding on the London stage. Indeed, the very notion of a one-off non-dramatic poem in print being cast in blank verse pentameter must still have had the sheen of novelty or at least rarity, since its use in that form was still

---

17 These are antedatings of *OED* 'shape' v. 16d, where the first citation is from a later work by Peele.

18 See *Life and Works of Peele*, ed. Prouty, ii. 276–8.

unusual and, excepting the first printing of Surrey's translation of Virgil by Tottel in 1557, was no older than Gascoigne's *The Steele Glas* of 1576.

As so often in early modern print culture, Peele's title-page fuses the functional with the allusive. It establishes the credentials of authorship and imprint—with Peele's customary preferred styling as *'Master of Artes in Oxforde'* to lend cultural weight. Its short and full titles—bluntly, *'A Farewell'*, plus the subjoined note of 'entitlement'—set out a generic and occasional frame of reference and public dedication for the poem. Additionally the *Tale* is advertised as *'annexed'*. As a poetic 'farewell' to departing men of arms or to a heroic venture it takes its place in a class of compositions which might lack a definitive name in the formal schemata of generic types (the *apobaterion* comes close), but which is a kind of more or less vivid and immediate public poetic address of leave-taking to balance the better-known private, amatory occasions of valediction rendered by Donne, for example. The class includes Henry Roberts's *A Most Friendly Farewell, Given by a Welwiller to the Right Worshipful Sir Frauncis Drake Knight . . . and to all the Gentlemen His Followers, and Captaines* (1585), occasioned by the departure of Drake's Caribbean voyage. Peele might almost be designingly updating and revamping that kind of public verse 'farewell': amplified echoes of the shop-worn fourteeners of Roberts's penultimate line (*'Aboard my mates, your warning peace is shot, thē hoise vp saile'*) run through Peele's declamatory rhetoric. A decade later the veteran Thomas Churchyard, quite possibly aware of Peele's heroic *Farewell*, published his own verse *Fortunate Farevvel to the Most Forward and Noble Earle of Essex*, on the occasion of the departure of Essex's expedition to Ireland.

The title-page epigraph of Peele's *Farewell*—'Parue nec inuidio sine me (liber) ibis ad arma, | Hei mihi, quod domino non licet ire tuo' ('O little book—and I do not envy you—without me you shall go to the wars; Woe is me, for it is not permitted for your master to go with you')—is taken and lightly adapted from Ovid's *Tristia* I, where the exiled poet anticipates his book's passage into the town, 'in urbem'. Peele turns it to anticipate his own book going to the wars, 'ad arma', and he can through Ovid rue his own absence from the company he addresses. (This distich, with yet another creative misprision at the end of the first line, was also used on the title page of William Percy's *Sonnets to the Fairest Coelia* in 1594.) The entire production—patched together in some ways though it is, with the uneasily appended *Tale* to fill it out—from title-page details, through dedicatory epistle, to the tonal register and wider implications of the poems, shows Peele reaching for a distinctively public idiom, a public form, a public projection of authorship, and specifically printed poetic authorship, as a characteristically public phenomenon. Around this time Peele (probably living somewhere in Bankside) was a productive playwright—though not, so far as we know, a professional man of the theatre in any fixed capacity. He had made money also from devising civic pageants—but he did not make any kind of living from his links with the City authorities. He was about to produce a series of encomiastic poems directed at courtiers and recording spectacles at court; but he comes across as being much more a flattering spectator of than participant

24   HUGH GAZZARD

in the court scene, and there is no record of his being the beneficiary of any sustained individual or institutional patronage. He seems at this juncture to be casting about for a triumphal mode and theme which might serve to sustain his writing career.[19]

On 1 August 1589, four weeks after the expedition's return, Peele's *An Eglogue. Gratulatorie* was entered in the Stationers' Register.[20] It was printed by John Windet for Richard Jones, who himself printed Peele's *Polyhymnia* the following year. The full title states that it is '*Entituled:* | ¶ To the right honorable, and renowmed | *Shepheard of Albions Arcadia:* Robert | Earle of *Essex* and *Ewe*, for his welcome | *into England from* Portugall'. '*Entituled*' here again carries the sense of 'inscribed, dedicated' (*OED*, 'entitle' *v.* 1b). In this choice of word Peele is echoing the *Farewell*; and, in both this choice and the very layout of this dedicatory inscription, he is emulating the work which had most influence upon his *Eglogue*, Spenser's *The Shepheardes Calender*. Spenser's 1579 title page states that his book is '*Entitled* | TO THE NOBLE AND VERTV- | *ous Gentleman most worthy of all titles* | both of learning and cheualrie M. | Philip Sidney'. As we shall see, the link between Sidney and the earl of Essex is one of the principal epideictic, encomiastic themes in Peele's poem.

Such slight attention as this poem has attracted has tended to dismiss it as a piece of failed pastoral patched up with tired and hollow triumphalism. Thus, it 'has little interest'; it is 'somewhat overdone', 'mechanical', and with 'no sense of a genuine pastoral world'; or, conversely, 'the entire expedition to Cadiz [*sic*] which Peele is celebrating' *has* 'become part of the pastoral world', although the '*tenuis avena* is no medium for heroic poetry'.[21] These responses misconstrue the work entirely, and ignore or misunderstand the important effect upon Peele's composition of the occasion prompting it, which is of paramount importance. After all, in some senses the occasion *is* the work; it gives the work its whole warrant. The notable thing about the *Eglogue* is that, where we might have expected a noisy victory ode, an *epinikion*, Peele has produced an intermittently muted and carefully qualified celebration of the exploits of Essex, his dedicatee, during the expedition, and of the expedition itself.

19 The fullest biography of Peele is in *Life and Works of Peele*, ed. Prouty, i. 3–146, 65–109 for the years in London.

20 George Peele, *An Eglogue. Gratulatorie* (London, 1589; STC 19534). Only one copy of the edition survives, at the Bodleian Library, Oxford (shelf-mark Malone 818). For some reason Horne, in vol. i of *Life and Works of Peele*, ed. Prouty, silently alters both spelling and punctuation of the poem's title, to *An Eglogue Gratulatory*. It is possible that the stop after *Eglogue* on the title page of the quite careless Windet printing of 1589 is an error for a comma, or is perhaps intended for a medial period. The entry in the Register renders the title with a comma, as 'an *Eglogue, gratulatorie*'. *A Transcript of the Registers of the Company of Stationers of London; 1554–1640 A.D.*, ed. E. Arber, 5 vols. (London, 1875–94), ii. 526.

21 W. W. Greg, *Pastoral Poetry and Pastoral Drama: A Literary Inquiry, with Special Reference to the Pre-Restoration Stage in England* (New York, 1959), 110; S. Chaudhuri, *Renaissance Pastoral and its English Developments* (Oxford, 1989), 187–8; H. Cooper, *Pastoral: Medieval into Renaissance* (Ipswich, and Totowa, NJ, 1977), 130.

'MANY A *HERDSMAN* MORE DISPOSDE TO MORNE'   25

The title is, of course, an immediate indication of the work's epideictic cast. There is a clear generic marker, '*Eglogue*', modified by this striking word, '*Gratulatorie*'. If the evidence of the *OED* and of the searchable text database of Early English Books Online is to be trusted, this word was, firstly, a relatively new (perhaps no older than three decades) importation into the language. The adjective *gratulatorius* (*-a*, *-um*) seems not to be recorded from classical but rather in patristic and later Latin. A simple search of bibliographical databases shows that self-styled single and collected *Carmina gratulatoria* abound in the corpus of encomiastic printed and public Latin poetry of the second half of the sixteenth century. (I have found no trace of an *Ecloga gratulatoria*, however.) Old French *gratulatoire* is attested by dictionaries—but, beyond the styling (which looks to be purely coincidental, the product of the like-mindedness of literary cultures in the European Renaissance) of *Amyntas pastorelle gratulatoire dedié à son excellence Monseigneur Iean Charles comte de Schonburg... sur son heureux voyage d'Allemagne en Espagne* (Luxemburg, 1634), 'par la Ieunesse du College de IESVS à Luxembourg', I do not know where it occurs. Peele's seems to be the first example in English of the word's direct descriptive application to an entire, distinctly literary composition, and he seems to be one of the first too to apply it in English in any purely secular context. The very first I have found is its appearance—describing a rhetorical 'member', or constitutive element, of a published letter by Roger Ascham—in Abraham Fleming's letter-writing manual, *A Panoplie of Epistles* (1576).[22] It is plausible to imagine Peele incidentally having cast an eye over Fleming's book during his time at Oxford in the 1570s—after all, words do not come from nowhere, and they can insinuate themselves from book to book. Whatever the case, Peele was sufficiently struck by the word to use it again to describe his *The Honour of the Garter. Displaied in a Poeme Gratulatorie* in 1593, and others—Drayton, Sir John Davies—took it up for use in poetic designation in succeeding decades. Above all, it is another way of connoting the epideictic; and, given the Latin titles already pointed to, Peele's title is interpretable as an attempt to confer upon his vernacular work a Latinate *gravitas* and impression of generic and occasional precision. As for 'eglogue', or 'eclogue': that word, and either spelling of it, were sufficiently current by this time as a name for a species of pastoral: compare Thomas Watson's pastoral elegy, *An Eglogue vpon the Death of the Right Honorable Sir Francis Walsingham* (1590), his own translation of his Latin *Meliboeus* of the same year.

After its half-title the poem is headed by a Latin epigraph: '*Dicite Io Pæan, & Io bis dicite Pæan,* | *In Patriam rediit magnus* Apollo *suam*' ('Cry "Io Paean", and cry twice "Io Paean", | Great Apollo has returned to his homeland'), a resoundingly heroic welcome back to Essex—the first line of which is the triumphal shout at the outset of the second book of Ovid's *Ars amatoria*. The *Eglogue* comprises a debate

---

22 This usage antedates *OED* 'gratulatory' *a.* 1 by one year: Abraham Fleming, *A Panoplie of Epistles, or, A Looking Glasse for the Vnlearned* (London, 1576; STC 11049), 2G3[b].

26   HUGH GAZZARD

between Piers (who is at one point more or less explicitly promoted as a poetic persona for Peele himself) and Palinode, namesakes of the interlocutors in Spenser's 'Maye' eclogue. Indeed, the diction throughout Peele's poem echoes that of *The Shepheardes Calender*. *Herdgroome*, *gars* ('causes'), *crancke* ('lively, brisk, merry'), *wunne* ('dwell'), *well thewed* ('of good character'), *swinck*, *foemans*, *accoyed* ('daunted'), and *witned* ('blamed'), from the *Eglogue*, are all found in substantially the same form and sense in Spenser's work (and 'foeman' and 'well-thewed' are given glosses by E.K. in the 'Februarie' eclogue). The perceived Spenserian texture of Peele's verse can only have been heightened by its scattering of 'thilke', 'mickle', and verbal forms with *y*- prefixes and *-en* terminations. In seeking to render a rustic and quasi-dialectal register for pastoral Peele looked to the example of Spenser, and even what seem to be his own coinages or importations—*smicker* ('smirking'); *sonizance* ('Obscure: perh. an error', says *OED*, but where the sense intended should be something like 'resounding noise'); *rumaricke* ('rendering rheumatic': not in *OED*)—even these have a Spenserian ring. Beyond that, in its stanzaic, metrical (although it is relatively more irregular than Spenser generally is there), and dialogic patterning, the *Eglogue* generally looks very much like something out of Spenser's pastoral. The only other discernible influence is Marlowe: Peele has 'royalize' in the sense of 'to render famous, celebrate', most likely an echo of *1 Tamburlaine* II. iii. 8.

The debate in the *Eglogue* between Piers and Palinode is about the fitness of their own pastoral mode to accommodate the praise which Piers wants to lavish on Essex. Piers is a sketchily delineated 'Herdgrome' whose affliction by 'cares' and admission that he was 'Yborne ... to be infortunate' recall the plaintive woes of Spenser's pastoral speakers. He intends to 'make my crowd speake' and

> To pipe lowd *Pæans* as my *Stanzaes* end.
> *Io Io Paean*[23]

in honour of Essex, but Palinode in effect objects to the generic impropriety of such heroic pastoral:

> So ill sitteth this straine, this loftie note,
> With thy rude tire, and gray russet cote. . . .
>
> (Man) if *Triumphals* heere be in request,
> Then let them chaunt them, that can chaunt them best. . . .
>
> *Warres Laud*, is matter for the brasen Trumpe. . . .
>
> Thy Reed to rough, thy seat is all to lowe.
> To writen sike praise, hadst thou blithe *Homers* quil
> Thou moughtest haue matter equall with thy skill.[24]

---

23 Peele, *An Eglogue*, A2ᵃ, A3ᵃ.
24 Ibid. A2ᵃ, A2ᵇ, B1ᵇ.

Piers replies that his 'Bagpipe vaunteth not of victorie'; eschewing 'Of Armes to sing', he will instead, 'For chiualrie, and louely learnings sake' (perhaps a recollection of the coupled 'learning and cheualrie' ascribed to Sidney in Spenser's earlier dedication to that hero), welcome back Essex, figured pastorally as 'One of the iolliest *Shepherds* of our Greene'. This is the cue for Piers to heap panegyric upon that 'great *Herdgroome*, certes, but no swaine'.[25] In the praise for Essex are assembled all the main elements of the cult of personality surrounding the earl as it was beginning to be elaborated at that time. He is the royal favourite; 'He is wel alied and loued of the best', and 'Well thewed, faire and francke'; his retinue is splendid. Mighty mythological and historical parallels are proposed for him: he tends the 'flocke' of his family and followers 'As when *Apollo* kept in *Arcadie*'—a comparison that echoes the poem's epigraph. His 'dread aduentures' in war are 'Equiuolent with the *Punic Chiualrie*' of Hannibal. Most of all, he was the ally, and is now the legatee, of Sidney:

> Fellow in Armes he was, in their flowing deies,
> With that great *Shepherd* good *Philisides:* . . .
>
> Yet in this louelie swaine, source of our glee,
> Mun all his Vertues sweet reuiuen bee.[26]

Had Peele been reading the *Arcadia* in manuscript? This seems to be the first identification of Sidney as 'Philisides' on record, anticipating by a year the appearance of the *New Arcadia* in print and also Spenser's references to Sidney as 'Philisides' in *The Ruines of Time*.

Essex is the returning hero whose service in the wars, winning him 'Honors spoile', is undertaken in the name of nationalistic and Protestant knighthood: in the Low Countries with Sidney he had warded the Catholic 'Wolfe from *Elizaes* gate', and now from Portugal he returns to '*Nue reared Troy*'.[27] All of this compresses into idealized encomium the awkward actuality of the expedition and Essex's participation in it: the storm-tossed voyage out; the overland march through sweltering heat, soldiers dropping or disappearing in their hundreds along the way; and the militarily unproductive but personally typical episode of chivalric posturing when Essex, camped out before the gates of Lisbon, issued a personal challenge to its governor for each to maintain the honour of his cause in single combat—a challenge which was ignored.[28] This was 'Honors spoile'.

25 Ibid. A2[b], A3[a].

26 Ibid., A3[b], A4[b].

27 Ibid., A4[a], A3[b].

28 P. E. J. Hammer, *The Polarisation of Elizabethan Politics: The Political Career of Robert Devereux, 2nd Earl of Essex, 1585–1597* Cambridge Studies in Early Modern British History (Cambridge, 1999), 231.

28   HUGH GAZZARD

Palinode has a new objection to Piers' glorification of Essex:

> If he be one come new fro *Westerne* coast,
> Small cause hath he or thou for him to boast.
>
> I see no Palme, I see no Laurell bowes,
> Circle his temples, or adorne his browes,
> I heare no Triumphes for this late returne,
> But many a *Herdsman* more disposde to morne.[29]

Here, of course, is the nub of the problem which Piers (and Peele) has been facing all along. The scope for sounding a triumphal tone, and for fully celebrating the expedition as well as Essex's part in it, was severely restricted by the controversy and criticisms that beset its return. These precluded the possibility of setting in a thoroughly apt form such acclamation and celebration as might have been warranted by the poem's occasion—in the heroic address of the *Farewell*, for example. Instead, Peele tempered things with pastoral, and he borrowed not only the studied rusticity of *The Shepheardes Calender*, but also that work's potentially perilous engagement with contemporary affairs.

The use of Piers as a public poetic persona for Peele prompts an obvious comparison with Spenser's adoption of the guise of Colin Clout. The poem's pastoral cast, strengthened by its Spenserian colouring, and its engagement with current affairs, would surely not necessarily have appeared stale or Parnassian in the charged atmosphere of late summer 1589. But it is also worth noting just how derivative and imitative Peele's literary imagination was. Just as his dramatic and non-dramatic blank verse seems essentially fashioned from the same fabric as Marlowe's, so when he came to compose topical pastoral he looked to the obvious example of Spenser.

But the poem is not an otherwise empty echo chamber of received and ornamental language; it engages with contemporary realities, or at least with contemporary constructions of reality. Piers defends his praise for Essex by defending the Portuguese venture generally. War is dangerous: 'Venter doth losse, and warre dothe danger bode'. Palinode, he thinks, expects too much from one expedition:

> But thou art of those *Haruesters* I see,
> Would at one shocke, spoile all the *Philberd-Tree*.[30]

Moreover, 'fames full of lies', and 'Enuie doth ay true honors deeds despise'. This is just the kind of rhetoric which the expedition's apologists deployed. Thus Anthony Wingfield, in his wholly defensive chronicle of the venture, noted of the expedition's detractors that 'euerie vertue findeth her direct opposit, and actions worthy of all memory, are in danger to be enuiouslie obscured'.

---

29 Peele, *An Eglogue*, A4[a].
30 Ibid., A4[b]; '*Philberd-*' emended from '*Philherd-*'.

Extenuating its fatalities, Wingfield also emphasized war's dangers: 'one hazard brought on another: and . . . though one escaped the bullet this day it might light vpon him to morrow, the next day, or any day'.[31]

Peele and Piers also have to face the problem that their hero's participation in the venture was in any case unauthorized. Palinode indeed remembers Peele's *Farewell*, but finds no mention of Essex in it:

> Did not thilk Bagpipe man which thou dost blow
> A farewell on our Souldiers erst bestow?
>
> How yst then, thilke great *Shepherd* of the field . . .
> Was in that worke, not mencioned speciallie.[32]

The uncomfortable and publicly reported reality was that Essex had, without leave, ridden away from court, evading pursuers, and had purloined (with the connivance of the expedition's colonel-general, Sir Roger Williams) one of the queen's ships, the *Swiftsure*, to join the expedition, infuriating the queen. In the face of this Peele makes Piers resort to some diplomatic mystification, conscious of the delicate ground on which they both tread:

> Harke *Palinode*, me dare not speake to lowd,
> Hence was he raught, wrapt in a fierie cloud:
> With Mars his *Viceroy*, and *a golden Drake*,
> So that of him, me durst no notice take.

Piers then reverts to more encomium of the earl, and of his 'dread aduentures', like Hannibal's,

> That brake his Launce, with terror and renowne,
> Against the gates of slaughtered *Rhemus Towne*

just as Essex struck his lance into the gates of Lisbon at the lifting of the English siege of the city.[33] Essex

> was the first of many thousands more,
> That at *Penechia* waded to the shore:

and Peele records this as stirringly as it must have been popularly reported on the strength of the dispatches home from the landing at Peniche: 'parte of o^{r}men landed . . . the Earle of Essex was the first that landed, who by reason the Billowes weare highe waidide to the shoulders to Come on shoare', as one representative example put it.[34]

---

31 A. Wingfield, *A True Coppie of a Discourse Written by a Gentleman, Employed in the Late Voyage of Spaine and Portingale* (London, 1589; STC 6790), B4^b–C1^a, C1^b.

32 Peele, *An Eglogue*, B1^a; 'thilk' and 'thilke' emended from 'thick' and 'thicke'.

33 Peele, *An Eglogue*, B1^a, B1^b. Hammer, *Polarisation of Elizabethan Politics*, 231.

34 National Archives (Public Record Office), London, SP 12/224/86.

30   HUGH GAZZARD

The *Farewell* and the *Eglogue* can be understood as two parts of a trio of specifically dedicated encomiastic poems by Peele from around this time, all of them constituting concerted appeals for aristocratic and courtly reward and patronage. *The Honour of the Garter* (1593) was 'Entitled', this time to the earl of Northumberland, on the occasion of his installation in the Order of the Garter. The verso of that book's title page carries the same engraving of the royal arms, surmounting the same Latin tetrastich on the monarch's heraldic flowers and lions, as those on the verso of the *Farewell*'s title page. There is no record of what the response by Norris, Drake, or Essex to the books dedicated to them might have been. In the case of *The Honour of the Garter*, however, Northumberland is known to have given Peele £3 in reward for his poem: the most immediately palpable fruits, after all, of the whole reciprocal business of public praise and reward.[35]

Alongside these three individual encomia might be placed Peele's *Polyhymnia* (1590), commending the courtiers who rode in tournament at the Accession Day tilt of 1590. Essex appears in that poem too, in a passage with echoes of the *Eglogue*, illustrating Peele's habit—shown also in the correspondences between the *Farewell* and *The Battle of Alcazar*—of recycling words, phrases, and images across the range of his works. 'Sable sad' and 'fairest shepheard of our greene' repeat, with variations, phrasing from the *Eglogue*, and the poet's interpretation of Essex's black-clad appearance at the 1590 tilt as a tribute to Sidney recalls Piers' memory of Essex in black 'Morning the misse of *Pallas* peereless Knight', itself evidently Peele's recollection of an earlier public appearance by the earl. And Peele borrows 'Yclad in mightie Armes' from close to the very beginning of the newly published *Faerie Queene*, making of Essex a suitably valorized and virtuous Spenserian questing knight.

The *Farewell* and *Eglogue*, apparently slight productions, have largely been overlooked precisely because of their connection with current affairs, as though the interest of public occasional poetry extends no further than merely noting its occasional character. In truth the events occasioning these poems loomed momentously enough in the collective consciousness of 1589—this expedition was, as I have noted, England's Counter-Armada. If we pay sufficiently close attention to the shaping influence of that contemporary context, or occasional pretext, and also to the subtleties of the poems themselves, the works assume a piquancy and complexity they might at first seem to lack.

35 Historical Manuscripts Commission, *Sixth Report of the Royal Commission on Historical Manuscripts. Part I. Report and Appendix* (London, 1877), 227. Cf. £5 awarded to John Case for 'a booke' by the earl of Leicester in 1585; the same amount given later that year by Leicester to Robert Greene for *Planetomachia*; and £10 given by Essex himself to the Cambridge academic Andrew Downes for a substantial work of scholarship. See H. Gazzard, 'The Patronage of Robert Devereux, Second Earl of Essex, *c.*1577–1596', D.Phil. thesis, University of Oxford, 1999 (2000), 47–8.

Comparable questions concerning generic propriety and the poetic mediation of public life can be asked of the only other contemporary attempt to commemorate poetically the expedition and the earl of Essex's participation in it. This was Thomas Campion's 'Ad Daphnin', printed in the 1595 edition of his *Poemata*, but evidently written and possibly circulated in the immediate aftermath of the return from Portugal.[36] It is conceivable that Campion had himself served on the expedition, just as he very probably participated (like Peele) in some capacity in Essex's venture in France in 1591; but he was in any case unmistakably exploiting the event's topicality for poetic purposes.[37]

Some of Campion's English poems had already been anthologized in the miscellanea appended to Newman's 1591 *Astrophel and Stella*; beyond that, his service in France, and his continuing connection with Gray's Inn, nothing substantial is known of Campion's life during the early to mid-1590s. *Poemata* was his first collection of work, including pieces composed over at least the preceding seven years: 'Ad Thamesin', Campion's mini-epic on the defeat of the Armada; 'Vmbra', an unfinished encomiastic vision of the Elizabethan court; nineteen elegies, chiefly amatory; and 122 epigrams, mainly addressed to Campion's friends and contemporaries at Gray's Inn, but including also epigrams addressed to Nashe, to Nicholas Breton, George Chapman, John Davies, and Robert Dowland, imparting a sense of the up-to-the-minute London 'high' literary culture. It bears traces too of Campion's probable service in France and of encomium of the earl of Essex's circle generally: an elegy for the earl's brother, Walter Devereux, killed at Rouen in 1591 ('In obitum fratris clariss. comitis Essexij'); and an epigram 'De Th. Grimstono & Io. Goringo'—Grimeston and Goring were captains on the French venture. The whole book is a kind of self-advertising *recueil* of the work of an emergent public poet, and stood as the sole published embodiment of Campion's neo-Latin literary ambitions until he extensively recast it for the much-expanded edition of 1619.

The occasional encomium 'Ad Daphnin' is addressed to Essex under the figuring of this persona, and is one of a pair of poems (the other, 'Ad Dianam', addressed to the queen) which serve, although they are not announced as such, as dedicatory verses for the volume. It has scarcely attracted any published comment in 400 years. J. W. Binns, in the only general study of Campion's Latin verse, simply calls 'Ad Daphnin' 'conventional', and Campion's most authoritative editor mistakes its occasion altogether.[38] Yet here again

---

36 Thomas Campion, *Tomæ Campiani Poemata* (London, 1595; STC 4544), B1^b–2^a.

37 *Campion's Works*, ed. P. Vivian (Oxford, 1909), pp. xxxi–xxxv.

38 J. W. Binns (ed.), *The Latin Poetry of English Poets* (London and Boston, Mass., 1974), 24; *Campion's Works*, ed. Vivian, 375: 'This poem appears to have been written at the time of the Queen's reconciliation with Essex in April, 1592, and his return home soon after from the French wars.'

32   HUGH GAZZARD

an ostensibly straightforward poem becomes, when read in the frame of
its literary antecedents and of the events which occasioned it, unexpectedly
complex and nuanced. Discussion of Campion's Latin verse is so rare
that I need make no apology for pursuing a close reading at some
length. The poem is short, relatively inaccessible and unfamiliar, and
nowhere reliably edited, so I offer a text and supporting material for my
close reading here.

AD *DAPHNIN

Ecquis atat superum? nec enim terrestris in illo
Effulsit splendor, certe aut Latous Apollo
Per uirides saltus teneros sectatur amores,
Aut Daphnis formosus adest, quem sordida terra,
Quem nemus abductum, quem si fas Cynthia fleuit.
Illi nequiquam Fauni, Charitesque quotannis   5
Ornarunt, festosque dies suauesque Hymenaeos,
Montibus et siluis immania lustra ferarum
Eruit, innuptae veneratus sacra Dianae.
Ah nimium intrepidus toruo occursare leoni   10
Gestit, et ingentes ad pugnam incendere tauros.
Quam modo qua Tagus auriferis incumbit arenis,
Per uaga dorsa freti iuuenum longo agmine cinctus,
Uastatoris apri fugientia terga cecidit!
Non Atlante satae (foelicia sydera munus   15
Hoc pietatis habent) magis infoelicis Hyantis
Confusae ex abitu steterunt, trepidaeque uolarunt
Per siluas, resonantibus undique Hyantida siluis;
Quam te, Daphni, super duplicantes uota Britanni,
Quam te, Daphni, super pendentibus anxia fatis   20
Diua, Notos metuens, longumque quod aestuat aequor.
Sed postquam sospes tandem patria arua reuisas,
Terra nemusque uiret, ueteresque ex ordine cultus
Solemni instituunt siluestria numina pompa,
Nec tibi tantum ausit decus inuidisse Menalcas.   25

*Claris-
simus
Essexiae
comes sub
Daphnidis
persona
adum-
bratur.

Textual Notes

Contractions—*i.e.*, -*q;* for -*que*—have been silently expanded.

14 cecidit!] *this text*; cecidit? *1595*
16 Hyantis] *Vivian*; Hyanti *1595*
21 Notos] *this text*; notos *1595, Vivian*
24 Solemni] *this text*; Solenni *1595, Vivian*

Expository Notes

7 Ornarunt] Contracted form of *ornauerunt.*

14 terga] Poetic plural for singular.

16 Hyantis] There is some confusion over the proper name here and in l. 18. The forms attested in antiquity show that in both Greek and Latin *Hyas* was declined regularly as a masculine noun of the third declension with stem in *-nt-*, so 'Hyanti' is plainly an error (perhaps by misprinting) for the Latin genitive *Hyantis.*

18 resonantibus undique Hyantida siluis] Ablative absolute—'the woods everywhere re-echoing'—with accusative of a name called repeatedly. In classical Latin the accusative of *Hyas* is always *Hyantem*, save that Ovid, in the passage drawn on here by Campion, has the contracted or heteroclitic 'Hyan' (*Fasti* 5. 179). Campion's odd-looking 'Hyantida' conflates the regular *-nt-* stem with the third declension for imperfectly Latinized names of Greek origin (compare Latin acc. *Parida* (or *-im* or *-in*), from nom. and voc. *Paris*, gen. *Paridis* (or *-os*), etc.). This questionable expedient is forced by metrical requirements. The name '*Ὕας* appears nowhere in ancient Greek verse, but where '*Ὕαδες* appears (e.g. *Iliad* 18. 486) it usually has three short syllables (unless the last is long by position): so also with *Hyades* in Latin. In Latin verse, the name *Hyas* appears only as the collective singular for *Hyades* (Statius, *Siluae* 1. 6. 21) and, as the character intended here, in Ovid's *Fasti* (see my discussion); its first syllable is always short. So, in l. 16, Campion scans

— ˘˘ — ˘ ˘ — ˘˘ — — ˘ ˘ — —

hoc pietatis habent) magis infoelicis Hyantis

In l. 18, Campion needs a trisyllabic dactyl in the fifth foot, precluding *Hyantem* or *Hyan*, so *-que* and *(H)y-* merge by *synaloephe* (compare *Aeneid* 3. 516, 'pluuiasque Hyadas', and *Metamorphoses* 13. 293,'Pleiadasque Hyadasque'), and he scans

— — — ˘ ˘ — ˘ ˘ — ˘ — ˘ ˘ — —

per siluas, resonantibus undiqu(e) Hyantida siluis;

One reordering of the line is metrically possible, and might be preferred for its orthodox inflection of *Hyas* and its more pointed *figura etymologica*:

per siluas, siluis resonantibus undique Hyantem

Campion perhaps rejected this as making for a harsher accentual scheme in the first half of the line. (See D. Attridge, *Well-Weighed Syllables: Elizabethan Verse in Classical Metres* (Cambridge, 1974), 30–68, on the likely importance of accent in Elizabethan reading of Latin poetry.)

21 Notos] The accusative plural *nōtos* from *nōtus*, 'acquaintance', is impossible metrically, and scarcely yields sense; Campion must intend the plural from *Notus*, the south wind, or, poetically (as in Virgil), the wind from any direction.

34   HUGH GAZZARD

TO*DAPHNIS

*The most illustrious Earl of Essex is shadowed under the person of Daphnis.

Ah! Is it anyone heavenly? For surely no earthly splendour shone in that man, certainly either Leto's son Apollo chases young loves through the green glades, or lovely Daphnis is here, for whom, were it right, the soiled earth, for whom the distant wood, for whom Cynthia has wept. In vain have the Fauns and Charites every year honoured him on both festal days and at merry marriages; having venerated the shrines of single Diana he destroys, in the mountains and woods, the wild haunts of beasts. Ah, too too intrepid, he yearns to encounter with the fierce lion, and to inflame huge bulls to fight. As, just now, where Tagus weighs down on gold-bearing sands, through the shifting sea-ridges long begirt by a troop of young men, he has hewn the fleeing back of the boar. The daughters of Atlas (who bear this happy gift, to be stars for love), after the passing of unfortunate Hyas, stood not more confounded, nor sped through the woods more alarmed—the woods everywhere re-echoing 'Hyas'—than for you, Daphnis (besides the huge hopes of Britain), than for you, Daphnis (besides fate in the balance), the goddess was anxious, fearing the winds, and because the sea long seethed. But since at length unscathed you see dry lands at home, both the wood turns green in the ground, and the ancient reverences orderly instruct the wood-gods in solemn procession, and Menalcas has not dared envy you such glory.

At first sight these hexameters might seem a simply heroic *epibaterion*, the poem for the returning hero; but Campion has 'shadowed' his returning hero under the persona of one who was, famously, a subject for pastoral elegy. Daphnis was the herdsman, the great inventor and exponent of bucolic song, mourned in the first Idyll of Theocritus; but it is the Daphnis of Virgil's *Ecloga* 5, albeit largely lacking the amatory associations customarily (as in Theocritus, and elsewhere in Virgil) attached to his name, whom Campion is recalling.[39] Virgil's Daphnis is mourned in a pastoral dialogue by Menalcas and Mopsus, and Campion evokes Virgil not only by including a Menalcas (whose name ends both his and Virgil's poem) but structurally, too: 'Ad Daphnin' has twenty-five lines, the exact length of each of the laments for Daphnis sung by Virgil's shepherds in *Ecloga* 5. And in making Essex the topical counterpart of his Daphnis Campion could scarcely have been unaware of the critical tradition (recorded as early as Servius, routinely recounted in Renaissance scholia on Virgil, and mentioned in Abraham Fraunce's translation of the *Ecloga*[40]) which interpreted the Daphnis of *Ecloga* 5 as an allegorical or quasi-allegorical figuration of the recently slain Julius Caesar.[41] Was Campion perhaps also influenced by the publication in 1589 of Fraunce's translation?

39 See *Theocritus*, ed. A. S. F. Gow, 2nd edn., 2 vols. (Cambridge, 1952), ii. 1–2, on surviving evidence for the ancient legends of Daphnis.

40 See *The Bucoliks of Publius Virgilius* Maro, trans. Abraham Fraunce (London, 1589), C3ª. Fraunce rehearses the alternative contenders, too.

41 On which see e.g. E. Coleiro, *An Introduction to Virgil's Bucolics with a Critical Edition of the Text* (Amsterdam, 1979), 147–9, and, for a sceptical examination, H. J. Rose, *The Eclogues of Vergil* (Berkeley and Los Angeles, 1942), 117–38.

After the exclamatory ellipsis of Campion's beginning, his Daphnis is seen to be so divinely *formosus* as to be confused with Apollo (a vivid and novel feature of Virgil's heroic Daphnis was his apotheosis) (ll. 1–4). Phonic associations might be at work here: the juxtaposition of Campion's Daphnis with an enamoured and pursuant Apollo was very likely suggested by a recollection of that god's pursuit of Daphne—and, as we shall see, memories of Ovid loom large later in the poem. The poem modulates to an elegiac register, with the reference, enigmatic as yet, to the widespread weeping for Daphnis (ll. 4–5); and it is noted, apparently mournfully, that the *festa* and *Hymenaei* have been observed for his sake *nequiquam*, in vain (ll. 6–7). The succeeding images of destruction wrought on the *immania lustra ferarum* (in this context, a suitably bestial collocation for the Spanish), and of the *intrepidus* hero yearning to brave wild beasts, come straight out of epic, but they are given an elegiac distance by the deploring *Ah nimium*—as though such bravery had cost this hero his life (ll. 10–11)—as also by the very choice of an elegized hero to suggest Essex.

Then, midway through the poem, when this intrepidity is instanced, we learn the compositional occasion. Campion's reference to the *Tagus* (Tèjo), couched as it is in the recent past (*modo*), and taken with the poem's verbs of arrival and return (*adest*, *reuisas*, ll. 4, 22), makes it plain that, *pace* Vivian, Campion is celebrating Essex's exploits at and homecoming from Portugal. He gives them a complicated poetic resonance: *aurifer Tagus* he might have remembered from Catullus (*Carmina* 29. 19) and from Ovid (*Amores* 1. 15. 34); it was in any case a formulaic phrase in Latin poetry of the Renaissance. Classically, the collocation emblematized the importance to the Romans of Iberian mineral wealth, and more generally of course connoted great riches.[42] In Campion, the allusion gains contemporary piquancy from the thought of the *flota* laden with New World bullion destined for Spain. The well-versed sixteenth-century reader would surely also have heard here an echo of Sir Thomas Wyatt's lyric—famous to Elizabethans from its inclusion in Tottel's *Songes and Sonettes*—beginning 'Tagus, fare well, that westward with thy stremes | Torns up the grayns off gold alredy tryd'; that poem strikes a similar tone of heroic homecoming shot through with muted, valedictory poignancy.[43] There is another Ovidian echo in *vastator aper*—Ovid has the dying Hercules boast of having vanquished *vastator aper* (*Metamorphoses* 9. 191–2), here adopted by Campion as a formidable and bestial guise for Spain.

Then comes the poem's longest sentence—a careful, set-piece, antenantiotic and paradigmatic comparison: national and divine anxiety on account of Daphnis was not less than the confusion and trepidation, visualized by the poet, of the

---

42 On which see Publius Ovidius Naso, *Amores: Text, Prolegomena and Commentary*, ed. J. C. McKeown, 2 vols. to date, ARCA Classical and Medieval Texts, Papers and Monographs 20, 22 (Leeds, 1987–), ii. 415–16.

43 I would like to thank Professor Katherine Duncan-Jones for pointing out the probability of the allusion to Wyatt.

daughters of Atlas after the passing of Hyas (ll. 15–21). We can infer that the queen is comprehended by *diua* both from the poem's intrinsic allegorical scheme and from the book's preceding poem, dedicatorily addressed to Elizabeth *sub* (as the marginal annotation has it) *Dianae nomine*, 'under the name of Diana'. The *Atlante satae* are the Hyades, the sisters of the lion-slain huntsman Hyas (the children of Atlas and a nymph), who were metamorphosed, for grief at his loss, into stars. The story of Hyas and the Hyades was told by the ancient mythographers—by Hellicanus, Timaeus, and scholiasts on Homer and Hesiod; by Hyginus in *Fabulae* and *De astronomia*; by Alexander Polyhistor in *Cretica*; by Servius; and by scholiasts on the *Phaenomena* of Aratus: all with some variations—and told in most detail and at greatest length by Ovid in *Fasti* (5. 159–82). It is on Ovid's version of the myth that Campion demonstrably draws in this, the poem's most significant use of or allusion to the Roman poet. Campion echoes Ovid's diction: Ovid has *fleuere*, and *satus* (albeit as a different part of speech), and, crucially, he records the sisters' *pietas*, similarly cited by Campion as the mainspring of their metamorphosis; the sixteenth-century editions of Ovid emphasized the word in their marginalia upon this passage. We might also compare the Ovidian passage's plangent diacope—'mater Hyan et Hyan maestae fleuere sorores'—with the doubly repetitive onomastic peal—*Hyantis . . . Hyantida*, and *Daphni . . . Daphni*—in Campion; and the emphasis on women's sadness in both pieces; and the collocation in both of the Hyas fable with animal names and with the ocean. The precise depiction of the Hyades' confusion and clamorous flight, and its sylvan setting, are original to Campion.

The actual congruity of this comparison between the perturbed Hyades and the queen was, as we shall see, questionable, to say the least; but there may be another, cryptic, allusiveness at work favouring its aptness. *Fasti* is a calendrical poem, calibrating the Ovidian universe of myth and lore by the rhythms of the Roman year. The story of the Hyades is fixed at 2 May, and elsewhere in the poem there are references to the morning or evening appearances of the star cluster on other dates, from 17 April (4. 677–8) through to 16 June (6. 711). This, roughly speaking, is the period covered by the expedition to Portugal—indeed, the English fleet finally set sail on 17 and 18 April. And Campion must very probably have seen the Ptolemaic ephemeris usually appended to Renaissance editions of the *Fasti*, which also gave ancient dates for the morning rising of the Hyades from April to June, the first of which is 6 April; the earl of Essex sailed from Plymouth in the night of 5/6 April, and the English fleet made its first attempt at departure on the morning of the 6th.[44] Moreover, the prominence of

---

44 There would have been an even more pointed coincidence of dates had Campion known that Ovid was in fact mistaken in the *Fasti*: in Ovid's time, the morning rising at Rome of the Hyades actually happened on 16 May—the day of the landing at Peniche. But Ovid's error seems not to have been detected before the nineteenth century: see *Publii Ouidii Nasonis Fastorum libri sex*, ed. and trans. J. G. Frazer, 5 vols (London, 1929), v. 19.

the Hyades around these dates (as well as one version of their name's etymology) associated them in the classical and post-classical poetic imagination with the kind of rainy and windy weather which had confined the English fleet within Plymouth Sound through much of March and April. It is not hard to believe that these connotations would have guided so learned and deliberate a poet as Campion in his choice and shaping of mythological material, because they furnish the kind of additionally esoteric allusiveness which the makers and readers of wrought, courtly poetry so often delighted in. It is even possible to suppose that he scanned the topical section of *Fasti* precisely to find such material. Wrought poetry—and poetry that is at least courtly to the extent of having the queen and the earl amongst its implied, because dedicatory, readers—Campion's Latin verses in *Poemata* certainly are.

The poem concludes by celebrating the return of its hero (with a final Ovidian echo, if Campion remembered *patria arua* from *Ibis*, 501), which has ensured renewal and revival in the natural world and in the *solemni pompa* (ll. 22–5). This picks up on the earlier religious images of shrines and festal days, and finally clarifies the key figural scheme governing the poem, for it is apparent that Campion represents the national elite of crown and court as being invested with a kind of numinous power, and as binding society ritualistically and religiously into a harmonious whole of *Charites* and *Fauni*: a harmonious whole of, as it were, all orders. It is this disposition of things (figured as the *sacra* of Diana/Elizabeth) which the heroic and semi-divine Daphnis/Essex upholds by his presence in England.

There are suggestions of this numinously charged nationalism elsewhere in Campion's poetry: in 'Ad Dianam', for one; and in the nearly contemporary 'Ad Thamesin' Campion celebrates the nation as 'Brutique nepotibus, & diis | O vetus hospitium, sanctumque Britannia nomen' ('the ancient lodging of the heirs of Brutus and of the gods; and the holy name, Britannia'), its reformed religion preserved from Catholicism and the Armada by divine providence, figured as Neptune, who

> Nec Romana feret purgata Orgia fanis
> Reffluere, aut vetitas fieri libamen ad aras.
> O pietas odiosa deo, scelerataque sacra,
> Quae magis inficiunt (damnosa piacula) sontes.[45]

At one level, all this was consonant with the more fevered manifestations of the cult of the Virgin Queen and the apocalypticism which increasingly inflected the struggle against Spain in the 1580s and 1590s; but Campion's mythos of

---

45 Campion, *Poemata*, B3ᵃ: 'Nor will he [Neptune] allow the Roman Orgies to flow back into the cleansed shrines, or a sacrifice to be made at forbidden altars. O piety hateful to the god, and scandalous rituals (destructive sacraments) which the wicked corrupt even more.' *The Works of Thomas Campion: Complete Songs, Masques, and Treatises with a Selection of the Latin Verse*, ed. W. R. Davis (Garden City, NY, 1967), 363.

nationhood is noteworthy for its heightened classical colouring. 'Ad Daphnin', then, typifies Davis's apt characterization of Campion as a Latin poet 'working in both the epic and the erotic Ovidian traditions, with a strong sense of the meaning of myth'—and with, it might be added, a strong urge to hammer the material of contemporary history into shapely mythology, and, more generally, to give his Latin poetry public and political themes.[46] That is what he did with the defeat of the Armada in 'Ad Thamesin', with the Elizabethan court as a whole in 'Vmbra', and with the Gunpowder Plot in the late *De puluerea coniuratione*. It was an urge he shared with other Anglo-Latin poets of the 1580s and 1590s: Peele, for one, constructed his own Latin mini-epic *Pareus* (1585)—which may have had some influence on 'Ad Thamesin'—out of the recent events of the Parry plot; the Oxford press of Joseph Barnes published university-produced miscellanea of Latin verse on the Parry and Babington conspiracies in the mid-1580s; and in the 1590s William Alabaster planned but failed to execute a Latin epic of the Elizabethan age.[47] These, on a more modest scale but also in a culturally prestigious idiom, were the counterparts of Spenser's mighty, contemporary mythopoeia.

It must be admitted that, with its coupling of the current and the mythological, and, even more, with its odd fusion of—or perhaps indecision amongst—the languages of pastoral, elegy, and epic, 'Ad Daphnin' shows a poet struggling to find an idiom either thoroughly appropriate or sufficiently complex to contain the topical occasion. The strength of the poem's elegiac element is especially unexpected: it almost looks as though Campion had anticipated having to write an epicede for a slain earl of Essex. I suggest that, as with the example of Peele's *Eglogue*, this sense of instability, of generic slippage, is a product of the fact that, in the event, the aftermath of the Portugal expedition proved too troubled for these poets to attempt a straightforwardly heroic and panegyric mode. It seems that Campion was striving to find a diplomatic way of representing what had actually been (as he surely knew) the highly controversial involvement of Essex in the expedition, and that it was this that dictated his figuration of Essex's departure in such ambiguous terms, and led Campion, as it were, to lament elegiacally, rather than triumphally to laud, Essex's valour ('Ah nimium intrepidus...'). Of course, the earl's actions were controversial with nobody so much as with

46 *Works*, 359.

47 On contemporary history and mythology in *De puluerea coniuratione* see Thomas Campion, *De puluerea coniuratione—(On the Gunpowder Plot): Sidney Sussex MS 59*, ed. D. Lindley, trans. R. Sowerby, Leeds Texts and Monographs, NS 10 (Leeds, 1987), 5–14, 22–3. For the influence of *Pareus* on 'Ad Thamesin', see *Oxford Poetry by Richard Eedes and George Peele*, ed. D. F. Sutton, The Renaissance Imagination (New York and London, 1995), 215. On Oxford's public poetry of the 1580s see ibid. 157–60, and William Gager, *The Complete Works*, ed. D. F. Sutton, 4 vols., The Renaissance Imagination (New York and London, 1994), iii, pp. v–xi. For Alabaster see *The Elisaeis of William Alabaster*, ed. and trans. M. O'Connell, Studies in Philology Texts and Studies (Chapel Hill, NC, 1979).

the queen, who (as was, so far as we can tell, widely known)—far from being *anxia* or as *confusa* and *trepida* as the Hyades—was furious. Her well-known letter of 4 May to Norris and Drake actually threatened Sir Roger Williams with death for having helped Essex to decamp, ending icily:

> And if Essex be now come into company of the fleet we straightly charge you that, all dilatory excuses set apart, you cause him safely to be sent hither forthwith, which if you do not, you shall look to answer for the same to your smart, for these be weighty actions nor matters wherein you are to deal by cunning of devices to seek evasions as the custom of lawyers is; neither will we be so satisfied at your hands. Therefore consider well of your doings herein.[48]

The affair did not, in the end, affect Essex's status as royal favourite after his return, but it must have contributed to the public sensitivity over the entire expedition. In his depiction of the goddess Diana anxious for the absent Daphnis, Campion is recasting the awkward actuality of the occasion into an almost absurdly wishful idealization. Presumably this was calculated to appeal to Essex and, perhaps, to the queen: the volume was after all dedicated, and perhaps presented, to both.

So much for the poem's topical content; beyond that, there is its formal and technical accomplishment. It exemplifies an artistry that inevitably is largely inaccessible to us now, but whose careful construction achieves the sort of finish prized in Renaissance Latin verse. Clauses and cadencing are weighed and tiered; apposition and antithesis, and sparing anaphora, lend the poem its rhetorical rigour. And the poem exemplifies Campion's controlled and enriching consciousness of the classical paradigm.

* * *

Both Campion and Peele, in piecing together a printed literature of the public event, were striving after a public vehicle and public tenor for a poetry which, although it might court and be supported by the individual patron, might also imply a sustaining public readership. Peele in some ways may be affecting a kind of popular voice, but both his and Campion's are still essentially the productions of Elizabethan 'high' literary culture. Peele's was the only immediately contemporaneous poetic marking of this public occasion either to survive or to be entered in the Stationers' Register. There is simply no trace of any spontaneous outpouring of something like a popular literary response to the expedition, as there had been after the defeat of the Armada, and as there would be in the immediate aftermath of the earl of Essex's expedition to Cadiz in 1596, for example. This silence might in its own right be invested with a certain eloquence.

---

48 *Expedition of Norris and Drake*, ed. Wernham, 137 (omitting transcription of draft corrections).

Years later, in the popular elegiac poetry circulated in print and in manuscript—and quite possibly improvised and transmitted orally—following Essex's execution, his service in Portugal, and above all his challenge at the gates of Lisbon, were remembered:

> The Portingale can witness be
>   his Dagger at Lisbon gate he flung,
> And, like a Knight of Chivalry,
>   his Chain upon the same he hung

as *A Lamentable New Ballad vpon the Earle of Essex His Death* has it.[49] But 1589 was no second *annus mirabilis* to celebrate.

In Peele's case, taking an overview both of his extant work and of the records (sparse enough) of his life, it is easy to come away with the impression of a hard-pressed literary talent restlessly striving for novelty of form or effect, for literary currency, for cultural authority, and for marketability all at once—and struggling to find the right medium and the right readership, fighting all the while to keep his writerly head above water. The pathos of Peele's deathbed begging letter to Lord Treasurer Burghley, sent as cover for the *Tale of Troy* (revamped and pressed into service yet again), brings that home.

No doubt also the *Eglogue*, at least, will strike most readers today as mediocre poetry, and quite possibly so struck most readers in 1589. It might even come perilously—and instructively—close to being downright bad poetry: bad because of its technical clumsiness, and bad, arguably, because of its bad faith. There is its literary bad faith, from its being so nervelessly derivative; but there is its ethical bad faith too, since it puts such a specious gloss on the chaos and squandered lives of the Portugal expedition. It can register only out of the corner of its vision the 'many a *Herdsman* more disposde to morne', and it can register the swart flies busy about the bodies beside a dusty path near the Tèjo not at all. This same charge might be levelled against Campion's poem. They were at odds not just with the fortunes of the voyage, but with the hard facts of its aftermath, too. Ten days before the *Eglogue*'s entry in the Register, a royal proclamation was issued prohibiting any unauthorized personnel from the forces from approaching the court, for fear of plague. A further proclamation on 24 August prohibited unlawful assembly by the soldiers and sailors (the authorities feared rioting), and on 13 November there was a threat of martial law against 'vagrant' 'Souldiers, Mariners, Maisterlesse men'.[50]

---

49 *The Roxburghe Ballads*, vol. i, ed. W. Chappell (1871), 572; and see *Ballads from Manuscripts*, vol. ii, ed. F. J. Furnivall and W. R. Morfill (1873), 247–8.

50 P. L. Hughes and J. F. Larkin (edd.), *Tudor Royal Proclamations*, 3 vols. (New Haven and London, 1964–9), iii. 39–40, 44–6, 46–8. A proclamation of 23 January had threatened deserters from the forces with martial law.

The poems' studied evasiveness, their specious gloss, runs through the contemporary published, public, and, as it were, authorized discourse on this military venture, as through that on so many other affairs of the Elizabethan state. In fact, there was scarcely any public discourse on the venture, no doubt because of its disastrous outcome. (Much of the topical printed output of 1589 related rather to French affairs.) *A Declaration of the Causes*... (London, 1589)— anonymous, but evidently an official production—defended the expedition's seizure of Hanseatic merchants' ships, and doubled as an anti-Hispanic and anti-Catholic diatribe, and defence of domestic religious policy. Anthony Wingfield's embattled and tendentious account and defence of the venture was authorized for the press by Burghley, and appeared anonymously, but may well have been called in by the authorities in December—though it was also included by Hakluyt in his *Principall Nauigations, Voiages and Discoueries* (where it was attributed to Wingfield) in the same year. A Latin abridgement for the European market was also published. The entry in the Stationers' Register on 13 August 1589 of a ballad, not extant,

> intytuled, Discrybinge the vallure of our Englishe Archers and shott that accompanied the Blacke Prince of Portugall their governor into the feildes on tuesdaie the 12 of August with the welcome into Lymestreete by master HUGH OFFLEY[51]

presumably commemorates a civic entertainment (Offley was Sheriff of London) which might have been a populist and celebratory attempt at topicality.

A cleric, Thomas Nun, appended 'The Apologie of the Portingall Voyage' to his sermon *A Comfort against the Spaniard*, printed in 1596. The 'Apologie'—most likely also originally delivered from the pulpit, and presumably soon after the expedition's return—states the voyage's aims, justifies English support for Dom António, and extols its dubious outcome. Nun concedes that there had been great loss of life, and concedes that 'this voyage is euill spoken off of some, whome nothing contenteth, and bitter to others that lost their friends'; but, being of the godly, he can console his congregation with the thought that 'to the godly death is no curse, and as for the rest it is a great blessing to the land that they neuer returned'.[52] (This same Thomas Nun in 1599 beat his stepdaughter, Abigail, to death with a pair of tongs; he was pardoned by the queen.[53])

Faced with the inglorious failure of an expedition which had embarked with so loud a fanfare from Peele, the only two poets who tried to commemorate it did so in decidedly equivocal terms. In the *Eglogue* Peele's dialogue subsumes

---

51 *A Transcript*, ed. Arber, ii. 528.

52 Thomas Nun, *A Comfort against the Spaniard* (London, 1596; STC 18748), C2[b], C4[a].

53 National Archives (Public Record Office), London, SP 12/270/118. See also *Calendar of State Papers, Domestic Series... Elizabeth, 1598–1601* (London, 1869), 199; L. Stephen and S. Lee (edd.), *Dictionary of National Biography*, 22 vols. (repr. Oxford, 1998), xlv. 102–3, s.v. 'Peter Pett'.

the heroic into pastoral, and balances disquiet about events with the drive to find something—and someone—praiseworthy. Campion fuses, or at least juxtaposes, the heroic with pastoral elegy and both with panegyric, and suffuses the whole with an Ovidian colouring. Both Peele and Campion were debarred an uncomplicatedly heroic register, yet still there is a jarring mismatch between the triumphant version of national identity (and therefore poetic self-identity) which both are trying to promote, and the terrible reality of events. These poets might have heard, but certainly sought to silence, the complaints and laments of the many mournful herdsmen.

Exeter College, Oxford

Part II
The Arraignment of Paris

[3]

GIFTS AND REASONS: THE CONTEXTS OF PEELE'S *ARAYGNEMENT OF PARIS*

BY LOUIS ADRIAN MONTROSE

George Peele's *Araygnement of Paris* claims attention as a courtly performance and a printed text, an ephemeral social event and a monument of literary history. It has secured a prominent place in the modern canon of Elizabethan literature precisely because it is so characteristic and compendious a production of Elizabethan court culture. The *Araygnement* has been made to exemplify not only hyperbolic royal entertainment but also humble pastoral retirement; it has been interpreted not only as a glorification of power but as a repudiation of ambition. These divergent critical responses point to the ideological complexity of Elizabethan culture and Peele's play. The play's setting is pastoral, its dramaturgy is spectacular, and its royal sentiments are fulsome. Its action repeatedly involves the humble and the great in rites of homage or strategies of coercion. *The Araygnement of Paris* recreates the culture which creates it. Acts of gift-giving and relationships of power within the fiction reproduce basic characteristics of the social world in which the play is written and performed. I shall explore some of the symbolic forms which typify Elizabethan court culture and Peele's play: pastoral conventions, myths of royal power, and acts of prestation.* If my exploration of these forms appears as much concerned with the contexts of Peele's play as with the play itself, this is because "text" and "context" define and illuminate each other.

---

* *The Oxford English Dictionary* defines *prestation* as "the action of paying, in money or service, what is due by law or custom, or in recognition of feudal superiority; a payment or the performance of a service so imposed or exacted; also, the performance of something promised." The earliest usage cited is in the Parliamentary rolls of 1473. The word is obsolete in English, though still current in French. *Prestation* is a central term in Marcel Mauss' ethnological classic, *Essai sur le don* (1925), where it is used of material and symbolic objects given within a network of social exchanges. The translator of the English edition (*The Gift*, trans. Ian Cunnison [New York, 1967]), uses *prestation* for want of an adequate modern English equivalent. I use *prestation* to connote an implicitly obligatory or coercive act of giving.

I PASTORAL

Hallett Smith opens his historical and critical study of Elizabethan poetry with a seminal chapter on pastoral, in which he takes as his paradigm Peele's *Araygnement of Paris:* "The Elizabethan attitude toward Paris reveals much of the meaning and significance of pastoral in the poetry of the age"; as "the major Elizabethan treatment of the Paris story, George Peele's play . . . is so important as an indication of the significance of pastoral in the Elizabethan mind that it must be discussed" in a study otherwise confined to non-dramatic poetry.[1] Peele's Paris says that he gave the prize to Venus rather than to Juno or Pallas because the only virtue in consideration was beauty; and because, as a shepherd, he is susceptible to the attractions of love and beauty but immune to those of power and riches, chivalry and martial prowess. Smith concludes that

> Paris is the judge precisely because the conditions of the pastoral life provide the greatest independence, the greatest security. The shepherd is not motivated by ambition or greed. Free from these two common passions, he enjoys "content," or the good life. Elizabethan pastoral poetry is essentially a celebration of this ideal of content or *otium.* The contemplative state enjoys a freedom, not only from ambition or greed, but from the vicissitudes of fortune. (*Elizabethan Poetry*, pp. 8-9)

Thus the "central meaning" of Elizabethan pastoral is defined as "the rejection of the aspiring mind. The shepherd demonstrates that true content is to be found in this renunciation" (p. 10). Smith's questionable though influential thesis invites an antithetical reading of Peele's play; and it provides a basis for fruitful disagreement about "the central meaning" of the Elizabethan pastoral kind.

In the sixteenth century, Paris's meeting with the three goddesses was commonly expounded as a choice among life patterns faced by a young man on the threshold of maturity:

> Hee beginneth nowe to discourse within himselfe, what kinde of life he were best to followe as the most noble in account amongst men: whether that which is grounded uppon knowledge, which the Philosophers were wont to cal a contemplative kind of life: or otherwise, yt which guideth a man that addicteth himself only to worldly matters, which they terme active: or else that which consisteth wholy in pleasure, which they name delightfull.[2]

Smith's argument tends to collapse the threefold Choice of Paris into the prevailing binary oppositions of Renaissance ethics, and to conflate the opposition between *otium* and *negotium* with that between contemplation and action. He turns concupiscible Paris into a philosopher—a lover of flesh into a lover of wisdom. Renaissance moralizers of myth usually opt for Juno or Pallas, or for a Humanist reconciliation of Action and Contemplation; they censure the Venerean alternative which was Paris's choice. Although he makes much of the young man's freedom to choose among all the options, Nenna concludes sternly that "he that is caried away to follow the delightfull kind of life, doth bring unto him selfe unspeakable detriment."

The fable is given an entirely different emphasis in the poetic theology of Florentine Neoplatonism. In a supplement to his commentary on Plato's *Philebus,* Ficino interprets the figure of Paris, tending his flocks on Mount Ida, as an allegory of the soul "nourishing the senses in the disordered matter of the elements."[3] According to Ficino, Paris's choice among the three goddesses is an allegory of the soul's option to pursue wisdom, power, or sensual pleasure. Ficino understands the pursuit of pleasure to be innate in human creatures; his concern is to discriminate among the forms of pleasure. Paris pursues the concupiscible pleasure of the lower senses; Ficino approves the pursuit of a rational pleasure in contemplative tranquility, a pursuit synonymous with Neoplatonic philosophy itself. In a dedicatory proem addressed to Lorenzo de' Medici, Ficino writes that concupiscible Paris, active Hercules, and contemplative Socrates all met with disaster because they were single-minded in the pursuit of sensual pleasure, power, and wisdom, respectively. But "our Lorenzo, having been taught by the oracle of Apollo, has neglected none of the god[desse]s. For he has . . . admired each one for her merits. On this account, he has won wisdom from Pallas and power from Juno and the graces and poetry and music from Venus" (p. 482). Like the Florentine court philosopher, the Elizabethan court poet turns the Choice of Paris into a lavish compliment for a Renaissance prince precisely by transcending the very act of choice: the point of the compliment is that the prince melds the alternatives into an harmonious *triplex vita.*

Of course, the differences between Peele's transformation of the myth and Ficino's are as important as the resemblances. Indeed, with its stress on a synthesis of pleasure and wisdom and its critique of the active life, Ficino's disquisition on the Judgment of Paris is better fitted to the terms of Smith's argument than is Peele's play. Peele's conceit is true to the prevailing temper of Elizabethan ethics in that it disapproves of the Epicurism and neglects the contemplative and mystical elements that are fundamental to Ficino's philosophy. The most significant innovation in Peele's treatment of the myth is to encompass Diana and the virtue of militant virginity. To proclaim that Elizabeth infolds the excellences of all the goddesses is to perfect the encomium in a manner that is possible only when the prince is a woman. By turning the Choice of Paris into a *Trionfo della Castità,* Peele is skillfully articulating the sexual politics of Elizabethan court culture.[4]

Although he is sometimes treated as a type of the shepherd, Paris is a Trojan prince who has been exiled in a foredoomed attempt to evade the prophecy that he will bring ruin to Troy. Paris's rape of Helen is the fruit of his choice of Venus, and it precipitates the war which destroys his civilization. Peele insists upon this fatal framework by presenting Ate herself as the prologue to his play, to prophesy "the Tragedie of Troie" (l. 29).[5] Paris chooses Venus over Juno and Pallas, and is arraigned by the Olympian gods at the insistence of the disgruntled losers. Diana is called upon to arbitrate because these events have occurred within her territories, and because the harried male gods think it politic for "a woman to be judge amonge her pheeres" (l. 1069). Diana rejudges the contest between the three goddesses; she awards the prize to her own votary, the "peereles nymphe" Eliza, whose country is Elizium and whose people are called Angeli. Eliza is

> In State Queene Junos peere, for power in armes,
> And vertues of the minde Minervaes mate:
> As fayre and lovely as the queene of love:
> As chast as Dian in her chast desires.

(ll. 1170-73)

In the culminating celebration of Elizabeth, fiction is absorbed into actuality and drama is absorbed into rite. Because the queen infolds their separate perfections, the goddesses gladly resign to her; because her virtues are "more than may belong, / By natures lawe to any earthly wight" (ll. 1221-1222), the Fates "lay downe their properties at the Queenes feete."

The play's extravagant compliment to Elizabeth is not an afterthought but a climax. What is significant about Paris is that he chooses wrongly; the movement and meaning of the drama work to discredit his pastoral perspective. Had Paris remained faithful to Oenone, the authentic shepherdess, he would have continued to enjoy the pastoral *otium* of which Smith writes. Paris's abandonment of rustic Oenone for "a face that hath no peere" (l. 490), "a lasse of Venus court" (l. 494), is a Venerean manifestation of the aspiring mind. Paris, as Spenser's Thomalin points out in *The Shepheardes Calender,* is an ironic type of the shepherd, a perverter of pastoral:

> For he was proude, that ill was payd,
>   (no such mought shepheards bee)
> And with lewde lust was overlayd.[6]

Peele's use of the myth of Paris is precisely opposed to Smith's interpretation: pastoral's offer of freedom from ambition, greed, and the vicissitudes of Fortune is an illusion, a deception.

The title page of the 1584 quarto of *The Araygnement of Paris* calls it "A PASTORALL." In Elizabethan literary theory and practice, the pastoral kind is constituted by a complex of formal features—conventions of character, setting, and theme—derived from the material objects and relations of rural life as well as from the traditions of literary history. The flexibility and allusiveness of this complex suit it to a variety of generic combinations and rhetorical strategies. Smith's pastoral formula—authentic contentment found in the renunciation of ambition—is an historical variant of Renato Poggioli's pastoral theory. For Poggioli, "the psychological root of the pastoral is a double longing after innocence and happiness, to be recovered not through conversion or regeneration but merely through a retreat."[7] Smith isolates "the central meaning" of pastoral in an ethical and political *theme;* Poggioli isolates it in the psycho-social *function* of Smith's theme: pastoral "performs with especial intensity the role that Freud assigns to art in general: that of acting as a vicarious compensation for the renunciations imposed by the social order on its individual members, and of reconciling men to the sacrifices they have made in civilization's behalf" (*The Oaten Flute,* p. 31). To mollify civilization's discontents in otiose fictions is to perform what Puttenham characterizes as the recreative function of literature: "the common solace of mankind in all his travails and cares of this transitory life."[8] But Puttenham is describing a function or effect that may be realized by any number of literary forms; it may include but is neither limited to nor wholly characteristic of the pastoral kind. Neither Smith's theme nor Poggioli's function exhausts the meaning of Elizabethan pastoral form.

The "central meaning" of Elizabethan pastoral forms like Peele's is not to be sought in their constitution of a "positive ideal" but in their performance of a social function: courtly pastorals are gracious and intimate cultural mediations of hierarchical political relationships.[9] The play's rustic setting, inhabited by creatures and deities

Louis Adrian Montrose 437

of fields and woods, provides an amenable meeting ground for the
humble and the mighty—mortals and goddesses, subjects and their
queen. Smith abstracts the Paris-motif from Peele's text and
abstracts Peele's text from the context of its performance. Similarly,
he abstracts an element of Elizabethan ideology—"the rejection of
the aspiring mind"—from its context in the Elizabethan social process. At the heart of orthodox Elizabethan cultural values was a
doctrine of divinely appointed, unchanging, hierarchical, and
analogical order. This conservative "Elizabethan world picture,"
however, was very much at odds with the facts of intellectual fer-
ment and social change so evident in the Elizabethan world. "The
rejection of the aspiring mind" may have been a requisite avowal of
piety but it was only a very partial expression of the spirit of the age.

In his study, *The aspiring mind of the Elizabethan younger generation*, Anthony Esler demonstrates that there were opposing attitudes toward ambition in Elizabethan England, and that the values of Elizabethan gentlemen and courtiers were often ambivalent.
He explains this complex and conflict-laden situation in terms of a
shift in the collective consciousness—the shared values and
experience—of successive generations:

> Two processes seem to have operated simultaneously in the de-
> velopment of this Elizabethan younger generation during the
> 1570's and early 1580's. First, there was a gradual process of
> alienation from the ideals of their fathers. Among the conse-
> quences of this alienation was an emotional rejection of the older
> generation's strictures against ambition. Secondly, there was a
> restless search for new values in a world of new and changing
> facts. Among the results of this quest for new ideals was the
> growth of a mood of high aspiration.[10]

The honors, power, and wealth rejected by Paris were ardently
pursued by the younger generation of Elizabethan gentleman
courtiers; the base-born writers who were their contemporaries and
had been educated with them pursued analogous goals within a far
more circumscribed range.

The literary sensibilities of these groups were pervasively Ovidian and Petrarchan, and vaguely Neoplatonic; the literature of
desire and amorous courtship they created is one of the characteristic expressions of their "mood of high aspiration." Their courtship
of Venus shadowed their courtships of Juno and Pallas. This amorous mode must have gained vitality from the fact that the ultimate
source of all preferments in Elizabethan society was "a most royall
Queene or Empresse . . . a most vertuous and beautiful Lady"

(Spenser, "Letter to Ralegh"). The ubiquitous persona of the plaintive and suppliant lover may project the aspiring courtier-poet's response to the impediments he faces: the patriarchal authoritarianism of an older generation who control policy and patronage; the tension between the sober values of Tudor Humanism and new or foreign tastes and values which implicitly challenge or undermine internalized norms; the Crown's severely limited and contracting resources, and its arbitrary bestowal of the rewards at its disposal.

The younger generation of ambitious gentlemen-courtiers and base-born writers aspiring to court patronage were the Elizabethans who most assiduously cultivated the humble pastoral kind. What appears to be a contradiction between ambition and pastoralism, between social value and cultural form, may in fact be a subtle rhetorical strategy. Puttenham dubs allegory "The Courtier or figure of faire semblant" (p. 299): "the Courtly figure *Allegoria* . . . is when we speake one thing and thinke another, and that our wordes and our meanings meete not. The use of this figure is so large, and his vertue of so great efficacie as it is supposed no man can pleasantly utter and perswade without it, but in effect is sure never or very seldome to thrive and prosper in the world, that cannot skilfully put it in use" (p. 186). Puttenham personifies his ironic figure of allegory as a Courtier; and the Elizabethan courtier incarnates such an allegory when he dons the mask of a shepherd. When the courtly poet's pastoral discourse rejects the aspiring mind, the politic shepherd may be speaking one thing and thinking another.

Consider the case of George Peele. A well educated but base-born and socially obscure member of the Elizabethan younger generation creates a lavish compliment to his prince. He is given an opportunity to serve his own interests by serving the Court. "The rejection of the aspiring mind" seems no more applicable to the personal motives of the humble poet than to those of the noble courtier or the prince herself. An expressive and compensatory psychological perspective which sees the function of Elizabethan pastoral as "the solace of mankind in all his travails and cares of this transitorie life" must be complemented by a rhetorical and dialectical social perspective. Such a perspective characterizes the third book of Puttenham's acute treatise on court culture and court conduct: courtly pastorals, like courtiers themselves, "do busily negotiat by coulor of otiation" (pp. 301-302).

Louis Adrian Montrose   439

II POWER

In his discussion of the eclogue, Puttenham makes a fundamental distinction between the pastoral of naive song and the pastoral of "artificiall poesie." In early ages, poetry was a spontaneous expression of actual shepherds, who enjoyed abundant leisure time in which to recreate themselves. Pastoral poets since Vergil, living in complex civilizations, have written artfully and obliquely about great persons and great affairs: "The Poet devised the *Eglogue* ... not of purpose to counterfait or represent the rusticall manner of loves and communication: but under the vaile of homely persons, and in rude speeches to insinuate and glaunce at greater matters, and such as perchance had not bene safe to have beene disclosed in any other sort" (p. 38). We do not know under what auspices *The Araygnement of Paris* was composed nor under what circumstances it was presented. It is apparent, however, that Peele's play belongs to a corpus of courtly texts and performances which shadowed the controversial issues of royal marriage and succession.[11] Courtly pastorals exemplify Puttenham's "Courtly figure *Allegoria*": in "the rusticall manner of loves and communication," Peele's mythological court pastoral insinuates and glances "at greater matters, and such as perchance had not bene safe to have bene disclosed in any other sort."

By an accident of fortune—or by the inscrutable will of Divine Providence—a profoundly and pervasively patriarchal society came to be governed by a virgin queen. The royal exception proved the patriarchal rule in society at large; even so, most of the men who surrounded the Queen wanted to see her married. There was a deeply felt and loudly voiced need to insure a legitimate succession, upon which the welfare of the whole nation depended. But there seems also to have been a more diffuse and obliquely expressed motivation: the political nation—which was wholly a nation of men—sometimes found it annoying or perturbing to serve a prince who was also a woman, a woman who was unsubjected to a man. Elizabeth was an anomaly. And her political genius manifested itself in her ability to turn to advantage the enormous political handicap of her gender.

Elizabeth's first parliament (1559) urged her to marry. In her reply, she discriminated pointedly between the humble petition of obedient subjects and the "very great presumption" of those who sought "to bind and limit" the sovereign's will—"To take upon you to draw my love to your liking or frame my will to your fantasies; for a guerdon constrained and a gift freely given can never agree together." She concluded that she was content to have as her epitaph "that a Queen, having reigned such a time, lived and died a virgin."[12] When she told her most assiduous suitor, the Earl of Leicester, "I will have here but one Mistress, and no Master,"[13] she was acknowledging the principle by which she retained political authority: the interdependence of her maidenhood and her mastery. The negative examples of her half-sister and her cousin—the fond doting of Mary Tudor, the violent passion of Mary Stuart—taught Elizabeth that the power of Venus might weaken the woman and corrupt the queen. The psychological factors in Elizabeth's choice of single life were also intrinsically social and political factors. The integrity and strength of the English body politic came to seem mystically dependent upon the integrity and strength—the intactness—of the Queen's body natural. The fantastic cult that celebrated the magical power of royal virginity was grounded in the most basic of socio-sexual realities: in a world otherwise governed by lords, fathers, and husbands, Elizabeth's power over access to her own person was a source of her political power. Her control of the realm was dependent upon her physical and symbolic control of her own body.

Common subjects were considered unfit to hold opinions about affairs of state. Even for courtiers, it was a risky business to offer advice to the prince. From the beginning of the reign, Elizabeth made it clear that she was hostile to discussion of her marital status or the royal succession, the intertwined destinies of her natural and political bodies. And from the beginning of the reign, courtiers and statesmen employed pagan myth to insinuate and glance at these intimate and awesome matters. In March 1565, the Earl of Leicester sponsored a pre-Lenten entertainment at court that included a mythological play. The Spanish ambassador is our witness: "The plot was founded on the question of marriage, discussed between Juno and Diana, Juno advocating marriage and Diana chastity. Jupiter gave the verdict in favour of matrimony. . . . The Queen turned to me and said, 'This is all against me'."[14] The Queen attended an aristocratic wedding in July 1566, at which a masque was performed. The gentleman masquers brought wedding gifts from the gods; Venus sent her golden apple. The presenter acknowledged the royal presence but pointedly bestowed the prize upon the bride. Juno sent word that wedlock was the most honorable state; Diana conceded that it was woman's destiny.[15] To glorify the bride was obliquely to criticize the fair vestal thronèd by the west, the guest of honor.

During the early years of the reign, the Earl of Leicester seems to have thought that Queen Elizabeth's person and the crown itself were within his reach. Although in time Leicester's vision of kingship faded away, the courtship continued until his death. Two of the entertainments he offered to the Queen on progress are of particular interest in connection with *The Araygnement of Paris: The Princely Pleasures at Kenelworth Castle* (1575); and *The Lady of May* (1578), a pastoral devised by Leicester's nephew, Philip Sidney, and performed at Wanstead.[16] The *Princely Pleasures* included a mythological show devised by Gascoigne; it was intent on "perswading the Queenes Majestie . . . that she consider all things by proofe, and then shee shall finde much greater cause to followe Juno then Dyana" (p. 107). Diana seeks her nymph, Zabeta, whom she has not seen for seventeen years; Zabeta is said to follow Juno now, though she remains constant to her maiden vows. Diana is a goddess of girlhood chastity, of princesses who live in maiden meditation, fancy-free; Juno is a goddess of womanly majesty, of marriage and matron queens. Zabeta has been a nominal follower of Juno since Elizabeth became Queen in 1558; the intent of the show is to bring the Queen to emulate Juno fully by fulfilling herself in marriage.

One of the most striking features of Gascoigne's text is that it gives full play to the topic of *maistrye,* to the maiden's fear—the maiden queen's fear—that for a woman, marriage means bondage. At the beginning of the play, Diana praises the virgin's estate:

> Rejoysing yet (much more) to drive your dayes,
> In life at large, that yeeldeth calme content,
> Then wilfully to treade the wayward wayes,
> Of wedded state, which is to thraldome bent.
>
> (p. 107)

Castibula, Diana's nymph, fears that Zabeta has been seduced:

> I dread Dame *Juno* with some gorgeous gift,
> Hath layde some snare, hyr fancie to entrap,
> And hopeth so hyr loftie mynde to lyft
> On *Hymens* bed, by height of worldly hap.
>
> (p. 110)

But Mercury reassures Diana and the nymphs:

> For though she finde the skil
> A kingdome for to weelde,

> Yet cannot *Juno* winne her will
> Nor make her once to yeelde
> Unto the wedded life,
> But still she lives at large
> And holdes her neck from any yoke,
> Without controll of charge.

(p. 115)

Diana is led to Elizabeth and praises her splendid fusion of "Princely port" and "Maiden's minde": "I joy with you, and leave it to your choice / What kinde of life you best shall like to holde" (p. 117).

Diana may leave the choice to Elizabeth but Gascoigne concludes his play with a presumptuous attempt to frame the Queen's will to Leicester's fantasy. Iris comes from Juno to discredit Mercury and Diana; she concludes the play with Juno's plea:

> O Queene, O worthy Queene,
> Yet never wight felt perfect blis,
> but such as wedded beene.

(p. 120)

The play "never came to execution," perhaps because the Queen's host thought his servants' efforts would give offence; in any case, the text would soon be in print for all to read.

In Sidney's Wanstead entertainment, Elizabeth is invited to choose a husband—a husband for the May Lady who is said to emulate the Queen. Elizabeth prefers the docile shepherd to the aggressive forester, even though Sidney has deliberately slanted the contest strongly in the forester's favor. Whether or not it pleased her host and his nephew, by her judgment Elizabeth had proved herself "Juno, Venus, Pallas *et profecto plus*" (p. 31). On Leicester's behalf, she was presented with "a chain of round agates something like beads," upon which he faithfully had said his *Ave Elizabeths*. The holy and inviolable virginity of the Queen is acknowledged in a tone of witty sacrilege and self-mockery reflecting a long personal intimacy. The whole entertainment seems to play out a delicately allegorical struggle for sexual and political mastery between a royal mistress and her ardent courtiers.[17]

Courtly entertainments constitute an elaborate sign system, a formation of figurative persons, actions, and topics in which loyal subjects may obliquely consider matters of state and subtly manipulate the royal will. Peele's *Araygnement of Paris* belongs within this tradition but its rhetorical motives are opposed to those which characterize most earlier texts. For example, Peele's play is an obvious antithesis to the 1566 wedding masque, in which the Judgment of Paris was re-judged in favor of the bride rather than the Queen. Entertainments such as those sponsored by the Earl of Leicester at Kenilworth and Wanstead in the 1570's ostensibly offered a choice to the Queen but it was one in which the options were skewed against female independence or dominion. Compared to these, Peele's offering is not "a guerdon constrained" but "a gift freely given." *The Araygnement of Paris* is typical of royal entertainments in its hyperbolic treatment of the royal spectator and her fictional personae. But it differs from many of the entertainments of the previous two decades in that it fully acknowledges and celebrates the Queen's own choice, her complex transcendence of the simplistic oppositions contrived by her courtiers. This Eliza, "whom some Zabeta call" (l. 1176), "is shee, / In whom do mete so manie giftes in One" (ll. 1167-68).

The play begins with Ate's grim prophecy of the fate of Troy, a civilization bound to the cycle of desire and destruction. Diana describes Elizium as "an ancient seat of kinges, a seconde Troie," where Eliza "giveth lawes of justice and of peace" (ll. 1153, 1157). The play ends with the providential Elizabethan fulfillment of Troy's promise, a civilization achieved by the virtuous and gentle discipline of holiness and temperance, chastity and justice. The dynastic and imperial myth which traces Elizabeth's lineage to Aeneas affirms that her state does not merely recapitulate but transcends the glories of Troy and Rome. Lustful Paris and the three covetous, contentious goddesses give way to Diana and Eliza. Like many another Elizabethan text, *The Araygnement of Paris* is concerned with the establishment and maintenance of order, and with the constant threat of disorder. Paris is the instrument of discord and is subject to the Fates; he is inscribed within a tragic, pagan world. Elizabeth rules the Fates and, like the virgin goddess of Vergil's prophetic fourth eclogue, she redeems history; she masters and harmonizes the contending forces within herself, her court, her realm.[18]

The analogical principle that pervades Elizabethan modes of thought structures Peele's play: order in the body politic depends upon and resembles order in the body natural; ordered selves create ordered states. *The Araygnement of Paris* abounds in examples of ungoverned and destructive passions. Not only does Peele's Venus personify seductive lust but his Juno is ceaselessly jealous and his Pallas is bloody (l. 117). When Paris urges Oenone to sing, she catalogues thirteen classical myths as possible subjects. Almost all of these involve rape or rebellion, violent acts of mastery and illicit desires which incur terrible punishments (ll. 252-77). Peele's double plot concerns the destructiveness of passion: "Poor Colin, that is ill for thee, that art as true in trust / To thy sweete smerte, as to his Nymphe Paris hath bin unjust" (ll. 597-98). The parallel courtships of Oenone and Paris and Colin and Thestylis end tragically, one in desertion and the other in indifference. The Choice of Paris and the Fall of Troy exemplify a cycle of love and death, violence and subversion, in the self and in the state. Elizabeth breaks the cycle; she is "the noble Phoenix of our age" (l. 1235), unique, unmated, and self-renewing. Elizabeth is "As fayre and lovely as the queene of love" but she is also "As chast as Dian in her chast desires" (ll. 1172-73). The play's Epilogue concludes with a simple *credo:* the Queen is "Corpore, mente, libro, doctissima, candida, casta."

A painting of Queen Elizabeth and the three goddesses, formerly attributed to Hans Eworth, gave the prize to the Queen a dozen or more years before Peele's *Araygnement of Paris* was performed.[19] Although this painting has been cited often as an analogue to Peele's play, there has been no comparison of how these two "texts" treat their common subject. The painting is characterized by oppositions, whereas the play achieves overwhelming harmony in the collective worship of the Queen. In royal performance, Elizabeth herself actually became the drama's incarnate resolution; she was the cynosure of both the characters and the audience. Of course, the Queen could only be represented in the painting; she could hardly be present within it. But perhaps the most striking compositional feature of the painting is that the center is occupied by the figure of Juno rather than the representation of Elizabeth. Juno looks toward Elizabeth; for the spectator, however, it is not Elizabeth but Juno who is the painting's cynosure. Elizabeth and her two ladies-in-waiting are heavily clothed; only their hands and faces are visible. The Queen's black, cross-hatched, and armor-like gown falls heavily in straight lines. It is quite unlike the multi-colored finery she wore on state occasions and in most of her portraits, and unlike the simple gowns of vestal white in which she often dressed.[20] The artist seems deliberately to have avoided brilliant effects in his treatment of the royal image. Comparison of the painting with the final pageant of Peele's play suggests that the

"Elizabeth I And the Three Goddesses," by "HE," 1569. COPYRIGHT RESERVED.

painting's stylistic and spatial details are at odds with its overt gesture of royal praise.

Juno's position as the focal point of the painting is reinforced by her dynamic pose: the torsion of her body; the swirling and flying of her gown and mantle; the emphatic gesturing of her hands; the intersecting planes formed by her bent and upraised arm, boldly marking the center of the canvas. Juno is equidistant from the Queen of England and the Queen of Love; her head turns back and her eyes fix upon Elizabeth, even as her feet move toward Venus. In the right half of the canvas, Pallas is the mediatory figure in a triad of goddesses; at the center, Juno is the mediatrix between Elizabeth and Venus, the paired and opposed figures on either side of the canvas. Elizabeth stands erect at the top of the stairs; Venus is seated, her feet touching the grass; and Juno stands between them, upon the lowest stair. The glances of these three figures lie in the same plane, which slopes downward across the painting, between Elizabeth and Venus. Venus is appropriately nude but is seated upon what appears to be a white gown. She and Cupid are tenderly embracing, though both look toward Elizabeth. At their feet lie his golden bow and quiver, and a broken arrow that points away from Elizabeth. The artist's treatment of the Goddess of Love is elegant and dignified; the emphasis is decidedly maternal.

The two groups of figures are placed in a sharply contrasted background of enclosed and open spaces, court and country, art and nature. Conspicuously absent are the figures, attributes, and woodland setting of the Diana cult, all of which are essential elements in the iconography of Peele's play. The iconography of the right half of the painting delicately suggests that the flamboyant majesty of Juno is joined to the fecund and protective motherhood of Venus by the heroic wisdom of Pallas. In the absence of Diana, Peele's mediatrix, the goddesses form a reconciled triad in their collective opposition to Elizabeth and her two attendant "nymphs." I am suggesting that the painter equivocates in his handling of the royal theme; and that its equivocations relate the painting to those contemporaneous mythological court entertainments of the 1560's and 1570's which, even as they glorified the Queen, obliquely criticized her obstinate persistence in single blessedness.

The painting of Queen Elizabeth and the Three Goddesses does not provide a visual translation of Peele's play so much as a foil for its unequivocal celebration of the royal virgin cult. The attitude of Peele's play was uncommon in royal entertainments before the 1580's. But by 1582, the prolonged courtship between the Queen and the Duke of Alençon, perhaps her most serious prospect for marriage, was finally at an end. Elizabeth was now entering her sixth decade, and the expectation that she would marry and produce an heir had almost faded away. Peele's play, performed and printed in the early 1580's, is responding to an altered view of the political horizon. His retrial of the Judgment of Paris epitomizes and celebrates a major reorientation in the form of Elizabethan court culture.

III PRESTATION

The central meaning of Peele's play is not to be found in the arraignment of Paris but in the apotheosis of Elizabeth. The presentation of a golden ball to the Queen climaxes a series of courtships involving the offering of gifts. In the first four scenes of the play, the lowly make symbolic offerings to the great. It is good to "give a thing, / A signe of love, unto a mightie person, or a king" (ll. 56-57). Pan, Faunus, and Silvanus—the "poore countrie gods"

(l. 69) of shepherds, hunters, and woodsmen—bring votive offerings to their respective goddesses: a lamb for Juno, a faun for Venus, an oaken bough for Minerva. Flora offers an emblematic display of flowers for each goddess. Pomona's offering of apples to all the goddesses balances Ate's demonic gift. The "fatall frute / Raught from the golden tree of Proserpine" (ll. 6-7) is cast among the goddesses in the form of "a ball of golde, a faire and worthie prize" (l. 357). In their competition for Ate's offering, the goddesses themselves offer worthy prizes to a mortal: riches, honors, and sexual favors. Collectively, they invest Paris as their judge; then, individually, they offer bribes to him for his partisanship.

The final offerings and collective act of homage infold and transcend the preceding rites and contests: "This Paragon, this onely this is shee, / In whom do meete so manie giftes in one" (ll. 1166-1167). Accompanying their ritual actions with a solemn Latin chant, the three Fates perform a "sacrifice" (l. 1238) to the Queen; they offer up unto her their distaff, spindle, and fatal knife. Diana offers to Elizabeth "This prize from heaven and heavenly goddesses" (l. 1241). A trio of humble rustic gods pays tribute to a trio of great goddesses, who in turn join a trio of Fates in paying tribute to a figure who is paradoxically human and divine. Peele's scenario suggests an Epiphany scene, in which shepherds and magi bring symbolic gifts to an incarnate deity, a prince of peace.[21] *The Araygnement of Paris* is a gift to the Queen, a rhetorical vehicle of royal courtship, which repeatedly thematizes its own social function.

The gift forms and the motives for giving incorporated into Peele's play recreate characteristic practises of Elizabethan culture. A few examples of Elizabethan prestation will suggest the scope of this dialectic between text and context. Elizabeth's triumphal entry into London on the day before her coronation was conceived and presented as the embodiment of "two gyftes": "blessing tonges, which many a welcome say" and "true hertes, which love thee from their roote."[22] Elizabeth was also presented with material signs of love: "a purse of crimosin sattin richly wrought with gold, wherein the citie gave unto the Quene's majestie a thousand markes in gold . . . The Lord maior, hys brethren, and comminaltie of the citie, to declare their gladnes and good wille towardes the Quene's majestie, did present her grace with that gold, desyring her grace to continue their good and gracious Quene, and not to esteme the value of the gift, but the mynd of the gevers" (pp. 26-27).

The Queen received these gifts graciously and requited them liberally; she responded "merveilous pithilie": "I thanke my lord maior, his brethren, and you all. . . . Perswade yourselves, that for the safetie and quietnes of you all, I will not spare, if nede be to spend my blood. God thanke you all" (p. 27). A pageant of Time and Truth culminated in Truth's presentation of the English Bible to Elizabeth. As restorer of the Reformed religion, the Queen herself was *Veritas, filia Temporis*: "Tyme? sayth she, and Tyme hath brought me hether" (p. 26). "She as soone as she had received the booke, kyssed it, and with both her handes held up the same, and so laid it upon her breast, with great thankes to the citie therfore" (pp. 28-29). The pageant following the presentation of the Bible purposed "to put her grace in remembrance of the state of the commonweale, which Time with Truth his doughter doth revele, which Truth also her grace hath received, and therfore cannot but be merciful and careful for the good government thereof" (p. 30). The narrative logic of the pageant conveys the moral coerciveness of the gift. Acceptance of a purse and a bible from the citizens of London puts Elizabeth under obligation to look to their material and spiritual welfare.

The authorized record of the entry, in print within ten days of the event, was an early example of the regime's cultivation of popular opinion. Appended to the narrative were "Certain notes of the quene's majestie's great mercie, clemencie, and wisdom used in this passage." One of them is particularly striking:

> What more famous thing doe we reade in auncient histories of olde time, then that mightye princes have gentlie received presentes offered them by base and low personages. . . . Let me se any writer that in any one prince's life is able to recount so manie presidentes of this vertue, as her grace shewed in that one passage through the citie. How many nosegaies did her grace receive at poore women's handes? how ofttimes staied she her chariot, when she saw any simple body offer to speake to her grace? A branche of Rosemarie given to her grace with supplication by a poore woman about fleetebridge, was sene in her chariot till her grace came to westminster, not without the mervaillous wondring of such as knew the presenter and noted the Quene's most gracious receiving and keping the same.
>
> (p. 38)

The reciprocal actions of the poor woman and the mighty prince introduce touches of calculating improvisation into standardized ritual gestures. The branch offered as a gift is also a symbolic admonition to the petition's recipient: "There's rosemary, that's for remembrance" (*Hamlet*, IV.v.171). Elizabeth showed herself gracefully mindful of the message and the expected response. The episode was a token of "What hope the poore and nedie may looke for at her grace's hande" (p. 38).

"The Quene's Majestie's passage through the citie of London to westminster the daye before her coronacion" was a veritable rite of passage for the new sovereign and for her new subjects. The stations of the journey occasioned a coherent program of allegorical pageants which confirmed the royal succession; affirmed principles of good government and reformed religion; and encouraged the young, female, and virgin ruler with demonstrations of public support and citations of biblical precendent. Like Elizabeth's entry into her capital and her reign, the royal progresses which later took her to aristocratic estates and provincial towns were great social dramas. They repeatedly affirmed the Queen's mystical power, her control over her domains; and they demonstrated the love and devotion of her subjects, both the humble and the great.

The shows performed during royal progresses, M. C. Bradbrook has felicitously called "drama as offering."[23] As in Sidney's *Lady of May*, an integral or culminating feature of these festivities was usually the explicit offering of gifts to the Queen. For example, as the Queen crossed a bridge on her way to the inner court of Kenilworth Castle during the Progress of 1575, she found upon the posts "sundrie presents, and giftes of provision" (Gascoigne, *Works*, II, 95). These had been left for her by Bacchus, Ceres, Pomona, Neptune, Sylvanus, Phoebus, and Mars. Later in the visit, the gifts were recalled and their significance unfolded in a coy dialogue between a Savage Man and Eccho that was overheard by the Queen (p. 99):

> Gifts? what? sent from the Gods?
>   as presents from above?
> Or pleasures of provision,
>   as tokens of true love?
>   *Eccho.*   True love
> And who gave all those gifts?
>   I pray thee (*Eccho*) say?
> Was it not he? who (but of late)
>   this building here did lay?
>   *Eccho.*   *Dudley*
> O *Dudley*, so me thought:
>   he gave him selfe and all,

> A worthy gift to be received,
>   and so I trust it shall.
>   *Eccho.*   It shall

Robert Dudley, Earl of Leicester, who had been offering himself to Elizabeth Tudor for a good many years, gave in order to receive.

The process of prestation was traditionally allegorized in the dancing Graces, "otherwise called Charites, that is thanks. Whom the Poetes . . . make three, to wete, that men first ought to be gracious and bountiful to other freely, then to receive benefits at other mens hands curteously, and thirdly to requite them thankfully: which are three sundry Actions in liberalitye."[24] In the fourth eclogue of *The Shepheardes Calender,* Colin Clout (Spenser's pastoral persona) advances Elisa (Elizabeth's pastoral persona) to be "a fourth grace . . . And reigne with the rest in heaven" ("Aprill," ll. 113, 117). Spenser's Elisa, like Peele's Eliza, is the only She, "in whom do mete so manie giftes in one" (*AP,* l. 1167). All gifts meet in Elizabeth because her manifold virtues elicit manifold acts of homage; and because, in the symbolic economy of court and monarchy, the Queen is the ultimate source and the ultimate recipient of gifts. This Spenser suggests in the Proem to his Legend of Courtesy:

> Then pardon me, most dreaded Soveraine,
> That from your selfe I do this vertue bring,
> And to your selfe doe it returne againe:
> So from the Ocean all rivers spring,
> And tribute backe repay as to their King.
> Right so from you all goodly vertues well
> Into the rest, which round about you ring,
> Faire Lords and Ladies, which about you dwell,
> And doe adorne your Court, where courtesies excell.
>   (*FQ,* VI.proem.7)

The rhythm of reciprocal giving that was exemplified in such formal rites as the exchange of New Years' gifts at Court also gave symbolic form to the patronage system upon which the Court itself was organized. Where gifts flowed, power flowed.

E. K. Chambers notes that "on New Year's Day it was etiquette for the lords and ladies at Court and many of the officers of the household to present the Queen with New Year gifts . . . while she in turn rewarded the donors with gilt plate from the royal jewel house and distributed largesse amongst her personal attendants and other customary recipients."[25] These exchanges were meticulously inventoried on great rolls signed by the Queen. The Queen's gifts came from magnates and from menials; they ranged from jewels and rich furnishings to finely bound books and fanciful constructions in marzipan. Each gave according to his ability: in 1578/79, for example, Robert Dudley, Earl of Leicester and Master of the Horse, gave "a very fair jewel of gold, being a clock garnished fully with diamonds and rubies," while John Dudley, Sergeant of the Pastry, gave "a very fair pye of quynces."[26] One's vital personal relationship to the sovereign could be renewed symbolically by an exchange of gifts at the threshold between the old court year and the new. But the rite was not without its elements of calculation and cynicism. In his discussion of profit and corruption on "The Elizabethan Political Scene," J. E. Neale remarks that "New Year's gifts were no negligible part of a patron's perquisites—nor, for that matter, of the Queen's." He records that "in December 1595 there was a rumour that the Queen 'will make both councillors and officers of Household.' A courtier was sceptical; 'but,' said he, 'it will increase the Queen's New Year gifts.'"[27] To an office-seeker, giving might bring a return of preferment; to a parsimonious and insolvent monarch, a gift might be less welcome for its sentimental than for its cash value.

In his study of "Place and Patronage in Elizabethan Politics," Wallace T. MacCaffrey explains that, although in theory "all decisions depended ultimately upon the pleasure of the sovereign lady," in fact the Elizabethan regime lacked "coercive power"; "the stability of the system demanded the arduous and constant wooing of the body politic." The monarchy "secured men's loyal service not only by appeals to their moral sense or through the wiles of the royal charmer but also by offering them material advantages. By the expert sharing of those gifts of office, prestige, or wealth at its command, the government could secure the continuing goodwill of the politically pre-eminent classes."[28] The fruits of patronage were unevenly distributed among great courtiers and government officials; their servingmen and assistants; and a large and heterogeneous group of gentry, professionals, and artisans. Suitors in this last group negotiated their indirect claims on royal munificence with the great courtiers who were not only recipients but sources of patronage.

The workings of an increasingly competitive and corrupt courtly marketplace were imaged in the harmonious order of dance and gift. In practise, the patronage system "produced a host of middlemen of all ranks who stood, hands outstretched for gratuities, between suitors and their goals" (Smith, *Government of Elizabethan England,* p. 63). If Spenser offered an idealized image of the Elizabethan court in the Proem to his Legend of Courtesy, in *Mother Hubberds Tale* he bitterly exposed how sordid and "pitifull" was "Suters state": "To fawne, to crowche, to waite, to ride, to ronne, / To spend, to give, to want, to be undone" (ll. 905-06). A correspondent of Lord Burghley observed that the buying and selling of offices "is winked at, and the mart kept within the Court"; and Michael Hicks, Burghley's secretary and one of the busiest of patronage middlemen, in writing to a friend about possible appointments referred to "us poor bribers here in Court" (Neale, *Essays in Elizabethan History,* pp. 65-67). In a society in which modern bureaucratic and economic structures were in the very process of formation, it was sometimes difficult or undesirable to make precise distinctions between salaries and gifts, between gifts and bribes.[29]

Let us now reconsider the prestation principle formulated at the beginning of *The Araygnement of Paris.* Pomona asks Faunus if "these goddesses will take our giftes in woorth"; he replies,

> Yea doubtles, for shall tel thee dame, twere better
> give a thing,
> A signe of love, unto a mightie person, or a king:
> Then to a rude and barbarous swayne but bad and baselie
> borne,
> For gentlie takes the gentleman that oft the clowne will
> scorne.
>
> (ll. 55-59)

The significance of the offering is not in the material value of the gift but in the symbolic value of the act of giving. The material gift is a sign of love, an offering of self and an initiation or reaffirmation of a bond between giver and recipient. Marcel Mauss echoes ancient philosophy in his study of symbolic exchange. He stresses that an act of gift-giving is part of a larger social situation, a dialectical process of prestation which "not only carries with it the obligation to repay gifts received, but implies two others equally important: the obligation to give presents and the obligation to receive them" (*The Gift,* pp. 10-11). As Pierre Bourdieu observes, "the operation of gift exchange presupposes (individual and collective) misrecognition . . . of the objective 'mechanism' of the exchange."[30] E. K. concludes his gloss on Spenser's Graces by noting that they are often represented with "one having her backe toward us, and her face fromwarde, as proceeding from us; the other two toward us, noting double thanke to be due to us for the benefit, we have done." Prestation is a tacitly coercive and vitally interested process predicated on the fiction that it is free and disinterested. Gift-giving is a kind of negotiation "by coulor of otiation."

According to Peele's Faunus, it is far better to give to the great than to the base because the social hierarchy is congruent with the moral hierarchy. In *The Winter's Tale*, this notion leads the ingenuous old shepherd to tell his clownish son, "We must be gentle, now we are gentlemen" (V.ii.152-153). Because gentlemen are gentle, they will accept humble gifts and thus acknowledge a bond to the giver; and because they are "mightie" persons, the signs of love which they return may materially benefit their social inferiors. Such institutionalized forms of giving are gestures in a system of symbolic exchange. Sacrificial offerings open a two-way channel between gods and mortals; and offerings of objects, services, and respects open a two-way channel between lords and subjects, patrons and suitors.

The Araygnement of Paris is an offering to Peele's sovereign that incorporates within it a variety of gifts; it is an epitome of the forms and motives of Elizabethan prestation. At the beginning of the play, the country gods make offerings of homage to the great goddesses; and at the end, the great goddesses in all humility pay tribute to the Queen. The *Araygnement*'s encomium takes the form of an epiphany; its rhetorical motive is simply to acknowledge the Queen's greatness, to worship her. In their offering of tangible signs of loyalty and submission, the Fates and Goddesses stand proxy for all the Queen's subjects. Hierarchical social relationships are ritually defined and affirmed in the offering and acceptance of gifts.

Between the ritual acts of celebration at the beginning and the end is a dramatic action focused upon two contrasting formal scenes of judgment: the Choice of Paris and the Arraignment of Paris. Paris, a mere mortal, is invested as "umpier in [the] controversie" (l. 416) between the goddesses: "Then if you will to avoyde a tedious grudge, / Refer it to the sentence of a judge" (ll. 407-08). At his arraignment, Paris pleads the difficulty of maintaining impartiality under pressure from superiors who possess power to coerce and gifts to corrupt:

> (Yee gods) alas what can a mortall man
> Decerne, betwixt the sacred guiftes of heaven.

Or, if I may with reverence reason thus:
Suppose I gave, and judgd corruptly then,
For hope of that, that best did please my thought,
This apple not for beauties prayse alone:
I might offende, sithe I was gardoned,
And tempted, more than ever creature was,
With wealth, with beautie and with chivalrie.

(ll. 924-930)

The exchanges between Paris and the goddesses suggest forms of patronage and clientage; they equivocate between gifts and bribes, between praise and flattery. They echo both the social relationships within the Court and Peele's own relationship to his courtly audience.

During a royal performance of *The Araygnement of Paris*, the Queen would have sat in state, perhaps sharing the stage with the actors. The actors always played to her; the others in attendance were not only watching a play but watching the Queen watching a play.[31] Whatever boundary exists between the reality within the fiction and that within the Court dissolves when Diana "delivereth the ball of golde to the Queenes owne hands." The Queen participates in mythic and material worlds simultaneously. The golden ball offered to her is the apple intended "unto the fayrest" (l. 365); it is the golden orb of Christian and British empire; and it is a synecdoche for *The Araygnement of Paris*. The performance offers a cultural form in which Queen and Court may legitimate and celebrate themselves. The negotiations of author, performers, and sponsors for the favor of their superiors and their royal mistress are mediated by the reciprocal wooings of mortals and gods in a pastoral fiction. Although Eliza is Diana's votary, Diana herself is the dramatic agent of Peele's royal compliment. In the world that revolves around Queen Elizabeth, Diana proves to be the exemplary courtier; the ironic fate of Paris and the pathetic fate of Colin exemplify the dangers and the frustrations of courtship.

The Araygnement of Paris manifests those intellectual gifts which recommended George Peele to the Elizabethan regime. Peele, who came from a family of London tradesmen and clerks, prepared to advance himself by a university education and a financially advantageous marriage. A gentleman only by virtue of his Master of Arts degree, he sought the substance of status by writing in hope of Court preferment. In *The Araygnement of Paris*, his first major work, Peele emulates the Vergilian progression by writing a pastoral with epic implications; he emulates Spenser by including

Louis Adrian Montrose   455

a pastoral subplot that makes a conspicuous allusion to the recent *Shepheardes Calender* (1579). In his Epistle to the *Calender*, E. K. remarks that it is the figure of Colin "under whose person the Author selfe is shadowed." The poet begins with pastoral because it allows him to advertise himself to the courtly source of power and reward without violating the decorum of humility and deference required both of social inferiors and of the younger generation. Within the humble pastoral poem which boldly announces his claim to be "our new Poete," Spenser incorporates Colin Clout to project a pattern of failure.[32] Like Spenser's persona, Peele's Colin is a shepherd-poet whose amorous desires are rejected and whose literary gifts are wasted.

Peele himself experienced the social failure which haunted the "University Wits" of his generation. He continued to pen occasional and celebratory courtly poems (often pastoral in form) throughout his short career. But, because he needed a larger audience for his works and a larger market for his wares, he also wrote Lord Mayor's shows for the City of London and bombastic plays for the common stage. By the late 1580's, Peele was in considerable financial difficulty. In 1593, he wrote "The Honour of the Garter" to celebrate the Earl of Northumberland's election to that exclusive order. The prologue begins with lavish praise of the Earl, who had given Peele £ 3. But it quickly becomes a bitter complaint, on behalf of all Elizabethan poets, against the aristocracy and the courtly culture which Peele is ostensibly celebrating:

> Why goe not all into th'Elisian fieldes,
> And leave this Center, barren of repast,
> Unlesse in hope Augusta will restore,
> The wrongs that learning beares of covetousnes
> And Courts disdaine, the enemie to Arte.
>
> (ll. 64-68)[33]

In 1596, Peele refurbished a poem from his college days (first printed in 1589) for a desperate offering: "To the r. honorable & woorthie Patrone of Learninge the L. Burleigh L. highe Theasorer of England . . . Georg. Peele mr of Arts Presents ye tale of Troy" (*Life and Minor Works*, p. 105). It was from *The Tale of Troy* that Peele had developed *The Araygnement of Paris* at the auspicious beginning of his career. It now made a humble gift indeed for the great minister of Elizabeth's Troynovant. Burghley, who by the 1590's virtually controlled the flow of patronage from the Crown, appears to have had little sympathy for contemporary poetry and poets. His response to Peele's begging letter was to file it "with others from cranks and crackpots, such as . . . 'Austin Metcalf's mad incoherent jargon, addressed to the Queen and Lord Bughley, by way of petition' " (*Life and Minor Works*, p. 108). Peele's gift went unrequited. Within a few months, he was dead.

IV EPILOGUE

The Araygnement of Paris is a cultural manifestation of the Elizabethan Court; the court itself provides the code in which Peele entertains it. Peele's apparent concern is not to anatomize but to praise and please an audience whose approval and favor he earnestly desires. The courtly pastoral with which Peele began his career makes an apposite contrast to Spenser's Legend of Courtesy, a late pastoral reprise which is markedly analytical and critical in its reproduction of Elizabethan court culture. The tension of values in Book Six of *The Faerie Queene* is epitomized in the contrast of two images of courtship: the heroic poet's courtship of his royal mistress in the proem and the pastoral piper's courtship of his country lass in canto ten. In effect, Spenser establishes two rival courts, the centers of political and poetic power, patronage and love; and the latter emerges late in the poem as the model of grace and courtesy by which courtly culture itself is measured and found wanting.[34] "Of Court it seemes, men Courtesie doe call" (VI.i.1), but Spenser knows not "seemes": "vertues seat is deepe within the mynde. / And not in outward shows, but inward thoughts defynd" (VI.proem.5).

Sir Calidore, the flower of Gloriana's court, sojourns among the shepherds in order to practice his courtship upon Pastorella; like other Elizabethan courtiers, he puts on a pastoral mask:

> That who had seene him then, would have bethought
> On *Phrygian Paris* by *Plexippus* brooke,
> When he the love of fayre *Oenone* sought,
> What time the golden apple was unto him brought.
>
> (VI.ix.36)

The resonant and ominous simile heralds Spenser's transformation of The Choice of Paris in the following canto. While hunting on a wooded hilltop, the shepherd-knight happens upon a most rare vision: "An hundred naked maidens lilly white, / All raunged in a ring, and dauncing in delight." In the midst of them, the Three Graces dance and sing;

Louis Adrian Montrose 457

> And in the middest of those same three, was placed
>   Another Damzell, as a precious gemme,
>   Amidst a ring most richly well enchaced,
> And with her goodly presence all the rest much graced.
>
> (VI.x.12)

"All gifts of grace" (x.15) emanate in concentric circles from this central figure:

> Another Grace she well deserves to be,
>   In whom so many Graces gathered are,
>   Exceling much the meane of her degree;
>   Divine resemblaunce, beauty soveraine rare,
>   Firme Chastity, that spite ne blemish dare.
>
> (x.27)

The maiden who infolds all the Graces is both a humble "countrey lasse" and "a goddesse graced / With heavenly gifts from heven first enraced" (x.25); Colin Clout, who plays to her alone (x.15), is both a rustic piper and a hierophant.

"All gracious gifts . . . / Which decke the body or adorne the mynde" are bestowed on men by the Three Graces, whose own powers seem now to emanate from the maiden who has replaced Venus at the center of their dance.

> They teach us, how to each degree and kynde
>   We should our selves demeane, to low, to hie;
> To friends, to foes, which skil men call Civility.
>
> (VI.x.23)

Courtesy makes human society possible, and imposes a civilizing form upon the predatory instincts of the courtier. Spenser's great icon infolds a metaphysics, a politics, and an ethics of reciprocity; it is the "true glorious type" of the Elizabethan court and its patronage system:

> Right so from you all goodly vertues well
>   Into the rest, which round about you ring,
>   Faire Lords and Ladies, which about you dwell,
> And doe adorne your Court, where courtesies excell.
>
> (VI.proem.7)

Spenser brings together pastoral conventions, myths of royal power, and acts of prestation to create an encomium conspicuously rivaling his own celebrations of Elisa (*The Shepheardes Calender*, "Aprill") and Gloriana—and rivaling, too, the culminating device of Peele's *The Araygnement of Paris*. The rustic maiden who replaces

Venus as the cynosure of the vision also supplants Elizabeth as the cynosure of the poem. Colin, who has been addressing Calidore within the fiction, turns to address directly the royal reader to whom the poem is ostensibly dedicated. The voice of the heroic poet, heard in the proems, now speaks through the pastoral poet:

> Great *Gloriana,* greatest Majesty,
> Pardon thy shepheard, mongst so many layes,
> As he hath sung of thee in all his dayes,
> To make one minime of thy poore handmayd.
>
> (x.28)

The shepherd-courtier's very apology is an oblique acknowledgment that Spenser's pastoral mythopoeia subverts the heroic poet's claim that the Queen and the Court are the authentic sources of his inspiration and reward.

In the proem, the weary poet claims scornfully that what now passes for courtesy "is nought but forgerie, / Fashion'd to please the eies of them that pas" (proem.5); and in the last line of the book, the embittered poet cautions his verse to "seeke to please, that now is counted wisemens threasure" (xii.41). The poet must begin and end as an entertainer and celebrant of the Court, as a maker of "fayned shows" for his social betters. But "deepe within the mynd"—within the pastoral fiction that bodies forth "inward thoughts"—the poet teaches "true courtesie" to the Knight, and celebrates Gloriana's rustic handmaid as the only she in whom do meet so many gifts in one.

University of California, San Diego

FOOTNOTES

[1] *Elizabethan Poetry* (1952; rpt., Ann Arbor, 1968), pp. 4, 7.

[2] *Nennio, or a Treatise of Nobility,* trans. William Jones (London, 1595), sig. H3^v (quoted in Smith, *Elizabethan Poetry,* pp. 5-6, n. 13). I have modified obsolete typographical conventions in quotations from this and other Elizabethan texts. See the discussion of "Virtue reconciled with Pleasure," in Edgar Wind, *Pagan Mysteries in the Renaissance,* rev. ed. (Harmondsworth, 1967), pp. 81-96.

[3] *Marsilio Ficino: The* Philebus *Commentary,* ed. and trans. Michael J. B. Allen (Berkeley, 1975), p. 446. I do not imply that Ficino's work is a "source" for Peele's. Other Tudor treatments of the Choice of Paris device are catalogued in John D. Reeves, "The Judgment of Paris as a Device of Tudor Flattery," *N&Q,* N.S. 1 (1954), 7-11; and Inga-Stina Ekeblad, "On the Background of Peele's 'Araygnement of Paris,' " *N&Q,* N.S. 3 (1956), 246-49.

[4] On the theme of Chastity in Peele's play (to be discussed more fully below), compare Andrew Von Hendy, "The Triumph of Chastity: Form and Meaning in *The Arraignment of Paris,*" *RenD,* N.S. 1 (1968), 87-101; on the motif of the *trionfo* in

Louis Adrian Montrose 459

Elizabethan iconography, see Frances A. Yates, *Astraea* (London, 1975), pp. 112-20. On Peele's spectacular dramaturgy, see Inga-Stina Ewbank, " 'What words, what looks, what wonders?': Language and Spectacle in the Theatre of George Peele," in *The Elizabethan Theatre V*, ed. G. R. Hibbard (Hamden, Conn., 1975), pp. 124-54, esp. pp. 136-41.

[5] *The Araygnement of Paris*, ed. R. Mark Benbow, in *The Dramatic Works of George Peele*, C. T. Prouty, gen. ed. (New Haven, Conn., 1970). My quotations follow the text and lineation of this edition.

[6] *Julye*, ll. 149-51. All quotations are from *Spenser: Poetical Works*, ed. J. C. Smith and E. De Selincourt (1912; rpt. Oxford, 1975).

[7] Renato Poggioli, *The Oaten Flute* (Cambridge, Mass., 1975), p. 1.

[8] George Puttenham, *The Arte of English Poesie* (1589), ed. G. D. Willcock and Alice Walker (Cambridge, 1936), p. 24. All quotations will be from this edition.

[9] For a detailed discussion of the politics of royal pastoral, see my study, " 'Eliza, Queen of shepheardes' and the Pastoral of Power," forthcoming in *ELR*, 10 (1980).

[10] Anthony Esler, *The aspiring mind of the Elizabethan younger generation* (Durham, N.C., 1966), p. 51. Esler's study is provocative and enlightening for students of Elizabethan literary history, even though it overstates its case. Esler pays insufficient attention to occupational and other categories of social status which cut across the generational categories. See Lawrence Stone, "Social Mobility in England, 1500-1700," *Past & Present*, 33 (1966), 16-55, for facts, figures, and a model of social change.

[11] This corpus is well discussed in David Bevington, *Tudor Drama and Politics* (Cambridge, Mass., 1968), pp. 141-86; and Marie Axton, *The Queen's Two Bodies* (London, 1977), pp. 38-115.

[12] Quoted in J. E. Neale, *Elizabeth I and Her Parliaments 1559-1581* (New York, 1958), p. 49. On the sixteenth century debate about gynarchy, see James E. Phillips, Jr., "The Background of Spenser's Attitude Toward Women Rulers," *HLQ*, 5 (1941-42), 5-32.

[13] Sir Robert Nauton, *Fragmenta Regalia* (written ca. 1630; printed 1641), ed. Edward Arber (London, 1870), p. 17.

[14] *Calendar of State Papers, Spanish* (1558-67), pp. 404-05; quoted in Axton, *The Queen's Two Bodies*, p. 49.

[15] Bodley MS Rawlinson Poet 108. The masque has long been cited in connection with *AP*; it is quoted and discussed in Axton, *The Queen's Two Bodies*, pp. 50-51.

[16] I quote the text of the Kenilworth entertainment (first printed 1576) from vol. 2 of *The Complete Works of George Gascoigne*, ed. J. W. Cunliffe, (Cambridge, 1910); and the text of the Wanstead entertainment (first printed 1598) from *Miscellaneous Prose of Sir Philip Sidney*, ed. Katherine Duncan-Jones and Jan Van Dorsten (Oxford, 1973).

[17] I have studied this text in greater detail, from the perspective of the author rather than the sponsor, in "Celebration and Insinuation: Sir Philip Sidney and the Motives of Elizabethan Courtship," *RenD*, N.S. 8 (1977), 3-35.

[18] Henry G. Lesnick suggests some "historico-mythical" elements in "The Structural Significance of Myth and Flattery in Peele's *Arraignment of Paris*," *SP*, 65 (1968), 163-70. The ideology and iconography of the Elizabeth cult are discussed suggestively in Yates, *Astraea*, pp. 29-111; and Roy Strong, *The Cult of Elizabeth* (London, 1977).

[19] "Elizabeth I and the Three Goddesses" (formerly at Hampton Court; presently in the collection of The Queen's Pictures, Buckingham Palace), monogrammed "HE" and dated 1569. The painting is catalogued in Roy C. Strong, *Portraits of Queen Elizabeth I* (Oxford, 1963), p. 79, and reproduced as Plate VI; it is reproduced in color, with details, in Roy Strong, *The English Icon* (London, 1969), pp. 143-45. I reproduce the painting by gracious permission of H. M. Queen Elizabeth II.

[20] On the Queen's wardrobe, see Neville Williams, *Elizabeth: Queen of England*

(London, 1967), pp. 226-27; and Paul Johnson, *Elizabeth I: A Study in Power and Intellect* (London, 1974), p. 197.

²¹ On the Elizabethan transformation of Nativity pastoral into royal pastoral, see my " 'Eliza, Queene of shepheardes' and the Pastoral of Power."

²² *The Queene's Majestie's Passage* (1559), rpt. in *Elizabethan Backgrounds*, ed. Arthur F. Kinney (Hamden, Conn., 1975), pp. 16-17; all quotations will be from this edition. I am indebted to Kinney's Introduction, pp. 7-9; and to Sydney Anglo, *Spectacle, Pageantry, and Early Tudor Policy* (Oxford, 1969), pp. 344-59.

²³ See *The Rise of the Common Player* (Cambridge, Mass., 1962), pp. 243-64.

²⁴ E. K.'s gloss on "The Graces," in the "Aprill" eclogue of Spenser's *Shepheardes Calender*. The fundamental iconographic study of the Graces is Wind, *Pagan Mysteries*, pp. 26-52.

²⁵ *The Elizabethan Stage* (Oxford, 1923), I, 19.

²⁶ John Nichols, *The Progresses and Public Processions of Queen Elizabeth* (1823; rpt., New York, 1966), I, xxxviii. In his collection, Nichols prints full rolls for five years of the reign.

²⁷ In Neale, *Essays in Elizabethan History* (London, 1958), p. 71.

²⁸ Wallace T. MacCaffrey, "Place and Patronage in Elizabethan Politics," in *Elizabethan Government and Society*, ed. S. T. Bindoff, J. Hurstfield, and C. H. Williams (London, 1961), pp. 96-97. See also Lawrence Stone, *The Crisis of the Aristocracy 1558-1641* (Oxford, 1965), pp. 385-504; and, for a good overview, Alan G. R. Smith, *The Government of Elizabethan England* (New York, 1967), pp. 57-69.

²⁹ See Joel Hurstfield, *Freedom, Corruption and Government in Elizabethan England* (London, 1973), pp. 137-62.

³⁰ Pierre Bourdieu, *Outline of a Theory of Practice*, trans. Richard Nice (Cambridge, 1977), pp. 5-6. I have also benefitted from Esther Goody, " 'Greeting,' 'begging,' and the presentation of respect," in *The Interpretation of Ritual*, ed. J. S. La Fontaine (London, 1972), pp. 39-71; and Raymond Firth, *Symbols: Public and Private* (Ithaca, 1973), pp. 368-402.

³¹ See Stephen Orgel, *The Illusion of Power* (Berkeley, 1975), pp. 9-11.

³² I have advanced this interpretation in " 'The perfecte paterne of a Poete': The Poetics of Courtship in *The Shepheardes Calender*," *TSLL*, 21 (1979), 34-67. Also see Richard Helgerson, "The New Poet Presents Himself: Spenser and the Idea of a Literary Career," *PMLA*, 93 (1978), 893-911.

³³ Quotations are from the text in David H. Horne, *The Life and Minor Works of George Peele* (New Haven, 1952). Horne's study is the source of biographical information.

³⁴ The introspection, disillusionment, and social criticism of Book Six have received considerable attention in recent studies: See, for example, Michael O'Connell, *Mirror and Veil: The Historical Dimension of Spenser's* Faerie Queene (Chapel Hill, 1977), pp. 161-89; and Daniel Javitch, *Poetry and Courtliness in Renaissance England* (Princeton, 1978), pp. 137-59. I have discussed *FQ*, VI.x from the perspective of Spenser's poetic career, in " 'The perfecte paterne of a Poete,' " pp. 55-58.

Louis Adrian Montrose 461

[4]

The Triumph of Chastity: Form and Meaning in The Arraignment of Paris

ANDREW VON HENDY

I N SPITE OF ITS CHARM, *The Arraignment of Paris* is usually dismissed by criticism as either disorganized or trivial.[1] This treatment is understandable if the play is judged by standards appropriate to more mimetic forms of drama. It appears both significant and well-designed, however, if we recognize how strongly it has been affected by the conventions of masques and entertainments. Peele responded to a specific occasion with a beautiful compliment to the Queen. This compliment is the formal intention of his play. He constructs *The Arraignment* to culminate, as masques do, in a scene which will absorb the audience into its imaginary

1. For typical complaints about the play's formlessness see Paul Reyher, *Les Masques anglais* (Paris, 1909), pp. 135–138; Enid Welsford, *The Court Masque* (Cambridge, Eng., 1927), pp. 277–278; Tucker Brooke in *A Literary History of England* (New York, 1948), pp. 455–456. Dismissals of the play as frivolous are generally connected with eighteenth- and nineteenth-century assumptions about the essentially frivolous nature of masque and pastoral. See, for example, W. W. Greg's discussion of the play in *Pastoral Poetry and Pastoral Drama* (London, 1906), pp. 216–224. The only commentary I know which recognizes both the "moral earnestness . . . at all times characteristic of Peele's work" and his "constructive dramatic skill" is Thorleif Larsen's in "The Early Years of George Peele, Dramatist, 1558–1588," *Transactions of the Royal Society of Canada* (1928), pp. 294–311.

world. The plot inclines us to accept the moral and political ideals with which the climactic moment invests the Queen. When she resolves the pastoral dilemma within the play, we witness a formal "triumph," the triumph of chastity over moral and political subversion.

The resemblance of the play to a masque is indicated on the title page of the 1584 quarto.[2] There *The Arraignment* is called a "pastorall." Our literary historians find the essence of Renaissance pastoral in the self-conscious contrast between the natural and the artificial.[3] The poet withdraws from the world to contemplate the problems of his everyday existence. Spenser and Milton meditated in a form which encouraged the projection of their ideal aspirations. I think both masque and pastoral are species of what Northrop Frye calls "romance," a mood in literature of dreamlike wish fulfillment.[4] Romance moves away from mimetic representation of the "real" world. The unfulfilled wish usually appears as the goal of a quest, and romance plots in general have a way of suggesting allegory. The characters are general types, sometimes clearly fragments of a single personality. Their actions are often absurd or puzzling by realistic standards. A psychologist might call their behavior "compulsive." The setting of romance is nearly always remote in time and space, a magic world where suspension of the natural laws is taken for granted. Romantic narrative is apt to seem sporadic, since the author is never far from his besetting abstractions. He introduces meditations on matters like fortune

2. We have no satisfactory edition of *The Arraignment of Paris*. Except for modernizing spelling for consistency with other editions from which I quote, I have followed throughout the text of the 1584 quarto, ed. H. H. Child (Malone Society Reprints; London, 1910). Child, however, follows previous modern editors in numbering lines according to altered divisions of act and scene. I have consulted for line numbering, therefore, the edition of the play in *English Drama 1580–1642*, ed. C. F. T. Brooke and H. B. Paradise (New York, 1933), which is unusual in honoring the divisions of the quarto.

3. See, for example, William Empson, *Some Versions of Pastoral* (London, 1935), especially his first two chapters; Frank Kermode's introduction to *English Pastoral Poetry from the Beginnings to Marvell* (London, 1952); Hallett Smith, *Elizabethan Poetry* (Cambridge, Mass., 1952), pp. 1–63; Edward Tayler, *Nature and Art in Renaissance Literature* (New York, 1964).

4. *Anatomy of Criticism* (Princeton, 1957), especially pp. 36–37, 186–203, 304–307. My description of the form is based on Frye but considerably modified by my own opinions. If "romance" is understood in its wide signification, pastoral and masque are species of this kind of narrative fiction.

The Arraignment of Paris   89

and justice or explicit debates, as between love and honor. Finally, to borrow a term from current politics, romance is radically conservative; it
contrasts an ideal society that never was or will be to the actual society in
which the writer lives.

The Arraignment opens with a prologue best explained, I think, by the
political implications of romance. Ate introduces the gold ball which will
cause the goddesses' quarrel. But her appearance is in unexplained contrast to the mood of the scenes which follow. Enid Welsford describes the
problem in *The Court Masque:* "The appearance of Ate 'from lowest
hell' should surely prelude the 'tragedy of Troy,' instead of leading to a
piece of extravagant flattery written in pastoral style" (p. 278). This objection seems to me valid if we see no connection between the appearance
of Ate and the "extravagant flattery" which follows it. I think we do find
such a connection, however, in the political implications of *The Arraignment*'s romantic plot. We can recognize these implications by recalling
some commonplaces of Elizabethan literature. First, Tudor history identified Trojan Brute as the founder of England and London as Troynovant.
The "tale of Troy" had nationalistic consequences. Second, the poets inherited from antiquity an association of the pastoral world with the Golden
Age of Saturn's reign. Third, Elizabeth was frequently identified with
Astraea, goddess of justice, who fled the world at the end of the Golden
Age. The famous line in Virgil's fourth eclogue, *"iam redit et Virgo,
redeunt Saturnia regna,"* is obviously ready for application to the Virgin
Queen. Fourth, political unrest was often represented as an anti-Olympian
principle of evil. The Titans frequently appear, for example, in the role
Ate takes in *The Arraignment.*

These four considerations are associated with each other in various
combinations in Peele's nondramatic works, especially in *The Tale of
Troy, The Device of the Pageant Borne Before Wolstan Dixi, Descensus
Astraeae,* and *Anglorum Feriae.* In the most elaborate grouping, *Descensus Astraeae,* the Lord Mayor's Pageant of 1591, "Astraea with hir sheephook on the top of the pageant" is identified with the Queen.[5] Euphrosyne,
guarding Astraea with the other Graces, explains the device:

5. For *Descensus Astraeae* see *The Life and Minor Works of George Peele,* ed.
David H. Horne (New Haven, 1952), pp. 214–219. I cite in the text lines as num-
bered in this edition. The Web in the pageant is a play on the name of the new
Lord Mayor, Sir William Webbe.

> Whilom when Saturnes golden raigne did cease,
>   and yron age had kindled cruel warres:
> Envie in wrath, perturbing common peace,
>   engendring cancred hate and bloody jarres:
> Lo then Olympus king, the thundring Jove,
>   raught hence this gracious nymph Astraea faire,
> Now once again he sands hir from above.

(ll. 66–72)

Astraea is threatened by "malecontents" who "strive and cannot strike." Elizabeth is preserved by miracle from the mortal condition. *"In the hinder part of the Pageant did sit a Child, representing Nature, holding in her hand a distaffe, and spinning a Web, which passed through the hand of Fortune and was wheeled up by Time . . ."* (p. 218).

>   And Time and Kinde
> Produce hir yeares to make them numberlesse
> While Fortune for hir service and hir sake,
> With golden hands doth strengthen and enrich
> The Web that they for faire Astraea weave.

(ll. 33–37)

Thus, in *The Arraignment,* Ate provokes a whole cycle of war and injustice, but she fails to disturb seriously the order of the gods, and she cannot affect at all a nymph served by the Fates themselves. *The Arraignment* follows the pattern of political myth summarized in Euphrosyne's speech.

The prologue, then, stands in much the same relationship to the scenes which follow it as an antimasque does to the masque proper. That is why Peele considers it decorous to change so abruptly from Ate to an ideal landscape across which the gods move in formal progress. (Their procession resembles a summer pageant greeting the Queen on the grounds of an estate.) Though the reign of Saturn is past, the Iron Age has not yet come and will not come till Ate prevails. Death and unrequited love have already appeared "even in Arcadia," but the natural world still keeps about it some of its unfallen glory. The setting of the first four scenes derives obviously from the *locus amoenus* of medieval dream vision, the earthly paradise just below the moon. The minor deities bring their gifts as Diana's vassals, but these gifts also signify the abundance of nature in

The Arraignment of Paris   91

the paradisal garden.[6] This traditional mode of symbolism shows most clearly, perhaps, in Flora's lovely catalogue of her jewels (I.iii.17–32). This ordered nature, governed by Diana, will become especially significant in the fifth act.

The procession of minor deities culminates in a spectacular burst of song and dance. A "quier within" responds antiphonally to a choir outside, that is, off stage. The latter is composed of the country gods, whereas the former, we are told, consists of the Muses themselves. This suggests again how far we are from a fallen world. The three goddesses march in "like to the pompe of heaven above" (l. 85), but as they exchange compliments we discover they have a further goal. They leave the stage moving toward a meeting with Diana herself. This procession will not reach its goal, however, until the last act. Its movement is interrupted by the disturbances that comprise the center of the play.

Act I concludes ominously with an interview between Paris and Oenone. The scene is superficially idyllic. Before the famous roundelay, "Faire and fayre and twise so faire," Paris assures Oenone that their music is "figure of the love that growes twixt thee and me" (I.iii.54). But Oenone is worried. In deciding what he should play, Paris has raised sinister topics:

> How Saturne did devide his kingdome . . .
> How mightie men made foule succesles warre,
> Against the gods and state of Jupiter.
>
> (I.v.19–22)

This catalogue proceeds (as the play does) from political rebellion to "love offence." Peele foreshadows the fate of Paris in terms of Ovid moralized. Paris' repertoire, both political and amatory, consists of tales of infidelity later corrected by justice. Oenone wisely invokes Cupid's curse: "They that do chaunge olde love for new, pray gods they chaunge for worse."

Act II opens *ex abrupto,* as the stage direction has it, with a fight among the goddesses on their way to Diana. Nothing in the first act has pre-

6. For a good exposition of this symbolism see J. A. W. Bennett, *The Parlement of Foules* (Oxford, 1957), especially pp. 140–142. See also E. R. Curtius, *European Literature and the Latin Middle Ages* (New York, 1953), pp. 183–202. Curtius shows explicitly that this topic was still a commonplace to Shakespeare.

pared us for the low tone and diction of the participants. Discord has invaded even the society of the gods. Its personification, Ate, appears in a thunderstorm and places before the goddesses the fatal apple, to be given "to the fayrest." They agree only to make the next person who appears "umpier in this controversie," and in walks Paris.

His judgment had long been a popular topic for moral allegory. In Montemayor's *Diana,* for example, "Delia and Andronius spend the greater part of a night arguing the question whether Paris gave the apple to the right goddess or not and whether the inscription on it referred to physical or mental beauty." [7] In England the topic had even been applied traditionally to royal compliment. "The Paris story was a common subject of the pageants—for Queen Margaret at Edinburgh in 1503, for the coronation of Anne Boleyn in 1533, and at a marriage masque in 1566." [8] I would guess that the topic was common on such occasions not only because Paris made the most famous pastoral choice but also because of the connection of Troy with the Tudor political myth.

Paris' three temptations are symbolized in the elaborate "shows" with which each goddess accompanies her claim. Juno offers gold and empire, Pallas wisdom and martial glory. Venus offers both herself and Helen, whom she introduces with a significant change of diction as

> A gallant girle, a lustie minion trull,
> That can give sporte to thee thy bellyfull,
> To ravish all thy beating vaines with joye.
>
> (II.ii.75–77)

Helen's song is itself a relevant piece of wit. Its language recalls the great Tuscan celebrators of courtly love, but it is a song against Diana as the personification of chastity. Diana, as Helen sings, is the goddess of a love

7. Hallett Smith, *Elizabethan Poetry*, p. 6. Smith discusses Peele's play on pp. 3–9, primarily in connection with the significance of Paris' pastoral choice.

8. *Ibid.,* p. 7. Smith follows T. S. Graves, *"The Arraignment of Paris* and Sixteenth Century Flattery," *MLN*, XXVIII (1913), 48–49. As Graves points out, the pageant at Anne's coronation is especially significant, for Elizabeth's mother also received the gold ball from the goddesses. In "The Source of Peele's 'Arraignment of Paris,'" *MLN*, VIII (1893), pp. 206–207, Felix Schelling shows that the topic is applied to Elizabeth in the works of Gascoigne, including an unacted pageant at Kenilworth in 1575. Larsen, in "The Early Years of George Peele," pp. 298–299, adds to the evidence a Latin epigraph addressed to Elizabeth in Lyly's *Euphues His England*. As Larsen observes, it is unlikely that Peele knew none of these allusions.

The Arraignment of Paris 93

very different in kind from Helen's. As queen of nymphs and flowers, woodland and forest, Diana deals death to shepherds. But as queen of hell she comforts the damned who died for love, and as queen of heaven she tenders light to weary hearts. She is a goddess of the Platonic ladder. Helen, however, calls herself a "Diana" who can make war with her very glances on this triple goddess of chastity. And Paris gives Venus the ball.

Now, it is quite possible to argue that Paris makes the correct pastoral choice. Paris himself makes this claim in his speech before the Council of the Gods. Hallett Smith summarizes his argument:

The simplicity of the shepherd's conditions makes for an invulnerability to appeals in the name of wealth or of chivalry. It is only beauty, of the three ideals represented by the goddesses, which has any significant power in a pastoral life.[9]

The structure of the play, however, frames this bold assertion in an ironic moral perspective. Helen's song clarifies the issue. All three of the goddesses represent forms of beauty; Paris chooses the lowest form. At the end of Act II he exits with Venus, but Act III consists almost entirely of choral commentary on his lack of wisdom. At the end of Act II Ate has succeeded in making the goddesses forget their purpose; the Diana against whom Helen sings is the very goal of their progress. From now on, however, the rift widens between gods and men in the post-Saturnian world. After Paris has been arraigned and judged, the gods will remember Diana.

The contrast between "the two loves" determines, I think, Peele's famous plagiarism at the beginning of Act III where he introduces a cast of characters out of *The Shepherd's Calendar*. As Peele conceives their conduct, it resembles the behavior of Lyly's lovers, the behavior Shakespeare remembered with a certain irony in *A Midsummer-Night's Dream* and *As You Like It*. "As all is mortall in nature, so is all nature in love, mortall in folly." Love is midsummer madness, lunacy induced by the elixir of a flower called "Love in idlenesse." Lyly's treatment of the theme in *Endymion* is especially appropriate for comparison with *The Arraignment;* in it, too, the presence of the Queen at the performance actually affects the meaning of the play. And Lyly, as usual, makes his antitheses crystal clear. Cynthia is the Moon, chaste affection, true friendship, and Elizabeth. Tellus is the Earth, physical sex, perfidy, and (perhaps) Mary,

9. Smith, *Elizabethan Poetry*, p. 8.

Queen of Scots. Eumenides must decide between the two extremes. He must choose between love and honor, attaining his lady, Semele, or freeing Endymion from his fatal sleep. Of course he elects honor: "Vertue shall subdue affections, wisedome lust, friendship beautie." Eumenides has to make the so-called choice of Hercules prominent in medieval and Renaissance iconography.

Paris' choice in *The Arraignment* is built on a similar dichotomy, although the presence of three alternatives rather obscures the two contraries. Montemayor's characters see the Platonic dualism when they dispute whether the inscription on the apple refers to physical or mental beauty. In his narrative poem, *The Tale of Troy*, Peele himself reduced the three possibilities to two:

> Ah Paris, hadst thou had but equall eyes,
> Indifferent in bestowing of the pryze,
> Thy humaine wits might have discerned well,
> Where the true beautie of the mind did dwell.
> But men must erre, because but men they bee.
> And men with love yblinded may not see.[10]

Act III demonstrates the folly of Paris' blindness to "true beautie of the mind" and the consequences of his erring choice.

It opens with Colin himself exhibiting his famous wares. He sings a medieval "complaint" which will soon be matched by Oenone's venture in the same form. Hobinol, Digon, and Thenot, who succeed Colin on stage, make the connection between his fate and Oenone's. Paris' choice offends all true lovers: "Poore *Colin,* that is ill for thee, that art as true in trust / To thy sweete smerte, as to his Nymphe *Paris* hath bin unjust" (III.iii.19–20). When Mercury enters to summon Paris, Oenone imagines "th'unpertiall skyes" have answered her prayer.[11] She does not realize that he comes at the partial behests of Juno, Pallas, and Vulcan and that injustice seems now to prevail above as below.

10. Horne, *Life and Minor Works,* pp. 187–188. These are ll. 113–118.

11. *Mercu. entr. with Vulcans Cyclops.* The Cyclops have no speaking role. They are apparently an iconographic representation for Peele of Vulcan's jealousy. In the fragment of Peele's *The Hunting of Cupid* anthologized in *Englands Parnassus,* the last two lines read, "Fourth, Jealousie in basest mindes doth dwell,/ This mettall Vulcans Cyclops sent from hell" (Horne, *Life and Minor Works,* p. 208). Within the play, Venus' scornful remark about *"Chimnysweepers"* seems to suggest the same sort of thing (III.vi.29–30).

The Arraignment of Paris   95

This state of affairs is reiterated in the curious scene which follows. A group of shepherds begs Venus for revenge on Thestylis. She has finally murdered Colin by her disdain. Venus promises justice for Paris' sake. She blames her son "that ever love was blinde." Paris has been listening quietly, but now he objects. If Venus would handle Cupid's bow, justice could be done in love. Venus immediately counterattacks by asking Paris if he has ever been in love. In reply to his evasive answer, "Lady, a little once," she seems to insist that true lovers, unlike wantons, will their own condition and cannot be cured by external causes. Paris is worried. Can Venus and Cupid excuse a slight past offence? Venus replies sardonically with a description of the torments false lovers suffer in hell. Paris is astounded: "Is Venus and her sonne so full of justice and severytye" (III.v.31)? The answer sounds even more like something out of a medieval dream vision. Venus explains that her son is not only a boy but also a "mighty god." He is, in fact, the Eros of classical tradition: "His shafts keepe heaven and earth in awe" (l. 38). Paris, however, sees the fallacy (ll. 39–44):

PARIS
And hathe he reason to mantayne why Colin died for love.
VENUS
Yea, reason good I warrant thee, in right it might beehove.
PARIS
Then be the name of love adored, his bow is full of mighte,
His woundes are all but for desert, his lawes are all but right:
well for this once me lyst apply my speeches to thy sense,
And *Thestilis* shall feele the paine for loves supposed offence.[12]

Venus' reply is analogous to the traditional Christian explanation of evil as God's will. Cupid's "right" can only seem like "might" to a mere mortal. Venus shrugs off Paris' sarcasm. This one time she will take a position he can understand; she will punish Thestylis according to Paris' standard.

The rest of the scene marks the working of her justice. The chant of the shepherds bearing Colin's hearse is matched by Thestylis' singing of "an olde songe called the woing of Colman" and of the complaint which fol-

---

12. I assume, with modern editors, that ll. 43 and 44 belong to Venus. Does the lower case opening of l. 43 indicate some larger typographical confusion about the beginning of this line?

lows it. The shepherds pick up the refrain of the complaint, "the grace
of this song" being, as Peele says in his stage direction, "in the Shepherds
Ecco to her verse." In other words, everyone sympathizes with her suffering, even Paris. Or perhaps I should say especially Paris. He has discovered that romantic love is a lord of terrible aspect. There is an undercur-
rent of threat in Venus' relationship with Paris. When he pities Thestylis
aloud, Venus says, "Her fortune not unlyke to his whome cruell thow hast
slaine" (l. 57).[13] She had only been toying with him, then, when she asked
if he had ever been in love. Paris is already plunged in melancholy when
Mercury enters. And when he sees Venus' fury he realizes at last that his
folly is an instrument of destiny: "The angrye heavens for this fatall jar,
Name me the instrument of dire and deadly war" (III.vi.39–40).

The scenes of low humor which open Act IV parody in the usual manner the serious plot. Diana's nymph repulses Vulcan who thinks he can
"treade awry as well as *Venus* doth" (IV.ii.2). At least this country jig
quickly gives way to the Assembly of the Gods. I use Lydgate's title deliberately, to emphasize the medieval tradition behind this scene. The
cosmological implications have their sources probably in the late Latin
encyclopedists. They were popular in European literature at least from
the time of the twelfth-century school of Chartres. The Olympians are
not in this scene merely the gods Peele found in his Latin school texts.
They are the planetary powers these deities had come to represent in the
Middle Ages. In medieval literature they frequently pass judgment upon
changeable men from a realm of changeless values. E. M. W. Tillyard
describes this convention in speaking of the descent of the gods in *The
Testament of Cresseid:*

The Middle Ages looked on the stars as an organic part of God's creation and
as the perpetual instruments and diffusers of his will. . . . When Henryson
used the planets as the instruments of Cresseid's punishment he . . . implied
that her punishment was by God's will.[14]

---

13. I accept the logic of modern editors who change "his" to "hers," but it is
possible that Venus refers not to Oenone but to Colin. The shepherds have pointed
out that Paris is unjust to all true lovers, and only Colin at this point is literally
dead.

14. E. M. W. Tillyard, *Five Poems 1470–1870* (London, 1948), pp. 20–21. The
essay on Henryson's poem contains the best basic exposition I know of "the Assembly of the Gods." See especially pp. 19–22.

The Arraignment of Paris 97

Peele's point is no more explicitly Christian, of course, than Henryson's, or Spenser's in the Mutability Cantos. Peele's gods, like Spenser's, convene in a place like the Garden of Eden, an earthly paradise presided over by the goddess Natura, who is called Diana in Peele's play.

The arraignment itself is modeled on the form of the law case, which was nearly as popular for literary analogies as the parliament. Peele probably considered "Paris oration to the Councell of the gods" the major set-piece of the play. It is marked by the specious argument, the handsome elaboration of topics customary in traditional rhetoric. Paris defends himself principally by pleading, as Smith points out, that he made the correct choice for a shepherd. He excuses his moral blindness: "beauties blaze" is physical for him. Peele, however, does not excuse it any more than the Spenser of *Four Hymns* would. After Paris has withdrawn to await the verdict, the gods concur that by his own standards he is innocent. Juno merely pouts, but Pallas comes up with the crucial distinction of the play: "Whether the man be guiltie yea or noe, / That doth not hinder our appeale, I troe" (IV.iv.141–142). The choice of an erring mortal has not decided, and indeed could not decide, which is the greatest sort of beauty.

The sequence of events immediately following the oration has been frequently disregarded. It is crucial, however, to the unity of the plot and to the moral significance of the play. Paris is recalled and dismissed, but the gods do not imagine that in dismissing him they approve his argument. They send him forth to the fate his nature guarantees, to what Apollo calls "his never-dying payne." Paris' choice is its own punishment. Venus will stand by her promise of "luck in love," but Paris is now aware that he has made a tragic error, destined somehow to cause the destruction of his city: "My lucke is losse, howe ere my love do speede" (l. 166). Paris is shut out of the Garden forever. But in the pastoral world of man's fulfilled wish the gods can still triumph. Discord has darkened their counsel, but Apollo, the god of poetry and prophecy, restores them to light. Jurisdiction in the appeal belongs, he says, to Diana, in whose realm the affair took place. As in the Mutability Cantos, the threat of disorder above the moon is to be handled by the goddess of nature. Apollo recalls the gods to their festal progress toward Diana. As they "rise and goe foorth," the processional movement of the play resumes, proceeding brilliantly now toward a goal off stage.

Act V is a single scene. After Diana receives the goddesses' pledges to

98   ANDREW VON HENDY

support her decision, she *"describeth the Nymphe Eliza a figure of the Queene."* The goddesses agree; Elizabeth combines their wisdom, charm, and majesty. It happens to be the time of year when the Fates, the true "unpartiall dames" of Oenone's world, pay "their yearely due" to Elizabeth. So the goddesses follow them before the Queen, and Diana delivers, amid general acclaim, the ball of gold.

If this scene really strikes us as inconsequential "extravagant flattery," then Peele has failed to lure us sufficiently inside the masquelike mood and structure of the play. By "masque" I mean a spectacular, romantic form of drama which culminates in a dance integrating actors with audience. Masque is spectacular in its use of a full range of auditory and visual effects. It is romantic in plot (what Peele called the "device," Jonson the "hinge"). Its dancing leads to the exaltation of the audience who have been from the beginning the goal of the dancers' processional movement. Both their unmasking and selection of partners are meant to be gestures toward union. The successful masque must somehow incorporate the audience into its imaginary world.[15] The masque usually attempts a compliment which will equate the social harmony of its ideal world with the actual hierarchy of the court. In *The Arraignment* Peele wants Elizabeth to share for a golden moment of fantasy the pastoral world of the goddesses. Even granted the Tudor appetite for flattery, a moment of this sort would be indecorous if the mood were not perfect. The mood of an actual dramatic performance is as irrevocable as the mood of a dream, and this is particularly true of a masquelike play written for a specific occasion. But perhaps we can remind ourselves abstractly of the importance of mood in *The Arraignment* by considering briefly a masque in which Ben Jonson actually allegorizes the psychology of the revels.

A Vision of Delight opens with the arrival of Delight "accompanied with *Grace, Love, Harmonie, Revell, Sport, Laughter.* WONDER *following*" (ll. 4–6).[16] Delight represents the determination of the court to

15. My attempt to define "masque" owes much to E. K. Chambers' discussion of the form in *The Elizabethan Stage* (Oxford, 1923), I, pp. 149–212, and to Northrop Frye's comments on masque in *The Anatomy of Criticism*, pp. 287–293. For an interpretation of some of Jonson's masques which uses as an aesthetic criterion the success of the "hinge" in joining actors and audience, see Stephen Orgel's *The Jonsonian Masque* (Cambridge, Mass., 1965).

16. For the text of *A Vision of Delight* see Ben Jonson, *Works*, ed. C. H. Herford and P. and E. Simpson, 11 vols. (Oxford, 1925–1952), VII, 463–471.

The Arraignment of Paris

enjoy itself within the form of the revels. He announces directly (ll. 9–12) that the performance to follow is intended to unite the Christmas festivities of the court with the pastoral atmosphere of the masque. The occasion, even the time of day, must be special. Delight dismisses the clowns of the first antimasque as "all sowre and sullen looks away / that are the servants of the day" (ll. 26–27). He summons up Night instead, "to help the vision of DELIGHT" (l. 31) by keeping "all awake with *Phantomes*" (l. 40). And Night, to accomplish this, conjures up "Phant'sie" while the "Quire" invokes her mood:

> Yet let it like an odour rise
> to all the Sences here,
> And fall like sleep upon their eies,
> or musick in their eare.
>
> (ll. 51–54)

These lines express the intention behind the successive regressions from the "real" world. Phant'sie, so to speak, is the audience's willing participation in the "hinge" of the poet. After she first breaks forth with a tumultuous speech, a second antimasque "of Phantasmes" portrays the mental dangers of Night which correspond to the "sowre and sullen looks" of Day. Fancy can be dangerous, even lunatic, if not controlled by the decorum of the occasion. Phant'sie herself dismisses her phantasms and produces a new scene. "The gold-haird *Houre*" descends, to the song of Peace, bringing with her *"the Bower of* Zephyrus." The speech of Wonder which follows praises in descriptive detail this new marvel of Art and Nature. Wonder represents the willingness of the courtiers to exclaim over the spectacular sets. When she concludes, Phant'sie remarks significantly, "How better then they are, are all things made / By WONDER!" (ll. 166–167). Phant'sie, however, immediately surpasses her previous achievement. *"Here (to a loud musicke) the Bower opens, and the Maskers [are] discovered, as the glories of the Spring"* (ll. 170–171). Wonder marvels over the details of this scene as she did the preceding one, concluding, "Whose power is this? what God?" (l. 199). And Phant'sie replies, "Behold a King / Whose presence maketh this perpetuall *Spring*" (ll. 201–202). After the Quire confirms her assertion, the maskers advance, singing and dancing *"their entry"* and *"their maine Dance."* Then *"they Danc'd with Ladies, and the whole Revells followed"* (l. 232). While the "gold-haird Houre" lasts King James does make, in the vision of delight, "perpetuall Spring." But Night and the Moone descend and Aurora appears "to bid you come away." As the maskers dance their *"going off"* the Quire sings, "They yield to Time, and so must all" (l. 244). Only the excited interplay of Phant'sie and Wonder could evoke a vision of a garden court where King James reigns in a timeless world. Our revels now are ended, and the mood melts into air, into thin air.

We can see by comparison that Peele's play is not a proper masque. Its spectacle, though plentiful, is relatively incidental; it does not end in formal dance; and its romantic plot is too rich in action and even in character development. We can also see, however, that it is constructed like a masque to induce the willing suspension of disbelief necessary to the compliment. Act V of *The Arraignment* is in no sense merely tacked on for the occasion; rather, the occasion shapes the play. The festive social conventions affect the literary ones. To resolve the action Elizabeth must be taken into the pastoral as queen of the triumphing gods.

In the forms of Renaissance romance where a social compliment of this type is intended, political allegory nearly always suggests itself. The works I have mentioned because of their relevance to the conventions of *The Arraignment* all have political implications. Even Spenser's generalized allegory in the Mutability Cantos contains the archetypal pattern of revolt which haunted the Elizabethan mind. Spenser's mythopoeic use of the traditional Platonic cosmology implies a highly conservative politics. The same is true of Jonson's masques, where the favorite themes, as in medieval dream vision, are the triumph of reason over sensuality and of order over disorder. These are the explicit themes, too, of Lyly's *Endymion,* yet Tellus is suspected of being someone like Mary, Queen of Scots in contrast to Cynthia's Elizabeth. One might almost say that the presence of the Queen attracts a political application.

In fact, I believe we can safely reverse the causal relationship and say that where we find this masquelike theme, the presence of the Queen is probable. I have referred, in connection with "Love in idlenesse," to the famous "faire Vestall, throned by the West" passage in *A Midsummer-Night's Dream* (II.i.148–169). The allegory in this passage closely resembles that in both *Endymion* and *The Arraignment,* which we know were affected by the Queen's presence. Cupid, flying between earth and moon, thinks he shoots at an appropriate sublunary target. But the time, the person, and his aim are all misjudged. The song of a mysterious mer-

The Arraignment of Paris

maid enraptures nature, and in this brief restoration of the Golden Age
the "imperiall Votresse" to Diana walks in a realm apart. Cupid's arrow
is analogous to Ate's golden ball. Among fallen mortals it produces the
maddening moral blindness called "Love in idlenesse," but Elizabeth is
above the sting of sensuality as she is above every assault from below. She
passes on, "in maiden meditation, fancy free." Recognition of this theme
will not help to resolve the voluminous controversy about the occasion
for the first composition of *A Midsummer-Night's Dream* or the occasion alluded to in the passage above, but I think it does support the probability that the play was written for a performance at which the Queen
presided.

So in the case of *The Arraignment,* the intention to compliment the
Queen seems to draw Peele to a plot with political overtones. He may
have chosen the story of Paris for his "device" because it combined with
its choice-of-Hercules parable some specific associations with Tudor history. As Tillyard finds in Shakespeare's history plays a kind of secularized mystery cycle, we can find in *The Arraignment* suggestions of a
political analogue to the Fall and the Redemption. Paris is the first parent
of England. His choice of the lesser good inaugurates a cycle of history
in the fallen world which will lead to Brute's settlement of England and
to the establishment of the Tudors on the throne after a century of civil
broils. Elizabeth's reign in the New Troy restores at last the social harmony and justice which Paris lost. This restoration is symbolized in the
play by the course of the golden ball from the hand of Ate to the hand
of Elizabeth. Ate first rises at the bidding of Tellus. Whether or not
Tellus represents Mary, Queen of Scots as she is sometimes said to do in
Endymion, Ate does represent the recurrent threat of political chaos in
postlapsarian society. But evil is dreamlike in romance. The malcontents
are powerless to strike. The revolt of the disordered passions cannot touch
a Queen enthroned in the sphere of the moon, changeable like mortals,
but changeless like the gods. Peele saw chastity, the predominant virtue of
romance, as the symbol not only of the Queen's majesty in general, but
of her political stability in particular. And I like to think that by the time
the full effect of his beautiful "device" had worked upon her, the old
Queen could rest for a moment in the fiction that she *had* restored the
order of the world, and deserved the poet's golden ball.

[5]

PASTORAL POETRY

The Vitality and Versatility
of a Convention

Hallett Smith

THE Elizabethan poet usually began, as Virgil had done, by writing pastoral poetry. And, since many poets begin and not all of them continue, the proportion of pastoral to the whole literary production of the Elizabethan period is fairly high. There have been many attempts to account for this prominence of the shepherd in the literature of an age of sea dogs and explorers, of courtiers and usurers, of magnificent Leicester, dashing Essex, and staid Burleigh.

One critic maintains that pastoral is always a vehicle for something else: "The pastoral, whatever its form, always needed and assumed some external circumstance to give point to its actual content. The interest seldom arises directly from the narrative itself." ¹ Another commentator shakes his head over the whole pastoral tradition and seems to think that in the Elizabethan period it is merely a literary fad which got out of hand. "The exquisitely artificial convention of the pastoral poetry of the late sixteenth century and its stylized vocabulary, at times so dazzling and yet so often monotonous, gave little scope for original expression." ² A more sensitive critic finds the reason for the popularity of pastoral in artistic

¹ W. W. Greg, *Pastoral Poetry and Drama* (London, 1906) , p. 67.
² Anonymous review of *England's Helicon*, ed. Hyder E. Rollins, 2 vols. (Cambridge: Harvard University Press) , in *TLS*, April 11, 1935, p. 240.

2   *Elizabethan Poetry*

considerations: "It was the peculiarly combined satisfaction
of freedom and formalism which attracted so many Elizabethans to pastoral." [3] Probably the most commonly held view
is that pastoral is merely escape literature, especially attractive at a time when populations are shifting, life is becoming
more complex, and the townsman dreams nostalgically of life
in the country.

It is certainly true that pastoral was a convention. Shepherds thronged in the entertainments for royalty, in the
pageants and devices like those presented at Kenilworth in
1575 and in the royal entertainments of 1578. These shows
are in part literature, and they had their influence on works
which were more purely literature.[4] But to establish the occasion, and even the fashion, of a work of art is not to explain
its significance. The more conventional it is, the more likely
it is to have some central core of meaning from which individual treatments may originate. "Originality" cannot be
estimated until we know what the convention meant to the
writers working in it.

Whatever may be said of other times and places, Elizabethan England saw a meaning in pastoral. This meaning
was, or constituted, a positive ideal. It was an ideal of the good
life, of the state of content and mental self-sufficiency which
had been known in classical antiquity as *otium*. The revival
of this ideal is a characteristic Renaissance achievement; it
would have been impossible in the Middle Ages, when time
spent in neither work nor communion with God was felt to
be sinful. By projecting this ideal, poets of the age of Shakespeare were able to criticize life as it is and portray it as it
might be. Their shepherds are citizens of the same Arcadia as
that inhabited by the shepherds of Milton and Matthew
Arnold.

The Elizabethan mind took over its conception of pastoral

---

[3] Kathleen Tillotson in *The Works of Michael Drayton*, ed J. W. Hebel,
5 vols. (Oxford, 1931–1941), V, 4.

[4] See, for example, Thomas Blenerhasset's *Revelation of the True Minerva*,
ed. J. W. Bennett (New York, 1941), and I. L. Schulze, "Blenerhasset's *A
Revelation*, Spenser's *Shepheardes Calender*, and the Kenilworth Pageants,"
ELH, XI (1944), 85–91.

Pastoral Poetry 3

from many sources. The most general and the most obvious of these sources was the Bible. In Genesis, the first great event after the fall of man is one which involves a shepherd; it is the story of Cain and Abel. What it meant to the Elizabethans is explained by Bacon:

We see (as the Scriptures have infinite mysteries, not violating at all the 'truth of the story or letter), an image of the two estates, the contemplative state and the active state, figured in the two persons of Abel and Cain, and in the two simplest and most primitive trades of life; that of the shepherd, (who, by reason of his leisure, rest in a place, and living in view of heaven, is a lively image of a contemplative life,) and that of the husbandman: where we see again the favour and election of God went to the shepherd, and not to the tiller of the ground.[5]

Moreover, David, perhaps the most romantic figure in the Old Testament, was a shepherd, as well as being the principal poet and singer of songs among the ancient Hebrews. Of his psalms, the twenty-third was of course a special favorite. It reflected not only the atmosphere of green pastures but also the doctrine of content as the greatest of God's blessings. "The Lord is my shepherd; I shall not want" was explained by the preachers as a pastoral metaphor expressing the truth of Christian content.[6]

In the New Testament there is the central pastoral imagery of Christ the Good Shepherd, and of course the episode of the shepherds hearing from heaven the good tidings of Christ's birth. As Michael Drayton wrote, "In the Angels Song to Shepheards at our Saviours Nativitie Pastorall Poesie seemes consecrated." [7]

Characteristically, the Renaissance mixed examples of the shepherd from Greek and Roman tradition and history with those from the Bible. In Mantuan's seventh eclogue, Moses and Apollo are mentioned in pastoral roles.[8] Paris, the son of

---

[5] *Sir Francis Bacon, Works*, ed. James Spedding, R. L. Ellis, and D. D. Heath, 15 vols. (Boston, 1860–1864), VI, 138.

[6] See, for example, *Davids Pastorall Poeme: or Sheepeheards Song. Seven Sermons, on the 23. Psalme of Dauid*, by Thomas Jackson (1603).

[7] "To the Reader of his Pastorals" in *Works*, ed. Hebel, II, 517.

[8] *The Eclogues of Baptista Mantuanus*, ed. W. P. Mustard (Baltimore, 1911), p. 97. Translations or adaptations of this passage are in Alexander

4 *Elizabethan Poetry*

Priam, King of Troy, was the most famous of all classical shepherds because from his actions sprang the whole epic narrative of the siege of Troy. Besides Paris, James Sandford's translation of Cornelius Agrippa (1569) cites Romulus and Remus, Anchises, and the emperor Diocletian as shepherds. Thomas Fortescue's translation from Pedro Mexía, *The Foreste* (1586) adds Galerius and Tamburlaine. A shepherd in Drayton's "Dowsabell" is described as resembling Tamburlaine in looks and Abel in temper.[9]

The Elizabethan attitude toward Paris reveals much of the meaning and significance of pastoral in the poetry of the age. The story of Paris is of course one of the great stories: how a king's son, living as a shepherd, is in love with the nymph Oenone; how he is chosen to be umpire among the three goddesses, Juno, Venus, and Pallas Athena, to decide which of them deserves the golden apple inscribed "For the fairest"; how he decides in favor of Venus and is given as a reward the love of the most beautiful of women, Helen; how he deserts Oenone, brings Helen to Troy, and precipitates the Trojan War with all of its consequences—this plot is surely one of the great achievements of the Western imagination.

Dramatic treatments of the story of Paris are mentioned by Saint Augustine;[10] the subject is inherently dramatic, both for the power of the rival claims of the goddesses and for the world-shaking consequences of Paris' choice. The death of Hector and Achilles, the destruction of Troy, the wanderings of Ulysses and of Aeneas, the founding of Rome (and of Britain, too, as the Elizabethans thought), all resulted from this one simple decision by a shepherd on the hills of Ida.

Purely as plot, then, the story of the shepherd's choice had color and vitality. But it was also symbolic, and an understanding of what was represented to the Elizabethan mind by the offers of Juno, Pallas, and Venus while Paris was trying

---

Barclay's fifth eclogue (before 1530), lines 469–492; in Turbervile's translation (1567), sig. K2ᵛ; in Spenser's July eclogue in *The Shepheardes Calender* (1579), lines 131–160; and in Francis Sabie's *Pan's Pipe* (1595), sigs. D2ᵛ–D3ʳ.

[9] *Works*, ed. Hebel, I, 89.

[10] *De civitate Dei*, XVIII, 10.

Pastoral Poetry   5

to make up his mind is essential to an appreciation of poetic treatments of the myth. From classical times on down, the principal myths had been interpreted morally, if not allegorically, and the Judgment of Paris was one which lent itself to such treatment in a very natural way. Athenaeus says, in the *Deipnosophistae,* "And I for one affirm also that the Judgment of Paris, as told in poetry by the writers of an older time, is really a trial of pleasure against virtue. Aphrodite, for example—and she represents pleasure—was given the preference, and so everything was thrown into turmoil." [11]

Fulgentius, Bishop of Carthage, also moralized the myth of the Judgment of Paris. The three goddesses, he says, represent the three ways of life: the active, the contemplative, and the voluptuous. Jove himself, continues Fulgentius, could not make judgment among the three contending goddesses or the ways of life they represent; it is essentially a human dilemma. A shepherd, in Fulgentius' opinion, is the most suitable of all men to be the judge, though of course, according to the bishop, Paris made a foolish choice. Spenser agrees, and in the July eclogue of *The Shepheardes Calender* goes out of his way to condemn Paris:

> For he was proude, that ill was payd,
> (no such mought shepheards bee)
> And with lewde lust was ouerlayd:
> tway things doen ill agree.[12]

To the Renaissance, Paris' mistake was intended as a powerful warning. Italian treatises on nobility considered the Judgment of Paris story to represent the choice which must actually be made by the young man deciding upon a course of life.[13]

[11] *The Deipnosophists,* XII, 510 c, trans. C. B. Gulick, Loeb Classical Library, 7 vols. (1922–1949), V, 295.

[12] The same point had been emphasized by Horace in *Epistles,* II, 10. The idea was also familiar to Renaissance Platonists and was elaborated by Ficino, for example, in his commentary on Plato's *Philebus.* See P. O. Kristeller, *The Philosophy of Marsilio Ficino* (New York, 1943), pp. 358–359.

[13] The passage in G. B. Nenna's treatise is so typical, and the reputation of his book in England is so amply attested to by Edmund Spenser, Samuel Daniel, George Chapman, and Angel Day, that it must be quoted: "Now let

6   *Elizabethan Poetry*

In the most popular of the pastoral romances, the Judgment of Paris is a subject for debate; in Montemayor's *Diana*, for example, Delia and Andronius spend the greater part of a night in arguing the question whether Paris gave the apple to the right goddess or not and whether the inscription on it referred to physical or mental beauty.[14] The shepherds and shepherdesses in Elizabethan pastoral poetry often allude to the Paris story or compare themselves with figures in it. An example is from "Phillidaes Loue-Call to her Coridon, and his replying," by "Ignoto" in *England's Helicon;*[15] another is Willye's compliment to Cuddie, the umpire of the singing match in Spenser's August eclogue:

> Neuer dempt more right of beautye I weene,
> The shepheard of Ida, that iudged beauties Queene.[16]

Drayton's Rowland, on the other hand, compares himself to the deserted Oenone.[17]

Whatever the faults of Paris' decision, the son of Priam remained, for the Elizabethan, the archetype of the shepherd. Spenser's Sir Calidore, when he takes off his armor and puts

vs consider what fruit may be gathered by the shadowe of fables, especially of this which I euen now recited. For indeed vnder those vailes we may receiue no lesse pleasant then profitable instruction . . . After that a man is once framed, and that he hath attained to that age, that hee beginneth nowe to discourse within himselfe, what kinde of life hee were best to followe as the most noble in account amongst men: whether that which is grounded vppon knowledge, which the Philosophers were wont to cal a contemplatiue kind of life: or otherwise, yt which guideth a man that addicteth himself only to worldly matters, which they terme actiue: or else that which consisteth wholy in pleasure, which they name delightfull. Then straightwaie discord entreth: of which three sortes of liues, Soueraigne Iupiter will not giue sentence which is the best, least that in approuing the one, he should condemne the other two; and so the life of man should rather be constrained then free, but hee leaueth them to the judgement of man, to the end that he may as pleaseth him, tie himselfe to that kind of life that shall best like him; it may be, shewing vs thereby, the free choice which is granted to vs by him. Of the which notwithstanding he that is caried away to follow the delightfull kind of life, doth bring vnto him selfe vnspeakeable detriment" (*Nennio, or a Treatise of Nobility*, trans. William Jones, 1595, sig. H3ᵛ) .

[14] Trans. Bartholomew Yong (1598) , p. 53.
[15] Rollins ed., I, 70.
[16] Lines 137–138.
[17] *Idea The Shepheards Garland* (1593) , Eclogue IX, lines 55–60.

Pastoral Poetry 7

on shepherd's weeds in order to woo Pastorella, suggests the obvious model, "Phrygian Paris by Plexippus brooke." [18]

The Judgment of Paris had of course been treated in medieval love allegories such as Froissart's *L'Espinette Amoureuse,* Machaut's *Le Dit de la Fontaine Amoureuse,* and Lydgate's *Reson and Sensuallyte;* there had been continental dramas on the subject in the fifteenth and early sixteenth centuries; and most important of all for the English pastoral, the Paris story was a common subject of the pageants—for Queen Margaret at Edinburgh in 1503, for the coronation of Anne Boleyn in 1533, and at a marriage masque in 1566.[19] It also appeared in the emblem-books. In Whitney's *Choice of Emblemes* the account of the Judgment is much abbreviated, but full justice is done to the interpretation.[20]

It is obvious, then, that the major Elizabethan treatment of the Paris story, George Peele's play *The Arraignment of Paris* (1584), is in a well-established tradition. It is in dramatic form, but it is so important as an indication of the significance of pastoral in the Elizabethan mind that it must be discussed briefly here.

In the temptation scene, when the three goddesses in turn offer their rewards to Paris, they are more abstract than personal. Juno offers the shepherd "great monarchies, Empires, and kingdomes, heapes of massye golde, scepters and diadems," symbolized theatrically by the appearance of a golden tree, the fruit of which is diadems. Pallas offers fame, wisdom, honor of chivalry and victory, "but yf thou haue a minde to fly aboue." The reward is symbolized by nine knights in armor treading a warlike Almain. Venus offers Paris the services of Cupid, kisses from herself, and finally (here the reward and the symbol become the same thing) Helen.[21] Paris is

[18] *Faerie Queene,* VI, ix, xxxvi.
[19] See C. R. Baskervill, "Early Romantic Plays in England," *MP,* XIV (1916–17), 483; T. S. Graves, "*The Arraignment of Paris* and Sixteenth Century Flattery," *MLN,* XXVIII (1913), 48–49; A. H. Gilbert, 'The Source of Peele's *Arraignment of Paris,*" *MLN,* XLI (1926), 36; and Douglas Bush, *Mythology and the Renaissance Tradition in English Poetry* (Minneapolis, 1932), pp. 51–52.
[20] Ed. of 1586, p. 83.
[21] Sig. Cʳ.

8   *Elizabethan Poetry*

constantly a symbolic figure; he is suggestive. I do not mean
that the artist had nothing to do with this suggestiveness and
that the audience could be counted upon to do it all. A sixteenth-century Italian treatise on painting makes clear the
artist's obligation in the matter and uses Paris as an example:

> Hence then the painter may learne how to expresse not onely the
> proper and naturall motions, but also the accidentall; wherein con-
> sisteth no small part of the difficulty of the Arte, namelie in represent-
> ing diversities of affections and passions in one bodie: A thing much
> practized, by the ancient Painters (though with greate difficulty) who
> ever indevored to leaue no iott∂ of the *life* vnexpressed.
>
> It is recorded that *Euphranor* gaue such a touch to the counterfeit
> of *Paris,* that therein the behoulder might at once collect, that hee was
> *Vmpire* of the three *Goddesses,* the *Courter of Helena,* and the slaier of
> *Achilles.*[22]

But Paris, with the alternatives clearly before him, chooses
Venus. When he defends himself before the court of the gods,
in Peele's play, he speaks first as a man, blaming his fault, if
any, on the judgment of his eye. Then he adds a *reason:* that
it was only for beauty he gave the ball, and if other virtues
had been concerned he would have chosen Pallas or Juno.
Furthermore, he says, he was tempted more than man ever
was, and as a shepherd he was relatively immune to offers
other than that of Venus.[23] The simplicity of the shepherd's
conditions makes for an invulnerability to appeals in the
name of wealth or of chivalry. It is only beauty, of the three
ideals represented by the goddesses, which has any significant
power in a pastoral life.

Paris is the judge precisely because the conditions of the
pastoral life provide the greatest independence, the greatest
security. The shepherd is not motivated by ambition or by
greed. Free from these two common human passions, he enjoys "content," or the good life. Elizabethan pastoral poetry
is essentially a celebration of this ideal of content, of *otium.*
The contemplative state enjoyed a freedom, not only from

[22] G. P. Lomazzo, *A Tracte Containing the Artes of Curious Paintinge,*
trans. Richard Haydocke (1598), sig. Bb6ʳ.
[23] Sig. D4ʳ.

Pastoral Poetry   9

ambition or greed, but from the vicissitudes of fortune. The
popular tradition of the fall of princes, represented in Elizabethan literature by the *Mirror for Magistrates* and the poems
added to it, had stressed ominously the dangers in the turn
of Fortune's wheel. Kings and princes, the high and mighty,
were exhibited in tragic circumstances, the victims of their
own high position, their ambition, or their greed. The poetic
tragedies of the *Mirror* therefore supported, negatively, the
same ideal celebrated by pastoral. Occasionally the warning
in a *Mirror* tragedy concludes with a direct endorsement of
the quiet life of content. In one of the tragedies in Blenerhasset's *Mirror,* for example, the herdsman who kills Sigebert
and is hanged for it concludes with the lesson:

> And happy he, who voyde of hope can leade
> A quiet lyfe, all voyde of Fortunes dread.

This makes the following Induction deal with the question
of why it is that formerly the wisest men were content to be
shepherds, but now "in these our dayes, none bee Heardmen
but fooles, and euery man though his witte be but meane, yet
he cannot liue with a contented mind, except he hath the
degree of a Lorde." [24]

In order to respond adequately to the appeal of the Elizabethan ideal of the mean estate, content, and *otium,* it is
necessary to feel the force of its opposite, a form of ambition
which the sixteenth century called most commonly the aspiring mind. Marlowe's Tamburlaine is of course the great representative of the aspiring mind, as he is its philosopher:

> Nature that fram'd vs of foure Elements,
> Warring within our breasts for regiment,
> Doth teach vs all to haue aspyring minds.[25]

But there are many other examples of the concept in Elizabethan England. Mr. Secretary Walsingham, summing up the

[24] *Parts Added to the Mirror for Magistrates,* ed. L. B. Campbell (Cambridge, England, 1946), pp. 462–463.

[25] Lines 869–871. For evidence that Tamburlaine was a symbol of this Renaissance spirit before he appeared in Marlowe's play, see my "Tamburlaine
and the Renaissance," *Elizabethan Studies in Honor of George F. Reynolds*
(Boulder, Colo., 1945), pp. 128–129.

1 0   *Elizabethan Poetry*

personal charges against Mary Queen of Scots, said that she
had an aspiring mind; [26] and Queen Elizabeth herself, writing
a poem about Mary, included the line

> But clowds of tois vntried, do cloake aspiring mindes.[27]

Blue, as the color of the sky, was symbolic of the aspiring
mind, according to Lomazzo:

> Persius sat. 1. speaking of Blew garments, sheweth that they belong
> only to such persons, as aspire vnto high matters: and Cicero vsed some-
> times to weare this color, giuing men thereby to vnderstand, that he bare
> an aspiring minde.[28]

There were many other Roman examples of the aspiring
mind; a typical one is Pompey.[29] That the aspiring mind was
a dangerous and possibly sinful state is made clear by Du
Bartas, who contrasts it to the attitude of the angels.[30] The
first example of the aspiring mind, according to Du Bartas,
was in the hunter, Nimrod, "that was the first Tyrant of the
world, after the time of Noah, the first Admiral of the worlde:
his aspiring minde & practises in seeking the peoples fauour,
his proud and subtle attempt in building the Tower of Babel,
& Gods iust punishment thereof in confounding the language
of the builders." [31]

The central meaning of pastoral is the rejection of the
aspiring mind. The shepherd demonstrates that true content
is to be found in this renunciation. Sidney expresses the preference in terms of a contrast between pastoral and court life:

> Greater was that shepheards treasure,
> Then this false, fine, Courtly pleasure.[32]

[26] Conyers Read, *Mr. Secretary Walsingham and the Policy of Queen Elizabeth*, 3 vols. (Oxford, 1925), I, 69.

[27] George Puttenham, *The Arte of English Poesie*, ed. Gladys D. Willcock
and Alice Walker (Cambridge, England, 1936), p. 248.

[28] *The Artes of Curious Paintinge*, trans. Haydocke, p. 122.

[29] *Fennes Frutes* (1590), sig. E3ᵛ.

[30] *The First Day of the Worldes Creation*, trans. Joshua Sylvester (1595),
sig. El ᵛ.

[31] *Babilon*, trans. William L'Isle (1595), sig. A3ᵛ.

[32] "Disprayse of a Courtly life," first published in *A Poetical Rhapsody*
(1602), ed. Hyder E. Rollins, 2 vols. (Cambridge: Harvard University Press,
1931, 1932), I, 9–12.

Pastoral Poetry 11

In the pastoral episode in Book VI of *The Faerie Queene*, Sir Calidore envies the apparent happiness of the shepherds; he comments that their life seems free from the "warres, and wreckes, and wicked enmitie" which afflict the rest of the world.[33] In reply to this, the sage old Meliboee then answers with an analysis of the pastoral existence which is in effect a definition of "the good life." It consists of four elements: (1) being content with what you have, however small it is —this is the way taught by nature (contrast Tamburlaine's statement that nature teaches us to have aspiring minds); (2) enjoying freedom from envy of others and from excessive care for your own possessions (the flocks multiply without your doing much about it); (3) avoiding the dangers of pride and ambition and also the insomnia that plagues those who hold positions of responsibility (see the testimony of Shakespeare's kings in 2 *Henry IV*, III, i, 1–31, and IV, v, 20–27; *Henry V*, IV, i, 266–290); (4) doing what you like. Old Meliboee does not speak from provincial ignorance, either. He once spent ten years at court, but returned to the pastoral life from choice.

The question of the moral validity of pastoral life when compared with life at court is not difficult to answer: the long tradition of dispraise of the court is always, by implication or by direct statement, an endorsement of the pastoral life. But there is a more difficult question when the alternatives are the quiet, retired life of the shepherd on the one hand or a mission of chivalric and honorable achievement on the other. The pastoral romance, both in Sidney and in his sources like Montemayor's *Diana*, mingles pastoral and heroic elements. The question of the relative value of the two kinds of life is naturally raised. The pastoral sojourn of Erminia in the seventh book of Tasso's *Jerusalem Delivered* is used as a contrast to the heroic actions of the main part of the poem. It is also obvious that pastoral and heroic put a different light upon the feelings of love; these might or might not be a detriment to the heroic life, but they are sanctioned in the world of pastoral.

[33] VI, ix, xix.

[6]

ELIZABETHAN EPIDEICTIC DRAMA:

PRAISE AND BLAME IN THE PLAYS OF PEELE AND LYLY

R. Headlam Wells

There is no topic which illustrates more pointedly the difference between Renaissance and modern poetics than that of praise. For the twentieth-century reader, and indeed many twentieth-century critics, the literature of praise is more or less synonymous with venality. And not without reason. There is, after all, some justice in the fact that Waller, that most representative of neo-classical panegyrists, is remembered chiefly, not for a handful of exquisite lyrics, but for Johnson's acid complaint that

> *It is not possible to read, without some contempt and indignation, poems of the same author, ascribing the highest degree of* power and piety *to Charles the First, then transferring the same* power and piety *to Oliver Cromwell, now inviting Oliver to take the Crown, and then congratulating Charles the Second on his recovered right. Neither Cromwell nor Charles could value his testimony as the effect of conviction, or receive his praises as effusions of reverence; they could consider them but as the labour of invention, the tribute of dependence.*[1]

Time has reversed the judgment of Waller's immediate contemporaries; but if we no longer regard him as one of the greatest poets of the seventeenth century, it cannot be said that Dryden does much to restore our belief in the value of epideictic literature either. Panegyric, it must be admitted, did not inspire the acknowledged master of the age to his greatest efforts.

A century earlier, however, this was not the case. *A prince of poets in his time*, Spenser was also a poet of princes. In an age—indeed the last age—when most people still believed in the concept of an orderly hierarchical universe and when the idea that princes were God's anointed deputies on earth was only just beginning seriously to be questioned, praise was a fundamental article in the credo of the humanist literary critic. Puttenham, for example, in his defence of the dignity of poetry, claims that, second only to poetry composed in praise of the immortal gods, is that which honours *the worthy gests of*

R. *Headlam Wells*   **EPIDEICTIC DRAMA**   16

noble princes.[2]   The task of an author who undertook such a work of praise was *to yeeld a like ratable honour to all such amongst men as most resembled the gods by excellencie of function and had a certaine affinitie with them, by more then humane and ordinarie vertues shewed in their actions here vpon earth* (p. 35).   In doing so his object was essentially a moral one.   The special nature of the responsibilities assumed by the panegyrist is perhaps best explained by Erasmus in a letter he wrote some twelve years before the composition of his own epideictic treatise on kingship, *The Education of a Christian Prince* (1516).   *Those who believe panegyrics are nothing but flattery*, writes Erasmus, *seem to be unaware of the purpose and aim of the extremely far-sighted men who invented this kind of composition, which consists in presenting princes with a pattern of goodness, in such a way as to reform bad rulers, improve the good, educate the boorish, reprove the erring, arouse the indolent, and cause even the hopelessly vicious to feel some inward stirrings of shame.*[3]

Such was the theory of praise which the Renaissance inherited from the rhetoricians of the ancient world.[4]   It is true that not every Elizabethan panegyrist is successful in observing Aristotle's important distinction between praise and flattery,[5] that is to say, between the celebration of a moral ideal through the vehicle of a person, a city or an institution and the defence of a particular individual's conduct or policies.   (It is one of the chief faults of the fifth book of *The Faerie Queene* that it descends from the former to the latter.)   Nevertheless, it was a belief which was fundamental to a didactic theory of literature that, by giving *praise, the reward of vertue, to vertuous acts...*[6] the poet might in turn inspire acts of virtue.

In view of the importance of praise in Renaissance poetics it is surprising that Elizabethan epideictic drama has received comparatively little scholarly attention.   Indeed, it is remarkable that, in his eloquent and persuasive defence of the Stuart masque, Orgel ignores altogether the Elizabethan forerunners of these royalist extravagazas.[7]   In this article I shall consider a group of plays by two underrated Elizabethan playwrights, Peele and Lyly.   (In the recent *Revels History of Drama in English*, for example, Peele and Lyly are allocated a mere four pages between them.)   It would be foolish to claim that all these plays achieve the status of great art; but though my object is principally to show that their epideictic intention does not necessarily preclude the serious dramatic treatment of moral questions, I suggest that, at their best these Elizabethan plays possess greater intrinsic literary interest than the masques which they in some measure adumbrate.

Peele and Lyly were both members of a group of Oxford graduates living in London in the early 1580s who aspired to positions at court.   Both wrote plays which were performed before the Queen by the Children of the Chapel. But whereas Lyly, after the success of his first play, *Campaspe*, went on to write a series of courtly comedies in which royal compliment is barely concealed, Peele appears to have had only one play performed at court. This was *The Arraignment of Paris*.

The Arraignment of Paris incorporates two sixteenth-century traditions— the tradition of royal pageantry and the *debat* tradition of the Tudor expository interlude.   A brief account of Peele's debt to the conventions associated with these traditions may help to define his purpose.

R. *Headlam Wells*   **EPIDEICTIC DRAMA**   17

Elizabethan royal pageantry was frankly propagandist. Its purpose was to present an image of the perfect prince appointed by providence to rule a chosen people. It employed a variety of means to promote this idea: triumphal arches decorated with emblematic devices, formal orations complimentary verses, songs, tableaux and masques. At the royal entry of 1559 the Queen was addressed as a prince of peace, the symbolic representative of the united houses of Lancaster and York:

> *Therefore as civill warre, and fuede of blood did cease*
> *When these two Houses were united into one,*
> *So now that jarrs shall stint, and quietnes encrease,*
> *We trust, O noble Quene, thou wilt be cause alone.*[8]

As her reign wore on these expressions of pious hope were naturally transformed into confident tributes to Elizabeth's statemanship.

A popular feature of the civic pageant was the use of historical or mythical figures who, acknowledging Elizabeth's superior virtue, gladly resign to her their pre-eminence. For example, in 1578 the city of Norwich offered an entertainment in which five women addressed the Queen in turn from an elaborate stage built in the form of a triple arch. The five figures, of whom *the first was the City of Norwich, the second Debora, the third Judeth, the fourth Esther, the fifth Martia, sometime Queene of England* each complimented the Queen by inviting comparison between their achievements and her own.

These speeches concluded, the Queen was then entertained with a consort song. The song tells of a strife in heaven. The rival claims to supremacy of Juno, Venus, Diana, Ceres, Pallas and Minerva are adjudicated by Jove who resolves the contention by reporting the existence of a *Soveraign Wight* in whom are to be found united the several virtues of the six goddesses. Jove's discovery is greeted with universal approval, and the song ends with a tribute to the Queen.[9]

Although Paris does not appear in the Norwich pageant, the quarrelling goddesses clearly perform precisely the same complimentary function as Peele's deities.[10] However this does not mean that the device should be regarded as a source for *The Arraignment of Paris*. Variations of one kind or another on the Judgment of Paris theme were so frequently employed in sixteenth-century pageantry as a means of flattering royal personages that it is impossible to specify a source for any one particular example of its use.[11] The central device of *The Arraignment of Paris* was traditional.

Traditional also was the *debat* motif used by Peele. In his edition of *The Arraignment of Paris* Benbow traces the development of a new kind of dramatic entertainment in the 1560s and the '70s which grew out of the earlier tradition of expository drama exemplified in the Tudor interludes and moralities. In plays such as Edwardes' *Damon and Pithias* or Farrant's *The Wars of Cyrus* historical or legendary material is used to illustrate an intellectual problem that is discussed and analyzed throughout the play. «The new expository drama», writes Benbow, «is similar to the morality; and the rhetorical debates on love, honour, and friendship recall the tirades and exhortations of the virtues in the moralities. The basic allegorical structure of the morality is disguised by the historical story, and the use of the historical framework is supported by the substitution of concrete characters for the older personifications».[12]

Although the new drama was considerably more sophisticated than the interlude from which it in part derived, its principal concern lay not in the development of character, but in the exposition of a central idea.   In *The Wars of Cyrus*, for example, the love-interest, the intrigue against Cyrus' life and the tragic death of Panthea are all subservient to the play's main object, which is to illustrate the nature of true magnanimity.   When Araspas confesses to his attempted seduction of Panthea, Cyrus tells him:

> *Araspas, they that would be conquerors*
> *Should chiefly learne to conquer their desire,*
> *Least while they seeke dominion over others*
> *They prove but slaves and bondmen to themselves.*   (IV.3.1276-9)[13]

In presenting a dramatic portrait of the perfect prince *The Wars of Cyrus*, like Lyly's *Campaspe* (which it clearly anticipates), lays great emphasis on sexual self-restraint.   Indeed for the Elizabethan court dramatist princely virtue became, for obvious reasons, more or less synonymous with chastity.

Elements of both the *debat* tradition and the tradition of Elizabethan civic pageantry were combined in a masque which Sidney wrote for the Queen's visit to Wanstead in 1578.   What slight dramatic structure *The Lady of May* might be said to possess springs from the rivalry between Therion the forester and Espilus the shepherd for the hand of their May queen.   However, Sidney's treatment of the debate between these unheroic representatives of the active life and the retired life shows that he was not interested in offering a solution to the problem. His primary object was to entertain the Queen and at the same time to flatter her. Having been 'surprised' in Wanstead gardens by a distraught mother, the Queen is requested to judge between the rival claimants to the daughter's hand.   While she listens to the evidence she is entertained first with the songs of the two contenders and then by the malapropisms of Lalus and the inkhorn pedantry of Rhombus.   Gracious flattery is provided by the May Lady herself who confesses that *you excel me in that wherein I desire most to excel, and that makes me give this homage unto you, as the beautifullest lady these woods have ever received.*[14] When judgment has been passed Rhombus presents a final compliment in which he claims that Elizabeth surpasses the united virtues of Juno, Venus and Pallas.

The Lady of May is more elaborate than the traditional pageant masque with its stiff allegorical figures and its formal encomiums of the Queen.   But although characterization is more fully developed, the piece can scarcely be called a play. It is an entertainment with music and songs designed for a specific situation, and its interest, for the modern reader, lies largely in the verbal comedy of Rhombus, forerunner of many an Elizabethan pedant.   Insofar as it combines certain elements of an expository dramatic tradition with the conventions of royal pageantry, it is tempting to see *The Lady of May* as a kind of transitional work forming a link, with *The Arraignment of Paris*, between the pageant masque and the truly dramatic works of a court playwright such as Lyly.   Certainly Peele's play has much in common with *The Lady of May*: both employ the device of a debate as a means of drawing the Queen into the action; both make the traditional comparison between Elizabeth and the three classical goddesses; and both use music and song as an essential part of the entertainment.   But although the two works are informed by the need to flatter their royal audience, this should not disguise the fact that their dramatic modes are quite different.   Sidney's piece is essentially occasional: it was written to meet the needs of a particular royal progress. Peele's was not.   Indeed it is because *The Arraignment of Paris* was not actually part of a pageant entertainment that Peele goes out of his way to imitate the setting of a royal progress in the first Act of the play.

The short first scene of *The Arraignment of Paris* is reminiscent of *The Lady of May*.   This time the rivals are three in number: a shepherd, a hunter and a woodman.   But the object of their rivalry is nothing as serious as the hand of a May queen, and they argue good-humouredly about whose gift will be preferred by the goddesses they are awaiting.   After two more scenes in which we see other rustics preparing for the arrival of the Olympians, Pallas, Juno and Venus make their entry to the accompaniment of a song.   The three goddesses express their appreciation of the *rare delights* which have been arranged in their honour, and a welcoming oration is delivered.   This done, the rustics present their gifts.

These opening scenes serve a twofold function: first, Peele adumbrates in the rustics' lighthearted banter the more portentous quarrel between the goddesses which Ate provokes in the next Act, and second, he evokes the setting of a provincial progress.   By giving his drama a thinly disguised English rural setting and showing a group of local characters making ready for a royal visitation, Peele prepares us for the inevitable entry of the Queen herself.   When the play is seen against the background of the pageant conventions it conspicuously imitates, it is impossible to criticize the appearance of Elizabeth in Act V as a violation of dramatic detachment.[15]   Nor is it a very pertinent objection to say that Peele fails to give us any resolution of what Benbow sees as the play's central problem, that is the debate concerning the true nature of beauty.[16]   Like Sidney, Peele is plainly not interested in the intellectual problem *per se*, only in the occasion it provides for the introduction of Elizabeth as arbiter.

A far more serious criticism of the play is the objection that the tradition within which it was written restricted the dramatist to the presentation of conventional problems in a world removed from reality.[17]   There is some truth in this claim.   It cannot be denied that there is little intrinsic merit in a tradition of royal panegyric which fostered a national myth for purely propagandist reasons.   However, Peele's play teaches an important political lesson at the same time that it pays a gracious compliment to the Queen.   The underlying seriousness of the Paris story is announced in the portentous words of Ate's prologue:

> *Beholde I come in place, and bring beside*
> *The bane of Troie: beholde the fatall frute*
> *Raught from the golden tree of Proserpine.*
> *Proude Troy must fall, so bidde the gods above,*
> *And statelie Iliums loftie towers be racet*
> *By conquering handes of the victorious foe:*   (5-10)

For the Elizabethan, as for the Roman poet, the sack of Troy was quite simply the most important event in the legendary history of the ancient world.[18] Since the achievements of Elizabeth, like those of Augustus, were foreshadowed in the story of Aeneas, any attempt rightly to interpret the significance of the present must begin with its prefigurations in the past.   Thus from one point of view Troy could be regarded as the inevitable starting point for a history of Rome (as it was for Livy) and consequently of Britain (as it was for Camden).

From another point of view the story of Troy could be seen as embodying an important moral lesson.   If providence had ordained that from this calamity there would follow a long train of events leading ultimately to the founding of two great civilizations, it was believed that their establishment was only made possible through the subjection of passion by the rule of reason.   The lesson of Troy, as Golding succintly explains in his commentary on Ovid's *Metamorphoses*, is the dangers of sensuality.

> *The seege of Troy, the death of men, the razing of the citie,*
> *And slaughter of king Priams stock without remors of pitie,*
> *Which in the xii. and xiii. bookes bee written, doo declare*
> *How heynous wilfull perjurie and filthie whoredome are*
> *In syght of God.*
>
> (Dedicatory *Epistle.* 242-6)[19]

The sack of Troy was the supreme example of a state overthrown by lust. Shakespeare's Thersites reflects the Elizabethan attitude to Troy in his complete identification of *wars and lechery*.   As Ralegh laconically puts in in his *History of the World: All writers consent with* Homer; *that the rape of* Helen *by* Paris *the son of* Priamus, *was the cause of taking armes...*[20]

It is important when we read *The Arraignment of Paris* that we keep in mind both the historical and the moral aspects of the Troy story, for in the play itself the two are interwoven with some subtlety.   The Trojan myth enjoyed such widespread currency in Elizabethan England that when Ate predicts the sack of Troy in her prologue Peele could be certain of his audience's knowing that from this disorder there would eventually emerge a new order, first under Augustus and then under his 'descendant' Elizabeth.   In this way the prologue looks forward directly to Diana's encomium in Act V in which the goddess tells of

> *A kingdome that may well compare with mine.*
> *An aunciest seat of kinges, a second Troie,*
> *Ycompast rounde with a commodious sea:*   (V.1.1152-4)

The action of the play is thus timeless: although it appears to be set both immediately before the Trojan war and also in the present time, no attempt is made to give realistic treatment either to the remote past or to present-day England.   Indeed Peele deliberately confuses our sense of chronology.   On the one hand he characterizes his country gods preparing for their Olympian visitation as English swains, while on the other his evocation of Elizabeth's England reads more like a classical account of the Golden Age.

Although discord is resolved in the general harmony of the play's conclusion, Peele does not allow us to forget that Troy was an historical fact. When Mercury informs Venus that her favourite has been summoned to appear

R. *Headlam Wells*   **EPIDEICTIC DRAMA**   21

before the court of heaven, she objects:

> *What heere I have, I woone it by deserte:*
> *And heaven and earthe shall bothe confounded bee,*
> *Ere wronge in this be donne to him or me.*   (III.6.772-4)

But Mercury, perceiving the unconscious irony of her words, remarks:

> *This little fruite, yf Mercury can spell,*
> *Will sende I feare a world of soules to hell.*   (III.6.775-6)

Paris appears before the gods and confesses that, being dazzled by Venus's beauty, he had allowed his fancy to rule his judgment.   After the arraignment, Jupiter passes sentence and instructs Paris to *take thy way to Troie, and there abide thy fate.*   Once again we are reminded what the consequences of Venus's gift will be, for, as Paris leaves the stage, Apollo pronounces the most memorable lines of the play:

> *From Ida woods now wends the shepherds boye,*
> *That in his bosome caries fire to Troy.*   (IV.4.990-1)

The fire that Paris carries in his bosom is, of course, both the fire of love and also the literal flames of Troy: the one is the direct cause of the other.   This is the reason why in *The Arraignment of Paris* love is consistently presented as ignoble and capricious, the cause of suffering and even death.   The greater part of Act III is concerned with the unhappy affairs of Colin and Oenone, both betrayed by Venus.   Though their complaints are beautiful, their fate is not. Oenone is left to pine away under her poplar tree—symbol of love's inconstancy —while Colin dies of grief.   If Colin and Oenone represent the tragic side of love, its grotesque aspect is symbolized by Venus's lecherous and unlovely husband attempting the seduction of one of Diana's nymphs (IV.1).

In the little pastoral world of the play Venus's capacity for mischief and injustice is limited to the disruption of individual lives.   But one of the functions of pastoral is to *glaunce greater matters*[21] and if we see in the petty conflicts of the play the historical events which they adumbrate, then it becomes clear that it is Venus, who, as Paris's patron, is ultimately responsible for the Trojan war.   The story of Troy, then, contains this important truth: if Elizabeth is Astraea *rediviva* and her London a new Troy, it is only by the disciplined subjection of passion that a repetition of the tragedy can be avoided.

Although Peele treats his material in a light-hearted manner befitting a court entertainment, his play is certainly not, as Benbow suggests, «fundamentally nonserious».[22]   *The Arraignment of Paris* performs a dual function: it flatters the Queen in terms of the popular myth which saw her as a Christian Prince inaugurating the new Golden Age prophesied by Virgil; but on another level it employs Elizabeth as a symbolic representative of the justice and order which alone can prevent history repeating itself.   Peele presents passionate love as the most powerful threat to civilized order partly, of course, because the woman whom his play was designed to compliment never married, but also because, as a humanist, he believed that civilization depended upon the rule of reason.

The dangers of erotic love is also a prominent theme in Lyly's plays. His most explicit dramatic tributes to Elizabeth are *Sapho and Phao* (c.1582-3) and *Endimion* (c.1585). Like *The Arraignment of Paris*, these plays present idealized portraits of the Queen. But this time she appears not as a miraculous *dea ex machina* graciously condescending to intervene in the disordered affairs of men and gods, but as one of the central characters in the drama. In both plays Elizabeth is portrayed as a queen of love worshipped by an adoring court. *Beleeue me Pandion*, remarks one of Sapho's courtiers to the scholar recently arrived in court, *in Athens you haue but tombs, we in court the bodies, you the pictures of Venus & the wise Goddesses, we the persons & the vertues* (I.2.17-20).[23]

Lyly was not, of course, alone in portraying the Queen as an idealized object of universal quasi-sexual admiration. From the earliest years of her reign Elizabeth's charms had been celebrated by ballad makers commemorating important contemporary events. But in 1579 a precedent was established for depicting her as the object of a poet's love when Spenser included a song of praise to *fayre Eliza, Queene of shepheardes all* in the *April* eclogue of *The Shepeardes Calender*. In the following years Elizabeth was idealized in dozens of lyrics as the very incarnation of feminine beauty and virtue. Constable's address *to the Queene: touching the cruell effects of her perfections* is an example of the way the traditional conceits of literary convention were applied to Elizabeth:

> *Most Sacred Prince ! why should I thee this prayse*
> *Which both of sin and sorrow cause hast beene*
> *Proude hast thow made thy land of such a Queene*
> *Thy neighboures enviouse of thy happie dayes.*
>
> *Whoe neuer saw the sunshine of thy rayes,*
> *An everlasting night this life doth ween*
> *And he whose eyes thy eyes but once haue seene*
> *A thowsand signes of burning thoughts bewrayes*
>
> *Thus sin thou caused envye I mean and pride*
> *Thus fire and darknesse doe proceed from thee*
> *The very paynes which men in hell abide*
>
> *Oh no not hell but purgatorie this*
> *Whose sowles some say by Angells punish'd be*
> *For thow art shee from whome this torment is.*[24]

In addition to such overt royal tributes as Puttenham's *Partheniades* (1579), Ralegh's *Cynthia* (c.1592), Drayton's *Ideas Mirror* (1594) and Davies' *Hymns of Astraea* (1599) are the numberless sonnets which pay oblique compliments to the Queen while praising the lesser virtues of some other real or imaginary lady.[25] So complete was the popular identification of Elizabeth with an abstract ideal of beauty that when Ralegh wrote his commendatory sonnet on *The Faerie Queene* he claimed that Petrarch's Laura had been deposed from her throne in the temple of fame by Spenser's mistress:

> *Me thought I saw the graue, where* Laura *lay,*
> *Within that Temple, where the vestall flame,*
> *Was wont to burne, and passing by that way,*
> *To see that buried dust of liuing fame,*
> *Whose tombe faire loue, and fairer vertue kept,*
> *All suddenly I saw the Faery Queene:*
> *At whose approch the soule of* Petrarke *wept,*
> *And from thenceforth these graces were not seene.*
> *For they this Queene attended, in whose steed*
> *Obliuion laid him downe on* Lauras *herse:*
> *Hereat the hardest stones were seene to bleed*
> *And grones of buried ghostes the heauens did perse.*
> *Where* Homers *spright did tremble all for griefe,*
> *And curst th'accesse of that celestiall theife.*[26]

It is this tradition of idealizing Elizabeth as a queen of love upon which Lyly is drawing in *Sapho and Phao*. Like her royal audience this queen is *faire by nature, by birth royall, learned by education, by gouernment politike, rich by peace: insomuch as it is hard to judge, whether she be more beautifull or wise, vertuous or fortunate* (I.2.7-10). Because the parallels between Sapho and Elizabeth are of a fairly explicit nature, Lyly is careful to avoid any imputation of moral weakness by suggesting that her passion for Phao is brought about by means beyond her control. Phao's beauty, the whimsical gift of Venus, is no earthly beauty; and when the humble ferryman appears at court, Sapho, though conscious, like him, of the impropriety of her passion, cannot resist the challenge of a linguistic game. Both are in love, both see through the other's verbal disguise, yet both must sustain the deception for form's sake:

Phao.	*It were best...that your Ladyship giue mee* *leaue to be gone: for I can but sigh.*
Sapho.	*Nay stay: for now I beginne to sighe, I shall* *not leaue though you be gone. But what do you thinke* *best for your sighing to take it away ?*
Phao.	*Yew Madame.*
Sapho.	*Mee ?*
Phao.	*No Madame, yewe of the tree.*
Sapho.	*Then will I loue yewe the better. And indeed* *I think it would make mee sleepe too, therfore all* *other simples set aside, I will simply vse onely yewe.*
Phao.	*Doe madame: for I think nothing in the world so* *good as yewe.*
Sapho.	*Farewell for this time.* (III.4.72-85)

Princes, it is discovered, are not immune to the passions which afflict lesser mortals.   As Alexander says in the earlier play *Campaspe: none can conceiue the torments of a king, vnless hee be a king, whose desires are not inferior to their dignities* (II.2.83-5).   But *fancie, thogh it commeth by hazard, is ruled by wisdome* (*Sapho and Phao*, II.4.56).   So Sapho renounces her love.   Although it is Cupid's dart which causes the cessation of her passion for Phao, we are given to understand that the change is due, in part at least, to Sapho's own moral determination: *Mee thinkes I feele an alteration in my minde,* she tells Cupid, *and as it were a withstanding in my self of mine own affections* (V.2.3-4).

As the embodiment of chaste decorum, Sapho is contrasted with her divine but shameless rival.   An ageing coquette who unscrupulously uses her husband for her own irresponsible ends, Venus has much in common with Peele's deity. In both *The Arraignment of Paris* and *Sapho and Phao* it is erotic love which is ultimately responsible for the ironies and confusions which go up to make the comedy.   The responsibility of princes in matters of love is an important theme in *Sapho and Phao*.   However, Lyly does not develop its political implications.   In Peele's play we are never allowed to forget the historical consequences of Paris's irresponsible conduct.   But although the immediate effects of Sapho's passion are seen in her whimsical and indecorous conduct (III.3), its social consequences are not stressed.   Dramatic emphasis is placed on the unique character of Sapho herself.   In reproving Venus for her indiscretions she arrogates Venus's own role and becomes herself a kind of *Goddess of affections* (V.2.64).   The final picture of Sapho as a queen of love, leading Venus *in chaines like a captiue* (V.2.66-7) and ruling the fancies of men without allowing herself to become compromised is an overt allusion to Elizabeth's practice of encouraging the amorous attention of her poets and courtiers in what was almost a parody of a medieval court of love.

If *Sapho and Phao* lacks political dimension, this is also true of Lyly's most explicit dramatic tribute to Elizabeth: for the world of *Endimion* is, if anything, more stylized and self-enclosed than that of the earlier play.   *Endimion* has much in common with *Sapho and Phao*.   Lyly's principal object is to present a dramatic portrait of Elizabeth, and once again we have a plot which concerns the relationship between a queen and her adoring courtier.   Unlike Sapho, however, Cynthia is never tempted by love.   Although Endimion himself speaks of the difference which heaven has set between them (V.3.168), the question of decorum in sexual choice is not really an important issue in the play.

The dramatic contrast between chastity and erotic love is another motif which Lyly repeats in *Endimion*.   In *Sapho and Phao* he had presented a variation on the familiar royal pageant motif of the earthly queen who usurps the place of her divine counterpart.   This time the drama deals with the rivalry between two deities, the moon and the earth.   In rejecting a topical reading of Lyly's allegory, Bevington has argued that the real subject of *Endimion* is the cosmic struggle between chaste and earthly affection.[27]   There is clearly much truth in this suggestion.   Both *Sapho and Phao* and *Endimion* exalt chastity over erotic love.   But while it is true that any attempt to establish the historical counterparts of Lyly's characters is likely to be a distraction from the main point of the plays, it is misleading to describe *Endimion* as a philosophic drama. There is no elaboration in the play of the initial evocation of the two goddesses and their respective spheres of influence (I.2.19-32).   Neither does the theme of chastity versus erotic lover ever become the subject of serious debate.   The superiority of chaste affection is certainly an important part of the play's meaning; but we are scarcely justified in dignifying such a commonplace of conventional Renaissance thought with the title of philosophy.   The real object of the play is not to examine the meaning of Platonic love, but to explore a paradox, the paradox of the Elizabeth of popular myth, that *myracle of Nature, of tyme, of Fortune* (I.4.36-7).

Lyly does not concern himself with the individual personality traits of his central character.   Like an Elizabethan portrait painter, he depicts not an individual, but an idea.   As a prince Cynthia lacks the humanity of Alexander or even Sapho; as a goddess she has none of the engaging sprightliness of Drayton's Phœbe.   She takes little part in the action and she is given none of the ironic dialogue which enlivens *Campaspe* and *Sapho and Phao* and which is seen in its most brilliant form in *Gallathea*.   Cynthia's character is evoked through report rather than realized in dialogue or action.   A good example of Lyly's technique is Endimion's first apostrophe to his goddess.   The speech is a long one, but is best quoted in its entirety, since its effect is cumulative:

> *O fayre Cynthia, why doe others terme thee vnconstant,*
> *whom I haue ever found vnmoueable ?   Iniurious tyme, corrupt*
> *manners, vnkind men, who finding a constancy not to be*
> *matched in my sweete Mistris, haue christned her with*
> *the name of wauering, waxing, and waning.   Is shee*
> *inconstant that keepeth a setled course, which since her*
> *first creation altereth not one minute in her mouing ?*
> *There is nothing thought more admirable or commendable*
> *in the sea, then the ebbing and flowing; and shall the*
> *Moone, from whom the Sea taketh this vertue, be accounted*
> *fickle for encreasing, & decreasing ?   Flowers in theyr*
> *buds are nothing worth till they be blowne, nor blossomes*
> *accounted till they be ripe fruite: and shal we then say*
> *they be changeable, for that they growe from seedes to*
> *leaues, from leaues to buds, from buds to theyr perfection ?*
> *then, why be not twigs that become trees, children that*
> *become men, and Mornings that grow to Euenings, termed*
> *wauering, for that they continue not at one stay ?*
> *I, but Cynthia, being in her fulnes, decayeth, as not*
> *delighting in her greatest beautie, or withering when*
> *she should be most honoured.   When mallice cannot obiect*
> *any thing, folly will, making that a vice, which is the*
> *greatest vertue.   What thing (my Mistris excepted) being*
> *in the pride of her beauty, & latter minute of her age,*
> *that waxeth young againe ?   Tell mee Eumenides, what is*
> *hee that hauing a Mistris of ripe yeeres, & infinite*
> *vertues, great honors, and vnspeakable beauty, but woulde*
> *wish that shee might grow tender againe ?   getting youth*
> *by yeeres, and neuer decaying beauty by time, whose*

> *fayre face, neyther the Summers blase can scorch, nor*
> *Winters blast chappe, nor the numbring of yeeres breed*
> *altering of colours.   Such is my sweete* Cynthia, *whom*
> *tyme cannot touch, because she is diuine, nor will*
> *offend because she is delicate.   O* Cynthia, *if thou*
> *shouldest alwaies continue at thy fulnes, both Gods and*
> *men would conspire to rauish thee.   But thou to abate*
> *the pride of our affections, dost detract from thy*
> *perfections, thinking it sufficient, if once in a month*
> *we enioy a glymse of thy maiestie, and then, to*
> *encrease our greefes, thou doost decrease thy glemes,*
> *comming out of thy royall robes, wherewith thou dazelist*
> *our eyes, downe into thy swath clowtes, beguiling our eyes,*

> (I.1.30-65)

Endimion's speech is a virtuoso performance and a marvellous piece of Elizabethan invention.   Its length is an essential part of its point, for its effect depends upon our appreciation of the speaker's skill in discovering so many points of artful correspondence in a simple analogy.   The whole piece is an extended conceit.   The speech is important because it is an index of Lyly's method in the play as a whole, and it is perhaps a mark of its weakness as a stage play that *Endimion* is really no more than a *Labyrinth of Conceits* (Epilogue to *Sapho and Phao*) expressive of Elizabeth's paradoxical nature. The play portrays her as the remote idealized object of men's affections, inspiring noble deeds, condescending to favour her loyal courtiers with chaste approval, but never allowing herself to become entangled in amatory affairs.   Cynthia, in short, embodies an ideal of womanhood which had been firmly fixed in the European imagination by two centuries of poets writing in the Petrarchan tradition.   Lyly's great gift to the Elizabethan stage was his unerring dramatic sense.   The interminable flyting and the ponderous humour of the Tudor interludes are gone; and out of the materials of rhetorical debate Lyly creates truly dramatic dialogue.   He is at his best when evoking the delicate and subtle confusions which arise when two characters are prevented for social or political reasons from declaring a mutual passion.   Comedy has come into its own. For all their elegance, their poise and their stylized sophistication, however, it must be admitted that *Sapho and Phao* and *Endimion* are limited by their subject matter.   Since their moral and psychological interest is slight, their principal importance will always be a technical and historical one.   The same cannot be said of *Campaspe* (1581-2).   Like the two later plays, *Campaspe* represents an idealized portrait of Elizabeth.   But in this case, rather than excluding any independent ethical interest, royal compliment is actually the vehicle of the play's moral, as it is in *The Arraignment of Paris*.

Where *Sapho and Phao* and *Endimion* portray Elizabeth as a chaste queen of love, *Campaspe* depicts her, through the character of Alexander, as a Renaissance prince.   The duties and accomplishments of the Renaissance prince were well defined.   A long tradition of humanist conduct books dealt with every aspect of the subject.   Among the most popular and influential sixteenth-century treatises were Castiglione's *Il Libro del Cortegiano* (1528), translated into English by Sir Thomas Hoby in 1561, and Sir Thomas Elyot's *The Boke Named the Governour* (1531). Both these treatises owed much to Cicero's *De Officiis* and they stimulated, in their turn, many imitations.[28]

Renaissance humanists were inspired by a wish to create a civilization which would rival the classical civilizations of the ancient world. The perfect state was to be ruled by an enlightened prince served by wise and virtuous counsellors, and it was in order to promote this ideal that manuals were written prescribing the education, accomplishments and virtues of princes and their courtiers. The prince is seen as a microcosm of the state; its virtues are his, and on him depends the well-being of his court. He is accomplished in all the arts and social graces; he is comely and decorous in his speech, his carriage, his dress and his conduct. But his accomplishments are worth nothing if they are not devoted to the cause of realizing the humanist ideal of the just society. It is axiomatic, however, that the man who governs others must first learn to govern himself. Thus the cardinal virtues to be observed by a prince or governor are wisdom, fortitude, justice and temperance. He must be indifferent to the vicissitudes of fortune; he must be prepared to undertake arduous tasks in the public interest; he must exercise impartiality in his judgment of his subjects; and in all his conduct he must display *mezzura*—the avoidance of excess of any kind.

This traditional body of thought is of particular importance to a discussion of *Campaspe*, for although the play is set in antiquity it is clearly a Renaissance humanist ideal against which Alexander's conduct is measured. *Campaspe* is a debate play of deceptive simplicity. Lyly's professed object is to mix *mirth with counsell, and discipline with delight* (Prologue at the Black Fryers) and he announces his topic of debate in the opening lines of the play: what is more becoming in a prince, courage or courtesy ? As the action unfolds and Alexander discusses with his general his love for Campaspe we are reminded repeatedly of the issues raised by this question. Campaspe herself knows that *In kinges there can be no loue, but to Queenes: for as neere must they meete in maiestie, as they doe in affection* (IV.4.30-1). It is Alexander who, having finally subdued his passion for his beautiful prisoner, concludes the debate in the play's final speech: *It were a shame Alexander should desire to commaund the world, if he could not commaund himselfe* (V.4.150-1). The moral, which is virtually identical with that of *The Wars of Cyrus*, is unequivocal: the cardinal virtue in a humanist prince is self-control.

If *Campaspe* belongs to a clearly-defined *débat* tradition, it also owes something to the pageant conventions which inform *The Arraignment of Paris*. This time, however, pageantry is no more than a dramatic motif in an economically constructed stage play, and *Campaspe* has none of the episodic quality which *The Arraignment of Paris* shares with the royal Progress entertainment.

Like *The Arraignment of Paris*, *Campaspe* begins with a triumphal entry. As the play opens we watch two of Alexander's men discussing their prince and anatomizing his virtues. Their talk is interrupted by a procession of Theban captives accompanied by their guards with other soldiers bearing the spoils of war. As Parmenio and Clito engage in light gallantries with their captives, the tone is immediately set for the drama which is to follow:

> Par.   *Madame, you neede not doubt, it is* Alexander, *that*
>   *is the conqueror.*
> Timo.   *Alex. hath ouercome, not conquered.*
> Par.   *To bring al vnder his subiection is to conquer.*
> Timo.   *He cannot subdue that which is diuine.*
> Par.   *Thebes was not.*
> Timo.   *Vertue is.*   (I.1.41-7)

This elegant verbal sparring in which serious matters are treated with studied
negligence is the very essence of *Campaspe*'s comedy.   The interchange is a
public display performed before an audience of minor characters, and Timoclea's witty replies are a necessary device for concealing emotions which she
cannot afford to indulge.

When the subject of their debate makes his entry the focus of attention
shifts, and Alexander, like a Tudor prince in a provincial progress, acts the part
of himself and asks the question which is expected of him and to which he
already knows the answer: *Clitus, are these prisoners ? of whence these
spoiles ?* (I.1.58).   The question is not a piece of dramatic *gaucherie*; it is
part of a script established by custom.   As the character of the conversation
between Parmenio and Timoclea was determined by its dramatic context, so
Alexander's role is fixed by the expectation of his stage audience.   What Lyly's
opening scene with its formal entries and emblematic displays of power serves
to emphasize is the public nature of Alexander's position.   He is the focus of
his audience's attention because their fate depends on his conduct.   As the
story develops we discover that this is true of his own court no less than of
his prisoners.   Ambiguity and confusion arise only when Alexander begins to
depart from his script and act out of character—the character, that is, of an
enlightened prince.

Act I sees the victorious Alexander turning from military affairs to the
art of peaceful government:

> Hephestion, *it resteth now that we haue as great care to*
> *gouerne in peace, as conquer in war: that whilest armes*
> *cease, artes may flourish, and ioyning letters with launces,*
> *we endeuor to be as good Philosophers as soldiers, knowing*
> *it no lesse praise to be wise, then commendable to be valiant.* (I.1.80-4)

His proposals for the establishment of a humanist court are met with the
warmest approval:

> *Your Maiestie therin sheweth that you haue as great desire*
> *to rule as to subdue: & needs must that common wealth be*
> *fortunate, whose captaine is a Philosopher, and whose*
> *Philosopher is a Captaine.*   (I.1.85-8)

Hephaestion's chiasmic reply emphasizes the importance of balancing the rival claims of the active life and the retired life.   If philosophy is the servant of virtuous action, scene iii shows the folly of allowing learning to become an end in itself.   Alexander's chamberlain summons the philosophers to court. But his first encounter is not a sanguine one:

> *First, I cam to* Crisippus, *a tall leane old man,*
> *willing him presently to appeare before* Alexander; *he*
> *stoode staring on my face, neither mouing his eies nor*
> *his body; I vrging him to giue some answer, hee tooke*
> *vp a booke, sate downe, and saide nothing:*
> Melissa *his maid told me it was his manner, and that*
> *oftentimes she was fain to thrust meate into his*
> *mouth: for that he wold rather starue then ceasse studie.*   (I.3.2-8)

Lyly's satire is directed not at learning, but its abuse, and later in the same scene we see Alexander reaffirming his humanist proposals:

> *sithence my comming from Thebes to Athens, from a place*
> *of conquest to a pallace of quiet, I haue resolued with*
> *my self in my court to haue as many Philosophers, as*
> *I had in my camp soldiers.   My court shalbe a schole,*
> *wherein I wil haue vsed as great doctrine in peace, as*
> *I did in warre discipline.*   (I.3.59-63)

However, *Campaspe* tells the story of a court ruled not by reason, but by a passion which affects the lives of prisoner and courtier alike.   When Alexander confesses his love for Campaspe, Hephaestion warns him of its impropriety:

> *Remember* Alexander *that thou hast a campe to gouerne, not*
> *a chamber; fall not from the armour of* Mars *to the armes*
> *of* Venus...*I sighe* Alexander *that where fortune could*
> *not conquer, folly should ouercome.*   (II.2.57-62)

By Act IV Hephaestion's fears have been realized, for instead of an academy of learning Alexander's court has become a Bower of Bliss:

> *Sithence* Alexander *fell from his harde armour to his*
> *softe robes, beholde the face of his court, youthes*
> *that were woont to carry deuises of victory in their*
> *shieldes, engraue now posies of loue in their ringes: they*
> *that were accustomed on trotting horses to charge*
> *the enimy with a launce, now in easie coches ride*
> *vp and downe to court Ladies: In steede of sword and*
> *target to hazard their liues, vse pen and paper to*
> *paint their loues.   Yea, such a feare and faintnes*
> *is growne in courte, that they wish rather to heare*
> *the blowing of a horne to hunt, then the sound of a*
> *trumpet to fight.*   (IV.2.11-20)

Eventually Alexander discovers where Campaspe's own affections lie, and, as he graciously resigns all claims on her, Lyly returns to the entry motif of the play's opening scene: *enioy one an other, I giue her thee franckly,* Appelles. *Thou shalt see that* Alexander *maketh but a toye of loue, and leadeth affection in fetters...*(IV.4.131-3). In renouncing his passion Alexander thus settles the question which the play began with. Self-command is shown to be nobler than military conquest. As Hephaestion remarks: *The conquering of Thebes was not so honourable as the subdueing of these thoughts* (V.4.48-9). But behind the simple debating topic lies a larger issue. The processional image in which Alexander announces his resolve serves to remind us that, like all his deeds, this is a public act with public consequences. If the final scene of the play is a demonstration of courtesy in action, it is not sufficient to define this virtue simply as «graceful self-deprecation».[29] Repeatedly the play has emphasized by dramatic means the dependence of the court on the conduct of its prince. Implied in the debate concerning the nature of true kingliness, therefore, is the question of the nature of the ideal court. For the prince who displays true courtesy is not merely one who knows when to give up gracefully; he is an upholder of humanist values. Courtesy is shown to be synonymous with true courtliness, as the etymological connection suggests.

The prince who graciously resigns personal interests for the higher good is clearly intended to evoke Elizabeth, *that good Pelican that to feede hir people spareth not to rend hir owne personne.*[30] Hunter and Bevington have warned that it is unwise to look for specific court allegory in *Campaspe.*[31] But while it is true that analogies between Elizabeth's court and the world of the play are general and typical rather than precise and particular, the virtues of Lyly's prince are naturally shown to have a special relevance for the royal audience before whom the play was first performed. Praise of great men was traditionally the province of epic and lyric poetry, and Lyly shows a typically Elizabethan disregard for classical precept in his choice of a form associated with the correction of folly rather than the honouring of noble deeds. Nevertheless, his object was essentially epideictic. He was not concerned to dramatize a specific event in the life of the court, still less to admonish Elizabeth for some amatory indiscretion. His purpose, like Spenser's, was to create a pattern of princely virtue both as a model for imitation and also as a tribute to his royal patron; his method was to temper *discipline with delight.*

Campaspe was first performed during the Court celebrations of Christmas 1581-2 when the Queen was at the height of her powers. It was a time when, in the words of Cranmer's sentimental prophecy from *Henry VIII, Her foes* [would] *shake like a field of beaten corn,/ And hang their heads with sorrow* (V.5.31-2). When *Henry VIII* was written the Queen had, of course, already been dead ten years and Shakespeare was obliged to respect the susceptibilities of her successor. So Cranmer prophesies that

> *as when*
> *The bird of wonder dies, the maiden phœnix,*
> *Her ashes now create another heir*
> *As great in admiration as herself,*
> *So shall she leave her blessedness to one*

R. Headlam Wells   **EPIDEICTIC DRAMA**   31

> [...] *Who from the sacred ashes of her honour*
> *Shall star-like rise, as great in fame as she was.*   (V.5.39-46)

Although James diligently cultivated the myth of a predestinate monarch appointed by heaven to rule a chosen people,[32] there was no poet of stature comparable with Spenser's to clothe what was already beginning to be seen as an anachronistic fiction; while those theatrical works which did seek to perpetuate the myth were not, in an important sense, truly dramatic.[33]   For the Stuart court masque has no meaning outside its immediate topical concerns. Its sole object was glorification of the monarchy.   When Orgel invites us to consider the reason for the enormous investment—both financial and artistic— in these prodigal expressions of baroque magnificence, our answer is a simple one.   It is precisely that the principles and beliefs which the court masque sought to promote were becoming increasingly remote from contemporary political realities.   As Orgel himself admits, the masque provided the monarchy with «an impenetrable insulation against the attitudes of the governed.   Year after year designer and poet recreated an ideal commonwealth, all its forces under rational control, its people uniquely happy and endlessly grateful».[34]

Unlike the Stuart court masque, the entertainments of Peele and Lyly were not simply «illusions of power»: these humanist plays were dramatic expressions of a moral and political ideal which, for a brief period, seemed to have become a reality.   The balance they achieved between gracious compliment and reverence for a divine principle was a delicate one.   When their subject died it was lost.

R. HEADLAM WELLS

NOTES

1.   Samuel Johnson, *Lives of the English Poets*, Everyman edition, 2 vols. (London, n.d.), I, 160.

2.   George Puttenham, *The Arte of English Poesie*, edited by Gladys Doidge Willcock and Alice Walker (Cambridge, 1936), p. 24.

3.   Letter to Jean Desmarez, *The Correspondence of Erasmus*, translated by R.A.B. Mynors and D.F.S. Thomson, 2 vols. (Toronto, 1975), II, 81.

4.   See O.B. Hardison, *The Enduring Monument: A Study of the Idea of Praise in Renaissance Literary Theory and Practice* (Westport, Conn., 1962).

5.   *The Art of Rhetoric*, I.9.33.

6.   Sir Philip Sidney, *The Defence of Poetry, Miscellaneous Prose of Sir Philip Sidney*, edited by Katherine Duncan-Jones and Jan Van Dorsten (Oxford, 1973), p. 97.

7.   Stephen Orgel, *The Illusion of Power: A Political Theater in the English Renaissance* (Berkeley, 1975).

8.   *The Progresses and Public Processions of Queen Elizabeth*, edited by John Nichols, 3 vols. (1788-1805; rpt. London, 1823), I, 43.

9.   Nichols, II, 145-50.

10. Parallels between the Norwich pageant of 1578 and *The Arraignment of Paris* are
     noted by Inga-Stina Ekeblad, «On the Background of Peele's *Araygnement of Paris*»,
     NQ, 201 (1956), 248.

11. For discussion of the Paris story in sixteenth-century literature see Felix E. Schelling,
     «The Source of Peele's *Arraignment of Paris*», *MLN*, 8 (1893), 103-4; T.S. Graves,
     «*The Arraignment of Paris* and Sixteenth Century Flattery», *MLN*, 28 (1913), 48-9;
     John D. Reeves, «The Judgment of Paris as a Device of Tudor Flattery», *NQ*, 199
     (1954), 7-11; Ekeblad, «On the Background of Peele's *Araygnment of Paris*», pp.
     246-9.

12. R. Mark Benbow, Introduction to *The Araygnement of Paris*, *The Life and Works
     of George Peele*, edited by Charles Tyler Prouty, 3 vols (New Haven, Conn., 1970),
     III, 36.   All quotations from Peele are from this edition.

13. *The Wars of Cyrus*, edited by James Paul Brawner, *Illinois Studies in Language and
     Literature* (Urbana, Illinois, 1942).

14. *The Lady of May, Miscellaneous Prose of Sir Philip Sidney*, p. 24.

15. See Enid Welsford, *The Court Masque* (Cambridge, 1937), p. 287.   Ekeblad («On
     the Background of Peele's *Araygnement of Paris*», p. 249) and Benbow (Introduction
     to *The Araygnement of Paris*, pp. 46-7) defend the dramatic propriety of the play's
     conclusion on grounds similar to those I have adduced.   See also Louis Adrian Mont-
     rose, «Gifts and Reasons: The Contexts of Peele's *Araygnement of Paris*», *ELH*, 47
     (1980), 433-61.

16. Benbow, p. 46.

17. Benbow, p. 13.

18. The significance of Peele's use of the Troy story is discussed by Henry G. Lesnick,
     «The Structural Significance of Myth and Flattery in Peele's *Arraignment of Paris*,
     SP, 65 (1968), 163-70.

19. *Shakespeare's Ovid, Being Arthur Golding's Translation of the Metamorphoses*, edited
     by W.H.D. Rouse (London, 1961), p. 6.

20. *The History of the World* (London, 1614), p. 382.

21. Puttenham, *The Arte of English Poesie*, p. 38.

22. Benbow, p. 49.

23. All quotations from Lyly are from *The Complete Works of John Lyly*, edited by
     R. Warwick Bond, 3 vols. (1902; rpt. Oxford, 1973).

24. *The Poems of Henry Constable*, edited by Joan Grundy (Liverpool, 1960), p. 138.

25. See Elkin Calhoun Wilson, *England's Eliza*, Harvard Studies in English, XX (1939;
     rpt. London, 1966), p. 245.

26. *The Poetical Works of Edmund Spenser*, edited by J.C. Smith and E. de Selincourt,
     one vol. ed. (Oxford, 1924), p. 409.

R. *Headlam Wells* **EPIDEICTIC DRAMA** 33

27. David Bevington, *Tudor Drama and Politics: A Critical Approach to Topical Meaning* (Cambridge, Mass., 1968), p. 181.

28. A bibliography of over nine hundred titles is contained in Ruth Kelso, *The Doctrine of the English Gentleman in the Sixteenth Century*, University of Illinois Studies in Language and Literature, XIV (Urbana, Illinois, 1929), pp. 169-277. See also John E. Mason, *Gentlefolk in the Making; Studies in the History of English Courtesy Literature and Related Topics from 1531-1774* (Philadelphia, 1935) and Sir Ernest Barker, «The Education of the English Gentleman in the Sixteenth Century» in *Traditions of Civility* (Cambridge, 1948).

29. G.K. Hunter, *John Lyly: The Humanist as Courtier* (London, 1962), p. 166.

30. *Euphues' Glass for Europe*, Bond, II, 215.

31. Hunter, pp. 145-52; Bevington, pp. 173-5.

32. See Charles Bowie Millican, *Spenser and the Table Round*, Harvard Studies in Comparative Literature, VIII (Cambridge, Mass., 1932), pp. 127-41 and Glynne Wickham, *Shakespeare's Dramatic Heritage* (London, 1969), pp. 250-8.

33. See Orgel, pp. 37-8. Those Jacobean plays which did incorporate the Tudor myth of an elect nation took the form either of retrospective panegyrics to an apotheosized queen (e.g. Heywood's *If You Know Not Me You Know Nobody* and Dekker's *The Whore of Babylon*) or of historical plays whose purpose was political rather than epideictic (e.g. Rowley's *When You See Me You Know Me* and Dekker and Webster's *Famous History of Sir Thomas Wyat*) (See Judith Doolin Spikes, «The Jacobean History Play and the Myth of the Elect Nation», *Renaissance Drama*, N.S., 8 (1977), 117-49).

34. Orgel, p. 88.

Part III
The Old Wives Tale

[7]

The Protestant Context of George Peele's "Pleasant Conceited" *Old Wives Tale*

FRANK ARDOLINO

THE first eight decades of scholarship on *The Old Wives Tale* left us with a play that is a naive and pleasant conceited comedy, or a satire of romantic comedies, or a flawed representation of the language, methods, and ethos of folk literature.[1] However, in 1978, John Cox established as central to the play two related themes: the use of Eumenides' prophecies by some of the characters who, through the practice of charity, bring about the defeat of the evil conjurer Sacrapant.[2] Cox's article led directly to the most fruitful period of scholarship on the play at the beginning of the 1980s when four major articles by Marx, Viguers, Renwick, and Cope appeared, which have not as yet been supplanted. In these works, the play emerged as a unified festive comedy in which the induction is related in theme and method to the framed play, the various plots are carefully coordinated and presented through developed stagecraft, and the characters form a hierarchy based on their relationship to the providential order.[3]

Criticism of *The Old Wives Tale* has not progressed much beyond these articles because no critic has attempted to relate the play to Peele's oeuvre and his perennial theme of the celebration of Protestant England under Elizabeth. Jenkins noted the presence of Peele's anti-Spanish bias, but he did not connect it to any developed political context.[4] Horne asserted, "*The Old Wives Tale* is the *Arraignment of Paris* brought down to the hearthside level," but he provided no further amplification of this interesting idea.[5] In 1983, Braunmuller summed up the situation by saying that the absence of a historical context has served "to conceal Peele's connection with the play, that is, to hide the dramatist or any other 'source' from our view."[6]

Two decades later, the play remains essentially, as Braumuller said, "mysterious" and "*sui generis*." However, a new direction has been indicated by Scott McMillin and Sally-Beth MacLean. In *The Queen's Men and Their Plays*, they trace the origin of the Queen's Men acting company to the nationalistic agenda of Sir Francis Walsingham, who assembled the all-star company in the name of service to the Elizabethan government and a Protestant ideology. The original company employed three actors from Lord Leicester's

Men, and as a result Leicester maintained close ties with the Queen's Men. Some of the plays performed by the company include Greene's *Friar Bacon and Friar Bungay*, *The Old Wives Tale*, *The Famous Victories of Henry V*, and Wilson's *Three Lords and Ladies of London*, which are marked by allegorical characterization and staging and are directed toward the praise of Elizabeth and her government.[7]

It will be the purpose of this article to recover the neglected subtextual religio-political context of Peele's play. I will show how he uses the folklore, romance, and ritual elements and themes to depict the struggle between Protestant England and Catholicism as represented by Sacrapant. When viewed from this perspective, *The Old Wives Tale* becomes less mysterious and joins Peele's other works as a celebration of the English Protestant settlement under Elizabeth.

I

The primary theme of all of Peele's works is the praise of Protestant England under Elizabeth. Peele was a courtier poet who used pageantry, myth, allegory, history, and spectacle to create patriotic shows that demonstrate the rightness of Elizabeth's reign. His first important work, *The Arraignment of Paris*, which was published in 1584 and is based on his long poem *The Tale of Troy*, is an allegorical and patriotic play that, in many ways, anticipates the rest of his career. Peele appropriates the classical myth of the "choice of Paris" and transports it to England where Elizabeth, who presumably served as privileged audience at the first performance, is awarded the prize by Paris as befitting her role as the all-powerful goddess of the second Troy. As Montrose argues, this play is part of a gift-giving cycle in which Peele offers his play as the gift to Eliza, a mirror image of the action in the play itself: "The play ends with the providential Elizabethan fulfillment of Troy's promise, a civilization achieved by the virtuous and gentle discipline of holiness and temperance, chastity and justice."[8]

Peele's pageants for the lord mayor of London are intended for the same patriotic purposes. In 1585, he wrote the *Device of the Pageant borne before Woolstone Dixi*, in which actors embody Country, Thames, and London, whose patriotic values and natural riches are praised, and Elizabeth is extolled as the preserver and salvation of the body politic. Similarly, in *Descensus Astraea* (1591), Peele presents Elizabeth as Astraea, the goddess of justice, who has returned to England to usher in the golden age despite the attempts of Catholic villains to defeat her.

In 1589, in the aftermath of the defeat of the Spanish Armada, Peele wrote a patriotic pamphlet, *A Farewell. Entituled to the famous and fortunate Generalls of our English forces Sir John Norris and Sir Frauncis Drake Knights,* to celebrate the launching of another strike against Spain. Peele salutes these Armada heroes as the descendants of Classical heroes and urges them to go "to loftie Rome / There to deface the pryde of Antechrist,/ And pull his Paper walles and popery downe" (34–36). The anti-Catholicism and anti-Hispanic sentiments expressed in *Descensus Astraea* and *Farewell* are also present in his plays, *The Battle of Alcazar* (1589?) and *Edward I* (1593). *The Battle of Alcazar* concerns the attempt by Norris and Drake, which was celebrated in *A Farewell*, to burn the Spanish fleet, seize the Azores, and place Don Antonio of Crato on the throne of Portugal. Peele attacks Philip II and the pope as representatives of Babylon who are determined to enslave England, just as in *Edward I* he castigates Queen Elinor of Castile as the representative of Spanish Catholic perfidy.

Finally, in 1595, the same year that he published *The Old Wives Tale*, Peele wrote *Anglorum Feriae* to celebrate, on the occasion of the queen's Accession Day, her recent escape from an assassination plot reputedly masterminded by Dr. Lopez, her physician. Peele invokes Clio to chronicle Elizabeth's escape from death during her adolescence when she was imprisoned by Mary and throughout the continuing attempts by Spain to subvert her reign, culminating with the attack of the Armada against England in 1588. In honor of her accession "were Eglantine / And wreathes of Roses red and white put on" (40–41). The Elizabethan Tudor rose has created an age of concord and fruitfulness for her people and country.

The Old Wives Tale contains the same methods and themes as the rest of Peele's oeuvre. The major difference is that in *The Old Wives Tale* the political context is hidden behind the facade of the "pleasant conceited comedy." By delineating this context, it will be possible to see that the play is not *sui generis* but of a piece with his praise of Elizabeth and the Protestant English settlement throughout his career. Peele has translated the fundamental political and religious conflicts of his age into folk, romance, and ritual elements. The importance of the recovery of the politico-religious context lies in the recognition that a play that has been perceived as having no relationship to the contemporary contexts is in fact thoroughly involved with them. Peele uses the popular drama to reconfigure the age's most dominant conflicts and present them under the guise of a pleasant conceited comedy.

In *Staging Reform, Reforming the Stage: Protestantism and Popular Theatre in Early Modern England*, Huston Diehl has argued that Protestantism was not hostile to the use of the imagination in dramas, and she has traced the presence of a Protestant aesthetics in Elizabethan tragedies. Drawing upon the work of Paul White, John King, and Robert Knapp, among others, she maintains "that the popular London theater . . . in the years after Elizabeth reestablished Protestantism . . . rehearses the religious crisis that disrupted, divided, energized, and in many ways revolutionized English society."[9] The tragedies of Marlowe, Kyd, Webster, Shakespeare, and Middleton contain rhetoric, rituals, spectacles, and material objects associated with Catholicism in order to condemn it and at the same time promote Protestantism and English nationalism.[10]

Similarly, Peele, like Dekker in *The Shoemaker's Holiday*, Protestantizes comedy by employing allegorical methods and plots to attack Catholic imperialism, simony, and the Eucharist.[11] The best way to reveal the Protestant English context of *The Old Wives Tale* is to demonstrate through close reading how the four related plots, Erestus as the old man at the crossroads and the white bear of England's wood; Lampriscus and his two daughters; Eumenides and Jack versus Sacrapant; and Delia and Venelia, convey meanings related to the matter of Elizabethan England. These plots are allegorical retellings of the coming to power of Elizabeth and the rise of Protestant England. By casting them in a popular dramatic form, Peele is presenting both a light and serious entertainment that invites his audiences to respond to the conflicts that England has experienced before achieving power and independence under Elizabeth. The audiences seeing Peele's comedy as performed by the Queen's Men would feel a sense of community and a renewal of their commitment to face the continuing threats from Catholicism.[12]

II

Each of the intertwined successful quest plots tells a story of balance achieved through the charitable cooperation with providence as represented by Erestus and Jack. The play is grounded in the efficacy of the English countryside. All of the questers come to England where they participate in events directly related to figures connected with the English ground—Jack, the Harvesters, the Heads at the well, the white bear of England's wood. These figures constitute the English elements of the play, and they are paralleled by the characters and the action of the induction. As Cope, Viguers, and Renwick have pointed out, the three lost courtiers, Antic, Frantic, and Frolick, whose names represent figures of the imagination, regain their direction as a result of their contact with the old wife Madge and her husband Clunch and by attending the dramatic reenactment of the tale told by the Mage figure.[13] Clunch, the simple English blacksmith whose last name refers to a simple person and a limestone building material, appears with his guiding light in the woods to lead the three characters to his humble cottage.[14] Madge and Clunch are an earthy English couple who serve simple English fare which proves to be restorative. Before she begins her tale, Clunch and Antic go off to bed, while the other two characters serve as the audience for Madge. The joining of Antic and Clunch represents the emblem of Peele's ethos in the play: he will join the simple artisan, the English pastoral Vulcan, with the spirit of the antic or romantic to create this play. As a result of seeing the play and partaking of the Mage's fare, the courtiers are reinvigorated and sent on their way in the morning. Madge and Clunch have changed dark to light as they have passed from night to the early morning of the English countryside.

The action and the characters of the induction mirror the action and characters of the framed play; just as the three courtiers regain their way, so too the successful questers gain their goals and rescue the lost characters as a result of their journey to England and their contact with English soil and the English spirit under Elizabeth. Similarly, the theater audience is expected to undergo the same journey toward understanding how the pleasant conceited comedy concerns in the guise of its folk, romance, and ritual elements an encomium to Elizabeth and Protestant England.

The most important character of the play proper is Erestus, whose significance, as Viguers notes, is demonstrated by the centrality of his stage locus, which "marks the crossroads between Madge's hearth and Sacrapant's cell, the confrontation at the center of the play."[15] Erestus possesses a number of identities which are related to the folk and political contexts of the play. He is the old man at the crossroads during the day, who greets and delivers his prophecies to the characters. Although he appears old—the aged conjurer has switched heads with him—he is in the "Aprill of my age" (196). Sacrapant has stolen Erestus's youthful identity, his springtime, and it will only be restored when the magician is killed.

Even though he has enchanted Erestus and stolen his identity, Sacrapant can not prevent his ability to prophesy in riddles. Cope has remarked that Erestus has transmuted Sacrapant's malevolent power to salutary attributes of insight and foresight.[16] Erestus is the presiding force for good who opposes Sacrapant's evil magic through his role as crossroads deity. Being at the crossroads—a traditional motif representing destiny—Erestus enjoys a special role identified with the Roman goddess Trivia and the triune goddess of Hecate, Diana, and Luna/Cynthia to whom charitable offerings were made in the form of food and honey pots to placate the deity and influence the future.[17] In Elizabethan iconography, the queen was associated with the triune goddess as an expression of her symbolic control over the underworld, the earth, and the moon.[18] Erestus's position at the crossroads invests him with the providential power associated with Elizabeth as iconic figure.

Erestus's second important identity is as the white bear of England's wood at night. On one level, this is a folk story of the type 425A, the "Monster animal as Bridegroom."[19] On the political level, the white bear as used by Peele conveys patriotic English significance. Bradbrook has traced the motif to a medieval romance which has as its hero William of Palerne, who is changed into a white bear.[20] Further, Crow has identified Merlin as the last of England's bears, and, as Traister has indicated, Merlin was associated with shape-shifting and prophecy.[21] Bale saw Merlin as a prophet of the Reformation, and in the *Mirror of Magistrates*, Merlin's prophecies were depicted as divinely inspired: "And learned Merlin whom God gave the sprite, / To know, and utter princes actes to cum, / Like to the Jewish prophetes."[22]

The most important poltical meaning of the motif of the white bear is its allusion to the Earl of Leicester. When the Leicester family assumed the War-wick title, their heraldic symbol became the white bear and the ragged staff, which was the chief heraldic image of the Elizabethan period.[23] Elizabeth's favorite, Robert Dudley, the Earl of Leicester, was identified in court circles as the bear.[24] In *The Ruines of Time*, Spenser praises the Earls of Warwick and Leicester as "two beares, as white as anie milke, / . . . Two fairer beasts might not elswhere be found, / Although the compast world were sought around."[25] Also, in the October eclogue, Piers refers to Leicester and his device: "Advaunce the worthy whome shee [Elizabeth] loveth best, / That first the white beare to the stake did bring" (47–48). As King has pointed out, this allusion signals Spenser's support of the anti-Alençon Protestant faction led by Leicester.[26]

As the leader of the Protestant faction in Elizabeth's court, Leicester be-came the dedicatee of a number of works connected with the promotion of the Protestant Reformation.[27] These books contained Leicester's device of the bear and the ragged staff, which became a symbol of his politico-religious role as Protestant champion. Geoffrey Whitney's *A Choice of Emblemes and Other Devises* represents the definitive linking of Leicester's device with his role as protector of Elizabeth and the Protestant cause. Part 2 contains a sepa-rate title page bearing Leicester's insignia and a prefatory poem praising Leicester and Warwick as two celestial and earthly bears in charge of direct-ing the public weal:

> Two noble peeres, who both doth giue the beare, . . .
> In English courte doe spend their blessed daies:
> Of publique weale, two greate, and mightie staies.[28]

They receive their heavenly light from the royal "Phoebe brighte," and their fame "while that the Beares in skye shall showe, / Within this lande, all fu-ture times shall knowe." Moreover, Leicester was not only celebrated as ur-sine religious and political hero, he was also symbolically present in dramas of the late sixteenth century where his relationship to Elizabeth and his role as Protestant champion were the subject of the conflicts depicted.[29] Thus, in his use of Erestus as the senex at the crossroads and the white bear of En-gland's wood, Peele is drawing upon the politico-religious, literary, and iconographic network of meanings associated with the queen and Leicester in the late sixteenth century. Erestus is the touchstone, the prophetic figure at the center of the play who guides the characters to the successful completion of their quests. The symbolic exaltation of the queen and Leicester is appropriate for a play performed by the Queen's Men.

III

The second plot concerns Lampriscus, under whose nexus are included his two daughters, Zantippa and Celanta, the two men they marry, respectively, Huanebango and Corebus/Booby, and the allegorical figures of the Heads at the Well of Life. Lampriscus had two wives who died and left him with two problematic daughters whose marriage prospects are dim. Zantippa, named after Socrates' scolding wife, is a proud and overbearing beauty whose unpleasant voice "afflictes me with her continuall clamoures" (223). His second daughter Celanta "is so foule and ill faced, that I thinke a grove full of golden trees, and the leaves of Rubies and Diamonds, would not bee a dowrie aunswerable to her deformitie" (234–36). This is ironically prophetic considering what happens to Celanta at the Well of Life, which is where Erestus tells him to send his daughters for the fulfillment of their fortunes. Immediately after Erestus's pronouncement, the Harvesters enter singing of the fulfillments that await "lovely lovers" (250).

After this, Huanebango stomps in armed with his two-handed sword and braggadocio. This braggart traditionally has been seen as a satire on Gabriel Harvey, Spenser's scholarly friend.[30] But Huanebango is more than a personal satire; he, like the various evil giants in *The Faerie Queene*, can be seen as an analogy to Spanish Catholicism and its imperialistic posture. The self-described "great and mighty" Huanebango traces his lineage to Spain, Dionara de Sardinia (303), and Bradbrook suggests that his name is "Juan Y Bango," a type of the Spanish *miles gloriosus* and fantastique, like Don Adriano de Armado in *Love's Labours Lost*.[31] He sees himself as totally self-sufficient, able to control his destiny (308–9), and when Erestus asks him for the propitiatory offering, he stoutly refuses: "Huanebango giveth no Cakes for Almes, aske of them that give giftes for poor beggars" (314–15). His companion Corebus does give a cake to Erestus, who predicts that in the final accounting Corebus will be wealthy but Huanebango will not (330–32).

When the Head at the Well of Life gives her the opportunity to gain riches—"Combe me smooth and stroke my head: / And thou shalt have some cockell bread" (639–40)—Zantippa is insulted by the obvious sexual connotations and rejects the offering by smashing her pitcher on the Head. Whereupon it thunders, suddenly waking Huanebango, who rises up in a mock resurrection to be joined with Zantippa in a union of thunderers and non-cooperators with destiny. Zantippa knows he is a fool and promises to make him a cuckold (682–83).

Their uneasy marriage is countered by that of the blind Corebus and the homely Celanta: he is blind to her ugliness and she serves to counter his foolishness by providing fruitful wifely support. She cooperates with the Head and reaps corn and gold. Unlike Sacrapant who forces Delia's brothers to dig for gold, Celanta just combs it into her lap, a sign of female fertility. They cooperate with good fortune, reap the reward, and go off together, in a perfectly balanced union. And Corebus, in an echo of Erestus's earlier prediction, says "Thou hast gotten wealth to mend thy wit" (794).

On one level, this is a pleasant tale of two types of balance achieved, a folk hybrid that combines two tales, the "Water of Life" and the "Three Heads at the Well."[32] But the story is not just a simple folk tale; rather, it is central to the Protestant Reformation context Peele allegorically presents. Lampriscus, whose name means the original light—the *prisca theologica*, the ancient or original religion—has two daughters, who represent the related but divergent religions of Roman Catholicism and Protestantism.

The concept of the original church or religion implicit in Lampriscus' name involves the idea that the old apostolic faith, the original religion, was usurped by the Roman Catholic Church, which introduced a number of ills which the Protestant Reformation was determined to remedy and thus restore the original religion in as unadulterated fashion as possible. As Betteridge has stated about the consanguinous relationship between the two religions, "Protestantism is the creation of an idealized social identity dependent on an understanding of papistry as its other. Without papists there can be no Protestants. And, of course, there can be no papists without Protestants."[33]

The Elizabethan church was intent on reviving the original practices and fervor of the original Saxon church. Drawing upon Eusebius's distinction between the corruption of the outward church and the sanctity of the inner church in *Auncient Ecclesiastical Histories*, English reformers denounced the ills that the Roman Catholic Church had created over the centuries. As Richey points out, this dichotomy served as the major aspect of John Jewel's essential *An Apology of the Church of England* (1562).[34] Bishop John Jewel argued that the Protestant Church was returning to the original religion of the first six hundred years, which was based on the Scriptures and simple faith of the apostles and the old catholic fathers, before Rome asserted its full and corrupting primacy.[35] He attacked the vain exterior shows of Catholicism as corrupt and empty, declaring that the bishops of Rome "have brought the sacraments of Christ to be used now as a stage play and a solemn sight to the end that men's eyes should be fed with nothing else but . . . mad gazings and foolish gauds."[36] For Jewel, as John Wall points out, "the conflict was not between two independent traditions whose relative merits and claims might be assessed, but between two parts of one community. . . . [D]ifferences between the two were to be accounted for in terms of Rome's departure from the church's ancient and universal practice, to which the English church had returned."[37] Analogously, Peele depicts the two sisters with different looks, personalities, and husbands as images of the related but opposed religions of Catholicism and Protestantism.

Another way to understand this opposition is to consider the Protestant dichotomy between hearing and seeing. The reformers believed that hearing the word of God was of the utmost importance, and they dismissed the visual imagery of the Catholic Church as "a vain pageant to gaze upon."[38] As Kingdon has remarked, "For Protestants the central religious experience became the sermon. For Catholics the central religious experience remained the Mass. . . . Catholics gained essential religious truth primarily by watching a priest. Protestants gained essential religious truth primarily by listening to a preacher."[39]

If we consider the play in the context of these Protestant concerns, we can see how Peele has translated them into dramatic folk action. The hubristic declarations and deafness of Huanebango represent the Protestant view of Catholicism in broad terms. Jewel presents the pope as a vain braggart à la Huanebango, all bluster and violence: "Why doth he . . . suffer himself to be called of his flatterers Lord of Lords, as though he would have all kings and princes . . . to be his underlings?"[40] Zantippa and Huanebango are loud, overbearing, vainglorious, and, in the final analysis, bankrupt, and impotent. They embody, from the Protestant viewpoint, the combination of Roman Catholicism and Spanish pride and militarism, all rodomontade and devoted to visual shows. By contrast, Corebus is blind to outward appearances, and he and Celanta accept the riches from the Head at the well.

The religious primacy of hearing is also shown by the fact that, immediately before their attack on Sacrapant, Jack stuffs Eumenides' ears so he will not succumb to Sacrapant's power. Once Sacrapant recognizes that Eumenides is deaf to him, he realizes that his "timeless date is come to end" (814). This scene is related to Ulysees protecting his men from the Sirens' song by stuffing their ears with wax. As Vredeveld has explained, the motif was given an allegorical Christian interpretation concerning the wise and virtuous man's ability to turn away from heretical teachings and sensuality.[41] When Jack stuffs Eumenides' ears, he is protecting him from the siren-like words of the evil Catholic conjurer.

The central Protestant motif in this segment is the Well and Water of Life, which comes from Jeremiah 2:13, Revelations 22:1, and John 4:10 and served as a Reformation commonplace symbolizing the word of God or the Gospel.[42] When Jewel attacked Catholics for having dispensed with the word of God, he used the image of their breaking a life-giving fountain into pieces: "Even so these men have broken in peeces all the pipes and conduits: they have stopped up all the springs and choked up the fountain of living water with dirt and mire. . . . [T]hese men, by damming up all the fountains of God's word, have brought the people into a pitiful thirst . . . of hearing the word of God."[43] Protestants believed it was necessary to cooperate with the proferred grace to be reborn.[44] By smashing the pitcher and not cooperating with the Head at the Well of Life, Zantippa is an image of Catholicism refusing the waters of life. In contrast, by giving charity to Erestus, whose prophecies turn out to be true, Lampriscus gains the disposition of his daughters, one in a beneficial Protestant union which cooperates with grace, the other in an unfruitful Catholic relationship that rejects it.

IV

Eumenides and Jack form another nexus and quest group. The name *Eumenides* originates with the "right-thinking" ones who, at the conclusion to Aeschylus's *Oresteia*, replace the Furies as the resident spirits of the city of Athens and represent a new form of justice under the guidance of the androgynous goddess Pallas Athene. Peele also draws upon the character Eumenides from Lyly's *Endymion*, which influenced *The Old Wives Tale*.[45] Eumenides is a moral character with traits of loyalty and generosity as friend and lover. Significantly, he breaks the spell over his friend Endymion by the proper use of a magic fountain.

Eumenides has come from Thessaly to rescue Delia from Sacrapant. When he encounters Erestus, whom he calls "just time" (432), the senex tells him that in order to rescue Delia he must achieve "wisdome govern'd by advise" (443) and must repent that he has given more money than he has as alms "Till dead mens bones come at thy call" (446). This advice leaves him perplexed, but a scene unfolds before him that is directly related to Erestus's prophecy. The sexton and the churchwarden are demanding more offerings for the proper burial in sanctified ground of Jack, and Jack's brother and his friend Corebus/Booby are attacking their venality vociferously. Eumenides attempts to calm the explosive situation by paying the final fee of fifteen or sixteen shillings, which leaves him with a three-half-pence.

Jack's simple name and heroic role are central to the theme of Protestant England overcoming Catholic Spain or Roman Catholicism. Jack is described by his brother Wiggen as "the frollick'st frannion amongst you" (470), and the churchwarden Steven Loach says, "He was not worth a halfepenny, and drunke out every penny." Jack represents an antic and rebellious spirit, associated with a series of folkloric figures, including the Green Man, Jack in the Green, Jack à Lent, Robin Hood, and King of the May.[46] Cox has characterized *The Old Wives Tale* as a medieval mystery play in which Jack is the supernatural hero.[47] Jack's life cycle can best be characterized as a burial followed by his own resurrection and that of the characters he helps to rescue from Sacrapant's unnatural sway. Jack has sown the seeds for all of those who are in the April of their age.[48]

After the testing of Eumenides' loyalty in the proposed halving of Delia,

Jack leaps back into the ground, the English soil, the source of his power and the place from which the water of the Well of Life emanates.[49] As a chthonic spirit, Jack can also be linked with the Redcrosse Knight and St. George (*Georgeos*), both of whom are Protestant heroes connected with the English earth. Redcrosse is the resurrected seed of the visible church who defeats the antichristian dragon.[50] Similarly, Jack comes from the ground and fulfills the same function as the beheader of the Catholic dragon, Sacrapant.

The demand by the avaricious church officials that the exorbitant funerary dues be paid for Jack's sanctified burial is directly connected with anticlerical satire and the Reformation attack on simony, the buying and selling of ecclesiastical blessings, pardons, and offices. Significantly, Peele changes the traditional motif of Jack's generalized debts in the "Grateful Dead" tales to funeral dues instead.[51] English anticlericalism specifically directed its attack against the church's collection of tithes and mortuary dues and the sale of indulgences.[52] Bishop Jewel attacked the sale of indulgences by the Catholic church as a crime against true spirituality: "[W]hat one is there of all the fathers which hath taught you to distribute Christ's blood and the holy martyr's merits, and to sell openly as merchandises your pardons and all the rooms and lodgings of purgatory?"[53] As a result of these attacks, Parliament put pressure on the church to regulate mortuary and probate fees according to the ability of the people to pay commensurate with their financial condition.[54]

Simony was named after Simon Magis, the magician who challenged St. Peter in Acts 8:20 by offering the apostles money to obtain their seemingly magical powers. That Peele is attacking simony is indicated by the use of the name *Simon* for the churchwarden, which appears in the first and only quarto of 1595. The churchwarden's first speech at line 459 has a speech prefix indicating his name is Simon. But he is subsequently identified twice as the Churchwarden, and in lines 495–96 he refers to himself and is referred to as Stephen Loach. Hook conjectured that *Simon* may indicate the actor playing the role, John Symons, who joined the Queen's Men about 1588 or 1589.[55] More recently, McMillin and MacLean have suggested that *Simon* may refer to Simon Jewell, who was probably a member of the Queen's Men.[56] While it is true that sometimes actors' names were substituted in Elizabethan play quartos for the characters they played, it is more probable that by identifying the greedy churchwarden as Simon, Peele is directing his reader to understand this incident in the Protestant context of attacking simony.

Protestantism championed the giving of voluntary charitable acts in place of enforced payments.[57] Good works freely tendered promote a good community; simony, however, implies a loss of honor for those forced to pay.[58] In *The Old Wives Tale*, Peele shows the benefits of a voluntary system of charity as opposed to the coercion practiced by the churchwarden. Those characters who freely give Erestus offerings or, as in the case of Eumenides, bestow alms according to his bidding, receive beneficent prophecies.

V

Sacrapant is a conjuring villain who seemingly controls the action by dominating the characters whose identities he has stolen or arrested, but he can not prevent destiny in the form of the questers, Erestus and Jack, from accomplishing his defeat.[59] Sacrapant is the son of Meroe, a famous Thessalian witch, who taught him to shapeshift, especially into a dragon, in which form he kidnapped Delia, daughter of the king. He keeps her under his control "with a potion [which] . . . hath made her to forget her selfe" (423–24). The purpose of his magic is the restoration of his youth, but, although he has exchanged faces with Erestus and "seemeth yong and pleasant to behold" (348), he remains "aged, crooked, weake and numbe" (349). He also declares that the source of his success is the glass with the internal light which is buried in the ground and has a Macbeth-like fate surrounding it:

> And never none shall breake this little glasse,
> But she that's neither wife, widow, nor maide.
> Then cheere thy selfe, this is thy destinie,
> Never to die, but by a dead man's hand.

> (426–31)

The name and nature of Sacrapant are important for the interpretation of his politico-religious significance.[60] Sacrapant's priest-like name and his conjuring and dark magical arts make him an image of Catholicism, which was associated with witchcraft and evil magic.[61] For Protestant apologists, Rome was Babylon, the kingdom of sorcery, which was attempting to enslave the world.[62] Popes and priests were pilloried for their witch-like activities. Spenser attacked the pope as a conjurer in the February eclogue (207–11) and gloss of the *Shepheardes Calender*, and in the July eclogue (197–200) Roman Catholic pastors are excoriated as wizards. The Catholic necromancers threaten Elizabeth and England with their evil machinations. James Aske in *Elizabetha Triumphans* (1588) declares that the "Pope doth send Magitians to her land / To seeke her death, by their devilish arte."[63]

Sacrapant's transformation into a dragon also associates him with Catholicism. Watson has traced the Catholic meanings Protestants attached to dragons such as the Holy Roman Empire, Rome and its seven hills, the papacy and papists, and the Counter-Reformation as directed by the Jesuits.[64] Pope Gregory XIII's (1572–1585) *impresa* was a dragon, which was interpreted by the Protestants as proof of his wickedness. Spenser used monstrous dragons throughout *The Faerie Queene*, especially at I.vii.44 and I.xi.3, to symbolize the Roman Catholic Church holding the Protestant religion, the equivalent of the early and true church, hostage.[65] Thus, when Sacrapant tells us that he turned himself into a dragon, it is not just a simple folk motif of the evil magician whisking away the heroine, but it fits the political and religious context of the play. Sacrapant as the magical shape shifter represents the evils of Catholicism holding Delia and Venelia hostage and depriving Erestus and them of their identities.

The satire on Sacrapant also concerns his devising vain shows to appeal to Delia. These conjurations are compared by Peele to the way the Mass was perceived by Protestants, who scorned the Catholic ceremony as a false show and a form of witchcraft. Bishop Ridley in *A Farewell Letter to his Friends* (1555) fulminates against the vain pageantry and essential trickery of the Catholic Mass as opposed to the simple virtue of the Protestant service: "'In the stead of the Lord's holy Table, they give the people, with much solemn disguising, a thing which they call their mass; but . . . it is a very masking and mockery of the true Supper of the Lord, or rather . . . a crafty juggling, wherby these false thieves and juggelers have bewitched the minds of the simple people, so that they have brought them from the true worship of God, unto pernicious idolatry.'"[66]

Ridley's attack applies to the displays that Sacrapant puts on to keep Delia under his influence. Delia, an example of an audience corrupted by the priest-figure, asks for "the best meate from the king of England's table, and the best wine in all France, brought in by the veriest knave in all Spaine" (362–64). Sacrapant complies with an act of conjuration in which he makes appear on his table (altar) "Meat, drinke and bred" (368). The veriest knave appropriately turns out to be a Spanish friar who delivers the food and wine to the altar in a parody of the Mass as a conjuring trick.

The principal objection to the Mass by Protestants concerned the controversy over Christ's real presence in the Eucharist. Catholicism maintained that the bread and the wine were miraculously changed into Christ's body and blood through the process of transubstantiation. On the other hand, Protestants believed that the substance does not change; only the accidents are present which merely represent or signify the body and blood.[67] As Jewel explains, "[B]read and wine are holy and heavenly mysteries of the body and blood of Christ, and . . . by them Christ himself, being the true blood of eternal life is so presently given over unto us as that by faith we verily receive his body and blood. Yet say we not this as though we thought the very nature of bread is changed and goeth to nothing."[68] The reformers attacked transubstantiation because it confused the visible sign (the bread) for the thing it is meant to signify (Christ's body), deluding worshippers into imagining a body is present when there is none and forcing them to focus on corporeal and external matters.[69] Hence, Protestants saw Holy Communion as a sham, a mere deception, as Cranmer rhetorically asserted: "'Whye then is not in the ministration of the holy communion an illusion of our senses, if our senses take for bread and wine that whiche is not so indeed?'"[70] As Diehl concludes,

"Magic thus becomes inseparably linked to Roman Catholicism in Protestant discourse and associated with fraud, illusion, superstition, and error."[71]

This issue is present in the play through the exchanging of the heads between Sacrapant and Erestus, with the result that Erestus appears to be an old man while Sacrapant seems young. However, only the accidents have changed and not their substances. Erestus is still the same good person, even though he has an old man's head and changes into a bear at night. As he says, "Seeming an olde and miserable man / . . . yet I am in Aprill of my age" (195–96). On the other hand, Sacrapant admits that "by inchaunting spells I doo deceive, / Those that behold and looke upon my face" (350–51). He employs magic to maintain the illusion that he has really become a young man. After he decapitates Sacrapant, Jack displays the conjurer's aged head as the means of finally dispelling the controlling illusion.

VI

The fourth and final plot concerns the role of the entranced women, Delia and Venelia, who form a dual image of arrested identity. Venelia was the betrothed/wife of Erestus, but she, like Delia, was abducted and changed into a madwoman who "[r]uns . . . all inrag'd about the woods" (198). Venelia enters the story most significantly when she is called upon to break the glass and blow out the light in Sacrapant's life index after he he has been dispatched by Jack. She is the only one who can do this because of her special status as "neither wife, widow, nor maide" (429). These materials translate into Protestant meaning when we understand that the imprisoned women, with their quasi-homophonic names, are a composite analogue to Elizabeth in her various paradoxical domestic and political guises as virgin queen and wife and mother to her country.

Delia's name is significant, being connected with the neoplatonic and Petrarchan woman of sonnet sequences such as Maurice Scève's *Délie* (1544). Délie, an anagram of *L'Idée*, is the name of Scève's beloved, whom he endows with Marian associations, mythological resonances of Diana and the triune goddess Hecate, and, finally, with the love emanating from the Christian godhead.[72] Peele's Delia is the beloved virginal princess whose chastity is under attack, a role that, as Berry has argued, "was closely associated . . . , in the context of Elizabethan courtly literature, with the monarch herself."[73]

Foxe depicted Elizabeth's troubled accession to the throne as a romance narrative with the royal Protestant heroine "erected out of thrall to Libertie, out of daunger to Peace and quietnesse . . . , of a prisoner made a Princesse, and placed in her throne Royal."[74] The various accounts of her imprisonment during her sister's reign and her narrow escape from death, which resembled the narrative of a young princess rescued from imprisonment in a castle, be-

came a central part of Elizabeth's mythos, especially when the idea of miraculous delivery was added.[75] Frye has summarized the importance of this
scenario: "Insofar as Elizabeth was concerned, her imprisonment had formed
a supreme test of her character that explained God's endorsement of her
claim to the throne."[76] Peele draws upon similar romance elements of the
imprisoned women Delia/Venelia receiving their freedom through the combination of charitable acts and the supernatural intercession of Jack. Sacrapant
futilely attempts to control time and nature, but he is defeated by a destiny
that dictates his overthrow and the restoration of Princess Delia and Venelia
to their rightful identities and relationships.

Another onomastic indication of Delia's providential status is provided by
her alternate name. Sacrapant administers a potion to Delia that will make
her forget herself and subjugate her brothers. He will call her Berecynthia,
and she will not know herself until he dies: "Faire Berecynthia so this Country calls you" (582). Hook glosses this line by citing Virgil's *Aeneid* (6.784)
where "*Berecynthia mater*" serves as another name of Cybele.[77] Peele
equates Delia with Elizabeth as the earth mother from whom the second
Troy, Troynovaunt, is born. Again, this shows how Sacrapant is contributing
to the larger destiny beyond his control; he is giving her the very name that
indicates her triumph over his control. In *The Faerie Queene* (4.11.27–28),
Spenser used this Vergilian context to signify the coming of the Elizabethan
golden age.[78] Similarly, Peele's use of Berecynthia/Cybele implies the imperial destiny of Britain and its ultimate source in the glory of the classical past.

Despite her lack of specific identity or because of it, Venelia is also instrumental in defeating Sacrapant, who has said that his life index can never be
broken by anyone "But she that's neither wife, widow, nor maide" (429).
This raises the question of Venelia's status: Is she married or betrothed and
how can she be considered to be outside the various roles of women?

Erestus first says he "wedded was unto a dame"(183), but a little later he
remarks that she was "his betrothed love"(197). In addition, Jack salutes her
as the "betrothed love [of him] that keeps the crosse" (840–41). Braunmuller
says that "[t]he woman who is neither maid, wife, nor widow is a proverbial
Elizabethan conundrum . . . [which] only makes the play more mysterious
and more magical."[79] Viguers points out that a similar paradox is introduced
in the prologue in which the true love or woman sings of giving birth and
then becoming a maid again.[80]

On one level, Venelia has been deprived of her identity and therefore does
not fulfill any feminine roles. On another level, Venelia combines with Delia
to represent a series of female roles with significant application to the political context. They are analogues to Elizabeth as the Virgin Queen who assumed a series of paradoxical identities which formed a central aspect of her
reign and its attendant iconography. In adapting the traditional roles of womanhood—virgin, spouse, and mother—Elizabeth became all women in a

sense. Marcus maintains that Eliza used a multiform female status to set herself apart from usual female activities and gain access to a more transcendent power as a result.[81] Montrose contends that Eliza's creation of her multi-role image can be seen as a mystery: "[B]y fashioning herself into a singular combination of Maiden, Matron, and Mother, the queen transformed the normal domestic life-cycle of an Elizabethan female into what was at once a social paradox and a religious mystery."[82] These are the identifications that Peele invests Delia/Venelia with; although the women are entranced by Sacrapant for most of the play, they prove to be instrumental in his final overthrow.

The Old Wives Tale belongs to the nationalistic literature developed to praise Elizabeth and Protestant England. As Helgerson has developed, Peele and other writers, including Daniel, Drayton, Greene, Hakluyt, Lyly, Marlowe, and Spenser, among others, "sought to articulate a national community whose existence and eminence would then justify their desire to become its literary spokesmen."[83] In *The Old Wives Tale*, Peele has transformed "a pleasant conceited comedie" composed of folk tales into the history of Protestant England's struggle to cast off the baleful influence of Catholicism. The play has the classical characters coming to England, where through the supernatural assistance of Jack, the chthonic repesentative of the English ground, Delia is reunited with Eumenides and her brothers, Venelia returns to Erestus, whose youth is restored, and Sacrapant and his attendant Furies are dispelled to institute an Astraean age reminiscent of the justice created at the conclusion of the *Oresteia*, which also ends with the triumph of the light over the dark.

Notes

1. For a summary of the scholarship up to 1970, see Frank Hook, ed., *The Old Wives Tale*, in *The Dramatic Works of George Peele*, vol. 3 (New Haven: Yale University Press, 1970),356–73. This will be the edition used in this article, and all subsequent references will be cited with line numbers in the text.

2. John Cox, "Homely Matter and Multiple Plots in Peele's *Old Wives Tale*," *Texas Studies in Language and Literature* 20 (1978): 330–46.

3. Joan Marx, "'Soft, who have we here?': The Dramatic Techniques of *The Old Wives Tale*," *Renaissance Drama* 12 (1981): 117–43; Susan Viguers, "The Hearth and the Cell:Art in *The Old Wives Tale*," *SEL* 21(1981): 209–21; Roger De V. Renwick, "The Mummers' Play and *The Old Wives Tale*," *Journal of American Folklore* 94(1981): 433–55; Jackson Cope, "Peele's *Old Wives Tale*: Folk Stuff into Ritual Form," *ELH* 49(1982): 326–38.

4. Harold Jenkins, "Peele's *Old Wives Tale*," *MLR* 34(1939): 23.

5. *The Life and Minor Works of George Peele*, ed. David Horne 3 vols.(New

Haven: Yale University Press, 1952) 1:91. This is the edition of Peele's poetic works I have used, and all subsequent references will cite line numbers in my text.

6. A. R. Braunmuller, *George Peele* (Boston: Twayne, 1983), 47, 46.

7. Scott McMillin and Sally-Beth MacLean, *The Queen's Men and their Plays* (Cambridge: Cambridge University Press, 1998), 33, 36, 110, 166, and *passim*.

8. Louis Montrose, "Gifts and Reasons: The Contents of Peele's *Araygnement of Paris*," *ELH* 47(1980): 444.

9. Huston Diehl, *Staging Reform, Reforming the Stage: Protestantism and Popular Theatre in Early Modern England* (Ithaca: Cornell University Press, 1997), 1. See also John King, *Spenser's Poetry and the Reformation Tradition* (Princeton: Princeton University Press, 1990; Robert Knapp, *Shakespeare—The Theater and the Book* (Princeton: Princeton University Press, 1989); and Paul Whitfield White, *Theatre and Reformation: Protestantism, Patronage, and Playing in Tudor England* (New York: Cambridge University Press, 1993).

10. Diehl, *Staging Reform*, 5.

11. See my article "Hans and Hammon: Dekker's Use of Hans Sachs and Purim in *The Shoemaker's Holiday*," *Medieval and Renaissance Drama in England* 14(2001): 144–67.

12. McMillin and Maclean have remarked that the play reinforces the value of communal relationships over selfish behavior: "The entire play can be read (and produced) as a thematization of the idea that identities can arise in . . . miraculous ways if one has faith in maintaining relationships rather than in seeking one's own advantage" (112).

13. Cope, "Folk Stuff," 328, Viguers, "Hearth and the Cell," 212, 221, and Renwick, "Mummer's Play," 453.

14. *OED* sb.1,5.

15. Viguers, "Hearth and the Cell," 211.

16. Cope, "Folk Stuff," 330.

17. "Hecate," in *Funk and Wagnalls Standard Dictionary of Folklore, Mythology and Legend*, ed. Maria Leach (New York: Funk and Wagnalls, 1972), 487.

18. Peter Mortenson, "*Friar Bacon and Friar Bungay*: Festive Comedy and Three-Form'd Luna," *ELR* 2(1972): 207.

19. James Bratcher, "Peele's *Old Wives Tale* and Tale-Type 425 A," in *Studies in Medieval, Renaissance, and American Literature . . .* , ed. Betsy Colquist (Fort Worth: Texas Christian University Press, 1971), 96.

20. Muriel Bradbrook, "Peele's *The Old Wives Tale*," in *Aspects of Dramatic Form in the English and the Irish Renaissance: The Collected Papers of Muriel Bradbrook*, vol. 3 (New Jersey: Barnes and Noble, 1983),10 n.8.

21. John Crow, "Folklore in Elizabethan Drama," *Folklore* 58(1947):305; Barbara Traister, *Heavenly Necromancers* (Columbia: University of Missouri Press, 1984), 23.

22. *The Mirror for Magistrates*, ed. Lily Bess Campbell (1938; rpt. New York: Barnes and Noble, 1970), 228.

23. Anthony Petti, "Beasts and Politics in Elizabethan Literature," *Essays and Studies* 16(1963): 76. For an excellent treatment of the roles of literary and real white bears in Elizabethan and Jacobean England, see Barbara Ravelhofer, "'Beasts of Recreacion': Henslowe's White Bears," *ELR* 32(2002): 287–318.

24. Edwin Greenlaw, "Spenser and the Earl of Leicester," *PMLA* 25(1910): 542.

25. Edmund Spenser, *The Complete Poetical Works of Spenser*, ed. R. E. Neil Dodge (Boston: Houghton Mifflin, 1908), lines 561,566–67. All quotations of Spenser will be from this edition and will be cited within the text.

26. John King, "Queen Elizabeth I: Representations of the Virgin Queen," *RQ* 42(1990): 49.

27. Eleanor Rosenberg, *Leicester Patron of Letters* (New York: Columbia University Press, 1953). Rosenberg has pointed out that two-thirds of the religious works sponsored by Leicester occurred in the crucial decade culminating in the victory over the Spanish Armada (275). For example, in a 1581 pamphlet directed against a treatise by the Jesuit Father Parsons, *A Brief Discourse contayning certayne Reasons why Catholiques refuse to goe to Church*, John Feild summarizes the value of Leicester as defender of the Protestant cause: "'[B]ecause . . . as God hath set you in a cheefe place ouer this his church, so you and all the rest of his calling, might watch against such enemies, and discharge that trust he hath committed vnto you, both to stoppe them from vndermining the Church of God . . . and also stande for the preseruation of the Queene'" (qtd. 252).

28. Geoffrey Whitney, *A Choice of Emblemes and Other Devises* (Leyden, 1586; rpt. New York: Da Capo Press, 1969), 106.

29. Susan Doran, "Juno Versus Diana: The Treatment of Elizabeth I's Marriage in Plays and Entertainments, 1561–1581," *The Historical Journal* 38(1995): 257–74; see also Marie Axton, "Robert Dudley and the Inner Temple Revels," *The Historical Journal* 13(1970): 365–78.

30. In his edition of *The Old Wives Tale*, Hook, 311–19, cites all the evidence and rules against the parallel.

31. Bradbrook, "*The Old Wives Tale*," 5.

32. Patricia Binney, ed. *The Old Wives Tale* (Manchester: Manchester University Press, 1980), 21.

33. Thomas Betteridge, *Tudor Histories of the English Reformation 1530–83* (Brookfield, VT.: Ashgate, 1999), 19.

34. Esther Richey, *The Politics of Revelation in the English Renaissance* (Columbia: University of Missouri Press, 1998), 109 n.

35. John Jewel, *An Apology of the Church of England* (1564), ed. J. E. Booty (Ithaca: Cornell University Press, 1963), xxviii, xxxiii.

36. Jewel, *Apology*, 35–36.

37. John Wall, "Church of Rome," in *The Spenser Encyclopedia*, ed. A. C. Hamilton and others (Toronto: University of Toronto Press, 1997), 162.

38. Jewel, *Apology*, 101.

39. Robert Kingdon, review of Thierry Wanagffelen, *Une difficile fidelité: Catholiques malgré le concile en France, xvi–xvii siècles*. *Sixteenth Century Journal* 32(2001): 570–71.

40. Jewel, *Apology*, 59.

41. Harry Vredeveld, "'Deaf as Ulysees to the Siren's Song': The Story of a Forgotten Topos," *Renaissance Quarterly* 54(2001): 858.

42. D. Douglas Waters, *Duessa as Theological Satire* (Columbia: University of Missouri Press, 1970), 116.

43. Jewel, *Apology*, 98–99.

44. See Sarah Plant, "Spenser's Praise of English Rites for the Sick and Dying," *Sixteenth Century Journal* 32(2001): 414–19.

45. For the similarities between *Endymion* and *The Old Wives Tale*, see John Doebler, "The Tone of George Peele's *The Old Wives Tale*," *English Studies* 53(1972): 417; Cox, "Homely Matter," 339.

46. Roy Judge, *The Jack-in-the-Green: A May Day Custom* (Cambridge, England: D. S. Brewer, 1979), 73–76. E. K. Chambers, *The English Folk-Play* (1933; rpt. New York: Russell and Russell, 1964), 65–66, points out that Jack is a character in the traditional mummer's play who collects money and is a bigger fool than anyone else, a role which parallels that of Peele's character. Norman Simms has indicated that Jack Straw was the name of the reviving character in death and resurrection games. "Nero and Jack Straw in Chaucer's *Nun's Priest's Tale*," *Parergon* 8(1974): 8.

47. Cox, "Homely Matter," 332.

48. Cope, "Folk Stuff," 332, 334.

49. In *Forms of Nationhood: The Elizabethan Writing of England* (Chicago: University of Chicago Press, 1992), 149, Richard Helgerson states that "[t]he land did . . . emerge in Elizabethan . . . cartographies as a primary source of national identity."

50. Richey, *The Politics of Revelation*, 31.

51. Hook, *Old Wives Tale*, 325.

52. A. G. Dickens, *The English Reformation* (New York: Schocken Books, 1964), 92.

53. Jewel, *Apology*, 92.

54. Dickens, *English Reformation*, 95.

55. Hook, 3:349.

56. McMillin and MacLean, 111.

57. Conrad Russell, "The Reformation and the Creation of the Church of England, 1500–1640," in *The Oxford Illustrated History of Tudor and Stuart Britain*, ed. John Morrill (Oxford: Oxford University Press, 1996), 267.

58. Wall, "Church of Rome," in *The Spenser Encyclopedia*, 158.

59. Renwick, "Mummers' Play," 448.

60. Sacrapant is somewhat similar to his namesake in Greene's *Orlando Furioso*, who pursues Angelica and in order to eliminate his rival brings on Orlando's magical enchantment. In Ariosto's *Orlando Furioso*, Sacrepant is a suitor of Angelica, and in Greene's *Perymedes*, he is a good king.

61. Peterson, "Witches," in *Spenser Encyclopedia*, 729–30.

62. Waters, *Duessa*, 10.

63. James Aske, *Elizabetha Triumphans* (London, 1588), 8.

64. Elizabeth Watson, "Spenser's Flying Dragon and Pope Gregory XIII," *Spenser Studies* 14(2000): 294.

65. Watson, "Flying Dragon," 296–97.

66. Quoted in Waters, *Duessa*, 13.

67. Mark Greengrass, *The Longman Companion to The European Reformation* (London and New York: Longman, 1998), 231.

68. Jewel, *Apology*, 33.

69. Diehl, *Staging Reform*, 75, 106.

70. Quoted in White, *Theatre and Reformation*, 126.

71. Diehl, *Staging Reform*, 131.

72. Gérard Defaux, "(Re)visiting Délie: Maurice Scève and Marian Poetry," *RQ* 54(2001): 732–33.

73. Philippa Berry, *Of Chastity and Power: Elizabethan Literature and the Unmarried Queen* (London: Routledge, 1989), 37.

74. John Foxe, *Actes and Monuments* (London, 1583), 2096–97.

75. Susan Frye, *Elizabeth I: The Competition for Representation* (London: Oxford University Press, 1993), 77, 117.

76. Ibid., 74.

77. Hook, *Old Wives Tale*, 436 n.

78. Peter Hawkins, "From Mythography to Myth-making: Spenser and the *Magna Mater* Cybele," *Sixteenth Century Journal* 12 (1981): 58. Delia's / Cybele's symbolic import is also connected with the role of Britomart as the maiden who is proleptically the mother of Britain and the Tudor dynasty. She is the *Magna Mater* as Merlin announces:

> For from [her] wombe a famous Progenie
> Shall spring, out of the auncient *Troian* blood,
> Which shall reuiue the sleeping memorie
> Of those same antique Peres, the heauens brood,
> Which *Greeke* and *Asian* riuers stained with their blood.
>
> (3.3.22)

79. Braunmuller, *George Peele*, 56.

80. Viguers, "Hearth and the Cell," 218–19.

81. Leah Marcus, *Puzzling Shakespeare: Local Reading and Its Discontents* (Los Angeles: University of California Press, 1988), 61.

82. Louis Montrose, "'Shaping Fantasies': Figurations of Gender and Power in Elizabethan Culture," in *Representing the English Renaissance*, ed. Stephen Greenblatt (Los Angeles: University of California Press, 1988), 50.

83. Helgerson, *Forms of Nationhood*, 2.

[8]

Homely Matter and Multiple Plots in

Peele's *Old Wives Tale*

John D. Cox

"Once uppon a time there was a King or Lord, or a Duke that had
a fair daughter, the fairest that ever was; as white as snowe, and as
redd as bloud."[1] So begins the tale of Gammer Madge, George Peele's
"old Wife," a tale as familiar as its formulaic opening, and apparently as familiar in the sixteenth century as it is today, if the response of one of Madge's listeners is any indication: "I have seen
the day when I was a little one, you might have drawne mee a mile
after you with such a discourse" (ll. 88–90). Naturally its exclusively folkloric subject matter has attracted more attention than
any other aspect of the play, particularly among the folklorists.[2]
The time seems to have come, however, to save the play from its
friends—those whose earnest endeavor to mine it as a valuable re-
pository of folk motives prevents them from seeing that the play is
a play. For *The Old Wives Tale* is a robust piece with dramaturgical
substance, not an "artless," "delicate structure," as it has been pa-
tronizingly described; and the key to acknowledging its substance
is recognizing that Peele adapted folkloric motives to the conventions of Elizabethan drama.

To be sure, the play has also been seen as something more than
a folklore miscellany by those who read it as satire or self-parody.
Indeed the play's latest editor sees opinion neatly dividing: "The
critical lines are drawn, the cleavage absolute: on the one hand,
those who see the play as a sophisticated juxtaposition of romance
and idealism for the purpose of satire; on the other, those who see
it as a childlike retelling of old tales."[3] What this summary fails to
note is that a common element shared by those who read the play
as folklore or satire makes the cleavage between them less absolute
than it appears to be: both presuppose a patronizing attitude toward the play's material. Either the playwright is parodying the
hackneyed conventions, or he is presenting them with an indulgent

air of superiority. This patronizing attitude is almost certainly a
consequence of the play's unusual source material, seemingly misplaced anywhere outside of the kindergarten classroom. Besides
its sentimentally erroneous (and relatively recent) assumption that
fairy stories are inherently suited to children, the patronizing attitude necessarily extends to other plays as well, where we normally
feel less confident about it. In the Shakespearean canon the closest
parallel to *The Old Wives Tale* is *A Midsummer Night's Dream*: both
plays deal with popular folk material; both apologize disingenu-
ously for themselves in their titles; both have been slow to win serious critical consideration, thus demonstrating that modern critics
are sometimes more naive than Elizabethan dramatists. This article
attempts to give due consideration to Peele's play, as recent criticism has admirably done for *A Midsummer Night's Dream*.[4]

"Who drest his dinner then?" Frolicke asks impertinently when
Madge tells her guests that the king sent all the men out of the
kingdom in search of his kidnapped daughter (l. 116). Frolicke's
question has been echoed in spirit if not in substance by almost
every critic who has faced the play's jumble of seemingly unac-
countable detail. We would do well to heed Madge's no-nonsense
reply, "Nay either heare my tale, or kisse my taile" (l. 117), for
the play's method becomes evident in the unfolding of the plot itself. If we set aside our preoccupation with the content of the play
—its "antic fables" and its "fairy toys"—we begin to see conventional formal elements that give the content artistic shape. One
such shape, without doubt the most basic, is that of romantic comedy, which we can clearly trace to the play's popular heritage. The
fair daughter, as white as snow and as red as blood, is one pole of
dramatic interest, together with her captor, a "cursed sorcerer."
Our attention is focused on the other pole: her brothers, her lover,
and a braggart knight, who attempt to overcome the sorcerer's
power and reclaim the maid. In the end the lover is successful, pre-
cipitating the death of the enchanter, releasing the king's daughter,
and incidentally releasing her brothers as well, who have been captured in the meantime. Thus the end of the play unites the two
poles of comic interest. Egeon is similarly reunited with Emilia at
the end of *Comedy of Errors*, just as Pericles is reunited with Thaisa
at the end of *Pericles, Prince of Tyre*.

In short, *The Old Wives Tale* can be seen to move through the
traditional phases of popular romance on the Elizabethan stage:
separation, wandering, and reunion. This is a pattern, as David
Bevington has shown, that derives from the medieval religious drama, the archetypal comedy involving a fall from grace, a period of
wandering in evil, and finally divine reconciliation.[5] The influence

of this heritage is evident in the source of separation and misfortune in *The Old Wives Tale*; for they are caused by a sorcerer who talks like Satan in the play world's Eden:

> The day is cleare, the Welkin bright and gray,
> The Larke is merrie, and records hir notes:
> Each thing rejoyseth underneath the Skie,
> But onely I whom heaven hath in hate:
> Wretched and miserable Sacrapant.   (ll. 335–39)

He is a dragon and a deceiver, and his power is dissolved when harmony is restored at the end, an image of the eternal harmony that marked the end of the divine comedy in the mystery plays: the dissolution of the fallen world and the establishment of a new creation. In *The Old Wives Tale* we find a secularized version of the medieval comic pattern, just as we do in Shakespearean comedy.

Complementing the elemental comic shape in Peele's play is his artistry in weaving several different strands of the plot into a single thread. Here his achievement is perhaps most noteworthy, for many of the plot elements are separate folklore motives which had apparently not been combined in Peele's sources. Gordon Gerould has pointed out, for instance, that no literary source had combined the motif of the Grateful Dead with that of the Poisoned Maiden for 1500 years before *The Old Wives Tale*.[6] This seems fair evidence that Peele made the association on his own. The mere fact of making these motives work together in a single plot, then, is a signal accomplishment; but Peele also makes them work together significantly—that is, to borrow Richard Levin's terms, he creates not only an efficient relationship between the plot strands, but a formal and final relationship as well.[7]

Levin uses these terms to describe the "modes of integration" that are possible between various plots. Analogous to Aristotle's material cause, for example, is a static relationship—such as kinship or master and servant—between characters in different plots. This arbitrary link is less complex than the "efficient" mode of integration, whereby a direct causal link is established between two characters, or sets of characters, as the plots unfold. The "formal" connection increases the complexity still more, since it involves a "comprehensive analogy in the structure of each plot and the work as a whole" (p. 14). This sort of analogy is usually thought of as thematic unity by critics of Renaissance drama, but Levin eschews the common parlance because he maintains it has become associated with too much loose thinking about dramatic construction.[8] Finally, corresponding roughly to Aristotle's final cause, is the "affective" relationship between plots, that is, the comparison or contrast between them in terms of emotional quality. In using Aristotle's terms, Levin acknowledges that the Stagirite disapproved of multiple plots; nor, one might add, did Aristotle ever suggest a relationship between his logical analysis of causation and his analysis of plot. Nonetheless, Aristotle's terms provide a useful analytical scheme, as Levin has shown in his intensive and sustained analysis of Renaissance dramas with multiple plots.

The Old Wives Tale combines five distinguishable plot lines whose only material relationship is through the homespun prophet Erestus, "the white Beare of Englands wood," who foretells each character's destiny in more or less oracular terms. Even this simple means of connecting the plots is not as arbitrary as it may seem. For one thing, Erestus himself belongs to one of the five plot lines; he is not added merely for the sake of uttering the prophecies. Moreover, his line is one of only two which are essential to the resolution of the principal romantic action, and his prophecies therefore provide a less perfunctory link between all the plots than would the same prophecies if uttered by a less functional or less important character. Finally, the prophecies are more than descriptions of what will happen in the action to follow: they actually come very near to establishing an efficient relationship between the plots, when various characters subsequently allude to the prophecies as a source of moral support or (more important) as a determining factor in making their decisions. Eumenides uses Erestus' prophecy in the first way, for instance, when he comforts himself after having given away his last bit of money in order to pay for Jack's burial (ll. 516–19); while Delia's brothers exemplify a use of prophecy as a determinant of their own action when they decide to assault Sacrapant's cell:

> *2 Bro.* Brother remember you the white Beare of Englands
> wood:
>> Start not aside for every danger,
>> Be not afeard of every stranger;
>> Things that seeme, are not the same.
> *1 Bro.* Brother, why do we not then coragiously enter?
> *2 Bro.* Then brother draw thy sword and follow me.
>> (ll. 409–15)

Since the resolution of comic uncertainty in *The Old Wives Tale* depends on the successful romantic union of Delia and her lover Eumenides ("the wandring knight"), whatever makes their union possible is the principal motivation of the main plot. As already noticed, two such factors emerge in the play. The first is Eumenides himself who, with Jack's help, is able to destroy the sorcerer and expose his light, the real secret of his power. Since Sacrapant is the source of romantic disequilibrium—having kidnapped Delia long before—his removal is essential to the romantic resolution; but even with Sacrapant dead, his light remains an obstacle, for as long as it burns, the power of his spell remains unbroken. Because Eumenides is incapable of extinguishing this light, a second factor is essential to comic harmony, and this we find in Venelia, who is betrothed (but not married) to Erestus, and is therefore "neither wife, widow, nor maide" (1. 429). This special status enables her to extinguish the lamp and release all of the sorcerer's enchanted victims, including herself. In this way, the plot line of Erestus and Venelia is made as essential to the comic ending as the plot line of Eumenides and Delia—though one might argue for the precedence of Eumenides' story because he makes the first move by destroying the sorcerer, and because he summons Venelia to her task with his horn. In any case, these two plot lines are clearly the only essential instruments in effecting the denouement, and they therefore constitute together the play's main plot. Consequently the other three stories—that of Delia's two brothers, of Lampriscus and his daughters, and of Huanebango—constitute a subplot or subplots, though the case of Delia's brothers is somewhat anomalous, as we shall see.

The essential task in arguing the unity of all these plots is to show that they exist in some relationship which is not wholly arbitrary. We have already noticed one such relationship in the prophecies of Erestus, but other more substantial and more significant relationships exist as well. Of these the most important is the definition of each character according to his attitude toward fortune and charity. This is what Levin calls a formal relationship, and he illustrates it with reference to *1 Henry IV.* where Prince Hal, Hotspur, and Falstaff are all defined by their attitudes toward honor (*Multiple Plot*, p. 12). A similar procedure—if small things may be compared to great—is evident in *The Old Wives Tale*.

The first characters to define themselves in this way, when Madge begins her "tale," are Delia's brothers, who perceive themselves and their sister as the victims of adverse fate:

> O fortune cruell, cruell and unkind,
> Unkind in that we cannot find our sister:
> Our sister haples in hir cruell chance.   (ll. 137–39)

Despite their misfortune, the brothers are not incapable of considering the needs of others, specifically Erestus, to whom they each offer an alms-penny and the promise of greater gifts if their quest is successful (ll. 148–53). The idea that courtesy consists in the free offer of charity, no matter what one's fortune, is an idea that appears elsewhere in medieval and Elizabethan literature, especially in Book VI of *The Faerie Queene* where the distinction between essence and appearance is crucial, as it is in Peele's play: "Things that seeme are not the same," Erestus tells the brothers (l. 160), a line that is repeated twice more in the play (ll. 169 and 413). The principle that connects fortune, charity, and deceptive appearances is spelled out by Spenser's Calidore:

> All flesh is frayle, and full of fickleness,
>   Subiect to fortunes chance, still chaunging new;
> What haps to day to me, to morrow may to you.   (*Faerie Queene*, 6.1.41)

The pattern of the brothers' meeting with Erestus occurs again as each strand of the plot is sequentially introduced: first Lampriscus, then Huanebango, finally Eumenides. In each case the characters describe their situation (unhappy in every case but Huanebango's), react charitably to Erestus (or uncharitably, in the case of Huanebango), and finally receive Erestus' response. Since the prophecy in each case is geared to the characters' attitudes toward fortune and charity, we can see that Erestus' prophecies play a crucial role in the formal relationships between the plots, however perfunctory his utterances may be otherwise.

When the pattern of response to fortune and charity is repeated the fifth time, it is slightly different, because the complaint against fortune is made in soliloquy by Erestus himself:

> Here sit thee now and to thy selfe relate,
> The hard mishap of thy most wretched state.
> In Thessalie I liv'd in sweete content,
> Untill that Fortune wrought my overthrow.   (ll. 179–82)

Erestus' charity, moreover, is not offered in tangible gifts, but in riddling advice to those who encounter him. We notice that this slight variation in the formal relationship between Erestus' story and the others' parallels the slight variation between his story and Eumenides' in the main plot. Though both are lovers who have had their sweethearts stolen by the sorcerer, in Erestus' case the

lover himself has fallen victim to Sacrapant as well, having been
constrained to take on the appearance of the sorcerer's old age by
day and the form of a white bear by night. This is why Erestus
tells the brothers that "things that seeme are not the same," and
this is also why charity to Erestus is important, no matter how he
appears. Though he too is a romantic lover in search of his sweet-
heart, he does not look like it or act like it. Yet he is actually pursuing his quest by giving advice to those who are able to resolve
the spell, for only if they act on what he tells them can the spell
be broken and Venelia restored to him. In the end, of course, his
patience and charity are rewarded.

Though all the characters in *The Old Wives Tale* define themselves by their attitude toward fortune and charity, no strand of
the plot is an exact repetition of any other. We have just noticed
variations in the stories of Erestus and Eumenides, and a pattern
of formal variations emerges in the other plot lines as well. Each
character's unfortunate situation is different, each character's response to fortune is different, and each character's charity takes a
different form. The least varied plot line is that of Delia's brothers,
Thelea and Calypha. As victims of Sacrapant and charitable donors
to the white bear, they do not differ significantly from Eumenides
and Erestus. Moreover, they play no part in effecting their sister's
release; on the contrary, their attempt to carry out dutifully the
advice Erestus gives them only results in their further victimization
by the sorcerer, who enslaves them and inflicts their sister with amnesia so she can play the part of their taskmistress. This wholly
gratuitous punishment is out of keeping with a general pattern of
adapting each character's destiny to his charitable gestures. In almost every respect, then, the brothers' story is the least well integrated aspect of the plot in *The Old Wives Tale*. It is the only aspect, in fact, which would not alter any of the relationships between the several plots if it were withdrawn from the play entirely.

In contrast to Thelea and Calypha, Eumenides is clearly the central figure of the play. The demands made of him are greater than
those made of any other character, but the rewards are greater too,
as Erestus suggests in his "old spell":

Sonne I do see in thy face,
Thy blessed fortune worke apace;
I do perceive that thou hast wit,
Beg of thy fate to governe it,
For wisdome govern'd by advise,
Makes many fortunate and wise.
Bestowe thy almes, give more than all,

> Till dead mens bones come at thy call:
> Farewell my sonne, dreame of no rest,
> Til thou repent that thou didst best.   (ll. 439–48)

Though Eumenides gives Erestus nothing and is puzzled by the conundrum that he must "give more than all," he charitably beggars
himself when the first opportunity arises, paying off the corrupt
church officials so that Jack can be buried, and recalling Erestus'
advice after doing so, as we noticed earlier:

> Now do I remember the wordes the old man spake at the crosse:
> Bestowe all thou hast, and this is all,
> Till dead mens bones come at thy call.   (ll. 516–19)

As a matter of fact, Eumenides misremembers Erestus' advice (he
had said, "give *more* than all"), but this is only the first test of Eumenides' generosity. The real trial comes at the end of the play
when Jack demands half of Delia after Eumenides has kissed away
her amnesia. In response to Jack's demand, Eumenides first says,
"take her all," but Jack refuses him (ll. 893-95). For this is the
point at which Eumenides must "give more than all": after having
won his lady he must not merely give her away but kill her. Though
fortune has dealt him her most cruel blow at the very moment of
his triumph, he is nevertheless true to his generous spirit: "Before
I will falsifie my faith unto my friend, I will divide hir, Jack thou
shalt have halfe" (ll. 896-97). Then, past all hope, Jack mercifully
relents, thus granting Eumenides the "rest" from fortune promised
by Erestus, a rest to be won only when "thou repent that thou
didst best."

Thus far we have been concerned solely with the formal relationships between the stories of Eumenides, Erestus, and Delia's
brothers. While the latter seem to be a special case—being too little
differentiated from the romantic principals—all three of these plot
lines have more in common with each other than they do with the
two stories we have not yet examined: those of Lampriscus and
Huanebango. We noticed earlier that these two characters effect
nothing in the play's denouement and therefore seem properly to
constitute a subplot. This kind of differentiation can be seen in
terms of their formal relationship to the romantic plot as well.

Neither Lampriscus nor Huanebango begins the play as a victim
of Sacrapant or fortune—a major distinguishing characteristic of
their stories. Lampriscus, to be sure, complains bitterly to Erestus,
but his troubles are clearly of his own making, the consequence of
his foolish inability to rule either of his now deceased wives. In his

present situation, he is left with two daughters who cannot find husbands: one beautiful but "curst as a waspe," the other "foule and ill faced" (ll. 229, 234). In spite of his poverty and unhappiness, Lampriscus' charity is analogous to that of the romantic principles, for he generously offers a pot of honey to Erestus, who acknowledges that "Honny is alwaies welcome to the Bear" (ll. 208–09). This humble, rather comical, donation has a homely thoughtfulness about it that Erestus recognizes, but the gift lacks the relative weightiness of prophetic advice offered by Erestus himself, or the "more than all" that Eumenides gives. Though this is all we see of Lampriscus in *The Old Wives Tale*, his story is continued and concluded in the stories of his daughters whom Erestus advises to go to the well for the water of life: "there shall they find their fortunes unlooked for" (ll. 238–40). We shall return to their story in a moment.

The dominant figure in the subplot of *The Old Wives Tale* is Huanebango, the huffing braggart who has consistently been the focus of attention in arguments that Peele's play is a satirical parody of romance and folk motives. The grounds for seeing Huanebango as a vehicle of parody have been found in the broad analogy between his story and Eumenides'. Like Eumenides, he is a wandering knight, one of the "Kinges men" whom Madge described as embarking on the quest for the kidnapped princess: "I have abandoned the Court and honourable company, to doo my devoyre against this sore Sorcerer and mighty Magitian; if this Ladie be so faire as she is said to bee, she is mine, she is mine" (ll. 278–81). Despite this analogy between Eumenides' plot and Huanebango's, the picture that emerges has more of contrast in it than parallel. In short, Huanebango does not parody Eumenides; rather, he exemplifies what Levin calls a "direct contrast plot," where the effect is to display some of the characteristics of the main plot by default (*Multiple Plot*, pp. 21–54). Levin offers an example in *The Second Shepherds' Play* where Mak makes a fool of himself, not of the holy family; but a closer analogue to *The Old Wives Tale* can be found in Lyly's *Endimion*.

For in Lyly's play we again meet a romantic lead called Eumenides, who may well be the original for Peele's character.[9] Given its meaning—"the kindly ones," denoting a beneficent aspect of the Furies—Peele's choice of "Eumenides" seems more than coincidence, since the name is attached to similar characters in *Endimion* and *The Old Wives Tale*. In Lyly's play Eumenides is a companion of the hero, Endimion. Because of his true heart as lover and friend, Eumenides is enabled to discover the secret that can break the spell cast over Endimion by the witch Dipsas. At the end of

the play Eumenides is rewarded with the love of his hardhearted
mistress, because he generously offers to take on himself the punishment she has incurred of having her tongue cut out. Though the
analogy with the hero of the Grateful Dead motif (the folk origin
of Peele's Eumenides) is not perfect, it is close enough to have suggested the name to Peele: the outstanding characteristic in each
case is faithfulness and generosity as lover and friend. Furthermore,
Endimion presents multiple plots that turn on the influence of a
sorcerer, a denouement that depends on mercy, a hierarchy of
moral awareness and award, and (most importantly) a simple contrast to Endimion in Sir Tophas who, like Huanebango, is a "Foolish braggart."[10]

Huanebango can most profitably be understood by analogy to
Sir Tophas, whose inverse imitation of Endimion is clearly designed
to reveal the folly of the earthly knight, not to parody the aspirations of the idealistic lover. Thus Endimion falls in love with the
goddess Cynthia, while Tophas falls in love with the witch Dipsas.
By the end of the play Endimion is content to maintain a platonic
relationship with Cynthia, while the fleshly Tophas remarks of the
woman he wins: "a true loue or false, so shee be a wench I care
not" (5.3.279-80). Similarly, Huanebango's imitation of Eumenides in *The Old Wives Tale* is designed to reveal the braggart's de-
ficiency in every respect. When Huanebango first enters, he is the
only character who perceives himself as the master of fortune: "I
will followe Fortune after mine owne fancie, and doo according
to mine owne discretion" (ll. 308-09). Unlike Eumenides, he is
rude to Erestus, arrogantly refusing to offer alms despite the good
example of his squire, Bobby: "Huanebango giveth no Cakes for
Almes, aske of them that give giftes for poore Beggars" (ll. 314-
15).[11] When Erestus recites his old spell to Booby, it is more ominous than his other responses: "He shall be deafe when thou shalt
not see" (l. 330).

This contrast between Huanebango and Eumenides goes beyond
the formal relationship that is revealed in each character's response
to fortune and charity, for the two are contrasted as romantic
questers as well. Indeed, here the relationship between subplot
and main plot achieves its most complex integration. The bump-
tious self-assertion with which Huanebango announces his quest
("if this Ladie be so faire as she is said to bee, she is mine, she is
mine") seems more likely designed to conceal romantic inadequacy
than to convince anyone of romantic worth. The same is true of
Huanebango's huge, two-handed sword, wielded suggestively as a
compensatory appendage: "Hence base cullion, heere is he that
commaundeth ingresse and egresse with his weapon, and will enter

at his voluntary, whosoever saith no" (ll. 553-55). The impotence
of this claim is ironically confirmed by a disembodied voice that
immediately says "No," while a flame of fire knocks the boaster
down. The end of Huanebango's romantic quest is like Eumenides'
in that both win a maid; but whereas Eumenides eloquently woos
the king's daughter whom Huanebango had been seeking, the braggart himself has a slapstick conversation with Zantippa, Lampriscus' "curst" daughter, whom Huanebango mistakes for the real
prize. Now deaf (as Erestus had predicted), the braggart comically
misunderstands his mate's verbal abuse as endearments, and again
suggests his sexual inadequacy in a hexameter couplet that also
suggests the poetic impotence of the lines Peele is parodying:[12]

> O that I might but I may not, woe to my destenie therefore:
> Kisse that I claspe but I cannot, tell mee my destenie where-
> fore?   (ll. 654-55)

If Huanebango's destiny is impotence, we can see that he has made
it for himself. Thus when Zantippa affirms her betrothal to Huanebango with the assurance "Cuckold bee your destenie" (l. 683),
we recognize that the braggart has indeed followed fortune according to his own fancy, ending his quest with a mate who is determined to ignore the hierarchy that ought to obtain between the
sexes. She bears the name of Socrates' wife, a traditional name for
the shrew; and her view has been complementary to Huanebango's
since she first entered the play: "Now my father sayes I must rule
my tongue: why alas what am I then? a woman without a tongue
is as a souldier without his weapon" (ll. 632-34).

Huanebango's romantic failure may seem irrelevant to the pattern we have been following thus far—the pattern of response to
fortune and charity—but in fact the two are closely related. For
Huanebango's impotence belongs to a pattern of barrenness and
fertility which is a subthesis, as it were, of the characters' response
to fortune and charity. The two patterns are related through the
metaphor of sowing what one reaps—common alike to charity and
romance. This metaphor occurs in the song of the mysterious harvest men, who suddenly appear without explanation and disappear
as suddenly after their song is done:

> All yee that lovely lovers be, pray you for me,
>
> Loe here we come asowing, asowing,
> And sowe sweete fruites of love:
> In your sweete hearts well may it proove.   (ll. 250-53)

"Whatsoeuer a man soweth, that shal he also reape," writes St. Paul (Gal. 6:7, Geneva translation). Sowing sweet fruits of love is what we see all but one of the characters doing in the first half of the play as they react charitably to those around them and also as they pursue the romantic quest for a "sweete heart." The equivocal use of love to suggest both charity and romance is not without a certain subtlety, however traditional it may be. Since the lovers reap their romantic reward only by sowing the fruits of charity, a hierarchical relationship is established between the two loves, *caritas* governing *eros*, as it had always done in the Platonized Christianity that Peele knew. The vision of harmony we see at the end is thus a vision of the two loves united in a renewed society, a vision familiar from Shakespearean comedy and romance.

The sole exception to the pattern of sowing love is, of course, Huanebango. His nastiness to Erestus is appropriately complemented by his reward: impotence and cuckoldom. He is the first to reap what he has sown, being struck down by the flame of fire immediately after the second entry of the harvest men:

> Loe heere we come areaping, areaping,
> To reape our harvest fruite,
> And thus we passe the yeare so long
> And never be we mute.   (ll. 535–38)

This song is sung near the play's midpoint, after all the strands of the plot have been introduced in their "sowing" phase. In the succeeding scenes each of the groups of characters comes on again to "reap." The order of their appearance is not identical to the order of their appearance in the first half, and the scenes are not so completely insulated from one another, but the business certainly gets done. None of the promises made by Erestus in the first half is left unfulfilled, and he also reaps his reward at the end by having Venelia and his true youthfulness restored to him.

Peele's differentiation of his plots with respect to both charity and romance is his most effective stroke in *The Old Wives Tale*, since it successfully preserves the fertility implications inherent in his folkloric sources. Perhaps nothing else better characterizes the play as Elizabethan than this combination of *joie de vivre* with a celebration of great creating nature and a strong sense of moral obligation. This, as Alfred Harbage showed long ago, is how they liked it. The same kind of differentiation extends to the story of Lampriscus' daughters, Zantippa and Celanta, who complement Huanebango in the subplot. They proceed to the well for the water of life, as Erestus bade them, mindful that they must speak "faire wordes" if they want a husband (ll. 613-14, 618). Zantippa irrationally breaks her pitcher against Celanta's and then complains, as we have noticed, about the requirement that she rule her tongue. When she proceeds to draw water, the head in the well begins to speak:

> Gently dip, but not too deepe,
> For feare you make the golden beard to weepe,
> Faire maiden white and red,
> Stroke me smoothe and combe my head,
> And thou shalt have some cockell bread.   (ll. 635-39)

Again Zantippa irrationally breaks her pitcher, this time against the head in the well. Her reward is quickly forthcoming: the deaf Huanebango rises up behind the well and begins the ridiculous courtship we noticed earlier. Zantippa thus sows and reaps her own reward, as everyone else does. The song of the head in the well is clearly related to a fertility charm of some sort;[13] in rejecting it, Zantippa rejects "the water of life" and appropriately wins an impotent husband. The scene is intelligible enough in itself, but a possible Biblical echo adds to its resonance: "For my people haue committed two euils: they haue forsaken me the fountaine of liuing waters, to digge them pittes, euen broken pitts, that can holde no water" (Jer. 2:13, Geneva translation).

Celanta's experience at the well shows what Zantippa's might have been, just as Eumenides' quest shows what Huanebango's might have been. Celanta is the ugly sister who appropriately finds her husband in Booby, Huanebango's squire who was struck blind when his master was made deaf. Though Booby's affliction is earned only through guilt by association with Huanebango, this evident injustice is allowed to stand in the interest of making the more important point that the clown's blindness emblematizes his loving response to the "foule and ill faced" Celanta. She affectionately leads her stricken husband to the well, where the head sings the same song it had sung for Zantippa. When Celanta combs the head, it yields ears of corn, and a second head appears, laden with gold, to vary the song:

> Faire maiden, white, and redde,
> Combe me smooth, and stroke my head;
> And every haire, a sheave shall be,
> And every sheave a goulden tree.   (ll. 783-86)

Having reaped a rich reward, the two depart to seek a coiner for
their gold. Though Booby's lot is not an easy one, it is clearly better than Huanebango's. Both were free of Sacrapant's enchantment
in the first half of the play, but they become spellbound in the second by enchantments that can never be broken: deafness in one
case and blindness in the other. Yet Booby has a considerate companion whose uncomely appearance is of no consequence because
he is blind to it: they have the substance of a profitable relationship, even if appearances are against them. In this they share the
blessings won by Eumenides, Erestus, and Delia's brothers who,
by the substance of their deeds, have also made their way against
the uncertainty of fortune and the deceptions of Sacrapant to a
successful completion of their quest.

     Just as the romantic action of Madge's tale has traditionally
been seen as little else than a charming anthology of folktales, so
the realistic induction (Madge herself) has been explained as an
elaboration of the title, simply a means of introducing the seemingly pointless tale. Who looks for art in an old wife's tale? If this
way of reading *The Old Wives Tale* were also applied to *The Winter's
Tale*, we would have to read the title and the Chorus of Time literally as Shakespeare's idea of the play rather than disingenuous
inventions, a position few would still be willing to defend. While
no one would claim that Peele's play has the richness of Shakespeare's, it is certainly of the same kind: not like the trinkets and
tall tales of Autolychus but like the art defended by Polixenes,
"an art / Which does mend nature—change it rather—but / The art
itself is nature" (*WT*, IV.iv.95–97). For the induction of *The Old
Wives Tale* presents a clear analogy to the tale itself, suggesting a
significant interaction between romance and reality.

     "What though wee have lost our way in the woodes?" asks An-
ticke with forced aplomb in the first speech of the induction, as he
attempts to cheer up Frolicke. Fantasticke speculates that the dog
they hear is mad, and Frolicke doubts the nature of the light ahead
of them: is it "the glymring of a Gloworme, a Candle, or a Cats
eye?" The creature who then emerges is challenged as an "oxe or
Asse." All this helps to establish a facetiously hair-raising atmosphere, appropriate to wandering lost in the dark among "the owlets
and Hobgoblins of the Forrest." Spenser's prayer to the night in
the *Epithalamion* includes a request not to let "hob Goblins, names
whose sence we see not, / Fray vs with things that be not" (ll. 343–
44). The lines suggest that Peele's three travelers have good reason
to fear the evidence of their senses. Their fears prove to be chimer-
ical, however, as Clunch quickly offers friendly reassurances and

an invitation to "house roome, and a good fire to sit by." In the
comforting reality of the smith's cottage, the travelers are offered
cheese and pudding, "Lambes-wooll," some fireside singing, a bit
of cheerful bawdy, and finally "a merry winters tale." Then the
cottage itself becomes the scene of a world filled with uncertainty
and disorder, where "things that seeme are not the same," though
all finally assumes the order of comic stability.

Like the tale, the induction thus moves through wandering and
uncertainty to a comic conclusion and "rest." One of the tale's
most important characters is the "white Bear of Englands wood"
who helps bring order out of chaos, just as Clunch does, another
English forest dweller. Frolicke begs Clunch for "hospitalities," as
Lampriscus will later beg Erestus for "charitie." In both induction
and tale, evil is the source of disorder. The three travelers' uncertainty springs from fear of what hobgoblins do to one in the forest
at night. Similarly a sorcerer is responsible for things seeming what
they are not in the tale. Simple kindness functions conversely to restore order in induction and tale, so that charity becomes the play's
ruling virtue. Clunch's hospitality reduces the uncertainty of Anticke, Fantasticke, and Frolicke, enabling them to hear a tale in
which charity again brings uncertainties to a stable conclusion.

The supreme irony of *The Old Wives Tale* is that the realistic induction derives its artistic significance from the fanciful tale. Madge's
visitors are as patronizing of her tale as the play's critics have been,
but we can see by the end that in spite of the realistic language
and detail of the induction, its rudimentary comic shape is the
shape of the primeval romance that comes to life before the pages'
eyes. Though they never indicate their awareness of this irony,
they seem comparable to the mocking lovers at the end of *A Midsummer Night's Dream*, who also fail to see that their laughter at
bully Bottom's play is unconscious laughter at their own inept an-
tics in the forest the night before. *The Old Wives Tale* has been compared to the kind of rustic production that Shakespeare gently parodies in the tragical mirth of Pyramus and Thisbe, but Peele's play
seems rather to stand midway between the likes of *Common Conditions* or *Cambises* and a sophisticated comedy like *A Midsummer
Night's Dream*. *The Old Wives Tale* is not an attempt to reproduce
or to satirize popular ineptitude but to adapt folk material to the
conventions of popular drama as well as the thematic organization
of court comedy and masque. Shakespeare went much further in
the same direction, exploiting the play-within-the-play as a statement of the stage/world parallel in a way that Peele's choice of the
tale metaphor made difficult. Nevertheless, Peele's play seems to

suggest, as *A Midsummer Night's Dream* clearly does, that the truth about reality may not be only in what we see but also in what we imagine.

Harvard University
Cambridge, Massachusetts

Notes

1. *The Old Wives Tale*, ed. Frank S. Hook, in *The Life and Works of George Peele*, gen. ed. Charles T. Prouty (New Haven: Yale Univ. Press, 1970), III, 297-443, lines 110-12. This edition of the play is cited throughout by line number; editorial matter is cited by page number.

2. *The Old Wives Tale* is the true subject of John Crow's purported survey, "Folklore in Elizabethan Drama," *Folk-lore*, 58 (1947), 297-311. The most recent study is by James T. Bratcher, "Peele's *Old Wive's Tale* and Tale-Type 425A," in Betsy F. Colquitt, ed., *Studies in Medieval, Renaissance, American Literature* (Fort Worth: Texas Christian Univ. Press, 1971), pp. 95-102. Earlier work on the play's folkloric background is thoroughly reviewed and evaluated by Hook, pp. 319-41.

3. Hook, p. 359. Hook's edition offers a complete review of criticism before 1965 (pp. 356-73). For more recent studies that view the play as satirical, see B. W. Ball, "George Peele's Huanebango: A Caricature of Gabriel Harvey," *RenP*, 1968, pp. 29-39; Laurilyn J. Rockey, "*The Old Wives Tale* as Dramatic Satire," *ETJ*, 22 (1970), 268-75; John Doebler, "The Tone of George Peele's *The Old Wives Tale*," *ES*, 53 (1972), 412-21. I have not been able to see a suggestively titled article by Mark Gelber, "The Unity of George Peele's *The Old Wives' Tale*," *New York-Pennsylvania MLA Newsletter*, 2 (1969), 3-9.

4. See especially David P. Young, *Something of Great Constancy* (New Haven: Yale Univ. Press, 1966). Since the publication of Young's book, hardly a year has passed without the appearance of substantial articles on *A Midsummer Night's Dream*.

5. David M. Bevington, *From Mankind to Marlowe* (Cambridge, Mass.: Harvard Univ. Press, 1962), pp. 190-98.

6. Gordon Gerould, *The Grateful Dead* (1907; rpt. Nendeln, Lichtenstein: Kraus Reprint, 1967), p. 169.

7. Richard Levin, *The Multiple Plot in English Renaissance Drama* (Chicago: Univ. of Chicago Press, 1971), pp. 1-20. An incidental virtue of Levin's Aristotelian analysis is that he takes his terms from the *Physics* rather than the *Poetics*, thus avoiding the implication that dramatists consciously designed their plays on the principles by which he analyzes them. In other words, his argument sidesteps the historical question of neoclassical critical influence. Though he does not say so, the Renaissance penchant for integrated actions —particularly for formal integration—pretty certainly derives from the medieval predisposition for multiplicity: the stylistic impulse to imitate the interconnectedness of the universe in a work of art. This impulse is evident, for example, in Shakespeare's most rigorously Plautine comedy, *The Comedy of Errors*, where the expansion of the original single-plot play is part of a drive toward plenitude: besides a nascent below-stairs plot, Shakespeare also adds

a frame that expands his characters' history, a romantic element, and—however facetious and farcical—allusive suggestions of redemption history: "After so long grief, such nativity" (V.i.407).

8. Levin has carried on a fervent campaign against thematic criticism—sometimes more persuasively than others—in a series of articles published since *The Multiple Plot*. See "Some Second Thoughts on Central Themes," *MLR*, 67 (1972), 1-10; "Thematic Unity and the Homogenization of Character," *MLQ*, 33 (1972), 23-29; "My Theme Can Lick Your Theme," *CE*, 37 (1975), 307-12; and "Third Thoughts on Thematics," *MLR*, 70 (1975), 481-96.

9. The parallel has been noted in passing by Hook (line 686n), and more extensively by Doebler, "The Tone of George Peele's *Old Wives' Tale*," pp. 414-18, who concludes that Peele's play is probably a parody of Lyly's.

10. John Lyly, *Endymion, The Man in the Moon* in R. Warwick Bond, ed., *The Complete Works of John Lyly* (1902; rpt. Oxford: Clarendon Press, 1967), III, 17-79. Hereafter cited by act, scene, and line number in the text. J. A. Bryant first argued that Divine Mercy is effective in the denouement of *Endimion*, "The Nature of the Allegory in Lyly's *Endimion*," *RenP*, 1956, pp. 7-9. His argument has been confirmed and enlarged by Peter Saccio, *The Court Comedies of John Lyly* (Princeton: Princeton Univ. Press, 1969), pp. 197 ff. Peter Weltner discusses the relationship Lyly establishes between the main plot and the parodic subplot in "The Antinomic Vision of Lyly's *Endimion*," *ELR*, 3 (1973), 5-29.

11. I am assuming that lines 311-12 are properly spoken by Booby, not by Huanebango, as the Quarto indicates. In these lines Erestus is addressed as "father" and offered a piece of cake. In subsequent lines Booby addresses Erestus as "father" three times, though Huanebango never does; moreover, Booby is clearly the only character who has cake to offer (ll. 320-21 and 327-28). Hook notes that lines 311-12 "would perhaps be more fitting for the Clown," but he assigns them to Huanebango nonetheless (l. 311n).

12. Dyce recognized the first line of this couplet as a quotation from Gabriel Harvey's "Encomium Lauri." Subsequent attempts to make *The Old Wives Tale* part of the Nashe-Harvey controversy by identifying Huanebango as Harvey are summarized and convincingly refuted by Hook (pp. 311-19). Peele seems more interested in poking fun at poetic ineptitude in general than in creating a satiric portrait; he also uses Huanebango to parody the Latin translation of Stanyhurst, for instance (l. 647), and the conventional blazon of Petrarchan love poetry (ll. 370-75).

13. Following the authority of W. J. Thomas, Hook identifies the making of cockell bread as a rustic fertility custom (p. 438). The erotic vitality of the song in Peele's play is particularly evident in contrast to a modern version in Joseph Jacobs' *English Fairy Tales* (New York, 1907), p. 234:

> Wash me and comb me,
> And lay me down softly.
> And lay me on a bank to dry,
> That I may look pretty,
> When somebody passes by.

[9]

'Seeing is believing': action and narration in *The Old Wives Tale* and *The Winter's Tale*

PHILIP EDWARDS

Whether or not Shakespeare had Peele's *Old Wives Tale* in mind when he was writing *The Winter's Tale*, the resemblances are striking.[1] Peele's play (of uncertain date, published in 1595) twice mentions 'winter's tale' in its induction:

> a merry winter's tale would drive away the time trimly. (85–6)

> I am content to drive away the time with an old wives winter's tale. (98–9)[2]

Here we see the affinity of the offhand titles of the two plays; they both imply an idle and foolish tale to which you couldn't give credence. Shakespeare, of course, has an extra level of meaning in his title; and when Mamilius, chief victim in the *wintry* tale, gives the play its ambiguous name, the passage seems to hark back to the first of Peele's phrases just quoted.

Hermione	'Pray you sit by us,
	And tell's a tale.
Mamilius	Merry, or sad, shall't be?
Hermione	As merry as you will.
Mamilius	A sad tale's best for winter ...	(II.i. 22–5)

In starting to tell his tale, Mamilius only gets as far as 'There was a man ... dwelt by a churchyard' when Leontes, the real-life man of winter, storms in. Is this interruption an allusion to the most famous element in Peele's play, the electrifying appearance of Madge's characters as she begins to tell her tale?

Other resemblances between the plays include the prominence of references to the passage of the seasons, the appearance of a figure representing Time in the middle of the play, and the theme of resurrection. Much more important than these, however, is the resemblance which gives rise to this essay: the sudden shifts of focus in presenting what is proclaimed to be a very unlikely story, and especially the movement between narration and performance.

We should look first, however, at an important feature of *The Winter's*

Tale which came directly from Peele, though not from *The Old Wives Tale*. This link makes it more likely that the resemblances already noted are not fortuitous. The feature in question is the handing out of appropriate flowers by Perdita, costumed as Flora.[3] In *The Arraignment of Paris*, the goddess Flora is literally preparing the ground for the entry of Pallas, Juno and Venus:

> The primrose and the purple hyacinth,
> The dainty violet and the wholesome mint,
> The double daisy and the cowslip, queen
> Of summer flowers, do overpeer the green.   (I.iii. 23–6)

Like Perdita, by sheer force of language, 'the queen of flowers prepares a second spring' (I.iii. 32). Flora then describes the flowers which she has prepared for the individual goddesses; for example, for Juno 'yellow oxlips bright as burnished gold'; for Pallas 'flowers of hue and colours red' including 'Julie-flowers'; for Venus 'sweet violets in blue, / With other flowers infixed for change of hue'. There is a curious additional premonition of *The Winter's Tale* when in admiring these gifts Venus says:

> Hadst thou a lover, Flora, credit me,
> I think thou wouldst bedeck him gallantly.   (I.iv. 50–1)

It is hard at this point not to think of Perdita making a garland for Florizel 'to strew him o'er and o'er'. Florizel is, like Paris, the hero of Peele's play, a prince in the guise of a shepherd.

It is common for Peele to use framing techniques in his plays to suggest different layers and levels in the fiction. The most sophisticated example is in *The Arraignment of Paris*. The play starts with a grim prologue by Ate, who explains that the play we are about to witness is the first stage of the destined destruction of Troy. The 'fatal fruit', the golden apple which is to begin it all, is in her hand. This beautiful play therefore has both its own nature and a much changed nature when viewed as part of a whole cycle of events. The light which bathes it is the strange light of a sunlit landscape seen against the intense black of an approaching storm. But by a sleight of hand, Peele makes the storm disappear from our minds. Paris is arraigned before the gods for awarding the golden fruit to Venus, and Diana is given the task of resolving the quarrel. Diana moves to the centre of the hall and gives the apple to Queen Elizabeth in person. By making her thus step out of the fiction into the life of the audience, Peele changes the status of his play from an induction to the collapse of Troy to an induction to the self-created destiny of the second Troy. The fiction of the play is given threefold definition: as itself, as modified by the prologue, as modified by the conclusion.

In both *The Battle of Alcazar* and *David and Bethsabe*, Peele uses a presenter to comment on and explain the action, and to fill in bits of the story. From *David and Bethsabe*, for example:

81   'Seeing is believing'

> Urias in the forefront of the wars
> Is murdered by the hateful heathen's sword,
> And David joys his too dear Bethsabe.
> Suppose this past, and that the child is born,
> Whose death the prophet solemnly doth mourn.   (570–4)

The presenter in *Alcazar* uses dumbshows, mostly allegorical, to underline the moral significance of the action. The use made of the presenters in these two plays looks forward to the use of Gower, the presenter of *Pericles Prince of Tyre*, and by this route establishes another important link between Peele and *The Winter's Tale*.[4] By means of Gower, Shakespeare ostentatiously places *Pericles* as a medieval romance, a very old tale which gives perennial delight. Gower moves his play forward by varying means of presentation: narration, dumbshow, and performance. In the Chorus to Act III, for example, he introduces a dumbshow in which it is revealed that the distressed knight is a prince, who is then summoned home with his bride to Tyre. Gower then tells of their perilous sea-journey, and concludes:

> And what ensues in this fell storm
> Shall for itself itself perform.
> I nill relate, action may
> Conveniently the rest convey.

('Action' means, as usual, 'acting'.) Narrative is an integral part of the play; it is offered as an alternative to performance, which is to vivify the most important parts of the story. *The Winter's Tale* handles its alternation of narration and performance very differently, but the arrow which points from Peele's presenters to Gower points directly forward to *The Winter's Tale*.

To return to Peele, everyone agrees that the technique of the frame which Peele uses in *The Old Wives Tale* is unique. Three young men are lost at night in a wood, and they are given shelter in a cottage. The old woman begins to tell them a tale to pass the time, and the characters in her tale suddenly materialise on stage and act the story out. It is an imaginative opening for a very subtle work. In general, critics have made heavy weather of trying to describe its strange blend of artlessness and sophistication, though some recent studies have considerably deepened our understanding of how the play works.[5]

Part of the difficulty in getting to grips with the play comes from a misunderstanding of the frame. The three who are lost in the wood are called Frolic, Antic and Fantastic, and for some reason editors and critics have always called them 'pages'. They are evidently young men, and they refer to 'our young master'. But when Clunch their rescuer answers their question, 'tell us what thou art', with a firm 'I am Clunch the smith. What are you?', they are pointedly evasive (37–40). It is repeatedly said that they are lost in the wood, and their words, as Susan Viguers says, 'conjure despair and figurative death'.[6] ('No hope to live till tomorrow'; 'never in all my life was I so dead slain' (4, 6–7).) Fantastic wonders that Frolic should be surprised at their situation 'seeing Cupid hath led our young master to the fair lady, and she is the only saint that he hath sworn to serve' (11–13). Surely these three are figurative characters, as much shadows as the eerie beings who materialise in the main action – indeed, more shadowy, since those characters have real names: even the ghost is called Jack. The only characters in the play who have proper substance are Clunch and Madge. There is great force in Clunch's solid words: 'What am I? Why, I am Clunch the smith. What are you? What make you in my territories at this time of the night?' For his visitors have strayed out of allegory into realism. They are personifications of qualities which the 'young master' has discarded now he is dedicated to serving his lady and which are withering away, deprived of their life-support. They are the qualities that Mercutio was sorry to lose in Romeo, the high spirits of unattached young men out to enjoy themselves: 'Cupid . . . hath cozened us all' (44). It is not anything so gross as food they want to revive them, and they rather rudely refuse Madge's 'piece of cheese and a pudding'. It is 'chat' they want, and a song, and 'a merry winter's tale'. The tale they are provided with shows an extraordinary medley of characters seeking and finding love, then returning home. When it is over, Madge offers her guests the cheese once more, for breakfast. And we assume they are reconciled to their master's inevitable enlistment in the ranks of love and will take ordinary food and accommodate themselves to his new life.

A second important point about the play which is not always understood is that the tale is not Madge's. As (again) Susan Viguers recognises, 'her tale has a reality not wholly dependent on her . . . The tale moves by its own energy'.[7] Everyone notices that Madge makes a mistake in saying that the harvesters at their first entry 'will sing a song of mowing' when their song is in fact about *sowing* (258–64). This is a bad mistake! For the two entries of the harvesters are fundamental to the structure and meaning of the play. Their first entry is spring:

> All ye that lovely lovers be,
> Pray you for me.
> Lo, here we come a-sowing, a-sowing,
> And sow sweet fruits of love.
> In your sweet hearts well may it prove.   (260–4)

Their second entry is autumn; they enter *'with women in their hands'*:

> Lo, here we come a-reaping, a-reaping,
> To reap our harvest fruit;
> And thus we pass the year so long,
> And never be we mute.   (561–4)

Madge, who knows about the harvesters, hasn't comprehended the significance of the order of the entries. This haziness is reflected in the opening of her narrative – all that she is allowed to tell.

> Once upon a time there was a king – or a lord – or a duke – that had a fair daughter . . .
>
> O Lord, I quite forgot! There was a conjurer . . .
>
> O, I forget! She (he, I would say) turned a proper young man to a bear in the night . . .   (113–14, 122, 128–9)

Given this incompetence, it is little wonder that the characters come alive to take over from her and put the record straight, telling the story as it really was. At the end of the play, it is discovered that Madge is fast asleep (956), though as she awakes she has no difficulty in continuing with her hazy explanations. Finally, Fantastic asks (with a note of irony in his voice?): 'Then you have made an end of your tale, gammer?' and she replies: 'Yes, faith. When this was done, I took a piece of bread and cheese, and came my way. . . .' The phrase 'when this was done' is extraordinary. What she has haltingly tried to relate was something that actually happened, which she observed; and when it was done she took a piece of bread and cheese and came her way. As she hesitates in re-telling it to her audience, the indignant story re-enacts itself – as does the story of the terrible bridal night in Yeats's play, *Purgatory*. This of course is our retrospective view, with the hindsight of Madge's closing words. As in *The Arraignment of Paris*, the bracket which closes the play is not one of a pair with the bracket which opens it.

'Why, this goes round without a fiddling stick', marvels Frolic as the characters act out their story. But what is it that the characters are so anxious to demonstrate the truth of? It is still only an old wives' tale, a bagful of folk-tales, individually and collectively beyond the bounds of credibility. The blithe way in which Peele has airily piled folk-tale on top of folk-tale quadruples the absurdity of the story.[8] The enchanter with his secret lamp, the old man at the cross who is really a youth, the abducted maiden, the heads in the well, the wandering knight, the grateful corpse – Peele's bland stitching together of these and the other folk narratives from which he has made his play has produced something unique in our literature, as amusing as it is beautiful, a great joke that derides nothing. It might seem that the braggart Huanebango is being used to debunk the world of romance and folk-tale as he assumes the role of questing knight, seeking his fortune 'among brazen gates, enchanted towers, fire and brimstone, thunder and lightning' (275–6), looking for precious beauty whom 'none must inherit but he that can monsters tame, labours achieve, riddles absolve, loose enchantments, murder magic, and kill conjuring' (280–3). But Huanebango is only at the extreme edge of an attitude to folk/romance material which is *never* serious but which never attempts to capsize or explode the subject.

When Huanebango, who has become deaf, is married off to the good-look-ing daughter with the shrewish tongue, and Corebus, who has become blind, is married off to the ugly daughter with the heart of gold, it is more than a good joke, and one is really quite perplexed and uncertain about one's response. There is something here which survives and outlasts the banter and the ridicule, and we feel this throughout the play.

Undoubtedly it is the language which in part at least gives the folk material its power to endure the treatment it is subjected to.

> *First Brother*. . . . If I speed in my journey, I will give thee a palmer's staff of ivory
>   and a scallop shell of beaten gold.
> *Erestus*.   Was she fair?
> *Second Brother*.   Ay, the fairest for white and the purest for red, as the blood of
>   the deer or the driven snow.   (156–60)

Erestus has not been told what the object of the journey is. (One scholar thought that his question was a sign of textual corruption.) The play is full of magical and evocative phrases, from the riddles of Erestus to the song of the three lost youths, the speeches of the Head in the well, and quite ordinary exchanges:

> – How now, fair Delia, where you have been?
> –At the foot of the rock for running water . . .   (371–2)

'Gently dip, but not too deep', says the Head in the well where is the water of life. Peele is dipping with the utmost gentleness in the deepest waters.

If Madge is not in control of the story, who is? One of the remarkable features of this ingenious conglomeration of folk-tales is that although many people seem to be directing its progress, there is really no one in charge. Certainly not Sacrapant the sorcerer, who has the most uneasy control over his victims and who is overcome with staggering ease by Jack and Venelia. The Ghost of Jack is in charge some of the time, directing Eumenides to Delia, outwitting and killing Sacrapant, and also interpreting the action. There is then the strange figure of Erestus, the young man on whom Sacrapant has forced his own aged and ugly visage, and who becomes a bear at night. He stands at the cross roads, issuing his riddling prophecies to all who pass. He seems to know the future as well as he knows the past. When Eumenides the wandering Knight enters (452), he addresses the empty air:

> Tell me, Time; tell me, just Time,
> When shall I Delia see?

Catching sight of Erestus, he asks him to tell him his fortune, and Erestus gives him the riddling advice which eventually leads him to Delia.[9] And then there is also the Head in the well of life, who has the power to award good and bad fortunes.

Peele seems to organise his play on the principle of superfetation. There is an abundance of plots, an abundance of quests, an abundance of presenters – and an abundance of deliverances, in that the sorcerer is defeated twice (Jack kills him and Venelia blows out the magic light). Since its light-hearted irresponsibility is part of the secret of its enchantment, how can we possibly ask serious questions about it?

In an important lecture in 1975, Inga-Stina Ewbank spoke of the relation between *word* and *show*, or language and spectacle, in Peele's plays.[10] She was particularly interested in the arousing of wonder, and several times pointed to resemblances between Peele's work and Shakespeare's final romances in the counterpointing of word and vision to create wonder in the audience. She said: 'At the heart of all living theatrical experience there is a kind of mystery: a creation, through what we see and hear, of a world which we accept as possible.'[11] In the published lecture there is at this point a footnote: ' "Possible" seems to me a more adequate word in this context than "real", with its misleading associations of "suspension of disbelief" '. It seems to me that 'possible' is in fact a very dangerous word to use, and I would be happier with that always misleading word, real. For Peele in *The Old Wives Tale* has strongly urged not merely the improbability but the *impossibility* of his story, while at the same time using all his powers as a dramatist to give that impossible fiction a vitality, a *life*, which has the power to interrogate, though it cannot challenge, the more sober range of happenings which makes up our 'possible' life. The tale which the old woman starts to narrate is a poor thing indeed, but as the characters arrive unsummoned to *perform* it, the vagueness and casualness disappear in favour of something wonderfully bright and magical – though still an old wives tale so far as possibility goes. 'Gently dip, but not too deep.' There is no need to be portentous or apologetic about folk-tales. *The Old Wives Tale* is a brilliant success in achieving the lightest conceivable treatment of folk-tale without betraying or ridiculing those deeper things which folk-tale may be held to represent and incorporate. J. D. Cox is quite right to point to Peele's 'combination of *joie de vivre* with a celebration of great creating nature', and to say that Peele 'successfully preserves the fertility implications inherent in his folklore sources'. The end of the play, he wrote, gives us 'a vision familiar from Shakespearean comedy and romance'. There is a problem here, however, in that the familiar vision of Shakespearean romance is itself full of perplexity, at least so far as *The Winter's Tale* is concerned.

The text for our discussion of *The Winter's Tale* is Paulina's remark in the final scene, when the statue of Hermione is revealed to be Hermione herself.

> That she is living,
> Were it but told you, should be hooted at
> Like an old tale, but it appears she lives . . .   (V.iii. 115–17)

Seeing is believing. Narration would be hooted at, but it *appears* she lives.
There are three narrations in *The Winter's Tale* which are of outstanding
importance: the Clown's account of the shipwreck and of the bear devour-
ing Antigonus at the end of Act III; the words of Time as chorus at the
beginning of Act IV; and the account given by the Third Gentleman in Act V
of the meeting of the kings and the recognition of Perdita.

To begin with 'Time, the chorus'. *The Winter's Tale* has no frame, but
Time is the concealed presenter, and the play is his tale as *Pericles* is Gower's
tale. He does not appear until Act IV, but then he calls the play 'my tale' (14),
and 'my scene' (15). 'Remember well', he says 'I mentioned a son o' th'
king's, which Florizel / I now name to you.' It was Hermione, Leontes and
Polixenes who spoke of the son in Act I. Time is clearly the tale-teller. Or
rather, the tale-teller adopts the guise of Time; he says he will 'Now take
upon me, in the name of Time, / To use my wings' (3–4). This is his little
joke. As a tale-teller, he is proposing to miss out sixteen years altogether,
which is the one thing Time cannot possibly do, and he justifies it as the sort
of thing that Time *can* do, on the specious analogy that 'it is in my power / To
o'erthrow law' (7–8). This master tale-teller, masquerading as Time, does
not reappear. The entire story, however, is his contrivance. Things happen
as he wills them; the play is his tale. He has two subordinates who do some
tale-telling for him, the Clown and the Third Gentleman.

The narrations by the Clown and the Third Gentleman are always recognised as perplexing in their tone. There is in both cases a great incongruity
between the quality of the event and the manner in which it is narrated. The
Clown has to tell the story of a ship being wrecked with the loss of all
aboard, and of the death of Antigonus, attacked and eaten by a bear. The
Clown is distressed and shocked by what he has seen, but his account of it is
embarrassingly comic.

> – How the poor souls roared, and the sea mocked them; and how the poor
> gentleman roared, and the bear mocked him, both roaring louder than the sea or
> weather.
>
> – Name of mercy, when was this, boy?
>
> – Now, now; I have not winked since I saw these sights; the men are not yet cold
> under water, nor the bear half dined on the gentleman; he's at it now!
>
> (III.iii. 96–103)

The emotions of the Shepherd and the Clown are not made fun of. The
gravity of the deaths and the awe at discovering the baby come over to
everyone. And yet the coincidence of the bear and the shipwreck is really
preposterous, and is made to seem more so by the Clown's ludicrous
account. Not even the burial of Antigonus is free from black humour: 'If
there be any of him left, I'll bury it', says the Clown.

In the later narration, the assertion of the First Gentleman (who wasn't a
witness) that 'the dignity of this act was worth the audience of kings and

princes, for by such was it acted' (77–8) only emphasises the cheapness given
to the momentous events by the prattle of the Third Gentleman, who is
over-articulate as the Clown was inarticulate.

> One of the prettiest touches of all, and that which angled for mine eyes – caught
> the water though not the fish – was, when at the relation of the queen's death, with
> the manner how she came to 't bravely confessed and lamented by the king, how
> attentiveness wounded his daughter; till, from one sign of dolour to another, she
> did, with an 'Alas' – I would fain say – bleed tears; for I am sure my heart wept
> blood.   (V.ii. 79–86)

It is notable that the Third Gentleman re-tells the incidents of the bear and
the shipwreck related by the Clown (61–76). It is notable also that both the
bear–shipwreck episode and the meeting of the kings with the opening of the
fardel were not in Greene's *Pandosto*. The first episode is entirely new
material created by Shakespeare; the second a re-working of Greene. It is not
a question, that is, of Shakespeare hurrying over a necessary part of the story
as told in his source. To create these incidents and to have them related in a
particular way is a single act of free artistic choice.

The arresting coincidence of the bear and the shipwreck is required in
order to destroy all the evidence of witnesses to the abandoning of Perdita:
'so that all the instruments which aided to expose the child were even then
lost when it was found', as the Third Gentleman puts it (68–70). This
destruction of the witnesses is necessary only because Shakespeare has
provided the witnesses; in *Pandosto* the babe is set adrift in a boat which is
washed up on the shore for the shepherd to find and no one has to be
liquidated. Shakespeare seems to have set up the problem in order to
produce its far-fetched solution. Similarly, the pell-mell of greetings and
discoveries in V.ii is entirely Shakespeare's choice.

> There was casting up of eyes, holding up of hands, with countenance of such
> distraction that they were to be known by garment, not by favour. Our king, being
> ready to leap out of himself for his found daughter, as if that joy were now become
> a loss, cries, 'Oh, thy mother, thy mother'; then asks Bohemia forgiveness, then
> embraces his son-in-law; then again worries he his daughter with clipping her.
>   (V.ii. 45–52)

It is the Third Gentleman who says plainly that what he is relating is
incredible, and beggars *description*. Of the meeting of the kings, he says it
was 'a sight which was to be seen, cannot be spoken of'. It 'lames report to
follow it, and undoes description to do it' (41–2; 54–5). Of the bear and the
shipwreck he says, 'Like an old tale still, which will have matter to rehearse,
though credit be asleep and not an ear open'. These old wives tales maunder
on though the audience, and belief, have fallen asleep and are paying no
attention. It won't do to say that Shakespeare is using the old device in
fiction of disarming incredulity by saying it's so improbable you'd think it
were fiction. He has increased the improbabilities of his source, and then

Philip Edwards

further intensified them by the 'lame' reports, the 'broken delivery', of the Clown and the Third Gentleman.

Why should Shakespeare emphasise the absurdity of his story every time that it is narrated? In proposing an answer to this, I want to make an excursus to the sheep-shearing feast in IV.iv.

Perdita, we recognise, has a great passion for what is natural. There is not only her absolute refusal to grow 'streaked gillyvors', whatever Polixenes says, because in setting them human art has to assist 'great creating nature', but also her discomfort with the costume she is wearing, her 'unusual weeds', making her 'most goddess-like pranked up' with her 'borrowed flaunts'. She is afraid her character is changing because of the garments she is wearing.

> Methinks I play as I have seen them do
> In Whitsun pastorals: sure this robe of mine
> Does change my disposition.   (IV.iv. 133–5)

Just as Polixenes' theory about the value of grafting is contradicted by his prejudices in the matter of Florizel marrying Perdita, so (on the other side of the argument) Perdita's commitment to naturalness in conduct and speech is contradicted by the fatal ease with which her unstudied talents translate her into another being. The sheep-shearing feast takes place (oddly enough) towards the end of summer, but, magnificently, Perdita creates spring in her words:

> Daffodils
> That come before the swallow dares, and take
> The winds of March with beauty –   (IV.iv. 118–20)

ending with her vision of the flowered bank, with Florizel 'quick and in mine arms'. It is the vivid reality of her own imaginative recreation of spring which alarms her. But Florizel steps in to reassure her: 'What you do / Still betters what is done' (135–6). This phrase is often misunderstood to mean 'is an improvement on what you last did'. The ending of the speech explains the beginning:

> Each your doing,
> So singular in each particular,
> Crowns what you are doing in the present deeds,
> That all your acts are queens.   (143–6)

As Dr Johnson put it, 'Your manner in each act crowns the act'. 'What you do / Still *betters* what is done.' That is to say, whatever you do always improves, or raises in value, the thing that is done. There is speaking, singing, buying, selling, giving alms, praying, ordering affairs, dancing. None of these is anything much in itself; everything depends on the way it is done. And everything that Perdita does finds its justification in the grace with which she does it. For Florizel, the acted presentation of the spring is as beautiful and real as anything else that Perdita has done; her role as 'no shepherdess, but Flora / Peering in April's front' as beautiful and real as anything else that Perdita has been.

By the brilliance of his art, and that of his boy actor, Shakespeare presents us Perdita, the princess-shepherdess who is all naturalness; and he emphasises the extent to which 'we are mocked by art'[12] by showing us how she, who is all naturalness, can bring alive by words and action a different being and a different season, making it real and convincing to her hearers in Bohemia, and in every theatre where the play is well acted.

'What the imagination seizes as beauty must be truth . . .' That is really the import of Florizel's speech, and is the underlying meaning not only of Perdita's impersonation of the spring-goddess but of the whole play.[13] The vividness of what is brought before us by speech and action in performance is its own certificate of credibility and acceptability. Shakespeare chooses to give emotional credence to particular scenes in *The Winter's Tale* by having them acted out in scenes which he has written with his full powers – particularly Leontes's jealousy, the springtime love of Perdita and Florizel, and the statue scene. But these scenes he so positions and illuminates that each is left with a very frail support in its before and after. Seeing is believing, and *only* seeing is believing. Those passages of the story which are not privileged with performance are relegated to the status of old wives tales.

It is not we who point to the fragility of the fiction in *The Winter's Tale*; it is Shakespeare. 'Such a deal of wonder is broken out within this hour that ballad-makers cannot be able to express it' (V.ii. 23–5). We have been told what colossal absurdities ballad-makers can get away with in Autolycus's description of the outrageous lies contained in the ballads he is selling at the feast. It is a mischievous stroke for Shakespeare to make Autolycus introduce the scene of the reunion of father and daughter as narrated by the various gentlemen. The reunion of Leontes and Perdita is narrated; the reunion of Leontes and Hermione is performed. Neither is likely; each is 'like an old tale still, which *will* have matter to rehearse, though credit be asleep and not an ear open'. But for some scenes credit is to be awakened, while for others it remains asleep. The most intriguing moment in this context is when Shakespeare suddenly materialises what is essentially narrated matter: 'Exit pursued by a bear'. Is credit here meant to be awake or asleep? It's a kind of after-dinner sleep, at the join between narration and action; a deliberate confusion of the two modes, and thus a pointer to their existence.

There is one very small piece of the story of *The Winter's Tale* which shows what by comparison seems a strange anxiety in Shakespeare to obtain credence for his story. The 'opening of the fardel' – the bundle in which the old shepherd had wrapped the clues to Perdita's identity – is a critical moment in the play. It happens when everyone is on Sicilian soil. I cannot think that any member of an audience has ever asked why the shepherd waited so long to open the fardel. If any question is asked, it is why the shepherd and his son consented to sail with Florizel, when their mission had been to Polixenes; in *Pandosto* it is described in detail how the shepherd is shanghaied aboard. On this matter, all that Autolycus says is that 'I brought the old man and his son aboard the prince'. (It is the audience he is giving this information to, at V.ii. 110, at the close of the Third Gentleman's narration.) He then enters into particulars about the fardel. He told the prince, he says, that 'I heard them talk of a fardel and I know not what'; but because both Perdita and Florizel *began to be sea-sick* 'this mystery remained unsolved'.

Why should Shakespeare be so concerned to give verisimilitude to his story just at this minor point when he has so ostentatiously refused it over much greater matters? It is curious that it is Autolycus who is so active here; he comes to look more and more like a surrogate of the tale-teller. Perhaps he is throwing dust in our eyes here: establishing the credibility of the tale just as we are being taken to the greatest improbability of all.

I refer of course to the sixteen-year concealment of Hermione. All that time, Paulina and Hermione have collaborated in pretending that Hermione has died.[14] After the revelation that the statue is in fact the living queen, only four lines of explanation or justification are given. Hermione says to Perdita:

> Thou shalt hear that I,
> Knowing by Paulina that the oracle
> Gave hope thou wast in being, have preserved
> Myself to see the issue.   (V.iii. 125–8)

This explains nothing: the question is not why Hermione has preserved herself but why she has kept Leontes in ignorance of her existence all these years. But even this explanation is cut short by Paulina.

> There's time enough for that,
> Lest they desire upon the push *to trouble*
> *Your joys* with like relation.   (V.iii. 128–30; my italics)

At the very end of the play, Leontes says:

> Good Paulina,
> Lead us from hence, where we may leisurely
> Each one demand and answer to his part
> Performed in this wide gap of time since first
> We were disseevered. Hastily lead away.

Those are the last words spoken. The emphasis in these extracts on explanations still to be given – but *not* in the play – is striking. How terrible this demand and answer would be! What Leontes had done came as near to the unforgivable as the mind can conceive. His contrition and penitence are complete and unquestioned. Even after all this time, however, he fears that recollection of his responsibility for the death of Mamilius might 'unfurnish me of reason' (V.i. 123). For sixteen years his wife goes on punishing him, punishing herself as she punishes him. Where in the last scene is the exchange of forgiveness – that most Shakespearean feature – between Hermione and Leontes? Shakespeare could not conceivably have put it in, because what it would have awakened would have destroyed the joy of the final scene. 'Hastily lead away!'

Shakespeare put everything into the intensely moving reunion between Leontes and Hermione. For the original audience, who might well have known Greene's *Pandosto*, in which the calumniated queen did indeed die, the surprise that she was still living would have been as great as that of Leontes. The surge of their pleasure would have mingled with the joy of the dramatis personae, and quite submerged the questions that might have been asked. Shakespeare placed the beauty of the statue scene over a void of questioning, and pointed to the void. Leontes saw Hermione 'as I thought, dead'. What was in her coffin at the double funeral with Mamilius (III.ii. 233) is anyone's guess. Never before in his career as a dramatist had Shakespeare kept secret from his audience a main element of the plot, as here in 1611 he kept secret from them the fact that Hermione had not died. It is an arresting innovation: it became absolutely commonplace in the tragicomedies of Fletcher and Massinger, and that is one reason why their plays are inferior to Shakespeare's.

Of course, it's only a play. But to accept the improbability of Oberon and his love-juice, or Portia's take-over of Venetian law, is very different from accepting the improbabilities and the plot manoeuvring of *The Winter's Tale*. What is so interesting is Shakespeare's keenness to impress on us that we have been cheated.

> That she is living,
> Were it but told you, should be hooted at
> Like an old tale, but it *appears* she lives . . .

The beauty of *The Winter's Tale* is its insubstantiality, to be compared with 'the uncertain glory of an April day', or the vanishing glory of the masque in *The Tempest*. The play consists basically of three extended actions: calumny and rejection; love in the younger generation; reunion and restoration. Each of these actions is brilliantly realised before us. But they are brought before us as make-believe, and their status insisted on by those parts of the story that are narrated rather than performed. They are moments in a most improbable tale, moments that a supreme dramatic artist has chosen to make real and convincing. It is not in any way a new thing for Shakespeare to demonstrate how 'we are mocked by art', and an ironical or quizzical presentation of the artist at work, in *The Winter's Tale* as elsewhere, serves

Philip Edwards   92

to affirm rather than sabotage the power of art. Much of Shakespeare's greatness, it can be argued, derives from the balancing of what I have called elsewhere the epic and the burlesque visions of his own activity.[15] The opposed visions are remarkably demonstrated in the self-images of the artist in the last plays. Beside the heroic image of the brooding, careworn Prospero, we have the anti-heroic image of Autolycus, the man who depends for his living on his protean resourcefulness and the gullibility of the public.

In both Peele's *Old Wives Tale* and Shakespeare's *The Winter's Tale*, segments of a very tall story are snatched from the inadequacies of narration and realised before us in action. Each dramatist tells us in his own way that this realisation does not one whit alter the improbability of the fiction. Life is 'not like that', whether we are talking about heads in a well or the preservation of Hermione and Perdita. In spite of the dramatist's care, you will find critics inattentively referring to 'the miracle' at the end of *The Winter's Tale*. What miracle there is is just there: in our being so convinced by what the dramatist keeps assuring us is an old wives winter's tale. In the end, those who claim so little for their fictions turn out to be their best advocates.

NOTES

1 The general similarity is noted by J. D. Cox, 'Homely matter and multiple plots in Peele's *Old Wives Tale*', *Texas Studies in Literature and Language*, 20 (1978), p. 343.

2 Text (with minor modifications) and line references for *The Old Wives Tale* are from the Revels Plays edition by Patricia Binnie, 1980.

3 The parallel is pointed out by C. Frey in *Shakespeare's Vast Romance: A Study of 'The Winter's Tale'* (Missouri, 1980), p. 99.

4 On Shakespeare's responsibility for the design and shape of *Pericles*, see the introduction to the New Penguin edition of the play by Philip Edwards (1976), pp. 31–41.

5 E.g., J. D. Cox as cited in n. 1; Joan C. Marx, ' "Soft, who have we here?": the dramatic technique of *The Old Wives Tale*', *Renaissance Drama*, N.S. 12 (1981), pp. 117–43; Susan T. Viguers, 'The hearth and the cell: art in *The Old Wives Tale*', *Studies in English Literature*, 21 (1981), pp. 209–21.

6 Viguers, 'The hearth and the cell' (n. 5), pp. 219–20.

7 *Ibid.* (n. 5), p. 212.

8 For the folk-tale material in the play with reference to earlier studies, see F. S. Hook's introduction to his edition in Vol. 3 of the Yale Peele, 1970.

9 Erestus's assumption of the role of Time (which I suggest above provides a link with *The Winter's Tale*) is pointed out by Susan Viguers in the article cited in n. 5, p. 217.

10 ' "What words, what looks, what wonders?": language and spectacle in the theatre of George Peele', *The Elizabethan Theatre*, V, ed. G. R. Hibbard (Toronto, 1975), pp. 124–54.

11 p. 125.

12 Leontes' phrase (V.iii. 68) when he is marvelling at the 'motion' in the eye of what he thinks is Julio Romano's statue. This is a brilliant double-cross by Shakespeare, for Leontes is mistaken; it is not a triumph of art that Leontes is beholding, but Hermione herself. It is in that 'Hermione herself' that the mockery

93 'Seeing is believing'

lies, for Hermione is a boy-actor pretending to be Hermione pretending to be a statue.

13 Keats's phrase is quoted by E. A. J. Honigmann in his chapter on *The Winter's Tale* in *Shakespeare's Impact on his Contemporaries* (London 1982), pp. 111–20, in the footsteps of which the present article treads. Honigmann argues that the assertion of unlikelihood in the play is an answer to the crudity of Jonson's demand for fidelity to life in art. Shakespeare's conclusion is 'more complicated than Keats's famous compromise that Beauty is Truth' (p. 115).

14 The morality of the deception is discussed in the context of the 'good deceivers' in Shakespeare in Philip Edwards, 'Shakespeare and the healing power of deceit', *Shakespeare Survey*, 31 (1978), p. 117.

15 See *Shakespeare and the Confines of Art* (1968), chapter 1.

[10]

Old Wives' Tales, George Peele, and Narrative Abjection

MARY ELLEN LAMB

> I have heard aged mumping beldams as they sat warming their knees
> over a coale scratch over the argument verie curiously, and they would
> bid yong folks beware on what day they par'd their nayles, tell what luck
> everie one should have by the day of the weeke he was borne on…When
> I was a little childe, I was a great auditor of theirs, and had all their witch-
> crafts at my fingers endes, as perfit as good morrow and good even.[1]

Included in a work revealingly titled *Terrors of the Night*, Nashe's
reminiscence from childhood reveals the extent to which he had
become a full communicant in the superstitious mysteries shared by
the old women of his childhood. As Adam Fox has noted for this and
other passages, 'At the juvenile level… the repertoire of unlearned
village women coincided for a brief but significant period with that of
the educated male elite'.[2] As Nashe's evocative title suggests, however, these repertoires did more than coincide. The 'witchcrafts' that
Nashe valued enough as a boy to learn by rote not only lost their use-
fulness: they became objects of contempt. The more common use of
the phrase 'old wives' tales' to refer to the lore of unlearned women
conveys a similar sense of stigma. In this essay, I discuss various
texts, finally focussing on Peele's *Old Wives Tale*, to explore the
implications of this shared repertoire within the wider context of a
culture whose antagonism to illiterate old women participated in ideologies deeply formative to early moderns and their literatures.

The phrase 'old wives' tales' serves an ideological as well as a
descriptive function. Adam Fox has traced how writers of the Protestant Reformation dismissed the alleged superstitions of the Catholic
church as old wives' tales; proponents of academic disciplines similarly denigrated ideas not sufficiently based on empirical inquiry
(175–7). The terms of these dismissals reveal, as Fox notes, the
views of 'a prevailing, male-dominated culture which typically characterized women as creatures of the spoken word'.[3] This early
modern binary opposing a literate male culture to an oral female

culture presents an obvious distortion: it excludes illiterate males as well as literate females. This binary also ignores the dense interrelationships between printed texts and oral tales demonstrated so well by scholars such as Fox, Robert Chartier, and Marina Warner.[4] Such distortions reveal that the purpose of this binary was never to reflect a complex social reality; like most binaries, it functioned instead to promote a social agenda. Deriving early modern 'truth-value' from the similarly distorting binaries of prevailing gender ideologies, the phrase 'old wives' tales' helped to naturalize a concept of authorship appropriate for literate males. Rather than the communal circulation of a common body of old wives' tales often in the performance of repetitive household tasks, authorship by male writers increasingly valorized the individual – his thoughts, his learning, his authority – as defining the nature and even the quality of a work. Whether used to denigrate Catholic doctrines or to express nostalgic yearning, the phrase 'old wives' tales' produced, and was produced by, social practices instituting the cultural capital of a developed and empowering literacy as primarily a male prerogative.

The contempt for women's lore expressed in the phrase 'old wives' tales' reflected a gender system structuring not only the content, but the experience, of the early modern grammar schools burgeoning in England between 1560 and 1660.[5] Since Walter Ong's often quoted representation of early modern education as 'puberty rites', scholars have thoroughly researched the rigorous process through which the attainment of Latin literacy was to internalize within schoolboys a disciplined rationality fitting them to assume authority over others as adults.[6] The homoeroticism within the schoolroom culture further supported a humanist pedagogy designed not only to distance boys from women but to remediate any ill effects remaining from this earlier period of female domination.[7] According to Frederic Jameson's definition of culture as an 'objective mirage...a nimbus perceived by one group when it comes into contact with and observes another one',[8] it would have been in their withdrawal from this intimate space of childhood to learn Latin from a schoolmaster that boys most directly encountered powerful binaries structuring early modern gender as inflected by social status: nurses vs. schoolmasters, androgynous childhood vs. masculine youth, vernacular vs. Latin, old wives' tales vs. classical myths. The understanding and perhaps even some childhood memories of boys who, like Nashe, learned the lore of an oral culture from 'mumping beldams' would have generally taken shape within this schoolroom environment. As becomes explicit in this statement by Erasmus, humanist hostility to 'old wives' fairy rubbish' was part of a larger conflict waged by the Latinate culture of the schoolroom for control over the minds of young boys:

> A boy <may> learn a pretty story from the ancient poets, or a memorable tale from history, just as readily as the stupid and vulgar ballad, or the old wives' fairy rubbish such as most children are steeped in nowadays by nurses and serving women.[9]

Within this contest between cultures, tales told by women took on ideological meanings they had not possessed in childhood. Contempt for old wives' tales, disparaged as 'rubbish', signified loyalty to humanist agendas; alternatively, a continuing appreciation for these tales provided a space of resistance. These two extremes defined an emotional spectrum with many points in between. The strategies for managing dissonance between the cultures known in childhood and in the schoolroom were undoubtedly as local and various as the experiences of individual schoolboys. For those who interpreted the tensions between these cultures as destructive, competing allegiances represented threats to the integrity of selfhood; and a clear-cut choice between the two was necessary. For others, the tensions between cultures remained more conflicted and more productive. Since strong social pressures mediated against any boy's admission – not to mention his written expression – of his continuing love for his nurse, few or no texts by schoolboys survive to express these cultural conflicts directly. But the variety of ways that the clashes between these cultures could be resolved, or left unresolved, emerges from the wide range of attitudes towards this oral tradition later expressed by adults. An investment in the classical curriculum predictable for a Cambridge don underlies Gabriel Harvey's utter incomprehension of Spenser's intention to write an epic including a fairy queen: 'If so be the *Faerye Queene* be fairer in your eie than the *Nine Muses,* and *Hobgoblin* runne away with the Garland from *Apollo...* fare you well, till God or some good Aungell putte you in a better minde'.[10] For John Aubrey, on the other hand, the 'fabulous stories nightimes, of sprights and walking of ghosts' told by the 'old women and mayds' of his early seventeenth-century childhood elicited nostalgia.[11] Rather than a pleasurable frisson, tales told by his mothers' maids evoked a terror for Reginald Scot that generalized to a distrust of all fictional narratives. The jumble of classical figures (satyrs, pans, tritons) among native figures (the Man-in-the-Oak, Tom Thumb, Boneless) in Scot's list of 'bugbears' categorizes even classical myths as 'old wives' tales' devoid of any merit or purpose beyond frightening children.[12] Ben Jonson took an opposite approach. Noting that the word 'faeries' might derive from a greek word 'pheras' for satyr, Jonson mingled fairies and satyrs together as equivalent subjects for a display of his impressive classical learning.[13] Whether they led to resolutions or to refusals of resolution, these individual negotiations between dissonant cultures often bring into play deep memories of childhood that may be at the source of adult creativity.[14]

William Wager's *The Longer Thou Livest, the More Fool Thou Art* (1568–9) provides insight into the challenges confronting a school-room culture even within a straight-forward example of humanist propaganda. The audience imagined for Wager's play is primarily schoolboys, according to the subtitle pronouncing it 'verie necessarie for youth, and specially for such as are like to come to dignitie and promotion'.[15] Stressing the necessity of 'good schoolmasters' to correct youth with 'reason' for the benefit of the commonweal (5), the Prologue expresses the play's sympathies with teachers such as Discipline and Exercitation in their futile struggles to win the loyalty of Moros, or 'fool.' The play foregrounds the destructive effects of the female domain of childhood at Moros's first appearance singing lines from at least eight ballads learned from 'A fond woman to my mother,/ As I war wont in her lap to sit' (8). Refusing to heed Discipline's stern advice ('Forget your babish vanity' 9), he later sings another ballad learned of his 'dame,/ When she taught me mustard seed to grind' (40) as Idleness and two other unworthy companions dance. The play represents Moros' enjoyment of ballads, games, and sensual pleasures in general as a refusal to 'grow up' to assume the sober responsibilities appropriate for adult males. As the small excesses of youth become large tyrannies in his more advanced age, Moros becomes a bad ruler of others. At the conclusion of the play, God's Judgement enters 'with a terrible visure' to strike Moros down with the stern declaration: 'The longer thou livest, the more fool thou art'(70). Confusion carries him on his back to the devil. Moros' terrible end is, no doubt, implicit from his entrance.

The actual performance of the play, especially before an audience of schoolboys, undoubtedly unsettled its explicit moral. The sober speeches by Discipline, Piety, and Exercitation are undeniably tedious. The most enjoyable moments of this play occur precisely when Moros and his unseemly companions rebel against their authority. These moments set up a counter-text opposing the explicitly stated intentions of the prologue. Moros's jumbled repetition of a Discipline's dry lecture on the complexities of Arius' heresy, for example, elevates play, name-calling, and pleasure in food. Moros's transformation of Discipline's sentence, 'Pray unto him to give you sapience', to 'Play now and then in thy master's absence' (16) displays delightful wit. Less witty but perhaps even more amusing is Moros' old comic gag of repeating phrases Discipline does not intend to be repeated, such as the instructions, 'Say the same verses alone together/ Like as you said them after me', until Discipline beats him savagely. But even as Moros cries out his obedience – 'For God's sake leave, mine arse is sore./ I will say as you will have me say now' – he still cannot resist the temptation to repeat 'Say thus' to Discipline's order 'Say thus' (19). Perhaps most evocative is Moros' renaming of these pedagogues. The emphasis on 'arse' in the renaming of Exercitation, for example, as 'Arse-out-of-fashion' (24) removes the teacher's privilege, rendering him vulnerable to the pain he inflicts through discipline and perhaps through sexual penetration. And within the queer economy of Moros's topsy-turvy grammar school, this old 'Arse-out-of-fashion' is 'out of fashion' – sexually undesireable – at the bottom of the heap in a youth's libidinal hierarchy. In all of these droll deviations from schoolroom authority, the irrepressible Moros draws on the oral, as opposed to written, skills honed at an earlier time. Despite the humanist moral of its prologue, *The Longer Thou Livest* sets up a contest not only between characters, but between cultures, for the loyalty of schoolboys. For some, the play's structure may have evoked horror, or perhaps grim satisfaction, as Moros received his just deserts in hell.[16] Others may have indulged their own desires to resist authority by laughing along with Moros' comic tricks. Some may have had it both ways, reliving their own narrative pleasures in Moros' defiance while finally abjuring these 'follies' to enjoy moral superiority in his punishment at the end of the play.

George Peele's *Old Wives Tale* (1595) challenges the pedagogical agenda of Wager's prologue in various ways. In its title, *Old Wives Tale* expresses a connection with women's oral traditions. It pays serious attention to folktales – the Abducted Maiden, the Grateful

Dead, the Heads in the Well – by arranging them in artful patterns.[17] It parodies the learned culture through the eminently silly Huanebango and his Latin nonsense. But, as with Wager's play, it is the contest, more than the outcome, of the conflict between oral and learned cultures that constitutes its primary engagement. In *Old Wives Tale,* negotiations between the perspectives of a learned culture on the one hand and, on the other, an oral culture reveal the shaping presence of a hybrid consciousness. This consciousness is located most visibly in the boys of the play's framing device, as they sit on stage to watch the play. Earlier critics have explored the implications of the on-stage presence of Frolicke and Fantasticke as a cue for the reception of the play by its larger audience.[18] Countering views of *Old Wives Tale* as a satire, Frank Hook, editor of the Yale edition, posits the 'uncomplicated and sympathetic acceptance' of these tales by the 'entranced' young Frolicke and Fantasticke as an invitation for us the audience similarly to 'give ourselves up like children to the story to be unfolded by the actors' (362, 359). Patricia Binnie also claims that Peele 'consciously recreates the basic aim of folklore – to recall to the hearer the instinct and images of his childhood' (20), yet she modifies this view with a double-perspective: 'If the audience, upon seeing it, re-enters the realm of childhood, it does so with adult understanding' (15). In none of these discussions do critics consider the circumstances of a distinctively early modern childhood, and specifically the transitional period between early childhood and young adulthood attained by the young pages. This transitional period is precisely the locus, I argue, of the consciousness structuring this play. The boys are hybrids of two cultures. In its staging of material from the Latin schoolroom as well as from folklore, *Old Wives Tale* reveals two cultures that sometimes cooperate but more often conflict in important ways. This contest between learned and oral cultures waged within the subjectivity of these boys becomes a primary subject of Peele's play.[19]

From its first scene, *Old Wives Tale* humorously evokes an instability of perspectives proceeding from this transitional state between cultures. The wandering of these boys, lost in the woods, may itself evoke a sense of an anxious middle-state between worlds, neither of which is yet, or any longer, truly their home. Their names – Anticke Frolicke, and Fantasticke – suggest that they, like Moros, have not become fully inculturated within the sober humanist system. Frolicke comforts himself by citing Latin;

but as he calls out the female name 'Maria!' his misquotation from
Terence's *Adelphoe* IV, 1.790 ('O maria! O Neptune!' for 'O maria
Neptuni') shows his imperfect understanding of the line.[20] Anticke,
on the other hand, turns to a homely proverb to relieve his anxiety
about sleeping outdoors: 'Three merrie men,and three merrie men,/
And three merrie men be wee, / I in the wood, and thou on the
ground,/ And Jacke sleepes in the tree'. Their divergent frame-
works produce competing perspectives. Fantasticke describes their
young master as led by Cupid to serve a 'faire Lady' as a saint; to
Frolicke, however, she is only 'his wench'. It is Frolicke, whoever, who hails their rescuer, the smith Clunch, as the Roman fire
god Vulcan. In a spate of collision-allusions, Frolicke inserts English folk hobgoblins into this world of classical mythology: 'We
are like to wander with a sorrowfull hey ho, among the owlets, and
Hobgoblins of the Forrest: good Vulcan, for Cupids sake that has
cousned us all: befriend us as thou maiest'. When Clunch offers
them hospitality in his cottage, all Latinate pretensions that Clunch
is Vulcan disappear, and they cry out together: 'O blessed Smith, O
bountifull Clunch' (l. 51).

Welcomed to their home by Clunch's wife Madge and offered
cheese and pudding (which they politely decline), the boys first sing
a round with Clunch, and then, after Anticke retires with Clunch
with an inappropriately Latin *'Bona nox* Gammer' (100), they ask
Madge for a story. This frame for *Old Wives Tale* provides a rich
source of early modern understandings of the female oral tradition.
Frolicke's request for a story shows his assumption that as a woman
of lower social station, she must know many such tales: 'Me thinkes
Gammer, a merry winters tale would drive away the time trimly,
come I am sure you are not without a score'. Like a child at bedtime,
Fantasticke equates a tale with sleep: 'I faith Gammer a tale of an
howre long were as good as an howres sleepe.' Frolicke explicitly
relates a tale with his childhood: 'Looke you Gammer, of the Gyant
and the Kings Daughter, and I know not what, I have seene the day
when I was a litle one, you might have drawne mee a mile after you
with such a discourse'. Perceiving such 'Gammers' as stand-ins for
the nurses of childhood, the boys' desire for a story conveys a sense
of the solace associated with old wives' tales. This sense of well-
being, so at odds with their wandering in a cold and frightening
woods, is an integral component this scene of narration, and a primary social meaning of her tale.

Peele's play does not sentimentalize Madge's narrative skills. Her awkward introduction marks her lower social status. As critics have noted, the sixteen lines of Madge's story of an abducted maiden fall far short of conventional standards of written texts.[21] Hers is an unpolished story filled with oral markers, beginning with her formulaic phrase, 'Once uppon a time', then repeated again in the same first sentence. She revises the rank of the maiden's father – 'a King or a Lord, or a Duke'. Twice she backtracks to relate a necessary and earlier point of plot with exclamations 'O Lord I quite forgot' and 'O I forget'. The structure of all three of her sentences is clumsily additive, piling up 'and' clauses with minimal subordination: 'Once uppon a time there was a King… *and* once uppon a time his daughter was stollen away, *and* hee sent all his men to seeke out his daughter, *and* hee sent so long that he sent all his men out of his Land' (ll. 110–115). Her narration fades into the play as the two brothers of her tale come to life on stage to announce their search for their missing sister Delia.

Critics have debated the dissonance between Madge's awkward beginning and the graceful performances composing the rest of Peele's play.[22] For Stephen Young, the staged performances of Madge's 'unintelligible' tale represent a 'rescue rather than a continuation'; by establishing the old woman as 'an object of fun', Peele points up 'the superiority of the dramatic action he supplies over mere storytelling.'[23] Frolicke himself is not uncritical. As he points out the illogic of her fantasy, he reveals his self-identification with the ruler-figure: if the King (or lord or duke) sent all his men to seek for his daughter, 'Who drest his dinner then?' (l. 116). Reducing him to child status, Madge's insulting ultimatum evokes a physical intimacy, an association between her story and her abundant and sexual bodiliness that was the source of the power as well as the anxiety later elicited by women's stories: 'Nay either heare my tale, or kisse my taile' (l. 117). Frolicke's critical attitude quickly subsides, and his next reply is more respectful. His gentle explanation of the sudden appearance of the two brothers – 'Soft Gammer, here some come to tell your tale for you' – locates her story as the origin of these performances. Yet Madge's astonished outburst – 'Gods me bones, who comes here?' – reveals that she did not invoke these apparitions, and that these staged actions have passed beyond her narrative control.

Exceeding the plausible influence of printed texts, the specialized knowledges of Latin culture confirm that Peele's *Old Wives Tale* does not attempt an unmediated representation of Madge's tale, or of a women's oral culture. As Margaret Dean-Smith has noted, 'This is not a fairy-tale for a child, but adult fantasy compounded of romantic allusions comprehensible to an Elizabethan audience familiar with Apuleius and Ariosto, constructed upon the recognizable materials of folklore, legend and classical myth'.[24] The play not only displays but uses classical learning in sophisticated ways. Eumenides, the name of a benevolent knight who pays for the burial of an indigent corpse, for example, means 'the kindly ones', and Braunmuller points out that this name was 'a propitiary or euphemistic name for the furies, or Erinyes' in ancient Greece (58). Peele's play balances the kindness of Eumenides with the malice of the actual furies assisting the evil conjurer Sacrapant who was, like the Sacrapant of Apuleius's *Golden Ass*, born in Thessaly to a famous witch Meroe (ll. 340–1). Yet Peele's play also revels in the customs of an irreverently physical culture at a far remove from the schoolroom. Drawing on a reference to a dance described by John Aubrey, Hook explains why the shrewish Zantippa broke her pitcher against a mysterious head rising from a well to plead: 'Stroke me smoothe, and combe my head,/ And thou shalt have some cockell bread' (ll. 642–3). Apparently 'cockell bread' was molded in women's private parts, possibly as a love charm. The play also celebrates the seasonal cycles of the agrarian year with the singing harvest men who inexplicably interrupt the action twice, once to sow and once, with 'women in their hands' (l. 532), to reap.

Rather than setting up a counter-text as in Wager's play, the folk elements of *Old Wives Tale* surround and absorb the classical referents. Even heroes with classical names like Eumenides conquer by goodness, a form of agency described by Hook as distinguishing folk heroes from romantic heroes, who usually succeed through strength or wit (360). The evil Sacrapant's magic is more folk than classical: he turns Erestus to an old man by day and to 'the white Beare of Englands wood' (l. 165) by night. Malevolent as they are, the furies function as a simple moving device to carry off Delia's two brothers and then Huanebango. The clown's name change from Booby to Corebus passes without remark or corresponding transformation in character. In none of these displays of classical knowledges does *Old Wives Tale* present learning as a positive value. The compulsively Latinate Huanebango is a figure of humor rather than of admiration. Huanebango's quotation of an execrable

hexameter by Gabriel Harvey: 'O that I might but I may not, woe to
my destinie therefore' (1. 654), identifies him with the learned pretensions of that Cambridge don.[25] But this form of Harvey-bombast
functions, I believe, not so much to devalue the learned experiment
of naturalizing classical hexameters in English, as for the sheer fun
of exaggerated caricature. Huanebango's arrogance takes on the
zaniness of a schoolboy parody, as he declines his possessive pronoun in his ecstasy of erotic optimism:

> If this Ladie be so faire as she is said to bee, she is mine, she is mine.
> Meus, mea, meum, in contemptum omnium Grammaticorum. (ll. 282–3)

Even as a parody of Stanyhurst's hexameters, Huanebango's vows to
Zantippa are delightful not for their aesthetic commentary, but for
their innate absurdity:

> Phylyda phylerydos, Pamphylyda floryda flortos,
> Dub dub a dub, bounce quoth the guns, with a sulpherous
>   huffe snuffe:
> Wakte with a wench, pretty peat, pretty love, and my
>   sweet prettie pigsnie;
> Just by thy side shall sit surnamed great Huanebango,
> Safe in my armes will I keepe thee, threat Mars or thunder
>   Olympus. (ll. 645–0)

Ultimately deriving from Plautus, the names of Huanebango's
father, Pergopolyneo, and grandfather, Polimackeroeplacydus,
sound, in context, more silly than learned (ll. 289–90). Paradoxically, these nonsense sounds bring Huanebango's language
perilously close to the nonsense sounds ('dub dub a dub') of nurs-
ery rhymes. Yet unlike Moros, Huanebango is not carried down to
hell. Instead, he marries the beautiful Zantippa, whose shrewish
words he is too deaf to hear. Within Peele's forgiving play, even
Huanebango leaves the stage happy.

   In all of its several plots, *Old Wives Tale* advocates kindness not
only as the highest virtue, but even as the most effective action.[26]
Conferring almost magical power, generosity to those less fortunate
is more important than learning, social position, or even sheer intel-
ligence to the outcome of the plots. When Delia's brothers give alms
to Erestus, his riddling prophecy provides the key to their rescue of
their sister. Erestus' neighbor Lampriscus brings him honey, always
welcome, as Erestus slyly notes, to the bear he becomes at night

(l. 208). When Eumenides spends his last money to bury a pauper, the corpse's grateful ghost Jack fills his purse with money and enables his rescue of Delia and her brothers from the evil Sacrapant. When Zantippa's good sister Celanta strokes the head in the well and combs his hair, the corn and gold poured into her lap provides for her marriage to her beloved Corebus. It is this high value placed on kindness that provides the most significant link between the play and its frame. The generosity of the characters in *Old Wives Tale* participates in the generosity that was a fundamental meaning of Madge's narrative act itself. It is in this way that Peele's play finally pays tribute to the oral tradition of old wives' tales: while her style was admittedly unrefined, Madge's hospitality to needy boys was outstanding. As any ten year old boy will tell you, what is really important is not silly declensions of 'meus, mea, meum', but the breakfast Madge provides before the pages depart. The play ends on this happy dramatic climax:

> Fantasticke: Then you have made an end of your tale, Gammer?
> Old Woman: Yes faith: When this was done I tooke a peece of bread and cheese, and came my way, and so shall you have too before you goe, to your breakfast. (ll. 926–8)

Peele's *Old Wives Tale* is unusual in the directness of its treatment of this oral culture transmitted by women. Self-identifications with this tradition are, for the most part, fraught with ambivalence. Whether blissful or nightmarish, the childhood dependency on women signified by old wives' tales challenged the hard-won masculinity achieved in the schoolroom. Casual use of the phrase 'old wives' tale' suggests a widely shared experience, yet few writers acknowledged directly the influence of fictions spell-binding enough to have drawn them, like little Frolicke, after their nurses for a mile. These storytellers are not, to my knowledge, mentioned by their own full names: they remain 'aged mumping beldams', Madge, or Mother Bunches. For authors as well as for the learned culture as a whole, old wives' tales become material for abjection, as described by Julia Kristeva as that often despised but necessary 'thing' that must be rejected, but which is too much a part of the self for rejection to be possible (4).

As one of the few other English works to present an actual tale told by a woman of lower status, Sir Philip Sidney's *Countess of Pembroke's Arcadia* provides a likely example of authorial

abjection. Strong cues in Sidney's text invite readerly disdain for
Mopsa's tale. She slobbers: she wipes her mouth 'as there was good
cause' before she 'tumbled into her matter'.[27] After only a few minutes, even the 'sweet Philoclea' has lost patience, and she bribes
Mopsa to desist with the offer of a gown. Yet except for Languet's
political beast fable, Mopsa's tale is the only fictional narrative in
either version of the *Arcadia*. The tales told by other characters are
all in some sense 'true', requiring an action, such as the rescue of a
maiden or the punishment of a villain. While Sidney's profound and
elegant work lies at the opposite end of the aesthetic spectrum, both
works are, finally, fictional. Both are even arguably a form of chivalric romance. Does this contempt lavished on Mopsa's tale, then,
signify an abjection of old wives tales within the *Arcadia*, a work
described in its dedication as a 'trifle' and consigned to the flames at
its author's death?

A cursory view of Shakespeare's plays reveals a range of authorial
identifications with old wives' tales. As I have argued earlier, Lady
Macbeth's disdain for her husband's 'flaws and starts' at Banquo's
ghost as appropriate to 'a woman's story at a winter's fire/ Authorized
by her grandam' (III. iv. 64–6) implicates the wider play. With its
walking ghosts, phantom daggers, and witches' cauldrons, *Macbeth*
arguably owes substantial portions of its plot, and perhaps some of its
creepy-crawly feeling, to just such old wives' tales. [28] As suggested in
its title, Shakespeare's *Winter's Tale* is more forthright in its debt to
this oral tradition circulated between women and children, staged as
the boy Mamillius whispers his tale of 'sprites and goblins' (II. i.
25–6) in his mother's ear ('Engendering', 532). Old wives' tales also
took ballad form. In *Twelfth Night*, Orsino's call for a song, 'old and
plain' chanted by 'spinsters and knitters in the sun' swerves unexpectedly when Feste complies with the tonally complex art song,
'Come away, come away, death'. Desdemona's song of 'Willow',
learned from her mother's maid Barbary, dignifies this women's tradition as her preparation for death. As Eve Sanders has ably argued,
Ophelia's use of ballads and old tales frees her for a time from the
tyranny of a print culture molding her as an 'icon of piety' (70);
within *Hamlet*, however, hers is the space of madness and death.

The uses of old wives' tales in these works by canonical authors
suggests the continuing power of this experience, rendered all the
more powerful by the cultural pressures to forget it. Elizabeth Mazzola has argued for the 'afterlife for abandoned symbols' of the

Roman Catholic church within Protestant England by observing that a deliberate forgetting entails an even stronger awareness of what must be forgotten.[29] This argument applies at least as strongly to old wives' tales. The denigration implicit within the phrase 'old wives' tales' indicates a cultural rhetoric that was never entirely successful. The memory of these tales, and even more, the memory of the once cherished 'mumping beldams' who told them, challenged dominant ideologies of class as well as of gender. This challenge offered an opportunity to engage – or to refuse to engage – in a deep synthesis of highly disparate modes of thinking and feeling. Through their rich and multivalent afterlives, these tales may well have contributed to the unusual outpouring of literary masterpieces of this period.

Notes

1. Thomas Nashe, 'The Terrors of the Night', *Works of Thomas Nashe,* ed. Ronald B. McKerrow (Oxford: Blackwell, 1966), I, 369.

2. Adam Fox, *Oral and Literate Culture in England 1500–1700* (Oxford: Clarendon P, 2000), 192. Fox's insight reinforces an earlier representation by the social historian Burke, *Popular Culture in Early Modern Europe* (New York: New York University Press, 1978), 28, describing educated males as 'amphibious, bicultural and also bilingual', knowledgeable in popular traditions regarded as 'play', as well as in 'great' or high-status traditions regarded as 'serious.'

3. Fox 177; Helen Hackett, *Women and Romance Fiction in the English Renaissance* (Cambridge: Cambridge University Press, 2000), 15–6 also describes the contempt for 'fantastic stories' associated with women as exemplifying a 'low' oral culture in the mapping of binaries configuring patriarchal culture. For extensive and able discussions of ideologies structuring female literacy, see Margaret Ferguson, *Female Literacies and Ideologies of Empire: Stories from England and France, 1400–1690,* forthcoming.

4. Marina Warner, *From the Beast to the Blonde: On Fairy Stories and Their Tellers* (New York: Farrer, Straus and Giroux, 1994), 24 describes 'an airy suspension bridge, swinging slightly under different breezes of opinion and economy, between the learned, literary and print culture in which famous fairy tales have come down to us, and the oral, illiterate, people's culture of the veillee, and on this bridge traffic moves in both directions.' This essay is generally indebted to Warner's discussion of old wives' tales (12–65) and *passim.* See also Roger Chartier, 'The *Bibliotheque bleue* and Popular Reading', in *Cultural Uses of Print in Early Modern France,* trans. Lydia Cochrane (Princeton: Princeton University Press, 1987), 240–64.

5. Anthony Fletcher, *Gender, Sex, and Subordination in England, 1500–1800* (New Haven: Yale University Press, 1995), 299.

6. Walter Ong, 'Latin Language Study as a Renaissance Puberty Rite', *Studies in Philology* 56 (1959), 103–24; Fletcher 87, 297–321; Keith Thomas, *Rule and Misrule in the Schools*

of Early Modern England (Reading: for the University of Reading, 1976), 8 on 'instinctual renunciation'; T.W. Baldwin, *William Shakspere's Small Latine and Lesse Greeke* (Urbana: University of Illinois Press, 1944), I,561; William Kerrigan, 'The Articulation of the Ego in the English Renaissance' in *The Literary Freud,* ed. Joseph Smith (New Haven: Yale University Press, 1980); Jonathan Goldberg, *Writing Matter: From the Hands of the English Renaissance* (Stanford: Stanford University Press, 1990), 42–8, 116; Eve Rachele Sanders, *Gender and Literacy on Stage in Early Modern England* (Cambridge: Cambridge University Press, 1998), 14–30; Anthony Grafton and Lisa Jardine, *From Humanism to the Humanities: Education and the Liberal Arts in Fifteenth-and Sixteenth-Century Europe* (Cambridge: Harvard University Press, 1986); Mary Thomas Crane, *Framing Authority: Sayings, Self, and Society in Sixteenth Century England* (Princeton: Princeton University Press, 1993); Coppelia Kahn, *Roman Shakespeare* (New York: Routledge, 1997), 20 explores how 'humanism made Romanness as manly virtue a widely known ideal of masculinity.' Rebecca Bushnell, *A Culture of Teaching: Early Modern Humanism in Theory and Practice* (Ithaca: Cornell University Press, 1996), 23–72 discusses cultural ambivalence towards the disciplinary processes of the schoolroom (23–72). In Richard Halpern, *Poetics of Primitive Accumulation* (Ithaca: Cornell University Press, 1991) a competing view of humanist restraint does not invalidate the general purpose to instill discipline (26–9; but see also 35–6).

7.   Bruce Smith, *Homosexual Desire in Shakespeare's England* (Chicago: University of Chicago Press, 1991), 79–115; Alan Stewart, '"Traitors to boyes buttockes": the Erotics of Humanist Education' in *Close Readers: Humanism and Sodomy in Early Modern England* (Princeton: Princeton University Press, 1997), 84–121. Wendy Wall, '"Household Stuff': The Sexual Politics of Domesticity and the Adventof English Comedy,' *ELH* 65 (1998), 5 notes the function of humanist education 'to correct the faults inculcated in the female and vernacular world of childhood.' Louis Montrose, *The Purpose of Playing: Shakespeare and the Cultural Politics of the Elizabethan Theatre* (Chicago: University of Chicago Press, 1996), 125 ably discusses the passage of boys from the 'world of mothers and nurses into the world of fathers and masters.'

8.   Frederic Jameson, 'On Cultural Studies,' *Social Text* 34 (1993), 33.

9.   Desiderius Erasmus, *De pueris statim ac liberaliter instituendis* (1529); quoted from William Harrison Woodward, *Desiderius Erasmus concerning the Aim and Method Of Education* (Cambridge: Cambridge University Press, 1904), 214.

10.   Gabriel Harvey, 'Three Proper and wittie, familiar letters' in Edmund Spenser, *Poetical Works,* ed. J.C.Smith and E.de Selincourt (1912; Oxford: Oxford University Press, 1991), 628.

11.   MS quoted Fox,189.

12.   Reginald Scot, *The Discovery of Witchcraft* (1584) (Carbondale: Southern Illinois University Press, 1964), VII, xv, 139. It is possible that this inclusion of satyrs, pans, fauns, tritons and centaurs suggests maids appropriated classical figures into the tales they told to Scot as a child. If productive exchanges between literate and oral cultures took place in his early household, they did not change Scot's contempt for the lot of them. For Scot, it was not the origin of the tales that mattered, but their mode of transmission. Whatever the cultural capital of their content, tales told by his mother's maids were simply women's stories, designed to keep children such as his earlier self in subjection through fear. From an historical perspective, of course, Scot was correct. Centaurs and fauns were in fact the creatures of old wives' tales of a much earlier age; and female caretakers of ancient Greece and Rome apparently used tales to terrify, as well as to comfort, the children in their care, as pointed out

eloquently by Diane Purkiss, *At the Bottom of the Garden: A Dark History of Fairies, Hobgoblins, and other Troublesome Things* (New York: New York University Press, 2000), 11–36. Warner is also most informative on the old wives' tales of ancient Greece and Rome. But this was hardly the point of Scot's diatribe.

13. Ben Jonson, *Works,* ed. C.H. Hereford and Percy and Evelyn Simpson (Oxford: Clarendon, 1941), VII, 343.

14. Another example is presented in Wall's excellent discussion of the way in which *Gammer Gurton's Needle* erodes the differences between domestic and learned spheres to create 'a national effect' linked 'to the world of women' (30). Julia Kristeva, *Powers of Horror: An Essay on Abjection,* trans. Leon S. Roudiez (New York: Columbia University Press, 1982), 75 posits a connection between creativity and dominant females of childhood:

> Writing causes the subject who ventures in it to confront an archaic authority, on the nether side of the proper Name. The maternal connotations of this authority have never escaped great writers.

15. T.W. Craik, *The Tudor Interlude: Stage, Costume, and Acting* (Leicester: Leicester University Press, 1967), 34, see also 29, speculates that Wager's play was written to be acted by boy actors as well as before an audience of boys, as a 'schoolboy performance.' All quotations from Wager's play will be taken from W. Wager, *The Longer Thou Livest and Enough Is as Good as a Feast,* ed. R. Mark Benbow, Regents Renaissance Drama (Lincoln: University of Nebraska Press, 1967).

16. In his discussion of *TLTL* with others as pedagogical plays designed to promote a 'humanist educational vision' (49), Kent Cartwright, *Theatre and Humanism* (Cambridge: Cambridge Univeristy Press, 1999), 55 notes the attempt to portray humanist knowledge as divine grace, so that 'the story of learning repeats the story of redemption.' David Bevington, *From Mankind to Marlowe* (Cambridge: Harvard University Press 1962), 163–4 describes Moros as presenting a 'fearful example' for auditors, who are supposed to 'recognize and scorn their own depraved instincts.' Bevington, 152, links the portrayal of characters who are 'irreparably damned' to the influence of Calvinism in Reformation England.

17. These separate tales are described well by Frank S. Hook, editor of George Peele, 'The Old Wives Tale' in *The Dramatic Works of George Peele* (New Haven: Yale University Press, 1970), 319–339, who notes that except for their appearance in Peele's play, several tales are not extant before the eighteenth century (319). See also Patricia Binnie, ed. *George Peele: the Old Wives Tale,* Revels Plays (Baltimore: Johns Hopkins University Press, 1980), 20–24, and John D. Cox, 'Homely Matter and Multiple Plots in Peele's *Old Wives Tale*', *Texas Studies in Literature and Language* 20.3 (1978), 330–346, who ably sets out the formal relationships between the plots. A.R.Braunmuller, *George Peele* (Boston: Twayne, 1983), 57–62 discusses folkloric elements. All quotations from Peele's play will be taken from Hook's edition.

18. Most critics discuss the audience for this play. Mary G. Free, 'Audience within Audience in *The Old Wives Tale*', *Renaissance Papers, 1983* (Southeastern Renaissance Conference, 1984), 55 describes Peele as sustaining a 'double view' by addressing the onstage pages and the larger audience simultaneously. Cox, 344, perceives 'Madge's visitors as patronizing of her tale as the play's critics' in spite of the sophisticated patterning of the plot. Jackson Cope, 'Peele's *Old Wives Tale*: Folk Stuff into Ritual Form', *ELH* 49 (1982), 327 claims that 'the ultimate audience was Peele's view of a timeless viewer.'

19. This hybridity or double perspective may explain the sharply divided views within the scholarship. Hook traces the 'cleavage absolute' of two critical perspectives, one rep-

resenting the play 'as a sophisticated juxtaposition of romance and realism for the purpose
of satire' and the other as 'a childlike retelling of old tales' (359). More recently, Kevin
Donovan, 'Recent Studies in George Peele', *English Literary Renaissance* 23.1 (1993), 213
has summarized the 'longstanding debate over the tone of the play – whether or not the
romantic and folkloric elements are used satirically.'

20.   Binnie 37.

21.   See, for example, Hackett 15–6.

22.   Braunmuller, 62, explains this disjunction of frame and main plot as a 'combination
of high art and simplicity' in terms of 'Elizabethan courtly values'; Susan T. Viguers, 'The
Hearth and the Cell: Art in *Old Wives Tale*,' *SEL* 21 (1981), 209–11 breaks down the distinction between the frame and the play by claiming various plots as belonging to Madge,
whose art is poised against the sinister sorceries of Sacrapant.

23.   Steven C. Young, *The Frame Structure in Tudor and Stuart Drama,* Salzburg Studies in English Literature (Salzburg: Institut fur Englische Sprache und literatur, 1974), 71–3.

24.   Margaret Dean-Smith, 'The Ominous Wood' in *The Witch Figure: Folklore Essays
by a group of scholars in England honoring the 75th birthday of Katharine M. Briggs,* ed.
Venetia Newall (London: Routledge & Kegan Paul, 1973), 54.

25.   Cox interprets this quoted line as implying sexual inadequacy (340). W.W.Greg, ed.,
George Peele, *Old Wives Tale 1595.* Malone Society Reprint (Oxford: Oxford University
Press, 1909), vi notes that among the "burlesque hexameters' of Huanebango, lines 813–4
are quoted directly from Harvey's *Encomium Lauri*, while ll. 801–2 consist of 'tags' from
Stanyhurst's translation of the *Aeneid* (1582). The critical literature identifying Huanebango
with Harvey is thoroughly summarized by Hook 309–19 who, however, argues that he is a
'stock figure adapted from the ruffler tradition' rather than 'personal satire' (319). See also
B.W.Ball, 'George Peele's Huanebango: a Caricature of Gabriel Harvey', *Renaissance
Papers 1968* (Southeastern Renaissance Conference, 1969), 29–39. Muriel Bradbrook,
'Peele's *Old Wives' Tale*: A Play of Enchantment' in *Shakespeare'sContemporaries*, ed. Max
Bluestone and Norman Rabkin (Englewood Cliffs: Prentice-Hall, 1970), 23–41associates
Huanebango with the Turkish slashers of mummer plays.

26.   The role of charity or generosity in this play is noted by Cox (336) and Braunuller
(57,59). Bradbrook represents this charity as a desired outcome of a possible performance by
players from Queen's Company down on their luck, acting this play before country folk.

27.   Philip Sidney, *Countess of Pembroke's Arcadia,* ed. Maurice Evans (New York: Penguin, 1977), 311.

28.   Mary Ellen Lamb, 'Engendering the Narrative Act: Old Wives' Tales in *The Winter's
Tale, Macbeth* and *The Tempest,*' *Criticism* 40.4 (1998), 537–542. I have developed a similar argument for *Midsummer Night's Dream* in 'Taken by the Fairies: Fairy Practices and the
Production of Culture in *A Midsummer Night's Dream,*' *Shakespeare Quarterly* 51.3 (2000)
277–312; for Spenser in 'Gloriana, Acrasia, and the House of Busyrane: Gendered Fictions
and the *Faerie Queen* as Fairy Tale,' in *World-Making Spenser: Essays on the Faerie Queene
and Early Modern Culture,* ed. Patrick Cheney and Lauren Silberman (Lexington: University of Kentucky Press, 2000), 81–100; and for Sidney's *Apology* in 'Apologizing for
Pleasure in Sidney's *Apology for Poetry,*' *Criticism.* 36.4 (1994): 499–520.

29.   Elizabeth Mazzola, *The Pathology of the English Renaissance: Sacred Remains
and Holy Ghosts* (Leiden: Brill, 1998), 1, 34.

[11]

"Soft, Who Have We Here?": The Dramatic Technique of The Old Wives Tale

JOAN C. MARX

I N RECENT YEARS critics have celebrated the folk narrative of *The Old Wives Tale*. In a country where many folktales of magic and "faierie" disappeared before nineteenth-century collectors could find them, Peele's play offers some of the earliest English evidence of these oral folk traditions,[1] and commentators have suggested that modern audiences "succumb to . . . [the play's] fairy-like atmosphere" and enjoy the "naïve" spell of old and powerful stories: of a young man compelled to assume a bear's form at night, of Golden Heads who rise from a well to reward two daughters, one selfish, the other kind; and of a hero who generously gives all he owns for a stranger's burial and is then guided by a magic helper.[2]

---

1. Katharine M. Briggs, Introduction to *A Dictionary of British Folk-Tales in the English Language* (Bloomington, Ind., 1971), I, A, 4.

2. A. K. McIlwraith, ed., *Five Elizabethan* Comedies (Oxford, 1934), p. xiii; and Frank Hook, ed., *The Old Wives Tale* by George Peele, in *The Life and Works of George Peele*, ed. Charles T. Prouty (New Haven, Conn., 1970), III, 365–366. See also Gwenan Jones, "The Intention of Peele's 'Old Wives' Tale,'" *Aberystwyth Studies*, VII (1925), 79–93; Thorleif Larsen, "'The Old Wives' Tale' by George Peele," *Transactions of the Royal Society of Canada*, Ser. 3, XXIX, sec. 2 (1935), 157–170; and M. C. Bradbrook, "Peele's *The Old Wives Tale*," ES, XLIII (1962), 323–330. The narratives incorporate the tale types of "The Kind and Unkind Girls" and "The Grateful Dead" and Motif D621.1.1, "Man by day, animal by night." Hook points out these folktale types and motifs (pp. 324–335) which have been classified by Antii Aarne and Stith Thompson in *The Types of the Folk-Tale*, 2d rev. ed. (Helsinki, 1961), and by Stith Thompson in *Motif-Index of Folk-Literature*, rev. ed. (Bloomington, Ind., 1955).

118   JOAN C. MARX

But one of the most remarkable qualities of this "pleasant, conceited Comedie," as its publisher called it, has been its ability to evoke another major and quite different critical view, one dominant in the first half of this century and still reappearing. In 1903 F. B. Gummere suggested that the play is "a saucy challenge of romance, where art turns, however timidly, upon itself."[3] The frame characters and mockery of Huanebango's boasts—his battles against "brasen gates, inchanted towers, . . . thunder and lightning"—make the play a remarkable predecessor to *The Knight of the Burning Pestle*: it is a gay spoof, a parody of romance.

I suggest that both of these perceptions, in some measure, are true. One group describes the play's genre as folktale and celebrates its enchantment, the audience's relaxation into "the cloudy fabric of a dream,"[4] the second sees the play as parody, focused on romance, and enjoys its sauciness and comic spirit. But each of these received critical views assumes that the play consists of only one genre. I propose instead that *The Old Wives Tale* is a comedy composed of several genres: folktale, romance, folk ritual, and farce.[5] Each of the genres appears in "straight," unparodied form,[6] and is juxtaposed with the others; no one of them rules the entire play. Instead, the play's extraordinary dramatic technique consists in slipping suddenly

3. F. B. Gummere, ed., *The Old Wives Tale* in *Representative English Comedies*, ed. C. M. Gayley (New York, 1903), I, 346. Others include: Felix Schelling, *Elizabethan Drama 1558–1642* (Boston, 1908), I, 136; G. P. Baker, "The Plays of the University Wits," *CHEL* (1910), V, 145–147; C. F. Tucker Brooke, *The Tudor Drama* (Boston, 1911), p. 242; Leonard R. N. Ashley, *George Peele* (New York, 1970), pp. 127 ff; John Doebler, "The Tone of George Peele's *The Old Wives Tale*," *ES*, LIII (1972), 412–421.

4. Janet Spens's image of a dream for *The Old Wives Tale* appears in *Elizabethan Drama* (London, 1922), pp. 53–54, and recurs in David H. Horne, Introduction to *The Life and Works of George Peele*, ed. Prouty, I, 90, and Bradbrook, p. 329.

5. It is one form of "threshold work," to use the terms of Gary Saul Morson, one where "mutually exclusive sets of conventions govern a work," and where "generic incompatibility" is created by "embedding or juxtaposing sections of radically heterogeneous material. The generic conventions governing individual sections may be clear, but the laws of their combination are not." "Threshold Art," in *The Boundaries of Genre: Doestoevsky's Diary of a Writer and the Traditions of Literary Utopia* (Austin, Tex., Forthcoming, 1981).

6. Huanebango's parody is an exception which will be discussed.

The Dramatic Technique of The Old Wives Tale   119

from one genre to another.[7] Such unexpected shifts create a mixture of surprise and daring—a comic sauciness—closely resembling, though differing from, the effect of parody.

If we consider the song of the Golden Head, for example, its chant creates the conventional spell of folktale. The magic head which rises from a well is a folk motif, part of a folktale type, "The Heads in the Well,"[8] and the song evokes folktale's style and mood:

> Gently dip, but not too deepe,
> For feare you make the golden beard to weepe,
> Faire maiden white and red,
> Stroke me smoothe, and combe my head,
> And thou shalt have some cockell bread.[9]

The chant addresses the maiden with the familiar "white and red," and the song's short rhythms, full and half rhymes, recur in the lulling insistence of a magic charm.[10] Wooing and demanding in the same moment, the Head asks for certain gestures from the girl—"stroke me smoothe," "dip, but not too deepe"—for the virile, literally disembodied, golden beard. Like the demands of the frog who must be taken up and placed by the girl's plate or laid on her pillow, these requests are imbued with a powerful yet unacknowledged sexuality, one that often marks the gestures required of maidens by the animals and monsters of folktale.[11]

The same kind of straight, unparodied rendering of generic convention appears at the moment the "wandring knight," Eumenides, rescues the princess and sues for her hand. Yet the genre embodied is not folktale but romance.

---

7. I will stress the "tale," but its generic shifts are prepared for by the mild stylistic shifts of the Induction, from "*O coelum! O terra! O maria!*" to "Hearke this is Ball my dogge," from "Cupid hath led our yong master to the faire Lady and she is the only Saint that he hath sworne to serve" to "wee commit him to his wench."

8. "The Heads in the Well" is a subtype of "The Kind and Unkind Girls"; see Warren E. Roberts, *The Tale of the Kind and the Unkind Girls* (Berlin, 1958).

9. *The Old Wives Tale*, ed. Frank Hook; all following references will be to this edition.

10. This recalls Madge's "white as snowe, and as redd as bloud," Motif Z65.1.

11. Bruno Bettelheim suggests this sexuality in Grimm's "The Frog-King" and other fairytales, in *The Uses of Enchantment* (New York, 1976), pp. 277 ff.

120   JOAN C. MARX

> Thou fairest flower of these westerne parts:
> Whose beautie so reflecteth in my sight,
> As doth a Christall mirror in the sonne:
> For thy sweet sake I have crost the frosen Rhine,
> Leaving faire Po, I saild up Danuby . . .[12]
>
>   (ll. 850–854)

The knight can express the maiden's beauty in a self-conscious rhetoric of "Christall mirror" and "fairest flower," and her "sweet" self focuses his vision and quest.[13] His stance is individual and heroic, and he sails a far-ranging, exotic, and yet a known world, one of "Po" and "Danuby."[14] He is not a careful walker in the fields of folk magic, bending to the rhythmic instructions of old men and singing Heads, traveling in a dark, unmapped territory to find a well of the "water of life."

But each such conventional moment in the play is continually being cut short; one mood, one range of style suddenly changes to another. The pleasure at abruptly arriving in new territory is akin to the comic liberation described by Freud; it is a burst of unexpected freedom, a sudden release from the expected tones and gestures—the conventional restraints—of a genre.

The change in mood may be as great and the translation of terms as neat as Zantippa's response to the Golden Head. In the folktale action of "the Kind and Unkind Girls" the shrewish daughter, seeking a husband, approaches the magic well with her pitcher; as she nears, the Golden Head rises and chants, "Stroke me smoothe, and combe my head, / And thou shalt have some cockell bread."[15] Zantippa draws back, cries, "Cockell callest thou it boy, faith ile give you cockell bread," and delivers the Head a blow with the pitcher. Both the rude "boy" and rough blow go much

---

12. The last two lines as well as ll. 855–856 are imitated from Robert Greene's *Orlando Furioso* (Hook, pp. 307, 442).

13. Eugène Vinaver describes the rise of a portrayal of "feeling" in medieval romance, *The Rise of Romance* (Oxford, 1971), p. 26; Erich Auerbach explores the knight's concentration of his quest on "feats of arms, and love" in *Mimesis* (Princeton, N.J., 1953), p. 140.

14. R. W. Southern discusses the knight's individual stance in *Making of the Middle Ages*, p. 244, cited by Vinaver, p. 2; this is the landscape of Italian rather than medieval romance, as the latter is described by Auerbach, pp. 128–129.

15. Roberts describes the conventional action, p. 119.

The Dramatic Technique of The Old Wives Tale   121

beyond the sister's conventional unkindness; in addition Zantippa is promising a comic transformation of the love charm of the Golden Head, its offered "cockell bread." These loaves had a crust which rose in sexually suggestive swells; Zantippa's "cockell bread" will be the bumps she can raise on the enchanted Head. [16] Funny, crude, and disrespectful, her action breaks the spell of folk magic. But folktale and folk magic are no more travestied by their disappearance and the sudden advent of farce than romance is satirized at the moment Sacrapant calls his spirits. Having shown himself a romance enchanter by falling in love with and courting a beautiful woman, idealizing her power in Renaissance terms ("See where she coms from whence my sorrows grow"), [17] Sacrapant offers his captive mistress whatever she desires. But when he turns to fulfill her request, his summons is a folktale charm.

> Spred table spred;
> Meat, drinke and bred

16. It seems clear from the context that "cockell bread" had some associations with marriage, love, or sexuality, but its range of associations during the Renaissance is not known. We can assume that it looked like the *pain coquillé* of the French, with swellings in the crust, described by Paul Robert, "coquiller," in *Dictionnaire alphabétique et analogique*, 6 vols. (Paris, 1951). Aubrey's comment of 1697, usually cited to explain the bread, describes young maids drawing up their skirts and rocking back and forth, singing of the "moulding of Cockle-bread." He also refers to an early medieval text describing bread used as a love charm and made while a woman exposed her naked buttocks; see William J. Thoms. ed., *Anecdotes and Traditions* (London, 1839), pp. 94–95. The association of buttocks with the bread is easy to make, but it is not evident that "moulding cockle-bread" is the bread's only or major association. During the fifteenth century such bread was being sold by French bakers and regulated in price; in the sixteenth, "coquillé" is used to describe an attractive stomach; see Emile Littré, "coquiller," in *Dictionnaire de la langue française*, 7 vols. (Paris, 1956). Cake and bread, including *gateaux phalliques*, were still being used symbolically during courtship in France, in recent years; see Arnold van Gennep, *Manuel de Folklore français Contemporain* (Paris, 1946), vol. I, pt. 1, pp. 265, 275. I would tentatively suggest that the reference is not obscene. Cockell bread is again included in the Head's second song, again an incantation, but this time it occurs within, rather than at the end of the chant; a lewd reference here would break the spell very awkwardly.

17. Folktale's enchanters may, however, have an implicit sexual bond with their princesses, as in "Beauty of the World," in *West Irish Folk-Tales and Romances*, ed. and trans. William Larminie (London, 1893), pp. 155–167.

122   JOAN C. MARX

> Ever may I have,
> What I ever crave:
> When I am spred,
> For meate for my black cock,
> And meate for my red.
>
> (ll. 367–73)

This is no vision of heaven or demons, but a spell with country roosters, the same call for a small feast in the fields that appears in Grimm's folktale of "The Wishing-Table, the Gold-Ass, and the Cudgel in the Sack." [18]

Like parody, this technique creates a gay mood and an awareness of form. But if the familiar image of parody is that of a distorted mirror, offering an exaggerated view of something outside the work itself—the true, substantial figure—then this play is more like several clowns gesturing at each other. [19] Each bit has its own life and substance, and the true is followed by "something else" rather than an insubstantial reflection of itself. What was there goes back in the well and is replaced by the new; the switch may cause a sense of loss, but the major sensation it produces is a mixture of surprise and daring, a sense of "Soft, who have we here?" to be asked by the audience as well as the Pages. [20]

Herbert Goldstone has been one critic to resist classifying the play as either naïve folktale or romance parody; yet for him these shifts serve such unlikely ends as rendering the characters more humane and highly artificial genres, such as folktale, more believable. [21] Instead the play has the slip and whirl of a fast carnival ride or the funny and graceful ice skating of the vaudeville comic, Ben Blue; an audience poised on the tip of romance, "Berecynthia, let us in . . . / And heare the Nightingale," suddenly whips into the sturdy "Now for a husband, house and home" (ll. 609–611).

---

18. Sylvia Lyons-Render cites the motif, the "magic table supplies food and drink" (D1472.1.7), in "Folk Motifs in George Peele's *The Old Wives Tale, TFSB,* XXVI (1960), 62–71.

19. See, for example, "Burlesque and parody," in M. H. Abrams's *A Glossary of Literary Terms* (New York, 1957).

20. Ll. 140, 533, 539, Madge's variant (l. 129), and Sacrapant's question (l. 393).

21. Herbert Goldstone, "Interplay in Peele's *The Old Wives Tale,*" *Boston Univ. Studies in English,* IV (1960), 205 ff.

The Dramatic Technique of The Old Wives Tale   123

These effects may feel more "real"; critics from Gummere onward have talked about "realism in diction" and its undercutting of romance.[22] Yet the change may be to a homelier but equally artificial style. When the Two Brothers enter, the formal rhetoric of their lament heightens their apostrophe to the power of fortune above, "O fortune cruell, cruell and unkind, / Unkind in that we cannot find our sister," and when Erestus appears, his short, heavy rhythms and earthbound concerns, "Hips and Hawes, and stickes and strawes, and thinges that I gather on the ground my sonne," create a small tumble from romance to folktale, one made more humorous by the Brothers' new attention to food, "Hips and Hawes, and stickes and strawes, why is that all your foode father?" But the new style is equally patterned, equally artificial.

The shift will also consist in a change of attitude as much as verbal style. When Huanebango courts Zantippa at the well of the water of life, theirs is a courtship molded by folktale justice; the beautiful "unkind" shrew has been awarded the deaf man who can appreciate her beauty but not her tongue. Yet her acceptance suddenly glimpses both a cynicism and a mutability foreign to folktale. She shrugs, "Lobb be your comfort, and Cuckold bee your destenie: Heare you sir; and if you will have us, you had best say so betime." The change in diction is less marked than the new attitude; instead of the folktale finality "they lived together in peace and contentment" or "they quarrelled for the rest of their lives," her resignation to a fool and "Cuckold" envisions compromise and an unsettled life, a future with other men.

To register the necessary surprise at such changes, Peele's audience would have needed a knowledge of the play's genres and boundaries, an awareness they would in fact have possessed even as they jostled into seats or standing room.[23] For such an awareness of each of the play's generic groups would have been awakened by a wide variety of experiences. The play does not depend on an acquaintance with one specific work in a given genre, on Greene's *Orlando Furioso* or "The Wal at the Warld's End," but

---

22. Gummere, p. 341.

23. An audience, like Guillén's writer beginning to compose, would have *a priori* notions of genre; see Claudio Guillén, *Literature as System* (Princeton, N.J., 1971), pp. 125–128.

124   JOAN C. MARX

merely on an exposure to some members of each general group: to *Olyver of Castylle* or *Guy of Warwick*, to their own village's Plough Monday or a mother's report of it, to the clown's jigs at The Theatre or *A Hundred Merry Tales*, to "The Robber Bridegroom" or "Snow-White and Rose-Red," told by an uncle or nurse.[24] Such experience of the members of a generic group would in turn create an awareness of the group's characteristics and its boundary, that limit which demarcates its characteristics and excludes others.[25] (This does not mean that there is a prescribed list of characteristics which marks every member of a generic group, for characteristics are shared in a partial way. Among three folktales, for example, the first and second might share talking animals, the second and third, a stepdaughter's quest. But even with such sharing, there is a family grouping of characteristics and a boundary to the group.)[26] My imagined Elizabethan in Peele's audience could expect certain gestures and styles of a particular genre and know that others are excluded: introspection is not part of folktale.

Tilting the play, readying it for shifts across these generic boundaries, are the small surprises within the genres. Conventional, expected gestures are frequently skewed, and create in turn a constant precariousness. There may be too many motifs—Erestus is transformed to an old-man *and* a bear; or a sequence of motifs is reversed—Celanta finds her husband before she encounters the magic donor, the Golden Head; or what is simply "not done" is done—Erestus thanks Lampriscus for his quite apropos gift, "Thankes neighbor, . . . Honny is alwaies welcome to the Beare," and in

24. Briggs gives two English analogies to Peele's "Kind and Unkind Girls": "The Wal at the Warld's End" and "Three Gold Heads." *Olyver of Castylle* was published in English in 1518 and known in 1575; see "*The Hystorye of Olyver of Castylle*," ed. Gail Orgelfinger, (Ph.D. dissertation, University of Chicago, 1978), pp. 83, 108. (I have modernized the "v".) Charles Baskervill describes the farce plots of the jigs, used as afterpieces and found in the jestbooks, in *The Elizabethan Jig* (Chicago, 1929), pp. 95, 233, and *passim*. "The Robber Bridegroom" is referred to in *Much Ado about Nothing*, I.i.216; "Snow-White and Rose-Red" seems to lie behind this play (Briggs, I, A, 4).

25. E. D. Hirsch describes the generic group as one form of "type," in *Validity in Interpretation* (New Haven, Conn., 1967); for "type," see pp. 64 and Appendix III.A, for "genre," see pp. 71 ff., 114–115.

26. As Robert C. Elliott points out in "The Definition of Satire," the boundary is a "*decision*" rather than a "*factual*" question (quoted by Guillén, pp. 130–131).

The Dramatic Technique of The Old Wives Tale   125

that second seems to bring his nighttime transformation into daylight, to casually acknowledge a dark, binding enchantment as an alternative image of himself.[27]

The most colorful and striking examples of such shifts within scenes may well be the Huanebango scenes: his two encounters of Erestus and Sacrapant and his courtship of Zantippa at the well. Their vividness is due partly to Huanebango's exaggeration as a figure of romance, partly to the triple variety of genres—romance, farce, and folktale—rapidly exchanged.

The mighty Juan y Bango is an apparent exception to the general notion that the play's technique lies in generic shifts rather than parody.[28] With his soaring, hollow boasts, his combat with "thunder and lightning" and search for peerless "Beautie," he clearly undercuts the assumptions of romance, its individual heroism and quests, and parodies the genre. Yet as a comic braggart, Huanebango is only weakly parodic. If *he* frames the objections to romance's assumptions, then romance, rather than being laughed at, is reasserted.[29] Analogously, when the braggart soldier, Sir Tophas, worships his hag in Lyly's *Endimion*, he deflects ridicule from the hero's adoration of Cynthia. In the end, even as a figure of parody, Huanebango serves the play's generic shifts: essentially he functions as a figure of romance, his parody making him only a more extravagant, colorful representative.[30] Eumenides, for example, could replace Huanebango at the well. Zantippa's replies would seem cruder, her suitor less comic and more vulnerable, but the basic scheme would remain: a romance knight courting "peerelesse" Beauty would still kneel before a folktale girl seeking "husband, house and home." But since Huanebango is exaggerated, he makes the distance between genres, e.g., between

27. Most folktale animals cannot mention their enchantments; see, for example, Grimm's "The Frog Prince" and "The Golden Bird." Sarah Clapp notes a number of such changes in "Peele's Use of Folk-Lore in *The Old Wives' Tale*," *Univ. of Texas Studies in English*, VI (1926), pp. 146–156.

28. Bradbrook gives his name its Spanish form, p. 328.

29. William Empson points out that a play of "heroic swashbucklers" will include "a comic cowardly swashbuckler" in order to keep the audience from mocking the heroes, *Some Versions of Pastoral* (Norfolk, Conn., n.d.), p. 30.

30. As John Felstiner says, "because all art entails some exaggeration of neutral fact, caricature and parody exemplify the larger genres they fall within," *The Lies of Art* (New York, 1972), p. 136.

romance and folktale—the territory sped over, as it were—greater and more apparent, more vivid and comic. He also helps romance accommodate farce. For the two genres sit oddly together; the cynicism, coarseness, and hunger for physical things in farce are often romance's direct enemies.[31] But as a comic extreme of romance, Huanebango can tolerate farce's vulgarity and shoves. Erestus's aside about Huan's mistress, "Faire inough, and farre inough from thy fingering sonne," is crude as it is, but its humor when addressed to the grand Huanebango, lauding an "earthly Goddesse," would be lost if directed at Eumenides.

The most remarkable achievement of these scenes is their coherence. Even with swift, broad shifts, from the exaggeration of romance on the one hand to farce on the other, there is no muddle; the genres remain clear, the slips evident. The quick switches in Booby's roles form one of the most striking instances. When Huanebango first enters with Booby, for example, the knight is manifestly a braggart soldier, accompanied like Lyly's Sir Tophas by a companion and subordinate. Like Epiton, Sir Tophas's page, Booby furnishes his knight with "straight lines" which make him reveal his foolishness.

> BOOBY
> Doo you heare sir; had not you a Cosen, that was called Gustecerydis?
> HUANEBANGO
> Indeede I had a Cosen, that somtime followed the Court infortunately, and his name Bustegustecerydis.
> BOOBY
> O Lord I know him well: hee is the knight of the neates feete.

31. Anthony Caputi suggests that among the essential qualities of "vulgar comedy" are its emphasis on physicality and its coarseness (both a "coarseness of grain in the image" presented and a "relatively simple and uncomplicated" response from the beholder), in *Buffo* (Detroit, 1978), pp. 175–185. An example of the strikingly different viewpoints of romance and farce toward the same action is the dwarf's awakening of a household as a young knight leaves a girl's bedroom in *Amadis of Gaul*. This is the stuff of farce, but the dwarf is seen as contemptible; trans. Edwin B. Place and Herbert C. Behn (Lexington, Ky., 1974), Book I, chap. 12, pp. 132–135. The conflict of the two when juxtaposed is illustrated by Delia's magic wishes (e.g., for "the veriest knave in all Spaine"); set against romance they seem low and unworthy of her. This is one shift in the play which fails.

The Dramatic Technique of The Old Wives Tale   127

HUANEBANGO
O he lov'd no Capon better, he hath oftentimes deceived his boy
of his dinner, that was his fault, good Bustegustecerydis.

(ll. 291–296)

Yet the moment before, Booby appeared not as a petite Epiton, a younger, cleverer version of Sir Tophas, one who shares his knight's assumptions that great deeds, love, wit, and rhetoric are important, but as a simple, coarse "countriman," leagues away from Huanebango's aspirations, someone who, when he heard of adventures with "thunder and lightning" and the search for "Beautie," replied, "Nowe sir if it bee no more but running through a little lightning and thunder, and riddle me riddle me whats this, Ile have the wench from the Conjurer if he were ten Conjurers." At one minute, in Epiton's style, Booby is parrying false Latin with the knight; in the next he is complaining—simple, good-natured lout that he is—that he cannot understand phrases like "foyson of the earth." (With hindsight Booby may be said to shift between Moth and Dull of *Love's Labor's Lost*.) In addition to these shifts, by the end of the scene Erestus has asked the knight to share his food, a conventional folktale test.[32] Huan fails, and in his place, Booby, the generous country lad, wins. In the next second, the new folktale hero calls good-bye, quits Erestus and his novel role, and runs to catch his commander, the grandiloquent Huanebango. The shifts are dizzying yet clear.

M. C. Bradbrook has suggested that *The Old Wives Tale* should be considered a "medley play," one whose structure consists only in cramming in as many "brief sequences, with as much scenic variety and multiplication of characters" as possible.[33] But what distinguishes Peele's play from her two examples, the *Rare Triumphs of Love and Fortune* and *The Cobler's Prophecy*, and serves to argue the artful, rather than hotchpotch, nature of *The Old Wives Tale*, is the fact that the other plays make no attempt to contrast different styles or highlight strange meetings. *Love and Fortune* does not display the same variety of characters as *The Old Wives Tale*, but *The Cobler's Prophecy* does; it includes such characters in its cast

32. Food must be given everyone on journey, Motif C675.
33. Bradbrook, p. 326.

128   JOAN C. MARX

as: Mercury, Gray Friar, Folly, Cobler's Wife, and Charon.[34] Yet these
characters move in a gray, common air. Almost anyone could come onstage, and almost anyone does, but the meeting of the Souldier and the
Muses, for example, is marked only by the momentary, coy surprise of the
Muses: "O sisters shift we are betraid, / Another man I see" (ll. 481–
482). There is none of the vivid, colorful incongruity of Huanebango, heir
to Polimackeroeplacydus, swirling his Latin around a folktale girl at the
well of the water of life, while she replies, "Foe, what greasie groome have
wee here?"[35]

However, such frequent, multiple incongruities require some continuities in order not to fragment the play into a collection of bits. To this end,
besides the weaving of plots, there are recurring phrases and rhythms.[36]
"Frollicke franion" and "Aprill of my age" fall from different lips, and as
Frank Hook has remarked, even when long lines like "Fortune cruell,
cruell and unkind" change to the quick "Hips and Hawes, and stickes and
strawes," or when verse changes to prose, from "Hips and Hawes" to "I
will give thee as good a Gowne of gray as ever thou diddest weare," the
strong effects of meter and patterning continue.[37] Clunch, bewildered by

34. In *Love and Fortune* the characters range from courtiers to a hermit and his servant to
the gods; plot lines are few and basically clear, and the worlds of gods and men are clearly
separated; *The Rare Triumphs of Love and Fortune*, in *A Select Collection of Old English Plays*,
ed. W. Carew Hazlitt (London, 1874), vol. VI. Robert Wilson, *The Cobler's Prophecy*, ed.
A. C. Wood (n.p., 1914); I have modernized the long *s*.

35. How extraordinary this combination is may be suggested in part by other braggarts:
Don Armado exercises himself and his Latin in a court transplanted to the country but not a
landscape with a magic well, and Sir Brian le Foy of the early romance, *Clyomon and
Clamydes*, though allied with a magic dragon, never appears with the dragon or any other
supernatural apparatus.

36. Hook points out that the "essential" threads of the narratives are neatly woven and
sustained, p. 343. But the omission of Huanebango's release from enchantment has been
claimed as evidence of textual abridgment; see, for example, Harold Jenkins, "Peele's Old
Wives Tale," *MLR*, XXXIV (1939), 177–185, and Bradbrook, p. 325. Even Hook
suggests that seeing Huanebango released would be "dramatically satisfying." Yet this is a
misunderstanding of the folktale of the play. It would not be satisfying to annul the
marriages, find the two daughters once more without husbands, and the folktale achievement of evenhanded justice an illusion. It would be worse to preserve the marriages and
witness the respective pain and disappointment.

37. Hook, pp. 361–364.

The Dramatic Technique of The Old Wives Tale   129

others' references to Vulcan and hobgoblins, still manages a graceful, unsmithlike, "What make you in my territories at this time of the night?" and the rowdy Wiggen threatens the Churchwarden with both pikestaff and Latin. There is a certain Lylian harmony to the language although it is never toned to Lyly's single, silver pitch.

The frame characters (the Pages and Madge) provide another major continuity during the Tale, for they serve as a kind of neutral ground for characters and styles. Unlike other frame characters—the Grocer and his Wife in *The Knight of the Burning Pestle* or the courtiers who watch "Pyramus and Thisbe" in *Midsummer Night's Dream*, for instance—they question and explain at breaks in the action, rather than interrupting it, and their comments serve first to voice the theater audience's surprise, its concurrent reaction of "Soft, who have we here?" and then to accept—and in that way draw together—the play's discrete sequences, e.g., Erestus and Lampriscus discussing dowries and the singing Harvesters.

The play also limits its generic contrasts. Rather than being an open-ended series of styles,[38] the play slips among the closely related genres of romance, folktale, folk ritual, and farce. Although each of these genres has its own boundary, they share characteristics so that their tangent, common boundaries are "thick"; folktale will share a man in bear's shape with romance, and folk ritual, like folktale, will manifest a Golden Head.[39] (Romance and farce, as I have suggested, are quite disparate, but each of these genres is closely related to the other two.) Such sharing of motifs and attitudes offers a coherence to *The Old Wives Tale*, even as it shifts, which would be missing from a play with slips among more unlike genres, e.g., pastoral, satire, and tragedy.[40]

38. Goldstone describes such an open-ended series.

39. Hirsch discusses thick boundaries, p. 45. "Snow-White and Rose-Red" has a prince as bear, and Bradbrook notes William of Palerne's similar enchantment, p. 325n. Brand reports a "Harvest Queen" with ears of corn in *Brand's Popular Antiquities of Great Britian*, ed. W. Carew Hazlitt (London, 1905), p. 308. Farce, which owes much of its origins to folk ritual (see Caputi, pp. 40–94), shares with it themes and styles, e.g., the revolt of the young against old and sexual ribaldry.

40. Eugene M. Waith discusses the conflict of attitudes which arises from a combination of pastoral and satire in *The Pattern of Tragicomedy in Beaumont and Fletcher* (New Haven, Conn., 1952), pp. 71 ff.

130   JOAN C. MARX

But an emphasis on the thick boundaries of the play's genres brings us close to where we began: the critical views of the play which have blurred those boundaries by perceiving the play as one rather than several distinct genres. The major, obvious result of losing this distinction of genres has been the loss of the play's incongruities and shifts. Less evident and lost with them, as a further and ironic consequence, has been the fresh awareness of different genres—their discrete or shared attitudes and values—which such incongruities afford.[41]

Folk ritual, for example, manifest largely in the Harvester scenes, has been barely noted.[42] Instead this genre's moments have been thought "extraneous" to the play's structure; they offered incidental opportunities for "costly display" of costumes or "rustic atmosphere."[43] The anonymous figures of the Harvesters appear early in the Tale, first, after the beggar, Lampriscus, has consulted with Erestus about his daughters, and then again after Wiggen's rowdy chase of the Churchwarden. They interact with no other characters of the Tale and have no part in any of the plots. Each time they appear singing; the second time, when they come in "with women in their hands," they may dance as well.[44]

> All yee that lovely lovers be, pray you for me,
> Loe here we come asowing, asowing,
> And sowe sweete fruites of love:
> In your sweete hearts well may it prove.
>
> (ll. 250–253)

> Loe heere we come areaping, areaping,
> To reape our harvest fruite,
> And thus we passe the yeare so long,
> And never be we mute.
>
> (ll. 535–538)

41. An essential point of the Russian Formalists, e.g., Shklovsky, was: "whenever a text can be firmly classed as anomalous, the outlines of the class or classes that exclude it are themselves sharpened . . . a good way to illustrate a rule is to violate it strategically and ostentatiously. Transgressions *mark* boundaries," Morson, "Threshold Art."

42. Bradbrook notes the "rural seasonal games" of the Harvesters, p. 326.

43. Doebler, p. 418; Hook, p. 372; Larsen, p. 168.

44. Hook, p. 337. Such figures on a stage, with several women instead of folk ritual's one or two, would probably be associated with the masques as well; Hook suggests the likeness.

The Dramatic Technique of The Old Wives Tale   131

The songs address the audience more directly than the speeches of other characters,[45] and their immediacy is emphasized by the punning bisexuality of the first lyric: "your sweete heartes" courts the women in the audience and enlists the men as allies. Since each of these songs consists of a single stanza repeated (as the stage directions point out), they have a mild incantatory effect, and their metaphor of sowing and reaping—which portrays men's search for women—envisions human sexuality as part of nature's fertility.[46]

Such folk figures, once as familiar in English life as Father Nicholas is today, and though still surviving in such rare groups as the Marshfield Paper Boys,[47] have almost completely disappeared. The "guizers" or "plough jacks" would appear in their own villages in processions and stationary ceremonies.[48] They might be clothed in "normal" or working dress or in the more extraordinary folk costume of the Marshfield players, their bodies covered with shreds of paper until they resemble vaguely conical, haystack-shaped masses.[49] Contemporary Elizabethan references allow glimpses of them: Spenser describes June as a procession of "players" carrying plough irons and dressed in "leaves," the originals of the Marshfield paper shreds;[50] Nashe's Harvest, referred to as a "Plough-Swain," is dressed in "thatch," and his Reapers, calling a traditional harvest cry, demand the conventional quête of offering.[51] Such plough jacks, chanting and moving in a familiar ritual, would be both members of

45. There are brief one-line addresses to the audience, but none is sustained.

46. Goldstone suggests that the Harvesters create "a parallel between reaping and sowing in the cycle of seasons and in love, both of which are parts of nature," p. 212.

47. The Marshfield players are pictured in Alan Brody's *The English Mummers and Their Plays* (Philadelphia, 1970), pp. 33 ff.

48. *Ibid.*, p. 4, and *passim.*

49. T. F. Ordish describes ploughmen "in clean smock-frocks" as well as "reapers with sickles" in a Plough Monday procession (quoted by Hook, p. 427).

50. Michael J. Preston, "The Folk Play: An Influence on the *Faerie Queene*," *AN&Q*, VIII (1969), 38–39. Margaret Dean-Smith discusses the relationship of leaves and paper in "Folk-Play Origins of the English Masque," *Folk-Lore*, LV, (1954), 74–86.

51. R. B. McKerrow notes their folk-ritual cry in his edition of Thomas Nashe's *Summer's Last Will and Testament*, in *The Works of Thomas Nashe* (Oxford, 1958), vol. III. Bradbrook points out a general resemblance of Peele's figures to Nashe's, p. 327. Brody discusses the quête as a ritual practice, p. 14 n.

132   JOAN C. MARX

the community and removed from it, special luck-bringers set apart by ritual action.[52]

In *The Old Wives Tale* this anonymous group of chanting men, who sing of fertility and confront the audience directly, offer some of the boldest discontinuities of the play. Each time they appear, their lyricism directly follows a scene of folktale which has flashed into the cynical or raucous tone of farce (Lampriscus's thankfulness that his two wives are dead, Wiggen's threats to the "whorson scald Sexton"), and each time their melodic songs precede a Huanebango-and-Booby scene which shifts between parodied romance, folktale, and farce. With their first appearance, the Harvesters can make it clear that the shifts which have constantly been occurring, but in milder forms, are the deliberate, major technique of the play.

Yet the Harvesters also share two important attitudes with romance and folktale, respectively: a celebration of lovers and an awareness of a supernatural presence in nature. Their shaping of these attitudes, their particular vision, is peculiar to themselves—a point we will return to—but the Harvesters' songs reinforce the positive, ideal, and supernatural in the other genres and, in so doing, help to preserve the distinct presences of folktale and romance in the play. This is particularly true in the first scenes, when the range of the play is being established and when, at the same time, folktale is frequently replaced by farce and romance usually appears as parody. Without some reassertion, the celebration of lovers and the acknowledgment of the supernatural might well be corroded and dissolved by the cynical and everyday. To take a specific instance: if Erestus and Lampriscus were immediately followed by Huanebango and Booby, without the Harvesters' first song, it is likely that future moments of lyricism and enchantment—Sacrapant's admiration of Delia or the chant of the Golden Head—would be heard as parody. As it is, the Harvesters are essential in maintaining the play's wide range in tone and attitude and the consequent distinction of its genres.

Unlike folk ritual, folktale and romance have been perceived, but they have then been obscured in a different way. They have been blended together either by describing the two genres as one, as in "an old-fashioned

52. Brody, pp. 16, 21, 28.

The Dramatic Technique of The Old Wives Tale   133

romantic tale, a fairy story,"[53] or, in a more Procrustean style, by relegat-
ing all motifs to one genre or the other, e.g., "all that Peele has borrowed
from romantic sources are the names of some of his persons."[54] The two
have such a thick boundary that romance not only owes many of its
individual motifs to folktale, but an entire tale type like the Grateful
Dead, which appears in *The Old Wives Tale*, can occur both in romance—in
Olyver of Castylle and *Sir Amadace*—and in folktale—in "Beauty of the
World," "Jack the Master," and "The King of Ireland's Son."[55] It is
possible as a result to have a moment which could belong to either genre,
e.g., Eumenides' speech, "This man hath left me in a Laborinth"
(ll. 449 ff.), after his encounter with Erestus. Here Eumenides, bewildered by Erestus's mysterious instructions, could be either a folklore
hero or a knight on a quest; it would be unprofitable to apportion such a
moment to one genre or the other. Nevertheless, even with their thick
boundary, the two genres are distinct: most scenes or moments, even of a
tale type common to both genres, are visibly rendered in one or the other
genre, are characterized by one or the other's attitude and style. Perceiving
these differences in generic moments, in their attitudes and styles, will
allow in turn an awareness of the genres' differing values.

   G. H. Gerould has abstracted the conventional action of the Grateful
Dead:

> A man finds a corpse lying unburied, and out of pure philanthropy procures
> interment for it at great personal inconvenience. Later he is met by the ghost of
> the dead man, who in many cases promises him help on condition of receiving, in
> return, half of whatever he gets. The hero obtains a wife (or some other reward),
> and, when called upon, is ready to fulfil his bargain as to sharing his possessions.
>
>   (p. x)

Two of these "grateful dead" scenes in *The Old Wives Tale*, the discovery of
the body and the magic helper's first reward of the hero, can be identified
as folktale rather than romance. The scene in which Wiggen and Corebus
quarrel with church officials, who claim that burial fees are needed to roof

---

53. McIlwraith, p. xii. Doebler speaks of "fairy-tale chivalric romance," p. 418.
54. Larsen, p. 161; see also Hook, p. 360.
55. G. H. Gerould, *The Grateful Dead*, Pub. 60 of the Folk-Lore Society (London,
1908), pp. 7–25.

134   JOAN C. MARX

a church, is marked by an everyday practicality. This same quality characterizes the simple discovery of the body in "The King of Ireland's Son,"
where a knight sees a funeral procession coming down the road and a man
puts "a writ down on the corpse for five pounds," and that in "Jack the
Master," where Jack stumbles on an unburied coffin as he prepares to bed
down for the night in a churchyard.[56] In the romance of *Sir Amadace*, in
contrast, the knight traveling in a forest comes on a mysterious chapel lit
by candles, and he must send first his servant, then his squire, and finally
go himself before he can comprehend the inner scene: a lone, sorrowing
mourner and a bier.[57] Again, when Eumenides and Jack arrive at the inn,
instead of the helper's providing romance gifts—armor and a horse, as in
Sir Amadace and *Olyver*—Jack offers the homely present of a purse filled
with money for a meal at an inn, much as the red man provides the prince
and himself with a simple breakfast, in "Beauty of the World." (The purse
filled with money is itself a folktale motif.)[58]

One of Peele's most provocative manipulations of generic boundaries
depends both on the thickness of romance and folktale's common boundary
and the two genres' final distinction. As Gerould suggests, the hero of the
Grateful Dead must often promise the magic helper to share any winnings,
and at the penultimate moment, before the magic helper will reveal himself as the grateful spirit, he demands his half of the hero's gains. (Thus in
The Old Wives Tale, after Eumenides has wakened Delia and been granted
her hand, Jack reminds him, "You know you and I were partners, I to
have halfe in all you got.") In the tale type, whether rendered in folktale or
romance, the hero must respond by agreeing to "share" his wife (or
child)—and thereby kill her—in order to fulfill his test and show his
truth. However, because of their differing values, folktale and romance
portray this action, the hero's response to the helper's demand, in contrasting ways. In *The Old Wives Tale*, the moment of Eumenides' response
crystallizes, in an extraordinary suspension, both of these alternative
portrayals.

56. "The King of Ireland's Son," in *Beside the Fire*, ed. Douglas Hyde (London, 1890),
pp. 18–47; "Jack the Master and Jack the Servant," *Legendary Fictions of the Irish Celts*, ed.
P. Kennedy (London, 1866), pp. 32–38.

57. *Sir Amadace and the Avowing of Arthur*, ed. Christopher Brookhouse, *Anglistica*, XV
(Copenhagen, 1968), ll. 61–132.

58. This is the motif of the "magic purse," D1192.

The Dramatic Technique of The Old Wives Tale   135

In folktale, which focuses on the hero's achievement of his own potential, gaining possession of a woman with good qualities and status and making her a wife is part of the hero's self-realization; agreeing to "share" her at the helper's demand represents an ability to give up what he holds dear in order to further prove himself, his "truth." In romance the knight's truth is bound up with his vision of the woman; his quest for the ideal may be vested in a search for her, and she becomes—to use Eumenides' phrase—the "loadstar of his life." As a result, where folktale can stress the hero's ability to "come through," to make the choice at the helper's demand, for romance the moment is agonizing and almost irresolvable.

In "Beauty of the World," for example, the British folktale closest to Peele's promise, the hero responds with reluctance but with a clear sense of priorities. The red man, the magic helper, announces that his time for leaving has come:

> "I don't know what I'll do after you," said the king's son.
> "Oh, make no delay," said the red man; "the hire is just."
> "It is just," said the king's son.
> He made two halves of all he gained since he hired him. "I will give you my child all," said he; "I think it a pity to go to cut him in two."
> "I will not take him all," said the red man; "I will not take but my bargain."
> The king's son took a knife and was going to cut. "Stop your hand," said the red man.

In *Olyver of Castylle* when the hero falls on his knees before his wife, praying her to forgive him, she kisses him and begs God and the Virgin to forgive her husband if killing her should be a sin.[59] When he approaches her, he is like "a man halfe oute of his wytte." In Sir Amadace, the "dividing" of the woman is transmuted by constant references to the sacrifice of Christ, "þat me dere boȝte," on the part of the hero, his mistress, and even the magic helper, the White Knight.[60] In this romance the hero cannot resolve his dilemma, and it is his mistress "myld of mode" who precipitates the action by freely offering herself, in another loving sacrifice.

59. *The Hystorye of Olyver of Castylle*, pp. 329–334.
60. *Sir Amadace*, ll. 703 ff.

136   JOAN C. MARX

In *The Old Wives Tale* the moment before Jack's demand is sustained romance: Eumenides has wakened Delia and avowed his quest for the "fairest flower of these westerne parts." The princess has acknowledged him her knight and granted her love:

> Thou gentle knight, whose fortune is so good
> To finde me out, and set my brothers free,
> My faith, my heart, my hand, I give to thee.
>
> (ll. 859–861)

With Jack's demand the play slips into folktale.

> JACK
> Why then maister draw your sworde, part your Lady, let mee have halfe of her presently.
> EUMENIDES
> Why I hope Jack thou doost but jest, I promist thee halfe I got, but not halfe my Lady.
> JACK
> But what else maister, have you not gotten her, therefore devide her straight, for I will have halfe, there is no remedie.
> EUMENIDES
> Well ere I will falsifie my word unto my friend, take her all, heere Jack ile give her thee.
> JACK
> Nay neither more nor lesse Maister, but even just halfe.
> EUMENIDES
> Before I will falsifie my faith unto my friend I will divide hir, Jacke thou shalt have halfe.
> 1 BRO.
> Bee not so cruell unto our sister gentle Knight.
> 2 BRO.
> O spare faire Delia, shee deserves no death.
> EUMENIDES
> Content your selves, my word is past to him, therefore prepare thy selfe Delya for thou must die.
> DELIA
> Then farewell worlde, adew Eumenides.
>
> (ll. 886–903)

The exchanges have folktale's directness and lack of psychological rendering; the conflict for Eumenides, as for the prince of "Beauty,"

The Dramatic Technique of The Old Wives Tale   137

appears only in decisive, though changed, responses. But with the romance scene which precedes it, the folktale dialogue seems too quick, too casual, and too decisive. Eumenides' seems a shrug of resignation, Delia's a hasty adieu. The scene's possible romance version, with its idealization of the woman and the knight's elaborated, torturous difficulty, seems to accompany the dialogue as a faint reverberation, a missing possibility. Such an awareness of romance is reinforced by the Two Brothers, since they in fact express romance in the midst of folktale, as they plead for a vision of "faire Delia" and a "gentle Knight." It is no wonder that for Gwenan Jones the moment is perfect folktale and for Tucker Brooke it seems a parody of romance.[61] Eumenides' answer to Jack is both quite right and oddly, humorously, wrong; one genre is present, the other vibrates in the air. Unconventionally, this brief conventional scene reveals the incongruity in values of the two genres.

Such playful manipulations of genres may also suggest the rich variety with which fiction can seize human experience. The play is light and merry, and I am not proposing that it suggests the variety of human life of a Shakespeare play, with its intertwined human motives, the interaction of history and individual lives, or even the quick insights into character, Cleopatra's "I shall see / Some squeaking Cleopatra boy my greatness." Yet as *The Old Wives Tale* slips from one genre into another, crosses a generic boundary, it releases the audience from the confines of the first, its objects and tones, and suggests a new country with its new vision lying just beyond. The Harvesters' simple lyrics portray a male search for women in which human relationships are subsumed into nature's harmony and renewal: the men sow, the women bear "frute"; they claim a yearly cycle which leaps "mute" death to pass again into the quick and fertile. When their folk ritual shifts to romance, one man and one woman claim supreme earthly importance for each other, emotional desire mates with the physical, and nature dwindles to frozen obstacles and thorny beds. As folktale thrusts romance aside, it claims the need of men and women for gold and home, and offers a world of voices—for those who venture out—of animals and water, speaking and caressing, a nature animate with human emotion and sexuality re-embodied.

61. Gwenan Jones, p. 89; G. F. Tucker Brooke, p. 279.

138   JOAN C. MARX

From the beginning the play has been aware of fiction's power. Frolicke suggests its attraction in his eager hush, when the Characters appear: "Let them alone, let us heare what they will say," and the old storyteller awakens attention to fiction's rules by violating them with good-humored ease. Madge omits essential plot details ("O Lord I quite forgot, there was a Conjurer"), confuses her characters ("she [he I would say]") and refuses to choose their identities ("there was a King or a Lord, or a Duke"). The Characters appear onstage to tell their story better—in a manner like Pirandello's centuries later[62]—and their amiable storyteller is found asleep when they have finished. The tale seems to have a life, an autonomy, of its own, to go "rounde without a fiddling stick" as Frolicke says.

With the Harvesters, for their brief moments, an audience also seems to enter more deeply into a fictive life. There are no narrative threads to weave the figures into a familiar continuum of time and space; instead the audience is confronted and addressed directly. The Harvesters' metaphor of sowing and reaping is simple yet essential, the central point of their appearance, and it is directly presented. They are both closer to the audience than other characters and more fictive, and, momentarily, their pull into the circle transforms us into an audience resembling—not the confident group attending the *Knight of the Burning Pestle*—but rather the Grocer and his Wife, unsure of whether we are part of the stage's group or outside it.

It was once believed that such an artful structure, one of generic contrast created by a purposeful technique, would be beyond Peele's reach. In her study of "form in Elizabethan drama," for instance, Peele was one of Madeleine Doran's chief examples of an Elizabethan playwright seduced by a love of "abundant event" into creating plays of "shapeless unselectivity of incident."[63] There have been and still are great problems with Peele's texts, and even with their textual problems set aside, *Edward I* and *The Battle of Alcazar* remain episodic plays.[64] Nevertheless, the dramatic tech-

---

62. Allardyce Nicoll pointed out the resemblance to Pirandello (noted by Larsen, p. 165); Hook points out that Madge guesses wrong about the Harvesters' song, p. 427.

63. *Endeavors of Art* (Madison, Wis., 1954), p. 102.

64. See *Edward I*, ed. Frank S. Hook; *The Battle of Alcazar*, ed. John Yoklavich; *David and Bethsabe*, ed. Elmer M. Blistein, in *The Life and Works of George Peele*, ed. Prouty, II and III.

The Dramatic Technique of The Old Wives Tale   139

nique of *The Old Wives Tale* and the sensibility it requires accord with Peele's other works.

Recent studies by Inga-Stina Ewbank have persuasively argued for coherent structures in *David and Bethsabe* and *The Arraignment of Paris*.[65] In addition, she has suggested that to achieve these structures Peele deliberately employed techniques of abrupt reversal and contrast, techniques which resemble the shifts of *The Old Wives Tale*. For example, in order to portray "Paradise lost and regained" in *David and Bethsabe*, Peele created a structure with abrupt changes of mood for David, e.g., the King's brusque relinquishment of grief over his child's death, a sudden turn which can suggest David's change from helpless misery to a new conviction of grace.[66] For *The Arraignment*, Peele purposely contrasted the finale's joyful optimism with both the lament of Ate come from Hell, which opens the play, and the successive sorrows and forebodings of war which shadow the play throughout. As a result, the large and dramatic shift in mood celebrates the "mysterious power of royalty": "the wonder of the ending . . . is the defeat of a whole tragic and dynamic world order (its dynamism having provided the action of the play) by the simple, static presence of the queen."[67]

Complementary to these abrupt contrasts is Peele's fascination with replaying language and gesture with slight variations of form. A doubling of words (e.g., "all yee that lovely lovers be") is a hallmark of his phrases,[68] and a like repetition characterizes the pageant form in which he frequently wrote. Pageants more than plays or even masques are given to re-presenting an audience with images of itself, and such reflections may be double or even triple. Thus in Peele's *Descensus Astraeae*, a Lord Mayor's Show, one "web" is referred to in the Presenter's speech, another appears in a child's hands, and both are puns on the name of William Webbe, the

65. "The House of David in Renaissance Drama: A Comparative Study," *RenD*, VIII (1965), 3–40; and "'What words, what looks, what wonders?'" in *The Elizabethan Theatre V*, ed. G. R. Hibbard (Hamden, Conn., 1975), pp. 124–154.
66. "The House of David," pp. 14–15, 21, 29, 38.
67. "'What words, what looks,'" p. 138.
68. *Ibid.*, pp. 134–135. This repetition may ultimately derive, as Inga-Stina Ewbank suggests, from his attention to the match of word and spectacle, a sense that one doubles the other and need only point to it.

140   JOAN C. MARX

new mayor watching the pageant.[69] In the earlier *Pageant Borne before Wolstan Dixi*, a group of Londoners standing before Guildhall is faced first with "London" and then with a figure of London's "Loyaltie."[70] Such doubling becomes more dramatic in *The Arraignment*: the play centers first on the award of the apple and then replays that award, giving the prize to the queen of "a seconde Troie" (l. 1153).[71] This sense of reiteration is intensified by the play's attention to echo and refrain—the story of Echo is recited, lines of dialogue serve as lyrical refrains (e.g., ll. 382, 626 ff., 980), and the country gods "bestowe an Eccho" to a chorus until a choir echoes "within and without" (l. 166).

Yet more striking are Peele's playful repetitions in which the repeated form is slightly skewed or, the form unchanged, a new context creates an ironic difference. In *The Old Wives Tale*, for example, the repetition of the approach to the magic well is demanded by folktale, and conventionally the scene is unvaried until the moment when each sister shows her nature by responding differently to the Head. But instead of this strict repetition Peele changes both the song, by adding lines, and the physical appearance of the Head, e.g., by adding "eares of Corne." In a more general sense, the dramatic technique of the entire Tale consists, as we have seen, in repeating familiar conventions but changing them in odd ways, by a sudden suppression or a skewing of their form: the Golden Head chants and Zantippa responds with a blow, or Sacrapant is killed in not one but two different ways. Similarly, Peele emphasizes with a textual note a refrain in *The Arraignment* which is sung by a nymph and repeated by shepherds. In

69. *Descensus Astraeae*, ed. David H. Horne, in *The Life and Works of George Peele*, ed. Charles T. Prouty, vol. I. Bergeron notes the visual repetition in *English Civic Pageantry 1558–1642* (London, 1971), p. 136; Robert Withington notes the verbal in *English Pageantry* (Cambridge, Mass., 1920), II, 25. We have few details of the moment in which the shows were presented, but since speeches were directly addressed to the mayor (e.g., in Peele's Show of 1585), it seems safe to extend Withington's comment on the 1590 Show: "We may presume that the mayor stopped before the pageant to hear the speakers" (p. 25).

70. *Pageant Borne before Wolstan Dixi*, ed. David H. Horne, in *The Life and Works of George Peele*, ed. Prouty, vol. I. No setting for the spoken parts is named; the Guildhall as the place of arrival seems possible from von Wedel's description of the 1584 Lord Mayor's Show. See *Transactions of the Royal Historical Society*, N.S. IX (1895), 253–255.

71. *The Araygnement of Paris*, ed. R. Mark Benbow, in *The Life and Works of George Peele*, ed. Prouty, vol. III.

The Dramatic Technique of The Old Wives Tale   141

their mouths her words become a judgment on herself, an ironic "Ecco," caused by the changed context, which Peele points out as "the grace of this song."[72] In a like manner, near the end of *David and Bethsabe*, David addresses "faire Bersabe" (l. 1655), lauds her "sweet sight," and continues into a sustained praise of "beautie." His blazon is so like earlier reveries on Bethsabe that it comes as a shock when David explicitly names his subject as "faire peace" (l. 1668).[73] To underscore David's ability to look beyond earthly beauty, Peele has deliberately made the context ambiguous, played on the audience's sense of repetition, and then required a sudden re-framing and with it an awareness of the new and heavenly context.

The interest in fiction and its genres which is evident in *The Old Wives Tale* also characterizes both the ending of *The Arraignment*—with its deliberate move from fiction to reality, the Fates reaching forward to the Queen in the audience—and Peele's generic experimentation. *David and Bethsabe* is the only extant Elizabethan example of a "divine play"; it combines a religious theme with the techniques of a history play, taking the Bible as its chronicle source.[74] *The Arraignment* is known for synthesizing different styles and subject matters: R. Mark Benbow, the Yale editor, proposes pastoral, mythology, moralities, and masque among them.[75]

I would further suggest, without attempting to argue the point here, that the awareness of different genres which is required in order to combine them—as Peele does in *David and Bethsabe* and *The Arraignment*—demands a sensibility similar in kind and degree to that needed in order to contrast them—as he does in *The Old Wives Tale*. It would take another essay to propose that Elizabethan combinations of genre, as of comedy with tragedy, have been so visible and debated in literary history that these same combinations have silently—and mistakenly—been assumed to be

---

72. The Fates' reappearance and giving over of their instruments recalls the threat of Ate that Atropos is cutting the "threede of Troie."

73. The turn is indicated by "but" and a change of person, yet the intertwining of Bethsabe and "faire peace" is so skillful that for the moment of clarification Peele gives not only the name but an epithet, "goddesse of our graces here," to call attention to the change.

74. Lily B. Campbell, *Divine Poetry and Drama in Sixteenth Century England*, p. 260, referred to by Inga-Stina Ewbank, "The House of David," p. 5; and Elmer Blistein, Introduction, p. 175.

75. Benbow, Introduction, p. 26.

easier and more natural than the rarer contrast of genres. Here we may
only note briefly the awareness of distinct tones and gestures suggested by
the combination of *The Arraignment*. After Ate's appearance, for example,
the gods who follow are disposed in a clear and careful progression: from
country gods (as Pan), to earthly but more rarefied female divinities (as
Flora), to the celestial goddesses (as Juno). The tone ranges from Rhanis's
stately welcome of the goddesses to Juno's bickering with Venus; from the
mourning over a shepherd dead for love to the bawdy of Vulcan and a
nymph; from, finally, Ate's tragic lament to the rejoicing over Eliza. This
variety, in its careful modulation, suggests a sensibility which—instead of
gracefully blending the tones and gestures of pastoral, mythology, and
"comedy of ideas"[76]—could equally well distill and sharpen generic
moments, then gaily, abruptly, shift from one to another.

English dramatists of the 1580s and early 90s were faced with a wealth
of plots, jokes, rhetorical styles, and genres; the comedies of George Peele
and John Lyly suggest different approaches to this diversity. Each set a
play in the English countryside, employed clever servants, an old woman,
and magic. For *Mother Bombie* Lyly shaped, blended, and smoothed. He
borrowed clever Roman plots, selected magic and riddling prophecy, then
established them in Kent. The worldly sons of Terence and Plautus are
softened to the adolescent heirs of wealthy farmers. Mother Bombie is an
old woman who can see the future and interpret dreams, but her divination
is lightened by common sense: asked to account for a fantastic dream, she
suggests, "Belyke thou wentst supperlesse to bed."[77] Having molded a
coherent bourgeois scene, Lyly then transmutes it to an impossibly articulate, rarefied world, peculiarly his own. The invention of wit springs
forth at every sentence end; its phrasing, patterned and balanced, creates
an extraordinary grace. Even the materialism of the fathers, for whom
"marriage . . . is become a market," is distilled by a bargaining con-
ducted in the elegant Lylian style.

76. "Comedy of ideas" is Benbow's term, p. 26.
77. *Mother Bombie*, ed. R. Warwick Bond, in *The Complete Works of John Lyly* (Oxford,
1902), vol. III. G. K. Hunter points out that both the specific portrayal of a bourgeois
world and the lack of "shadow and the supernatural" are peculiar to *Mother Bombie* among
Lyly's plays, in *John Lyly* (London, 1962), pp. 220–229. Yet the shadows, even when
present, are of Lyly's own shaping; they are not direct imitations of folktale's Golden
Heads. Lyly of course is writing for the boys and Peele for an adult company.

The Dramatic Technique of The Old Wives Tale   143

Peele in contrast selected and rendered in order to suggest both the variety of his sources and the intrinsic power of each. His old country-woman retorts in a hearty, vulgar style, "Heare my tale or kisse my taile"; divination is given to Erestus, an enchanted, riddling old man who becomes a bear at night. A ghost, a princess, and the magic Head appear, but lumbering into their midst come Wiggen and the good-natured Booby. The lyric Harvesters dance and sing of "reaping"; then Huanebango demands "ingresse and egresse . . . whosoever saith no." A thunderous voice shouts "No," and the champion, in elegant slapstick, falls on his face.

As a result, *The Old Wives Tale* is pleasing partly for its simple "variety of spectacle" and its satisfaction of the old demands it embodies: a "Kinges Daughter" is rescued, generosity is rewarded, and lovers are reunited.[78] Yet in addition, unlike a Lyly comedy, a group of folktales, or even a self-conscious parody, Peele's play can awaken us to "the different levels of the imaginative life itself."[79] With its vivid incongruities, its vision of a Spanish braggart kneeling by the well of the water of life, *The Old Wives Tale* creates a passage through various fictions. As we change from folktale to romance to folk ritual, highly conventional forms removed from the everyday, tumble for an instant into the cynical or raucous and back, we seem to skate from one extraordinary possibility to another, to feel with delight the range of fiction.

78. Bradbrook, p. 325.

79. *Ibid.*, pp. 329–330. Goldstone proposes that the play is "dramatizing . . . the working of the imagination and showing how it enlarges, unifies, and yet refreshingly complicates human life," p. 213. I hope to have suggested the source of these perceptions. Earlier versions of this essay profited from the thoughtful criticisms of Phyllis Gorfain, Roberta Johnson, and the participants in David Bevington's NEH Seminar, 1978–79.

[12]

The Hearth and the Cell: Art in *The Old Wives Tale*

SUSAN T. VIGUERS

It is a commonplace that a play should be seen to be understood fully; directing an informal production of George Peele's *The Old Wives Tale*[1] (1595) convinced me that in that play, perhaps more than in most, the spatial dimension as it would have been defined by the original stage provides an essential key to the play's often misunderstood inner logic. Through my staging, the play's structure appears remarkably simple, in spite of the complex plot, and easy to diagram spatially. (This simplicity is by no means an accepted attribute of the play.[2]) Such staging not only helps make *The Old Wives Tale* accessible to a modern audience, but it reveals the play to be a rich and typically Renaissance exploration of the conflict between two fundamental kinds of art, represented by the two central figures in the play, Madge and Sacrapant. The stage diagram below, which includes three entrances[3] and five permanent locations or structures, represents the framework on which the discussion that follows will be built.

Susan T. Viguers is an Assistant Professor of Language and Literature at Philadelphia College of Art. This essay is part of a work in progress on the quintessentially Renaissance (more particularly, Shakespearean) theory of art implicit in the works of George Peele.

[1] The edition of *The Old Wives Tale* used in this paper is Frank S. Hook's in *The Life and Works of George Peele*, gen. ed. Charles Tyler Prouty, 3 vols. (New Haven: Yale Univ. Press, 1970), vol. 3. Citations are given by line numbers.

[2] See, for example, the Yale editor, Hook, who maintains that "there is not much point in trying to pretend that the play is really very clearly plotted" (p. 369), and Arthur M. Sampley, "Plot Structure in Peele's Play as a Test of Authorship," *PMLA* 51 (September 1936):697. Other critics, though none comes near making the demonstration I intend, are closer to my position. See John Doebler's review of the literature, "The Tone of George Peele's *The Old Wives' Tale*," *ES* 53 (October 1972):418, n.18. Even John D. Cox, whose "Homely Matter and Multiple Plots in Peele's *Old Wives Tale*," *TSLL* 20 (Fall 1978):330-46, is very suggestive, does not come to grips with the dramatic (rather than literary) plot nor with the staging.

[3] Textual evidence suggests the need for two entrances besides Sacrapant's cell: see especially after line 431. Moreover, throughout the play, blocking would be extremely awkward without a third entrance.

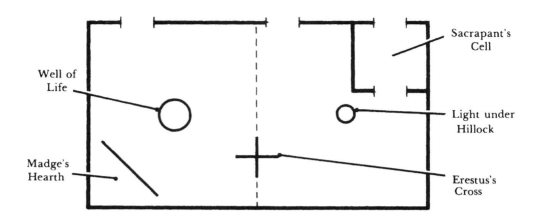

Although there is controversy about what the staging of the play would have been, there is agreement that the storyteller Madge and the sorcerer Sacrapant were each associated with a permanent location on stage. Sacrapant has a cell, which must be represented physically. Not only does his first entrance connect him to that mansion, but one stage direction indicates it is *his* cell even if he is not among the characters entering through it (after 629). The fire before which Madge sits and tells her tale at one point is tended, which suggests that there should be some structure representing the hearth. Whether there is a hearth is less important than that Madge, with her audience, Frolicke and Fantasticke, constitutes a permanent location for all but the opening of the play.

Where Madge tells her story (the hearth) and Sacrapant's cell are the features of the stage that take up the most space. They should be as far apart as possible. Necessities of blocking, as well as my interpretation of the play, dictate they be on opposite sides of the stage, dividing it vertically, and at opposite corners, creating a diagonal tension. The hearth and the cell set up the spatial tension for the stage.

Madge and Sacrapant each dominate the space and entrances nearest them. Thus one permanent structure, the Well of Life (in its fertility, associated with Madge's art), is near her, and another, the light under the hillock (an image of Sacrapant's art), is near Sacrapant. The three

SUSAN T. VIGUERS 211

entrances, as I see them, are not symmetrically placed.[4] One is on
Madge's side, one is Sacrapant's cell, and a third is near the center
upstage, but in Sacrapant's domain. Those characters in Madge's tale
on a journey to destroy Sacrapant and to rescue the princess Delya enter
through the opening nearest Madge and exit on Sacrapant's side. All
those under Sacrapant's control enter and exit through his cell or the
other opening associated with his art. Characters on their way to the
Well of Life enter on Madge's side[5] and, after their experience there,
exit the same way. This blocking not only simplifies the immensely numerous entrances and exits, but helps focus our attention on Madge and
Sacrapant as the two primary powers.

The final locus, positioned in the middle of the stage, is Erestus's
Cross. Erestus, the young man made old by Sacrapant, nonetheless affirms Madge's definition of reality. He marks the crossroads between
Madge's hearth and Sacrapant's cell, the confrontation at the center of
the play.

The Old Wives Tale consists of a frame play and an inner play.
Madge, in the frame, tells a story (the inner play) that includes Sacrapant. Spatially, however, Madge and Sacrapant are parallel; and that
parallelism, necessary if Madge and Sacrapant are to function dramatically as opposing forces, is supported by the imagery of the text.

Both major characters are in a wood (Sacrapant's wood is a wood
within a wood). As the frame play opens three Pages — Frolicke, Fantasticke, and Anticke, who will later be entertained by Madge and her
husband Clunch — are lost in a forest; and in the inner play, two characters under Sacrapant's enchantment, Erestus and his betrothed Venelia,
are explicitly connected to the woods. The woods in both outer and
inner tales, as is common in Renaissance literature, figures a realm of
illusion and magic, both wonderful and fearful.

It is in a dwelling within her wood that the Pages meet the imaginative
world of Madge's story. To the Pages at the beginning of the play, however, that wood is terrifying; it seems far from the rationality of daylight

---

[4]Little is known about stages at the time of The Old Wives Tale. It is possible to
suggest a curtain at the back of the stage — either covering the tiring house, or, if the
stage were a temporary, moveable playing booth, concealing the actors' dressing area —
which allows flexibility: entrances through slits could occur anywhere along the curtain.
The absence of a permanent inner stage (which would provide a center door) is reasonable since the play would have been performed by the Queen's Men in first-generation
London theaters and/or, more likely, in halls and innyards.

[5]There is one appropriate exception: when the unconscious Huanebango is carted in
by the Furies and laid by the Well of Life, they obviously enter through one of the
entrances on Sacrapant's side.

and the comfort of the everyday. In this world of "owlets, and Hobgoblins" (41), Anticke describes himself and his friends as making "faces for feare" (36). "Hush," cries his comrade Fantasticke on hearing the bark of a dog: "a dogge in the wood, or a wooden dogge" (23). "Wood" also means "mad," and the double meaning echoes through the play. Magic and the imaginative capacity are akin, in one way, to madness itself.

In Sacrapant's wood, full of marvels and strange magical beings, dwell prophecy, in the form of the Old Man, and madness, in the form of Venelia, each unfettered by "normal" rationality. His wood is even more obviously fraught with danger than Madge's. The young maiden Delya is imprisoned; her two brothers, who are searching for her, are enslaved; Huanebango and Booby, also engaged in that search, are struck deaf or blind; Erestus is transformed by day into the Old Man at the crossroads and by night into a bear; and Venelia is bewitched.

Not only Sacrapant, but the other master of a magical realm, Madge, as her name suggests, is a mage, a magician. Madge does not simply "tell" her story. Like a conjuror she seems more to summon than to create; her tale has a reality not wholly dependent on her. When, in Pirandellian fashion, the characters in her story take over their own tale, they are as much a surprise to the old woman as to her audience, Frolicke and Fantasticke (128). "Why this goes rounde without a fiddling sticke" (243), Frolicke exclaims later in the play; in other words, the tale moves by its own energy. Madge's story continues when she falls asleep, and, similarly, Sacrapant's death does not bring about the destruction of his art. That art has a reality of its own which must itself be confronted and destroyed; only when the light in the glass under the hillock is extinguished is his magic dispelled.

The autonomy of their illusions suggests that neither Madge nor Sacrapant is in complete control of what each creates. Madge's very introduction to her tale is disorganized and tentative. "Once uppon a time," she begins, "there was a King or a Lord, or a Duke" (110-11). Later she amends the order of the tale and even confuses the sex of Sacrapant (125). Her erroneous introduction of the Harvesters, when they come on the stage the first time, is again striking evidence of her failure to be absolute mistress of her tale. "O these are the harvest men," she says with confidence; "ten to one they sing a song of mowing" (248-49). But the Harvesters sing of sowing, not mowing.

The limitation of Sacrapant's control is particularly evident when Sacrapant conjures for Delya "A Frier with a chine of Beefe and a pot of wine" (after 373). The scene proceeds as Sacrapant desires until the Friar, in response to Delya's question as to who is the "greediest Englishman" (390), implicates the magician himself, who angrily and abruptly dismisses him.[6] Sacrapant's own illusion defies him. Though Sacrapant is capable of changing Delya so that she does not know herself (572), he mournfully admits he cannot make her responsive in the ultimate way he would like (357-58). In the scene leading up to the conjuring of the Friar, the formality of Delya's speech, echoed visually by her failure to sit and relax when Sacrapant first requests that she do so (353-66), helps us understand Sacrapant's dissatisfaction.

As creators of illusion, both Sacrapant and Madge demand or even depend on audience perception and response. Sacrapant "was a miserable, old, and crooked man," explains the spirit Jack at the end of the play, "though to each mans eye he seemed young and fresh" (868-69). Like Susanne Langer's "virtual object," Sacrapant's art "exists only for perception."[7] Thus, when Sacrapant's art is destroyed, those entrapped in his magic suddenly see themselves and those about them as they truly are.

Sacrapant's art is, in fact, so completely dependent on his audience that a lack of response can destroy him. Like Odysseus, who blocks the ears of his sailors so that they will not hear the Sirens' song, Jack puts wool into the ears of Eumenides, Delya's rescuer, and positions him so that he will neither hear nor see Sacrapant. Eumenides sits there unmoving,[8] unaware of Sacrapant when he addresses him. When Sacrapant sees he is having no effect on Eumenides, he realizes his defeat (805-808).

Madge's art similarly requires her audience. Most obviously, she tells her story to entertain her guests. Thus she insists that the Pages stay awake and respond to the story (106-108), and their comments periodically interrupt her tale. Furthermore, unless they accept her conventions, she refuses to continue her story (116-17). But the relationship of audience to tale extends even further. The worlds of the audience and of the characters in Madge's tale mirror each other. Not only are both worlds defined as a wood inhabited by a mage or creator of illusion, but,

---

[6]Critics such as H. Jenkins, "Peele's 'Old Wive's Tale,'" *MLR* 34 (April 1939):178, and Hook, pp. 341-42, are disturbed by the Friar's abrupt dismissal, which does, however, work dramatically if we see Sacrapant as disconcerted by how Delya's question is answered: "The most miserable and most covetous Usurer" (391). Sacrapant has just recently called himself "miserable" (339); his coveting Venelia and Delya is the source of the evil in the play; and like a usurer his creations are unnatural.

[7]Susanne Langer, *Feeling and Form: A Theory of Art* (New York: Charles Scribner's Sons, 1953), p. 47.

[8]Laurilyn J. Rockey's statement, in "*The Old Wives Tale* as Dramatic Satire," *Educational Theatre Journal* 22 (October 1970):268-75, that "Eumenides wanders around the stage with wool in his ears" (p. 271) contradicts the text (line 804).

as I shall discuss later, the movement of the tales within each wood is similar. Madge's work of art (the inner play) reflects her audience (the outer play). That audience, in more than one sense, is the *raison d'être* of her tale.

In defining Madge and Sacrapant as parallel characters, Peele delineates a typical Renaissance concept of the artist. Though as creators of illusion, Madge and Sacrapant are figures of power, they are not absolute masters of their creations; their art has a reality apart from them and a dependence on their audience. For Peele, as for others in the Renaissance, however, art has a potential for good *or* evil, and it is that difference between the art of Madge and of Sacrapant that creates the conflict in the play.

Nothing suggests both the parallel and the antithesis between Madge and Sacrapant more visually than the objects that symbolize their art. What the Pages lost in the woods first see of Madge's home is Clunch's lantern. The aura about Clunch is that of comforting familiarity, with which the Pages immediately identify, for Clunch's lantern embodies the reassurance of human order. The "Lanthorne and Candle," which the stage directions (after 27) tell us Clunch is carrying, were in fact words associated with the cry of the London night bellman.[9] Clunch's lantern soon expands to become the welcoming hearth of his home. "Well Masters it seemes to mee you have lost your waie in the wood," he says; "in consideration whereof, if you will goe with Clunch to his Cottage, you shall have house roome, and a good fire to sit by" (45–48). It is around that fire they gather for Madge's story. The fire associated with Clunch and Madge gives both light and warmth to the audience.

The image that represents Sacrapant's art, the flame in the glass under the turf, is an exact analogy to Clunch's lantern, yet diametrically opposed to it. Sacrapant's flame inverts the Christian parable of the candle which must not be covered up, but placed on a candlestick for all to see. That parable, as J. W. Lever remarks in his notes to *Measure for Measure*, was "a secular commonplace" in the Renaissance.[10] Sacrapant's hidden light is a perversion of the light that fights falsehood and despair, that is a spark of the heavenly flame. Sacrapant not only denies his audience guidance or protection, he endangers them.

How the two artists relate to space and how the structures with which they are associated are defined further delineate their differences. For Madge space is richly metamorphic: it is not static, but "becoming."

---

[9] See *O.E.D.*, s.v. "lantern."

[10] J. W. Lever, ed. *Measure for Measure*, Arden edn. (New York: Vintage Books, 1965), p. 6.

The stage directions tell us that the entrance of Clunch and the three young men into the cottage is indicated by Madge's coming on stage. Instead of Clunch and his guests entering a limited place, the stage becomes the cottage. Later the stage as cottage becomes the world of her tale; the hearth before which she tells her tale opens out and embraces all. Critics have either assumed Madge has a mansion or that she does not necessarily *have* to have one.[11] I feel, however, that Madge *cannot* have a mansion: such a form would not reflect her art.

On the other hand, it is appropriate that Sacrapant have a mansion. In its position at the back of the stage, his cell both dominates and, at least for most of the audience, is distant — consistent with our feeling of Sacrapant's power and isolation. (Madge's hearth, in contrast, is down-stage, close to the audience.) As a pavilion, the cell is a limited space, set apart from the rest of the stage. When the brothers are about to encounter Sacrapant, they speak of "enter[ing]" (414), as do Huanebango and Booby when they come to the same point (554), and that idea of entering accents the separateness of the structure confronting them. None of them successfully goes into that cell. At least for much of the play, it is actually sealed off with a curtain. In the end, after the sorcerer's death, it is that curtain behind which Eumenides discovers Delya as she "sitteth asleepe" (after 843): her location behind the curtain, as well as her sleep, figures her bondage. Significantly, there is no other such limited space, no other pavilion on stage.[12]

Typically in the Renaissance, as in such plays as *Doctor Faustus, The Jew of Malta,* and *Friar Bacon and Friar Bungay,* the kind of art that emerges from a cell, from a confined space, is profoundly sinister. Sacrapant's art presents illusion as though it were reality. That, contrary to appearance, Erestus is young and Sacrapant old is not something we see until Sacrapant's art is destroyed. Near the end of the play, Eumenides cannot believe the head Jack holds is Sacrapant's; and we, the play's audience, also need reassurance that the strange new head is the same as the very different one the magician previously possessed. For a similar reason, Erestus, when he enters at the end of the play as a young

[11]The following give Madge a pavilion: Robert Lee Blair, "An Edition of George Peele's *Old Wives' Tale*" (An Abstract of a Thesis, Univ. of Illinois, 1936), p. 14; M. C. Bradbrook, "Peele's *Old Wives' Tale*: A Play of Enchantment," *ES* 43 (October 1962):323; E. K. Chambers, *The Elizabethan Stage,* 4 vols. (Oxford: The Clarendon Press, 1923), 3: 48. Hook, pp. 375-76, feels that in some productions Madge's mansion could have been eliminated.
[12]Both Blair, p. 14, and Chambers, p. 48, imply a mansion for the inn where Eumenides eats. Hook, while considering that structure superfluous (p. 375), nonsensically suggests (p. 374) that Erestus's Cross could be a mansion.

man,[13] must be welcomed by name (873). Through most of the play, illusion is visually more real to us than truth. That kind of confusion informs Sacrapant's world. The word "deceive," used again and again in connection with Sacrapant's art, acknowledges that illusion is presented and experienced as reality. Sacrapant, indeed, sets up his fiction as an alternate reality not only for others, but for himself as well. Through his art he creates a magical world, and at the center of it all he places himself, metamorphosed so that he can enjoy what he has created.

Madge presents and relates to illusion in a very different way. The fantastic and parodic quality of her tale so clearly points up its fictional character that the story is distanced from both us and the audience in the frame play. Madge's story is a fabulous one, a tale of strange creatures and enchantments. Its plot, characterizations, and language, moreover, parody the popular chivalric romances of the era.[14] The idiomatic, homely quality of Madge's remark as her story characters appear on stage, "gods me bones, who comes here?" (128), puts in high relief the rhetorical bombast with which the two brothers begin the dramatization of her tale. The farcelike quality of Madge's tale climaxes in the scene at the end of the play in which Eumenides reveals his willingness to cut his beloved Delya in half in order to keep his promise that his friend Jack would receive "halfe in al . . . [he] got" (884). Such monstrous foolishness outdoes even Valentine's willingness in *Two Gentlemen of Verona* to give his beloved Silvia to his friend Proteus. The event in *The Old Wives Tale* is clearly a parody of such friendship stories. As a parody, Madge's tale calls attention to itself as an imitation of an imitation. It insists on its own unreality, on being a product of the imagination, and its humorous absurdity contrasts with the deadly earnestness of Sacrapant's art.

Nearly every time one of the characters in the frame play comments on the arrival of the characters within the tale, another immediately interjects, "Let them alone." The refusal of Frolicke, Fantasticke, and Madge to interfere in the play before them dramatizes their acceptance of the tale *as* a tale. For Peele, as for other Renaissance writers, a healthy artistic experience depends on understanding not only that a work of art is connected to the "real" world, but also that art, in consisting of shadows, of images, is different from that world. Indeed, it is only be-

---

[13]The text never mentions that Erestus is changed; but a careful reading makes it obvious.

[14]See Doebler, Rockey, and F. G. Gummere, "Critical Essay on *The Old Wives Tale*, in *Representative English Comedies*, ed. Charles Mills Gayley, 4 vols. (New York: Macmillan, 1903-1936), 1:335-48.

SUSAN T. VIGUERS   217

cause art *is* different that it can point up the "real." Madge requires that her audience appreciate that fact; Sacrapant demands that his audience deny it.

For the Renaissance, the work of man must not be confused with the work of God (i.e., reality); but that is not to deny that above man's art stands Nature, the hand of God. Art is artificial because it is created by man; yet healthy art is also profoundly natural, for the artistic creation and audience experience are in keeping with the laws of Nature. Thus Pico della Mirandola in his *Oration on the Dignity of Man* describes the magus as one who "does not so much work wonders as diligently serve a wonder-working nature."[15] In *The Old Wives Tale* the confrontation between Sacrapant's art and Madge's art is that between art that seeks to subvert the natural movement of life and art that seeks to realize the ultimate end of that movement.

Sacrapant can be associated with the usurer (as the Friar conjured by the magician implies), because, like the usurer who breeds money out of money, Sacrapant's creations are fundamentally out of tune with organic processes. In the same tradition, Dante speaks of the usurer as one who "scorns Nature."[16] In turning himself into a young man and reversing the age of Erestus, Sacrapant is defying that instrument of nature, time. His is an art of transformations that bind and impair, of unnatural stasis and paralysis. Time, moreover, is inextricably connected to truth, as the Renaissance commonplace, Truth is the Daughter of Time, suggests. Sacrapant's artifice is empty of any significance that would tie it to the realm of reality beyond it; in manipulating appearances, undermining identities, he is denying truth. That, however, is Sacrapant's undoing. Evil spells "weare out with time, that treadeth all things down but truth," warns the magician Dipsas in John Lyly's *Endimion.*[17] As Eumenides comes on stage, he cries to Time to tell him the future; and quite clearly Time is represented by Erestus when, soon after, he prophesies the hero's success and Sacrapant's destruction.

Sacrapant's art is undone by time; Madge's art is realized by time. Moreover, in three episodes—the prologue and the two Harvester scenes—Madge defines time as a profoundly natural movement. These

---

[15]Giovanni Pico della Mirandola, *Oration*, trans. Elizabeth Livermore Forbes, in *The Renaissance Philosophy of Man*, ed. Ernst Cassirer et al. (Chicago: Univ. of Chicago Press, 1948), p. 248.

[16]*The Divine Comedy*, trans. H. R. Huse (New York: Holt, Rinehart and Winston, 1954), *Inferno*, XI. 110.

[17]*The Complete Works*, ed. R. Warwick Bond, 3 vols. (Oxford: The Clarendon Press, 1902). 3: I.iv.47.

scenes are unusually important in setting up and ordering her tale. Before Madge is persuaded to begin her story, Frolicke and Clunch sing a
song of late summer, harvest, and fertility, which serves as the prologue.
The sexual overtones of the song's images of ripe cherries and strawber-
ries are reinforced by the general import of the last lines: the "true love"
in the song cannot live as a maiden because she is with child. Her child is
symbolically the tale itself. The concept of time as organic and creative,
introduced by the prologue, is developed and made structurally significant by the two Harvester episodes. Those two scenes, obvious lacunae
in Madge's story, order the sequence of events in that tale;[18] the pattern
of episodes and characters after the first of the two scenes is similar to
that after the second. The first time the Harvesters come on stage they
sing of sowing the fruits of love, and the second time, now joined by
women who symbolize what has been fulfilled, they sing of reaping that
fruit. The Harvester scenes, like the prologue, dramatize time as a
process of fruition.

    That definition of time is a key to Madge's art. Her art comprises both
her tale and her effect on her audience, and the movement in both her
tale and the world of her audience is natural and creative. Though both
worlds begin in want and despair, they move to rewards and restoration.

    The idea of a journey becomes for the audience an image of that
movement. Most of the major characters within Madge's tale are on a
quest, visually represented by their recurring movement across the
stage. Lampriscus and the two daughters whom he despairs of marrying
off are among the few not on a journey, but at the Well of Life his
daughters' fates connect with those of Huanebango and Booby, who *are*
among the travelers. The Well of Life, the importance of which is made
obvious by its emblematic presence on the stage, and the journey become conflated. Life is figured as a journey. It is, moreover, a journey to
appropriate rewards. The two Harvester episodes, we must remember,
act out the adage that what one sows one reaps.

    In the first part of Madge's tale the brothers, Lampriscus, Huane-
bango and Booby, and Eumenides, all meet the Old Man at the Cross as
he is gathering "Hips and Hawes, and stickes and strawes" (143). The
Old Man at the crossroads in the center of the stage is the touchstone and

---

[18]Hook considers Erestus's exit after line 240 just before the Harvesters enter the first
time as evidence of Peele's failure to think "through all the details" (p. 273) of the play,
since Erestus is needed on the stage in the scene after the Harvesters. To the contrary,
Erestus's exit, it seems to me, is necessary for it calls attention to the structural importance of the Harvester episode. Critics have not fully understood that importance. Hook
maintains that "the only function [of the Harvesters and their women] is to add to the
entertainment" (p. 372).

guide at the center of the play. All of the characters respond to him with kindness except for Huanebango: "Huanebango giveth no Cakes for Almes" (314), he says loftily. Eumenides is the last to meet Erestus; after that the Old Man disappears until the story's happy finale, and the spirit Jack (for whom Erestus, in veiled terms, prepares Eumenides) takes over the Old Man's role. It is Eumenides' generosity to Jack — his giving all his money so that young man whom he has never known can be buried — that is the climactic act of kindness in Madge's story. That scene comes at the end of the "sowing" section of the tale.

The Harvesters' reaping scene introduces what follows. The kind of people the characters in the tale have revealed themselves to be generates their rewards. At the beginning of the tale, Lampriscus receives directions on ridding himself of his two daughters, but it is not until after the Harvesters' second scene that the daughters do as their father bids. At the Well of Life the cursed daughter and the proud Huanebango find each other, and the union of the kind daughter and good-hearted Booby is blessed with gifts of corn and gold. But the culminating reward in the tale is Delya; and the play emphasizes that Eumenides has earned, not simply been given, that beautiful heroine (877-78, 905-909).

The paradox in the prologue and in the first Harvester episode is the same. The "true love" in the song looks ahead to the birth of her child and to becoming a maid again, and the Harvesters sing of planting. The fruits of autumn and the promise of spring co-exist. The movement of the story is not only to reward, but also from sorrow to restoration.

Most of the major characters in Madge's tale either begin in despair or are soon plunged into it. Erestus, Lampriscus, Eumenides, and Delya's two brothers all bewail their cruel fates. As the tale begins, we see love cut asunder (the separation of the betrothed Venelia and Erestus), love incomplete or frustrated (the searchers' unsuccessful efforts to find Delya, and also, perhaps, Delya's heart), and, most important, love perverted (Sacrapant's lust for Venelia and Delya). With the end of the tale, love transcends and is successful, and all but Sacrapant are made happy. When Erestus, the Old Man at the Cross, becomes a young man, age is even restored to youth. Delya herself, however, undergoes what is perhaps the most suggestive change. The "Castle . . . made of stone" (122), where Sacrapant keeps Delya, is an image of both a tomb and the hardness of the heart. When the hero Eumenides finally opens the curtains of the cell and awakes the maiden, he seems like the prince in "Sleeping Beauty" to have released her from a form of death.

That restoration in Madge's story is echoed by the frame play. The words of the Pages at the beginning of the play conjure despair and figurative death. "How nowe fellowe Frolicke, what all amort?" (1) asks Anticke; and Frolicke answers, "never in all my life was I so dead slain" (8). He proposes they sing to the tune of "O man in desperation" (16).

"Desperately spoken fellow Frollicke in the darke" (17), responds Anticke. The very identities of Frolicke and Fantasticke seem threatened.
Frolicke, whose name means "sportive mirth," is asked by Anticke,
"Doth this sadness become thy madnes?" (1-2); and Fantasticke, whose
name means one "having a lively imagination,"[19] shows unimaginative
fatalism when he remarks to Frolicke that he should have anticipated
their being lost, "seeing Cupid hath led our yong master to the faire
Lady and she is the only Saint that he has sworne to serve" (11-13). The
predicament in which the young men find themselves is somehow contingent on the loss of their master to love. As in the inner play, something
about love has gone wrong. Cupid represents a power, as Frolicke puts
it, "that hath cousned us all" (42).

Clunch and Madge, however, are themselves characters in the mythology of love. The smith Clunch is called "good Volcan" (41), making
Madge a comic Venus. The kindness Clunch and Madge show the young
men, moreover, is an example of a very different kind of love from the
Pages' image of their master's love affair, which they find isolating and
threatening. In Madge's tale itself the wandering knight does not divide
his world in the process of rescuing the saint he has sworn to serve. He
reunites it, destroying the evil that has held it in bondage.

The Pages' restoration begins when they are met by the kindly Clunch
and brought to his cottage. Anticke goes off to bed with Clunch. They
are to be renewed by sleep rather than by Madge's story; but those
characters who witness the tale are similarly involved in a process connected with sleep. As has frequently been noted,[20] there is a dream-like
quality to Madge's story. Fantasticke himself suggests the affinity of the
story to sleep when he remarks, "a tale of an howre long were as good as
an howres sleepe" (85-86). A few moments later he declares, "No better
hay in Devonshire, a my word Gammer, Ile be one of your audience"
(97-98): the tale is better than any bed.[21] Significantly, the ending of the
tale coincides with the crow of the cock and dawn.

Madge's tale, moreover, is restorative in the way sleep is. The play
ends with the two young men following Madge off the stage to have
something to eat and drink before they depart, an event which contrasts

---

[19]See *O.E.D.*

[20]See, e.g., Bradbrook, p. 328; David H. Horne, *The Life and Works of George Peele,*
gen. ed. Charles Tyler Prouty, 3 vols. (New Haven: Yale Univ. Press, 1952), 1:90; and
Jenkins, p. 178.

[21]Hook's note on this line (p. 424) misses the point: "Sounds proverbial, but I have not
found it elsewhere. If Peele's family were from Devon (See Horne, p. 10), he might have
preserved some local saying. McIlwaith notes: '"hay" may be either a country dance or
an abbreviation of "have you," but I do not understand this in either case.'"

to their turning away food when they arrive at the cottage. The weariness and negativity of the night before have vanished.

The artificial and elaborate divisions of the stage are dissolved in the resolution of Madge's tale. In the scene of Sacrapant's destruction, Jack positions Eumenides downstage and within Madge's part of the playing space. Not only does that blocking give room for the interaction between Sacrapant and Jack behind Eumenides, sitting deaf and blind to Sacrapant's art, but it puts Eumenides symbolically within Madge's power. When Sacrapant goes to Madge's part of the stage to address Eumenides, he is destroyed. Soon after, when the light that represents his art is blown out, his cell is breached in a way not possible before. Earlier, when the brothers and Huanebango and Booby start to enter the cell, they are struck down; yet the words Eumenides and Delya exchange when they first see each other underscore the fact that Eumenides has entered the cell successfully and is standing by her (844-47). The space previously closed to all but Sacrapant and his slaves is integrated into the rest of the stage. Sacrapant, who pretends his art is not a fiction and creates an art profoundly unnatural, acknowledges the superiority of Madge, who presents her art as artifice and imbues it with the process and laws of nature. Her audience's experience affirms the same recreative and restorative movement that informs her story. In that victory of hearth over cell, Peele dramatizes a reaffirmation of art.

Part IV
The Battle of Alcazar

[13]

ALCAZAR: The text and the sources

David Bradley

It is now a simple matter to rescue *Alcazar* from the implications of Greg's fanciful reduction of its cast to twelve. When we apply to this text the principles we have applied to others, it appears that there is no foundation at all for the idea. The Plotter calls for seventeen actors, and even if we follow his example by doubling the Queen of Morocco with Christopher de Tavora, and make things a little easier for ourselves by casting the Moor's son as a boy, we cannot reduce the adult cast required by the text below sixteen. Even then we will be in difficulties finding soldiers. The text, as we have seen, contains crucial scenes, and shows itself to be prescient about patterns of doubling that justify our counting the cast as of standard size. But it will not be easily fitted. In the original performance represented by the text, sometime about 1588 or 1589, there must have been a fair complement of boys. At I, ii, 230–3, we are treated to a description of the previous scene in which we are told that Abdilmelec's arrival at Tremissen was greeted by 'many Dames of Fesse in mourning weeds'. They do not appear in stage-directions, except perhaps as 'others' and 'the Ladies', but they are addressed at I, i, 123, and told to wipe their tears away. They must surely have been intended to appear; but there is not a sign of them in the Plot. Then, soldiers are needed for the first scene, to be addressed as 'ye Moors'. With sixteen men we can produce four actors (nos. 10, 11, 15, and 16 in the skeleton cast-plan on p. 244), but only if we had eighteen could we allow any of these to be black, as is their leader Zareo. Once again, the Plotter can provide no Moorish troops at all.

If, according to our rules, the text is in some difficulty, even with a standard cast, what is to be made of Greg's reconstruction? We must pause briefly on this, for his arguments in favour of it have been influential in creating a theory of indiscriminate doubling that is totally at odds with the facts as we have seen them. His cast is really only alleged to be of twelve men and four boys.[1] In fact it demands fifteen players to whom the Plotter in 1598 allots male roles. Greg makes only a small saving by doubling Ruben Arches, the widow of Abdelmunen, with Calipolis, the wife of her sworn enemy. He is not himself quite certain whether four boys are involved, or only two. He thus really allows for an adult cast of fourteen. If that were not so, his Portuguese court would have had a very juvenile appearance, three of Sebastian's four Lords having to be played by boys young enough to play women. Perhaps he felt justified in regarding such a possibility as a fall-back plan, because it is true of two of the five Portuguese Lords cast in the Plot. Attendants for the opposing Moroccan parties he also supplied by allowing two of Sebastian's Lords to alternate in their allegiance and to make immediate re-entrances on opposing sides.

To justify these admitted difficulties, Greg invoked a principle that when a character who is said to enter in the initial direction to a scene is allotted no speaking part, it may be suspected that there was an intention to delete him from the play, or at least from that section of it. The incidence of silent, named characters in good texts of the period is, of course, far too frequent to be any kind of key to corruption, and the wholesale application of Greg's theory would have depopulated the early drama to an alarming extent. Nevertheless, by judicious choice between the silent roles in his Plot of *Alcazar*, it was possible so to arrange the minimum cast as to suggest that the motive for excision in most cases was to eliminate the need for actors to make immediate re-entrances in changed costume in successive scenes.[2] Thus, at the expense of dodging the Presenter and Abdelmelec as the Ambassadors of Muly Mahamet, and dodging the latter as a Spanish Ambassador, he was able to avoid Barceles's change from an attendant Moor between II, iii and II, iv, on the grounds that the text's silent second Moor had been cut. Likewise de Silva must have been excised from III, i, where he does not speak, in order to appear as a Moorish attendant in III, ii.

These arguments are not quite disingenuous. On Greg's principles, there is no crisis for his hypothetical reviser in these scenes. He might have chosen to suppress any of the other non-speaking Lords, especially if, on identical grounds, he had suppressed the silent Muly Mahamet Seth in III, ii and cleared the way to double him as a Portuguese, which is an equally possible solution in other scenes as well. Greg's doubling patterns, therefore, are not truly revealing of limiting or crucial scenes. They are merely convenient possibilities. They cannot be shown to arise of necessity and they admit of too many exceptions to be convincing. They were, indeed, designed to support the proposition that the manuscript from which the text was printed had undergone a process of double revision.

First, Greg posited a reviser whose task was to make a fair copy of the original manuscript in which cuts had been carefully marked, and who wrote his directions in an italic hand. His careful copy would nevertheless have included odds and ends of the original directions that no longer applied. A second Stage-reviser then worked on this revised script, striking out speeches and omitting characters, and sometimes whole scenes, and roughly tidying up passages of dialogue where his cuts had left raw edges. Sometimes, where he had made wholesale revisions, he must have written new directions, but failed to alter the old ones in these scenes to accord with his own changes. Greg then discovered the signs of his activity in the roman stage-directions (both the roman and italic directions, we must assume, having been faithfully followed by the compositor) which he could then regard as more consistent with the revised text than the italic.

On these baseless hypotheses he was able to cast suspicion on the text in quite astonishing ways. For example, the one case that contravenes his observation that when a character is dropped from a scene the directions for his entry are always in italic is the direction for the death of the Duke of Avero in battle (*Malone Society Reprint*, line 1,367). This is easily explained as replacing a whole scene of the original – for at this point there is no parallel offered by the Plot. One is inclined to say with Dr Johnson that he who believes this may believe more. Greg himself saw that a quite different scenario was possible, but, rather than abandon his hypothesis of double revision he was prepared to allow for great inconsistency in the text and to doubt the thoroughness of both his hypothetical Stage-revisers. Thus, he also finds that Calipolis has been cut from an italic direction in which she is not mentioned, although she is addressed in the text and appears in the Plot. His argument for the original Vimioso having been deleted from Sebastian's Lords, in II, iv, is also curiously at odds with the argument that the Stage-reviser's actual intention in this and the subsequent Portuguese scene, III, i, was to remove the silent de Silva, whom he left prominently named, when both Vimioso and the Duke of Barceles have disappeared from the stage-directions without trace.

Suspicion falls on *Alcazar*, then, mainly because of its brevity. This, too, may simply be a matter of false perception. Hart's estimate of the average length of plays of the period as about 2,300 lines, obviously will not hold for plays printed between the opening of the Theatre and 1594, for which the figure is 1,623, just twelve lines longer than the text of our play. We may strongly suspect that *Alcazar*, like *Orlando*, began life as a Queen's play at about the same time as *Locrine*, *1 & 2 The Troublesome Reign of King John*, and *A Looking Glass for London and England*, all of which are sixteen-cast plays and much of a length. It is, perhaps, no accident that the first two share lines in common with *Alcazar* as well as other verbal echoes. It is also true of course that *The True Tragedy of Richard Duke of York* and others of the plays of the Strange's–Admiral's combination also echo *Alcazar*, but Queen's is the more likely company to have furnished the large number of boys Peele anticipates, and a drastic reduction of the men to sixteen from over twenty-five would surely have left gaping wounds. It is probable that either the dramatist himself or the Plotter who prepared the text of the 1594 Quarto did make adjustments to accommodate the text to the available cast, but those that we shall observe affect quite different passages of the text from those that concerned Greg and may be far more simply explained according to our alternative hypothesis. These changes are mainly the result of speeches being re-assigned to other speakers. They do not greatly affect the spoken text and the question of who made them will not be troublesome. As the text is prescient in many places about the casting problems, I propose for the sake of simplicity to speak of it as the dramatist's.

The story and the sources

By the fortunate chance that the source material for the greater part of the play is finite, we may now proceed straightforwardly to give an account of the playwright's strategy in adapting the historical record in sequence to the requirements of his stage and his cast, and thus to justify the text itself from the sources. *Alcazar* may be compared with its sources in a minuteness of detail that can hardly be matched in the case of any but some few of Shakespeare's historical tragedies. It is a highly instructive comparison, for this is a play about contemporary history written by a poet who, if something of a student in handling his historical material, had nothing of the imaginative passion that in Shakespeare transforms the moralised chronicles of Holinshed and Plutarch into the intellectual image of living creation.

Peele did a good job with *Alcazar*. He was writing, probably very rapidly, a popular pot-boiler about the most striking event of the recent past: more portentous in its way than the massacre of St Bartholomew because of its immediate importance for the expansion of Spain and the consequent threat to the precarious destiny of Protestant England. Possibly it had immediate relevance to the expedition of Drake and Norris in support of the pretender Don Antonio, an expedition which, whether the fact was widely known or not in England, had been jointly planned with that very Muly Hamet whose installation as King of Morocco ends the play.[3]

The playwright was clever at turning the historical record into popular spectacle and in giving it some marks of 'classical' prestige. His material itself was not lacking in excitement. It was already instinct with feeling, as the sources themselves indicate, and engaged an incurable bias in the mind of anyone who touched it. This fact is an advantage to the student.

The battle fought at El Ksar Kibir (Alcazar) on Monday, 4 August 1578 was one of the absolutely decisive and therefore forgotten battles of history. Its memory was so painful in Portugal that the true story could not be told. There was scarcely a family that did not mourn the loss of a son, and hardly an estate that had not either lost its heir or been ruined by his ransom. In the catastrophe, the country lost its king, the greater number of its nobility, and its national independence. The kingdom passed, after a brief interregnum, into the heritage of the hated Spaniard. It was not a pretty story for the self-esteem of the proud race of seafarers, the conquerors of the Indies. The nobility who set out from Arzilla on what was, with the Pope's official blessing, the last European Crusade, rolling bravely into Africa in their state coaches, ended it in the midst of a fearful slaughter, cringing under their silken cushions and begging for their lives on any terms. The expedition was in chaos before it sailed, its purpose confused, its leadership disastrous, its strategy incompetent, and its defeat overwhelming. Of the alleged 200,000 Portuguese, only half of them combatants, who made the dismal march to El Ksar Kibir, only some 200 regained the safety of the coastal fortresses.[4] The rest were either massacred or enslaved, a few hundreds of the nobility afterwards being ransomed.

The national reaction was silence and total disbelief, and the official accounts were never published either in Portugal or Spain until the Spanish archives were opened late in the nineteenth century. Philip II's motives in the affair were too much open to question for him to welcome any discussion of it. The Portuguese firmly refused to believe that the last of their Princes was dead, and the ready credence given to every rumour of his whereabouts created the semi-religious cult of the Sebastianists, who were still going strong in the last century, looking for the day when the mystic king should return, like Arthur from Avalon, to restore the national glories.

Accounts of the battle, some of them by eye-witnesses, were nevertheless written and filtered through to the rest of Europe, where they were published in French, Latin, and Italian, and, finally, in English. There are five sources from which Peele could have learnt the story, and it is probable that he knew and used three of them. He could not have known any others, for, before 1594, there quite certainly were none that were not mere transcripts of those already published. Those he had, he followed with such fidelity that there can be little doubt about what he had in front of him as he wrote. We are thus provided with a uniquely accurate check on his text in all the scenes, except the dumb-shows and those dealing with the notorious doings of the adventurer Thomas Stukeley. For the latter he might have drawn on all kinds of material, even including personal acquaintance, but his account of the facts differs so widely from the accepted tradition that it seems more probable that he invented most of it.

Of the 1,590 lines of text, 342 can be traced verbatim in the sources. At least as many more are mere commentary on this material or repetition of it in other ways. We can thus assign just under half the play with literal certainty to the source-materials. This half, moreover, contains the sum total of the information presented on any subject in the text, with the exceptions mentioned above, to which may be added a few incidents that appear to be picturesque inventions: the golden statue of Amurath in I, i, the 'lyones flesh' episode in II, iii, and the scene in which the Moorish ambassadors thrust their hand into a flame in token of good faith. Even some of these can, I believe, be traced to the source-material, at least for the germ of their invention. Ten more lines (lines 512–21) may be vouched for from their parodic misquotation in *Poetaster* (1602), and another six, attributed to Greene, from *England's Parnassus* (1608).

The earliest account to be published was in *Les Voyages et Conquestes des Roys de Portugal* (1578), allegedly the memoirs of a certain Sieur Joachim de Centellas. No such person appears to have existed. The work is almost certainly by Jean d'Ongoys, a Parisian printer and bookseller. His account cannot have been derived from eye-witness reports, for the details are so exceedingly inaccurate that they must simply have been invented, although invented by someone with a considerable knowledge of Portuguese history. Peele probably knew this work, but there is little evidence that he used it, except conceivably for Sebastian's speech to the Moorish ambassadors in II, iv.

The second and most important account for our purposes was written by a brother of the Order of Preaching Friars, Luis Nieto. He had lived some time in Morocco and probably spoke Arabic, for he is very well informed about the history and affairs of the Shareef Kings. In the dedication of his manuscript to Philip II he claims to have been present at the battle itself. His account was never published in Spanish, but a French translation was printed in Paris in 1579 under the title *Histoire véritable des dernières Guerres en Barbarie*. From this also a Latin version was made by Thomas Freigius, *Historia de Bello Africano* (1581), and published at Nuremburg. This, in turn, was translated into English by John Polemon and published in his *Second Booke of Battailes* (1587). It is certain that Peele used the English version and knew the Latin, for he borrows details from the poem prefacing Freigius's translation that was omitted by Polemon. He may also have known the French, for the French and Latin versions are very close and their account of events almost identical. They differ only in their spelling of a few names, in a scattering of mis-translations, and in omissions and additions that reveal their national bias.

The fourth and most authoritative account was published in Genoa in 1585, in a work entitled *Dell' Unione del Regno di Portogallo alla Corona de Castiglia* by Hieronimo Conestaggio, secretary to Cardinal Sforza. Conestaggio's version of the battle is so accurately informed and so critical of the Portuguese that it was immediately suspected of having been provided, if not written in its entirety, by Juan de Silva, the Spanish ambassador to Sebastian's court. Since the opening of the Spanish archives, it has been shown, by the close correspondence of *Dell' Unione* with de Silva's exactly similar but more outspoken despatches to Philip II, that such was almost certainly the case.

De Silva was an eye-witness of the whole train of events. It was he who watched the first levies of Portuguese exercising on the parade ground at Lisbon and wrote cynically back to his master that not one of them could handle a gun, the only instructor to be found being a Friar, who had himself never handled weapons, but had read up the theory from books. It was he who conveyed the frequent messages of dissuasion from Spain, and who understood the utter incompetence of the Portuguese nobility and the insensate chivalry of Sebastian. But Sebastian had his way with de Silva, as he had with most people, and the reluctant ambassador accompanied the expedition and fought valiantly in the king's entourage until the deluded young leader was dead and he himself wounded and forced to beg for his ransom.

The pro-Spanish flavour of Conestaggio's account is unmistakable and could hardly have attracted Peele, who, however, recognised its authoritative tone. On the whole, he used Nieto's account in Polemon's translation and took only the details from Conestaggio that are not vouched for by Nieto, and even then, only when the Spanish bias was not so obvious as to suggest real distortion.

Another account possibly known to Peele was a pamphlet called *A dolorous discourse of a most terrible and bloudy battel, fought in Barbarie* (1578). This is presumably a version of an account written by Don Duarte de Meneses that was known and circulating in London by October 1578. We cannot be certain that this is the exact version he saw, but it may be taken as typical of it. He does not use any of its details, but he may have checked the time-scheme of Nieto and Conestaggio against it, and it may have helped to confirm his imaginative picture of Muly Mahamet, who is called 'the blacke Kinge' throughout. No accounts of the battle other than those deriving from these five appeared in Europe before 1594, nor can the influence of any other accounts be detected in the very few histories or fictions concerning *Alcazar* written in Europe for at least the next hundred years. We may conclude that we have a complete account of all the material on the subject that could have been available to the playwright.

Peele had certainly done his homework, and his careful consideration of the documents is, paradoxically, illustrated by the confused pattern of allegiances his play follows. The sources all tend to be anti-Portuguese and highly favourable to Abdelmelec, the 'enemy'. There are many reasons for this. Muly Molocco was a cultivated ruler, wise, moderate, yet active in the exercise of arms, and proficient in Turkish, Spanish, and Latin. He was thought to be the best poet of his day in Arabic. He had an un-Moslem liking and admiration for Christians, and especially Spaniards, but the austerity of Protestantism attracted him more than the idolatrous worship of Rome. He was in secret correspondence with Queen Elizabeth, whom he much admired. He favoured her envoys, kept English musicians at his court and English dogs for his recreation. The Moroccan traffic with England, vital to the island kingdom as her sole source of saltpetre to furnish gunpowder for the fleet preparing to meet the threat of Spanish invasion, was equally important to Abdelmelec, and the goods that passed south in exchange, under the nose of Philip II, were also materials of war: muskets, firelocks, pikes, lances, heavy artillery, and iron shot. It is one of the major ironies of history that the forces of Portugal, England's oldest ally, were annihilated on the plains of Fez by firearms manufactured in the foundries of Kent and Surrey. It is a minor irony that the deforestation of those counties to feed the furnaces helped to establish the fortunes of Philip Henslowe, and to build the Rose theatre in which our play was performed.

If the personal stature and moderation of Abdelmelec forced Christian Europe to look critically at itself, even in the midst of its struggle with the empire of Suleiman the Magnificent, traditional allegiances were far too strong to represent him as other than an honourable exception to the rule of heathenish superstition and ignorance which it was the unique task of Christianity to confront and overcome. Sebastian's war was a Crusade, even if the Vatican had at first been made to think twice by pressure from

Philip II, whose truce with Amurath, forced on both of them by powerful religious and nationalistic revolutions at home, was endangered by the enterprise of Africa. The Bull for the Holy War had nevertheless arrived in Lisbon as early as 1573, and Philip had shown Sebastian remarkable signs of honour. Cynics might put down Philip's civility to a politic desire to appear attractive in the eyes of the Portuguese, whose king, given the inveterate disinclination of Sebastian to women and the virtually certain disaster of the expedition, he was quite likely to become. But there seems no doubt that he was genuinely fond of the young man. He wanted to stop him making a fool of himself, but was carried away, as everyone was, by the chivalric glamour of his ambitions. Even William of Orange, flattered to be approached with a request for help, allowed some companies of dissident German troops to sail for Lisbon at Sebastian's expense.

Sebastian is cast as the hero of the story: the last chivalric champion of medieval Europe. It is clear that whatever considerations of global strategy or differences in religion may have tempered the offers of practical support from the European princes, and whatever sober reflections about the folly of the expedition may have been provoked after the event by its failure, neither folly nor failure could inhibit the simpler emotional response accorded by everyone, including our playwright, to the ideals it evoked of honourable knight-errantry and the embattled unity of Christendom. It was Sebastian's destiny to live out those ideas, aroused in him by his Jesuit teachers from earliest boyhood, with particular intensity, and to become, only six years after the Spanish axe fell on the neck of the Inca king, Tupac Amaru, their last royal victim.

The villain is, in all accounts, Muly Mahamet. In this luxurious, cowardly, Christian-hating usurper, Sebastian's ally, the wounded sentiments of European chivalry found an apt and perhaps fitting scapegoat. The sources treat Mahamet with reasonable objectivity, commenting on his insignificant stature and indolent nature, but not attributing to him worse vices than might be expected of Moslem rulers. He took his complexion from his mother, who was black-skinned, and this taint was used by Moors and Christians alike to indicate the unreliability of his nature. Even Abdelmelec, his uncle, referred to him contemptuously as 'the negro'. He is thus an appropriate villain for our playwright, who dresses him in more devilish hues than the sources warrant.

This characterisation of Mahamet, however, leads to a conflict of loyalties within the play, because of Peele's peculiarly English pre-occupation with the legitimacy of rulers. It does not occur to the writers of the source material to put much emphasis on the tanist method of succession devised by the second of the Shareef Kings, but to the Elizabethan this abrogation of the right of primogeniture becomes a justification of importance for Sebastian's invasion. Mulei Shareef (Mahammed Ech-Cheikh, the *Muli zaref* of line 139 of the text) was the first king to unite Fez and Morocco under a single rule. He declared that the inheritance should always pass to the oldest surviving male member of the Shareef clan. He had thoughtfully put his own brother to death, so that in fact he was followed by his eldest son Abdallas (Abdullah el-Ghalib). Abdallas settled his position by disposing of his remaining cousins, and then, as Peele says, 'reigned his time', but his hand was also against the lives of his own brothers, Abdelmunen (Abd el-Moumen), Abdelmelec (Abd el-Malik), and Muly Mahamet Xeque or Seth (Ahmed el-Mansour) also called Muly Hamet in the play. The mother of two of the boys had taken them to Constantinople where they were brought up in the Turkish court. Abdelmunen had fled to Algiers. Abdallas then made clear his intention of settling the kingdom on his son, Muly Mahamet (Mohammed el-Mesloukh) and duly created him Viceroy of Fez. Abdelmunen was persuaded by promises of goodwill to return as far as Tlemcen (Tremissen) on the borders of Morocco, and there he was slain with an arrow, while at prayer in a mosque, by some followers of his nephew Mahamet.

Upon the death of Abdallas, Abdelmelec immediately begged support from Amurath, and, indeed, from Philip II, and set out for Tangier to assert his right to the crown. This is the point at which the play begins. Having defeated Mahamet in three rapid battles, he invested himself as king, at the same time naming his next brother, Muly Ahmed el-Mansour (Seth), his heir, thus upholding the legal manner of inheritance laid down by his father and ratified, as the play says, 'by voice of all his peers'.

It is a rather complicated story, and all accounts simplify it in one way or another; but all regard Abdelmelec as the rightful king and Mahamet as an usurper. Peele follows the sources in this, and allows Abdelmelec to set forth his claim to the throne in I, i as if the play had no intention of questioning it. At the same time he allows sentiment for the right of primogeniture to colour his emotional picture, and favourably interprets Sebastian's support for Mahamet as consistent with hereditary right 'according to … our wholesome Christian laws' (III, iv, 1,026). Sebastian's support of a wrongful king would put out all the emotional values of the play, but we are clearly told in the Presenter's first speech (I, Induction) that Mahamet is an usurper, and a murderous one at that, and so we must fall in with Peele's characterisation of him as a vicious and double-dyed hypocrite, without ever quite being able to put our finger on his actual acts of hypocrisy.[5] His offer of the Empire of Morocco to Sebastian is an obvious one, but we should think the less of Sebastian if it were allowed to appear that he had undertaken the expedition solely in hope of gain, and that enticement is rather played down as a motive. Mahamet then remains, like a pocket Iago, a creature of motiveless malignity, and on this rather infirm peg Peele hangs the interpretation of his story. 'Interpretation' is perhaps too positive a word, for he has nothing to say about the events, except for the journalistic comment, that, because of the Nemesis attendant on Mahamet's hypocrisy, so many tall men were 'destinate to dye in Afric here'.

The same confusion is evident in the playwright's treatment of

Stukeley, who speaks the words just quoted. He is allowed to die in Act V as a famous Englishman, and his dying soliloquy is a carefully neutral résumé of the major events of his life. Nothing more is alleged against him than that he was one of those

> that never could endure
> To hear God Mars his drum, but he must march,

and despite his sinister intention of invading Ireland, which brings him in the first place to Lisbon, he is treated throughout as a poor man's Tamburlaine. The typical note of his speeches is:

> Huff it brave mind, and never cease t'aspire
> Until thou raigne sole king of thy desire.

It would be absurd in such a play, where the characters are pasteboard and their motivations automatic, to look for any great subtlety in the handling of the sources, but as we shall see, Peele did criticise his material and tried to get the matter as clear as he could for an audience.

His first problem arose in deciding what to call his characters. This is rather a complex matter, and we had better deal with it at once. The story is to represent four parties: the Portuguese, the English adventurers, and two opposing teams of Moors, one led by Abdelmelec and the other by Muly Mahamet.

The Moroccan story offers four or five characters who have eminently confusable names. First there is 'the Moor', Muly Mahamet (Mahamet el-Mesloukh). In Nieto he is usually called *Muly Mahamet*, *Mahamet*, or *the Moor*, but sometimes the *Xerif*. In *The Dolorous Discourse* he is called *Mulla Sherriffa* or *the Blacke King*, and in Conestaggio, *the Moor*, the *Xariffe* or *Molei Mahamet*. To make things more confusing, Polemon sometimes calls him *Muly Hamet*, which is the commonest name for his youngest uncle.

Then there is the father of Abdelmelec, Mohammed Ech-Cheikh, who needs to be named as the instituter of the law of tanist succession. He is called *Muly Mahamet Xeque* in Nieto and also *Muly Mahamet*. In *The Dolorous Discourse* he is *Mully Hamet Shek*, and in Conestaggio *Molei Mahamet Xariffe*.

The Moor's son (another Mohammed Ech-Cheik) is called *Muly Xeq* (Nieto), *Muly Xeque* (Polemon) and *Moleixeque* (Conestaggio). In Freigius's table he appears merely as *Xequus*.

Abdelmelec's younger brother, Ahmet el-Mansour, who was the reigning king of Morocco at the time the play was written, is called *Muly Hamet* or *Muly Agmet* (Nieto), *Hamet* (Polemon and Conestaggio) and *Mulla Hamet* in *The Dolorous Discourse*.

Finally, there is the progenitor of the whole clan, Mohammed el-Kaim who is called *Xarif* by both Nieto and Conestaggio.

The reader will now be as confused as Peele undoubtedly was. He perhaps did not understand that *Xeque* is the Spanish transliteration of Sheikh, and he may have had no clearer idea than an average modern reader of what a Sheikh and a Mullah really are. He had no means of distinguishing the names of Ahmet (Hamet) and Mahamet from the sources. He appears to have taken the shorter form as a familiar name, much as Harry stands in relation to Henry, and allows that form of address to be used only by members of the family. But he still has three characters to represent with names so similar that they cannot be made clear, and others to mention who are equally confusable. So he begins to distinguish as best he can.

He keeps the title *Xarif* for the first king of Morocco and never uses it elsewhere. It appears as 'our grandsire *Mulizaref*'(I, i, 139). Then he decides to give the Moor's son no name at all in the spoken text. He is called 'boy', 'brave boy', 'my dearest son', 'this young Prince'. Peele *thought* of him as *Muly Mahamet*, however, for that is the form that occurs once in a stage-direction, and also in speech-headings when they vary from 'Moores son' or 'sonne'. He must call the Moor's grandfather *Muly Mahamet Xeque* because he has to be mentioned and there is nothing else to call him. The Moor himself he proposes to call *Muly Mahamet*, and here there will be no confusion, because the grandfather does not appear on stage. But he now has to distinguish Muly Mahamet the Moor from Muly Hamet (or Mahamet) his uncle. His first solution to that was to give the latter the distinguishing name, or title, *Xeque*. At his first entrance he is so called in the stage-direction and in two of his three speech-prefixes, the other being *Muly Mah*. There is no confusion here because the Moor is not on stage, but, as Hamet's grandfather of the same name is mentioned in the spoken text Peele allows the character on stage to remain unidentified, except by Abdelmelec's reference to 'my brother'. At his next appearance, his name has to be mentioned, for he is to be installed as heir to the throne. The dramatist, forced to make a decision and to find a name that can be pronounced (for what English actor could cope with 'Xeque'?), hits on the solution of calling him 'Seth'.

Greg takes this name to be a misreading of *Sech*, Peele's manner of writing the common Elizabethan transliteration *Seich* (Sheikh), but if that were so, we should have to suppose that the compositor misread it five times in an English hand, and once (according to Greg's theory) in an Italian hand. *Seich* is, of course, only one among many English forms for Sheikh. If Peele had wanted an alternative, the spelling *Shek* was available from *The Dolorous Discourse*. That he made a decision about the pronunciation may be guessed from the fact that as soon as Hamet is given that name, all trace of the original *Xeque* disappears from the speech-prefixes. He is listed as *Muly, Muly Mah.*, and eventually, after Mahamet is dead, simply as *Mah*. Peele had reason to infer from the sources that *Xeque* was a kind of title for the heir to the throne and he merely transferred it from the usurping family to the rightful tanist heir.[6] In the same way, he seems to have thought of the honorific *Muly* (Mullah) as the equivalent of 'Lord'.

We can now see how he solves the problem of the other Mahamets, distinguishing them quickly as he goes. He knew, as his audience did not, that there was a Muly Mahamet on stage in I, i. When, in I , ii, he is faced with two more, father and son, he calls them simply 'the Moore' and 'his sonne' in the stage–direction and adopts the expedient of using *Moore* for the father's speech–prefixes and *Muly Mah.* for the son's. This serves well enough. In the next scene, where Muly Mahamet Seth is named and speaks, he is now given the form *Muly Mah.* for his speech–prefix, for there can be no confusion with other Muly Mahamets, neither of whom is on stage. In II, iii the Moor enters as *the Moore*, but the son appears as *Muly Mahamet his sonne* and is *Mah.* in his speaking part. Upon the Moor's second entrance (with raw flesh spiked on his sword), *he* is now called *Muly Mahamet* and his first speech–prefix takes the form *Muly Mah.* This is clear enough for Peele's purposes, for the son has nothing more to say in the scene, but it is, of course, confusing for the reader.

In III, iv, where the Moor is addressed in the spoken text as *Muly Mahamet, Lord Mahamet*, and *the Arabian Muly Hamet*, the speech–prefix *Muly Mah.* for the son must be abandoned and he is given the elaborate heading *The moores sonne.* In IV, ii, where the son is not on stage, the Moor takes over the forms *Muly Mahamet* and *Muly Mah.*, but in Act V he becomes *Moore* once again. The reason is that in Peele's knowledge the 'boy' who enters with him *is* his son, although the fact that he is hysterically addressed as 'villain' gave Greg the impression that he was merely a servant. Moreover, Greg had been forced to double the son elsewhere in his hypothetical cast and was not disposed to interpret Mahamet's last speeches of neo-Senecan ranting as the work of a responsible dramatist.

After the Moor's speaking part has come to an end, the form *Muly* is taken over by Muly Mahamet Seth. On the report that the Moor is missing, his speech–prefix extends to *Muly Mah.*, and when it is virtually certain that the Moor is dead, he can be allowed the simple form *Mah.*, for he is now the only Mahamet of any shape or form left with a speaking role.

From an editorial point of view this is all totally irregular and, indeed, impossible to standardise, but it provides no grounds for doubting the text. All too often, the theories of textual bibliography can be sustained only by demanding of texts that were prepared for quite other purposes the consistency that is appropriate for the scholar in his study. As soon as we look backwards in this text we are, of course, confused by the haphazard duplication of speech-prefixes, but *au courant* they are clearly functional and explicable. It is very doubtful whether a reviser cutting this play could have maintained such a forward-running consistency. These directions are responsive to the dialogue at every point and must have come from a working dramatist in the act of composition.

One final question of nomenclature remains, that is, the alternative name for Abdelmelec: *Muly Molocco.* It is of some importance to determine whether this play was indeed the *mulomurco* performed by Strange's Men as an old play on 20 February 1592, and thereafter for

fourteen performances until 20 January 1593. The name is only twice used
of Abdelmelec: at line 15 and at line 418. In both cases it appears to be used
as a title with patriotic or thrilling overtones, and there is, of course, no
reason at all for it to appear in the Plot. It is not altogether clear from the
sources, and may never have dawned on the playwright, that *melec* and
Moluco are the same. The name occurs in Conestaggio as *Molei Moluco*,
and also as *il Moluco*, while Mahamet is called *Molei Mahamet Xariffe* and
il Xariffe Mahamet. This may well have suggested to Peele that the one had
the title *Xariffe* and the other *Moluco*. Greg did not know that the
dramatist was following a source in which *Moluco* is the standard form and
assumed that the appearance of *Molocco* in the text was some kind of sport,
deriving from *The Dolorous Discourse*, which has *Maluca*.[7] For the same
reason he failed to grasp the dramatist's intention in Act V, where
Abdelmelec's body is set up in a chair on stage 'with cunning props', so
that his soul may preside with joy over the defeat of the Christian army.
It is Conestaggio's account, alone of the sources, that records the
deception practised upon the Moorish army by which the dead
Abdelmelec was carried forward against the enemy in his litter as if still
alive and directing the operation.[8] Greg supposed that Abdelmelec played
only a minor role; but he has the fourth-largest speaking part, and
although mute in the fifth act he dominates the stage for the greater part
of it. *Muly Molocco* may very well have been the name under which the
play passed at the Rose: indeed I think there can be no doubt of its
identity, for there could not have been another play about Abdelmelec
based on the actual information available that was not exactly like this
one.

The doubt Greg cast on the ascription in *Orlando and Alcazar* was
provoked by his wish to sustain the roman–italic principle, which, as we
have seen, is false. In his edition of Henslowe he had been happy to let the
common identification stand, and Chambers followed him without
question. But the operation of the roman–italic argument makes it appear
that the excised portions of the play must have contained material relating
to Sebastian and Stukeley. He was thus inclined to look for the remains
of *mulomurco* in *The Famous Historie of Captain Thomas Stukeley*. This play
may well have excited the jibe in *Satiromastix* that the Admiral's Men has
'cut a poor Moor in the middle to serve him in twice', for the latter scenes
of *The Famous Historie* are a replay of some of the spectacular moments of
Alcazar. But the name *Molocco* is used only in the Spanish scenes of
Stukeley and these could not have appeared in the earlier *mulomurco*.
These matters having been disposed of, we may now follow the setting
up of the sources in action in somewhat greater comfort.

The sources in action

In the Presenter's first speech, the theme of the action is stated clearly
enough: this is to be an account of Portuguese honour and chivalry,
caught in the toils of the Nemesis that attends the murderous hypocrisy
of Muly Mahamet and his unjust usurpation of the throne from the 'brave
Barbarian Lord Muly Molocco'. The actual account of how that
usurpation came about is, as we have seen, more than a little difficult to
present, and has been further muddled by the attempt of the compositor
to rectify his second page. The first part of the speech runs thus:

> Honor the spurre that pricks the princely minde,
> To follow rule and climbe the stately chaire,
> With great desire inflames the Portingall,
> An honorable and couragious king,
> To vndertake a dangerous dreadfull warre,
> And aide with Christian armes the barbarous Moore,
> The Negro *Muley Hamet* that with-holds
> The kingdome from his vnkle *Abdilmelec*,
> Whom proud *Abdallas* wrongd,
> And in his throne instals his cruell sonne,
> That now vsurps vpon this prince,
> This braue Barbarian Lord *Muly Molocco.*
> The passage to the crowne by murder made,
> *Abdallas* dies, and deisnes this tyrant king,
> Of whom we treate sprong from the Arabian moore
> Blacke in his looke, and bloudie in his deeds,   16
> And in his shirt staind with a cloud of gore,
> Presents himself with naked sword in hand,
> Accompanied as now you may behold,
> With deuils coted in the shapes of men,
> Like those that were by kind of murther mumd.

The punctuation of the text is, of course, nowhere to be trusted, and in
the last two lines above I have reversed it in order to make a point. The
real confusion arises because of the page division. The last line of this
passage, which would otherwise have stood alone at the top of A2^v, is
printed following the direction for the first dumb-show in which the
Moor's young brethren are led to the bed in which they will later be
murdered. The reading thus appears to be:

> Like those that were by kind of murther mumd,
> Sit downe and see what hainous stratagems
> These damned wits contriue.

Now the murder of the young brethren has not yet taken place, and the
audience can hardly be asked to sit as still as the dead they have just seen
murdered when they cannot have seen any such thing. The dumb-shows
have clearly been inserted in the first convenient place, simply because
there is no exactly right place for them. The shows are almost continuous,

but the stage is cleared between them, and the time-continuum of the Presenter's commentary overlaps both, with appropriate pauses. There is no way of rectifying this as a written record, although it is perfectly simple to fit the parts together in performance. The real problem is the line

> Like those that were by kind of murther mumd.

One might attempt an emendation of this to read

> Like those that were of kind by murther mumd

but I am not sure that this makes any better grammatical sense in Elizabethan speech. The meaning, however, is tolerably clear. The words refer not to the young brethren who are about to suffer, but to their murderers, the 'devils' who accompany Mahamet. These have already been silenced forever because of their nearness to the throne.

The whole passage was troublesome to Greg, because it appeared to him that Abdallas's death is anticipated before the succession is secured. But this is not so. As long as we take 'deisnes' as a finite verb, almost certainly a misprint for the normal Elizabethan usage 'desines' (= nominates, or appoints) the combination of theatrical and historical sense works without obscurity. Peele has merely contracted the order of events for the sake of excitement. He turns at line 16, as it were, from the historical present tense to the theatrical present. *That* is the background to the action; *this* is what we are now to see; but the stage action he has planned causes some overlapping in the narrative.

In Nieto's account, the order of events begins with Abdallas's murder of his kindred, then the installation of Mahamet as heir at an assembly of peers, then Mahamet's murder of Abdelmunen, followed by the death of Abdallas, and finally the fates of the young brothers, one of whom in actuality was killed and the other imprisoned. Peele's intention is to represent the murders of Abdelmunen and the young brothers in his first dumb-shows, although the former event had in fact taken place before Mahamet's accession. These events, however, have nothing to do with 'the passage to the crowne by murther made'. *That* passage was created by the murder of Abdallas's uncle and cousins, and it is their devilish forms who now appear with Mahamet 'coted in the shapes of men'. There are only two of them, perhaps for the reason that two is a good number to carry Abdelmunen in his chair, but rather more probably because the dramatist is already counting his cast. The chair itself – as Greg did not see because it does not appear in the Plot – is an important property. It will later serve as Abdelmelec's litter in which his corpse will be propped up to oversee the battle sequence in Act V, and finally as the throne for Seth's installation.

In the remainder of the Presenter's speech we are returned to chapter IV of Nieto for the briefest possible explanation of Abdelmelec's life among the Turks and the slightly complex fact that the support of Amurath has been offered to him for services rendered to Amurath's predecessor,

Suleiman. We then pass to chapter V of Nieto to witness Abdelmelec's arrival at Algiers and at Tremissen where he meets with Muly Mahamet Xeque. That meeting and the setting out of Abdelmelec's claim to the throne are the principal concerns of I, i.

The characters to be brought on stage are partially drawn from Conestaggio's account, for, as we have seen, the dramatist would have been foolish to burden himself with Moors at this stage if he could have avoided it, and the Plotter could provide none at all. Nieto mentions only that Abdelmelec was given a commission to raise troops in Algiers. That he returned with Moorish troops is recorded only by Conestaggio:

He obtained three thousand soldiers of the Turke ... [and] with these forces and the Moores that followed him, which wanted not in Africk, he entered his Nephewes kingdom.[9]

Peele takes Conestaggio's word that the Turkish troops had come from the Porte and presumably decided on a name for the leader, Calcepius, before turning the page of Nieto where it is discovered that his name was Rabadan. There can be no doubt that Calcepius is original and was followed by the Plotter. Peele then borrowed Zareo from the later account of the battle, and made him Abdelmelec's chief lieutenant. He is called *Argerd* Zareo, but it is not necessary to think that this suggests some connection with Algiers. I should be tempted to suppose that the word in Peele's copy was *Vizeroie*, carelessly written in an English hand (Zareo is given that title in Polemon). A printing-house reviser, checking from the description of this scene offered in I, ii might have discovered the meeting to have taken place 'Neere to Argier' and invented the curious adjective. But I am reluctant to compete with the speculations of the bibliographers. What is certain is that Zareo is described as a Moor, but his soldiers are not certainly of the same complexion. Indeed, the singling out of Zareo in the stage-direction may suggest that they could not be. As I have said, there is no possibility of these soldiers being blackamoors in a sixteen-cast play, and the Plotter, once again, provides none at all.

The soldiers' welcome will inevitably be rather thin, but Polemon records that Abdelmelec was 'honourably received' at Tremissen. If this is to be represented on stage, it can only be by means of the boys. They appear only as 'others' in the stage-direction, entering with Muly Mahamet Xeque and the royal ladies at line 105, but they are vividly described in the following scene (I, ii):

> Rubyn our vnkles wife that wrings her hands
> For Abdilmunens death, accompanied
> By many dames of Fesse in mourning weeds,
> Neere to Argier encountred Abdilmelec.

As he cannot make a convincing military entrance, the playwright has turned the spectacle into a family occasion, dressing the Dames in black and possibly allowing Ruben to sing a dirge or 'tragicke song'. If so, it has not been preserved, just as songs in many printed texts and manuscripts are

'Alcazar': the text and the sources 143

missing, but Abdelmelec's rather dry-sounding comment is presumably a
response to it:

> Rubin these rights to Abdelmunens ghost
> Haue pearst by this to Plutos graue below.

The rest of the information in this scene is vouched for by the sources;
but, as the Plot is seriously in default here, and, by the application of
Greg's logic, the text has therefore been suspected, it may be worthwhile
to defend two brief passages against the charge of corruption. One
concerns the possibility of dropped lines following line 123. Here
Abdelmelec addresses the boys on stage as:

> Distressed ladies and yee dames of Fesse,
> Sprong from the true Arabian *Muly Xarif*
> The loadstarre and the honor of our line.

The playwright can hardly have thought this to be literally true. If a line
or two is not missing, we must take 'sprong' rather loosely, but that is not
at all inconsistent with the strong team spirit that characterises each party
in the play. 'Arabian' is, for the Moors, a word of approval. It recalls the
direct descent of the royal family from the Prophet Mahamet. Even the
black Mahamet is 'sprong from the Arabian moore' (line 18), but
Abdelmelec and the dames spring from the 'true Arabian'. I believe that
Peele intends to imply that the royal ladies and the dames of Fez are all 'on
our side' and are all white. He may possibly have been undecided about
whether the Shareef was, indeed, the progenitor of the whole race, or
merely the first king, for there is a possible ambiguity in the lines

> And of the Moores that now with vs do wend,
> Our grandsire *Mulizaref* was the first,

but I believe this is to be read as a grammatical inversion and that the
name is correctly used as a title by Peele, both here and in the quotation
above.

The second suspect passage, lines 111–117, throws some light on the
style of the verse. Muly Mahamet Xeque is speaking as one who has
arrived at Tremissen having just passed by the camp of the Turkish
Janissaries:

> Our Moores haue seen the siluer moons to wane,*
> In banners brauely spreading ouer the plaine,
> And in this semicircles haue descride
> All in a golden field a starre to rise,
> A glorious comet that begins to blase,
> Promising happie sorting to vs all.
>   [*sc. waue]

This metaphor, which fits together literal pieces of information and a
violent conceit is very offensive to the taste of modern critics. It is,
however, typical of the style of the play (cf. lines 125, 257–60, 267–72,
512–22, 550–1, 565–7, 574–5, 578–81, 584–609 – this, a gloriously inverted

example, parodied by Shakespeare – 752–5, 806–7, 817–18, 836–7, 888–93, 968–70, 973–5, 1,014–18, 1,021–2, 1,045–9, 1,406–9). The trick was perfected by Marlowe and is natural to the early drama that imitates him. Greg regarded the passage as corrupt because of the breakdown of rhyme after 'plaine / wane'. Yoklavitch correctly pointed out the turned letter in 'wane', but still attempted to support Greg's diagnosis of corruption by observing that the Ottoman flag did not bear a star within the crescent in the sixteenth century. That does not seem to have been recognised by Elizabethan illustrators and Portuguese mapmakers, or by the designer of the Turkish banner captured at the Battle of Lepanto and now in the Doge's Palace in Venice, but even if it were officially so, it is not necessarily relevant to the passage.

Peele is attempting to move from the Moors' observation of the presence of Turkish soldiers, which is literally true and demonstrated by the presence of some few of them on stage, to the abstract joy of the beholders at seeing them. To do so, he fixes on the waving banners of the Janissaries, which, it is the point of the metaphor to say, have put new heart into the Moorish nation. The crescent banners are then transferred, as it were in long-shot, to the (offstage) formation of the main body of the army as it spreads over the plain. Nieto mentions that typical 'demi-circulaire' disposition of a Turkish force, and Polemon translates it as 'new Moon'. De Silva (Conestaggio) well remembered the 'corni della luna' in which Abedelmelec drew up his army at Alcazar and which threw the Christian army into confusion and cut off its retreat. The golden field is, of course, the field of promised success, but also the heraldic field of the crescent banners. The star or comet is an omen of success, but it is also an actual comet that might have been seen rising above the army spread on the plain. This comet appeared in 1577, the year in which Peele took his B.A. at Oxford, and he may well have remembered it as a matter of personal experience. If not, he could not have missed it either in the Latin poem prefixed to Freigius's account, or in the amusing description in Conestaggio of its appearance over Lisbon on 9 November. I do not pretend it is a skilfully managed metaphor, but it is perfectly intelligible when one observes the elements of Peele's reading that went into it.

The dumb-shows, indeed, also spring from the same trick of sub-poetic thought, whereby a verbal allegory is merely made into a literal spectacle. If Mahamet is 'bloody', he appears in a shirt sprinkled with gore; if war is a 'fatal banquet', waited on by weapons, blood and death, a table appears, furnished with dishes of bones and severed heads, and attended by three garçons bearing symbolic properties; if kingdoms are falling, as in Act V, crowns are hung on a tree and persuaded one by one to drop off.

This innocent poetry of make-believe strikes critics as childish, as no doubt it is. The implication of the commentary on these passages is either that Peele could not have written them, or else that they are all corrupt. They are, of course, easily corrupted, for they are close to nonsense as they stand, and one compositorial error throws them into complete confusion.

They naturally excite editorial impatience, because they strain concepts of syntax and are almost totally resistant to modern punctuation.

One other semblance of confusion in this scene might be taken to indicate the omission of some previous action. Calcepius declares that he has come to make Abdelmelec Emperor (lines 99–101) and will say later that he is 'calld for by the Gods / To sit vpon the throne of Barbary', as if that is still to happen in the future. On the other hand, Muly Mahamet Xeque refers to Abdelmelec as 'your anointed king' (line 197). But nothing is missing. There can have been no coronation scene, nor is any suggestion of it included in the description of this scene that is offered in the next. There is, indeed, no mention of any ceremony of installation in the sources. What is involved here is simply the difficulty of keeping the time-sequence straight in a play where the choruses anticipate the action. We have been told in I, Induction that it is Abdelmelec who suffers the wrong of Mahamet's usurpation. We have seen an anonymous uncle strangled in his chair and are now told that Abdelmelec is fighting to revenge 'my deepe wrongs, and my deare brothers death'. The account we have been given, in between, of the tanist laws of inheritance, makes it clear that the man we saw strangled *was* Abdelmunen, the next legitimate heir, whose claim has now passed to Abdelmelec. Abdelmelec's 'anointing' may thus pass as a pardonable exaggeration, indicating merely that he is truly legitimate.

In I, ii we come to the first of the all-black scenes. The Moor appears in his celebrated chariot, counter-marching none too bravely against Abdelmelec's forces, who, we are told, are already encamped near Fez. Muly Mahamet's concern is to get his treasure safely past the enemy lines, but precisely where it is going cannot be made out. Peele routes it through Scyras, a place-name that has no equivalent in the sources, or in any map of North Africa that I have found. I believe it is merely a tag name, invented to serve the moment's need.[10] The treasure is to be captured and a report will arrive that the whole country is turning to Abdelmelec. At the end of the scene the Moor and his company are to leave the stage in flight.

All the sources agree about Mahamet's understanding of the importance of money in warfare. The subject of the treasure (it appears in the stage-direction) is therefore a useful device for the dramatist, for material is already running short and a great part of this scene is taken up with a description of the preceding one. Moreover, there can be no battle, for there are no troops. The dramatist envisages seven black actors, in all, but only three of them are available as soldiers, and two will presumably be necessary to move Mahamet's chariot. If pages were used for the purpose, as in the Plot, they are not mentioned. The other actors available as soldiers have all appeared in the preceding scene on Abdelmelec's side, and, except for Zareo, must all have been 'white'. Thus, the battle of Er-Roken in which Mahamet's treasure was captured, must be represented by a messenger, while Mahamet, his wife, his son and his two attendants remain on stage. It is rather absurd to suppose, as Greg does, that the treasure was a mere flourish of the dramatist's that could not have appeared (because there are no properties listed in the Plot). The treasure is the whole *raison d'être* of this scene and there is no reason why Pisano should not, if necessary, have carried it himself. I suspect that Greg may have assumed that it would need to be carried in the chariot, and, as the chariot does not leave the stage, this must have been another example of truncated spectacle. It is probably Greg, not the dramatist, who is confused here. Pisano is ordered to take a cornet of horse and other forces,

> And with our carriage march awaie before.

The impression is thus created that some form of vehicular transport has departed with Pisano, but a carriage is, of course, a sixteenth-century baggage-train, not a chariot.

The appearance of Mahamet's chariot is amusingly justified by the French translation. Mahamet was not personally courageous. He is said in the manuscript to have watched the battle from a *cerro*, or little hill. A copyist or translator mistook the word for *carro*, which Freigius renders as *carrui* [*insistans*], and Polemon as *wagon*. But the French version has *char*. It seems likely that Peele was happy to take the grander of the possible meanings of the French word, but it may also have been attractive because he knew Tamburlaine's chariot was available in the properties' store.

Nevertheless, this scene shows clear evidence of the dramatist's having been in difficulties. The absence of Calipolis from the stage-direction need not detain us, although it is made much of by Greg. There is no reason for cutting her from the scene. A more probable explanation is that she has been added to it. This was probably by the dramatist himself when he came to introduce her first as originally planned in II, iii. There he wrote the elaborate and probably initial direction: *with Calipolis his wife*. Then he realised that she might be called to appear to swell the numbers in the earlier treasure scene and introduced her there simply by adding an extra-metrical word of address to one line (line 221):

> Madame, gold is the glue, sinewes and strength of war.

Calipolis simply completes the tally of the six negro Moors who may be called to enter in this scene, but there are signs soon afterwards that the text did need revision because of a shortage of cast and that an impression of numbers was needful.

After the exit of Pisano (which is unmarked), the verse certainly goes to pieces for five lines, while we move into the speech of Young Mahamet's recapitulation of the events of I, i:

> (*Moore.*)   Now boy whats the newes?
> *Muly Mah.*   The newes my Lord is warre, warre and reuenge.
> And if I shall declare the circumstance,
> Tis thus.
> Rubyn our vnkles wife that wrings her hands
> For Abdilmunens death, accompanied

> With many dames of Fesse in mourning weeds,
> Neere to Argier encountred Abdilmelec,
> That bends his force puft vp with Amuraths aide
> Against your holds and castles of defence.
> The yonger brother Muly Mahamet Seth,
> Greets the great Bassa, that the king of Turkes
> Sends to inuade your right and royall realme,
> And basely beg reuenge, arch-rebels all,
> To be inflict vpon our progenie.

It teases us out of thought to know how the son came to have learned all this. Moreover, it seems that his reluctance to speak is an admission that he has no business to know it. The speech is really in Messenger language. It is inappropriate for the boy to refer to one of his great-uncles as 'our uncle', and to the other as 'the younger brother', and even more inappropriate for him to speak of '*our* progenie', for, while Peele sometimes uses that term in its widest application to refer to ancestors as well as descendants, the only surviving progeny of the Moor and his son in any sense are the arch-rebels themselves! The most natural conclusion is that the speech originally belonged to a Messenger. When re-allocated to the son, two changes of pronoun have been made. The original would have read: 'Rubyn *your* vncles wife' and 'To be inflict vpon *your* progenie'. The Messenger has more to say, but the boy at this point appears to react in fear, as if he were the progeny intended, and Mahamet's next speech is comforting:

> Why boy, is Amurath's Bassa such a bug,
> That he is markt to do this doubtie deed?

The son, nevertheless, continues with the Messenger's speech until interrupted by Mahamet with a line that might more appropriately have been addressed to the original Messenger, the change to the son being rectified by the addition of two extra-metrical addresses ('Why boy' and 'Boy') to the following lines :

> *Moore.*   Awaie, and let me heare no more of this,
> Why boy, are we successours to the great Abdilmelec,
> Descended from the Arabian Muly Zarif,
> And shall we be afraide of Bassas and of bugs,
> Rawe head and bloudie bone?
> Boy, seest here this semitarie by my side,
> Sith they begin to bath in blond, (sc. bloud)
> Bloud be the theame whereon our time shall tread.

'Abdilmelec' is, of course, an error for 'Abdallas'. This may suggest that the patching here was the work of a reviser, but the regularity of the speech-headings is more indicative of the author himself. A reviser is unlikely to have changed an original Messenger's speech-prefixes to *Muly Mah.* for the son in a scene where the father is the more prominent character. But patching there has probably been, and at least one line has dropped out of the text after line 258.

These signs of revision point to the excision of a first Messenger in the scene, and reveal that the playwright had given some thought to the identity of the second Messenger who is now to enter to report the loss of the baggage-train. There seems, on reflection, no reason why the three Moorish attendants should not have left the stage with the treasure, two of them returning subsequently as the two Messengers. The dramatist, however, did not arrange things this way. The speech of the second Messenger implies that more actors remain on stage than Mahamet's immediate family. He cries:

> *Mes.*   Flie king of Fesse, king of Moroccus flie,
>   Flie with they friends Emperour of Barbary

and, if this is so, there is no-one to enter but Pisano, unless the playwright had been prepared to use a white actor. The dialogue makes that most improbable, for the Messenger gives Mahamet his three royal titles, which no white Moor would do. Thus, it would appear that the dramatist wanted Mahamet to remain attended by his guard, and was even prepared to revise his text in order to permit it, roughly ironing out the rather gross improbability of characterisation in transferring these speeches to the son. There is probably a more compelling reason, concerning the status of the actors, that is hidden from us. When we plot out the roles of these attendants it appears that one is always mute and the other allotted only a very few lines. They are not of sufficient dignity to be allowed to speak these speeches. The Plotter of 1598 adopted precisely the same solution, using the mute William Cartwright as one attendant and Mr Hunt, who can have spoken at most ten lines, as the other, and returning Pisano (Sam Rowley) to the stage to report the loss of the baggage he was sent to guard.

There is no inkling in the remaining part of the scene that the original speech of the second Messenger has been tampered with. The verse is perfectly regular. It is merely perverse of Greg to argue (this being a crucial test of the roman–italic theory) that Pisano was originally recognisable as the El-Dogali of the sources, the captain whose defection at the battle of Er-Roken lost the day for Mahamet.[11] Greg's reason for this is that Pisano's speech implies that treachery has been at work in the surrender of the garrisons – and that is simply not true. The dramatist must also have envisaged the second Messenger as Pisano, just as the Plotter does, for he now had only one more black actor to call on – Zareo! – who is blocked here by having to enter in the next scene. The lack of another must certainly have caused the excision of the first Messenger from the scene. It is fairly clear that the playwright's understanding of the situation was identical with the Plotter's, although, as he was prepared to double Zareo in the Moor's party in a later scene, he may have had that alternative in mind here. The Plotter could not have followed him, for his Zareo is white.

In the Induction to the second Act there is no independent direction for a dumb-show, but one cannot believe that the Presenter's speech was unaccompanied by performance. The verbal cues: *Hearke Lords* ... *And now start vp* ... *Thus* ... *is a councell held*, imply that something is intended to take place. The pantomime is, indeed, essential to the dramatist's theme. The ghosts of the murdered brethren and Abdelmunen are heard crying for revenge, 'as in a hollow place a farre'. Their cries arouse Nemesis, who appears beating on her 'doubling drum'. A drum is not a conventional property of Nemesis, but the drummer-boy of the company is to be pressed into service, and his noise arouses the Furies, who appear with symbolic properties listed in the text. All this is followed to the letter by the Plotter. Despite Greg's suspicions of excisions here, it is difficult to see what could have been omitted. The verse is in need of little emendation, as long as we read the obvious *Dimme Architect*, for *Diuine Architect* at line 312.

The remainder of the Presenter's speech will be cause for comment in some later scenes, for, like I, Induction, it appears to muddle the order of events and to omit the Stukeley scenes altogether. This might give grounds for suspicion, were it not for the fact that lines 340–59 are a précis of chapter VI of Nieto and keep closely to the order of events there recounted. The only thing that is not in Nieto is the description of the ceremony of Calcepius's departure. The Plot contains no mention of the playwright's spectacular invention and it is worth noting:

> The dames of Fesse and ladies of the land,
> In honor of the sonne of Soliman,
> Erect a statue made of beaten gold,
> And sing to Amurath songs of lasting praise.

The scene in which this is enacted immediately follows. There is, admittedly, no mention of the golden statue in the stage-directions, and the Dames of Fesse are called on stage only by their generic name, 'the Ladies'. This is a common term for 'all the boys' and occurs twice, as we have seen, in *2 Seven Deadly Sins*. There may have been a distinction in the playwright's mind between 'the Ladies' who are Dames of Fesse, and enter at the beginning of the scene, and 'the noblest ladies of the land' to whom attention is drawn later in the scene, and who may have been intended to enter at that point, bearing gifts for Calcepius. If that is so, it was not grasped by the Plotter. He brings on all the ladies at the beginning, just as the stage-directions seem to require. From the text, we may picture this strange attempt at an oriental ceremony, in which, to the sounding of trumpets, incense and obeisance are offered to a golden statue of Amurath. This cannot have been another of Greg's vague gestures of the dramatist, for some of the lines will sound very odd without it. The Queen, for example, declares:

> As Rubin giues her sonne, so we ourselues
> To Amurath giue, and fall before his face.

Abdelmelec's payment of his 'due and duties' to Amurath must also be accompanied by some offering or gesture of a like kind.

All this is an attempt by Peele to represent three events of importance recorded in Nieto, chapter VI: the sending away of the Turkish Janissaries, the growing love towards Abdelmelec of all his subjects, who 'with liberall and bountifull mindes brought him verie great, rich, and honourable gifts and presents', and the swearing of 'all the peeres of the kingdom unto his brother Muley Hamet', followed by 'incredible feasts and triumphs'.

One further casting problem for the dramatist in this scene must be observed. We have seen that he had to introduce two white Moors in the very first scene, and might have introduced four if he had wished. It is perhaps more likely that he thought of four Janissaries and two Moors. In the present scene (II, i), he calls once again for Moors and Janissaries, and one might expect that this direction would bring on the same attendants who had appeared previously. But that can no longer be. A new set of characters altogether is to appear in the following scene (II, ii) – Diego Lopez, Governor of Lisbon, the English Captains, Stukeley, Jonas and Hercules, and an Irish Bishop. All but the Governor must have appeared either as Moors or Janissaries in I, i. Thus, in II, i, four of the original supporters of Abdelmelec are blocked from entering and only two actors can appear as Janissaries. They are the actors who will later be needed for the Dukes of Avero and Barceles, but they still have an intervening scene in which to change costume. If Sebastian himself did not double as a Janissary, there is no help for it but to call in the Presenter as the Governor of Lisbon, just as the Plotter does in 1598. The Presenter will, in any case, be needed in some capacity or other, for the only remaining members of cast who can swell this scene are black. The stage-direction for II, i reads:

Alarum within, and then enter Abdilmelec, Muley Mahamet Seth, Calsepius Bassa, with Moores and Ianizaries, and the Ladies.

The text, once again, shows the dramatist to have calculated the situation. We do not know precisely how many Moors he expected to appear. As this scene is imagined to be an entrance from battle, any number of the black cast may be brought on, but, whoever they are, apart from Zareo, they must be of Mahamet's party, and they will at least equal and probably outnumber the Janissaries. Greg, of course, was right in sensing some awkwardness here, but his suspicion that a speech of Abdelmelec's and other speeches of Zareo's had been excised was needless. To have included a victory speech by Zareo would have been insensitive, for he would have to speak as a black Moor who had triumphed over others of his race, whereas the given of the scene is that the victory has been won by the Janissaries. Abdelmelec himself speaks in diplomatic confusion of:

this fight happie and fortunate
Wherein our Moores have lost the day

for the black Moors are still *his* subjects, even if in defeat, and, as the scene must be filled, they are politicly addressed as *our* Moores and *Lords of Barbarie* (line 378).

'Alcazar': the text and the sources 151

The second business of the scene is to install Muley Mahamet Seth as heir to the throne. The dramatist could see from Nieto, chapter VI that this involved Abdelmelec's re-affirmation of the tanist law, and the confirmation of it by an oath of the nobility. But it is a little awkward to have a troop of defeated peers swearing allegiance to a man who has so recently been their enemy. Abdelmelec therefore does not ask for their franchise, but appeals to a higher power:

> Ye Gods of Heaven gratulate this deed,
> That men on earth may therewith stand content.

Here, as elsewhere, we can see the playwright giving the best account he can of the source-material with his available cast. He was probably also aware that Calcepius's generous words:

> This chosen gard of Amurath's Ienizaries
> I leaue to honor and attend on thee

would ring very hollow, for neither of the soldiers offered to the new king will ever be able to appear with him again. The story told in Conestaggio, however, has to be kept faith with.

Peele leaves aside the fortunes of Mahamet (described in Nieto, chapter IV) until the next scene, and skips forward to Chapter VII to introduce a scene in Portugal not accounted for in the Presenter's Induction – the arrival of Stukeley and his company at Lisbon. Stukeley's name is not given accurately in any of the sources. Nieto calls him both Count and Marquess of Ireland and Conestaggio corrupts his name to Esternulie, but Peele obviously knew something of his history by common report, and was able to make use of Conestaggio's fuller account, which he follows in general outline.

Conestaggio represents Stukeley as furnished with troops by the Pope at the instigation of Philip II, who, irritated at Elizabeth's secret help to the Netherlands, determined to follow her methods and secretly to abet the plots of the Earl of Desmond and the Catholic faction in Rome against Ireland. The party having been wrecked by a storm in the bay of Lisbon, however, their ship became subject under Portuguese law to the disposal of the crown, and Sebastian lost no time in persuading them to accompany him to Africa in return for promised help on their return. To this Philip could offer no public objection, for he wished his hand in the matter to remain secret, and the Pope was too far away for news of the detour to reach him until the army was already in Africa.

Nieto furnishes Stukeley with 600 Italian troops and three men of war, but he gives no reason for the expedition. Conestaggio gives him only one ship, but confirms the 600 troops, and this figure appears to be correct, for it is also confirmed by the deposition to Burghley of English merchants in Rome. The dramatist has multiplied it tenfold, for effect (line 723), and worked out that an army of 6,000 would need seven tall ships and two pinnaces for its transport.

Greg's feeling that the play once had much more to do with Stukeley

stands on very frail ground. Any unbiased reader must admit that the
existing Stukeley material is already spread extremely thin. There is much
material from which the dramatist might have gathered information
about the man, but scant evidence that he used any of it.[12] Stukeley's own
speeches are mostly the padded-out hyperboles of a wide-boy who has
recently been reading his *Tamburlaine*, and the facts of his life, as given in
his dying soliloquy, are few and inaccurate. There is no evidence that he
originally appeared in any of the dumb-shows where the Plotter has
introduced him.

Once Stukeley is dead, no further mention is made of him and we
cannot suppose that he ever had a more prominent part in the finale. The
sources are impressed by the spectacle of three kings dead in a day, or, as
one says, 'three kings *in re* and one *in spe*', and although Peele seems to
have prepared the ground for Stukeley to seek reputation by spilling his
blood in the company of kings, the idea is not carried through. The author
of *The Famous History* was fully and accurately informed about Stukeley's
early life, but when he comes to the affair of Alcazar he, too, goes directly
and independently to Polemon for the main details. Peele is able to eke out
a little more for Stukeley to say from Conestaggio, and he did know two
odd things that he could not have derived from any published source that
I have discovered. One is that the Bishop accompanying Stukeley's
expedition is made, apparently for the sake of a silly pun, the Bishop of
St Asaphs ('asses'). In fact, Bishop Cornelius Goldwell, with whom
Stukeley is known to have been associated when in Rome, was Bishop of
St Asaphs,[13] and a Bishop Cornelius was reported on the expedition.[14]
The other is that the play gives the point of departure from Italy as Ostia
('Austria', line 487), which, according to the reports of the English
merchants to Burghley, is more correct than the sources that give it as
Civita Vecchia.[15] Stukeley's murder by the Italian forces he commanded
is mentioned in both plays and in the ballad tradition, but there appears
to be no reliable source for the story.

In II, iii we return to Mahamet fleeing with his party into the
mountains. He is without his chariot, but since there are no details of any
intervening happening and his opening speech indicates that he is still in
flight from the battle, we must suppose that the scene is virtually
continuous in time with I, ii. The Presenter has already given us the
programme:

> By this imagine was this barbarous Moore
> Chased from his dignitie and his diademe,
> And liues forlorne among the mountaine shrubs,
> And makes his food the flesh of sauage beasts.

'The mountain shrubs' happily translates the French *aux plus espais et
touffus lieux de la montagne*, but although Nieto dwells on the hardships of
life amidst cold, snow, and perpetual fear, he does not suggest hunger or
wild beasts. Peele may have invented the idea of Mahamet's forcing the
lioness from her prey and returning with 'lyons flesh vpon his sworde',

but he may have found the germ of the idea in various ways. In Conestaggio there is a description of Sebastian's training for war: 'The king gave himself inordinately to the chase, and was never more elated than when he met with the savagest of animals in single combat.'[16] The lions of Barbary were also perhaps known from Drake's account of his voyage round the world, where the English sailors, standing off the Barbary coast near the ruins of the ancient city of Tit at the precise moment of the battle of Er-Roken, saw them to be inhabited by the beasts and could plainly hear their roaring from the sea. This may have given Peele the idea that lions might rend 'The breeding vaultes / Of proudest sauages'[17] (lines 593–4).

This notorious scene was much parodied, and there can be little doubt that it was played in 1598 in the form represented by the text. Pistol misquotes its refrain – 'Then feed and be fat (my faire *Calipolis*)' – in *2 Henry IV*, among much other fustian from play-ends, and, in Jonson's *Poetaster*, two theatre boys, riding one on the other's shoulders, stride round the stage in mimicry of Edward Alleyn's tall frame spouting seven of the ridiculous first ten lines.[18]

The elaborate identification of Calipolis is evidence enough that she was originally introduced here for the first time, in order to provide a motive for Mahamet's hunting. She is named six times in the scene and referred to by the son as 'mother' and possibly as 'my father's wife' (wise?). One may compare with this the case of Calsepius who is named twice on his first appearance and not at all on his second. Even Stukeley, who has a habit of repeating his own name, does so only three times in the first scene in which he appears.

The text, however, creates a mild suspicion that something has been left out, by having jumped ahead in the Act II Induction to give us the programme for the following scene as well:

> Now at last when sober thoughts renude,
> Care of his kingdome and desired crowne,
> The aide that once was offered and refusde
> By messengers, he furiously imployes,
> Sebastians aide braue king of Portugall.

We are told in II, iii that Mahamet has sent ambassadors to Sebastian, as we had previously been told by the Presenter, but the Presenter's list of events, although derived directly from the sources, does not accurately forecast what we are in fact to see. In this matter, as Greg pointedly observes, the text appears to depart from the sources: it should have read 'the aide that *twice* was offered and refusde'. But this is mere obfuscation. The dramatist knew from Conestaggio, as Greg did not, that these negotiations were protracted through many more stages than two. Peele obviously did not want to go into long explanations of how it occurred to Mahamet to seek aid from Portugal, or to probe deeper into Sebastian's motives than that he was 'forward in all armes and chiualrie'. To have done so would have thrown out all the emotional values of the play.

The ordering of the scenes, nevertheless, creates a casting problem. Two of the black actors must appear in II, iv as Mahamet's Ambassadors, and they are therefore precluded from appearing in this scene. Peele thus writes the direction for II, iii precisely:

Enter the Moore, with Calipolis his wife, Muly Mahamet his sonne, and two others.

One of these others has the speech-prefix '*Zareo*', and that is perfectly logical. One of the three black attendants is always mute. Pisano and the first 'devil' will therefore appear as Ambassadors and Zareo must be called in to speak in this scene. It may be that he was initially described as a Moor with this very purpose in mind, for even had Peele contemplated using Mahamet's Moors in two immediate re-entrances in the first three scenes (as Greg's reconstruction does), he would still not have been able to provide four black Moors for Mahamet's party in II, iii and II, iv, and would have had to call in a white actor; or else he would have been forced to what is almost an immediate re-entry for 'Zareo' as the Ambassador in the following scene. The latter solution is, in fact, adopted by the Plotter, who has fewer Moors to call on. His casting could not, of course, allow Zareo to appear in II, iii, because he is the wrong colour.

Re-ordering these scenes would not have solved the playwright's problem. There can be no doubt that by 'two others' he intended two black actors, for even Mahamet calls them negroes. Thus, the Ambassadors cannot be *sent*, physically, because the actors who will play them cannot be allowed to enter. Peele simply has to write his way out of it. The news that the embassy is on its way must first be given under colour of comfort for Calipolis who is fainting from weariness and hunger, and it is to Zareo that the speech falls.

In the Plot, Zareo's lines will fall to Thomas Hunt, who does appear immediately as one of the Ambassadors. To allow him to do so with some show of credibility, the Plotter's solution was to keep Mahamet on stage at the end of the scene with a 'manet muly'. There is no direction for this in the text, and as there is no obvious soliloquy for Mahamet to speak, Greg's suspicions are naturally aroused. The direction for the general exit at the end of this scene is also missing, and Greg fixes his attention on this as positive evidence of revision, even though the direction for the following scene is italic. Mahamet's scenes do tend to end up with rather pointless monologues, and although there appears to be nothing left for him to say in this scene, which is largely filled with his ranting, it does appear that something might be missing.

From the dramatist's point of view, we have seen that, even if there had been a soliloquy positioned here for Mahamet, it would make no difference to the casting. What Zareo speaks is the programme for the following scene, II, iv, and as the implication is that these scenes are concurrent in actual time, he could scarcely appear in it with any credibility, even if he were allowed space to do so. That Mahamet may have been intended to remain on stage briefly at the end of the scene, is, however, consistent with the text, if the reasons that can be offered for it are somewhat bizarre.

The psychology of the scene (if such a term may be applied properly to it) is not a little difficult to interpret. Calipolis appears to oppose Mahamet's cursing of their misfortune with a counsel of patience, submission, and the need for practical action. She is faint and weak, but she does not actually say (though she seems to imply it) that she is dying of hunger. Mahamet's response is to rail against patience and to seek some desperate and glorious action to restore their state. But he agrees, even in this elevated mood, to search for some food worthy of his mettle, and, indeed, to overcome Famine itself. He goes out to hunt lions. The son then also gently rebukes his mother, saying that thoughts of patience are unworthy of the hopes of happiness and ease that princes ought to cherish, and, to comfort her, he and 'Zareo' reveal the hypocritical plan that has been formed for engaging Sebastian's support. Calipolis's 'unhearty soule' fears that this will bring upon them the judgment of heaven. The Moor then returns with an appropriately grand meal of raw flesh that he has forced from a lioness, and offers it to Calipolis as

> Meate of a princesse, for a princesse meate,

and continues to press the grisly offering on her to the refrain, parodied by Shakespeare,

> Feede then and faint not faire Calipolis.

She replies, with thanks, that the virtue of her mind will prevent her from starving, and the Moor's final speech runs:

> Into the shades then faire Calypolis,
> And make thy sonne and Negros here good cheere,
> Feede and be fat that we may meete the foe
> With strength and terror to reuenge our wrong.

There is no happy way of reading these lines. The Moor may be understood to say that, if Calipolis cannot eat the meat herself, she had better take it into the shrubbery and cook it for the others. Clearly a direction to move off stage is implied. But does Calipolis actually take the meat from Mahamet? If she does, 'feede and be fat' must be addressed to the others, for she has declined to eat it. If she does not, then 'make good cheere' will read a little oddly. I believe that her thanks are to be interpreted as a polite refusal and that Mahamet keeps possession of the larder, such as it is. If that is so, his final soliloquy is not far to seek: it consists of the last two lines of the speech quoted above, which can logically be addressed to no-one but himself. If he remains on stage longer it is not to speak, but to eat — to demonstrate his beastly and self-indulgent feeding to the audience. The others will, no doubt, have to content themselves with Shakespeare's reflection that 'small cheer and great welcome maketh a merry feast'. But there is still an uncomfortable feeling that Mahamet's use of the royal plural here is out of key with the rest of his speeches in the scene.

The next scene, II, iv, ushers in the whole Portuguese Court and is imagined as taking place in Lisbon. The two events to be represented are the reception of the Moorish Ambassadors and the arrival of Stukeley and his party. By the end of the scene the whole of the 'white' cast, with the exception of Abdelmelec and Muly Mahamet Seth will be on stage. If the playwright thought of Christophero de Tavora as a man, even Seth would have been forced to appear here as a Portuguese. The other Portuguese lords will all have been Janissaries or white Moors in a previous incarnation. They cannot have been actors of much account, for they are virtually all mute. The Duke of Avero is later given eight lines to speak in IV, ii, and in the present scene eight lines are allotted to an unspecified attendant (the Plotter assigns these to Avero also) and one line to Christophero. No speeches fall to any others of these actors in their Portuguese roles, and as this scene is already the longest in the play, there is no likelihood that they ever had more to say.

Even as it stands, the scene is quite alarmingly short of matter. To make any show of its content, Sebastian is compelled to speak a long and quite improbable panegyric about Queen Elizabeth, which even Stukeley recognises to be somewhat irrelevant. Lines appear to have dropped out in several places from the longer speeches, but, apart from a double set of commands addressed to the Duke of Avero, which may be perfectly innocent, there is no sign that these concerned a revision of the cast. The Plotter here introduces an additional lord, the County Vinioso (properly Vimioso), who might have existed in the prompt-book, but is probably, as we shall see, a convenient addition made possible by the Plotter's white Zareo. It is of little significance either way, for all the Portuguese lords except Avero are merely attendants in fancy dress. There is, moreover, good reason for keeping them silent, for one of them will certainly have to speak as a Spanish Ambassador in the next act.

It is worth pausing at this stage to enquire how Peele derived the names of his Portuguese nobility. The tasks allotted to the lords are in every case unhistorical, except for that of Lewes de Silva, who actually was Sebastian's Ambassador in Madrid. Strangely enough, this fact could not have been gathered from any of the sources, and appears to be contradicted by Conestaggio, who correctly relates that the Ambassador sent to arrange the specific meeting at Guadalupe was Pietro d'Alcasova. The playwright's cast of attendants for Sebastian consists of the Dukes of Avero and Barcellos, Lewes de Silva and Christophero de Tavora. Conestaggio lists the names of four colonels who were charged with mustering the Portuguese troops, but only one of these appears in the play (Diego Lopez de Siqueira), and his name Peele had borrowed for the Governor of Lisbon. Nieto lists no lords until the battle, in which he records Alvares Peres de Tavora, Ludovicke Caesar, Duartes Meneses the governor of Tangier, the Duke of Avero, Don Antonio (later the pretender supported by the English), Christophero de Tavora, and the Bishops of Coimbra and Portua. Conestaggio records a number of other names in the battle and elsewhere, and Peele has pretty clearly chosen from among these those who were closest to the king. These are Luigi di Silva (*uno di piu favoriti del Re*), Cristofforo di Tavora (*suo cameriero e cavallerizo maggiore ch'egli amava oltre modo*), and the Duke of Barcellos, who, despite the fact that he was only about twelve years old and is called by Conestaggio a *giovanetto*, actually did fight beside Sebastian's standard at Alcazar. Apart from Avero he is the highest-ranking noble mentioned in the sources (the style belongs to the eldest son of the Duke of Braganza) and may be given a task worthy of his ancestors of raising soldiers in Antwerp, even if it may seem beyond the capacity of what Peele calls his 'forward youth'. Avero is made Sebastian's principal supporter, for it was his charge in the early stages of the battle that almost secured a Portuguese victory, and his death in the ensuing retreat that sealed their defeat.

Describing the dispositions for the battle, Peele will list, apart from these, Alvaro Peres de Tavora and Lodeuco (Lodovico – Conestaggio's form) Caesar. There is also a Lord Lodowicke addressed in the text in III, iv, who should, by rights be this man, but he does not speak and must have been played in the text, as in the Plot, by Lewes de Silva. His name is a useful combination of the two roles. The playwright will keep Don Duarte de Menysis as Governor of Tangier, although he is not identified in the spoken text. Peele knew, of course that de Menesses was the Master of the Camp, or Commander-in-Chief, but it is more convenient to cede that role to Avero. The case of Vinioso will be more conveniently considered in the discussion of the Plot in the next chapter. It is sufficient to say, here, that there are no Portuguese commanders at Peele's battle who are not vouched for by Conestaggio.

Returning to our scene (II, iv), we recall that the Moorish Ambassadors who appear at the beginning must have been played by Pisano and one of the former 'devils'. Their hypocritical purpose, as explained in the previous scene, is to offer Sebastian the Empire of Morocco. In demonstration of their good faith, they call for fire, and thrust their hands into the flame.[19]

This pantomime allows us to interpret the seemingly corrupt lines spoken by 'Zareo' in the previous scene (lines 562–7):

> His maiestie hath sent Sebastian
> The good and harmelesse king of Portugall,
> A promise to resigne the roialtie
> And kingdome of Marocco to his hands,
> But when this haughtie offer takes effect
> And workes affiance in Sebastian,
> My gracious Lord warnd wisely to aduise,
> I doubt not but will watch occasion,
> And take her fore-top by the slenderest haire,
> To rid vs of this miserable life.

They may be paraphrased: 'And when this high offer works as we intend, and Sebastian begins to show such signs of trust as my lord has

wisely given intructions to observe (and encourage), I have no doubt that
he will seize any opportunity of improving our wretched situation.'[20]
Peele does not take Sebastian for a complete fool. He is shown to be
suspicious of Mahamet's motives, but is instantly convinced by the
charming classical parallel, when the Ambassadors, like twin Scaevolae,
hold their hands to the fire.

The English party are called on stage only by the direction, 'Enter
Stukley and the rest'. As they have all been seen before and they all speak,
there is no doubt about their identity.

We now come to the Presenter's speech at the beginning of the third
act. There is no evidence in the text of the elaborate dumb-show that
accompanies this in the Plot, other than the first three lines:

> Lo thus into a lake of bloud and gore
> The braue couragious king of Portugal
> Hath drencht himself.

The unusual form of the preceding direction: *Enter the Presenter and
speaks*, does not necessarily suggest a show, and may simply refer to
Sebastian's decision at the end of the previous scene to leave immediately
for Africa. The purpose of the Induction is to give a brief account of the
meeting between Sebastian and Philip II at the monastery of Guadalupea
(Polemon's spelling, corrupted in the printing house to 'Sucor da Tupea').
The theme of the whole is the poisonous hypocrisy of Spain which is to
contribute to Sebastian's disaster. The rather tortuous expression is
brought about, not by excisions, as Greg supposed, but by the dramatist's
critical appraisal of his sources. Greg, as I have said, did not know
Conestaggio, and was puzzled by the lines referring to Philip II in the
Presenter's speech:

> And now doth Spaine promise with holy face,
> As favouring the honor of his cause,
> His aide of armes, and leuies men apace,
> But nothing lesse than king Sebastians good
> He means, yet at Sucor de Tupea,
> He met some saie in person with the Portugall,
> And treateth of a marriage with the king,
> But ware ambitious wiles and poisned eies,
> There was nor aide of armes nor marriage,
> For on his waie without those Spaniardes king Sebastian went.

It may, of course, seem puzzling to the literal-minded that, when the
Presenter has declared the Spanish promises to be lies, the next scene
should represent the Ambassadors promising those very things. There is
no real contradiction. Act III, scene ii is a scene played out 'with holy
face', a scene of bitter irony that will end with a shrewd comment from
Stukeley about the purpose of the Spanish levies:

> The Spaniard ready to embark himself
> Here gathers to a head, but all too sure,
> Flanders I fear shall feele the force of Spaine.

'Alcazar': the text and the sources 159

Both sources record the meeting at Guadalupe, but when the accounts of Nieto and Conestaggio are put together there are strong grounds for suspecting Philip of such hypocrisy that it is hard to imagine a personal meeting at which he could have made such patently false promises. The dramatist is, of course, eager, as a patriotic Englishman, to make the Spanish promises sound a little falser than they were. Both the French translation and Polemon suggest that Philip's concern for Sebastian was genuine, but in the fuller, vehemently pro-Philip, account in Conestaggio, Peele found cause for suspicion. Juan de Silva's account, based on his personal involvement in the negotiations, is concerned to justify Spanish policy and to lay to rest the scandalous imputation that Philip had failed the young king deliberately and sent him to his death. Peele naturally regarded this account with suspicion. He thought of it, with Protestant scepticism, as a 'Catholic case', and was also growing impatient with the usage 'the Catholic king', which is, of course, Conestaggio's ordinary way of referring to Philip II. He will cause Stukeley to say 'Philip whome some call the catholicke king' (line 876), possibly because Nieto does not use the Papal honorific and Polemon does not translate the words 'comme prince vrayement chrestien' that appear in the French.

Conestaggio's defence of Spanish policy, moreover, does leave a very strong smell of fish. The conditions Philip attached to his offer of aid were almost impossible of fulfilment. When the Portuguese inevitably failed to meet them, he did not, according to Conestaggio, allow a single regular soldier to leave Spain, except for the last-minute dispatch of Francesco d'Aldana as a military adviser. In the matter of the marriage, he offered Sebastian one of the Infantas, but did not say which. As both were below marriageable age, this contract too, appeared more likely to be honoured in the breach than the observance. Philip's temporising policy was no doubt intended by de Silva to appear as statesmanlike caution moderated by affability, but it is not surprising that Peele read it as rankest hypocrisy – and on that he builds his scene. He even takes the detail of Don John of Austria's appeal for reinforcements in the Netherlands, which de Silva wishes to represent as a necessary limitation on Philip's ability to engage himself in Africa, as evidence of his real intention in permitting military levies. Nevertheless, both sources record that Spanish troops finally did fight at Alcazar and Peele has simply skewed the account here and in two other places to omit them. In III, iii he will keep Sebastian fifteen days at Cadiz, waiting for Spanish reinforcements that fail to arrive, and in Act V he suppresses all mention of Spanish forces and allows their commander, Alonzo di Aguilar, to take charge of the German troops on the left wing.

There is possibly also a practical reason for misrepresenting the Spanish attitude. Peele cannot bring on the king of Spain, because he does not have an actor to play him. Even the Spanish ambassadors create a problem, although possibly a less acute one than appears in the Plot. The direction that introduces III, i reads :

Enter the king of Portugall and his Lordes, Lewes de Silua, and the Embassadors of Spaine.

Lewes de Silva was dispatched with letters to Spain at the end of II, iv, and it is naturally he who returns with the Ambassadors here, creating a sense of continuity with the earlier scene. It will be a purely visual impression, for in the former scene he is identified only by one word of address, and in this scene he is not identified at all in the spoken text. He shares this anonymity with all the other Lords, but the prominent appearance of his name in the stage-direction must surely indicate that he is important for some reason. The dramatist is showing no sign of strain here.[21] He can still write 'and his Lordes', just as he brings Stukeley on with 'the rest', and he can allot speeches to 'another' without calculating too precisely. For him, there can be several others who might serve the purpose. For the Plotter the other must be the Duke of Avero, because he is the only Portuguese Lord remaining. This shortage of white cast is, oddly enough, the mathematical result of changing Zareo's colour, and it is the Plotter, not the dramatist, who has to pay a heavy penalty. He will be forced to omit the next scene altogether.

The dramatist is much better off. He might have kept all Sebastian's Lords on stage by using Hercules and Jonas as the Spanish Ambassadors. He might even have used the Irish Bishop. He will have had to sacrifice one of the lords, but might seem to have one other recourse that is not open to the Plotter: he might have called in the Presenter as a replacement. The Presenter, as we have seen, probably played Diego Lopez in II, ii, as he does in the Plot. He might therefore have entered at II, iv, 701, conducting the English party, whom he is the first to meet, to Sebastian's court. But there is no sign of him there, and the direction that follows II, iv: *Enter the presenter and speakes*, indicates that he did not. His function in the play has begun to define itself otherwise.

It is the Presenter's task throughout to keep us in mind of the destiny of King Sebastian, and the very first words he speaks in the play establish that intention. But the playwright is following the order of events related in his sources. These all deal with the affairs of Barbary, before turning to the intervention of the Portuguese. Sebastian therefore does not appear in person until II, iv. It is perhaps as much for this reason as for the audience's advance knowledge of the failure of the expedition that the Inductions have been cast ironically. All the action preceding Sebastian's arrival at Tangier is interpreted as the gathering of the forces that will bring the Portuguese innocently to destruction. The irony is embodied neither in the action nor in character, but applied externally, as it were, through the words of the Presenter and the pantomimes of Devils and Furies roused by the drums of Nemesis.

The first appearances of Nemesis are connected with the hypocrisy of Muly Mahamet. In II, Induction, it is his appeal to Sebastian for help, and the hypocritical offer of the throne of Morocco that begins 'Sebastians tragedie in the tragicke warre', but other strands of irony are also at work.

The chance arrival of the English at Lisbon is the third. In this the Presenter himself will play a part as Diego Lopez, welcoming the reinforcements that encourage Sebastian's resolution. When the latter two events are in position, Sebastian will cry:

> Follow me Lords, Sebastian leads the way
> To plant the christian fa[i]th in Africa.

His words are immediately ironised once again by the Presenter in III, Induction:

> Lo thus into a lake of bloud and gore
> The brave courageous king of Portugall
> Hath drenched himself.

The fourth string of the fatal events is now to be shown: the failure of the Spanish promises of aid and the hypocrisy of Philip II. Act III, scene i is thus, in itself a pantomime. All the information in it is known to be false before it is played. There is thus no reason why the Presenter himself might not take part in it, acting out the ironies it has been his function to interpret. It is perhaps for this very reason that he warns the audience to beware 'ambitious wiles and poisned eies', before moving into the scene as one of the Spanish Ambassadors himself. The contrary situation will almost certainly occur at the end of III, iv, where the Presenter, now appearing as the Governor of Tangier, will have to move straight out of that scene to speak the Induction to Act IV. It is suggestive that whereas in every other instance the Presenter is said to 'Enter', in Act IV there appear only the words *The presenter speaketh*.

In III, i, then, we may suppose the dramatist meant all his European cast to be on stage. The natural consequence, of course, is that one of the Moorish parties must enter next, and, as there is nothing that can be told of Mahamet, who is merely waiting at or near Tangier for Sebastian's arrival, the following scene, III, ii, brings on Abdelmelec. The material is mostly taken from Polemon with some additions from Conestaggio, relating the secret negotiations between Abdelmelec and Philip II, which offer further proof of Spanish perfidy.

The Plotter, as we have seen, could not play this scene at all, and there is probably also a mild problem for the dramatist about who is to accompany Abdelmelec. The directions call for Muly Mahamet Seth, Zareo '*and their Traine*'. The train may be composed once again of Ladies, for there is nothing much to indicate a military scene. The Janissaries and white Moors have all been absorbed into the European party, so that unless Stukeley's dialogue with 'another' was long enough to allow a change of costume, Abdelmelec can have only black Moors and boys at this point. We may infer from the Plotter's behaviour that the twenty-one lines of dialogue were insufficient in 1598 to allow Zareo to dodge over this scene break, and thus the time was likely to have been too short in the dramatist's estimation for the European Lords to reappear as Abdelmelec's soldiers.[22]

The reference in the text to 'Zareo and ye manly moores' does probably mean that the three or four black actors who appeared with Abdelmelec in II, i are on stage again. 'Manly', like 'Arabian' is a white's term of approval for a blackamoor. It is used twice by Sebastian's captains of Muly Mahamet in the following scene and stands in contrast to 'Negro moore' which always implies contempt. Abdelmelec will later be able to recover one actor who appeared with him as a white Moor in I, i, but for the present that actor is blocked by having to appear as a Portuguese Captain in the next scene. There is no help for the embarrassment that may be caused to the black cast at hearing one of their own colour contemptuously referred to as a Negro.

At this point we can foresee dimly what the dramatist must always have known: that the battle of Alcazar will have to be fought and won for Muly Mahamet Seth almost wholly by troops of the opposing Moorish faction. The text of the battle scenes will divide the forces without any confusion into Christians and Moors.

Act III, scene iii presents no problems. There are only three actors who can possibly enter in it, for all the cast, with the exception of the three principals of the last scene – Abdelmelec, Muley Mahamet Seth, and Zareo – are to be on stage in III, iv, and the time-scheme is continuous. Peele has taken from Conestaggio the story of Sebastian's refusal to disembark at Lisbon once he had gone aboard, but he transfers the incident to Cadiz in order to underline the double-dealing of the Spaniards, whose expected troops do not arrive. The Governor of Tangier must be played by the Presenter whose long speech seems to have been written with just that situation in mind. It is pure narration material of the expedition's sailing, purporting to have arrived by letter, and narrowly saved from improbability (for where could such information have been sent *from*, and when?) only by the arrival of the fleet on the heels of the message itself. There is also a quite ingenious suggestion in the metaphor of Achilles cursing for want of wind in Aulis that the main fleet is late because it was becalmed. The subterfuge of putting this speech in the Governor's mouth is helped out by our knowledge that he is in fact the Presenter. This may also account for the rather perfunctory dramatisation of the remainder.

It is of some small consequence to note that Peele may have pondered the time-scheme of the voyage, which is not easy to gather from the sources, and that he produces an original version, once again emphasising the effect of the false promises of Spain. Sebastian certainly left Lisbon on 26 June 1578, but Peele keeps the ships at sea for twelve days on the short passage to Cadiz. He must have mistaken the date of the departure from Cadiz (8 July) for the date of the fleet's arrival. He then keeps Sebastian at Cadiz for fifteen days, in accord with Nieto, and thus appears almost to square the date of its departure with that given in *The Dolorous Discourse* (22 July). This is the only evidence I have found that Peele may have consulted the latter work, on which Greg places great reliance, and it is rather slight.[23]

Act III, scene iv, being very largely the playwright's own invention, is a formal reprise of information we already know. Peele turns the meeting of Sebastian and Mahamet into a discussion of hereditary right and allows Mahamet to speak his own condemnation with unconscious irony. The business, so far as it advances the story, is the offering of Young Mahamet to Sebastian as a hostage and his dispatch to Mazagan. Both sources describe the event, Conestaggio recording that the young prince was placed under the conduct of Martin Correa de Silva. Peele gives the task jointly to the Duke of Avero and 'Lord Lodowicke'. There can be no-one on stage for whom that name is fitting except Lewes de Silva, and thus my picture of the dramatist's casting plan gains some fragile support. If it is supposed that the lightly identified de Silva is the Lodovico Caesar who is mentioned in Act V it will not matter, and it is doubtful whether any audience would pick up the detail. If the Presenter is on stage, as I believe he is, he cannot be Lord Lodowicke, for Peele thinks of him, correctly, as Don Duarte de Meneses, and, in any case, he must remain on stage to speak the Induction to Act IV.

The Induction to Act IV adds nothing to our knowledge of events, but contains the direction *Enter to the bloudie banket*. If we may judge by the Plotter's response, this was to be a pantomime allegory based on the verbal cue (lines 1,063–4):

> And warre and weapons now, and bloud and death
> Wait on the counsels of this cursed king.

Although the Presenter's speech is brief, we may imagine that the show took some little time, for one actor at least must double into the role of Celybin.

The action now begins to move forward to the battle and Peele takes survey of the forces in IV, i. He has no option, of course, according to the conventional workings of the stage, but to do so through the eyes of Abdelmelec. In the historical record, the next action is the mustering of the Portuguese army before the walls of Arzilla, and this is therefore reported to Abdelmelec by the spy, Celybin, whose name, borrowed either from *Tamburlaine*, or from the account of the battle of Lepanto in Polemon, suggests that he is thought of as a revived Janissary. If he is a white actor, he can be doubled only with one of the Captains of Tangier, or with Lewes de Silva. The material is all taken from chapter IX of Nieto, but there is no doubt that Peele was here following Polemon's translation. He takes over Polemon's account verbatim for the first twenty lines and uses the figure of 1,500 wagons for the baggage-train that appears in no other source.

Having used the muster at Arzilla to get his scene going, Peele now skips on to the actual disposition of the forces on the day of the battle in Polemon's version of Nieto, chapter XI. To anyone following the sources, he gives the impression of having moved Sebastian to Alcazar in twenty-four lines, thus anticipating the following scene, but that, of course, is not the audience's case. The only change he makes in the battle positions is in placing Mahamet in the centre instead of the right wing, and surrounding him with 'twice three thousand needless armed pikes', instead of Polemon's 600 spears. The intention is, of course, to emphasise Mahamet's cowardice. For his troops, Peele has simply multiplied Polemon's figures by ten, as he did earlier with Stukeley's Italians. As for the personnel of the scene itself, the stage-directions call simply for '*Abdilmelec and his traine*'. This must be intended to call on those who appeared with him in III, ii, who, apart from such boys as there may have been, must have been Moors. With the addition of Celybin, however, he is now able, once again, to speak of his 'trustie gard / Of Ianizaries, fortunate in warre'.

We now pass in IV, ii to the Portuguese camp on the eve of battle. The programme is taken from Polemon (Nieto, chapter IX). Abdelmelec's letters mentioned in III, ii have now reached Sebastian, and his Council agrees that prudence demands avoiding a pitched battle, but Sebastian, being eager to test himself in personal combat, pays no heed. The Portuguese are momentarily dismayed by the huge numbers arrayed against them, until Mahamet arrives with the persuasive, but false, information that Abdelmelec's army is ready to desert to him. Sebastian and his Lords leave the stage as if to commence the fight and Mahamet remains to soliloquise in the hysterical vein of a triumphant Senecan villain.

This is the last scene contained in the Plot. It is of some importance to us, because of the questions raised by the decay of the paper as to who ought and who ought not to be on stage. The dramatist even seems to be mildly uncertain here, and brings on Sebastian, Avero, Stukely, *and others*. Hercules turns out to be one of the others, so that we may suppose Jonas also to be on stage. The other actors available are Lewes de Silva and one of the Portuguese Captains, but they have nothing to say. Peele must have known that the Portuguese who appeared in III, i are still, roughly speaking, available, with some subtractions, but he will not know precisely what name to give any of them at this stage. Even from the decayed fragments of the Plot, it is clear that the Plotter also treated this scene rather freely and had trouble in reconstituting Sebastian's powers, for he had doubled Celybin with Lewes de Silva and his Barceles had reverted to his original role as Zareo, while his Vinioso had been demoted to the status of a guard.

This last point is of some importance, for had Greg known that Vimioso played a role of some prominence in Conestaggio's account of the first Council at Arzilla, he would have had even greater confidence in supposing this scene to have been heavily cut. Peele is here paraphrasing and running together the end of Nieto, chapter IX and the beginning of chapter X, which make no mention of Vimioso, but, as the dramatist includes details of the Council at Arzilla in the account of the Council before the battle, it will be necessary to trace out the events in a little detail.

On meeting with Muly Mahamet at Tangier, Sebastian sent the major part of the fleet southward to Arzilla. His intention was to rejoin the ships there and to sail on to Alarache (Larissa), a Portuguese 'hold' that would be a convenient base for operations against Fez. The soldiers who left the ships at Arzilla, however, proved more willing to face the perils of the land than those of the sea and refused to re-embark. They were now in hostile territory, supplies were running low, and it was vital to press on to Larissa where arrangements had been made for provisioning them by sea. The question was, how to get there. To march southward along the coast presented great danger, for the route lay over marshy tidal flats and across difficult river mouths. To march on a detour inland to the east and far south would bring them to a convenient ford over the river Loukkos (Lixus), but near that ford, not far from the town of El Ksar Kibir, the main body of Abdelmelec's army was encamped. This was, nevertheless, the plan decided upon.

It was known at the Council at Arzilla that Abdelmelec was willing to avoid an engagement if the Portuguese would only return quietly to their ships and go home. Even when they arrived at Alcazar, he contrived to let them know that he would not attack if they would turn towards the sea. Both Councils, then, debated the question of whether to march back to Alarache, or to seek out the enemy and give battle, but at the time of the second Council the Portuguese were trapped in a fork of the river, with the Wadi-el-Mekhazen behind them. To march on to the ford over the Lixus would expose their flank dangerously, should Abdelmelec change his mind.

The dramatist sets his scene at this point. He follows Nieto in representing Mahamet as eager to encourage battle, lest the Portuguese should give over the enterprise and leave him to the mercy of his uncle's vastly superior forces. Mahamet therefore urges, untruthfully, that the great mass of Abdelmelec's troops will desert to him and fight for the Portuguese. This is for Nieto, and for Peele, the final proof of his murderous hypocrisy. Mahamet's advice, according to Nieto, was given on the Saturday evening. There may therefore be some justification for placing here a fragment of the Plot containing what appears to be a mention of torchlight ('y Tor'), on the assumption that the scene takes place at night. The Council itself, at which the lords advised retreat and Sebastian was adamant for battle, also took place, according to Nieto, at night on Sunday, although the other sources place it on Sunday morning. In the play, the Portuguese leave the stage as if to give immediate battle, but that may be mere theatrical enthusiasm: we still have to wait for the Presenter's description of the preliminaries and the dumb-show in the Induction to Act V.

The question of whether there might once have been additional material in this scene, derived from Conestaggio's account of the Council at Arzilla cannot, then, be solved, by reference to the sources. Vimioso might still have been original to the play, even though he was disgraced at Arzilla for the failure of the commissariat. The internal evidence of the argument, however, suggests that no further material could have been admitted. The dramatist is always unwilling to allow dishonourable behaviour in any of the European party. A debate in which some of the Lords must have appeared as cowards would not have been to his taste, nor could he have allowed any of the motives of favour and false flattery that Conestaggio attributes to Vimioso to appear.

There is, indeed, a dislocation in the text as it stands, directly attributable to this desire to keep European honour bright. Hercules has pretty clearly been thrust in as a speaker to take over half of the lines of the Duke of Avero counselling moderation. After Sebastian's declaration of berserk valour, Avero's speech would originally have run:

> So well become these words a kingly mouth
> That are of force to make a coward fight,
> But when aduice and prudent fore-sight,
> Is joynd with such magnanimitie,
> Troupes of victorie and kingly spoiles
> Adorn his crowne, his kingdome, and his fame.
> We haue descride vpon the mountaine tops
> A hugie companie of inuading Moores,
> And they my lord, as thicke as winters haile,
> Will fall vpon our heads at vnawares,
> Best then betimes t'auoide this gloomie storme,
> It is in vaine to striue with such a streame.

That is, Avero is arguing that advice and prudent foresight consists in recognising when you are outnumbered and when the enemy has the initiative and the advantage. Mahamet then enters with his false assurance of victory, and Avero is forced to recant even this eminently reasonable point of view:

> Shame be his share that flies when kings do fight,
> Auero laies his life before your feet.

Peele obviously disliked, on second thoughts, the faint imputation of cowardice in the first speech, and divided it, giving the last six lines to Hercules. He was presumably untroubled by the penalty (at least to a cynical, modern mind) that Avero is then left with the foolish appearance of praising Sebastian's berserk valour as prudent foresight. It is hard to believe that the scene ever ventured on a debate of more complex issues, when even this mild criticism of Sebastian's actions calls for such ignominious repentance. The interpolation of Hercules, of course, also cancels the sense of recantation from Avero's second speech quoted above, and allows it to read as hysterical enthusiasm. The Plotter was perhaps as puzzled as a modern critic by this curious arrangement of speeches, and decided to introduce Hercules as a kind of messenger, bursting on to the stage with his news, and thus to create an impression of 'dastard flight' more vividly than anything the dramatist appears to have had in mind.

'Alcazar': the text and the sources   167

The Plot now deserts us, but Act V follows chapter XII of Nieto so closely that there can be no doubt of the playwright's intention. He simplifies the battle, of course, and slightly changes the order of events for theatrical reasons, but he is so close to Polemon's narrative that he frequently reproduces phrases from it. We are thus able to supply with ease the missing material at the two or three places where lines have dropped out of the text.

The hiatus on either side of line 1,313, in the following passage, for example, is clearly to be supplied from within the passage of Polemon that is quoted below it:

Peele

My Lord, when with our ordenance fierce we sent
Our Moores with smaller shot as thick as haile   l. 1,313
Follows apace to charge the Portugall,
The valiant Duke the deuill of Auero,
The bane of Barbary, fraughted full of ire
Breakes through the rankes, and with fiue hundred horsse
Assaults the middle wing ...

Polemon

the Moores did first begin to shoote off their great ordenance against the Christians, but they had not shot off three, but that the Christians answered them with theirs. And straight waie the harquebusiers on foote on both sides discharged as thick as haile, with such a horrible, furious and terrible tempest, that the cracking and roaring of the Gunnes did make the earth so tremble, as though it would have sunk downe to hell, and the element seemed to burn with the fire, flames, lightning and thunder of the Gunnes. After that the storme of the shot was past five hundreth men of armes of the first battaile, whom the Duke *de Avero* lead, gave a charge on the left wing of the Moores, and brake and scattered them ...[24]

A second example, at line 1,585, reads:

Peele

His skin we will be parted from his flesh,
And being stifned out and stuft with strawe,
So to deterre and feare the lookers on,
From any such foule fact or bad attempt

Polemon

But as for the bodye of *Muley Mahamet*, the newe king his uncle commaunded the skinne to be pulled off (because he had beene the author of so many slaughters) and to bee salted, and then stuffed with strawe, and to be carried thorough out all the provinces of his kingdom, for to deterre all other for attempting the like at anie time after.[25]

It is clear that omissions of this kind do not result from theatrical cutting, for no attempt is made to tidy up the sense. They are simply the accidental omissions of a careless compositor and arise from the casual omission of one or two lines. Similar lacunae occur between lines 258–9, 395–6, 492–3, 717–18, 747–8 and 1,025–1,026. Three other passages that appear to dislocate the sense in the same way are probably in need only of literal emendation.

For some of the details of the spectacle, Peele drew on the Latin poem attached to Freigius's account. First, there is the dumb-show, a particularly elaborate affair involving lightning and thunder, the appearance of a tree and the descent of Fame to hang three crowns on it, the setting off of a huge Catherine-wheel representing the comet, and the falling of the three kingdoms, represented by the crowns. The passage from Freigius's poem is as follows:

> Lapsa trium quoque cernis humi diademata Regum.
> Quisnam magnanimo regi persuasit, ut ipse
> Insidos Mauros ferro tentarit inerti?
> Quam pia cura Deum? non hanc praenuncia cladem
> Signa e sublime (si mens non laeva fuisset)
> Dixerunt specula? an cauda candente Cometes
> Falsus erat vates splendenti extensus in aula
> Caelestis regni?[26]

Perhaps the most astonishing omission in Greg's account of the text is his failure to account for the existence of this dumb-show. To regard it as one of the 'odds and ends' accidentally copied by the reviser from the original Book is to stretch credulity to its limits. Would this not have been the first thing to go in preparation for a country tour? Admittedly it makes no great demands on the cast. Only the Presenter and one of the boys appear on stage, but the Presenter's Induction is essential to allow time for the re-grouping of forces that are immediately to appear in battle, and his lines would hardly make sense without the displays of stage-machinery that accompany them.

The cast is now divided simply into 'Christians', among whom Muly Mahamet and his son will be included, and 'Moors', that is to say, all the rest, including the former black troops of Mahamet who are now fighting on the side of Abdelmelec. The text represents the new alignment clearly. All the troops on Muly Mahamet Seth's side now become 'our Moores', while Stukely will complain of 'These barbarous Moores'. Hercules will murder him for having tied their fortunes to 'the ruthless furie of our heathen foe', while even Muly Mahamet and his son now fly in fear of 'these ruthlesse Moores' pursuing them at the heels. If this were not so, the installation of Muly Mahamet Seth as the new king could hardly have been attended by anyone but Zareo, and even being so, his train will be small, for two Portuguese and two Moors must be off stage, searching for the bodies of Mahamet and Sebastian with which they enter later in the scene. It is no doubt for this reason that Stukeley is given a long biographical soliloquy:

> Harke friends, and with the story of my life
> Let me beguile the torment of my death

and so on – for forty-nine lines! This must be spoken in order to give

Jonas and Hercules, and probably others of the slain Portuguese, time to change into Moorish attire for the impressive final exit with reversed arms bearing off the bodies of Sebastian and Abdelmelec. One cannot, of course, be certain that extras were not called in for the finale, but it is unlikely that they would have been called in for the battle itself. I have found in plotting through the texts that there is a tendency to level the numbers of opposing sides in battle scenes, and here there will be approximately eight 'Christians' (including Mahamet) and eight 'Moors' (including Abdelmelec) available.

The death of Muley Mahamet by drowning is mentioned in all the sources, but Peele appears to have taken the details from Freigius's Introduction (A4, A4^v):

Mulejus Mahametus, autor tot tantorumque malorum prostratis unique copiis fugae sese mandans, dum fluvium Mazagam trajicere conatur, ab equo ex caeno eluctante excussus, in lutulento aquae gurgite submersus periit.[27]

It is from this introduction that he must have gathered the odd (and false) information that the Moors commonly embalmed their dead with salt. But the reference to embalming was perhaps suggestive of a dramatic way of representing the battle scene. Greg failed to understand what Peele was up to here, for he did not grasp the significance of the direction at line 1,302 : 'Skirmish still, then enter Abdilmelec in his chaire.' This chair is undoubtedly the same chair as that in which Abdelmunen was brought in to be strangled (I, Induction), and it is the best the theatre can manage for the litter in which his brother Abdelmelec travelled from Morocco to the battle, and in which he died. The litter is mentioned in Nieto, but its full significance becomes apparent only in the account of Conestaggio.

Abdelmelec died at the crucial moment of the battle, from the accumulated effects of arsenical poisoning administered by his Turkish captains who feared he would send them back to Constantinople. He was taken from his horse and placed in his litter, but his death was dissembled and the litter was carried forward against the enemy as if Abdelmelec's commands still issued from it. Peele naturally could not represent him on his horse, but he invents a famous *coup de théâtre* by having him die calling for it; and he brings Hamet back from the fight a little earlier than in the sources so that Abdelmelec may be set up in his chair 'with cunning props', in his 'apparel as he dyed':

> That our Barbarians may beholde their King
> And think he doth repose him in his Tent.

The detail of the king's sumptuous apparel is taken from the general conclusion to Nieto's account. There can be no question that Peele intended the battle to sway to and fro on stage under the gaze of the glittering figure of the dead Abdelmelec whose 'soule', as Hamet says, is joyfully to 'sit and see the sight'.

When Mahamet Seth returns in victory and is to be proclaimed king, the chair in which Abdelmelec sits now represents the throne, in its usual central position under the hangings. In order to be installed, Hamet has, of course, to get Abdelmelec out of it, and he commands that his brother be taken down and laid upon the earth 'till further for his funeralls / We provide'. Hamet is then crowned by Zareo, Elizabethan-fashion, with the diadem that Moroccan kings did not wear.

Stukeley's part in the battle is not mentioned in any of the sources, but as, in the play, it is he who in reality has been the principal member of Sebastian's party throughout, his presence allows the reporting of the major incidents of the deaths of Avero and Sebastian. The latter report accounts, as it were, for the passage which, in Polemon and in the play, immediately precedes Mahamet Seth's installation. There is no basis for Greg's suggestion that Stukeley's soliloquy was added to replace a scene in which Sebastian was killed. *That* is better left as a mystery. All the sources point to Sebastian being sought for among the dead after the battle, and the playwright must have wished to follow them, in order to enhance the pathos of the later scene in which he is carried in, 'done to death with many a mortall wound' and wrapped in his country's colours. A precise dramatisation of Sebastian's death would certainly spoil this effect. That no such scene was intended is suggested by the fact that the manner of his death is not certainly known to the Moors (lines 1,526–7), who believe that he has been treacherously killed by his captors.

No conclusions about the reliability of the text can be of the highest degree of certainty, but I believe two things appear very clearly from the evidence presented in this chapter. The first is that the playwright is prescient and consistent in the calls he makes for actors and appears to have a clear casting scheme in mind. We have seen him carefully adjusting his text, and the very manner and order of telling his story, to the cast he knows to be available at each point. The second is that, in every case where Greg suspects some large excision, Peele is most often following his sources with fidelity and has used all the available material. On the occasions when we can see that there is more in the sources that might have been used, there are reasons of casting that can be advanced to show why it was not. It would, indeed, be astonishing, if a play that had originally contained a good deal of incidental matter, had been cut down, in all the relevant sections, in a way that accidentally brought it into such close and literal conformity with its sources as is the case with *Alcazar*.

What, then, was the nature of the copy for the text of *Alcazar*? There are signs, particularly in the spelling of unfamiliar names, that it was difficult to decipher. Almost certainly its punctuation was deficient or marked simply by slashes which the compositor has not often interpreted with insight. Rather a large number of its corruptions appear to arise from dictation ('Austria' for 'Ostia'; 'Aldest gulfe' for 'Aulis gulfe') rather than from copying by eye, although others that appeared corrupt to Greg (Efestian for Hephaestion) are common spellings found in other play-texts. Turned letters and minim errors are frequent, and passages of one or more lines have dropped out in several places, leaving gaps in the sense.

'*Alcazar*': *the text and the sources* 171

There may, of course, be other examples of all three kinds of error that we cannot detect, when the text makes reasonable sense.

Whether these stigmata may or may not be regarded as typical of a compositor's handling of an author's manuscript in the Elizabethan printing-house is a matter far from being settled by bibliographical analysis. *Alcazar*, in its printed form, is an infinitely superior text to the manuscript of *John of Bordeaux*, or to any edited version so far produced of the manuscript of *Sir Thomas More*, which Greg took as his exemplar. If we were to assume that the copy had been prepared by a scribe who worked with about the same degree of accuracy as the scribe of *John of Bordeaux*, we should have to allow for a very great deal of regularisation and tidying up in the printing-house, whatever we might guess of the competence of the compositor. If, on the other hand, we assume that the copy handed to the printer was as good as that of the manuscript of *John a Kent and John a Cumber*, we might suppose that he could have made a very good fist of it.

The record of Elizabethan compositors on play-texts is not wholly encouraging, however, even on good copy. Pollard himself pointed out that the reprint of *Richard II* is about three times as incorrect as Q. 1, and concluded: 'It is not possible to say in the case of the average first Quarto, duly entered ... that the blunders in it cannot all be due to the printers. The proved inaccuracy of the printers suffices to account for all the faults.'[28]

Alcazar was not duly entered, but that is not now thought to be automatically a ground for suspicion. The play was never reprinted, and collation reveals very few variants, so that it is difficult to form any opinion about the accuracy of the press-work from internal evidence. I believe I have provided good reason for concluding that, errors of carelessness in the transmission apart, the text represents with reasonable accuracy the copy as it left Peele's hands. Greg was, of course, committed to regarding the printer's copy as a prompt-book, whatever its treatment in the press, so that, whether the play was or was not cut down for a travelling company, his argument must allow for at least one stage of copying, with its consequential accumulation of error, before it reached the printing-house. The possibility that the prompt copy for the 1598 performance differed in many minor respects from the printed play cannot, of course, be ruled out. Such unimportant differences exist between the autograph version and the printed edition of Daborne's *The Poor Man's Comfort*. That the prompt-book of *Alcazar* may have differed in major respects is difficult to maintain in the light of the theatrical consistency of the printed text.

The only real ground on which the suspicion of wholesale shortening of *Alcazar* rests is its brevity, and even this, when compared with the majority of other plays of the 1580,s is not exceptional. If, then, we may assume that the Plotter was working from this very text, or something so close to it that it may, for all practical purposes, be regarded as identical,

The Plott of the Battell Of Alcazar

I. Cho.

Enter a Portingall [to him,] mr Rich: Allen to him
1   Domb shew   *found*

I.i   *f⟨e⟩nnett*

Enter Muly Mahamett mr Ed : Allen, his sonne
Antho : Jeffes : moores attendant : mr Sam, mr Hunt
& w . Cartwright : ij Pages to attend the moore
mr Allens boy, mr Townes boy : to them 2 .
young bretheren : Dab : & Harry : : to them
Abdel⟨m⟩enen w . Kendall : exeunt   *found*

Enter Abdelmelec : mr Doughton : Calcepius
bassa mr Jubie : Zareo mr Charles attendant
with ⟨th⟩e Bassa : w . Kendall : Re : Tailor :
George⟨e w⟩ them Muly mahamet Xeque
Abdula Rais & Ruben H Jeffes, dick Jubie
& Jeames : exeunt   *found*

I.ii   *found*   *sennett*

Enter in a Charriott Muly ⟨M⟩ahamett
& Calipolis : on each side ⟨a⟩ pag⟨e⟩
moores attendant Pisano mr Hunt
w . Cartwright and young Mahamet
Anthony Jeffes : exit mr Sam manett
the rest : to them mr Sam a gaine exeunt   *⟨A⟩larū*

II. Cho.   *⟨found sennett⟩*

E⟨n⟩ter the Presenter : to him
2 domb shew
En⟨te⟩r aboue Nemesis, Tho : Dro⟨m⟩ to
them 3 . ghosts wᵗ kendall Dab . & Harry :⟩
⟨l⟩ying behind the Curt⟨a⟩ines 3 .
Furies : Parsons : George & Re : T⟨ai⟩lor
one wᵗʰ a whipp : a nother wᵗʰ a ⟨b⟩lody
tor⟨ch⟩ : & the 3ᵈ wᵗʰ a Chop⟨ping⟩ kni⟨fe⟩ : exeunt
   ⟨a whipp⟩ brand   *Chopping knife :*

(lines 59–85)

and ⟨Robin Tailor :⟩ to them ⟨3 .⟩ diu⟨e⟩ills to
mr Sam : H Jeffes] Antho : Dab : & Harry
them 3 ghosts ⟨:⟩ w . kendall Dab & Harry
the Furies [Fech] First Fech in Sebastian
& Carrie him out againe, which done they
Fech in Stukeley & Carrie him out, then
bring in the Moo⟨re & Carrie him out : exeunt
   3 . violls of blood & a sheeps gather

III.i   *found*

Enter : 2 . bringing in a chair of state
[mr Hunt] : w . Kendall Dab & Harry
enter at one dore : Sebastian ⟨Duke⟩
of Auero : Stukeley : 1 Pa⟨ge[s] Jea⟩nes
Jonas : & Hercules [th] to ⟨them a⟩t anothe⟨r⟩
dore Embassadors of Spai⟨ne mr⟩ Jones
mr Charles : attendants of George & w
Cartwright : exeun⟨t manet Stu⟨kel⟩ey
& Duke of Auero : exeunt

III.ii

Enter Gouernor ⟨of⟩ Tange⟨r ⟨:⟩ a
Captains mr Sha⟨a H⟩ Jeffes : exeunt

III.iii   *found*

Enter at one d⟨ore the Portingall army with
dron & Cullors :⟨ Sebastian Christofobro
Duke of Auero : Stukeley Jonas
Hercules : Lodouico Caesar mr Jones :
att another dore Gouernor of Tanger
mr Shaa & 2 Captains H Jeffes
mr Sam from behind the Curtaines to
them mu⟨ly mahamet Calipol⟩is .
in their ⟨Charriott with⟩
o⟨n⟩e on ⟨each side & Cartw⟩right :
m⟨a⟩ham⟨e⟩t, & w . Cartw⟩right :
George : exeu⟨n⟩t

The Battle of Alcazar — transcript of Plot with fragments re-arranged and conjectured restorations

174 *From text to performance in the Elizabethan theatre*

we shall see that the result he achieves, although appearing to Greg to differ drastically from the intentions of the dramatist, actually arises from the very same logic we have seen to be at work in the text. In the consideration of the Plot, to which we now turn, we shall see that the Plotter's logic, like the dramatist's, is governed by principles identical with at least four of the five propositions from which we began.

Alcazar: the text and the sources

1. W. W. Greg, *Two Elizabethan Stage Abridgments: Alcazar and Orlando* (Oxford, 1923), facing p. 122.

2. Ibid., p. 213. Greg perfectly well understood Poel's principle that an actor on stage at the end of one scene does not enter immediately in the next, and, in fact, uses it here to subvert the text. In his imaginary casting for a reduced company, it will explain both the cutting of the silent Moor attendant from II, iii, on the grounds that he will be needed to appear as Barceles in the following scene, and (we are led to assume) the reviser's intention to remove de Silva in particular from the Portuguese party, because he cannot have been the 'other'who remains on stage with Stukeley at the end of III, i. Both interpretations contradict the stage-directions, and are, of course, entirely hypothetical.

3. Peele's panegyrical *Farewell* to this expedition (1589) possibly refers to *Alcazar* as one of the delights the departing troops are leaving behind. See C. T. Prouty (ed.), *The Life and Works of George Peele*, vol. I, pp. 220–3.

4. Modern historians reckon the force as between 16,000 and 17,000, accompanied by an almost equal number of camp-followers, but the sources known to Peele give absurdly large figures.

5. The germ of the idea of Mahamet's hypocrisy is not hard to derive from the sources, but it is given particular emphasis in J. Centellas, *Les Voyages et Conquestes des Roys de Portugal* (Paris, 1578), pp. 48–9.

6. See *A True Historicall discourse of Muly Hamets rising to the three Kingdoms of Moruecos, Fes and Sus* (London, 1609): 'There is another title of dignitie termed Sheck, attributed to the chiefe man of everie familie or cast. Neither doth the Kings eldest sonne scorne the title, signifying that he is the prime or best blood of the royal kindred.'

7. The German translation of Conestaggio (1589) has 'Molucco'.

8. H. F. Conestaggio, *Dell'Unione del Regno di Portogallo alla Corona di Castiglia* (Genova, 1585), Lib. 2, Istoria di Portogallo, p. 41.

9. Ibid., trans. Edward Blount? *The History of the Uniting of the Kingdom of Portugal to the Crown of Castile* (London, 1600), p. 41.

10. *The Famous History of Captain Thomas Stukeley* has 'Sirus'(= 'Sus'?), Malone Society Reprint, line 2,373, but the names in that play are worse garbled in

the printing-house than those in *Alcazar*, although it is not a suspect text. The Trojan stories, or, perhaps, the lines of his own lost play of *Iphigenia*, were clearly running in Peele's head as he wrote. The birthplace of Achilles may naturally have presented itself as a place-name.

11. Greg, *Alcazar and Orlando*, p. 106.

12. See R. Simpson, *The School of Shakespeare* (New York, 1878), vol. I.

13. A. Munday, *The English Roman Life* (London, 1590), ed. P. J. Ayres (Oxford, 1980), p. 50.

14. William Pullen's report to Burleigh, P.R.O., State Papers Domestic, Addenda, Elizabeth, vol. XXV, no. 95.

15. Thomas Mansell, writing from Pisa to Ed. Mansell, 15 March 1578. Cecil MSS. Hatfield House, vol. CLX, f. 120.

16. Conestaggio, *Dell' Unione*, Lib. 1, p. 15. My translation.

17. A more specific account of the destruction of the city is in B.M. Sloane MSS. 61, ff. 3.4: 'the inhabitants being proud and exceeding in all other wickedness, the Lord sent an army of lyons upon them, whoe sparing neither man woman nor child, but consuming all ... took the city in possession to themselves.'

18. Ben Jonson, *Poetaster*, III, iv, 346–52. C. H. Herford, P. Simpson and E. Simpson (eds.), *Ben Jonson* (Oxford, 1932, rep. 1954), vol. IV, p. 256.

19. An African flavour for this Roman scene may have been prompted by a passage about oath-taking among the Abyssinians derived from Peter Pigafetta's translation of Leo Africanus. Povy's translation (1600), ed. Robert Brown, Hakluyt Society, Series I, vols. XCII–XCIV (London, 1896), runs: 'the partie to be deposed goeth accompanied by two priests, carrying with them fire and incense to the church-doore, whereon he layeth his hand; and then the priests adjure him to tell the truth, saying: If thou swear falsely, as the lyon devoureth the beasts of the forest, so let the divell devoure thy soule ... and as fire burneth up wood, so may thy soule enter into Paradise'. The passage is not in Leo.

20. Thus showing that Sebastian's 'aide that once was offered and refusde' (II, Ind., 353), contrary to Greg's opinion, never had any part in the play. The dramatic *given* of the scene is Sebastian's *mistrust*, inconsistent with the report of a previous offer of help that has crept in from the source material at the earlier point.

21. Greg's suspicions are aroused by the speech prefix *Legate* for the second Ambassador. A Papal Legate had, indeed, brought to Portugal the customary Bull for operations against the Infidel in 1573, but the Legate in the play speaks for King Philip. He is surely so called because the word in Freigius is always 'legatus', and 'legate' is so perfectly common an alternative in Elizabethan usage that examples ought to be needless. In *Alphonsus, King of Aragon*, the lords in Act IV are sent as 'Legats to god Mahomet', and recall a visit from 'the stately legate of the Persian King'. Even Milton recalls being received in Paris by 'the noble Thomas Scudamore, Viscount Sligo, legate of King Charles' (*Second Defence of the English People*, 1654).

22. What may be sufficient time for a costume change will, of course, vary according to the kind of action implied, and is, as Gary Taylor remarks in *Modernising Shakespeare's Spelling with Three Studies of Henry V* (Oxford, 1979), pp. 73–4, 'a matter of judgment'. He cites Ringler's observation that Jessica changes into boys' attire in seventeen lines between II, v and II, vi in

The Merchant of Venice. There are, however, twenty-five lines allowed for this change. One does not have to suppose, as Ringler does (having deducted, by some odd arithmetic, seven lines for the ascent), that the boy playing Jessica changes and *then* climbs the stairs. It is a hasty change, and it will not matter if it looks like it. Jessica, moreover, is not disguising herself from the audience or from the characters on stage. I have not found cases of genuine changes of identity under about twenty-seven lines. A test case is Face in *The Alchemist* (1610), who is an expert at disguising, and the faster the funnier; but is never allowed less than twenty-seven lines to change, unless Tim Mares is correct (F. H. Mares (ed.), *The Alchemist*, The Revels edition, London, 1967, note. p. 123.) in ignoring the break between Acts III and IV; in which case Face has to change on stage from his Captain's outfit to his 'Lungs' costume in only twenty lines. I think this strains the dialogue and that Jonson's act divisions are intended.

23. The eccentric time-scheme that Peele adopts suggests either careful calculation or great carelessness. I believe he wanted to play up the suggestions of Spanish deceit by prolonging the delay at Cadiz, and to waste no time in moving on to the battle once the army was in Africa.

24. J. Polemon, *The Second Book of Battailes* (London, 1587, rep. Amsterdam, The English Experience Series, no. 483, 1972), X2^v.

25. Ibid., Y2^r.

26. T. Freigius, *Historia de Bello Africano* (Nuremberg, 1580) A5^r. 'See, too, the crowns of three kings, fallen to the ground! Who was it urged the noble king to attack the infidel Moors with untried sword? What kind of faith was this? Did not the signs in the heavenly watchtower presage this disaster to any enlightened mind? Was the Comet a false prophet, with its blazing tail stretched out through the house of the celestial realm?' I am indebted to Professor David Rankin for the elucidation of this rather obscure poem.

27. Ibid., A4^v.

28. A. W. Pollard, 'The Manuscripts of Shakespeare's Plays', *The Library*, 3rd Series, no. 26., 7 April 1916, p. 214.

[14]

Moors, Villainy and
The Battle of Alcazar

Peter Hyland

One of the most important effects of recent theoretical approaches to the culture of the English Renaissance has been the revaluation and relocation of repressed or marginalized perspectives, especially insofar as this work has shown how such voices have been misrepresented or even silenced both in literary and cultural texts and in their critical reception. This has particularly been the case with the drama of the Elizabethan period, which was centrally implicated in the construction of an English national identity at a time of European competition and expansionism. Much recent criticism has examined ways in which the conception of national identity located its values within boundaries that were marked and validated through the representation of racial and religious 'otherness', particularly in relation to blackness and Islam,

dramatized in the figure of the Moor.[1] While there can be no
question that this has revealed the racist underpinnings of much
Elizabethan drama, it has also resulted in a totalizing approach
that has misrepresented and distorted some of the texts. I want to
consider here one way in which George Peele's play *The Battle of
Alcazar*, and particularly its treatment of its Moorish villain Muly
Mahamet, has suffered from such distortion

Any attempt to interpret attitudes reflected in cultural texts
of the past, and especially attitudes in the sensitive area of racial
distinction, must deal with the complex set of differences generated
by temporal distance. The very term 'racist' is a recent coinage
(neither 'racist' nor 'racialist' appears in the 1933 edition of the
OED), and while this obviously does not mean that the conditions
and prejudices that we think of as racist did not exist within the
cultures that produced these texts, it does mean that we must be
very careful about how we construe them. In his book *Race and
Culture*, Thomas Sowell argues that the term 'racism', while widely
used in contemporary ideological discussion, is ill-defined. For
Sowell the word's 'straightforward meaning—a belief in innate

---

[1] Amongst the more important books on the construction of blackness
on the early English stage are: Eldred Jones, *Othello's Countrymen: The
African in English Renaissance Drama* (London: Oxford University Press,
1965); Elliot H. Tokson, *The Popular Image of the Black Man in English
Drama, 1550-1688* (Boston: G.K. Hall, 1982); Anthony Gerard
Barthelemy, *Black Face, Maligned Race: The Representation of Blacks in
English Drama from Shakespeare to Southerne* (Baton Rouge: Louisiana
State University Press, 1987); Jack D'Amico, *The Moor in English
Renaissance Drama* (Tampa: University of Florida Press, 1991; Ania
Loomba, *Gender, Race, Renaissance Drama* (Manchester and New York:
Manchester University Press, 1989; Kim F. Hall, *Things of Darkness:
Economies of Race and Gender in Early Modern England* (Ithaca and
London: Cornell University Press, 1995).

racial inferiority or superiority' is in danger of getting lost because
it has been contaminated by 'ideological redefinitions', to the
degree that 'political overuse of the word may destroy its
effectiveness as a warning against a very real danger.'[2]
        One of these 'ideological redefinitions' connects racial and
gender issues. Ania Loomba, a prominent analyst of the racial
implications of cultural documents, writes at the beginning of
Gender, Race, Renaissance Drama: 'The processes by which women
and black people are constructed as the "others" of white
patriarchal society are similar and connected....'[3] There are two
problems here. One lies in the shift from 'similar' to 'connected',
for if the processes are similar we can analyze them in comparative
terms, but if they are connected we cannot examine the
construction of race without also examining the construction of
gender, and the danger is that an agenda of discrediting white
patriarchy will stand in the way of empirical analysis. A second
and potentially more serious problem is that Loomba's implied
universalization of a contemporary truth takes insufficiently into
consideration the 'otherness' of the past. If, in trying to define the
'racism' we perceive in the cultural texts of past times, we read too
fully into them our present experience, we are likely to distort them
in the name of a superior moral understanding that might not, in
fact, have been available four hundred years ago.
        In her book Loomba delineates what she sees as the process
through which racism developed, contending that 'how colours
come to be invested with moral connotations is precisely the
history of racism.'[4] She is echoed in this by Kim F. Hall, who has

---

[2] Thomas Sowell, *Race and Culture: A World View* (New York: Basic Books,
     1994), p. 154.
[3] Loomba, p. 2.
[4] Loomba, P. 42.

also written extensively about the construction of the black 'other' in early modern England. At the opening of *Things of Darkness* Hall suggests that descriptions of light and dark were means whereby the English began to develop notions of 'self' and 'other', contending that 'white' and 'black' had developed a heavy load of meaning long before the English came into contact with black people, and that this meaning contributed to the 'demonology of race.'[5] She presents a powerful argument for this, but it is only part of the picture. Self-definition is a complex and dynamic process. The 'other' is also a 'self', and there is nothing inherent in the white/black binary (unlike, for example, the legitimate/illegitimate binary) that implies hierarchy. In *The Black Feet of the Peacock* Linda Van Norden outlines a tradition stretching from Theophrastus to the seventeenth-century heraldic writer Edmund Bolton that white and black are the 'common parents', the colours from which all the rest descend.[6] Van Norden stresses the inconsistency of the historical construction of the relationship between white and black, which is subject to a very complex set of philosophical negotiations. As we might expect, much of the evidence compiled in her exhaustive study confirms Hall's position, but there are enough exceptions to indicate the dangers of generalization.

The idea of 'self' implied by Hall is inseparable from the idea of a national identity, and its development in Tudor England was part of a long process. During that process many unfamiliar cultures and hostile nations, including other white European societies, were represented in terms of derogatory stereotypes.

---

[5] Hall, pp. 2, 9.

[6] Linda Van Norden, *The Black Feet of the Peacock: The Color-Concept 'Black' from the Greeks through the Renaissance*, compiled and edited by John Pollock (Lanham: University Press of America, 1985), p. 6.

Foreigners were brutal, devious, corrupt, transgressive, but Moors or Turks, followers of Islam, were not necessarily more so than Catholic Spaniards, Frenchmen or Italians, or, if we are to believe the Earl of Westmoreland, Welsh women.[7] So while nationalism perhaps inevitably leads to racism, the relationship between the two is predicated upon a broader set of impulses. As John Gillies has argued, 'The need to constitute an identity by excluding the other is not just primal, but perennial'.[8] When we approach non-white figures in Elizabethan plays, I would suggest, we need to understand them in a broader perspective that allows us to go beyond the potentially misleading black/white binary.

The Battle of Alcazar (1588/89) was one of the earliest plays to stage figures that were identified as both Islamic and black.[9] Most of its leading characters are Moors, and the plot concerns a generational struggle for the throne of Fez, to which a dimension of Christian/Islamic hostility is added by the involvement of Sebastian, king of Portugal. Although very few scholars have treated this play in any detail, it has generally been identified as

---

[7] William Shakespeare, *1 Henry IV*, I.i.45. Quotations from Shakespeare's plays are from Stephen Grenblatt et al (eds) *The Norton Shakespeare* (New York: W.W Norton and Co., 1997).

[8] John Gillies, *Shakespeare and the Geography of Difference*. (Cambridge: Cambridge University Press, 1994), p. 6.

[9] Peele's play is treated, usually briefly, in the books noted in fn. 1. Amongst the few extensive treatments are those by John Yoklavich in his introduction to *The Battle of Alcazar* in *The Dramatic Works of George Peele*, Vol. 2, ed. by Frank S. Hook and John Yoklavitch (New Haven and London: Yale University Press, 1961), from which all quotations from the text are taken; A.R. Braunmuller, *George Peele* (Boston: Twayne, 1983); David Bradley, *From Text to Performance in the Elizabethan Theatre: Preparing the Play for the Stage* (Cambridge: Cambridge University Press, 1992). Most journal articles concern local textual or historical questions.

having initiated, in the character of Muly Mahamet, the stereotype of the villainous Moor. Scholars interested in constructions of the racial or cultural 'other' and in Renaissance stage representations of the Moor or of Islam have tended to treat the play in the same way: it offered, in Muly Mahamet, a demonized prototype of a figure that reflected Elizabethan anxieties about Moorish and Turkish power and expansionism, about the Islamic threat to Christianity, and about miscegenation. While I do not wish to deny that Muly Mahamet is related to later stereotyped Moorish villains, I would argue that by removing him from the context of the play in which he appears and inserting him into the larger structural context of Elizabethan racial fears, critics have distorted both his significance in the play and the complexity of the perspectives that the play provides. *The Battle of Alcazar* is, to be sure, generally inept and frequently incoherent, and exhibits little actual knowledge of Islamic religion or culture. However, in attempting to read remote cultural concerns (both religious and ethnic) in the context of more immediate political issues related to the Protestant struggle against Catholicism, Peele's play presents a picture of the Islamic 'other' that is more complex, and perhaps more generous, than the preoccupation with the negative racial stereotype allows.

Peele's interest in the Alcazar story, I believe, has more to do with Elizabethan Protestant anxiety about Catholicism than with Moorish villainy. He wrote his play in the immediate context of the defeat of the Spanish Armada in 1588 and the expedition (the unsuccessful 'counter Armada', which Peele enthusiastically supported) of Norris and Drake in 1589 to burn the Spanish fleet and place Don Antonio on the Portuguese throne. As a staunch anti-Catholic Peele was quite ready to believe that Spanish designs on the English throne had not been extinguished. It is not surprising, therefore, that he took advantage of the revived popular interest in the events that led to the Portuguese king Sebastian's defeat at Alcazar in 1578.[10]

The headstrong Sebastian, promoting himself as Christ's agent against Islam, and hoping to gain political benefit from the civil war between Abd el-Malek and his nephew Mohammed el-Mesloukh (the play's 'Muly Mahamet'), had allied himself with the nephew in what turned out to be a disastrous campaign in which all three died and his army was massacred. The issues surrounding these events are murky now, and probably were at least as murky to Peele. Philip of Spain had first tried to dissuade Sebastian from aiding el-Mesloukh, but had promised him aid when Sebastian refused to listen. There is, however, evidence that Philip was in secret alliance with Abd el-Malek. There is also evidence, however partial, of a secret exchange of arms between Elizabeth and Abd el-Malek.[11] The consequence of the Battle of Alcazar was of great moment to the English, for after the defeat of Sebastian Portugal was absorbed by Spain, which troubled England's involvement in Barbary trade.

Although the English favored Abd el-Malek in his struggle with his nephew over the throne of Fez and Morocco, the rights of the issue could hardly have been clear to them. The struggle arose because in 1557 Moulay Mohammed ech-Cheikh, father of Abd el-Malek, established a law of succession whereby his eldest son Abdallah would inherit the crown, but the crown would then

---

[10] Most of the relevant historical material relevant is provided in Yoklavich's introduction to his edition and by Bradley in his thorough account of the play.

[11] Jones, pp. 138-9, n. 25, cites the *Calendar of State Papers, Rome, 1572-1576*, p. 495: 'there is no evil that is not devised by that woman, who, it is perfectly plain, succoured Muloco with arms and especially with artillery'.

pass to Abdallah's eldest brother, not to his son. Abdallah, who ruled from 1557 to 1574, wished to pass the crown on to his son Mohammed el-Mesloukh, and to do this he ordered the murder of his brothers; Abd el-Malek was one of two who escaped. Mohammed succeeded to the throne in 1574, but Abd el-Malek, with the aid of the Turkish leader Amurat III, deposed him. It was at this point that Sebastian became involved. For English observers the right of Abd el-Malek, established by his father, obviously prevailed; yet there must have been some discomfort, to a people accustomed to a patrilineal model of succession, at the exclusion of Mohammad.

To the patriotic dramatist the attraction of this material, providing for an anti-Catholic narrative in a distant and exotic setting, must have been great, but Peele also had to shape the material for his own theatrical context. He wrote the play for the Admiral's Men, who had recently had great success with Marlowe's Tamburlaine. It seems reasonable to assume that Peele, certainly an opportunist, would have picked up on the commercial possibilities of this new theatrical fashion, and must have seen the rich potential of bombasting out blank verses in a play that would combine chronicle history with revenge tragedy. In Muly Mahamet and Captain Thomas Stukeley the play offers two potential roles for Edward Alleyn, who had triumphed as Tamburlaine, but the person involved in the Alcazar story who presented the best excuse for flights of exotic emotional rhetoric was Mohammed el-Mesloukh; furthermore, his historical role as tempter of Sebastian had affinities with the theatrical role of villain-tempter that had developed in the Elizabethan theatre out of the morality Vice. Peele made him guilty of the murders that were actually instigated by his father, and turned him into the somewhat more despicable Muly Mahamet; thus the supposed progenitor of a line of Moor-villains may in the first place have been born out of nothing more sinister than theatrical need.

Most modern commentary on Peele's play has related Muly Mahamet's villainy to his blackness (a connection seen to reflect Elizabethan racist attitudes) rather than to the dramatic need to have a villain. It is true that, by all contemporary accounts, Mohammed el-Mesloukh was a villain. In addition, through his Negro mother he was darker than other Moors, and the taint of his black skin 'was used by Moors and Christians alike to indicate the unreliability of his nature. Even Abdelmelec, his uncle, referred to him contemptuously as "the negro"'.[12] (Bradley 134). This appears to show that he was as much a victim of Moorish as of English racism, and that Christians readily perceived that he was different from other Moors. The critical treatment of the figure has, however, distorted this perception. It seems to have begun with Eldred Jones in his book *Othello's Countrymen*. Pointing out that Mohammed el-Mesloukh was known as 'the black King', Jones makes the large claim that the Elizabethans generally distinguished between 'black' Moors like Muly Mahamet and 'white' Moors like Abd el-Malek.[13] This distinction has been accepted by some later scholars such as Braunmuller and, especially, Emily Bartels, who suggests that the 'white' Moor Abdelmelec might, in fact, have been a Christian.[14] What in effect has happened is that a special case has been generalized into a whole category. Only Elliot Tokson dismisses the idea of a black/white distinction, arguing that Moors in general were probably considered to be black.[15]

---

[12] Bradley, p. 134.

[13] Jones, pp. 14, 49.

[14] Braunmuller, p. 146, n. 33; Emily C. Bartels, 'Making More of the Moor: Aaron, Othello, and Renaissance Refashionings of Race', *Shakespeare Quarterly*, 41 (1990), 433-54 (p. 434, n. 49).

[15] Tokson, p. 39.

Having generated out of *The Battle of Alcazar* a category of
bad 'black' Moors and (presumably) good 'white' Moors most of
these critics go on to focus on the former category and effectively
ignore the latter. Jones thinks that 'Peele's play must have done a
good deal to fix the stereotype of the "Moor"', by which he means
the villain.[16] Ania Loomba, not so precise about the chronology of
plays with Moorish villains, notes that 'The tradition of the black
villain-hero in Elizabethan drama resulted in a series of negative
portrayals of black men, such as Muly Mahamet'.[17] Bartels
describes him as the 'prototypical cruel black Moor'.[18] All these
writers treat Peele's play in a very cursory manner as part of larger
discussions of Moors, Africans, or racial or cultural 'otherness', but
even Braunmuller, who examines the play at some length, says that
Peele 'virtually invented a stock character of the later drama, the
Moor-villain'.[19]

All of this agreement might seem conclusive, and certainly
it is impossible to deny that Peele might well have intended to
create a figure who reflected stereotyped public hostility to Moors,
or that the success of his play might have encouraged other
dramatists to create such figures. What is of crucial significance,
however, is the fact that Peele's Moor does not, in fact, contain most
of the representative characteristics of the stereotype as critics have
identified it. Jack D'Amico, while not writing specifically about
Muly Mahamet, elaborates on the significance of the stock figure:

[16] Jones, p. 14.
[17] Loomba, p. 46.
[18] Bartels, p. 434.
[19] Braunmuller, p. 79.

The Moor as villain becomes a convenient locus for those darkly subversive forces that threaten European society from within but that can be projected onto the outsider. The destructive forces of lust and violence are thus distanced by being identified with a cultural, religious, or racial source of evil perceived as the inversion of European norms.[20]

If Muly Mahamet is the prototype, he only vaguely fits D'Amico's summary of the stereotype: he is certainly not a figure of lust, and his violence (mainly verbal) is directed locally. In the other encapsulations of Muly Mahamet, too, we can perceive a certain confusion. Is he a villain or is he a villain-hero? Loomba's term indicates that she considers Muly Mahamet to be unquestionably the play's central character. She further implies that Muly Mahamet was the result of an Elizabethan theatrical stereotype of black men that already existed, though there is no evidence of any plays prior to Peele's that featured Moors. Jones and Braunmuller would appear to be more accurate in giving Peele the credit for inventing the stereotype. However, as early as 1937 Samuel Chew offered a more exact account of Peele's character: 'The tyrannical Moorish king is a typical stage villain, "black in his look and bloody in his deeds"'.[21] (526). Chew does not, as the others do, say that Muly Mahamet's villainy is connected to his blackness, but rather that he is a typical stage villain who in this case happens to be a Moor. The line Chew quotes, juxtaposing black looks and bloody deeds, appears to contradict this; however, Peele might have thought of the blackness of Muly Mahamet's looks in the same way as Shakespeare apparently did of the 'black-fac'd Clifford' in the bloody act of murdering Rutland (*Richard III*,

---

[20] D'Amico, p. 2.
[21] Samuel C. Chew, *The Crescent and the Rose: Islam and England during the Renaissance* (1937; repr. New York: Octagon Books, 1965) p. 526.

I.i.157); he does not refer to literal blackness, but to a metaphorical state of vicious hatred.

I do not wish here to appear to defy common sense. There were, as all the critics quoted above and many others have shown, racist representations on the Elizabethan stage, and we are reminded frequently by the play's Presenter that Muly Mahamet is 'this Negro', a 'barbarous Moor', an 'unbelieving Moor'. However, his black animosity is not directed against white enemies, but against his Moorish uncle, the 'courteous and honorable' Abdelmelec. So, if we are to blame Peele's play for the initiation of a stereotype, we are obliged also, I think, to examine carefully the degree to which the play itself subscribes to that stereotype, and to examine the other things that it does in dealing with racial and cultural 'otherness'. In other words, the fact that the play has a cruel Moor-villain is, surely, mitigated to a degree by the fact that it also has a noble, devout Moor-hero.

Against all the attention that has been paid to Muly Mahamet one might argue that Peele's primary interest was not in him as an evil Moor, but in a complex of competing religious and political positions centered on the figure of Sebastian. The title page of the 1594 quarto gives the play's full title as *The Battell of Alcazar, fought in Barbarie, betweene Sebastian king of Portugall, and Abdelmelec king of Morocco. With the death of Captaine Stukeley.* Muly Mahamet is the only one of the four main characters not mentioned, despite the fact that the role was played by Alleyn. If we examine the size of each of the main roles we find that Muly Mahamet and Abdelmelec have roughly the same number of lines (162 and 165 respectively), but Sebastian, with 218, has 33% more than either of them (the Presenter, who is not a character but a framing device, has 174 lines, and Stukeley only 132).

As we have seen, English interests were involved in

Sebastian's fate. In Peele's play Sebastian is a gullible opportunist, concerned mainly 'To propagate the fame of Portugall' (765) by aiding the usurper Muly Mahamet against his uncle. Sebastian believes that in return for this favor Muly Mahamet will hand over the 'kingdome of Maroccus' to the Portuguese. Christian justification for this is provided largely by ambassadors from Spain, who claim that the Spanish are willing 'To spend their blouds in honor of their Christ' to aid Portugal and 'plant religious truth in Affrica' (774, 767). They represent the Spanish king Philip, however, who has no real intention of supporting Sebastian, and Peele's own staunchly anti-Catholic views make it improbable that he intended his audience to sympathize with these crusading claims. Much of the play's praise of Sebastian (and most of the abuse of Muly Mahamet) comes through the Presenter. The play's Yale editor suggests that 'The Presenter's tone and viewpoint is European, not Moorish; he is practically to be identified with some eyewitness of the battle'.[22] The contradiction in the Presenter's enthusiasm for sweet Sebastian on the one hand, and his hostility to Sebastian's 'Catholike case' 'To plant this cursed Moor' (742-4) on the other, makes him somewhat suspect as a shaper of audience judgement, however, and he is best seen as a choral device with the primary function of controlling and explicating the play's most theatrical elements, the dumb shows.

In his dramatic relationship to Sebastian, Muly Mahamet clearly has roots in the morality Vice, and many of his villainous characteristics stem from this tradition. A plausible tempter whose grotesque excess at times verges on the comic, he offers Sebastian friendship and power while intending to betray him:

[22] Yoklavich, p. 236.

> He can submit himselfe and live below,
> Make shew of friendship, promise, vow and sweare,
> Till by the vertue of his faire pretence,
> Sebastian trusting his integritie,
> He makes himselfe possessor of such fruits,
> As grow upon such great advantages.   (525-30)

There is nothing particularly Moorish about this, however, for it simply aligns Muly Mahamet with many other smiling, damned villains of the Elizabethan stage. More immediately, it aligns him with the Spanish king, to whom Stukeley assigns a similar Vice-like treachery:

> For Spaine disguising with a double face,
> Flatters thy youth and forwardnes good king,
> Philip whome some call the catholike king,
> I feare me much thy faith will not be firme,
> But disagree with thy profession.   (808-12)

In effect, Peele's Protestant anxiety about Catholic duplicity is displaced on to the duplicitous Muly Mahamet.

Similarly, through the figure of Stukeley, Muly Mahamet is aligned with Catholic ambition. The Catholic adventurer Sir Thomas Stukeley had led an abortive expedition that aimed to restore Papal rule to Ireland, and had subsequently been romanticized into semi-legendary status. Although Peele makes his Stukeley comparatively attractive, he places him with care in the political structure of the play by identifying him at his first appearance as a 'valiant Catholike' (384). Like Milton's Satan in his unwillingness to be a subject, Stukeley asks himself 'Why should not I then looke to be a king?', and answers himself: 'never cease t'aspire,/Before thou raigne sole king of thy desire' (461, 466-7). His words are echoed only a few lines later by Muly Mahamet, setting up a clear parallel with this example of Catholic ambition: 'What patience is for him that lacks his crown?' (493).

Against this Catholic aggression, Abdelmelec stands almost like a Protestant defender of the True Faith. Although the Spanish Catholics describe the adventure against him as a 'warre with Moores and men of little faith' (777), the play hardly presents Abdelmelec as an unbeliever. At his first appearance, when he welcomes the support of the Turks, he throws up his trembling hands and prays to his god (56-7). At no point is he shown as anything other than devout, giving to his gods the credit for his victories, and at no point does the play mock his devotion or his religion. To be sure, the play does not understand Islam: the gods invoked by both Muly Mahamet and Abdelmelec are classical deities, echoing the Saracenic pantheon that Christians popularly understood constituted Islam, and nothing in the play suggests any familiarity with Mohammedanism. Nevertheless, the play gives us a good and a bad Moor, a good and a bad Mohammedan, and we cannot ignore Abdelmelec's heroic stature.

If it is true that Peele originated the stereotype of the villainous Moor there is irony in it, for the overall Moorish context presented in the play, of god-fearing leaders who are good husbands and fathers, suggests a different intention. It is necessary to reiterate that Muly Mahamet's villainy is not contingent upon his Moorishness or his religion, and comes as much from the stage history he inherited as from the cultural and political context in which he operates. By an act of displacement his villainy alerts Peele's audience to Catholic villainy. The true dark villain of this play, who never appears, is Philip of Spain, who stands silently outside the play but whose influence is felt everywhere in it. Peele's play reminds his audience where the feared and hated 'other' is actually located.

Huron College
University of Western Ontario

[15]

THE BATTLE OF ALCAZAR

Eldred Jones

The battle of Alcazar (El-ksar el Kebir), fought in Barbary in 1578, in which Sebastian of Portugal and his army were crushed by the Moors under Abd-el-Malek, provided the materials for a romantic tragedy well suited to Elizabethan tastes. Almost all the ingredients for such a tragedy were present in the numerous popular accounts of this battle: villainy—duly punished—in Muly Hamet, misguided chivalry in Sebastian and Captain Stukeley, virtue—justly rewarded—in Abd-el-Malek, and a large loss of life. All these elements simply invited dramatic treatment. The magnitude of the disaster alone made the subject sensational. Practically every able-bodied Portuguese nobleman had followed the foolhardy Sebastian to Africa, and had died in the battle. J. F. Connestaggio, on the consequences of the battle for Portugal, writes:

There was none in Lisbone, but had some interest in this warre, who so had not his sonne there, had his father; the one her husbande, the other her brother; the traders and handie-crafts men, who had not their kinsemen there (and yet many of them had) did venture their wealth in it, some of them for the desire of gaine, and others for that they could not call in that which they had lent to Gentlemen, and souldiers: by reason wereof all were in heaviness . . .[13]

Apart from the flower of Portugal, troops from Germany, the Low Countries, Spain, and Italy fought and died in the battle. For the ordinary Englishman, however, interest in the battle was centred on the figure of Sir Thomas Stukeley, who, rather contrary to his just deserts, became a popular hero. Stukeley, who in his lifetime had been twice imprisoned for treasonable activities against his country, had also been a privateer, and one of the heroes of Lepanto. All the hero-worship which was lavished on him at his death was doubly ironical because he was actually on his way to invade Ireland with the blessing of the Pope, when he was persuaded to join the expedition to Alcazar which he regarded as a breakfast on the Moors before a dinner on the English.

All these facts about Stukeley were either not popularly known or were interred with his bones, for he passed straight into legend.[14] He was celebrated in plays, ballads and pamphlets in all of which, unlike the official records, he was accounted a hero. One unfavourable Stukeley tale occurs, however, in Thomas Deloney's *The Gentle Craft*, in which he was beaten by the shoemaker Peachy and had to sue for peace.[15]

While ordinary Englishmen were extolling Stukeley in ballads, pamphlets, and plays, the Queen and her counsellors were preoccupied with the imminent danger of Philip of Spain's accession to the now vacant throne of Portugal, and with attempts to prevent it. These attempts also helped to keep the memory of Sebastian, Stukeley, and the battle alive in England for some time.[16]

Apart from all this human interest in the battle and its consequences for Europe, the setting—Africa—and the characters of the Moorish participants provided the ingredient of romance, as well as an opportunity to the dramatist to reproduce something of the exotic extravagance of *Tamburlaine*. Such, then, were the opportunities offered to Peele by this rich historical event.

The date of the play

The date of the play is important in this study because it appears to be the first full-length treatment of a Moorish character in English dramatic literature.

The facts relevant to the dating of the play are briefly these. On the title page of the quarto edition printed in 1594, appear the words 'as it was sundrie times plaid by the Lord High Admiral his servants'. W. W. Greg[17] points out that there is no reference in *Henslowe's Diary* to a performance in 1594, and concludes that it must have been performed earlier than that year. Another clue to the date is the reference in Peele's 'Farewel to Norris and Drake', a poem entered in *The Stationers' Register* on 18 April 1589, to Tom Stukeley as a popular stage hero:

> Bid theatres and proud tragedians,
> Bid Mahomet's Poo and mighty Tamburlaine,
> King Charlemagne, Tom Stukeley and the rest,
> Adieu.

If this reference is to *The Battle of Alcazar*, as Dyce,[18] Greg[19] and Chambers[20] take it to be, then the date is even earlier. Greg supports 'not later than Christmas 1588', while E. K. Chambers suggests 1589. Unless the identification of the reference in 'Farewell to Norris and Drake' is wrong,[21] later dates like F. E. Schelling's 1591[22] must be ruled out.

If Greg's early date is preferred—it seems the most satisfactory— then the play gives the earliest full treatment of Moors as dramatic characters.

Muly Hamet

The hero of *The Battle of Alcazar*, Muly Hamet, is called in the play 'the Moor'. This title is in itself significant in a play in which most of the characters are Moors. The explanation is that the historical counterpart of Muly Hamet—Mulai Mohammed—was born of a Negro mother.[23] The stage character thus attracts to himself the title 'Moor', which to the Elizabethan mind usually conveyed the image of a black person. In addition to this general title, Muly is also referred to as 'the Negro Muly Hamet' (10) and 'Negro Moore' (921).[24]

Muly Hamet was a novelty on the stage in that he was probably the earliest Moor-villain, but his character owes something to his white predecessors. In his boastful grandiloquence, for instance, he is reminiscent of Marlowe's Tamburlaine. Combined with this bombastic element, there is also in Muly a suggestion of craft—in his treacherous dealings with his brother, his uncle, and Sebastian— which reveals traces of the dramatic type of the Machiavel. This curious combination of the grandiloquent extrovert and the subtle plotter is a characteristic which other stage Moors, Aaron and Eleazer for example, were to demonstrate later.

Muly is presented from the outset in a totally unfavourable light, and in this he is contrasted with his light-skinned uncle, Abdilmelec,[25] against whom he is fighting.

The Presenter's speech at the beginning handily summarizes the play's attitude towards the chief characters:

> Honor the spurre that pricks the princely minde,
> To followe rule and climbe the stately chaire,
> With great desire inflames the Portingall
> An honorable and couragious king,
> To undertake a dangerous dreadfull warre,
> And aide with Christian armes the barbarous Moore,
> The Negro Muly Hamet that with-holds
> The Kingdome from his unkle Abdilmelec,
> Whom proud Abdallas wrongd,
> And in his throne instals his cruell sonne,
> That now usurps upon this prince,
> This brave Barbarian Lord Muly Molocco.

The passage to the crowne by murder made,
Abdallas dies, and [leaves]²⁶ this tyrant king,
Of whome we treate sprong from the Arabian moore
Blacke in his looke, and bloudie in his deeds,
And in his shirt staind with a cloud of gore,
Presents himselfe with naked sword in hand,
Accompanied as now you may behold,
With devils coted in the shapes of men.

(Alcazar, 1–23)

The cruelty of Muly suggested here is soon demonstrated in the dumb show in which he is shown treacherously supervising the murder of his two younger brothers and his uncle Abdelmenec. Thus the stage is set for a typical revenge play—crime to be followed by retribution—to which the Presenter actually looks forward in lines 49–54. The necessities of a chronicle play, however, rather blur the revenge theme.

After the opening dumb show, Muly's character is portrayed in a series of scenes in which his high-sounding terms rise far above his deeds. His first reaction to a setback of any kind is a spate of bombastic curses or equally bombastic yet empty boasts. In scene two, he is despatching his treasure for safe keeping, when his son brings news of the forces ranged against him, and of the fact that his opponents have received help from the Turks under the leadership of Bassa. Without waiting for details, Muly bursts out:

Why boy, is Amuraths Bassa such a bug,
That he is markt to do this doubtie deed?
Then Bassa, locke the winds in wards of brasse,
Thunder from heaven[,] damne wretched men to death
Barre [Bear] all the offices of Saturnes sonnes,
Be Pluto then in hell and barre the fiends,
Take Neptunes force to thee and calme the seas,
And execute Joves justice on the world,
Convey Tamberlaine into our Affrike here,
To chastice and to menace lawfull kings,
Tamberlaine triumph not, for thou must die
As Philip did, Caesar, and Caesars peeres.²⁷

(240–251)

This outburst is characteristic of the Moor's habit of dodging reality with pointless speeches in which the classical gods—frequently of the lower world—and their haunts are his favourite sources of imagery. Here his mind soon veers away from the uncomfortable reality of Bassa and his troops to the gods, Tamburlaine, Philip, and Caesar. Certainly, the rhetoric is Tamburlaine's; but Muly's character is no blind imitation of his predecessor's. Peele has cleverly adapted his character to the facts of history. His bombast and large curses are in his case a cloak; a refusal to come face to face with the fact that his cause is doomed from the start; merely an external show to blind himself to the reality of his inward fear and cowardice. Viewed in this way, Muly's character is not as simple as it appears on the surface. He is always next door to despair, and only keeps himself from surrendering completely to it by his own words.

He is not a man of action like Tamburlaine. Peele gives him only two positive acts: one is from history—his luring of Sebastian with promises, to fight on his behalf; the other, a superb effort of the playwright's own imagination, is the episode in which Muly obtains lion's flesh for the fainting Calipolis.

His dealings with Sebastian are used to illustrate both his treachery and his cowardice. He flatters the young king in his presence, eggs him on to fight, and then callously abandons him during the battle, retiring to a safe place to await the outcome. Thus having welcomed him, and sworn in his usual style by 'the hellish prince grim Pluto' to

> ... performe religiously to thee,
> That I have holyly earst undertane
>   (1007–1008),

and having burst in once again on the now wavering King to 'exclime [sic] upon this dastard flight' (1193) and to urge him to stand and fight, he takes no further part in the fighting, except by making fruitless invocations which by their very fury betray his inner lack of confidence:

> Now have I set these Portugals aworke,
> To hew a waie for me unto the crowne,

46   OTHELLO'S COUNTRYMEN

Or with your [their] weapons here to dig your [their] graves[.]
You dastards of the night and Erybus,
Fiends, Fairies, hags that fight in beds of steele,
Range through this armie with your yron whips,
Drive forward to this deed this christian crew,
And let me triumph in the tragedie,
Though it be seald and bonoured with my [the] bloud,
Both of the Portugall and barbarous Moore.
                                            (1227–1236)

Muly is a coward, but he is also a conscious manipulator of
others—a trait which Aaron and Eleazer (and of course white
villains, particularly Iago) were to cultivate with the relish of
amateurs in crime. The lines just quoted also prepare—in their
suggestions of cowardice—for Muly's next precipitate entrance in
which he calls Richard-like for a horse, but, unlike Richard, only
'To swimme the river . . . and to flie' (1390). In this extremity his
curses flow with their wonted vehemence; he seeks for

        Some uncouth walke where I may curse my fill,
        My starres, my dam, my planets and my nurse,
        The fire, the aire, the water, and the earth,
                            (1392–1394)

and indeed without waiting for the 'uncouth walke', he proceeds
to curse all these persons and objects (1398–1409). In his final lines,
as he disappears to an ignominious death by drowning while
running away, he vows revenge on Abdilmelec, again in words
which suggest his deeper consciousness that even this last revenge
will not materialize, for its venue swiftly changes, from here and
now, to
        If not on earth, yet when we meete in hell,
        Before grim Minos, Rodomant, and Eocus.
                            (1422–1423)

All this is a clever adaptation of recorded history in order to create
an effective stage character. Yet it is in the invented episode in
which Muly hunts for food for his wife, Calipolis, that Peele, in the
interplay of these two well contrasted characters, most effectively
demonstrates his skill in character portraiture.

This scene (III. iii) opens with Muly in a characteristic mood. He is in despair, is blind to all but his own predicament, and, as is usual with him in such circumstances, is hiding behind curses which are couched in language whose wild images, in their suggestions of death, betray his inner consciousness of the hopelessness of his cause:

> Some foule contagion of the infected heaven,
> Blast all the trees, and in their cursed tops,
> The dismall night raven and tragike owle
> Breed, and become fore-tellers of my fall,
> The fatall ruine of my name and me,
> Adders and serpents hisse at my disgrace,
> And wound the earth with anguish of their stings.
>
> (518–524)

To this Calipolis replies with a quiet sense of reality, enjoining Muly to address himself to their present 'distrest estate':

> I faint my Lord, and naught may cursing plaintes
> Refresh the fading substance of my life.
>
> (532–533)

Calipolis' speech does in fact succeed in bringing Muly sufficiently close to reality to make him go out and hunt for food. While Muly is absent from the stage, Peele uses the interval to develop further the tender character of Calipolis. Their son—a miniature of his father—tries to console his mother with the hope that their position will soon improve, since Muly has now succeeded in luring Sebastian with empty promises to fight for him—the son is as cynical as the father (569–575). Calipolis, without scolding, quietly refuses the comfort of such words:

> But more dishonor hangs on such misdeeds,
> Than all the profit their returne can beare.
>
> (576–577)

Her quiet integrity here glitters like the proverbial gold of Barbary against the dark background of Muly's perfidy. When Muly returns and proudly proffers food which turns out to be flesh forced from a lioness,[28] and with promises of even more extravagantly procured fare—

> I will provide thee of a princely ospraie,
> That as she flyeth over fish in pooles,
> The fish shall turne their glistering bellies up,
> And thou shalt take thy liberall choice of all—
>   (602–603)

Calipolis' reticent reception of this royal but unappetizing fare is eloquent of her good sense:

> Thankes good my Lord, and though my stomacke be
> Too queasie to disgest such bloudie meate,
> Yet strength I it with vertue of my minde,
> I doubt no whit but I shall live my Lord.
>   (610–615)

With these words Calipolis disappears from the play; but the firmness of her outline, the economy of her portrayal, as well as the veiled but eloquent commentary on Muly which is implied in her quiet sense of reality, all these make this character into a sensitive vignette, in a play which in other places shows cruder techniques. Beside her, the other ladies in this play—the Queen and Rubin Arches—are mere shadows, appearing in the more customary passive rôle of the subservient Moorish woman, and reflecting little personality. (Later portrayals of Moorish women who appear as Moors-in-exile in plays set outside Barbary—Zanche in Webster's *The White Devil* (1611) and Zanthia in Fletcher's *The Knight of Malta* (1616–1618), for example—are quite differently conceived.)

In contrast to Muly, his uncle Abdilmelec, whose historical counterpart stood higher in the estimation of Englishmen, is represented as a just defender of right, the instrument of Nemesis, quietly confident of victory. While Muly rants and curses in the name of the classical gods of the lower world, Abdilmelec, on reaching the borders of his native city, turns his thoughts and those of his followers to God:

> Cease ratling drums, and Abdilmelec here
> Throw up thy trembling hands to heavens throne[.]
> Pay to thy God due thankes, and thankes to him

> That strengthens thee with myghtie gracious armes,
> Against the proud usurper of thy right,
> The roiall seate and crowne of Barbarie.
>
> (73–78)

His attitude to Sebastian is not only free of spite, but is sympathetic to the point of condescension. He considers Sebastian's course misguided, and seeks to dissuade him by peaceful means from joining the cause of Muly:

> But for I have my selfe a souldier bin,
> I have in pittie to the Portugall
> Sent secret messengers to counsell him.
>
> (905–907)

Abdilmelec's attitude is thus in line with that of the Presenter towards Sebastian. His character is not, however, roundly drawn. Peele treats him primarily as the instrument of revenge and as a symbolic contrast to Muly.

We have then in this play two principal Moors. Abdilmelec emerges as the prototype of the dignified 'white' Moor, endowed with a romantic oriental dignity, wise and, according to his own lights, pious. If he is the forerunner of any other character it is of Shakespeare's Prince of Morocco. Muly is an altogether different conception. He is the type of the cruel Moor who is usually portrayed, as he is here, as black. Historical accident thus combined with popular rumour to produce Muly, who headed a line of black Moors on the stage, a line which included notably Aaron in *Titus Andronicus* (1589–1590),[29] Eleazer in *Lust's Dominion* (1599), and, in a striking reversal of the traditional portrayal, the hero of *Othello* (1604).

Notes

13. G. Connestaggio, *The Historie of the Uniting of the Kingdom of Portugall to the Crowne of Castil*, 1600, p. 55. (In quotations, i, u and v are modernized where necessary.) This book was first published in Genoa in 1585 and was very widely read in Europe. It was translated into several languages: French (1596), English (1600), Latin (1602), and Spanish (1610). The English translation was by Ed. Blount.

NOTES 137

14. Among the popular works on Stukeley which include treatments of his last battle are:

(i) 'The Life and Death of Famous Stukelie, an English Gallant in the time of Queen Elizabeth who ended his dayes in a battle of three kings in Barbary'. Richard Simpson reproduces this ballad (without the title) in *The School of Shakespere*, 1878, vol. i, pp. 144–51. The title is given with the text in a volume of ballads in the Wood Collection in the Bodleian Library (Shelfmark, Wood 401).

(ii) *The Famous History of Stout Stucley: or his valliant life and death.* A prose pamphlet also in the Wood Collection (Wood 254, 13).

(iii) At the end of the pamphlet mentioned in (ii) above, is a ballad on Stukeley beginning:

> In England in the west
> Where Phoebus takes his rest
> There lusty Stukeley he was born.

(iv) An anonymous play *The Famous History of the Life and Death of Captain Thomas Stukeley* (1596) treats the whole life of the hero, and includes a short biography spoken by the hero himself just before his death. (A number of commendatory references to Stukeley in works of the period are quoted by Alexander Dyce in his edition of Peele's Works, 1828, vol. ii, pp. 3–4.) Other accounts of this famous battle which are not primarily connected with Stukeley include:

(a) *A Dolorous Discourse of a most terrible battle, fought in Barbarie*, entered in *The Stationers' Register* to J. Charlwood, March 1579. The author is unknown. This account is reproduced in H. de Castries' *Les Sources Inedites D'Angleterre, de L'Histoire de Maroc*, 1918, vol. i, pp. 331–8.

(b) Edward White, *A Brief Rehersall of the bloodie Battel in Barbary*, entered in *The Stationers' Register*, Feb. 1579.

(c) *Historia de Bello Africano . . . in Latinum translata per Ioannem Thomam Freigium*, Nurnberg, 1580. Peele may have used this for his account of the battle. Warner G. Rice in 'A Principal Source of the Battle of Alcazar' *Modern Language Notes*, vol. lviii, 1943, pp. 428–31, thinks that Peele 'almost certainly read this work in the English translation printed by John Poleman' (in *The Second Part of the Booke of Battailes*, published 1587). The verbal correspondences between lines 1077–95 of the play and a section of folio U2b of Poleman's translation are almost conclusive proof of this.

(d) Ro. C., *A True Discourse of Muly Hamet's Rising*, 1609.

15. *Works*, ed. Mann, 1912, pp. 170–5.

16. Peele's 'Farewell to Norris and Drake' (1589), which contains a reference to Tom Stukeley among the popular stage heroes of the day, was written on the occasion of the two men's departure on an expedition to set Don Antonio on the Portuguese throne.

138   NOTES

17. *The Battle of Alcazar*, ed. W. W. Greg (Malone Society Reprints) 1907, Introduction, p.v.
18. Alexander Dyce, *The Works of George Peele*, 1828, vol. ii, p. 4
19. *The Battle of Alcazar*, 1907, p.v.
20. E. K. Chambers, *The Elizabethan Stage*, 1923, vol. iii, pp. 459–60.
21. Richard Simpson, *The School of Shakespere*, 1878, vol. i, pp. 153–4, thinks so.
22. F. E. Schelling, *Elizabethan Drama*, 1908, vol. i, p. 228.
23. This fact about Mulai's parentage was well known. The prose narrative 'A Dolorous Discourse' records this about the original of Muly: 'Now the cruel King Mulla Abdulla, amongst manye other, taking to his wife a bondwoman, that was a blacke Negro, had by her a sonne called Mulla Sheriffa [this is our Muly] who for that he was of his mothers complection was commonly called the Black King . . .' H. de Castries, *Les Sources Inedites, Angleterre*, vol. i, p. 332. Poleman's translation of Freigius' account of the battle also records of Muly that he was 'so blacke, that he was accompted of many for a Negro or black Moore.'
24. Quotations are from W. W. Greg's 1907 edition in which the lines are continuously numbered throughout. (The letters i, u and v are modernized where necessary.)
25. Abdilmelec in the play corresponds to the historical Abd-el-Malek, who in contrast to other Moors, and the Turks among whom he was brought up, was quite favourably disposed towards Christians. He encouraged trade with Christian countries and especially with England. The cannon balls with which the armies of Sebastian and Mulai Mohammed were shattered came from England—under a secret treaty between Elizabeth and Abd-el-Malek—in exchange for saltpetre. His reception of the Queen's ambassador, described in Hakluyt's *Principal Navigations*, 1904, vol. vi, pp. 285–94, was so warm that it aroused the jealousy of the Portuguese ambassador, who lodged a protest against it in London (*Calendar of State Papers, Foreign, 1577–1578*, p. 68). Elizabeth was in fact regarded by Catholics as being responsible for the defeat of Sebastian at Alcazar. In the words of the Papal Nuncio in Spain: 'there is no evil that is not devised by that woman, who, it is perfectly plain, succoured Muloco [Abd-el-Malek] with arms, and especially with artillery' (*Calendar of State Papers, Rome, 1572–1578*, p. 495).
26. 'leaves' is the result of Dyce's emendation of 'deisnes' which appears in the 1594 edition of the play.
27. Square brackets indicate emendations to the 1594 text accepted by A. H. Bullen in his edition of the play—*The Works of George Peele*, vol. i.
28. There is a slight confusion here. The stage directions call for 'lyons flesh on his sword', while Muly himself refers to the meat as 'This flesh I forced from a lyonesse' (584).
29. See p. 50 below for a discussion of this controversial date.

Part V
Edward I

[16]

Edward I:
In Peace Triumphant,
Fortunate in Wars

A.R. Braunmuller

Alone among Peele's dramatic works, *Edward I* appeared in two Elizabethan printings, the quartos of 1593 and 1599. Copyright records suggest that in 1600 yet another printer considered issuing the play.[1] Theatrical accounts confirm the play's popularity: Philip Henslowe's *Diary* lists fourteen performances of *Longshanks*, the king's nickname and apparently Henslowe's term for *Edward I*, between 29 August 1595 and 9 July 1596. "Longeshankes seute"—presumably the "suit of glass" Edward wears in scene 3—was still important enough to mention in two inventories of 1598.[2] As printed, *Edward I* has enough flaws to make acting it impossible without some rearrangement, cutting, or rewriting.[3] The existence of a printed text did not harm the play's theatrical success: Henslowe earned very respectable sums from *Longshanks* in 1595–96.[4]

Precisely when *Edward I* was written or first produced remains unknown, as it does for so many of Peele's plays. A text was certainly finished by 8 October 1593, when Abel Jeffes entered it as his property in the Register of the Stationers' Company. The likeliest period of composition (mid-1590–1592) falls in a stretch of very lean years for London theater companies. Many took to the road or dissolved and reformed or disappeared completely.[5] During this chaotic period, plays may have been cut and rewritten for smaller casts, or some may even have been stolen from their rightful owners or become the property of a united company which later divided, with each new company claiming ownership of a given play. In the confusion, certain facts remain: alone among Peele's accepted plays, *Edward I*'s title page neither mentions a theater company nor claims that the play was "publicly acted"; a play called *Longshanks* earned

the Admiral's Men good returns in 1595–96; *Edward I* appeared in
two editions before 1600. Thus, it is possible, if unlikely, that a
version reached print before it, or another, reached the stage.[6]

Critics have added many speculations to these facts. A popular
suggestion has been that the printed play includes partial revision,
either by Peele himself or by some anonymous hand.[7] One critic
has suggested that *Edward I* represents a "bad quarto," constructed
surreptitiously by individuals (perhaps actors) who had neither artistic nor commercial rights to the play.[8] Peele's signature on the
last page—"Yours. By George Peele . . ."—must mean that his
original script underlies at least some of the play. What (or how
much) of the 1593 quarto he hoped to see performed as a single
theatrical event we cannot know.

Multiplicity of Action

The play itself employs three basic plot elements, and the title
page promotes each, some rather sensationally. The first is more or
less accurate historical narrative which Peele has steeply compressed
and rearranged: "The Famous Chronicle of king Edward . . . with
his returne from the holy land"; a second group of materials derives
from popular tales of Robin Hood: "Also the Life of Lleuellen rebell
in Wales"; the third element is a completely unhistorical characterization of Queen Elinor as divinely judged murderess: "Lastly,
the sinking of Queene Elinor, who sunck at Charingcrosse, and rose
againe at Pottersith, now named Queenehith." Peele apparently
sought to subordinate the second and third plot elements within a
frame tracing Edward's glorious military triumphs over the Scots
and Welsh.[9] Despite a rather confused text, this plan can be seen
again and again. Scenes 1 through 5 embrace the first cycle of the
plot.[10] Informed of Henry III's death, "Triumphant Edward" (103)
returns from the Holy Land to be crowned and to advance English
domination over the British Isles. The Queen Mother, by way of
prologue, offers praise of "Illustrious Champions" who have awed
"neighbor realmes" (lines 11ff.). Edward rewards his loyal soldiers
and urges his queen and chief courtiers to do the same (lines 118–
80), but his daughter Joan (or "Jone")[11] worries about her mother's
pride:

> Let not your honour make your manners change,
> . . . .

Edward I: In Peace Triumphant, Fortunate in Wars   89

> That Prince were better live a private life,
> Then rule with tirannie and discontent. (246, 254–55)

Here, Joan both warns the Queen and praises her father. Throughout the play, Peele will contrast Edward with friends and enemies to create the image of a model king.[12] After this first contrast between Edward and Elinor, Peele introduces "Lluellen, alias Prince of Wales." Like the Queen Mother and welcoming English lords of scene 1, Lluellen also awaits a loved one, Elinor de Montfort, his English fiancée, who will help advance his political aims (lines 288–95). A group of comic characters—a Friar, his novice, his "wench," and a Welsh prophetic bard—appear. Incognito, Prince Lluellen cheerfully taunts his subjects until the Friar proves too good a cudgel-man and the Prince is forced to become friends with this ribald crew. Comic byplay ends abruptly when Lluellen learns that Edward has intercepted Elinor de Montfort's fleet. Open rebellion must follow: "To armes true Britaines sprong of Trojans seede, / And with your swordes write in the booke of Time" (610–11).

Contrasted with this Celtic rebellion is the loyal Scottish attitude of scene 3. Edward here resolves a dispute over who should rule Scotland. Following the English "Coronations due sollemnitie" (634), Edward chooses John Balliol as the true monarch of Scotland (lines 666–87). Like scene 1, this scene ends with an episode which juxtaposes Elinor's love for her husband (in a passage called "Queene Elinors speeche," lines 704–24) with her proud contempt for his subjects. When Queen Elinor meets the Lady Mayoress of London returning from her son's christening, she darkly threatens the poor woman, who can only wail, "Alas I am undone, it is the Queene, / The proudest Queene that ever England knew" (765–66).

In scene 4, Lluellen and his brother Sir David of Brecknock devise a plan to exchange David, a double agent whom Edward trusts, for the captured Elinor de Montfort, and the next scene shows the scheme's success. Edward releases Elinor and accepts an anonymous soldier's proposal for renewed peace and "A truce with honourable conditions"—"That none be Cambrias prince to governe us, / But he that is a Welshman borne in Wales" (996, 988–89). Only one character is displeased. Mortimer, earl of March, has fallen in love with Elinor, now Lluellen's bride (lines 1008–10). This scene ends the first cycle of the play's action, but several sources of future

conflict have been introduced: Queen Elinor's pride, Mortimer's
disappointed love, and the possibility of a new Welsh or, by analogy,
Scottish rebellion.

As history has it, so the play: Edward immediately sets about
meeting the Welsh demand for a native prince by summoning his
pregnant queen to Wales. She understands his plan: "So then it is
king Edwards pollicie, / To have his sonne, forsooth sonne if it be, /
A Welshman" (1095–97). When the King and Queen meet in
Wales, Elinor greets her husband angrily and strikes him (lines
1131ff.). This strange and unprovoked anger, so similar to her earlier
outbursts, is excused as sickness and justified by Edward as a husband's proper humility (lines 1137–38). Even as Edward plans to
circumvent the Welsh demands, Lluellen, his newly regained love,
and their supporters decide—rather unexpectedly—to imitate Robin Hood. They will rove the mountain of Mannock Denny disguised
as an outlaw crew, "men at armes and knights adventurous" (1217).
Scenes 7 and 8 establish their comic masquerade and reveal Mortimer
disguising himself as a potter to be near his beloved Elinor.[13]

Amidst this humorous and romantic disguising, a brief scene (9)
reveals new political dangers: John Balliol has decided that "Scotland
disdaines to carrie Englands yoke" (1413) and orders a courtier loyal
to Edward: "Beare thou defiaunce proudly to thy king" (1421). As
if in compensation for this new revolt, the future Edward II is born
and declared "Edward of Carnarvan . . . And Prince of Wales"
(1512–13). The scene of Edward II's birth also includes the happy
portent of a marriage agreement between Joan and the earl of
Gloucester, a union Elinor promoted and Edward heartily approves.
Elinor herself, at first loving and tender, becomes suddenly vicious
and requires her husband to order that all Englishmen's beards be
shaven and that all Englishwomen cut off their right breasts. This
sadistic demand, a new and more horrible example of Elinor's will-
fulness, is turned aside when Edward declares he will be the first
shaven man and his wife the first mutilated woman: "Princes ought
no other doe, / Faire ladie, then they would be done unto" (1676–
77).

Scene 11 concludes the second cycle of action by showing Edward
himself as a disguised member of Lluellen's band of outlaws. Edward
and Mortimer eventually battle Lluellen and David. Each leader
discovers that a trusted member of his entourage is in fact a traitor:
"what Davy is it possible thou shouldest be false to England?" (1887)

and "no Potter I, but Mortimer . . . whose comming . . . is to
deceive thee" (1893–94). At this point, both Welsh prince and
Scottish king have revealed their enmity. Like the political order,
Edward's family life, seemingly so happy and hopeful, will soon
break down as well.

A cheerful, ceremonial scene (12) marking Prince Edward's christening and Joan's wedding is interrupted by news of the Scottish
revolt, and Edward directs his forces against the two new threats:

> While wee with Edmund, Gloster, and the rest,
> With speedie journeis gather up our forces,
> And beat these braving Scots from Englands bounds,
> Mortimor thou shalt take the route in taske,
> That revell here and spoile faire Cambria. . . . (2011–15)

After a glimpse of Balliol's cruelty to Edward's messenger (scene
13), a truncated and incomplete scene shows Mortimer pursuing
the Welsh rebels. Havoc and cruelty also move from Edward's realm
into his family. Queen Elinor pursues the Lady Mayoress, whose
earlier joy had so offended her. With grotesque cruelty, the Queen
invites the Mayoress to become the nurse of young Prince Edward
and orders a servant, Katherine, to

> binde her in the chaire,
> And let me see how sheele become a Nurse,
> So now Katherin draw forth her brest
> And let the Serpent sucke his fil, why so
> Now shee is a Nurse, sucke on sweet Babe. (2092–96)

Edward's successful Scottish campaign and Mortimer's defeat and
beheading of Lluellen now appear in a series of short scenes (16,
17, 19). Interspersed with this reestablished political order are two
scenes (18, 20) showing Queen Elinor's spectacular punishment.
Thunder and lightning greet the Queen and her daughter on Charing
Green. When Joan accuses her mother of murdering the Mayoress,
Queen Elinor swears an unfortunate oath:

> Gape earth and swallow me, and let my soule
> Sincke downe to Hell if I were Autor of

92   GEORGE PEELE

> That womans Tragedy, Oh Jone, helpe Jone
> Thy mother sinckes. (2196–99)

No less spectacularly, the earth releases her (scene 20) amidst some splendidly blasé rural folk:

> *Potters wife.* . . . but staie John, whats that riseth out of the ground? Jesus blesse us John, look how it riseth higher and higher.
>
> *John.* By my troth mistres, tis a woman, good Lord do women grow, I never saw none grow before.
>
> *Potters wife.* Hold thy tongue, thou foolish knave, it is the spirite of some woman.
>
> *Queene.* Ha let me see, where am I, on Charing green? I on Charing greene here hard by Westminster, where I was crowned and Edward there made King, I tis true so it is, and therefore Edward kisse not me unlesse you will straight perfume your lips Edward.
>
> *Potters wife.* *Ora pro nobis,* John, I praie fall to your prayers, for my life it is the Queene that chafes thus, who suncke this daie on Charing greene, and now is risen up on Potters Hive, and therefore trulie John ile goe to her. (2266–81)

King Edward harangues the defeated Balliol in the short scene (19) between Elinor's sinking and rising. When Edward begins: "Now trothles King what fruites have braving boastes, / What end hath Treason but a soddaine fall?" (2208–9), it is hard to miss the parallel between political and moral "treason," between public and private rebellion against the king's peace. Balliol and Elinor both "fall."

Edward soon learns of his wife's "strange affright" (2330). Discovering that she has called for "secret conference with some Friers of France" (2332), Edward decides that he and his brother Edmund, duke of Lancaster, should "take the swete confession of my Nell, / We will have French enough to parlee with the Queene" (2334–35). At first, Edmund refuses to join this strange deception (lines 2337–45), but then reluctantly agrees. Scene 22 concludes the overt political plot of the play: the surviving Welsh rebels are dragged miserably toward London and execution.

Like the last act of *The Battle of Alcazar,* the final scene (23) of *Edward I* has suffered various unexplained textual indignities. If the opening stage direction is literally correct (*"Elinor in child-bed . . ."*), we may be meant to see the Queen returned once more to the point of her greatest happiness and the origin of her first violent anger toward the Lady Mayoress. Elinor's crime was a horrible parody of motherhood, and sexual crimes now fill her mind. Distraught and near death, Elinor wants to "repeat and so repent my sinnes" (2402). Edward and Edmund eventually arrive, *"in Friers weede,"* to hear Elinor confess "flocking troupes of sinne" (2447). She stuns her husband and brother-in-law:

> In pride of youth when I was yong and faire,
> And gracious in the king of Englands sight,
> The daie before that night his Highnes should,
> Possesse the pleasure of my wedlockes bed,
> Caitife accursed monster as I was,
> His brother Edmund beautifull and young,
> Uppon my bridall couch by my concent,
> Enjoied the flowre and favour of my love.
> And I becam a Traitresse to my Lord. (2469–77)

According to Elinor, "unto this sinne a worser doth succeede,"

> For Jone of Acon the supposed child,
> And daughter of my Lord the English King,
> Is baselie borne begotten of a Frier. . . . (2492–94)

Thus, Edward's "onelie true and lawfull sonne . . . his sonne that should succeed, / Is Edward of Carnarvan latelie borne" (2496–98). Her sins confessed, the Queen dies, and Edward orders Edmund away, promising, "Traitor thy head shal raunsome my disgrace" (2541). The King must now tell Joan of her mother's confession. Their meeting is poignant and painful for both ignorant child and too-knowing father. Elinor's adultery mortally wounds her daughter, and Joan first *"fals groveling on the ground"* and then *"dies at the Queenes beds feete."* Unfortunately, the text now becomes very confused and Edward is summoned offstage to deal with the Scottish and Welsh rebels we have already seen defeated.[14] Gloucester remains to lament his wife's death and is curiously interrupted by a silent *"Mortimor with the head"* (of Lluellen). Again, some textual confusion here gives the play a very lame and incoherent conclusion.

Extensive textual confusion appears before the play's finale. The 1593 quarto and the 1599 reprint have many signs of incomplete revision or rewriting. For example, Edward's seeming friend Sir David of Brecknock, Lluellen's brother, reveals his true allegiance in scene 11: "Edward I am true to Wales, and so have beene frendes since my birth" (1888–89). It comes as a surprise, therefore, to hear Edward say in the next scene, "Sir David you may commaund al ample welcome in our court, for your cuntreymen . . ." (1958–59). King Edward's enemies seem to possess miraculous powers of renewal, even resurrection. Lluellen, decapitated in scene 16, and Balliol, defeated in scene 19, both reappear as fresh threats in scene 23. There are many more inconsistencies and oversights.

Public and Private Life

Despite the textual confusion, we can detect a pattern designed to show Edward as a great English hero and model king who valiantly subdues his foreign and domestic enemies. To produce this clarity and symmetry, Peele has manipulated his historical sources very cleverly. Although Edward's tomb in Westminster Abbey calls him "Hammer of the Scots," he never lived to subjugate them entirely. At his death, his early Welsh campaigns—and his system of defensive castles which remain today—must have seemed a mockery of his later military failures. Peele has radically compressed and rearranged events to make the Welsh and Scottish rebellions coincide and to make Edward the undisputed victor in each. Time schemes and documented personal relations are juggled for most of the central characters: Queen Elinor died and her husband both remarried and died many years before Joan's death; although Joan reluctantly married Gloucester, she survived him and remarried. The contention for the Scottish throne among Balliol and eight other claimants actually postdates Elinor's and Lluellen's deaths by six years.[15]

Dramatic condensing of events and careers gives the opening five scenes their concise and sturdy structure. That group of scenes supports the many subsequent contrasts between Edward and his opponents. Peele develops this pattern in two directions, the public (Lluellen, David, Balliol) and the private (Elinor, Edmund, Joan). Although the lines probably belong elsewhere, Edward's final speech links these public and private threats:

How one affliction cals another over.
First death torments me, then I feele disgrace,
Again Lluellen he rebels in Wales,
And false Balioll meanes to brave me to,
But I will finde provision for them all,
My constancie shall conquer death and shame. . . . (2655–60)

Joan's and Edward's warnings to Queen Elinor (lines 246–55 and
1674–77, respectively) harp upon her responsibilities as both a
private person and a queen. Elinor's personal crimes have, as we
will see, very serious consequences for the royal succession not only
in Edward's time, but in Elizabeth's, too. Other challenges to Edward's reign appear in personal terms: the traitorous Sir David is a
trusted friend, the rebellious Balliol received his crown at Edward's
hands. Mortimer and later Edward must disguise themselves in order
to pursue personal aims (Mortimer's love for Elinor de Montfort)
and public ones (Edward's suppression of Lluellen's outlawry),
respectively.

Although Irving Ribner called *Edward I* "one of the crudest of
the early English history plays,"[16] the public-private split has many
dramatic advantages and also allows a good deal of covert political
commentary. Shakespeare's English history plays often contrast a
political figure's personal desires with his public responsibilities,
and Marlowe uses the dichotomy very effectively in *Edward II*, a
play written at precisely the same period as *Edward I*.[17] Given Peele's
characteristic nationalism, his hatred of Spain and of Roman Catholicism, his version of Edward's career naturally promotes a strong
central monarchy in recalling the Barons' Wars (lines 290–92), in
condemning Welsh and Scottish factionalism, and in ridiculing
Catholic piety through the licentious (and very amusing) Friar David.
Edward meets the various threats, of course, as both a public and
a private individual.

Contemporary Political Issues

Peele's introduction of Robin Hood has been condemned as a
corruption of true dramatic history,[18] but the episode has both
political and theatrical value. Temporarily defeated as a political
force, Lluellen and his crew adopt the entertaining fiction of "Robin
Hood and little John, / The Frier and the good Maide marrian"

(1521–22). Edward's reaction to their outlawry shows how different the Welsh imitators are from their originals. Masquerading as Robin Hood, Lluellen pursues his rebellious plans; unlike his legendary model, Lluellen does not benefit his society, nor can the forces of order accept him. The popular poem called *The Mery Geste of Robyn Hood* (London, ca. 1560) contains the most comprehensive known version of the Robin Hood saga and shows a king (identified as "Edward") disguising himself in order to meet and befriend Robin Hood; an identical episode (although the king is Richard the Lion-hearted) appears in Anthony Munday's play *The Downfall of Robert Earle of Huntingdon afterward called Robin Hood* (licensed for performance in March 1598 and printed in 1601).[19] Peele works against the tradition, then, when his disguised king fights the rebel disguised as Robin Hood. Like their illustrious popular models, they meet as private men rather than as king and subject, but the new masquerade fails just as open revolt had done. Tradition cannot make them friends and allies. Robin Hood legends were very popular and appear often in sixteenth-century ballads and plays, but pure entertainment cannot fully explain Peele's choice. By attaching the Robin Hood charade to Prince Lluellen, Peele assures that it will have a political valance: in Elizabeth's world, as in Edward's, independent armed groups were intolerable, no matter how charmingly decorated or seemingly innocent.

Peele has also been criticized for his completely unhistorical vilification of Queen Elinor. His chronicle sources portrayed her very differently, but here—as perhaps in the Robin Hood material—contemporary Elizabethan political issues have influenced the play. *The Battle of Alcazar* and *Anglorum Feriae* show how sensitively Peele responded to one of the major domestic problems of the 1580s and 1590s: who should or would succeed Queen Elizabeth? Marie Axton has recently recalled that one group of political writers answered this question with a candidate who must have horrified the nationalistic Peele: Isabella, the Spanish Infanta. From at least 1571, arguments favoring the Spanish claim had been put forward; in 1594–95 the pseudonymous R. Doleman (in fact the Jesuit Robert Parsons and other writers) published *A Conference about the Next Succession to the Crowne of Ingland.* This book earnestly discussed and seemed to approve the Infanta's rights, and plays like *Edward I* or *The Battle of Alcazar* or Robert Greene's *Friar Bacon and Friar Bungay* (which also concerns Edward and Elinor) can be seen as responses to such views.[20] Edward's queen formed part of the pro-Spanish argument, as did Edmund Crouchback, King Edward's brother and founder of the house of Lancaster. An artist who opposed that argument might rewrite history to poison the Spanish claim at its roots. Thus, Marie Axton holds that Peele "draws the portrait of a lustful fourteenth-century Spanish princess whose shameless incontinence before and after her marriage to Edward I leaves the entire genealogy (by which the sixteenth-century Infanta claimed) illegitimate. . . . Peele . . . asks the audience . . . to recognize the one sound branch of legitimate succession which will pass precariously through the weak Edward II."[21]

Peele stones two sinners, Elinor and her supposed paramour, Edmund, duke of Lancaster, because the Lancastrian line (through John of Gaunt) leads to the royal houses of both Portugal and Spain, including the late-sixteenth-century Infanta. Thus, Elinor conveniently confesses not only marital infidelity, but treason: she is a "Traitresse" (2477) and Edmund a "Traitor" (2541). That political interpretation of a private deed then extends forward in time to destroy the sixteenth-century Spanish claim. Should that claim still seem valid, Peele reminds his modern audience of their present monarch's "familiar majestie" (250) and the certainty of a foreigner's "Spanish yoake" (257). This argument and the related ones concerning the Robin Hood episodes or *The Battle of Alcazar* are of course not aesthetic or theatrical ones. Political convictions can neither explain nor justify Peele's dramatic success or failure. Fortunately, *Edward I* conveys its political and "Elizabethan" arguments rather well.

Edward's kingship and its public and private demands frame the entire action. Lluellen's masquerade as Robin Hood has a political motivation and continues his political conflict with Edward. The other large subsidiary set of events—Queen Elinor's crimes and their punishment—has political implications and, of course, affects Edward as an individual father and husband. Whether giving a close-up image of Edward as a loving husband or offering high-flown praise of his glorious English attributes, Peele generally concentrates on the public-private contrasts and on every action's political significance. A line from *Descensus Astraeae* might apply to Edward as well as to Elizabeth: "In peace triumphant, fortunate in wars."[22] The difficulties of triumph and victory form the play's substance.

98   GEORGE PEELE

Violence and History

A comparison of *Edward I* with *The Battle of Alcazar* identifies
the history play's many unusual features. Peele's sources for *Alcazar*
offered, if anything, too little action, while the chronicles of Edward's reign brimmed with complex events and manifold dangers.
Indeed, Peele adds to the sheer amount of material his play must
organize. *The Battle of Alcazar* seems to be a "tragedy" in Peele's
view, however odd that designation may seem today, but *Edward
I* did not need, in Elizabethan terms, to fit any precise generic
formula. Although Peele has very skillfully rearranged his historical
sources, his play need not provide any more causal explanation than
the implied one: this event followed that event in history. He does
provide a frame, of course, but it embraces more ample and varied
actions than does *The Battle of Alcazar*. While *Alcazar* seems to take,
at most, a few weeks, *Edward I* covers years. Variety of action
produced greater variety in language and in social classes, but both
plays regard their political and military subject matters as intensely
violent.

Alcazar's violence, of course, resides largely in the language and
in the dumb shows. We see Stukeley's murder and the quiet death
of Abdelmelec, but the slaughter of Sebastian's army and their
Moorish enemies, and the deaths of Sebastian himself and of Muly
Mahamet, are presented either in hasty battle scenes or reported by
others. *Edward I* is very different. To win Elinor de Montfort's
release, Lluellen tortures his brother Sir David in full view of his
English friends. According to the stage directions, David is stabbed
"into the armes and shoulders," threatened with *"hote Pinsers,"* and
finally has his nose slashed. The sadism becomes all the more remarkable when we recall that Sir David agreed to be tortured and
thus help Lluellen win back his love. When Balliol decides to throw
off English domination, he sends Lord Versses *"with a halter about
his necke"* as a messenger (scene 12). Edward replaces the halter with
his "chaine" (1986, 1999), a ceremonial golden badge of rank (see
line 2064), and tells Versses to "carrie" Balliol "this token that
thou sendst" (2000). The symbolic exchange so enrages Balliol—
"darst thou bring a halter to thy King?" (2061)—that he immediately orders Versses hanged on "a silver Gibbet . . . for fowles
to feede uppon" (2065–66). Elinor, of course, progresses from the
threatened mutilation of all the women in England to the torture

of the Lady Mayoress, left to die in full view of the audience. During the Welsh battles, successive rebels appear preparing to commit suicide, and Lluellen is first *"slaine with a Pike staffe"* and then beheaded. Our last glimpse of the Welsh rebels is of Sir David *"drawne on a hurdle,"* a sledge for the public humiliation of condemned traitors,[23] and of *"Lluellens head on a speare"* (scene 22).

Although Marlowe has a modern reputation for staging violence, *Edward I* exceeds in variety and number the scenes of torture and cruelty shown in Marlowe's plays. Part of the explanation lies, no doubt, in the audience's taste; after all, they liked Marlowe's violence and Shakespeare's. Peele's contemporary concerns also made degrading Queen Elinor important. Significantly, Edward is insulated from the violence: he suffers its effects, but never instigates it. His only acts of physical violence are sword play (scene 11) and warfare (scene 19), acceptable and "heroic" deeds very unlike the torture and petulant cruelty of his enemies and betrayers. Finally, the staged violence vividly portrays the dangers of political action, specifically rebellion against legitimate authority. That is, the play's violent episodes manifest Peele's authoritarianism and its obverse, his anxiety about social instability.

Language and Characters

Violence is never far away in *Edward I,* and it appears at every social level in the remarkably diversified cast of characters. Quite unlike *The Battle of Alcazar* or any other of Peele's plays, *Edward I* embraces social groups from royalty and aristocracy through the middle class (the Lady Mayoress) to farmers and skilled laborers. Peele exploits the Welsh scenes and the Robin Hood episode to bring in "Morgain Pigot, our good welsh prophet" (469), with his doggerel songs, as well as a farmer-victim of Friar David's con game (lines 1734ff.), and Friar David's own entourage of Jack, a novice, and Guenthian, his "wholsome Welsh wench" (365). When the Queen rises from the earth at Potter's Hithe, two concisely developed local characters forget their own comic argument to greet the royal apparition. Aristocratic characters in the play can be appropriately dignified (in scenes like the welcoming of Edward, or his choice among the Scottish claimants to the throne) or properly classical in their allusions (like Lluellen worrying about Elinor de Montfort's safety or seeing her in Edward's custody). Peele also presents these public figures' human qualities sympathetically (the sweating, slippered queen of lines 1016ff., for instance, or Edward commiserating with Gloucester at lines 2620ff.).

The history play's loose definition freed Peele to imagine a wide range of social types. So freed, he created distinctive languages for those different characters and used as many poetic meters as he had done in *The Araygnement of Paris*. Royalty and aristocratic characters usually employ iambic pentameter, but conversations will sometimes become iambic pentameter couplets. Fourteeners appear rarely, often as a way of pointing a warning or drawing a slightly aphoristic conclusion. The scenes of Robin Hood and the scene at Potter's Hithe are principally in prose, with irregular four-stress lines for some of the songs. Aristocratic characters get drawn into prose when they converse with comic or rural or lower-class prose-speakers, but rarefied allusions and diction remain an upper-class prerogative. Some of the repetitions of Pigot's prophecies recall the similar repetitions in *The Old Wives Tale,* and Peele will typically have serious characters repeat each other's words at moments of crisis.

Whatever the dramatic forces shaping Queen Elinor's fictional personality, her speech has more variety than any other principal character's. She can be homely and downright, or angry and shrewish, or conscience-stricken, or loving. The remains of a fine speech can be detected in a confused passage when she rejects Joan's consolation (lines 2417–31), but an earlier speech is a tour de force. To celebrate Edward's coronation, Elinor demands that he "weare a sute that shee shall give thy grace, / Of her owne cost and workmanship" (217–18). This gift proves to be the "sute of Glasse"— apparently a garment decorated with numerous globes—which the impresario Philip Henslowe recorded in his inventory of 1598. Gazing at her husband, Elinor delivers a complex speech which even has its own heading, *"Queene Elinors speeche"*:

> The welken spangled through with goulden spots,
> Reflects no finer in a frostie night,
> Then lovely Longshankes in his Elinors eye:
> So Ned thy Nell in every part of thee,
> Thy person's garded with a troope of Queenes,
> And every Queene as brave as Elinor,
> Gives glorie to these glorious christall quarries,
> Where every orbe an object entertaines,

> Of riche device and princelie majestie.
> Thus like Narcissus diving in the deepe,
> I die in honour and in Englands armes:
> And if I drowne, it is in my delight,
> Whose companie is cheefest life in death,
> From foorth whose currall lips I suck the sweete,
> Wherewith are daintie Cupids caudles made,
> Then live or die brave Ned, or sinke or swim,
> An earthlie blisse it is to looke on him.
> On thee sweete Ned, it shall become thy Nell,
> Bounteous to be unto the beauteous,
> Ore prie the palmes sweete fountaines of my blisse,
> And I will stand on tiptoe for a kisse. (704–24)

Frank Hook complains that this speech is "so extravagant that it verges at times on nonsense,"[24] but the dramatic situation justifies the extravagance and "nonsense" is unfair. The Queen's verbal play turns upon ideas of reflection: the image of what we see reflected in our eyes ("lovely Longshankes in his Elinors eye") and the image of herself reflected in the numerous glistening orbs of Edward's suit ("thy Nell in every part of thee"). Reflected images of the Queen— "riche device and princelie majestie"—"gard" (decorate, protect) the King. The glass seems a pool in which Elinor sees herself reflected, Narcissus-like, and may even drown, but living or dying is all the same so long as she has Edward's love. His beauty, enriched by all the reflected images of his queen, excuses her forwardness: "On thee sweete Ned, it shall become thy Nell, / Bounteous to be unto the beauteous," and the complicated puns of the final couplet ask for a kiss. "Ore prie" means "overpeer," that is, "excel" and "look over"; palm trees were a conventional Renaissance emblem of married happiness. The "fountaines" of Elinor's "blisse" are Edward's eyes, reflecting her image, her eyes reflecting his image, the "glorious christall quarries" of his suit, and finally the pool wherein Narcissus drowned himself in love.[25] Edward Longshanks was extremely tall and could therefore "look over" a queen who has to "stand on tiptoe for a kisse." Physically and emotionally, Edward overpeers or excels conventional wedded happiness when he kisses his wife. Although the mythologizing, the opulent language, and the complicated figurative thought all make the speech very formal and courtly, the use of nicknames, the homely image of a night

sky, and the proverbial phrase ("or sinke or swim") also make it
warmly intimate.

Peele may have added this speech when revising the play.[26]
Whether or not a late addition, the speech collects some important
ideas and presents them very theatrically. Elinor's deep love and
Edward's response are etched in the speech. Later he will say, almost
unwillingly, "Fast to those lookes are all my fancies tide [tied]"
(1629). The speech also hints at the dangers of Elinor's own pride:
Narcissus is an ambivalent mythological model. Theatrically, Peele
establishes the richness of scene, costumes, and court, and Edward's
most notable physical quality, his great height. Finally, the speech
images a happy and secure peace—wedded love, the coronation,
and the end of Scottish discord—which will be first disturbed and
then destroyed in coming scenes.

Edward I has many verbal styles besides the one in Elinor's speech;
the play ranges more widely than any other Peele wrote. Most
notable here—and it can be found elsewhere in the play—is the
way even a very formal speech also possesses dramatic value. We
admire the language, the allusions, the complicated puns, but we
also recognize that this speech will lose important qualities when
removed from its dramatic context. Nor is that context only the
immediate one: the speech summarizes what goes before and anchors
what follows it. This is language written for stage delivery, and
Peele shows here and elsewhere in the play his sense of drama as
well as his lyric gifts.

Theatricalism

All the verbal artistry of Elinor's speech depends, of course, on
a single spectacular fact: Edward's costume. Only if we imagine (or
see) this remarkable glass suit can we wholly appreciate Peele's lyric
skill. Lyric and dramatic cannot be separated. While the suit has a
bizarre fascination, the quarto allows us to deduce much more about
how the play might have appeared. Paradoxically, the text's uncertain auspices make it an intriguing source of information about
staging.[27] However close or distant Peele's connection with the
printed text (and his signature means he cannot be too far behind
at least some parts), the stage directions often provide a powerful
impression of a play on the stage. For example, the processional
stage direction (after line 40) mentions *"every man with his red Crosse*

on his coate." These red crosses are not just decorative or historical detail. Peele clearly has them in mind when Rice ap Meredith sadistically suggests that Lluellen "sacrifice" David of Brecknock in Elinor's presence "which beeing done, one of your souldiers may dip his foule shirt in his bloud, so shall you bee waited with as may crosses as king Edward" (944–47).

Even more interesting are stage directions which seem to describe an actual performance, or an imagined one firmly based in practical experience: for example, the directions after lines 1015, 1453, 1932, and 1940. These directions resemble those in *The Old Wives Tale* and *David and Bethsabe*. Like them, they imply simultaneous staging; several imaginary locales coexist on the stage. They further suggest that the Admiral's Men must have provided some fairly substantial props, like Elinor's "litter." It might be possible for Queen Elinor to display her infant son in an alcove or curtained doorway at the rear of the stage, but references to a "Tent" suggest a fabricated playing-space like King David's tent in *David and Bethsabe*. Directions often refer to geographical locales as if they had recognizable embodiments on stage:

Exeunt ambo from Wales. (after line 2175)

The Frier having song [sung] *his farewell to his Pikestaffe a* [he] *takes his leave of Cambria, and Exit the Frier.* (after line 2146)

Peele, or whoever wrote these directions, may have let his imagination run free, but the implication—again—is that the audience had some tangible reason to associate a place name with a certain structure on the stage, or a specific area on the stage.

Finally, some of the stage directions already mentioned and others make the text sound like that of *The Araygnement of Paris;* it becomes almost a production record meant to be read, like those we associate with masques. For example, the stage direction which ends *"Bishop speakes to her in her bed"* (after line 1940) is centered above the Bishop's speech, which lacks a separate speech prefix, and the same thing occurs after line 1964: ". . . *Longshanks speaketh.* / What tidings bringes Versses to our court?" Earlier, when Edward has persuaded Elinor not to pursue her vicious attack on English men and women, he rebukes her, "Leave these ungentle thoughts, put on a milder mind . . ." (1681). She replies angrily, dismissing him, and *"The*

104   GEORGE PEELE

Nurse closeth the Tent" (after line 1686). The 1593 quarto then prints
a quotation from Horace, italicized and centered in the middle of
the page:

Quo semel est imbuta recens servabit odorem Testa diu

(The jar will long keep the fragrance of what it was once steeped in when
new)[28]

This classical observation sounds like an author's comment to a
reader, since the next speech has its own prefix and concerns (appropriately in the dramatic context) Elinor's Spanish pride and her
insulting behavior to the King.

Masquerade and Politics

Just as uncertainties about the text qualify our conclusions on
how the Admiral's Men might have staged *Edward I,* so too textual
muddle prevents dogmatizing about the play's literary or aesthetic
values. After all, the 1593 quarto may include an anonymous reviser's work, and it certainly has some inconsistencies which neither
Peele nor a theater company would be likely to approve. Nonetheless, we may admire Peele's artful handling of his historical sources,
the way political issues link the Robin Hood and the Queen Elinor
episodes to the historical action, the play's wide range of verbal
styles, and the diversity of the characters who use them.

One other motif repays attention. When Shakespeare and Marlowe
dramatize the conflict between a politician's public and private
selves, their plays often become studies of deception and role-play-
ing. Thus, for example, Prince Hal declares he will pretend to be
worse than he is in order to appear still better when he publicly
renounces his old ways. On other occasions, a political design or
disaster will force a public character into some unwanted deceit. At
one such moment, Marlowe's Edward II and Peele's Edward I speak
the same line: "Hence faigned weedes unfaigned is my griefe" (2519,
and see *Edward II,* 4.6.96, substituting "woes" for "griefe"). Edward Longshanks's disguise as a French friar is only one among many
disguises—conscious and unconscious, literal and figurative—in the
play. As a rebel prince, Lluellen appears physically disguised from
the very start (scene 2) and eventually leads his entire entourage
into the Greenwood fantasy. Mortimer disguises himself for love,

Sir David of Brecknock for political advantage. Physical conflict and political crisis finally force both men to declare their true allegiances (scene 12). John Balliol appears a loyal dependent until he abruptly declares his true hatred (scene 9). In Peele's rewritten history, Elinor and Edmund disguise their moral natures until Edward's physical and spiritual disguising uncovers their guilt. Joan, of course, discovers that her status—royal princess and wife of Gloucester—is a fraud, and the discovery kills her. Indeed, deception revealed almost always causes violence, and the revelation often requires violence. Queen Elinor's attempt to deny murdering the Lady Mayoress leads to the most spectacular "revelation," the supernatural sinking and rising.

Disguise, masquerade, and deception are, in fact, endemic. The characters' announced or implied motives range from romance and lust to consolation, self-protection, and patriotism; consequences include comic entertainment, theater spectacle, and disillusionment. Amidst this variety, the pattern remains constant, too constant for chance, although the textual confusion prevents any unequivocal judgment about Peele's artistic design. Yet, Werner Senn has shown conclusively that Peele almost always uses repetition for emphasis and structure. Within *Edward I*'s slightly random action, multiple disguises do point out parallels and, sometimes, ironic contrasts. Does Peele use these episodes as more than a device to highlight and organize small units of his play? Part of the answer lies in what the play's disguises do not do. They do not serve conventional romantic or comic ends, as they do in Robert Greene's nearly contemporaneous *James IV* and *Friar Bacon and Friar Bungay*. Mortimer does not win the lovely Elinor de Montfort, for example, and Peele inverts the age-old story of the husband who poses as his wife's confessor.[29] In Peele's version, the deception produces unhappiness rather than comic embarrassment and reconciliation.

Although disguise does not serve traditional comic purposes, it does inevitably accompany political action. Edward finds again and again that political motives conceal or distort the true face of friends (Sir David), allies (John Balliol), and even wife and brother. In *The Battle of Alcazar*, we recall, Stukeley accuses Philip of "disguising with a double face" (808), and King Sebastian's other ally, Muly Mahamet the Moor, proves equally deceitful. Since Peele never uses disguise elsewhere—if we except the magical transformations of *The Old Wives Tale*—its concentrated presence in *Edward I* and the figurative mention in *The Battle of Alcazar* plausibly suggest that he regarded deceit, masquerade, and disguise as facts of political life. At the same time, however, disguise does not satisfactorily advance any political cause in *Edward I,* as it sometimes does in Shakespeare's history plays. Instead, violence almost always trails disguise, and deception leads to death.

Disguise does more than underline local parallels, then, but it hardly creates an overall dramatic statement. Indeed, for a modern taste, *Edward I* may try to encompass too much. Almost every separate element—the historical action, the Robin Hood and comic episodes, the love of Edward and Elinor, as well as the Queen's crimes and the diversified groups of characters, for example—is well and attractively developed. The play's contemporary success, in fact, suggests that modern critics decry precisely the qualities that pleased Elizabethans most. Neither Elizabethan generic conventions nor the public theater audience demanded intensity or concentration in a chronicle history play. If anything, the genre's loose definition and the audience's appetite for variety invited a rambling, excitement-filled production. Peele's play answers these implicit demands quite skillfully.

As the extensive, ahistorical revision of Elinor's life shows, *Edward I* also draws contemporary Elizabethan concerns parallel with historical or pseudohistorical events. Even without the succession issue, the play offers a grim account of political life. Violence, deceit, and a wearying course of troubles crowd the play. Although Edward himself appears a model king and model Englishman, his every success introduces a new challenge, despite Peele's careful selection and rearrangement of historical fact. Even the amusing comedy of Friar David and his fellows concludes with political defeat and death; Joan and Gloucester's marriage has been made unhistorically happy in order—it seems—to intensify their pathetic end. Peele's good theatrical sense accounts for this variety: the play includes something for everyone. His own political and social interests contribute a tone and presentation which are at once monarchist and insecure. Consequently, what might almost be nostalgia for the days of "Triumphant Edward" and "Illustrious England" coexists with pervasive violence and public chaos.

Part VI
David and Bathsheba

[17]

Peele's *David and Bethsabe*: Reconsidering Biblical Drama of the Long 1590s

Annaliese Connolly

Marlowe's influence upon the dramatic work of George Peele has frequently been noted in relation to Peele's *The Battle of Alcazar*. [1]The play is often grouped with those plays designated "The Sons of Tamburlaine", which were written in imitation of Marlowe's first theatrical smash hit. [2]In this paper I want to discuss in greater detail the specific nature of the relationship between Marlowe's *Tamburlaine* and those plays which sought to imitate it, beginning with *David and Bethsabe*, another of Peele's plays which also bears traces of Marlovian influence. Whilst critics such as G.K. Hunter and David Bevington have noted this connection, Peele's biblical play continues to be overlooked in this context, as criticism to date has tended to focus upon the play's anomalous position within Peele's body of dramatic works and amongst the work of his contemporaries. [3]My approach to *David and Bethsabe* and the biblical drama from the period c.1590 to c.1602 is influenced by recent work in repertory studies by Scott McMillin and Sally Beth MacLean in their seminal study *The Queen's Men and their plays* in which they advocate a fresh approach to Elizabethan drama by shifting the focus away from the dramatist and onto the theatre companies and their repertories. [4]I therefore devote some discussion to the place of biblical drama in the repertories of the theatre companies which performed at the Rose and Fortune theatres, so that they are considered in terms of their place within a commercial enterprise and not simply as an isolated, disparate group. Recently Roslyn Knutson, Susan Cerasano and John H. Astington have suggested that later Elizabethan biblical plays formed part of a wider repertorial policy, whereby companies such as the Admiral's Men, for example, could build on the success of existing plays in their repertory such as *Tamburlaine*, *The Jew of Malta* and *Doctor Faustus*, since many of these plays, including *David and Bethsabe*, recycle Marlovian themes and motifs such as exotic locations, charismatic protagonists and stage spectacle. They also provide comparable roles for their leading actor Edward Alleyn, whose celebrity status had been confirmed by his performances in the roles of Tamburlaine, Barabas and Faustus. My argument will, therefore, build on the work of Knutson and Cerasano, who have both argued that Elizabethan theatre

---

[1] See for example, Peter Berek, 'Tamburlaine's Weak Sons: Imitation as Interpretation Before 1593' in *Renaissance Drama*, 13 (1982), 55-82.

[2]   G.K. Hunter, 'The Emergence of the University Wits: Early Tragedy' in *English Drama 1586-1642 The Age of Shakespeare*, 49.

[3] G.K. Hunter, 'The Emergence of the University Wits: Early Tragedy' in *English Drama 1586-1642 The Age of Shakespeare* p. 49 and Bevington, David. *Tudor Drama and Politics: A Critical Approach to Topical Meaning* (Cambridge, Massachussetts:Harvard University Press,1968)

[4]   Scott McMillan and Sally Beth MacLean. *The Queen's Men and their Plays*. Cambridge, CUP, 1998.

companies used their repertories to market their most successful plays by staging revivals of their older plays, such as Marlowe's *Tamburlaine* and *Doctor Faustus*, and by commissioning new plays which would replicate their most popular features. Peele's *David and Bethsabe* is one example of this latter strategy and a survey of other biblical plays, including the now lost *Nebuchadnezzar* (1596), *Judas* (1601) and *Joshua* (1601) which were commissioned for the new Fortune Theatre between 1600 and 1602 and coincided with Alleyn's return to the stage, suggests that this continued to be a popular policy. The potential subject matter of these plays indicates that biblical kings and warriors were utilised with the primary function of appealing to Alleyn's paying public.

During the period between c.1590 and c.1602 contemporary records such as Philip Henslowe's *Diary* and the Stationers' register indicate that at least thirteen biblical plays were commissioned, written or performed for the Elizabethan theatre audience. Of these thirteen plays only two remain extant: *A Looking Glass for London and England* by Robert Greene and Thomas Lodge and George Peele's *David and Bethsabe*. Critics have certainly been puzzled by the sudden glut of biblical plays which appear between c.1590 and c.1602, particularly since medieval religious drama had been gradually phased out through the legislation of the Protestant Tudors. [5]The critical responses to Peele's *David and Bethsabe* summarise some of the difficulties critics have had in explaining why a series of plays which focus upon Old Testament patriarchs and warriors should have been written during the 1590s. Peele's biblical drama appears to sit awkwardly amongst his other extant works for the stage which include *The Arraignment of Paris*, a courtly entertainment, the two histories *The Battle of Alcazar* and *Edward I* and the pastoral comedy *The Old Wives Tale*. The play itself points up its resistance to generic classification in its title, *The Love of David and Fair Bethsabe with the Tragedy of Absalon*, since the emphasis upon the king and his lover has tended to wrong-foot critics who expect that the play will focus primarily upon David's relationship with Bethsabe, when in fact it is the king's relationship with his sons, particularly Absalon, with which the play is most concerned. A.H. Bullen describes it as "a mess of cloying sugar plums" (Bullen 1888, xli) while Murray Roston summarises the confused nature of the critical response when he notes that "What is really a fine biblical tragedy has thus often been judged as a drama of Renaissance love and been found wanting"(Roston 1968, 103).

Elmer Blistein in his edition of *David and Bethsabe* concludes his discussion of the figure of King David in English plays with the remark:

> David, then, plays a small part in the English drama before 1600. We should not be surprised, for biblical drama as a whole seemed to interest neither the Elizabethan dramatist nor his audience (Blistein 1970, 174).

Blistein supports his assertion by considering a small number of plays which were based either wholly or partially on the Bible and were either printed or entered in the Stationers' Register during Elizabeth's reign. There are five plays including *Jacob and Esau* which was entered in 1557/8, but not printed until 1568. The second is *Goodly Queen Hester* which was entered

[5]   See for example Michael O'Connell, *The Idolatrous Eye: Iconoclasm and Theater in Early-Modern England* Oxford: Oxford UP, 2000 and Paul Whitfield White, "Theater and Religious Culture" in *A New History of Early English Drama* ed. John D. Cox and David Scott Kastan. New York: Columbia University Press, 1997, 133-151.

in the Stationers' register in 1560/1 and printed in 1561 and the third is Thomas Garter's *Susanna* which was entered in 1568/9 and printed in 1578. William Golding's translation of Theodore Beza's *Abraham Sacrifant* is also considered, together with *A Looking Glass for London and England* by Robert Greene and Thomas Lodge which was entered in 1593/4 and printed in 1594 (Blistein 1970, 174-175). Peele's *David and Bethsabe* also fits this pattern here since it was entered in the Stationers' register in May 1594, with the first quarto printed in 1599. Blistein acknowledges that his criterion for identifying biblical plays of the period is potentially a restrictive one: Perhaps other plays on biblical subjects were written during the reign of Elizabeth, but they were neither entered in the Stationers' register nor, so far as we are able to discover, printed (Blistein 1970, 175).

A much clearer sense of the number of biblical plays written or performed during the later part of Elizabeth's reign is provided by the account book of the owner of the Rose Theatre, Philip Henslowe, a source which is not consulted by Blistein. The *Diary* is an invaluable resource since it provides details of plays commissioned and performed which perhaps were not printed and are now lost and had not been entered in the Stationers' register. Louis B. Wright in his early study of Elizabethan biblical drama compiles a survey of biblical plays using a range of source material, including Henslowe's *Diary*, and remarks: "That the Bible was a storehouse of material which dramatists at times used effectively on the full-grown Elizabethan stage is largely overlooked"(Wright 1928, 47). Wright stops short of suggesting a detailed response to the question of why these plays flourished, arguing simply that "the Bible was more useful in the theatres than we have been accustomed to believe"(Wright 1928, 47). Ruth H. Blackburn also notes the prevalence of these plays and identifies a pattern relating to the popularity of biblical plays, noting that from 1568/9 after the registration of Garter's *Susanna* until the early 1590s there are no records of "any native Biblical plays" and yet between c.1590 and c.1602 there were at least thirteen biblical plays written for the English stage (Blackburn 1971, 155-160). The significance of these statistics is revealed if we consider their place within the repertory of the Rose playhouse.

The thirteen biblical plays compiled in Table 1 of the appendix give an overview of the plays and provide a date for when they are first recorded either in Henslowe's *Diary* or in the Stationers' Register and the company with which they are associated. The information in the second table comes from the playlists provided in the *Diary* with information relating to the performances of biblical plays between March 1592 and March 1597. The table outlines the other plays performed in that particular weekly run, as well as the receipts received for individual plays, including the highest grossing play. The aim of using the information from the playlists demonstrates the way in which a fuller sense of the company's repertory facilitates the reassessment of these particular plays and indicates factors which contributed to their genesis. The earliest performance of a biblical play recorded by Henslowe was *A Looking Glass for London and England* which was performed twice at the Rose in March 1591, again in April that year and later in June 1592 by Lord Strange's Men (Henslowe, *Diary*, 16-17, 19). The play proved popular in print as it was published first in 1594 and again in 1598, 1602 and 1617, with five passages from the play appearing in *England's Parnassus* in 1600. Greene's other play on a biblical subject was *The History or Tragedy of Job* which was entered in the Stationers' register in 1594, although it was never printed and has not survived (Wright 1928, 53).

Henslowe's *Diary* refers to three lost biblical plays which were also performed at the Rose between 1591-1597, with the entries detailing the receipts for each performance. The first of these is *Abraham and Lot* which was performed three times at The Rose in January 1593 by Sussex's Men (Henslowe, *Diary*, 20-21). The second biblical play, *Esther and Ahasuerus*, was performed twice in June 1594 at Newington Butts by the Admiral's and Chamberlain's Men, (Henslowe, *Diary*, 21) while *Nebuchadnezzer* was performed eight times at The Rose between December 1596 and March 1597 by the Lord Admiral's Men (Henslowe, *Diary*, 55-57). The play appears to have been successful as the second and third performances brought in the highest returns of all the plays performed in those particular weeks.

Later payments made by Henslowe for biblical plays which have not survived include a payment in May 1600 to William Haughton for a play called *Judas* (Henslowe, *Diary*, 135) and in the December of the following year the accounts indicate money was given to Samuel Rowley for the completion of what appears to be Haughton's play (Henslowe, *Diary*, 185-186). In January 1601 there was a payment to Thomas Dekker for writing the prologue and epilogue to *Pontius Pilate* (Henslowe, *Diary*, 187). In addition to the completed *Judas*, 1602 saw at least six more plays written based on figures from the Old Testament. In May, June and July a series of payments were made for a play involving Antony Munday and Thomas Dekker called *Jephthah* (Henslowe, *Diary*, 200-203). In May 1602 Henry Chettle received the first of four payments for his play *Tobias* (Henslowe, *Diary*, 200, 202-203, 296), while in June Samuel Rowley and Edward Jewby were paid for their play *Samson* (Henslowe, *Diary*, 204). In September 1602 Rowley was also paid by Henslowe for his play entitled *Joshua* (Henslowe, *Diary*, 205).

Table 1 indicates that of those biblical plays listed the records point to their inclusion, firstly, in the repertories of those companies at the Rose such as the Lord Strange's Men, the Queen's Men and the combined companies of the Admiral's Men and the Chamberlain's Men. After 1594 when the Chamberlain's Men and the Admiral's Men emerged as the two dominant companies, biblical plays become associated almost exclusively with the repertory of the Admiral's Men. Together with the lost play *Job*, Peele's *David and Bethsabe* is the only biblical play not assigned to a specific company. The title page of the first quarto, published in 1599, indicates only its popularity: "As it hath been diuers times plaied on the stage".[6] There is a tantalising entry for stage properties by Henslowe in October 1602 for Worcester's Men in which fourteen pence was paid to workmen for "poleyes & worckmanshipp for to hang absolome" (Henslowe, *Diary*, 217), which has led to speculation that it relates to a performance of Peele's *David and Bethsabe*, but unfortunately there is no further evidence which indicates that the entry refers specifically to Peele's play or to a performance of that play.[7] The play was entered in the Stationers' register in May 1594 and apart from the suggestive reference to the stage properties in Henslowe's *Diary* and the appearance of three passages from the play in the anthology *England's Parnassus* in 1600 there are no further contemporary references to *David and Bethsabe*. Despite this apparent absence of material relating to the play in contemporary records, I will argue that there is evidence available which makes it possible to suggest that *David and Bethsabe* was written for the Admiral's Men, and that like the biblical

---

6   Roston, *Biblical Drama in England*, 100.

7   See Roston, *Biblical Drama* in England, 100

plays of his contemporaries, Peele's play was destined for performance at the Rose, with Alleyn in the title role.

Peele already had strong connections with the Rose and the companies which performed there, as both his histories, *The Battle of Alcazar* and *Edward I*, belonged to the repertory of plays staged between 1592 and 1596. The title page of the first quarto of *The Battle of Alcazar*, which was published in 1594, indicates that the play was performed by the Admiral's Men: "As it was sundrie times plaied by the Lord high Admirall his seruants". [8]Henslowe's *Diary* details entries for fourteen performances of a play called *Muly Mollocco* by Lord Strange's Men between February 1592 and January 1593. There has been some debate, however, as to whether *Muly Mollocco* is in fact Peele's play, referred to by Henslowe using the name of its villainous character, or whether it refers to a separate play, now lost. [9]If we keep an open mind as to the identity of *Muly Mullocco* and resist identifying it with Peele's play, it is still possible to make a number of useful points about the play's role in the repertory. Firstly, the play appears to have popular as on three occasions it was the highest grossing play during the weekly run of plays performed. Secondly, Roslyn L. Knutson has argued that one of the strategies employed by the companies which owned Marlowe's plays was to build "a complementary repertory that duplicated, exploited, or exaggerated certain of their features"(Knutson 2002, 25). One example of this strategy at work can be seen in relation to performances of *Muly Mullocco* and *The Jew of Malta* by Lord Strange's Men at the Rose between 1592 and 1593, when the company sought to capitalise on the success of Marlowe's play by pairing it with other plays in the repertory that would complement it. One such play is *Muly Mullocco* with its Mediterranean locale and a Machiavellian protagonist. Table three indicates that *The Jew of Malta* and *Muly Mullocco* were frequently performed during the same weekly run during this period, and Knutson notes that the scheduling of these plays indicates a deliberate strategy at work since on at least four occasions *The Jew of Malta* and *Muly Mullocco* are performed on consecutive days, thereby reinforcing the connections between the plays (Knutson 2002, 28-29).

Although Henslowe's play lists cannot furnish us with details of the performance history of *David and Bethsabe*, it is still possible to argue that the play is the product of the reportorial strategy suggested by Knutson. Peele deliberately replicates aspects of stage spectacle from Marlowe's *Tamburlaine*, including scenes of siege warfare with vaunting between characters upon city walls, together with the hanging of characters either from walls or, in the case of Absalon, from a tree. Peele's king shares a surprising number of qualities with Marlowe's Scythian and David's status as God's anointed warrior allows the play to recall Tamburlaine's epithet as "The Scourge of God" with its Old Testament origins whilst pointing up his ambiguous relationship with the Christian, Muslim and classical gods of the play. Such a strategy of alluding to Marlowe's *Tamburlaine* has been more readily identified in *The Battle of Alcazar* whilst the influence of Marlowe's first theatrical smash hit on *David and Bethsabe* has been comparatively overlooked. If we begin by briefly examining some of the strategies employed by Peele in *The Battle of Alcazar* to allude to *Tamburlaine* it allows us to recognise that this same strategy is also at work in *David and Bethsabe*. When Muly Mahamet [sic]

---

[8]   George Peele, *The Battle of Alcazar* in *The Stukeley Plays* edited by Charles Edelman (Manchester: Manchester University Press, 2005), 17.

[9]   See for example Charles Edelman (2005) and Roslyn Knutson (2002).

first appears on stage in Act 1, scene 2, he enters the stage in his chariot. This stage spectacle echoes those famous scenes from *Tamburlaine Part Two* when Tamburlaine appears on stage in his chariot drawn by the kings of Trebizon and Soria and then by Orcanes, King of Natolia and the King of Jerusalem. The fame of this scene is attested to by the fact that it is parodied by Shakespeare in *Henry IV part 2* when Pistol demands

> Shall pack-horses
> And hollow pamper'd jades of Asia,
> Which cannot go but thirty miles a day,
> Compare with Caesars and with Cannibals?[10]

Here Peele begins by making a visual homage to Tamburlaine, employing the iconic image of Tamburlaine in his chariot. To reinforce this visual connection with Marlowe's play Muly Mahamet's speech echoes Tamburlaine's dying words when he dismisses the power of the Turkish king to challenge his right to the throne:

> Convey Tamburlaine into our Afric here
> To chastise and to menace lawful kings.
> Tamburlaine triumph not, for thou must die.
> As Philip did, Caesar, and Caesar's peers.[11]

In *David and Bethsabe* Peele once again alludes to Marlowe's play with a visual homage in a scene which recalls several iconic moments from *Tamburlaine Part Two*. After the play's opening exchanges between David and Bethsabe the scene shifts to preparations for war against the Ammonites, as David's army, led by his captain Joab, lays siege to the city of Rabbah. As in *The Battle of Alcazar*, the parallel is made in the stage direction as the inhabitants appear on the city walls: "*Hanon with King Machaas, and others, upon the wals*".[12]The scene in which the leader of an attacking army addresses a besieged city is reminiscent firstly of *Tamburlaine Part Two* in Act 3, scene 3, when Theridamas and Techelles arrive at the walls of Balsera and speak to the Captain and his wife Olympia, and the stage directions note "*Summon the battle. [Enter above] Captain with his wife [OLYMPIA] and son*".[13]They refuse to surrender and the town is taken. The second and perhaps most famous example of this scenario is in Act 5, scene 1: "*Enter the GOVERNOR OF BABYLON upon the walls* with [MAXIMUS and] others". The governor refuses to agree to a truce and the town is taken; Tamburlaine then orders "Hang him in chains upon the city walls / And let my soldiers shoot the slave to death" (V.1.108-109). The

---

[10]   William Shakespeare, *Henry IV Part Two* ed. A.R. Humphreys (Walton-on-Thames: Thomas Nelson and Sons Ltd, 1966), I.4.160-163.

[11]   George Peele, *The Battle of Alcazar* in *The Stukeley Plays* ed. Charles Edelman (Manchester: Manchester University Press, 2005), I.2.35-38.

[12]   George Peele, *David and Bethsabe* edited by Elmer M. Blistein in *The Dramatic Works of George Peele* Volume III (Hew Haven: Yale University Press, 1970), line 186 sd. All further quotations from the play will be taken from this edition and reference will be given in the text.

[13]   Christopher Marlowe, *Tamburlaine the Great Parts One & Two* ed. J.S.Cunningham (Manchester: MUP, 1999), III.3. sd. All further quotations from the play will be taken from this edition and reference will be given in the text.

scene's dramatic impact is recorded in a letter from Philip Gaudy, a law student, to his father concerning a performance of a play in November 1587:

> My L. Admyrall his men and players having a devyse in ther playe to tye one of their fellows to a poste and so to shoote him to deathe, having borrowed their callyvers one of the players handes swerved his peece being charged with bullet missed the fellowe he aymed at and killed a child, and a woman great with child forthwith, and hurt an other man in the head very soore. [14]

It is not clear from the records which play was being performed, but the company was the Lord Admiral's Men and it is generally accepted that the play was *Tamburlaine Part Two*. [15]The violent fate of the Babylonian governor is recalled in Peele's play by the staging of the death of Absalon. During Absalon's rebellion against his father he becomes caught by the hair in a tree and is an easy target for David's soldiers. The stage directions indicate his predicament: "*The battell, and Absalon hangs by the haire*". Joab, David's captain, discovers the prince and stabs him for his treachery:

> But preach I to thee, while I should revenge
> Thy cursed sinne that staineth Israel,
> And makes her fields blush with her childrens bloud?
> Take that as part of thy deserved plague,
> Which worthily, no torment can inflict (ll.1524-1528).

Absalon continues to hang in the tree and lament, he is then stabbed again, this time by more of Joab's men, who finally kill him:

> Our captaine Joab hath begun to us,
> And heres an end to thee, and all thy sinnes.
> Come let us take the beauteous rebel downe,
> And in some ditch amids this darksome wood,
> Burie his bulke beneath a heape of stones (ll.1556-1560).

The parallels between David and Tamburlaine are developed further in Peele's play when David visits the city of Rabbah in person. Hanon once again appears on the city walls, as indicated by Joab's line "see where Hannon showes him on the wals" (l.777), thus recalling their encounter earlier in the play. The vaunting between David and Hanon underlines the parallels between David and Tamburlaine as Peele's king is described as the scourge of God by Joab, indicating that it is his destiny is to defeat the Gentiles in God's name: "Israel may, as it is promised, / Subdue the daughters of the Gentils Tribes" (ll. 779-780). Joab warns Hanon that

> the God of Israel hath said,
> David the King shall weare that crowne of thine,
> That weighs a Talent of the finest gold,
> And triumph in the spoile of Hannon's towne (ll.802-805).

---

[14] Andrew Gurr, *The Shakespearian Playing Companies* (Oxford: Clarendon Press, 1996), 232.
[15] Gurr, *The Shakespearian Playing Companies*, 232.

The stage direction then notes "*Alarum, excursions, assault. Exeunt omnes. Then the trumpets, and David with Hannon's crowne*"(l.14 sd). This scene which stages the transference of the crown from the king of the Ammonites to David is suggestive of the physical tussle between Tamburlaine and Mycetes in Part One for the crown of Persia. Mycetes begins by attempting to bury his crown in a hole in the ground, but then he is forced to engage in a tug-of-war with the Scythian for his crown. Although there are no stage directions given here it is clear that Tamburlaine has snatched the crown from Mycetes:

MYCETES:	Come, give it me.
TAMBURLAINE:	No, I took it prisoner.
MYCETES:	You lie, I gave it you.
TAMBURLAINE:	Then 'tis mine.
MYCETES:	No, I mean, I let you keep it.
TAMBURLAINE:	Well, I mean you shall have it again.
	Here, take it for a while, I lend it thee,
	Till I may see thee hemmed with armèd men.
	Then thou shalt see me pull it from thy head:
	Thou art no match for mighty Tamburlaine (I.II.iv.31-41).

The parallels, however, between *David and Bethsabe* and *Tamburlaine* extend beyond just the use of stage spectacle. On closer inspection there are a number of startling similarities between King David and Tamburlaine, including their humble origins as shepherds and their reputations as formidable soldiers and politicians. This unlikely alliance between them not only reflects the importance of the Old Testament as a source of inspiration for Elizabethan dramatists keen to cash in on the popularity of *Tamburlaine*, but also highlights the cultural currency of both David and Tamburlaine during the late 1580s and 1590s as both are used to renegotiate English national identity in the wake of a series of Armadas sent by the Spanish.

The defeat of the first Armada in the summer of 1588 by apparently providential winds was celebrated in a number of publications such as Edmund Bunny's *The Coronation of David* and John Prime's sermon "The Consolation of David, briefly applied to Queen Elizabeth". Each of these texts drew an analogy between the trials faced by England at the hands of the Spanish and their allies with the persecution of David and the Israelites at the hands of the Philistines. In Bunny's tract England is presented as the defender of the Protestant faith and like the young David before Goliath triumphs over a more powerful adversary:

> But now we also (God be praysed) haue our Dauid in the power of the Gospell, that Jesus Christ (the sonne of Dauid) hath now in these days sent unto us. When our brethren disdained to heare us talke of any such matter; when the wiser sort thought it impossible; without Sauls armour without any earthly helpe whatsoeuer: upon assurance of such like matters before achieved with a sling and a stone is Goliath with great courage incountered, and with as good success, in a manner cleane overthrowne (Bunny 1588, 12).

Prime's sermon makes explicit the parallels between the queen and King David when he describes Elizabeth as "a daughter of David [who] had as great deliuerances as ever Dauid had"(B2r).England's position as a nation favoured by God is emphasised by the defeat of the mighty Spanish fleet:

not an angel but God himself had a favourable eye toward us, an holy hand ouer us and that he was as much with us as euer any nation, when not withstanding all their crakes and famous Dons and duotie aduentures and painted hauntes, we lost by them who are now sent home a wrong way, neither man, nor ship nor boat, nor mast of ship (B7v).

Peele's play also taps into the political significance of the equivalence between David and Elizabeth as God's anointed servants to underline England's position as a providential nation and to celebrate their role as the underdogs in the war with Spain. In *David and Bethsabe* David's enemies insult the Israelites by referring to the humble origins of their leader. Hanon, the King of Ammon, sneers,

> What would the shepherds dogs of Israel
> Snatch from the mighty issue of King Ammon,
> The valiant Ammonites, and haughty Syrians? (ll.187-189)

King Machaas also insults Joab and David in this vein, emphasising David's role as a shepherd:

> Hence thou that bearst poor Israels shepherds hook,
> The prowd lieutenant of that base born King,
> And kep within the compasse of his fold,
> For if ye seeke to feed on Ammons fruits,
> And stray into the Syrian's fruitfull Medes,
> The mastives of our land shall werry ye,
> And pull the weesels from your greedy throtes (ll. 202-208).

In the opening scenes of the play it is clear that David has God's authorisation to pursue the war against the Ammonites and Joab's speech describes His involvement:

> He casts his sacred eyesight from on high,
> And sees your foes run seeking for their deaths,
> Laughing their labours and their hopes to scorn (II.12-14).

Divine sanction for this war indicates the ways in Peele's play appears to rehearse the Christian argument for a just war, which was based on the teachings of Saints Augustine and Thomas Aquinas which proposed that war could be sanctioned if it had the authority of the sovereign, if the cause was just and if it was carried out with aim of securing peace. [16]David's defeat of the Ammonites provides another example of the ways in which such biblical precedents could be utilised to chime with those feelings of English nationalism which intensified during the 1590s.

Like King David, Tamburlaine was celebrated as a great warrior in contemporary translated accounts of his career. In several of the sources available to Marlowe, including Sir Thomas Fortescue's *The Forest or Collection of Histories* (1571) and George Whetstone's *The English Mirror* (1586), Tamburlaine's military achievements are applauded. Fortescue, for example, offers a favourable comparison with Alexander the Great, an accolade all the more impressive since Tamburlaine began as "a poor labourer or husbandman":

---

[16]   Nick de Somogyi, *Shakespeare's Theatre of War* (Aldershot:Ashgate, 1998), 17.

In the end he became lord of such great kingdoms and seigniories, that he was in no point inferior to that prince of the world Alexander; or if he were, he yet came next him of any other that ever lived (Thomas & Tydeman 1994, 83).

Whetstone continues in a similar vein:

Among the illustrious captains Romans and Grecians none of all their martial arts deserve to be proclaimed with more renown than the conquest and military disciplines of Tamburlaine (Thomas & Tydeman 1994, 93).

Tamburlaine, like David, begins his career as a shepherd yet he goes on to establish a reputation as a successful military leader. In the opening scenes of Part One of Marlowe's play Tamburlaine appears in shepherd's clothing and his transformation from shepherd to warrior is enacted on stage as he removes his shepherd's garb and replaces it with armour: "Lie here, ye weeds that I disdain to wear! / This complete armour and this curtle-axe / Are adjuncts more beseeming Tamburlaine" (I.I.2.41-43). Tamburlaine's enemies also use his lowly origins to insult him. The kings and rulers whom Tamburlaine challenges curse him as "A Scythian shepherd"(I.I.2.154), a "devilish shepherd" (I.II.6.1) and a shepherd turned fox - "a fox in midst of harvest-time / Doth prey upon my flocks of passengers" (I.I.1.31-32) - and "shepherd's issue, base-born Tamburlaine" (2.III.5.77). Despite his humble origins it is Tamburlaine's skill on the battlefield and his political cunning which confirm his reputation and contemporary reactions to Marlowe's protagonist emphasise his power and success. Richard Levin argues that the play's handling of Tamburlaine's career was intended to prompt admiration in the audience rather than put forward a moral judgement and this is reflected in the ways in which many of the contemporary allusions to Tamburlaine make use of the epithet "mighty". [17]The address to the reader by the printer Richard Jones is a case in point:

Gentlemen and courteous readers whosoever: I have here published in print for your sakes the two tragical discourses of the Scythian shepherd Tamburlaine, that became so great a conqueror and so mighty a monarch.

The figure of Tamburlaine, therefore, had a particular resonance during the years of the Armada threat. James Shapiro has noted that despite being written a year before the first attempted invasion the play's "exploration of conquest, honour, social mobility and the representation of power made it in retrospect a paradigmatic Armada play" (Shapiro 1989, 352). The suggestion that Elizabethans regarded Tamburlaine as a figure to be admired and even emulated is further evidenced in Peele's poem "A Farewell to Norris and Drake" which was written on the occasion of England's counter-Armada to Portugal under Sir Francis Drake and Sir John Norris in 1589. Peele suggests that while the men may bid goodbye to life at home they should remember to emulate those figures who have graced the stage in their endeavours against the Spanish:

Bid Theaters and proude Tragedians,
Bid Mahomets Poo, and mightie Tamburlaine,

---

[17]   Richard Levin, "The Contemporary Perception of Marlowe's *Tamburlaine*.", 56.

King Charlemaine, Tom Stukeley and the rest
Adiewe (A3v).

The play itself invites its audience into a relationship of identification with Tamburlaine when it challenges them to "View but his picture in this tragic glass / And then applaud his fortunes as you please". The motif of reflection which begins in this first prologue suggests that in fact what we see is a mirror image of ourselves. This process of identification with Marlowe's protagonist, however, problematises the very issue of English national identity, since Tamburlaine is not simply an ambitious shepherd but a Scythian, and this had a specific set of negative associations for the Elizabethans since the Scythians were regarded as a barbarous nation and the antithesis of civilised society. The Irish were frequently described as being descended from the Scythians in order to justify the brutal programme of repression against the Irish during the sixteenth and seventeenth centuries. Tamburlaine's acts of conquest have also been identified with Spanish colonialism and it is possible that Marlowe may have been alluding to the career of the conquistador Lope de Aguirre when he depicts events from Tamburlaine's career (Cartelli 1996, 110-118). Like Tamburlaine, the Spanish conquistadors were used as models for English adventurers such as Sir Walter Ralegh in their undertakings in Ireland and the New World. In this way the desire for success aligns the English coloniser with the practices of the very enemy they have previously condemned. Marlowe, like Peele, also examines the competing theories of war by juxtaposing the Christian theory of a just war with the secular theory propounded by political theorist Niccolo Machiavelli. Machiavelli discounted the theory that war was a consequence of sin resulting in divine punishment and argued that war was a political instrument of will used directly by men and not God. Tamburlaine himself calls up the argument for war as the divine scourge of sin by the use of his epithet as the "Scourge of God", whilst his career makes the case for war as the political instrument of individual ambition (De Somogyi 1998, 21-22). Both plays therefore scrutinise the political expediency of using biblical precedents to legitimate war and whilst the power of divine sanction is acknowledged, ultimately it is the human qualities of the military leader which appeared to be prized above all in the case of both David and Tamburlaine. David, like Tamburlaine, is a charismatic leader; both exemplify military valour and both are prepared to perform acts of extreme violence to secure their aims. With this in mind it is possible to look at the relationship between David and Tamburlaine in the context of other subsequent biblical plays and to conjecture that it was these requirements which partly motivated the dramatists responsible for these plays.

The lost play *Nebuchadnezzar* is a case in point. Table 2 indicates that *Nebuchadnezzar* appears to have been a successful play for the Admiral's Men, with entries for a series of eight performances between December 1597 and March 1598, with several performances bringing in the highest receipts for that week. The play poses a number of difficulties however, as there are no existing documents which record either the date when it was composed or first performed. Despite the absence of an extant playtext or dates relating to its composition or first performance it is still possible to suggest reasons why the figure of Nebuchadnezzar may have been the subject of an Elizabethan play. The king appears in the Old Testament books of Daniel, Jeremiah and Judith in the Apocrypha. In the Book of Daniel Nebuchadnezzar is depicted as a proud king who is punished by God for bragging of his own power and capability. In Daniel 4:30 the king is cast out to live as a beast for seven years:

And he was driuen from men, and did eat grasse as the oxen, and his bodie was wet with dewe of heauen, til his heeres were growen as egles (feathers) and his nailes like birds (clawes) (*Geneva Bible* 1561, 325).

Nebuchadnezzar is frequently used in homiletic literature as an exemplar of pride, but it seems that the aspects of Nebuchadnezzar's story which would have had greater appeal for an Elizabethan dramatist are that like King David, Nebuchadnezzar was also famous as a warrior king and is remembered for his military campaigns against Egypt and the kingdom of Judah. Historical accounts of the king also record his siege and capture of the city of Jerusalem in 597 BC. [18]In the Book of Jeremiah he is described as God's instrument that will be used to punish the sinful city of Jerusalem. The prophet describes the coming of the Babylonian king in ways that would no doubt have appealed to a dramatist aiming to write a play which would recall Tamburlaine:

Beholde, he shal come vp as the cloudes, and his charets (shalbe) as a tempest: his horses are higher [than] eagles (*Geneva Bible* 1561, 291).

From the biblical sources it seems that the play about Nebuchadnezzar could easily reproduce those popular motifs of war, particularly siege warfare, as well as instances of physical violence. Jeremiah chapter 39 verses 5-5 provides one such example when he describes Nebuchadnezzar's treatment of Zedekiah, the king of Jerusalem, who is captured and tortured by his enemy:

They broght hym to Nebuchad-nezzar kyng of Babel vnto Riblah in the land of Hamath, where he gaue judgement vpon him. Then the king of Babel slew the sonnes of Zedekiah in Riblah before his eyes: also the kyng of Bable slewe all the nobles of Iudah. Moreover he put out Zedekiahs eyes, and bounde hym in chaynes, to carry him to Babel. Abnd the Chaldeans burnt the Kyngs house, and the houses of the people with fyre, and brake down the walles of Jerusalem (*Geneva Bible* 1561, 291).

Although discussion of the content of the play can only ever be based on speculation, if we look at the plays performed during the weeks that *Nebuchadnezzar* featured in the Admiral's repertory, we can see that it appears on four occasions with the play called *Stukeley*, an abbreviation for the play *The Famous History of the Death and Life of Captain Thomas Stukeley*. *Stukeley* had itself been written partly in response to Peele's *Alcazar* and is also concerned with war and battles of conquest in North Africa and the Mediterranean and would no doubt have served as a useful pairing with *Nebuchadnezzar*.

The repertory of the Admiral's Men was shaped not only by the popularity of Marlowe's plays, but also by the acting of Edward Alleyn, the company's leading man during the 1590s, who played the roles of Tamburlaine, Barabas and Doctor Faustus and had contributed to their success. Alleyn's physical presence and his acting style suggest that he was striking in these large central roles. Susan Cerasano has argued that based on the sizing of Alleyn's signet ring the actor was likely to be an imposing figure, probably above average Elizabethan height (Cerasano 1994, 171-179). The part of Tamburlaine would require that the actor was both physically impressive with vocal talents to match. Alleyn's depiction of Tamburlaine and

---

[18]   "Nebuchadnezzar II." Encyclopaedia Britannica. Retrieved August 1, 2007, from Encyclopaedia Online: http://search.eb.com/eb/article~9055140

the other Marlovian protagonists he played clearly made an impression upon his audience. In an important essay on the influence of Alleyn's celebrity status upon the repertory of the Admiral's men, Susan Cerasano has argued that based upon the roles Alleyn is known to have performed with the company, it is possible to conjecture that he may well have performed the central role in other plays in the repertory. Cerasano identifies the two biblical plays Greene's The *Tragedy of Job* and Peele's *David and Bethsabe* which she argues would have provided "iconic Alleyn-style roles" (Cerasano 2005, 49). Cerasano goes on to note that

> The biblical history, while not prominent in the company's repertory in 1587, soon became so, and it remained popular with the company's audience well into the early seventeenth century (Cerasano 2005, 49).

Further evidence that biblical plays like Peele's *David and Bethsabe* were written with Alleyn in mind can be traced if we return to the list of biblical plays listed in Table 1. Although it is difficult to date individual plays precisely it is possible to see from the table that they can be divided into two groups. The first contains those biblical plays written or performed between c. 1590 and 1597: *A Looking Glass for London and England, Abraham and Lot, Esther and Ahasuerus, The History or Tragedy of Job, David and Bethsabe* and *Nebuchadnezzer*. The second group belong to the period c. 1600-1602 including *Judas* (1600/1601), *Pontius Pilate, Jephthah, Tobias, Samson* and *Joshua*. In the autumn of 1597 Alleyn stepped down temporarily from his position as the leading actor for the Admiral's Men and "retired" from the stage. Henslowe alludes to his son-in-law's departure in an entry in his diary when summarising the expenditure for costumes which he records as a "not of all suche goods as I haue Bowght for playnge since my sonne Edward allen leafte lange [sic]" (Henslowe *Diary*, 83-84). Alleyn's retirement from the stage in 1597 is now thought to have been a calculated decision by Alleyn and his father-in-law Philip Henslowe as both were involved in a number of business ventures. Alleyn in particular was involved in attempts to secure the Mastership of the Bears and in negotiations for securing the lease for the site on which the new Fortune theatre would be constructed (Cerasano 1998, 98-112). In 1600 the Admiral's Men relocated from the Rose on the South Bank to the Fortune theatre in the parish of Cripplegate, which stood outside the jurisdiction of the City authorities with the older theatres such as the Theatre and the Curtain. When the new theatre opened Alleyn returned to the stage, no doubt to help draw the crowds away from the Chamberlain's Men at the Globe. The payments for the second group of biblical plays beginning in 1600 coincide with the opening of the Fortune and the need for new plays to satisfy audience demand. The Old Testament figures around whom the plays were organised indicate that dramatists were writing plays which would offer a platform for Alleyn's talents and his association with those earlier Marlovian roles he had made his own. Again, a brief examination of the figures selected indicate that this was the most likely strategy at work. It has been suggested by Michael O'Connell that the play called *Judas* which is begun by Haughton in 1600 and is completed in 1601 by Rowley is more likely to be concerned with the figure of Judas Maccabeus from the Apocrypha, rather than that of Judas Iscariot, since the latter's story would require the representation of Christ on stage, something which had been prohibited (O'Connell 2000, 111). Judas Maccabeus is a more likely choice since his story is one which would be more in keeping with the kinds of plays the Admiral's men favoured as he is a great warrior who is chosen by the Israelites to rise up against King Antiochus:

So he gate his people great honour: he put on a brestplate as a gyant, and armed him self, and set the battel in array, and defended the campe with the sworde. In his actes he was like a lyon, and as a lyons whelpe roaring after the pray (*Geneva Bible* 1561, 411).

John H. Astington in his discussion of Alleyn's final season at the Fortune theatre also notes that new biblical plays such as *Samson*, *Joshua* and *Jephthah* were written for Alleyn with an eye to reprising earlier roles:

> There seems to be little doubt that Alleyn would have played the title role in all these, and they may have been written with him in mind, in that Samson is a kind of Hercules, and Joshua a kind of Tamburlaine (Astington 2006, 133).

Joshua, as Moses' captain who leads the Israelites across the Jordan to establish by conquest the Promised Land, is another appropriate choice, as Astington points out, since the Book of Joshua provides the story of the siege and destruction of the city of Jericho, together with an alarming succession of wars and battles - indeed chapter 12 consists simply of a list of the thirty one kings defeated by Joshua. Both Judas and Joshua may have been suggested to Haughton and Rowley as potentially suitable figures from the Old Testament to dramatise from scrutinising the plays which existed in the repertory of the Admiral's Men. Judas and Joshua, like King David, belonged to the group known as the Nine Worthies, a list of men who exemplified martial valour and were drawn from Pagan, Old Testament and Christian sources. [19]The classical examples included Hector, Alexander the Great and Julius Caesar and the Christian examples were King Arthur, Charlemagne and Godfrey of Bouillon. Henslowe's *Diary* indicates that the Admiral's Men had performed the no longer extant play *Godfrey of Boulogne* between July 1594 and September 1595, which seems to have been a play in two parts as the entries refer to receipts for "2pte of godfrey of bullen" (Henslowe Diary, 22-25, 28, 31). Godfrey was the Duke of Lorraine and descendant of Charlemagne, who was famous for leading the first crusade in 1095 and ruled Jerusalem after the defeat of the Muslim forces. [20]There is some indication from the performance lists that *Godfrey of Boulogne*, like *Muly Mullocco* and *Nebuchadnezzar*, had been deliberately paired with the lost play *Mahomet*, so that they might complement one another. There were three occasions during August and September 1594 when a performance of *Godfrey* was followed by a performance of *Mohamet*, suggesting that the plays were grouped thematically to capitalise on their shared subject matter of foreign conquest and battles against the Turks.

Biblical drama performed on the public stage in the final decade of Elizabeth's reign, then, was written as part of a commercial strategy to complement and prolong the stage life of existing plays in the repertory. The biblical plays staged by the Admiral's Men at the Rose and Fortune theatres replicated the themes and motifs of older plays in their collection, particularly the most popular of Marlowe's plays such as *Tamburlaine* and *The Jew of Malta*. The eponymously titled plays are therefore characterised by accounts of soldier kings or conquering prophets whose campaigns are set against an ancient and exotic backdrop. Peele's

---

[19]   *he Concise Oxford Dictionary of English Literature* second edition (Oxford: Oxford University Press, 1970), 621-622.

[20]   "Godfrey of Bouillon." Encyclopaedia Britannica. Retrieved August 1, 2007, from Encyclopaedia Britannica Online: http://search.eb.com/eb/article~9037164

David and Bethsabe can clearly be located in the context of these reportorial strategies, while King David's identification both with Marlowe's Tamburlaine and with a besieged Protestant England also suggest some of the conflicting ways in which English national identity underwent a process of reconfiguration during the Long 1590s.

Appendix

Table 1: Elizabethan Biblical Plays

Date	Play	Theatre Company/ Theatre
c. 1590	*A Looking Glasse for London and England*	Rose
c. 1593	*Abraham and Lot*	Rose
c. 1594	*Esther and Ahasuerus*	Admiral and Chamberlain's Men, Newington Butts
c.1596	*Nebuchadnezzar*	Admiral's Men The Rose
	Tragedy of Job	Unknown
c. 1594	*David and Bathsheba*	Unknown
c. 1600	*Judas }*	Admiral's Men
c. 1601	*Judas }*	Admiral's Men
c.1601	*Pontius Pilate*	Admiral's Men
c. 1602	*Jephthah*	Admiral's Men
c. 1602	*Tobias*	Admiral's Men
c. 1602	*Samson*	Admiral's Men
c. 1602	*Joshua*	Admiral's Men

Table 2: Playlists for Biblical plays taken from Henslowe's Diary

Extant plays are in bold type face

Play	Date of Performance	Takings	Plays in Performance that week	Highest grossing play for that week
Looking Glass for London and England	8th March 1592	7s	*Four Plays in One,* **Henry VI** (x2), *Zenobia,* **The Jew of Malta**	**Henry VI** £3
	27th March	£2 s	**Henry VI, Muly Mullocco,** *Don Horatio***Jeronimo**	*Henry VI* £3 / 8s
	19th April	£1 / 4s	**Muly Mullocco, The Jew of Malta,** *Titus and Vespasian,* **Henry VI,** *Don Horatio*	*Titus and Vespasian* £2 / 16s
	7th June	£1 / 9s	*Bendo and Richardo, Titus and Vespasian, 2 Tamar Cham,* **Jeronimo, Knack to Know a Knave**	*Knack to Know a Knave* £3 / 12s
Abraham and Lot	9th January 1594	£2 / 12s	*Friar Francis, George a Green, Buckingham, Huon of Bordeaux, Fair Maid of Italy*	*Friar Francis* £3 / 1s
	17th January	£1 / 10s	*Friar Francis, George a Green, Richard the Confessor, King Lud*	*Friar Francis* £1 / 16s
	31st January	12s	*Buckingham,* **Titus Andronicus**	*Titus Andronicus* £2
Hesther and Ahasuerus	5th June 1594	8s	**The Jew of Malta, Titus Andronicus,** *Cutlack*	*Titus Andronicus* 12s
	12th June 1594	5s	*Bellendon, Hamlet, Taming of a Shrew,* **Titus Andronicus, The Jew of Malta**	*Bellendon* 17s
Nebuchadnezzar	19th December 1596	£1 / 10s	**Stukeley,** *Vortigern,* **Dr. Faustus**	*Stukeley* £2
	21st December	£1 / 6s	*Vortigern* (x2), *Blind Beggar of Alexandria*	*Nebuchadnezzar* £1 / 6s

27th December	£3 / 8s	**Stukeley**, *Vortigern, That Will Be Shall Be, Seven Days of the Week*	*Nebuchadnezzar* £3 / 8s
4th January 1597	16s	*That Will Be Shall Be* (x2), **Dr. Faustus**, **Jeronimo**, *Vortigern*	*Jeronimo* £3
12th January	13s	**Stukeley**, **Jeronimo**, *That Will Be Shall Be, Alexander and Lodowick, Blind Beggar of Alexandria*	*Alexander and Lodowick* £2 / 15s
19th January	10s	**Jeronimo** (x2), *That Will Be Shall Be*, **Stukeley**, *Vortigern*	**Jeronimo** (first perf.) £1
26th January	9s	*That will be Shall Be, Blind Beggar of Alexandria, Woman Hard to Please* (x2), *Long Meg of Westminster*	*Woman Hard to Please* £2 / 11s
22nd March	5s	*Alexander and Lodowick, Guido*	*Guido*, £1 / 4s

Table 3: Performance Details for Muly Mullocco taken from Henslowe's Diary

Extant plays are indicated in bold type face.

Play	Date of performance	Takings	Other plays in performance that week	Highest grossing play of the week
Muly Mullocco	21st February 1592	£1 / 9s	*Orlando, Don Horatio, Sir John Mandeville, Henry of Cornwall* and **The Jew of Malta**	*The Jew of Malta* £2 / 10s
	29th February	£1 / 14s	*Clorys and Orgasto*	*Muly Mulloco* £1 / 14s
	17th March	£1 / 8s and 6d	*Don Horatio,* **Jeronimo** (**The Spnaish Tragedy**), *Henry of Cornwall,* **The Jew of Malta**	*Jeronimo* £4 / 11s
	29th March	£3 / 2s	**Looking Glass for London, Henry VI,** *Don Horatio,* **Jeronimo**	*Henry VI* £3 / 8s
	8th April	£1 / 3s	*Machiavel,* **The Jew of Malta, Henry VI,** *Brandimer,* **Jeronimo**	*The Jew of Malta* £2 / 3s
	17th April	£1 / 10s	**The Jew of Malta, Looking Glass for London,** *Titus and Vespasian,* **Henry VI,** *Don Horatio*	*Titus and Vespasian* £2 / 16s
	27th April	£1 / 6s	**Jeronimo,** *Jerusalem, Friar Bacon, 2 Tamar Cham, Henry of Cornwall*	*2 Tamar Cham* £3 / 4s
	1st May	£2 / 18s	*Jeronimo, Titus and Vespasian, Henry VI, The Jew of Malta, Friar Bacon*	*Muly Mullocco* £2 / 18s
	19th May	£1 / 16s and 6d	**Jeronimo, Henry VI,** *Titus and Vespasian, Sir John Mandeville, Henry of Cornwall*	*Jeronimo* £3 / 4s
	3rd June	£1 / 3s	**Henry VI,** *2 Tamar Cham,* **Jeronimo,** *Machiavel,* **The Jew of Malta**	*2 Tamar Cham* £1 / 16s and 6d

	13th June	£1	**Henry VI**, **The Jew of Malta**, Knack to Know a Knave, Sir John Mandeville	**Knack to Know a Knave** £2 / 12 s
	29th December	£3 / 10s	Jeronimo	Muly Mullocco £3 / 10s
	9th January 1593	£1	**Jeronimo**, Friar Bacon, Cosmo, Sir John Mandeville, Knack to Know a Knave	Cosmo £2 / 4s
	20th January	£1	Titus and Vespasia, **Henry VI**, Friar Bacon, **The Jew of Malta**, 2 Tamar Cham	The Jew of Malta £3

Works Cited

- Astington, John H. "Playing the Man: Acting at the Red Bull and Fortune." *Early Theatre* 9.2 (2006): 130-143.

- Berek, Peter. "Tamburlaine's Weak Sons: Imitation as Interpretation Before 1593." *Renaissance Drama*, 13 (1982): 55-82.

- *The Bible and Holy Scriptures conteyned in the Olde and Newe Testament.* Geneva,1561.

- Blackburn, Ruth H. *Biblical Drama under the Tudors*. The Hague: Moutan and Company, 1971.

- Boas, Frederick S. *An Introduction to Tudor Drama*. Oxford: Clarendon Press, 1966.

- Braunmuller, A.R. *George Peele*. Boston: Twayne Publishers, 1983.

- Bullen, A.H. *The Works of George Peele Volume One*. London: Ballantyne Press, 1888.

- Edmund Bunny's *The Coronation of David*. London: 1588.

- Cartelli, Thomas. 'Marlowe and the New World' In *Christopher Marlowe and English Renaissance Culture*. eds. Darryll Grantley & Peter Roberts (Aldershot: Scolar Press, 1996), pp. 110-118.

- Carson, Neil. *A Companion to Henslowe's Diary*. Cambridge: CUP, 1988.

- Cerasano, S.P. "Edward Alleyn, the New Model Actor, and the Rise of the Celebrity in the 1590s" *Medieval and Renaissance Drama in England* 18 (2005): 47-58.

- Cerasano, S.P. "Edward Alleyn's 'Retirement' 1597-1600." *Medieval and Renaissance Drama in England*, 10 (1998): 98-112.

- Cerasano, S.P. "Tamburlaine and Edward Alleyn's Ring." *Shakespeare Survey* 47 (1994): 171-79.

- Chambers, E.K. *The Elizabethan Stage*. 4 Vols. Oxford: Oxford UP, 1923.

- Ekeblad, Inga-Stina. "*The Love of King David and Fair Bethsabe*: A Note on George Peele's Biblical Drama" *English Studies* 39 (1958): 57-62.

- Ewbank, Inga-Stina. "The House of David in Renaissance Drama. A Comparative Study" *Renaissance Drama* 8 (1965): 3-40.

- Foakes, R.A. ed. *Henslowe's Diary* 2nd edition. Cambridge: CUP, 2002.

- "Godfrey of Bouillon." *Encyclopaedia Britannica*. Retrieved August 1, 2007, from Encyclopaedia Britannica Online: http://search.eb.com/eb/article~9037164.

- Gurr, Andrew. *The Shakespearian Playing Companies* Oxford: Clarendon Press, 1996.

- Hopkins, Lisa. *Christopher Marlowe. A Literary Life* (Basingstoke: Palgrave, 2000)

- Hunter, G.K. "The Emergence of the University Wits: Early Tragedy" in *English Drama 1586-1642 The Age of Shakespeare* Oxford: Clarendon Press, 1997.

- Knutson, Roslyn L. "Marlowe Reruns: Repertorial Commerce and Marlowe's Plays in Revival" in *Marlowe's Empery: Expanding His Critical Contexts* ed. Sara Munson Deats and Robert A. Logan. London: Associated University Presses, 2002, 25-42.

- Knutson, Roslyn L. "The Repertory" in *A New History of Early English Drama* ed. John D. Cox and David Scott Kastan. New York: Columbia University Press, 1997, 461-480.

- Levin, Richard. "The Contemporary Perception of Marlowe's *Tamburlaine*." *Medieval and Renaissance Drama in England* 1 (1984): 51-70.

- McMillan, Scott and MacLean, Sally Beth. *The Queen's Men and their Plays*. Cambridge, CUP, 1998.

- Marlowe, Christopher. *Tamburlaine the Great* ed. J.S.Cunningham Manchester: MUP, 1991.

- "Nebuchadnezzar II." *Encyclopaedia Britannica*. Retrieved August 1, 2007, from Encyclopaedia Online: http://search.eb.com/eb/article~9055140.

- "The Nine Worthies." *The Concise Oxford Dictionary of English Literature* 2nd edition. 1970.

- O'Connell, Michael. *The Idolatrous Eye*: *Iconoclasm and Theater in Early-Modern England* Oxford: Oxford UP, 2000.

- Peele, George. "A farewell Entituled to the famous and fortunate generalls of our English forces: Sir Iohn Norris & Syr Frauncis Drake Knights, and all theyr braue and resolute followers" London 1589

- Peele, George. *David and Bethsabe* ed. Elmer M. Blistein in *The Dramatic Works of George Peele* Volume III Hew Haven: Yale UP, 1970.

- Peele, George. *The Battle of Alcazar* in *The Stukeley Plays* ed. Charles Edelman Manchester: MUP, 2005.

- Prime, John. "The Consolation of David, briefly applied to Queen Elizabeth" Oxford: 1588.

- Roston, Murray. *Biblical Drama in England. From the Middle Ages to the Present Day*. London: Faber and Faber, 1968.

- • Shakespeare, William. *Henry IV Part Two* ed. A.R. Humphreys Walton-on-Thames: Thomas Nelson and Sons Ltd, 1966.

- Shapiro, James. *Rival Playwrights*: *Marlowe, Jonson and Shakespeare* New York: Columbia UP, 1991.

- Shapiro, James. 'Revisiting Tamburlaine: *Henry V* as Shakespeare's Belated Armada Play', *Criticism*, 31 (1989), 351-366.

- Somogyi, Nick de. *Shakespeare's Theatre of War* Aldershot: Ashgate, 1998.

- Thomas, Vivien and Tydeman, William. ed. *Christopher Marlowe. The Plays and their sources* London: Routledge, 1994.

- White, Paul Whitfield "Theater and Religious Culture" in *A New History of Early English Drama* ed. John D. Cox and David Scott Kastan. New York: Columbia University Press, 1997, 133-151.

- Wright, Louis B. "The Scriptures and the Elizabethan Stage." *Modern Philology* (1928): 47-56.

[18]

The House of David in Renaissance Drama

A COMPARATIVE STUDY

Inga-Stina Ewbank

Si j'avais à . . . [exposer sur le théâtre] . . . [l'histoire] de David et de Bethsabée, je ne décrirais pas comme il en devint amoureux en la voyant se baigner dans une fontaine, de peur que l'image de cette nudité ne fît une impression trop chatouilleuse dans l'esprit de l'auditeur; mais je me contenterais de le peindre avec de l'amour pour elle, sans parler aucunement de quelle manière cet amour se serait emparé de son cœur.[1]

IT IS HIGHLY UNLIKELY that when Corneille wrote the above words, in his *Examen de Polyeucte,* he should have known of an English play, written some sixty or seventy years earlier, in which the episode of King David watching the bathing Bathsheba is not just described but actually put on the stage.[2] Corneille was discussing how to deal dramatically with religious, and especially biblical, material; and he was doing so at a time, well over a hundred years after Buchanan's *Jephthes,* when humanists all over Europe had proved the possibility of christianizing the Tragic Muse, of serving both the ancients (but more specifically the not-quite-so-ancient Seneca) and the Lord. French dramatists in particular had been quick to see that the Bible contained as much potentially tragic material as classical myth;[3] but at about the same time as Corneille was working on his play

1. *Oeuvres de P. Corneille,* nov. ed. (Paris, 1873), II, 113.

2. Corneille presumably had in mind Montchrestien's *David,* which is discussed later in this essay. Cf. *Les Tragédies de Montchrestien,* ed. L. Petit de Julleville (Paris, 1891), p. 306.

3. Cf. the Introduction to *The Poetical Works of Sir William Alexander,* ed. L. E. Kastner and H. B. Charlton (Manchester, 1921), p. cxxxv. (This essay remains

4 INGA-STINA EWBANK

about Polyeucte, saint and martyr, Milton was pondering over biblical topics for tragedy and noting down as possibilities, among others, "David Adulterous," "Tamar," and "Achitophel." The House of David might be as fruitful as the House of Atreus when it came to furnishing a tragic plot, and there was always the advantage that scriptural authority would, by definition, make the argument not less but more heroic.

> L'execrable Inceste d'Amnon
> Dont tu peints si bien la vengeance,
> Plus que la mort d'Agamemnon
> Tesmoigne de Dieu la puissance,

we read in a commendatory ode on N. Chrestien's play about how David's son Amnon raped his sister Tamar and was, in revenge, slain by his brother Absalom.[4] Corneille, too, assumes that biblical story has the sanctity of divine inspiration about it, so that a dramatist using such material may not change anything in his source. But his second point, and the one that leads up to the quotation above, deals with the *omissions* which may be made—provided always that one does not obscure "ces verités dictées par le Saint-Esprit." In the cause of dramatic decorum and unity of impact, he says, one must be selective. It is here that Corneille becomes immediately relevant to my main theme in this essay, because he shows how, in neoclassic theory, the standards of the "well-made" play are already looming up. He is in fact anticipating the criteria by which George Peele's play, *The Love of King David and Fair Bethsabe, With the Tragedie of Absalon*, is still most frequently judged—and by which,

---

the best work in English on the Renaissance Senecan tradition in Europe.) Cf. also Lancaster E. Dabney, *French Dramatic Literature in the Reign of Henri IV* (Austin, 1952), Chap. I; and Gustave Lanson, *Esquisse d'une Histoire de la Tragédie Française* (New York, 1920), pp. 15 ff.

4. "Ode" by O. du Mont-Sacré in commendation of *Tragédie d'Amnon, et Thamar*, in *Les Tragedies de N. Chretien* (Rouen, 1608).—In the case of both Chrestien and Montchrestien, whose names appear variously with or without an "s," I follow the spelling used by Raymond Lebègue in *La Tragédie française de la Renaissance*, 2nd ed. (Brussels, 1954).—This argument for the superiority of a biblical subject over a similar classical one was a commonplace. See, e.g., Christopherson on his *Jephthah* as against Euripides' *Iphigenia in Aulis*. (Quoted in F. S. Boas, *University Drama in the Tudor Age* [Oxford, 1914], pp. 48–49.)

The House of David 5

inevitably, it is seen as the result of "shapeless unselectivity of incidents."[5]

There has always been disagreement as to what kind of a play *David and Bethsabe* really is. Peele's own title page shows a happy disregard of genres. Restoration play-lists call it a tragicomedy.[6] Thomas Warton places it in the medieval miracle tradition.[7] F. S. Boas veers between "revenge tragedy" and an almost Polonian labeling of the play as "Scriptural chronicle-history."[8] Lily B. Campbell is practically alone in taking it seriously as a new departure in drama, "a divine play conscious of its place in divine literature"; but even she finds the structure "cluttered with episodes."[9] Scholars are, perhaps, no longer as anxious as they once were to father onto Peele every shapeless Elizabethan play of unknown authorship, but he still tends to be used as an example of someone who "cared little for structural consistency."[10] We might do well to listen to Wolfgang Clemen when he says that, in order to do justice to Peele's plays,

dürfen wir sie nicht mit den üblichen Masstäben dramatischer Einheit und Komposition beurteilen, sondern müssen nach ihrer Eigengesetzlichkeit fragen.[11]

In this essay I propose to work toward a definition of that "Eigengesetzlichkeit" in *David and Bethsabe* and to do so by looking at other dramatic treatments of Peele's source (i.e., 2 Samuel XI–XIX.8), as well as at

5. Madeleine Doran, *Endeavors of Art* (Madison, 1954), p. 102.

6. See Francis Kirkman, *A True, Perfect, and Exact Catalogue of all the Comedies, Tragedies, Tragi-Comedies* . . . (London, 1671), and William Winstanley, *The Lives of the Most Famous English Poets* (London, 1687), p. 97.

7. *The History of English Poetry*, rev. ed. (London, 1824), IV, 153, note e.

8. *An Introduction to Tudor Drama* (Oxford, 1933), p. 157, and *University Drama*, p. 363.

9. *Divine Poetry and Drama in Sixteenth Century England* (London, Berkeley, and Los Angeles, 1959), p. 260.

10. Arthus M. Sampley, "The Text of Peele's *David and Bethsabe*," *PMLA*, XLVI (1931), 670.

11. *Die Tragödie vor Shakespeare* (Heidelberg, 1955), p. 146.—In his translation of Clemen's book, T. S. Dorsch renders this passage as follows: "To do justice to Peele's plays, we must not judge them according to the normally accepted standards of dramatic unity and structure; they must be judged by criteria that are appropiate to their special character" (*English Tragedy before Shakespeare* [London, 1961], p. 163).

6   INGA-STINA EWBANK

nondramatic versions of the story, wherever they illuminate points in the plays under consideration.

Peele's is the only Elizabethan play on the subject of the House of David: if the fourteenpence paid by Henslowe in October 1602 for "poleyes & worckmanshipp for to hange absalome" were spent on a play other than Peele's, that play is now lost. We therefore have to go abroad for comparative material, and rightly so, for—as scholars like F. S. Boas, and more recently Lily B. Campbell and Marvin T. Herrick, have shown—the Renaissance desire to turn Bible story into drama was a European, rather than a localized, phenomenon.[12] If anything, the English dramatists, academic as well as popular, seem to have been more wary of tackling this type of drama than, for example, their Dutch and French contemporaries. Comparisons for comparison's sake are odious, but in this case I hope that a comparative method, while incidentally throwing some light on the ways in which the same source material is shaped by different individuals in different dramatic traditions, will mainly prove helpful toward defining the nature of the play we have before our eyes.

At the outset, however, something must be said about the *text* we have before our eyes.[13] There is no doubt that the text of the quarto of *David*

12. See Boas, *University Drama*; Campbell, *Divine Poetry and Drama*; and Marvin T. Herrick, *Tragicomedy: Its Origin and Development in Italy, France and England* (Urbana, 1955). See also Herrick's essay, "Susanna and the Elders in Sixteenth-Century Drama," in *Studies in Honor of T. W. Baldwin*, ed. D. C. Allen (Urbana, 1958), pp. 125–135.—I have been helped in my search for plays on the House of David by the bibliography in *Le Mistère du Viel Testament*, ed. James de Rothschild (Paris, 1882), IV, lvii ff.; and also by the list compiled by John McLaren McBryde, Jr., in his article, "A Study of Cowley's *Davideis*," *JEGP*, II (1899), 454–527. Invaluable bibliographies of neo-Latin drama are Alfred Harbage's "Census of Anglo-Latin Plays," *PMLA*, LIII (1938), 624–629; and the two works by Leicester Bradner: "A Check-List of Original Neo-Latin Dramas by Continental Writers Printed before 1650," *PMLA*, LVIII (1943), 621–633, and "List of Original Neo-Latin Plays Published before 1650," *Studies in the Renaissance*, IV (1957), 31–70.

13. For the purpose of this essay I have used, and quoted from, the Malone Society reprint of the 1599 quarto of *David and Bethsabe* (ed. W. W. Greg, 1912). —To minimize the confusion which might arise from the fact that each author tends to use his own form of the biblical names (and that in Peele's play the spelling sometimes varies from scene to scene), I have in all cases, except in direct quotations, used the form and spelling to be found in the Authorized Version; thus "Bathsheba," "Hushai," "Absalom," "Ahitophel," etc.

The House of David 7

and Bethsabe printed in 1599 is garbled. There are such flagrant corruptions and problems as the three misplaced lines, 1660-1662, which belong nowhere in the play as it stands; the "5. Chorus" which is the second, and last, in the play; and the reference in this chorus to "a third discourse of Dauids life," with its never fulfilled promise of showing us "his most renowmed death" (ll. 1654-1655). I cannot deal here with the textual riddles of the play, but for the purposes of my argument they seem to have been solved satisfactorily by A. M. Sampley's theory, which is that Peele originally wrote a five-act play dealing with the love of David and Bathsheba and the tragedy of Absalom.[14] This version was cut for stage performances and gradually got so mutilated that in the end it had to be revised to be brought back to a more reasonable length. The play, then, in its present form represents a drastically cut stage version of the play as Peele first wrote it, plus an addition (the Solomon scene) made by Peele before sending it to the printer. The important point, to my argument, is that we can be fairly certain, because of the homogeneity of the style throughout, that the final revision was carried out by Peele himself. That being so, the present text—apart from such obvious errors as undeleted lines—represents what Peele himself deemed ready for the stage and for the reader. To Sampley it stands as a proof that Peele was not interested in "structural consistency." I shall argue, however, that the play has virtues—a kind of imaginative shape and thematic unity—which have not been allowed for; and I hope to bring these out by discussing what qualities there are in Peele's play that are not also in others dealing with the same subject, and vice versa.

David and Bethsabe opens with a Prologue which takes the form of an epic invocation—

> Of Israels sweetest singer now I sing,
> His holy stile and happie victories—

but, as the "Prologus" "*drawes a curtaine, and discouers Bethsabe with her maid bathing ouer a spring: she sings, and Dauid sits aboue vewing her,*" it is hardly one of the happy victories he presents. Peele's audience would have been conditioned toward two kinds of response to this scene, and in his treatment of the love of David and Bathsheba, Peele draws on both.

14. See *PMLA*, XLVI (1931), 659-671.

8   INGA-STINA EWBANK

> Adam, Sansonem, Loth, David, sic Salomonem
> Femina decepit . . .

we read in the neo-Latin *Comedia Sancti Nicolai*,[15] and here we have in a nutshell the first attitude to David the lover, one which the sixteenth century had inherited from the Middle Ages. David's *sin* is emphasized and seen as another version of the Fall, with Bathsheba as another Eve. The David and Bathsheba story had become an *exemplum* to illustrate one of the great medieval moral-satirical themes. As late as 1581 there was printed in London a collection of the dialogues of Ravisius Textor, where in the *Dialogus* between "Troia," "Salomon," and "Sanson" we find the following well with three buckets:

> TROIA
> Quis generi humano Paradisi limina clausit?
> SALOMON
> Foemina. Quis lyrici cantus Davida peritum
> Fecit adulterium committere?
> SANSON
> Foemina. Sed quis
> Aeneam valido fecit confligere Turno?
> TROIA
> Foemina. Qui veteres fecit pugnare Sabinos
> Contra Romanes pastores?
> SALOMON
> Foemina . . .[16]

And so on, until the whole dialogue adds up to a flaming indictment of woman. Again, David's sin is linked with Adam's, as well as with that of the heroes of classical myth and history. David and Bathsheba form one of

15. This was written by a French Augustinian friar and printed about 1510. I have not seen this play but take my information about it, as well as the quotation, from Raymond Lebègue, *La Tragédie religieuse en France: les debuts (1514–1573)*, (Paris, 1929), p. 121.

16. *Ioan. Ravisii Textoris Nivernen Dialogi aliquot festivissimi* (London, 1581), fol. Cc 5ᵛ. The dialogues of Textor, written for his pupils at the Collège de Navarre, were well known in England; they were performed in Latin at the universities and in translations and adaptations elsewhere. Some of them were translated by Thomas Heywood as late as 1637 (*Pleasant Dialogues and Dramas, Selected out of Lucian, Erasmus, Textor, Ovid. & c.*).

The House of David 9

the examples of the Triumph of Love in Petrarch's *Trionfi* (together with such figures as Alexander the Great, Pyramus and Thisbe, and Hero and Leander), and of adultery ("true," historical, adultery as against the fictitious sins of classical myth) in Brant's *Narrenschiff*.[17]

To the less sophisticated members of the audience the image of David as the adulterous sinner would come from more familiar sources, fictional and homiletic. In a "pleasant fable" George Gascoigne showed how insidiously a would-be adulterer could use the example of David to argue his case; [18] and Vives, in his *Instruction of a Christen Woman*, used David as a warning example in his chapter "Of Loving." [19] In 1589 Henry Holland published a moral treatise called *Dauids Faith and Repentance*, in which is described how David saw Bathsheba washing herself,

whereby his filthie lustes became so vehement, and kindled in him such a fire, that he could not, as in his former assaults, call for the presence of Gods spirit.[20]

Although the play entered on the Stationers' Register in 1561 as "an new interlude of the ii synnes of kynge David" is not extant, one can well imagine what it must have contained, especially as John Bale, in his *Tragedy or enterlude manyfestyng the chefe promyses of God unto men*, had shown the Lord rebuking David:

> Of late dayes thou hast, mysused Bersabe,
> The wyfe of Vrye, and slayne hym in the fyelde.[21]

But, as in Bale, David was not only the representative sinner but also the archpenitent. In his poem to the queen, "Of King Dauid," Harington stresses this side of the moral image:

17. See *The Tryumphes of Fraunces Petrarcke, translated out of Italian into English by Henrye Parker knyght, Lorde Morley* (1565?), fol. D 1ᵛ; and *Narrenschiff* (Augsburg, 1498), fol. C 4ᵛ.

18. See *The Whole Woorkes of George Gascoigne* (London, 1587), pp. 195–196.

19. *A very Frutefull and Pleasant boke callyd the Instruction of a Christen woman* (London, 1541), fol. N 4ᵛ.

20. Henry Holland, *Dauids Faith and Repentance* (London, 1589), fol. C 3ʳ.

21. *A Tragedye or enterlude . . . manyfestyng the chefe promyses of God vnto man by all ages . . . Compyled by Iohan Bale. Anno Domini 1538*, fol. D 1ʳ.

Thou, thou great Prince, with so rare gifts replenished
Could'st not eschew blind Buzzard *Cupids* hookes,
Lapt in the bayt of Bersabees sweet lookes:
With which one fault, thy faultles life was blemished.
Yet hence we learne a document most ample,
That faln by fraillty we may rise by fayth,
And that the sinne forgiuen, the penance staieth.[22]

Nathan's fable, as the Lord's method of rousing David's conscience, had attracted many; and both Harington and Sidney had seen in it the best mousetrap of all for catching the conscience of the king, and accordingly used it as a proof of the moral justification of fiction:

the applycation most diuinelye true, but the discourse it selfe fayned; which made *Dauid* (I speake of the second and instrumentall cause) as in a glasse to see his own filthines, as that heauenlye Psalme of mercie wel testifieth.[23]

As Sidney's words also suggest, it was natural to see David as an example of penitence when there were the Penitential Psalms as a constant reminder. The "miserere mei" of the Fifty-first Psalm had indeed become a universalized cry of confession and repentance; yet one also knew that it was "A Psalm of David, when Nathan the prophet came unto him, after he had gone in to Bathsheba." Many translators of, and commentators on, the Psalms had analyzed David's sin and repentance at great length, but perhaps the greatest literary expression of the connection between the Penitential Psalms and the love of David and Bathsheba is Wyatt's version, where his own links between the individual psalms describe the background story and David's progress in penance.

Indicative of the association of the Penitential Psalms with the love story behind them is the fact that in the late Middle Ages—and in France well into the Renaissance—a picture of Bathsheba bathing and David "above viewing her" would often be used in illustrating Books of Hours, as an

22. *The Letters and Epigrams of Sir John Harington,* ed. N. E. McClure (Philadelphia and London, 1930), pp. 223–224. The epigram "Of King Dauid. Written to the Queene" is in both the 1600 and the 1603 MSS.

23. Sidney, *An Apologie for Poetrie,* in *Elizabethan Critical Essays,* ed. G. Gregory Smith (London, 1904), I, 174.—Cf. Harington's *Briefe Apologie of Poetrie* (1591), in which Nathan's parable is used to defend the poet's right to "lie" (*Elizabethan Critical Essays,* II, 205).

The House of David   II

introduction or frontispiece to the Penitential Psalms.[24] Here we are approaching the other form of response to the David and Bathsheba story —the delight in the sensuous beauty and sensual pleasure inherent in the scene as a human situation—for frequently the *Horae* illustrators seem to have taken more interest in the long, golden hair and other bodily charms of Bathsheba than in her representativeness as a vehicle of sin. In a typical Book of Hours, written in France in the early sixteenth century, we see David in contemplation of the carefully executed foreground figure of Bathsheba; she is standing in an ornate golden fountain, her equally golden hair falling over her shoulders, and with an arrow fired by a blind cupid heading straight for her breast (Figure 1). Bathsheba's bathing scene, we can see, was a natural meeting ground for Christian and pagan imagery. As Elizabeth Kunoth-Leifels has shown in her study of the David and Bathsheba motif in pictorial art, this motif—like its parallel, Susanna and the Elders—tended in the Renaissance to fuse with classical motifs, especially that of Venus and Adonis, into an image of earthly beauty.[25] The same tendency is obvious in verbal representations of the story: David appears torn between the Lord and Cupid, and Bathsheba's beauties are carefully catalogued. An English example of this is Francis Sabie's somewhat pedestrian epyllion, *Dauid and Beersheba* (1596), in which the poet, after entertaining us with Bathsheba's striptease act, cries out:

> O shut thine eies *Narcissus* come not neere,
> Least in the well a burning fire appeare.[26]

French poets were less restrained. In Remy Belleau's short epic, *Les Amours de David et de Bersabee* (1572), the emphasis is on the love story

24. Cf. Louis Réau, *Iconographie de l'art chrétien* (Paris, 1956), II, 273 ff. I have also found much valuable information on this subject in M. R. James, *The Illustration of the Old Testament in Early Times* (The Sanders Lectures for 1924; typewritten copy in the British Museum, pressmarked 03149.i.18).—In early printed books, a woodcut of the bathing scene was also extremely common. See Edward Hodnett, *English Woodcuts, 1480–1535* (London, 1935).

25. Elisabeth Kunoth-Leifels, *Über die Darstellungen der "Bathseba im Bade": Studien zur Geschichte des Bildthemas 4. bis 17. Jahrhundert* (Essen, 1962).—Cf. also Réau, *Iconographie*.

26. *Adams Complaint. The Olde Worldes Tragedie. Dauid and Bathsheba* (London, 1596), fol. F 1ʳ.

(for all that the poem ends with David's repentance) and above all on the bathing scene. The poet revels in Bathsheba's charms, and his lengthy catalogue of them becomes increasingly detailed and warmly sensual as he proceeds.[27] In Du Bartas, Bathsheba turns into an image of Venus:

> Elle oingt ses cheveux d'or: qu'elle plonge tantost
> De son corps bien formé l'albastre sous le flot,
> Telle qu'un lis qui tombe au creux d'une phiole,
> Telle qu'on peint Venus quand, lascivement molle,
> Elle naist dans la mer, et qu'avecques les thons
> Jà le feu de ses yeux embraze les Tritons.[28]

The same happens in the 1601 edition of Antoine de Montchrestien's play, *David ou l'adultère,* where David describes how he saw Bathsheba—

> . . . telle comme on dit qu'vne belle Déesse
> Poussa des flots feconds le thresor de sa tresse,
> Quand sur vne coquille à Cithere elle vint,
> Seiour plaisant & beau que depuis elle tint—

but a sense of decorum has made him remove these lines from the 1604 edition of the play.[29] Peele here shows more decorum than his French contemporaries, for, though his bathing scene is steeped in beauty, his imagery is taken from the Bible and especially from the Song of Songs, rather than from classical myth:

27. See *La Bergerie de R. Belleau* (Paris, 1572), p. 103.
28. *The Works of Guillaume De Salluste Sieur Du Bartas,* ed. Holmes, Lyons, and Linker (Chapel Hill, 1940), III, 363 (*Les Trophées,* ll. 907 ff.).—Cf. the delight with which Sylvester, translating Du Bartas, elaborates on this description: "[Bathseba] Perfumes, and combes, and curls her golden hair; / Another-while vnder the Crystall brinks, / Her Alabastrine well-shap't Limbs she shrinks / Like to a Lilly sunk into a glasse: / Like soft loose *Venus* (as they paint the Lasse) / Born in the Seas, when with her eyes sweet-flames, / Tonnies and *Tritons* she at-once inflames." (Quoted from the 1613 ed. of Sylvester's translation, *Du Bartas His Deuine Weekes and Workes,* p. 542.)
29. I quote from *Les Tragedies d'Ant. de Montchrestien* (Rouen, 1601), fol. Q 2ᵛ. In the 1604 ed. (also Rouen), described on the title page as "edition nouvelle augmentée par l'auteur," the play has lost its subtitle and become just *David.*

The House of David   13

Fairer then Isacs louer at the well,
Brighter then inside barke of new hewen Cædar,
Sweeter then flames of fine perfumed myrrhe.

(ll. 81–83)

I have already tried to show elsewhere [30] how much the opening scene of
David and Bethsabe is in the tradition of Ovidian sensual poetry of the
fifteen-nineties. No doubt the boy acting Bathsheba would have had to be
dressed rather the way Bathsheba is in those Dutch sixteenth-century
pictures where she is depicted as modestly washing her feet, her skirt
pulled up to barely reveal her knees; [31] but Peele's poetry provides all the
erotic atmosphere that later Rubens, for example, was to give to the scene.
It may not be altogether fanciful to suggest that the play on sense
impressions in Bathsheba's song—

Hot sunne, coole fire, temperd with sweet aire,
Black shade, fair nurse, shadow my white haire
Shine sun, burne fire, breath aire, and ease mee,
Black shade, fair nurse, shroud me and please me—

stems from the same impulse as that which introduced into paintings of
the scene either a colored handmaiden or a black messenger boy, to set off
the white-skinned and blonde-haired beauty of the bathing figure. There is
no moral condemnation within Peele's scene; it would be "placed" only by
the audience's awareness of its traditional moral implications. When David
says of Bathsheba,

Faire Eua, plac'd in perfect happinesse,

. . . .

30. I-S. Ekeblad, "The Love of King David and Fair Bethsabe," *English Studies,*
XXXIX (1958), 57–62.

31. See, for example, Hans Bol's "The Handing of the Message to Bathseba" in
the Amsterdam Rijksmuseum (1568); the same painter's drawing, under the same
title, in the H. Reitlinger Collection, London; and Maerten van Heemskerck's
"The Handing of the Message to Bathseba." All these are reproduced among the
excellent illustrations to Elisabeth Kunoth-Leifels' study (see her figs. 41–43). For
a colored messenger, see the Rubens painting, Dresden Gemäldegalerie, and for a
colored handmaiden, see Cornelisz van Haarlem, "Bathseba Bathing" (1594),
Amsterdam Rijksmuseum (Kunoth-Leifels, figs. 50 and 48).

14   INGA-STINA EWBANK

> Wrought not more pleasure to her husbands thoughts,
> Then this faire womans words and notes to mine,
>
> (ll. 57–61)

there is none of that irony in the image, placing the situation and anticipating its unhappy issue, which Marlowe uses so frequently—as when the Jew of Malta in Act I tells us that he holds his daughter as dear "As Agamemnon did his Iphigen." Like the illustrators of the Penitential Psalms, Peele is having his cake and eating it too: for, after using the first scene to celebrate the beauties of the flesh and the senses, he moves on to a strictly moral structure for the rest of the scenes dealing with the love story. Uriah is called home, and in a tragicomic scene (ll. 500–571) is made, ironically enough, to drink the health of "David's children"; and this is immediately followed by a chorus which underlines the sin of David—

> O prowd reuolt of a presumptious man,
> Laying his bridle in the necke of sin—

and goes on to point the general moral:

> If holy Dauid so shoke hands with sinne,
> What shall our baser spirits glorie in.
>
> (ll. 572–588)

The death of Uriah and the birth of the child, whether or not they had been enacted in an earlier version of the play, are summarized in the same chorus, leaving room for a scene of ritualistic lamentation of the sick child as a symbol of sin—

> The babe is sicke, and sad is Dauids heart,
> To see the guiltlesse beare the guilties paine;
>
> (ll. 625–626)

for Nathan's parable, which is taken almost verbatim from the Bible; and for David's penitence, with its echoes of the Psalms. Rapidly the rhythm of this scene brings David from penitence to purgation; as the child dies, retribution has been meted out, and David becomes the forgiven sinner:

The House of David 15

Let Dauids Harpe and Lute, his hand and voice,
Giue laud to him that loueth Israel,
And sing his praise, that shendeth Dauids fame,
That put away his sinne from out his sight.

(ll. 727–730)

The stage symbol of that forgiveness is the traditional *"Musike, and a banquet"*; its spiritual symbol is the conception of another son—

. . . decke faire Bersabe with ornaments,
That she may beare to me another sonne,
That may be loued of the Lord of hosts.

(ll. 735–737)

And so, by his treatment of the subject, Peele ultimately turns the love of King David and Fair Bathsheba into a kind of divine comedy.

We can find a very similar pattern in Hans Sachs's play on the same subject. His *Comedia: Der Dauid mit Batseba im Ehbruch* (written some time before 1561) follows the rhythm of sin, forgiveness, and ultimate triumph: he takes us from the adultery, via the death of Uriah, Nathan's fable, and the death of the child, to the birth of a second son, Solomon,

Herr König / Bathsheba ausserkorn
Hat dir ein andern Sohn geborn
Dich wider mit zu trösten thon.

(fol. 89ᵛ) [32]

Sachs treats the story with the same concreteness as in his *Fastnachtsspiele* he treated secular material—"dry brevity" is Creizenach's description of his style [33]—and so the total effect is much like that of a medieval mystery. There is none of the nymph-in-fountain atmosphere round Bathsheba's ablutions; they have the same style of domestic realism as in the second *Horae* illustration reproduced here (Figure 2):

32. *Das dritt vnd letzt Buch sehr Herrliche Schöne Tragedi / Komedi vnd schimpf Spil / Geistlich vnd Weltlich* (Nuremberg, 1561), I.

33. Wilhelm Creizenach, *Geschichte des Neueren Dramas* (Halle, 1903), III, 428.

16   I N G A - S T I N A   E W B A N K

> Nun so hab ich gewaschen mich
> Von meinem schweiss / nun so will ich
> Mein hauss beschliessen.

(fol. 85ʳ)

As always in Sachs's plays, all moralizing is kept away from the characters'
speeches; it is left for the end, where the Epilogue warns against adultery
but, above all, stresses that man must not despair, however great a sinner,
but must trust to God's forgiveness. For, God

> . . . durchs heilig Evangelion
> Zeigt vergebung der sünden an
> Der Sünder wider thut begnaden
> Und wendet im ewigen schaden
> Dass auss verzweiflung im nit wachs
> Der ewig todt / das wünscht H. Sachs.

(fol. 90ʳ)

The same material that was shaped by Sachs into a homiletic *comedia*
was used, some forty years later, by Antoine de Montchrestien, writing in
quite a different dramatic tradition,[34] for his neo-Senecan tragedy, *David
ou l'adultère*.[35] His is also a play about sin and punishment, but with the
stress on the sin and only a final gesture toward contrition in David.
Where Sachs's five-act structure served him mainly to chop up the action
into equal parts, Montchrestien's follows a formal pattern of exposition,
development, and catastrophe. Act I, as we have already seen, is one long
monologue by David, relating how he saw Bathsheba bathing, lusted for
her, and satisfied his lust; at the end the news of her pregnancy is brought,
and Uriah is sent for. Act II is virtually given over to Uriah, who returns
with shrewd suspicions of what is going on; in Act III David debates with
Nadab whether he should send Uriah to his death, and Uriah himself has a

34. A recent and valuable study of that tradition is *Les Tragédies de Sénèque
et le théâtre de la Renaissance,* ed. Jean Jacquot (Paris, 1964). I am also indebted—
apart from the studies of sixteenth-century French drama already cited—to H. C.
Lancaster, *A History of French Dramatic Literature in the Seventeenth Century*
(Baltimore, 1929) and Kosta Loukovitch, *L'Évolution de la tragédie religieuse
classique en France* (Paris, 1933).

35. Cf. n. 29, above. In what follows, I quote from de Julleville's edition of
Montchrestien (cf. n. 2, above).

The House of David 17

long speech in which he is shown as noble and loyal, as against the tyrannous king. In Act IV a messenger, in an elaborate account, relates the siege of Rabbah and Uriah's death. Act V opens with Bathsheba's lament over the death of Uriah and the sin of David, who "s'est montré trop homme et trop absolu Roy"; and David exhibits his hubris in sentences of extreme balance:

> On te rauit Vrie, et David t'est rendu;
> Tu gagnes beaucoup plus que tu n'auois perdu:
> Le Ciel t'oste vn soldat, vn Monarque il te donne.
>
> (p. 229)

But now the peripeteia occurs, as Nathan comes in and by his parable catches the conscience of David. The act and play end with Nathan's speech of absolution. A large proportion of the lines in each act is spoken by the chorus, which is significantly unspecified in nature and whose function is to provide lyrical-moralizing comments at the end of acts (or, in Act V, before the peripeteia). The subjects on which it meditates form, in order, a paradigm of the action. The chorus of Act I is on how *amor vincit omnia;* of Act II, on the sacredness of marriage; of Act III, on the terrible power of a tyrannical ruler; of Act IV, on the transitoriness of life; and of Act V, on how crimes will out and remorse will await the sinner.

As this will have indicated, in *David* the scriptural story has become purely a vehicle of moral generalizations. Nothing happens; all is said. Rhetoric is used to build the characters up into theoretically heroic positions. David in the first act, honor and love at war within him, has a lengthy, patterned sequence of lines, each starting "Suis-je ce grand Dauid qui . . . ?" which sets up the traditional figure of the Herculean hero conquered by love, and indeed the chorus comes in with the Hercules parallel:

> Hercvle auoit vaincu les monstres de la terre;
> Tout ce qui luy fist teste il le peut surmonter:
> Mais s'il fut indomptable au milieu de la guerre,
> Au milieu de la paix vn œil le sçeut donter.
> Amour n'est qu'vn enfant, mais sa puissance est grande.
> C'est vn aueugle Archer, mais il vise fort bien:
> C'est le plus grand des Rois puis qu'aux Rois il commande
> Et que de son seruage il ne s'exempte rien.
>
> (p. 207)

This is very much like the hubris of the David figure in one of Textor's dialogues, where David proudly declares his greatness and his scorn of any but divine love—

> Inter fatidicos prima est mihi gloria vates,
> Et mea prospiciunt praesagi verba prophetae,
> Ille ego sum David, tortae qui verbere fundae
> Magna Philistiae percussi membra gigantis.[36]

But there, too, Cupid shoots his arrow, and painfully David realizes, in the concluding words of the dialogue, that *Omnia vincit amor*. There is only one step from this image to the use of David in a *de casibus* tragedy; and thus we find him in Anthony Munday's *Mirrour of Mutabilitie* (1579), where he appears as a representative of the fall from high place through "Lecherye," warning the reader:

> You Princes great that rule in regall state,
> Beholde how I did blindly run astray:
> And brought my self unto destructions gate,
> But that my God redeemd me thence away.[37]

But Montchrestien does not seem to feel that the Fall of Princes is in itself a tragic enough subject, or that David is a satisfactory tragic hero, and so he places Uriah at the center of the tragic structure. He, even more than David, is allowed to build himself up to heroic stature:

> Mon cœur est grand et haut, mon ame ardente et pronte,
> Sensible au vitupere encor' plus qu'aux douleurs.

(p. 218)

The play, then, works as a kind of debate on the nature of heroism and of kingship, epitomized in the interchanges of David and Uriah and in the stichomythia between Nadab and David in Act III. Montchrestien did not want merely to teach a moral lesson. The biblical story would have appealed to him, too, because it was rich in situations of a potentially

---

36. *Dialogi* (cf. n. 16, above), fol. Bb 5ᵛ.

37. *The Mirrour of Mutabilitie, or the Principall Part of the Mirrour for Magistrates* (1579), fol. C 2ᵛ.

The House of David 19

antithetical kind—love versus honor in David, loyal soldier versus tyrannical ruler in Uriah's opposition to David, moral conscience versus exultant
sinner in Nathan versus David.[38] The play becomes a pattern of antithetical positions, fine stuff for rhetorical monologues, sharp stichomythia, and
choral meditations, but dramatically and spiritually stillborn.

What, in fact, we may see by comparing Montchrestien with Sachs, and
with Peele, is something of the inherent weakness of a narrowly academic
scriptural Seneca. The Senecan form was devised to accommodate the
internal struggles of heroic minds, the stichomythic debates where such
minds defined themselves more clearly, the violent physical actions which
issued from them, and the remorse, torment, and punishment which
followed. To achieve this out of the simple chronicle material of 2 Samuel
would mean an inflation of figures, motives, and situations only possible if
they were given a psychological depth which Montchrestien cannot master.
(Later we shall see how another neo-Senecan, Honerdius, achieves this.)

What Montchrestien has also lost, because of his formal concentration on
the single event, is the larger moral pattern which is implicit in the Bible
and which is Peele's guiding idea: the effects of David's sin on his House.
Seneca's is a drama of great individuals whose own tormented natures
matter more than any hereditary curse over their House; and Montchrestien, as indeed his chosen structure forces him to do, treats David in
isolation from his House. The play ends with Nathan's prophecy that the
child of David and Bathsheba will die—thus not only before the first
tangible occurrence of retribution but also well before the redemptory birth
of Solomon which forms the "comic" conclusion of Sachs's play.

Montchrestien is here outside the main stream of sixteenth-century
thought about David, for one of the fascinations his story held for the
contemporary mind seems to have been its more extended moral perspective: the sin of the father being visited on the children and hence revisited
onto the father himself. To some, David seemed the ideal hero of a moral
tragedy; while on the one hand he was "a most mightie King, and . . . a

---

38. It is interesting to note that all the plays in Montchrestien's 1601 collection
have exemplary subtitles—such as *Aman, ou la vanité* or *Les Lacénes, ou la
constance*—but that in the 1604 ed. these have been removed: perhaps an indication
that he did not want to think of himself as writing in a plainly homiletic vein. The
sensuous delight with which he elaborates the bathing scene in *David, ou l'adultère*
rather obscures the moralistic purpose.

most holie Prophet," the fortunes of his House, on the other hand, formed
an unequaled "monument . . . of so many and heinous crimes proceeding
out of one fact." [39] The connection between David's adultery, Amnon's
rape of his sister Tamar, Absalom's murder of Amnon, and finally
Absalom's rebellion and usurpation of the throne was used from the pulpit
as a stock example of the subtle way in which the Lord arranges his
retribution:

Even as he had dishonoured another mans childe / so sawe he shame upon his
owne children while he lyved / and that with greate wrechednesse. For Amnon
defloured Thamar his awne naturall sister. And they both were Dauids children
/ yet Absalom did miserably slaye Amnon his brother / for comytting that
wickednesse with his syster Thamar. Not long after / dyd the same Absalom
dryve his own naturall father Dauid out of his realme / & shamefully lay with
his fathers wifes. Whereupon there followed an horryble greate slaughter / in
the whych Absalom was slayne with many thousands mo of the comen people.[40]

Peele's structure shows that this connection between David's sins and the
sexual disorders within his House, as well as civil strife within his realm,
was his organizing principle. In the Bible the rape of Tamar is subsequent
to the whole David and Bathsheba story, whereas in Peele's play it is fitted
in between David's adultery and the Lord's judgment, so that the thematic
link is implicit. It is also made explicit by David's reaction to the rape:

> Sin with his seuenfold crowne and purple robe,
> Begins his triumphs in my guiltie throne.
>
> (ll. 402–403)

Again with a modification of scriptural chronology, the news that Absalom has murdered Amnon is brought to David just after the capture of
Rabbah. This scene of victory is lamented by Sampley as a "digression," [41]

39. *The Psalmes of Dauid . . . set forth in Latine by that excellent learned man
Theodore Beza. And faithfully translated into English, by Anthonie Gilbie* (London,
1581), p. 112.

40. Heinrich Bullinger, *The Christen State of Matrimonye*, trans. Myles Coverdale
(London, 1541), fol. 3ʳ⁻ᵛ.—Cf. the same Bullinger's *Fiftie Godlie and Learned
Sermons*, trans. "H. I." (London, 1587), p. 233, where the same point is made.

41. Arthur M. Sampley, "Plot Structure in Peele's Plays as a Test of Authorship,"
PMLA, LI (1936), 698.

and so it is from the "well-made" point of view; but it seems to me obvious
that Peele has here built up as effective a reversal—in visual and theatrical
as well as moral terms—as possible. David, having taken Rabbah (at whose
siege, we remember, Uriah was slain) and crowned himself with Hanun's
crown, is at the height of his power and glory—

> Beauteous and bright is he among the Tribes,
> As when the sunne attir'd in glist'ring robe,
> Comes dauncing from his orientall gate,
> And bridegroome-like hurles through the gloomy aire—
>
> (ll. 863–866)

when suddenly the glories of this Sun King are dashed by the message
that all his sons are dead. (A special poignancy is given here to that piece
of misreporting.) Similar reversals, theatrical and moral, form a leading
pattern in that part of the play which deals with Absalom's rebellion; and
I shall deal with these later on.

For the moment we must turn to the story of Tamar, Amnon, and
Absalom. Peele treats it concisely, with only two elaborations on the Bible
account. The first is Jonadab's speech while the rape is being committed. It
is out of character (as he had been the one to counsel Amnon to enjoy his
sister) and entirely choric; it aims not only to raise sympathy for Tamar—

> Now Thamar ripened are the holy fruits
> That grew on plants of thy virginitie,
> And rotten is thy name in Israel,
> Poore Thamar, little did thy louely hands
> Foretell an action of such violence,
> As to contend with Ammons lusty armes,
> Sinnewd with vigor of his kindlesse loue—
>
> (ll. 303–309)

but also, by implication, to relate Amnon's sexual crime to David's:

> Why should a Prince, whose power may command,
> Obey the rebell passions of his loue,
> When they contend but gainst his conscience,
> And may be gouernd or supprest by will.
>
> (ll. 296–299)

The second is Tamar's *Klagerede* after the rape, when she sees herself

> Cast as was Eua from that glorious soile
> (Where al delights sat bating wingd with thoughts,
> Ready to nestle in her naked breasts)
> To bare and barraine vales with floods made wast,
> To desart woods, and hils with lightening scorcht,
> With death, with shame, with hell, with horrour sit.
>
> (ll. 337–342)

The poetry here performs the function of realizing the emotional and moral state of a fall; and by the inversion of the Eden imagery from the bathing scene, the link with David's sin—as well as the sense that we are dealing with *all* sin—is kept.

Traditionally Amnon's rape was an *exemplum horrendum,* sometimes illustrating the Fall of Princes through lust,[42] sometimes a standard example of incest.[43] Peele, in concentrating on the plight of Tamar, shows more imagination. Dramatically his approach is a great deal more fruitful than that of Hans Sachs in his *Tragedia: Thamar die Tochter König Dauid mit irem Bruder Ammon vnd Absalom* (1556).[44] Sachs, too, connects the action with the David and Bathsheba story by giving David an opening speech about his guilt; and, as in Peele's play, the arrival of the news of the murder brings an ironic reversal into a scene where David muses on the happy and peaceful state of his kingdom. But his action leads up to an Epilogue which interprets the story typologically: David stands for God, who has two children; one—Tamar—is "die Christlich seel," the other—Amnon—is Satan. Absalom is God's vehicle of both retribution and consolation. The play is interesting to us chiefly, I think, as an indication that as late as 1556 a playwright could still ask his audience to keep together such (to us) disparate attitudes to a character as a cautionary and a typological one: David is, on the one hand, a human sinner and, on the other, a figure of God.

The story of David's children was obviously a subject which invited a

---

42. Munday, *Mirrour of Mutabilitie,* fol. I 3ᵛ.

43. Vives, *Instruction of a Christen Woman,* fol. M 1ᵛ.

44. *Das dritt vnd letzt Buch* . . . (1561; though the *Thamar* is dated, at the end, 1556), I, fol. 90ᵛ ff.

The House of David   23

Senecan treatment of passion, incest, revenge, and fratricide, while at the same time it had a built-in opportunity for combining "tragicos cum pietate modos." [45] In three plays first published within a few years of each other, it was thus used. N. Chrestien des Croix wrote in French a tragedy, *Amnon et Thamar* (Rouen, 1608); and from the Low Countries there are two neo-Latin tragedies on the subject: *Thamara* (Leyden, 1611) by Rochus Honerdius (Roch van den Honert, *c.* 1572–1638), and *Amnon* (Ghent, 1617), by Jacobus Cornelius Lummenaeus à Marca (Jaques-Corneille van Lummene van Marcke, 1570–1629). [46] A detailed analysis of all these plays is out of the question here; all I want to show is how a comparison of structure and thematic emphasis in the three plays may bring out the different ways in which the same subject could be treated in what is, to a large extent, the same dramatic tradition. All three plays are neo-Senecan. They use a five-act structure with a chorus kept apart as commentator, a fairly unified action, and a relatively small number of characters. All are rhetorical rather than theatrical. In all, Amnon is given much scope to speak about the torments of his passion, Tamar to lament the outrage done to her, and Absalom to deliberate his revenge.

What initially distinguishes Chrestien's play from the two neo-Latin ones is that, while they put David at the moral center, Chrestien is writing a drama balanced between the two immoral individuals, Amnon and Absalom. David appears at the beginning of *Amnon et Thamar,* and is referred to throughout, as the godlike standard from which his two sons are aberrations. The pattern of concentration on villainy needs an ideal governor as a foil. Amnon wants his sister, Absalom wants the crown, to which Amnon is immediate heir; Amnon's rape gives Absalom the chance to combine moral revenge with the pursuit of political ambition:

> Dieu m'ouvre le moyen, & sans nul vitupere,
> De me deffaire en fin de ce pariure frere:

45. See the epigram by Hugo Grotius, in commendation of Honerdius' *Thamara* (Leyden, 1611), no page ref. Cf. n. 4, above.

46. In discussing these three plays, I use, and quote from, the following editions: *Les Tragedies de N. Chretien, Sieur des Croix Argentenois* (Rouen, 1608); *Rochi Honerdii . . . Supremi in Hollandia Consistori Senatoris, Thamara Tragoedia* (Leyden, 1611); *Amnon Tragoedia Sacra. Autore Rdo. Domino D. Iacobo Cornelio Lvmmenaeo à Marca* (Ghent, 1617).

Frere mon premier né, & qui doit deuant moy
Succeder à l'Estat de Dauid nostre Roy.

(p. 87)

Chrestien, then, has built out of the Bible story at least the beginnings of an
intrigue play; the plot has some complexity, and motives and actions are
neatly intertwined. Both Amnon and Absalom are Senecan heroes, con-
templating with fascinated horror the deeds they are about to perpetrate.
Amnon can no longer be interesting after the rape, so he is dropped—only
to be brought on for a brisk on-stage murder in Act V—and Absalom
comes to the fore in the second half of the play. All of Acts I and II are
taken up with Amnon's struggles with his "Meurtriere Passion,"

Qui condamne mon ame, & destruit mon honneur;

and in Act III he even reads his confidant a love poem he has written about
Tamar.[47] In Act I, with a slight reminiscence of morality technique, he has
a dream where an angel and a "Megere" appear to him, respectively to
persuade him to sin and dissuade him from it. This parallelism of
contrasted counsel is made a structural principle for the whole play, which
is exceedingly symmetrically built up. Amnon has a good counselor—Ithai
—with whom he debates in Act I the problems of love versus honor, good
versus evil; he also has a bad counselor—Jonadab—with whom there is
much stichomythic debating in Act III on the subjects of suicide and
freedom of the will. Parallel to these deliberations are Absalom's two sets
of stichomythia in Act II, with one good and one evil counselor. The
dialogue between Absalom and Hushai becomes a debate on how to
govern a state, with Absalom as the rebel and revolutionary and Hushai as
the conservative speaker for king and country. In pointed contrast it is
followed by the dialogue between Absalom and Ahitophel:

ABSALON
Mon Pere vit encor, & Amnon qui me passe.
ARCHITOPHEL
Il faut trouver moyen que ce frere trespasse.
ABSALON
Comment, tüer mon frere! ô forfait inhumain!

47. These "stances" use the image of Tamar as the sun and Amnon himself as an
Icarus figure. Cf. the much more relevant use of this image in Peele's Prologue.

The House of David   25

ARCHITOPHEL
Qui veut libre s'esbatre, oste le cruel frein.
ABSALON
Mais cest ébat, de Dieu le courroux nous attire.
ARCHITOPHEL
Ne desire donc point d'acquerir vn Empire.
ABSALON
Pourquoy, s'il est permis?
ARCHITOPHEL
Tu n'en as point de tel.
ABSALON
Mon Pere peut mourir, Amnon n'est immortel?
ARCHITOPHEL
La vie de ton frere est ta mort bien certaine.

(pp. 42–43)

This symmetry of contrasts is observed on the plane of sexual morality too. The first part of Act II presents Tamar as extremely pious, full of "l'amour vers Dieu" and ironically praying for her brothers' welfare, thus establishing a contrast with the ungodly passions of Amnon and also making the outrage on her more heinous; and we are also given a discussion between her and her women in which she appears as the mirror of chastity. The theme is taken up at the end of the act by the chorus of "Filles Iuifues," who sing the praises of chastity. Again, after the rape, there is a debate between her and her women about whether the violation of the body can also sully the spirit.

Altogether, then, *Amnon et Thamar* shows us a playwright interested in the Bible as Senecan raw material and (rather like Montchrestien) in this particular story for its possibilities as a scaffold for antithetical arguments. It brings home to one the weaknesses of the post-Garnier Senecan tradition in France: A subject that could have lent itself to the psychological and moral tensions of a *Phèdre*, or the examinations of divine justice of an *Athalie*, never rises in its execution above a chess play of moral axioms and rhetorical posturing. Chrestien's chosen scope does not allow him to show justice done on Absalom and his rebellious ambitions; the play ends as David has reconciled himself to the death of Amnon. Thus it remains morally lopsided.

If one sets side by side with *Amnon et Thamar* the *Amnon* of Lummenaeus à Marca, the difference in moral structure becomes imme-

diately apparent. Lummenaeus' scope is almost identical with Chrestien's:
He starts with Amnon lamenting his infatuation and ends with David's
reception of the news of Amnon's death at Absalom's hand. But his action
is firmly held in relation to David's own guilt. Act IV is largely one long
monologue of David's:

> Peccaui! & an diffitear? & crimen meum est,
> Quod fecit Amnon, publicum exemplum dedi,
> Et Bethsabea strauit incaesto viam;
>
> (p. 29)

and the chorus which follows takes up the same idea. There is little
theatrical interest in his structure. Everything happens offstage; the short
acts are made up either entirely of monologues (Acts I and III) or of a
combination of monologues and stichomythia; the choruses (by unidentified speakers) are very long and meditate upon the situation by
giving examples—biblical and classical—of parallel situations. As in
Montchrestien's *David,* each act is in fact a static tableau. But within the
limits of a closet drama the play provides a dramatic tension between
human and divine revenge, Absalom's and the Lord's, with David as the
pivotal figure.

   Also, Lummenaeus à Marca's stichomythia, unlike Chrestien's, grows
from the situation rather than from theoretical concepts, and thus manages
to communicate a human content. In the following exchange between
Tamar and Absalom, the repetition of the words "frater" and "soror" is not
just rhetorical patterning; it acquires a symbolical value as an index to the
horror of the situation as it has to be spoken out by a sister and slowly
dawn on a brother:

> ABSALOMUS
> Quid me occupas insaniis? rursum iacet.
> THAMARA
> Crudelis Amnon!
> ABSALOMUS
> Tetigit.
> THAMARA
>   Atrox, impie,
> Incæste, abominabilis semper mihi!
> Amnon! Iuuentæ carnifex turpis meæ!

The House of David   27

ABSALOMUS
Frater?

THAMARA
Tacere liceat.

ABSALOMUS
& rursum implicas.

THAMARA
Frater pudorem rapuit incæstus meum.

ABSALOMUS
Frater? Sorori Virgini?

THAMARA
Parce obsecro.

ABSALOMUS
Amnon Thamaræ noxiam? & potuit ferus,
Et potuit? Amnon Virgini stuprum intulit?
Amnon? Sorori Virgini? . . .

(p. 16)

This exchange is, too, an ironic echo of Amnon's words in Act I, while he still struggles with his passion:

O sancta probitas! Virginem vt stupro occupem?
Frater sororem?

(p. 8)

The repetition of the phrase "Absalom omnes tulit," when in Act V David has got the false news that Absalom has killed all his sons, has the same quality of expanding the Bible story not just into rhetoric but into fully realized human moments.

Honerdius, in *Thamara*, carries this psychological probing one step further—so that Leicester Bradner can, with some justification, speak of him as a forerunner of Racine.[48] With even less external action than Lummenaeus à Marca, he has concentrated on the tension inside his characters even more, humanizing them rather than merely making them vehicles of rhetoric. The difference in titles between the two plays is significant, and is reflected in the way identical material has been handled. In *Amnon* the rape takes place between Acts I and III—before Tamar has appeared on the stage—and the revenge is thus made the central element in

48. "Latin Drama of the Renaissance," *Studies in the Renaissance*, IV (1957), 42-43.

the action. In *Thamara* the rape is delayed till between Acts III and IV, and the action stops short of the retributive murder of Amnon. (The last speech is Absalom's vow to avenge the crime against "nobis, sorori, legibus, regi, deo.") The structure thus gives a different emphasis to the story: Amnon's act is one which he has fought hard against and which, when it comes, is seen as done on a girl who is innocent, tender, and sympathetic. Also, unlike the case in *Amnon,* David impresses his sense of sin on the reader *before* the crime has been committed. Act II consists of a six-and-a-half-page monologue in which he speaks of the expiation of his sin; ironically he fears a fate for Amnon similar to that of his firstborn child with Bathsheba:

> Et morte pueri credidi falso scelus
> Satis piatum. poena sic iuxta suum
> Nefas stetisset . . .

                                                            (p. 21)

The play's emphasis, then, is thrown on Tamar, in herself innocent, expiating David's sin. This, together with the central position of David in the play, confirms the didactic purpose which Honerdius states in his preface "Ad Lectorem":

Tota namque haec actio nihil aliud est quam implexa disciplina. Quid enim? . . . Thamarae injuria, parentum libidinem, liberorum contumelia plerumque expiari?

Honerdius was not a professional divine, and, as far as I am aware,[49] he wrote only one other play, and that also a neo-Latin biblical one, *Moses nomoclastes* (Leyden, 1611). I have not seen this tragedy, but the title suggests that he may have chosen the subject for its moral, rather than inherently exciting, nature. On the other hand, Lummenaeus à Marca, who was first a Capuchin and then a Benedictine monk, was a prolific writer, especially of scriptural plays; and in the collection of his works published as *Musae Lacrymantes* (Douai, 1628), we find not only the almost inevitable *Jephtha* but also plays on such topics as *Bustum Sodomae* and *Samson.* He seems to have had a good eye for a sensational biblical

---

49. I take my information on Honerdius from the *Biographie Universelle* (Paris, 1857), XIX, 387.

The House of David   29

subject. That, however, he combined this with an interest in moral themes can be seen from his *Dives Epulo*—one of his *Tragoedia Sacra* (Ghent, 1617)—in which, though presented in richly classical imagery, all the characters apart from Dives and Lazarus are personified abstractions: Voluptas, Desperatio, Poenitentia, and so on.

After Chrestien's *Amnon et Thamar*, the two neo-Latin plays from the Low Countries would seem to go some way toward justifying a Christian Seneca. The tight form makes for a solemn, almost ritualistic acting out of the doom on the House of David; moral emphasis grows out of the action itself and is, especially in the case of Honerdius, supported by psychological realization of the human problems involved.

In his lines "Ad Lectorem" Honerdius also speaks of Absalom's *ambitio* as another of David's punishments, and thereby he provides a link with the next, and last, group of plays I want to deal with—plays treating the rebellion of Absalom, his usurpation of David's throne, David's flight, and Absalom's death. (This is the story of 2 Samuel XIV–XIX.) Obviously these events contain much material that is naturally dramatic—from the hubris of Absalom to the pity and terror of David's lament over his son.

In Peele's play, as I have already said, it is made clear that Absalom's insurrection is part of a pattern of personal guilt and civil disorder evolving from David's adultery and his misuse of kingly power in having Uriah killed. The pattern is emphasized by the very abruptness—a structural flaw if we look at it from the viewpoint of the "well-made" play—with which we move from the scene where David forgives Absalom's fratricide (scene ix) to that which follows: *"Enter Dauid . . . with others, Dauid barefoot, with some lose couering ouer his head, and all mourning"* (S.D., ll. 1020–1022). It is one of the many sudden and morally effective reversals typical of the play. David's opening speech here is a confession of sins, in which the body politic and the individual conscience are fused into one image:

> And to inflict a plague on Dauids sinne,
> He makes his bowels traitors to his breast,
> Winding about his heart with mortall gripes.
>
> (ll. 1033–1035)

By the use of Gospel imagery, Absalom is seen as the type of an anti-Christ:

30   INGA-STINA EWBANK

> Ah Absalon the wrath of heauen inflames
> Thy scorched bosome with ambitious heat,
> And Sathan sets thee on a lustie tower,
> Shewing thy thoughts the pride of Israel
> Of choice to cast thee on her ruthlesse stones.
>
>   (ll. 1035–1040)

David's guilt, then, in all its aspects—personal, domestic, national, and moral-allegorical—is the thematic unifier which makes the Absalom scenes an essential part of Peele's play. It functions in the totality of the play somewhat as the usurpation of Henry IV functions in the three *Henry VI* plays.[50] As in Shakespeare's trilogy, the underlying moral-political cause may be lost sight of within the individual scenes, but it is brought up at key points and it forms the framework of the whole. Some of Peele's scenes, like Ithai's demonstration of faithfulness or the cursing of Shimei, are in themselves moral tableaux, but they are not "digressions." Shimei's cursing, in particular, is very effectively and cogently handled: Not only is Shimei himself made the voice of David's conscience (unlike the source passage in the Bible where he merely refers to vengeance for the blood of Saul)—

> Euen as thy sinne hath still importund heauen,
> So shall thy murthers and adulterie
> Be punisht in the sight of Israel,
> As thou deserust with bloud, with death, and hell—
>
>   (ll. 1363–1366)

but he also gives the king the opportunity of appearing as David Penitens—

> The sinnes of Dauid, printed in his browes,
> With bloud that blusheth for his conscience guilt—
>
>   (ll. 1374–1375)

and above all as the Christian figure of Patience. The various episodes of this part of the play are, in fact, devoted to bringing out David's patience, as a refusal to despair:

50. Cf. E. M. W. Tillyard, *Shakespeare's History Plays* (London, Penguin, 1962), p. 147.

The House of David   31

> I am not desperate Semei like thy selfe,
> But trust vnto the couenant of my God,
> Founded on mercie with repentance built,
> And finisht with the glorie of my soule.
>
> (ll. 1382–1385)

Most clearly the juxtaposition of despair with patience is brought out in the contrast, implied by the structure, between David and Ahitophel. In the Bible Ahitophel's suicide is dealt with very briefly:

And when Ahitophel saw that his counsel was not followed, he saddled his ass, and arose, and gat him home to his house, to his city, and put his household in order, and hanged himself, and died.

In Peele he is given a scene to himself (xiii), in which he makes a speech of nihilistic despair, leading up to the climax,

> And now thou hellish instrument of heauen,
> Once execute th'arrest of Ioues iust doome,
> And stop his breast that curseth Israel. *Exit.*
>
> (ll. 1502–1504)

The "hellish instrument of heaven" is explained by the stage direction: *"Achitophel solus with a halter."* The halter, the instrument of Judas' self-destruction, was well known as a symbol of despair, from pictorial representations and from dramatic as well as nondramatic literature.[51] As Ahitophel exits, he is like Despayre in *The Faerie Queene*, who, from a collection of murderous instruments,

> . . . chose an halter from among the rest,
> And with it hong himself, unbid, unblest.
>
> (Bk. I, canto ix)

Another moral contrast theatrically pointed throughout these scenes is that between Absalom's pride and David's humility. We move, for example, from David's laudable *apatheia*—

---

51. See S. C. Chew, "Time and Fortune," *ELH*, VI (1939), 83–113.

> Here lie I armed with an humble heart,
> T'imbrace the paines that anger shall impose,
> And kisse the sword my lord shall kill me with—
>
> (ll. 1114–1116)

to the next scene: *"Absalon, Amasa, Achitophel, with the concubines of Dauid, and others in great state, Absalon crowned"* (S.D., ll. 1160–1161); and it becomes obvious that even without Absalom's proud and self-infatuated speeches this would have struck the audience with the force of a visual emblem—just as the sight of Absalom hanging by his hair hardly needs Joab's words to point the irony of moral retribution:

> Rebell to nature, hate to heauen and earth,
>
> . . . .
>
> Now see the Lord hath tangled in a tree
> The health and glorie of thy stubborne heart,
> And made thy pride curbd with a sencelesse plant.
>
> (ll. 1579–1585)

Similar in many ways to the Absalom section of Peele's play is a *Tragedia Spirituale* by an Italian Franciscan friar, Pergiovanni Brunetto. *David Sconsolato* was first published in Florence in 1556 and appeared in several later editions.[52] In external shape it is a regular five-act tragedy, but its internal form is almost as episodic as the Bible story. Brunetto starts with Absalom's recall from banishment, expanding the scene of the widow from Tekoah; in Act II we see Absalom's growing rebelliousness; and only in Act III does the rebellion proper break out. Between David's flight from Jerusalem and his encounter with Shimei, the Bible has the episodes of Ittai, Zadok, Hushai, and Ziba. Out of these Peele has only included that

---

52. I have used, and quoted from, the 1586 edition. There were at least three separate editions: 1556 (though Rothschild, *Le Mistère du Viel Testament*, IV, lxxii, disputes its existence), 1586, and 1588; and the play was also published in Vol. III of *Raccolta di Rappresentazioni sacre* (Venice, 1605 and 1606). Despite the kind assistance of Professor Carlo Dionisotti, I have been able to find out very little about Brunetto. The title page of *David Sconsolato* describes him as "Frate di S. Francesco osseruante"; and Mazzuchelli, in *Scrittoria d'Italia*, II (1758 ed.), p. 2178, only adds that he flourished around the middle of the sixteenth century and wrote poetry in the vernacular. The bibliographical information above is also taken from Mazzuchelli, who lists no further works by Brunetto—whom, incidentally, he calls Brunetti.

The House of David   33

of Ittai, the Gittite. He combines the others into the ritualized lamentation scene, ll. 1050–1071, where he gets the effect of a crowd of faithful followers round David, by lyrical rather than narrative or dramatic means. Brunetto, however, in a series of short scenes in Act III, includes and expands all the biblical episodes. In some ways, then, his structure is closer than Peele's to that of the mystery type of religious drama. But Brunetto's unifying theme, like Peele's—and as his title indicates—is that of David's sin; and here he makes effective use of a popular Senecan device. *David Sconsolato* opens with a prologue spoken by "Ombra del Figliuolo adulterino di Dauid," who expounds the whole tragic context in an atmosphere that is as much Senecan as biblical:

> Da le dannate grotte vscit' à luce
> Men vengo à voi presente ombra infelice,
> Del figlio adulterin, del Gran Dauide;
> Grande per certo per valor', & forte,
> Temuto, & ammirato in ciascun' Clima:
> Ma s'à le gent'indomite preualse,
> Epost'ha'l freno à molte ampie prouincie;
> Vinto si diede pur al van diletto,
> De le brutte bellezze d'vna Donna,
> Ne pote ritener in vita il figlio
> Che egli contra'l mondo, e contra'l Cielo
> Acquistò bruttamente, e chi puo mai
> Il voler impedir del grande Dio?
>
> (no sig.)

He also dwells on the intermediary tragedy—

> Amnon Tamarre stupra sua sorella
> Et Absalon l'vccide per vendetta—

and predicts "La morte d'Absalon ch'ambizioso." And the curse on David's House, and its origin in the adultery, is harked back to throughout the play—notably by Bathsheba on her first appearance (I.iii).

Despite the Senecan opening, the play does not develop into a horror tragedy: Absalom's death is reported; Ahitophel—though, Timon-fashion, he gives us his epitaph—hangs himself offstage. It is, though, a strongly emotional play, with a great deal of human interest gained out of the many episodes. Unlike the more formal French tragedies we have looked at, this play, with its wealth of characters and incidents, does create a strong sense of context—House and city—for David. Contributing to this effect is the chorus "di donne Gierosolimitane," which is used not only to provide meditative odes (like the "O' miseri mortali" at the end of Act II) but also to take part in the conversation and the action. Brunetto shows how effective, in relation to this material, is the tendency of Italian humanist tragedians of the sixteenth century to combine Senecan and Grecian dramatic techniques.[53] His moral theme also forces him toward a tragedy of double issue rather than a plain unhappy ending, in that the outcome is a fall for Absalom (and Ahitophel) but is at the same time ultimately happy—that is purgative—for David and his House. In the end David himself takes the place of the chorus:

> Mal può letizia dar trafitto core
> Dicesi, & è ben vero,
> Spesso'n cibo soaue
> Mosca noiosa, & importuna cade,
> Dauid tropp'era liet'hor è beato,
> Al Regno ritornato,
> Se non moriua'l figlio,
> Ma così'n questo esiglio
> Il mal si purga, e illustrasi bontade.

Good has ultimately issued from evil, David disconsolate has become David consoled; and in Hans Sachs's terms the play would be a *Comedia*,[54] but like Peele's it remains formally the tragedy of Absalom. Yet its real nature is best indicated by the woodcut which, twice repeated, illustrates the play in the 1586 edition—one often used, too, to illustrate the Penitential Psalms in *Horae* (cf. Figure 2). It represents David kneeling in contrition, his crown laid humbly aside, with God's grace, symbolized by the sun, streaming down upon him. Brunetto could be used by either side in the debate about the possibility of a Christian tragedy.

53. Cf. Kastner and Charlton, *Works of Sir William Alexander*, pp. lxiii–xciv; and Herrick, *Tragicomedy*, pp. 93 ff.

54. Sachs himself did write a play on the Absalom story: *Ein Tragedi . . . der auffrhüriske Absalom mit seinem Vatter König David (Das ander Buch . . .* [Nuremberg, 1560], I, fol. xvii' ff.). This is an allegorical morality about good fathers and bad children, good kings and rebellious subjects. The play itself is dated 1551.

The House of David 35

Clearly the ambitious Absalom, rather than the contrite David, was the more stimulating figure to anyone wanting to pour this particular biblical story into a neoclassical mould. We see this exemplified in the Latin MS play *Absalon*, of unknown authorship and date.[55] Whether it is by Bishop Watson or not is immaterial here, though it seems to me that the careful metrical annotations on the autograph manuscript would fit in with an author "who to this day would never suffer yet his *Absalon* to go abroad, and that onelie because, in *locis paribus, Anapestus* is twise or thrise vsed in stede of *Iambus*."[56] Boas, who compares this play with Peele's, thinks that it "profits by comparison," for "in dexterous arrangement of material, in concentration of interest, and, above all, in psychological insight, *Absalon* is the work of an abler and more original playwright than Peele."[57] Boas' comparison, however, neglects the fact that Peele's whole intention and direction in this, the third, movement of his play were different from those of the classical scholar who penned *Absalon* into a neat five-act structure. Though the author of *Absalon* has not pressed his material into artificial conformity with the unities—like Brunetto he starts with Absalom's return from exile and ends with David's lament over Absalom's death—he has yet treated the Bible chronicle very selectively. According to the plan of a "well-made" play, he has subordinated the chosen events to an over-all study of rebellion and of the casting out of a tyrant. Absalom emerges as a typical Senecan tyrant figure; Ahitophel, as the bad counselor hoist with his own petard, who wittily rationalizes his particular form of suicide:

> Ergo nocentis vinculo vocis viam
> Obstingere est equū. scelus cōcepit hec,
> Periat eadem. solū placeat suspendiū.
>
> (fol. 24ᵛ)

55. There is a unique manuscript in the British Museum: MS Stowe 957. It is discussed most fully by G. R. Churchill and Wolfgang Keller, "Die lateinischen Universitäts-Dramen in der Zeit der Königin Elisabeth," *Shakespeare Jahrbuch*, XXXIV (1898), 229-232, and by Boas, *University Drama*, Appendix I.—Unfortunately, a recent critical edition and translation of the play came to my notice too late for me to use it for this essay: John Hazel Smith, *A Humanist's "Trew Imitation": Thomas Watson's "Absalon"* (Urbana, 1964).

56. Ascham, *Scholemaster*, in *Elizabethan Critical Essays*, I, 24.

57. *University Drama*, p. 365.

We need only compare this situation to Peele's Ahitophel and his morally emblematic halter to see that the author's dramatic conception (as indeed Boas points out) is pagan rather than Christian. Although David is at one point (II.ii) made to recognize that what is happening is part of a retributive pattern, the structure itself does not bear out such a pattern. Although David is consoled at the end, he is so because Absalom deserved death rather than because Absalom's death was part of the ways of God to David. The author of *Absalon,* then, has admirably fulfilled his plan of constructing a classical tragedy out of biblical material; what he has not achieved, because he had no intention of doing so, is the creation of a spiritual pattern where, as in both Peele and Brunetto, divine comedy emerges out of tragedy. That this is the final direction of Peele's play becomes obvious when we turn to the scene which neither of the other Absalom plays dramatizes: that involving the accession of Solomon (xvii). To Boas and most other Peele critics, Peele's introduction of Solomon is particularly obnoxious; it "mars the emotional effect of Absalom's tragic fate and diverts the interest at a culminating point." [58] I would argue that, rather, it *directs* the interest—once we know what the interest is—*to* a culminating point.

Once we are clear—and I hope the preceding discussion has made that point—that it is not "the emotional effect of Absalom's tragic fate" Peele is primarily after, but the working out of moral and civil disorder within the House of David, then it also becomes clear that Solomon at the end of *David and Bethsabe* has a function that can be compared, however cautiously, with Richmond's at the end of *Richard III* or even Fortinbras' at the end of *Hamlet.* After the disorders in the House and the strife within the kingdom, here is the good son, figure of the future. Solomon's establishment in the succession of David means not merely the rooting out of evil from the House and realm of David but also the enthronement of good. Yet the use of Solomon, with the distortion of biblical chronology which it involves, has reverberations of a more general moral significance. Solomon is the son whom David begot on Bathsheba, with the Lord's blessing, after the child of adultery had died. We have already seen how his birth forms the resolution of Hans Sachs's *Comedia* on the adultery and how the conception of "another Sonne, That may be loued of the Lord of

58. *Ibid.*

The House of David   37

hosts" formed the happy resolution of the first movement of Peele's play. Nor would the audience have forgotten that this was the son who was to carry on the line of Jesse—the House of David—toward the Messiah. In Bale's interlude, *The chefe promyses of God unto men,* the Lord turns from rebuking David to his promise:

> A frute there shall come, forth yssuynge from thy bodye,
> Whom I wyll aduance, vpon thy seate for euer.
> Hys trone shall become, a seate of heauenlye glorye,
> Hys worthy scepture, from ryght wyll not dysseuer,
> Hys happye kyngedome, of faythe, shall perysh neuer.
> Of heauen and of earthe, he was autor pryncypall,
> And wyll contynue, though they do perysh all.[59]

Of this fruit, Solomon is a prefiguration; the promise embodied in him reaches forward to the end of all sin. But we have also seen how, through the imagery of the play and through the traditional associations of the audience, David's sin reaches back to Adam's, to the beginning of all sin. At this point, the particular form of the Solomon scene becomes of interest. It has long been known that Peele here shamelessly incorporates a large number of lines almost literally translated from Du Bartas' *Les Artifices.*[60] In *Les Artifices* Du Bartas presents Adam in a state of poetic-prophetic "fureur secrete," in which he sees the future of his race and describes it to his son Seth. Now, Seth was the son of Adam and Eve who represented *their* special promise:

For God, said she, hath appointed me another seed instead of Abel, whom Cain slew.

(Genesis IV.25)

And so Peele is not just plagiarizing when he modifies Du Bartas' words into what he would see as a parallel situation—for Adam showing the future of the world to Seth is like David handing over to Solomon his House and his vision,

59. *The chefe promyses of God,* fol. D 2ʳ.
60. See P. H. Cheffaud, *George Peele* (Paris, 1913), esp. p. 131; and H. D. Sykes, "Peele's Borrowings from Du Bartas," *NQ,* CXLVII (1924), 349–351, 368–369.

> Of all our actions now before thine eyes,
> From Adam to the end of Adams seed.
>
> (ll. 1821–1822)

He is using Du Bartas' material more organically than Du Bartas himself had done, for the "fureur secrete" which seizes Du Bartas' Adam is spiritually less motivated than the fury that moves David to prayer—

> Transforme me from this flesh, that I may liue
> Before my death, regenerate with thee.
> O thou great God, rauish my earthly sprite,
> That for the time a more then humane skill
> May feed the Organons of all my sence—
>
> (ll. 1829–1833)

and that "ravisheth" the soul of Solomon. Peele has given us the Psalmist, the inspired David of the Psalter, and in so doing he has linked the scene up with the invocation to the play:

> And when his consecrated fingers strooke
> The golden wiers of his rauishing harpe,
> He gaue alarum to the host of heauen,
> That wing'd with lightning, brake the clouds and cast
> Their christall armor, at his conquering feet.
>
> (ll. 10–14)

He has not simply improved on his source in using it; he has also given us an indication, by the Adam-David analogy, of the dramatic structure which his contemporary audience—whether they knew Du Bartas or not—would, I think, have sensed in the "epic" drama on "Israel's sweetest singer": the rhythm of God's promises, of Paradise lost and regained. It is at this point, I think, that we can see why Peele inserted the succession of Solomon before the reception of the news of Absalom's death: The final part of this scene gives in an epitome the spiritual progress that the whole play acts out.

With one of the sudden reversals which we have seen as typical of the play, Absalom's death sends David from the highest celestial communion to the lowest human despair, in which he sees his poetry, the link between him and God, as shattered:

The House of David 39

Then let them tosse my broken Lute to heauen,
Euen to his hands that beats me with the strings,
To shew how sadly his poore sheepeheard sings.
He goes to his pauillion, and sits close a while.

(ll. 1908–1911)

In the Bible, Nathan is not in this episode (2 Samuel XIX), but in the play
he is, to echo and complete his role as a moral conscience. It is he who
points out to David that he is sinking into the sin of despair:

These violent passions come not from aboue,
Dauid and Bethsabe offend the highest,
To mourne in this immeasurable sort.

(ll. 1922–1924)

And after Joab's persuasion (which follows the Bible in appealing on the
point of national unity), in defiance of psychological probability but in
fulfillment of the spiritual pattern, David "riseth up," to pronounce a
Lycidas-like apotheosis of Absalom. Boas finds this last move on Peele's
part "still more incongruous with the general scheme and spirit of the
play" and speaks of "David's amazing final rhapsody upon Absalom's joy
in the beatific vision of the Triune Deity."[61] But David's restoration to
spiritual health, and his vision of a forgiven and beatific Absalom, both
summarize and complete what I hope we have by now seen as the over-all
"scheme" of the play. Though infinitely more inarticulate, intellectually
and structurally, than Milton's mighty edifice, Peele's *David and Bethsabe*
yet anticipates the epic on the Fall and the Redemption.

In the end the closest parallel to *David and Bethsabe* among all the
documents I have discussed here may be the *Horae* illustration reproduced
in Figure 2: Both consist of fragments from the story of David, held
together under the one unifying vision of sin and grace. By the standards
of "well-made" structure, smooth-flowing story, and consistent characters,

61. *University Drama*, p. 365.—I should not like to conclude this essay without
thanking all the friends and colleagues who, over the last few years, have helped
me to collect David material—especially Mr. Bernard Harris, Professor G. K. Hunter,
Miss Joan Grundy, and Mr. Brian Nellist. I should also like to thank Mr. David
Cook for discussing *Horae* illustrations with me, and the staff of the Warburg
Institute for letting me look at the Institute's collection of Renaissance biblical
pictures.

40   **INGA-STINA EWBANK**

Peele's play is clearly inferior to the humanist tragedies on the same biblical subject written in other languages. But by the standards of its own elastic pattern—glorying in the sin as much as in the redemption—it is not less but more humanist. Perhaps his position in time and space, and the freedom from the tyranny of external form which it implied, gave Peele a better chance than any of the others who dramatized the story of the House of David—a chance to embody in a dramatic structure, however badly made, the glory that was the Renaissance.

[19]

"What words, what looks, what wonders?": Language and Spectacle in the Theatre of George Peele

INGA-STINA EWBANK

The title of this paper contains one of the more unrecognizable quotations of the conference; but I take heart when I am asked (as I have been) whether it refers to Shakespeare's Marina, or to T. S. Eliot's.[1] Such guesses help to confirm my feeling that there is, at times, in the theatrical art of George Peele a peculiar quality of wonder and, though that is not my main concern, that this makes him very occasionally anticipate certain Shakespearian moments. This "wonder" – Peele's version of *admiratio*[2] – is, I believe, produced by some notable combinations of visual and verbal effects. The quotation, then, is offered as a paradigm of the quest I propose: for it is a quest, rather than a thesis, and the most important part of the quotation is the question mark. What is the relationship between language and spectacle in the theatre of Peele?

1. I should point out that the quotation has been slightly tailored to suit the paper. Line 49 in *David and Bethsabe* reads: "What tunes, what words, what looks, what wonders pierce . . ."; but, as I cannot attempt to deal with the contribution made by music to the total theatrical effect, I have cut out the "tunes." All quotations from Peele are taken from the three volumes of *The Dramatic Works of George Peele*, general editor Charles Tyler Prouty (New Haven, Conn., 1952, 1961 and 1970).
2. For a discussion of Renaissance theory and practice of *admiratio*, see J. V. Cunningham, *Woe or Wonder: The Emotional Effect of Shakespearean Tragedy* (Denver, Colorado, 1951), esp. chapter IV.

Though this conference has dealt chiefly with issues of pre-Shakespearian stage history and stage conditions, I feel by now no need to apologize – as for a feminine ending to the mighty line of the other papers – for closing it with an apparently literary paper. For the proceedings of the conference have also made it clear that, whether we call ourselves theatre historians or dramatic scholars or literary critics, we are all deeply dependent on each other's work. And this, of course, only reflects the interdependence of the means whereby the theatre works. From the audience's point of view the basic interdependence is that of their own senses:

> The unique distinction of drama as an Art is that it appeals to eye and ear simultaneously. The emotions of the recipient are open to assault through two senses at once and, as his emotional temperature rises, the auditor-spectator has the focal length of his imagination steadily enlarged to a point where the mind may perceive truth, meaning, reality, unobtainable by processes of the intellect alone.[3]

There is an almost Wordsworthian sense of "something far more deeply interfused" in this passage which no doubt has to do with the fact that Professor Wickham is trying to account for the birth of drama out of the liturgy of the Christian church. But it also has to do, I think, with the fact that at the heart of all living theatrical experience there is a kind of mystery: a creation, through what we see and hear, of a world which we accept as possible.[4] We may, in Hippolita's words, see what is presented to us as "strange and admirable," but we also share her readiness to accept it as "something of great constancy." Situations of wonder offer an extreme form of such experience. Extreme, because they tend to present characters who themselves experience extremes of feeling: not only joy but also grief or horror; Macbeth as well as Miranda speaks of being rapt with "wonder." Extreme, too, because they involve a particularly keen sense of the possible *and* the impossible, best described by Pericles when he tells Marina

> I will believe thee,
> And make my senses credit thy relation
> To points that seem impossible. (V.i.121–3)

3. Glynne Wickham, *Early English Stages*, I (London, 1959), C310.
4. "Possible" seems to me a more adequate word in this context than "real," with its misleading associations of "suspension of disbelief."

Inga-Stina Ewbank   *126*

The experience of the impossible becoming possible is obviously central to Shakespeare's last plays: felt most keenly, perhaps, in the wordless wonder of the last scene of *The Winter's Tale* and described most fully in the penultimate scene of the same play:

> . . . the changes I perceived in the King and Camillo were *very notes of admiration.* They seem'd almost, with staring on one another, to tear the cases of their eyes; *there was speech in their dumbness, language in their very gesture;* they look'd as they had heard of a world ransom'd, or one destroyed. A notable passion of wonder appeared in them; but the wisest beholder that knew no more but seeing could not say if th' importance were *joy or sorrow* – but *in the extremity of one* it must needs be. . . . This news, which is call'd true, is so like an old tale that the verity of it is in strong suspicion. (V.ii.9–29)

It is also central to the beginning of post-classical theatre: the wonder of the three Marys discovering that Christ is not in the tomb, or the wonder of the shepherds at the Nativity. Here, too, it is a matter of an interaction between what we see and what we hear, what the "playwright" shows and what he says. "*Venite, et videte locum,*" the Angel urges the wondering women; and, before they can articulate their joy in the anthem "*Surrexit Dominus de sepulchre,/Qui pro nobis perpendit in ligno,*" the wonder must be visually dramatized:

> *Hec vero dicens, surgat, et erigat velum, ostendatque eis locum cruce nudatum, sed tantum linteamina posita quibus crux involuta erat.*[5]

The lifting of the veil, or the "discovery," or the drawing of a curtain which (as we shall see) marks the beginning and the end of Peele's *David and Bethsabe,* is, either literally or metaphorically, as much part of the experience of wonder as is the verbal articulation of extreme states: things dying and things new-born, or things transfigured by passion as in Belimperia's plea

> O let me goe, for in my troubled eyes,
> Now maist thou read that life in passion dies.
> (*The Spanish Tragedy,* II.iv.47–8)

---

5. From the *Regularis Concordia* of Ethelwold, usually assigned to the year 967. Quoted from John M. Manly, *Specimens of the Pre-Shakespearean Drama,* I (Dover Publications reprint, N.Y., 1967), p. xx.

Because of our unfamiliarity with most pre-Shakespearian plays
on stage, we tend to underestimate their theatrical *life*, as against
such verbal patternings and spectacular arrangements as we can
easily apprehend from the texts in front of us. In the summer of
1973, undergraduates at London University still believe that
Horatio and Belimperia go into the arbour for the express purpose
of having stychomythia.[6] The men writing for the London theatres
in the 1580s and early 1590s were particularly strongly subjected
to pulls in two directions: towards the word, in the shape of
exuberant and/or horrific rhetoric, and towards spectacle in every
sense, from the significant grouping to the bloody banquet or the
coronation pageant. They responded, not with the schizophrenia
of contemporary British theatre, but with a happy eclecticism.
Renaissance scholarship is increasingly emphasizing that this was
a period good at simultaneously entertaining apparently contra-
dictory impulses; and nowhere, perhaps, do we see this more
clearly than in the theatre. It is not only that a playwright like
Peele could both compose the delicate lyric which opens *David
and Bethsabe* and devise a dumb-show which needed "3. violls of
blood and a sheeps gather",[7] but that he and his contemporaries
were always trying out new ways of combining word and spectacle.

For such combination we are still quite short of a critical
language and therefore, as the two are related like the chicken and
the egg, of a sympathetic understanding. Anything short of the
mature Shakespearian interaction of visual and verbal poetry
tends too readily to be dismissed as spectacle decorated with
verse or, at best, to be set down as a kind of emblematic art in
which language and visual effects duplicate each other.[8] "That
which can be made Explicit to the Idiot is not worth my care,"

6. Those who were lucky enough to see the production by the Other Theatre
Company at the Mercury Theatre, London, in October 1973 (while this paper
was being prepared for the press), will no longer think so; for the performance
(despite – or because of – shoestring conditions) beautifully brought out the
human reality underlying the patterned speeches.
7. See the theatrical plot of *The Battle of Alcazar*, in W. W. Greg, *Two
Elizabethan Stage Abridgements* (Oxford, 1922), p. 32.
8. Dieter Mehl, "Visual and Rhetorical Imagery in Shakespeare's Plays," in
Essays and Studies (1972), p. 95. Professor Mehl's is one of the few sys-
tematic attempts at discussing this subject. I have published a few thoughts
on it in *Shakespeare Survey* 24 (1971), 13–18 (" 'More Pregnantly than
Words' ").

Blake says about such "Moral Painting";[9] and Peele and his contemporaries hardly saw their audiences as idiots. Though a great
deal of dramatic language in this period does act mainly as commentary on tableaux, to stop at this point is to blinker oneself
against the possibility of mutual illumination, of significant interaction, between "words" and "looks" which I wanted to hint at in
my title quotation. It seems important, then, to ask questions about
the relationship of word and show in the theatre immediately
before Shakespeare. But perhaps the first question that springs to
mind is whether Peele is an important enough playwright to ask
such questions about? His theatrical career, in its variety of genres
and audiences, seems largely opportunistic, lacking in the kind of
inner compulsion which lies behind the work of Marlowe, and
even Kyd. Therefore he has seemed, on the whole, unworthy of
serious scholarly or critical study (always excepting the splendid
Yale edition). Even those who have written on him have, in order
not to appear to claim too much for him, leant over backwards so
far as to make one wonder why they bother at all. In what follows,
I shall err, if anything, on the side of generosity. In the theatre, I
believe, there is room for an art which is mainly a search for what
audiences need and want; and there is another kind of compulsion
than an ideological-thematic one: a technical one, which involves
the sheer pleasure of accomplishing certain effects in the theatre,
doing certain things to audiences, being (in Emrys Jones' term)[10]
a "technician of the emotions." It is to Peele as an eclectic technician of the emotions that I turn, in order to explore his words,
looks and wonders.

My title quotation, of course, comes from the opening scene of
David and Bethsabe: The *Prologus*, departing,

> *drawes a curtaine, and discovers Bethsabe with her maid bathing
> over a spring: she sings, and David sits above vewing her.*

At this point, what the audience is viewing is a tableau with
familiar bearings. The motif of Bethsabe in the bath, from its
frequent use in medieval Books of Hours to a number of sixteenth-
century paintings, had become an image of earthly beauty, usually

9. Letter to the Revd. Dr. Trusler, August 23, 1799 (Nonesuch *Blake*, 4th
ed., London, 1967, pp. 834–5).
10. *Scenic Form in Shakespeare* (Oxford, 1971).

with the connotations of moral condemnation.[11] But iconographical familiarity does not make the visual image self-sufficient, any more than a dumb-show of Cleopatra at Cydnus could substitute for Enobarbus' barge speech. The wonder of "the flower of Israel," as of the "rare Egyptian," comes in an appeal to all the senses, communicated through words – though Enobarbus' speech can create its own scene, while David's, like Iachimo's in Imogen's bedchamber, has the task, probably more precarious, of helping to convey something which the audience actually and simultaneously sees. What a literal-minded audience, of course, sees at the opening of *David and Bethsabe* (that is, what they saw in the 1590s), is a boy dressed up as a girl with, presumably, no more visual sex appeal than those sixteenth-century Dutch pictures of the bathing scene where Bethsabe is depicted as modestly washing her feet, her skirt pulled up to reveal at most her knees.[12] But Peele does not give the audience a chance to remain literal-minded: we "see" the scene through its words. First there is Bethsabe's song, the purely musical effect of which we cannot recapture, as the setting is lost. But the lyrical poem which remains creates a whole landscape of sensuousness, in which she herself is the focus:

> Hot sunne, coole fire, temperd with sweet aire,
> Black shade, fair nurse, shadow my white haire.
> Shine sun, burne fire, breathe aire, and ease mee,
> Black shade, fair nurse, shroud me and please me.
> Shadow (my sweet nurse) keep me from burning,
> Make not my glad cause, cause of mourning.
> Let not my beauties fire,
> Enflame unstaied desire,
> Nor pierce any bright eye,
> That wandreth lightly.

The challenge of the situation has touched Peele's verbal imagination to particularly fine issues: the rhythm and the patterning give simple words a haunting suggestiveness far beyond their normal reach, and the total effect, rather than merely descriptive or celebratory, is of an awareness, as in a metaphysical poem, of

11. See my essay on "The House of David in Renaissance Drama," *Renaissance Drama*, VIII (1965), 3–40.
12. Ibid.. p. 13; and see Elisabeth Kunoth-Leifels, *Über die Darstellungen der "Bathseba im Bade": Studien zur Geschichte des Bildthemas 4. bis 17. Jahrhundert* (Essen, 1962).

many worlds.[13] One shudders to think that when William Poel revived *David and Bethsabe* in 1932, he told the actress who took the part of Bethsabe to compose her own song and enter singing any words she fancied.[14]

Then Bethsabe speaks, and in her invocation to Zephyr sensuousness changes into a Narcissistic sensuality which yet is so delicately balanced with innocence that no simplistic response is possible. Fair Bethsabe projects the wonder of irresistible physical beauty; we watch David watching her and having his whole consciousness pierced by the wonder:

> What tunes, what words, what looks, what wonders pierce
> My soule, incensed with a sudden fire?

Later in the play, David is going to look back on this scene and see it, as the illustrators of the Penitential Psalms did, as an emblem of concupiscence, sexual appetite. But within the dramatic present neither he nor the audience can take a coolly rational and moral view of the situation – any more than the scene in which Cleopatra helps to arm Antony could be circumscribed by the motto "The triple pillar of the world transform'd /Into a strumpet's fool." If Peele were a more respectable dramatist, we could use phrases like "visual and verbal ambivalence" about the climax of the scene, when David rhapsodizes in a rhetorical figure which itself enacts the whole sexual paradox,

> Bright Bethsabe gives earth to my desires,
> Verdure to earth and to that verdure flowers,
> To flowers, sweet Odors, and to Odors wings,
> That carrie pleasures to the hearts of Kings,

and when Bethsabe is brought up[15] to join him, elevated yet falling, representing both "earth" and "wings," flesh and spirit. As it is, we dare at least say that Peele's poetry feeds from the visual image and *vice versa*; and that he is making the theatre prove the wonder

13. Elizabeth Holmes, in *Aspects of Elizabethan Imagery* (Oxford, 1929), p. 16, draws attention to how "the quaint double suggestiveness of 'burning' catches even something of the metaphysical in its note."
14. See Robert Speaight, *William Poel and the Elizabethan Revival* (London, 1954), pp. 266–68.
15. Elmer Blistein, in his Yale edition of the play, believes that David *descends* to Bethsabe.

of being human and the impossibility of making simply moral responses to such wonder.

David's experience, in so far as it involves having his soul "pierced" with "wonders," is by no means unique in Peele's drama. He likes to subject his characters to experiences which "pierce" or "daze" or "dazzle" them; and, indeed, both in his dramatic and his non-dramatic poetry there is much explicit interest in wonder: what it is and how it affects a beholder. Thus in *Anglorum Feriae*, the poem written to commemorate the Accession Day festivities of 1595, he declares his intention to

> recommende to Tymes Eternitie
> Hir [i.e. the Queen's] honors heigthe and woonders of hir age;
> Woonders of hir that reasons reache transcend,
> Suche woonders as hathe sett the Worlde at gaze; (ll. 13–6)

and in those wonders "that reasons reache transcend" lies the key to the dramatic structure of *The Arraignment of Paris* (as I shall presently argue). In *Edward I*, even the Queen Mother is overcome with the wonders of triumphant kingship. She opens the play with forty eloquent lines in which she envisages the return of her sons from their Holy Wars; but when she is faced with the actual pageant (carefully described for us in the stage directions), words fail her and "*she fals and sounds.*" In *The Arraignment of Paris* the shows of the three goddesses leave the protagonist in a daze which, like states of confusion in *Macbeth*, can only be articulated in a paradox:

> Most heavenly dames, was never man as I
> Poore shepherde swaine, so happy and unhappy; (ll. 509–10)

and (as, again, I shall presently argue) shows of the supernatural, "able" (in Paris' words) "to wrape and dazle humaine eyes," become in *The Battle of Alcazar* the device through which Peele tries to dramatize the wonder of extreme evil. For horror and evil have their wonders, too. Priam in Peele's *Tale of Troy*, like the mother of Edward I, is "mazde" by what he sees; but in the case of the unfortunate king it is "with frights and feares":

> Ah what a piercing sight it was to see,
> So fair a towne as Troy was said to be,
> By quenchlesse fire layd levell with the soyle. (ll. 424–6)

Inga-Stina Ewbank   *132*

In all these examples, Peele is trying through words to communicate the effect of something seen. But sight is not the only sense involved in provoking an experience of wonder. In *The Honour of the Garter*, a poem apparently written to order, there is little excitement or evocativeness in the description of the garter procession as such; but where the poem comes alive is in the framework attempt to introduce that procession as a pageant in a dream. The wonder of the vision is rendered as an account of what used to be called "total theatre":

> Mine eyes, and eares, and senses all were served,
> With every object perfect in his kinde.
> And lo, a wonder to my senses all,
> For through the melting aire perfum'd with sweets,
> I might discerne a troope of Horse-men ride. . . . (ll. 34–8)

As in the *David and Bethsabe* passage which I have just been examining, Peele is interested in the whole banquet of sense; and this interest has a great deal to do with his qualities as a playwright.

One might have expected a young poet who had been at Oxford with neo-Latin dramatists like Richard Edes, Leonard Hutton and William Gager, to see drama primarily as a matter of verbal rhetoric. Nashe's praise of him as "the *Atlas* of Poetrie, and *primus verborum Artifex*" suggests that he was seen mainly as an artist in words.[16] But Christ Church had a theatrical tradition of spectacular entertainments; one remembers the cry of hounds in the quadrangle which so pleased the queen during the performance of Edwardes' *Palamon and Arcite* in 1566. And Peele himself, well after he had officially left Oxford, returned to stage-manage a scarcely less spectacular show put on before the visiting Polish Count Palatine, Alasco, in June 1583. This production of Gager's *Dido* contained the apparently indispensable hounds – "a goodlie sight of hunters with full crie of a kennell of hounds" – but it also involved such powerful appeals to various senses as

> Mercurie and Iris descending and ascending from and to an high place, the tempest wherein it hailed small confects, rained rosewater,

16. *The Works of Thomas Nashe*, ed. R. B. McKerrow (London, 1904–10), III, 323.

and snew an artificiall kind of snow, all strange, marvellous, abundant.[17]

Similar appeals are involved in many of the pageant occasions, at court or in the city, with which Peele came to be connected during his post-Oxford career. The records which remain of these suggest that he tended to respond more to the occasion than to its intellectual or moral meaning. In *Polyhymnia*, for example, the versified description of the couples who tilted in the 1590 accession tournament, the strength of the verse lies in its rendering of the visual delight of costumes, armour, and so on; whereas the attempts at moral allegory are thin and perfunctory. The fact is, of course, that even a *primus verborum Artifex* held a very secondary position at such occasions. He may be showing his hand in Sir Henry Lee's farewell sonnet, "His golden lockes, Time hath to Silver turn'd" (if we may assume it to be by Peele), but it is worth remembering what a grand occasion it was a small part of. Sir William Segar's account of the way the Queen's Champion took his leave of her –

> Her Majesty beholding these armed Knights comming toward her, did suddenly heare a musicke so sweete and secret, as every one thereat greatly marveiled. And hearkening to that excellent melodie, the earth as it were opening, there appeared a Pavilion, made of white Taffata, containing eight score elles, being in proportion like unto the sacred Temple of the Virgin Vestall. This Temple seemed to consist upon pillars of Pourferry, arched like unto a Church, within it were many Lampes burning[18]

– suggests stage marvels like the last two scenes of *Pericles* rolled into one, while Peele's sonnet is introduced into this account simply as verses which "accompanied . . . the musicke aforesayd" and were "sung by M. *Hales* her Majesties servant, a Gentleman in that Arte excellent, and for his voice both commendable and admirable." The poet receives no mention and his art is clearly regarded as the handmaiden of the other arts.

The same is basically true for the Lord Mayor's pageants, though in the later of the two which have been preserved, *Descensus Astreae* (1591), the verbal images (the web and the fountain) are

17. Described by Holinshed (1587), quoted from *The Life and Minor Works of George Peele* (vol. 1 of the Yale edition), p. 61.
18. Ibid., p. 167.

Inga-Stina Ewbank *134*

more intrinsic to the show than any in the earlier *Pageant borne before Woolstone Dixi* (1585): a reflection, possibly, of Peele's experience of playwriting in the intervening years. By definition, obviously, a pageant poet's verses have to be functional: to explain as directly as possible to a wide and varied audience (many of whom would probably not hear the words anyway) what is seen, what it means and what "wonders" are being celebrated. If, as there is some evidence to suggest,[19] Peele was involved in producing pageants as well as writing for them, these functional needs would seem natural and no strait-jacket. It is worth pointing out, too, that the relationship works both ways; if the words are subordinated to a mainly visual situation, they are also themselves given meaning and weight by that situation. A couplet in *Descensus Astreae,*

> O let hir princely daies never have fine,
> Whose vertues are immortal and devine, (ll. 84–5)

is not particularly evocative or memorable on the page; but, spoken by the figure of one of those "vertues" (Charitie) in the company of other virtues and of Astrea, the manifestation of the queen's "devine" qualities, it must have had a very different resonance. As for "immortal," a spectator need only move his eyes to "the hinder part of the Pageant," where

> *did sit a Child, representing Nature, holding in her hand a distaffe, and spinning a Web, which was wheeled up by Time,*

and the conceit, of the queen's divine independence of ordinary human nature and time, would come alive – even more so if he remembered that the Presenter of the pageant spoke of how "Time and Kinde/Produce hir yeares to make them numberlesse" (ll. 33–4).

One wonders if the pageant writer's attitude to language – as something which does not so much evoke meanings and create patterns in its own right as *refer* to a visual reality, existing already, before the very eyes of the spectator – may not help to explain one feature of Peele's dramatic style that has often come under attack. I am thinking of his tendency to repeat the same, often colourless, adjective time and time again, a tendency decried as "monotony,

19. See D. M. Bergeron, *English Civic Pageantry, 1580–1642* (London, 1972).

poverty . . . emptiness and affectation."[20] For example, in the midst
of the Coronation pageantry of *Edward I*, the queen appeals to the
king in lines which, read at the scholar's desk, suggest the poor
vocabulary of a modern teenager:

> And lovelie England to thy lovely Queene,
> Lovelie Queene Elinor, unto her turne thy eye,
> Whose honor cannot but love thee wel. (ll. 701–3)

Seen (and I use the verb advisedly) in context, the lines suggest a
sense of decorum (little as we may like it): Peele is envisaging,
rather than feeling into, the scene, and all the adjectives need do is
to point to what the spectator can see: two "lovely" people in state,
representing the honour and glory and growing unity of England.

I repeat that I am trying to explain, rather than excuse, what is
often an irritating feature in Peele. But it is worth remembering
how in the greatest moments of wonder in drama, language tends
to take on this quality of simply referring to what is seen, as when
the bystanders at Hermione's miraculous and silent reunion with
Leontes speak only stage directions ("She embraces him," etc.). In
The Tempest adjectives such as "strange" often function, like
Peele's "lovely," merely as dotted lines on which he who has eyes
to see and ears to hear may inscribe further meanings. And, of
course, in the court masque proper the language often serves as a
kind of incantatory pointer to what is seen. Jonson's *Vision of
Delight* (1617) is, I think, the masque which most explicitly con-
templates the wonder of its own devices (the main scene transformation into "the bower of Zephyrus," and the discovery of the
main masquers as "the glories of the spring") as well as the wonder
of monarchy. Ultimately the two wonders are fused: "Behold a
king/Whose presence maketh this perpetual spring," and the choir
turns what is seen into a litany of the King's power:

> The founts, the flowers, the birds, the bees,
> The herds, the flocks, the grass, the trees
> Do all confess him.

It is hardly necessary to point out how, outside the full context of
the occasion, this reads merely like an inventory. It is written for

20. See John Dover Wilson's introduction to his New Shakespeare edition of
Titus Andronicus (Cambridge, 1948), p. xxix.

Inga-Stina Ewbank 136

spectators, to embody a delight

> Which who once saw would ever see;
> And if they could the object prize,
> Would, while it lasts, not think to rise,
> But wish their bodies all were eyes.[21]

Now, I do not for a moment think that in approaching a Peele play we wish our "bodies all were eyes." Even without Nashe's description of him, it is clear that Peele saw drama very much as a vehicle for poetry. There is the obvious delight in the writing itself: in experimenting (with metres in *The Arraignment of Paris*, with varieties of style and tone in *The Old Wives Tale*, with biblical and oriental imagery in *David and Bethsabe*) and in imitating fashionable modes (trying to out-Tamburlaine Tamburlaine in *The Battle of Alcazar* and to fit stretches of almost literal translations from Du Bartas into the texture of *David and Bethsabe*). There is also the evidence of at least one text, that of *The Arraignment of Paris*, that he was anxious for it to be read as literature in the strictest sense.[22] Notes are appended, like the critical guide to the dialogue between Thestilis and the shepherds: *"The grace of this song is in the Shepherds Ecco to her verse"* (1.742 SD); captions draw attention to the importance of the two big set speeches (Paris' to the Council of the Gods, and Diana's on – and to – Queen Elizabeth); and the poetic plums are marked out as if Peele had anticipated the coming of Lamb's *Specimen* (and indeed Colin's Lament and Oenone's Complaint both appeared in its 1600 equivalent, *England's Helicon*). But we must, to put this emphasis on the literary nature of the play in perspective, remember that it is an exceptional play, based entirely on the presence of the queen at performance.[23] To explain it, as the Yale

21. *Ben Jonson: The Complete Masques*, ed. Stephen Orgel (New Haven, Conn., 1969), pp. 253–54.
22. We are safe in seeing Peele's hand in the preparation of the text, as "the evidence concerning the printers' copy indicates that it was probably either the autograph manuscript or a careful transcript of it that served as the prompt book" (R. Mark Benbow, in his edition of *The Arraignment of Paris*, vol. 3 of the Yale edition, p. 57).
23. Peter Saccio, in *The Court Comedies of John Lyly* (Princeton, New Jersey, 1969), p. 16, n. 17, discusses the nonce-quality of the play and points out that it is unprofitable to speculate on the possible existence of an alternative version suitable for Blackfriars performance. For, "in any case, another version would have been a very different play."

editor does, by Peele's "conforming to the sixteenth-century conception that poetry but not drama was proper to the gentleman" is to forget that here is a play which as soon as the occasion (the first and probably only night) is gone, becomes "the book of the play." When no longer a play *to* and *for* the queen, it becomes a poem *about* her. And besides, even as a reading text the play testifies to the contrary pull, towards spectacle. The great care taken over the stage directions (and this applies to other Peele texts, too) helps to point to the fact that the words exist in visual situations. Sometimes those situations are as spectacular, and the dependence of the words on what is seen as incontestable, as in *The Vision of Delight*. "Lo," says Juno to Paris, "this Tree of Golde will I bestowe on thee." The stage direction tells us that *"hereupon did rise a Tree of gold laden with Diadems and Crownes of golde"*; whereupon Juno proceeds to put its wonders into words: "The body and the bark of golde, all glistringe to beholde," etc. But even in the less spectacular scenes there is an unusual directness of speech. A reference to visual actuality is often all we need: "Pomona with her fruite comes time enough I see" (1. 53), or "Pallas in flowers of hue and collowers read" (1. 110). As in a masque, there is little need for verbal conceit: the conceit lies in plot – or, rather, in structure, which here is plot. Again we must remember the exceptional nature of this play; with a mythological and a pastoral world actually presented on stage, verbal metaphors have resolved themselves into visual figurations before the play starts. There is some conventional Petrarchan imagery around the two unhappy lovers, Colin and Oenone. But even that becomes curiously literal when the stage also holds a character who can speak of *"Cupid* my sonne" as a matter of fact.

However exceptional, Peele's first play yet suggests that he saw himself as an *"artifex"* both in words and in shows. Returning, at last, to the point I started from, I feel that at key moments of "wonder" in his plays he achieves a kind of mutual illumination between his visual and his verbal imagery. I want now to turn to such moments in four of his plays. Time will not permit an examination of *The Old Wives Tale*, which is so much a thing in itself, though it is worth pointing out that the frame construction makes the whole of that play into one continuous "wonder" enacted before its stage audience.

I return to *The Arraignment of Paris* where, I believe, wonder is

Inga-Stina Ewbank   **138**

the point of the whole play. Usually it is seen as a work with an interesting middle – modern critics agreeing with Nashe about the "manifold variety of invention" displayed – but a misleading beginning and an unsatisfactory end. This is, of course, a very damning criticism; for if "this final episode in which Diana gives the apple to the Queen does not follow inevitably from what goes before,"[24] then not only the unity but also the entire *raison d'être* of the play will collapse. Two recent critics have attempted a defence in terms of the play's political and moral themes, both in the process moving on to "historico-mythical" levels which seem to me to have little to do with the reality of the play as a piece of theatre.[25] Andrew von Hendy finds "its spectacle, though plentiful, . . . relatively incidental" and so in fact undermines his own argument that the play "is constructed like a masque to induce the willing suspension of disbelief necessary to the compliment." But, it seems to me, if there is a unity in this gallimaufry of a play, it lies exactly in the spectacle; and if there is a suspension of disbelief, it comes not through rational argument about Britain as the new Troy or through allegorical correspondencies between Elizabeth and Christ, but through our being "dazed" with wonder, even as Paris was "dazed" by the shows presented before him. Even Ben Jonson had to admit that it was the outward show of the masque in performance which could "steal away the spectators from themselves";[26] and in *The Arraignment of Paris* it is Peele's sense of theatre that makes our senses credit the denouement "to points that seem impossible."

The wonder of the ending, in so far as we can paraphrase it in words, is the defeat of a whole tragic and dynamic world order (its dynamism having provided the action of the play) by the simple, static presence of the queen. Ate Prologus, who has been much maligned for misleading us, opens the play by establishing that order:

> So loath and weerie of her heavie loade
> The Earth complaynes unto the hellish prince,

24. G. K. Hunter, *John Lyly: The Humanist as Courtier* (London, 1962), p. 155.
25. Andrew von Hendy, "The Triumph of Chastity: Form and Meaning in *The Arraignment of Paris*," *Renaissance Drama* n.s. I (1968), 87–101: and Henry G. Lesnick, "The Structural Significance of Myth and Flattery in Peele's *Arraignment of Paris*," SP, 65 (1968), 163–71.
26. Jonson's description of *Hymenaei*, in Orgel, *The Complete Masques*, p. 94.

> Surcharged with the burden that she nill sustaine.
> Th' unpartiall daughters of Necessitie
> Bin aydes in her sute: and so the twine
> That holdes olde Priams house, the threede of Troie
> Dame Atropos with knife in sunder cuttes.
> Done be the pleasure of the powers above,
> Whose hestes men must obey: and I my parte
> Performe in Ida vales . . .

To complain that this ought to, but does not, lead into a tragedy of Troy and not a pastoral-mythological-complimentary comedy, seems to me as irrelevant as it would be to berate Jonson for not making a scene of "an ugly hell, which flaming beneath, smoked unto the top of the roof" introduce a *Masque of Witches* rather than the *Masque of Queens*. We cannot tell how striking Ate looked, but her words are clearly meant to give a vivid image both of the hell she comes from,

> Where bloudles ghostes in paines of endles date
> Fill ruthles eares with never ceasing cries,

and the hell the gods are going to create on earth:

> Proude Troy must fall . . .
>
> .   .   .   .
>
> King Priams pallace waste with flaming fire,
> Whose thicke and foggie smoake piercing the skie,
> Must serve for messenger of sacrifice
> T'appeaze the anger of the angrie heavens.

The smoke and the cries give way to visual delight and musical harmony as the scene becomes "Ida vales," but they remain, as it were, in the periphery, as a sense of a world of discord elsewhere – and one which, so "Th'unpartiall daughters of Necessitie" have decreed, will eventually and inevitably take over. This sense is underpinned by the extraordinary amount of sadness in the Arcadian world of the play. By the final scene, Colin has been carried out on a bier, dead from a broken heart; Oenone, though still alive, has lamented and left (and, as Peele well knew, the two lyrics of lament are emotional centres of the play); and Paris, in a very moving exit, has left the stage as "the shepherd boye /That in his bosome carries fire to Troy." Now would seem the time for the world of discord to take over; the wonder (not the structural defect) is that it does not. Its rulers are there, including "th'un-partiall dames of destenie" (as Clotho now describes them) who have materialized from Ate's Prologue; but even the Fates are wearing "robes of cheerfull collours," and they are there only to submit to the real ruler, the Queen. There must have been a shock to the audience as she entered the action – as essential to the play as is the visual shock when Hermione's statue "comes alive" in *The Winter's Tale*.

The theatrical climax (and the real denouement) is not the goddesses' argued decision to present the apple to Elizabeth because she is "so wise and fayre," but the ritual of submission which bounces us into acceptance of the mysterious power of royalty. The entry of the Fates is carefully prepared by music –

> *The Musicke sounde and the Nimphes within singe or solfa with voyces and instruments awhile. Then enter Clotho, Lachesis and Atropos singing as followeth: The state being in place*

and staged as a kind of sung Eucharist, the relative unfamiliarity of the Latin adding to the sense of wonder. As they lay their fatal instruments at the queen's feet, they might simply be pageant figures whose lines illustrate an emblematic gesture:

> Dame Atropos according as her pheeres
> To thee fayre Queene resignes her fatall knife,

but in the full structural context, with the Queen *there* and with the knife of Atropos having hovered over the action since the Prologue, they become a dramatic image of monarchy rising above the powers of fate and time. We are not in the dreamlike world of relative time which surrounds the figure of the Queen in *Endimion* but much more in the kind of unquestioned double time to which the English theatre had been used in the days of the *Secunda Pastorum*. Even as Mac is tossed in a blanket, the shepherds turn to God's Lamb in the manger. Even as Paris goes to start the Troyan war, according to "the pleasure of the powers above/ Whose hestes men must obey" (Prologue), the Queen rises above those powers. There is indeed a jolt in the final scene,[27] and the

27. As Enid Welsford complains, in *The Court Masque* (Cambridge, 1927), p. 281.

jolt itself is essential. The Queen is not just a super shepherdess, or the most beautiful and wise lady ever, as the language tells us. She is, as the whole visual-verbal-musical structure of the ending shows us, *different*, part of a mystery beyond possibility.

The wonder of monarchy, Peele knew, would not make a play for the public stage; but, as *Tamburlaine* and possibly *The Spanish Tragedy* had just demonstrated, tyranny would. It is easy enough to be scathing about *The Battle of Alcazar*, for in Peele's attempt to dramatize the workings of political evil there is so much that seemed absurd even to his contemporaries. The exiled and starving tyrant enters *"with [raw] flesh upon his sword"*; and the unintentional parody of a Tamburlaine rhapsody which follows was in its turn parodied by Shakespeare and many others:

> Hold thee Calypolis feed and faint no more,
>
> .   .   .   .
>
> Feede then and faint not faire Calypolis. (ll. 537–61)

There is so much, too, that could have been in the play but is not. The nearly contemporary historical events which form the plot contain a number of interesting moral paradoxes: a justified ruler who yet had to make his way to the throne by violence, in Abdelmelec; a usurping ruler driven into exile, where he has some cause for feeling more sinned against than sinning, in Muly Mahamet; a good king, misled and forced into the position of a villain, in Sebastian of Portugal, and so on. But Peele does not have the language for moral discriminations which in Shakespeare's histories illuminates and patterns similar raw material. The most that he manages is a heavy-handed insistence on the essential innocence of Sebastian, and his misfortune of getting mixed up, together with the protean Stukeley, in the African venture. Nor can his imagination do much (apart from some spectacular scenes of battle or of triumphant entry, and from the eulogy of Queen Elizabeth and her nation put into the mouth of Sebastian) to transmute the factual material. The historical-political scene tends to be rendered with the prosaic dispassionateness of a news announcer, as in the following account of Sebastian's progress towards the scene of the battle:

> The 26. daie of June he left the bay of Lisborne,
> And with all his fleete at Cardis happily he

Inga-Stina Ewbank

> Arriv'de in Spain the eight of July, tarrying for the aide
> That Philip king of Spaine had promised,
> And fifteene daies he there remaind aboord. (ll. 883–7)

If then the historical plot as such did not fire Peele's imagination, what did was the general, ineluctable sense of retribution taking its course which he could derive from the plot and both "show" and discuss in the dumb-shows and the Presenter's speeches. The transition from the general vision to the particular situation often has the sinking effect of a "Tey Bridge Disaster," as in the dumb-show before the last act and the Presenter's comment,

> The crownes of Barbary and kingdomes fall,
> Ay me, that kingdomes may not stable stand,
> And now approching neere the dismall day,
> The bloudie daie wherein the battels joyne,
> Mondaie the fourth of August seventie eight. (ll. 1180–4)

In other words, if the language of the play is constantly letting us down, the imaginative core of the play is the framework of dumb-shows which show us how evil deeds set in motion an infernal machinery.

Because the 1594 Quarto represents such an imperfect and abbreviated version of the play, it has been difficult to get any sort of overall sense of its original structure. In the Quarto there is no trace of the third dumb-show, for example, and scarcely more than fragments of the second and the fourth. But W. W. Greg's invaluable edition of the theatrical plot of *The Battle of Alcazar*, and now also the heroic labours of the Yale editor, John Yoklavich, who sensibly incorporates information from the "plot" into the stage directions he prints, indicate that Peele is using the dumb-shows as a consistent fatalistic framework.[28] The real structure of the play is an overall visual pattern.

From the audience's point of view, the chief character in this play is the Presenter. Unlike Revenge in *The Spanish Tragedy*, who together with the Ghost of Andrea makes up a self-contained audience *within* the play, he maintains a very immediate relationship with us "lords" or "lordinges." This is established in his speech which opens the play,

28. Greg, *Two Elizabethan Stage Abridgements*, and Yoklavich, ed., *The Battle of Alcazar*, vol. 2 of the Yale edition.

Sit you and see this true and tragicke warr
A modern matter full of bloud and ruth (ll. 49–50)

and he makes no bones about the *de casibus* nature of this "modern matter":

Where three bolde kings confounded in their height,
Fall to the earth contending for a crowne. (ll. 51–2)

At the same time he is flexible in his approach to the matter he has to present. His first task is to provide a résumé of the action before the dramatic present: fifteen lines of exposition which, at first sight, are almost unintelligible to a reader, because of the dynastic complications and because everybody seems to have the same name. But then the first dumb-show takes over and shows us, in three separate scenes, how Muly Mahamet and his son, together with two Murderers, strangle the two young princes in their bed, "in sight of the uncle" Abdelmunen, and then proceed to strangle this unfortunate spectator in his chair. While we still measure the length of plays in numbers of lines instead of hours of traffic on the stage, it is worth reminding ourselves how long this would have taken to show – and, incidentally, how after this no one in the audience need be confused about which Muly Mahamet is which. At this stage, the Presenter's commentary is, if sensational, as directly related to what we see as that of a lantern slide lecturer:

this tyrant king,
Of whome we treate sprong from the Arabian moore
Blacke in his looke, and bloudie in his deeds,
And in his shirt staind with a cloud of gore,
Presents himselfe with naked sword in hand,
Accompanied as now you may behold,
With devils coted in the shapes of men. (ll. 14–20)

All the more effectively, therefore, he can warn us, at the end of this first dumb-show, against brushing aside what we see as mere fiction – "Saie not these things are faind, for true they are" – and also relate what we have seen to the universal pattern of "Nemesis high mistres of revenge." Then, at last, he can turn to the actual present of the play. His "now behold" introduces the first scene of the play proper, so that there is, at this stage in the play, no distinction felt between dumb-show and speaking show.

Inga-Stina Ewbank   *144*

The first dumb-show, then, shows nothing which has not happened in real life. But, as the action progresses, the dumb-shows come more and more to be of another world (one hesitates to use as presumptuous a phrase as "another level of reality"): their cast includes supernatural powers and their "plots" become increasingly allegorical. Nemesis, *"three ghosts crying* Vindicta" and three Furies appear at the beginning of Act II. In the third show we see the pulsations of unmerited pain as the innocent and misled are drawn into the infernal machine. At the beginning of Act IV Sebastian and Stukeley feast with the Moor, at "the bloudie banquet," on dead men's heads and similar delicacies. And the last dumb-show, of lightning and thunder, blazing stars and fireworks and the fall of two crowns from the tree where "Fame like an Angel" has deposited them, completes the allegorization of the "modern matter" into the *de casibus* pattern initially outlined by the Presenter. There is an interesting enjambement here, between the end of Act IV and the opening of Act V, for the dumb-show comes as an ironic visual response to the Moor's attempt to invoke "You bastards of the night, and Erybus,/ Fiends, Fairies, hags . . ." (ll. 1136–7), and to prescribe (like the Ghost of Andrea at the end of *The Spanish Tragedy*, but unsuccessfully) a detailed set of hellish punishments for his enemies.

It is as if Peele was beginning to feel his way towards counterpointing word and show, rather than merely having one illustrate the other – a way which, however remotely, leads towards the irony when Macbeth's assurance that Banquo, like all mortals, is "assailable" is translated, in the banquet scene, to the visual certainty that the dead "now . . . rise again." It is that sense of the mystery of evil which occasionally makes *The Battle of Alcazar* rise above cliché or parody; and, to me, the most undeniable of such occasions rests in the combination of language and visual effects around the dumb-show of Act II. The Presenter introduces Nemesis and goes on to say:

> Nor may the silence of the speechlesse night,
> Divine Architect of murthers and misdeeds,
> Of tragedies and tragicke tyrannies,
> Hide or containe this barbarous crueltie
> Of this usurper to his progenie. (ll. 279–83)

On the page, it looks like the kind of verbal statement about night
(like Lucrece's outcry to "comfort-killing Night, image of Hell! . . .
Black stage for tragedies and murders fell!" [ll. 764–6]) which the
literature of the period teems with. But night here really becomes
identified with the "black stage," as the theatre situation makes
manifest, through eyes and ears, the ghastly nature – the relentless
irony – of "the silence of the speechlesse night." (Three ghosts crying "Vindicta" might not look so funny on stage as they do in the
study.) If silk purses were ever made of sows' ears, one would
suggest that there is a germ of *Macbeth* here, in the confrontation
with the infernal machinery set in motion by, and therefore ironically working against, the "Traitor to kinne and kinde, to Gods and
men" (*Alcazar*, l. 287). The wonder of evil is epitomized in the
night which, in a hallucinatory way, both facilitates deeds and
brings about retribution for them.

Whatever *The Battle of Alcazar* achieves, it suggests that glories
rather than horrors are Peele's forte. A sense of this may be the
reason why, in his attempt at an English history play, he turned to
a king who started in the triumph of victorious Holy Wars and
went on, through encounters with a Welsh Greenwood world, to
the glory of national unity, and who, besides, was a great lover. I
am prepared to accept the persuasive argument of the Yale editor
of *Edward I*, Frank S. Hook, that the parts of the play vilifying
Queen Elinor were interpolations, to accommodate the contents
of the two ballads on "The lamentable fall of Queene Elnor" and
"Queen Eleanor's Confession."[29] There are absurdities in these
parts – like the wonder of the Queen sinking into the earth on
Charing Green and popping up again at Potters Hive – which
seem like (but are not) deliberate parodies on "wonder." There
are other textual problems, dealt with by Hook, which I cannot
go into here. But if, through these complications, we try to glimpse
the original and unrevised structure of the play, we find it to be,
like that of *The Battle of Alcazar*, a primarily visual one. The
action moves through a series of pageants: the triumphal entry at
the beginning, the coronation of Edward, the (dumb-show)
christening of the Prince of Wales and wedding of Jone and
Gloster, followed by revels (laconically referred to in the stage

29. See vol. 2 of the Yale edition, pp. 19–37.

Inga-Stina Ewbank   *146*

direction as "the showe": l. 1964). And, though we do not reach
Elinor's funeral, Edward's lament for her death is itself soon
deflected into an envisaged celebration:

> You peeres of England, see in roiall pompe,
> These breathles bodies be entombed straight,
> With tried colours covered all with blacke,
> Let Spanish steedes as swift as fleeting winde,
> Convaie these Princes to their funerall,
> Before them let a hundred mourners ride . . . (ll. 2630–5)

Suitably (in terms of the structure, rather than the character), the
last reference to Elinor is a sort of apotheosis, as Edward orders

> a rich and statelie carved Crosse,
> Whereon her stature shall with glorie shine. (ll. 2642–3)

Suitably, too, even after the revisions the play ends as a kind of
speaking show: Gloster alone on stage with the dead body of Jone,
giving us a *Klagerede* in which the language draws attention to
what is seen: "Thy eies thy lookes thy lippes and everie part" (l.
2674).

The revision theory clearly does not account for all the oddities
and unevennesses of the play. After the single-mindedness of *The
Battle of Alcazar*, *Edward I* provides a Greene-like hotch-potch of
emotions. Yet there are moments when the play seems to pull itself
together into amazing anticipations of dramatic and poetic modes
to come. The finest of these is in the coronation scene, in what the
text proudly marks out as "*Queene Elinors speeche.*" Its qualities
are such that I cannot believe the Yale editor when he puts it down
as another "Spanish pride" interpolation; nor can I agree with him
that "it is so extravagant that it verges at times on nonsense."[30] It
is necessary to quote the speech in full:

> The welken spangled through with goulden spots,
> Reflects no finer in a frostie night,
> Then lovely Longshankes in his Elinors eye:
> So Ned thy Nell in every part of thee,
> Thy person's garded with a troope of Queenes,
> And every Queene as brave as Elinor,

30. Ibid., p. 182 (note on ll. 704 ff.).

> Gives glorie to these glorious christall quarries,
> Where every orbe an object entertaines,
> Of riche device and princelie majestie.
> Thus like Narcissus diving in the deepe,
> I die in honour and in Englands armes:
> And if I drowne, it is in my delight,
> Whose companie is cheefest life in death,
> From forth whose currall lips I suck the sweete,
> Wherewith are daintie Cupids caudles made,
> Then live or die brave Ned, or sinke or swim,
> An earthlie blisse it is to looke on him.
> On thee sweete Ned, it shall become thy Nell,
> Bounteous to be unto the beauteous,
> Ore prie the palmes sweete fountaines of my blisse,
> And I will stand on tiptoe for a kisse. (ll. 704–24)

Well may we ask "What words, what looks, what wonders?" What is remarkable about this speech is, first, the interaction of words and looks and, second, the way the wonder is being experienced by the audience *through* the speaker. By this second point I do not so much mean that it is a characterizing, differentiating, speech (in the same play Lluellen, for one, speaks in a very similar tone, with similar vocabulary and imagery, when he sets eyes on *his* Elinor) as that we wonder with and at a human experience, not at a dramatic situation or concept, as we did in Peele's earlier plays. By the first, I mean the remarkable way in which visual excitement generates verbal excitement and *vice versa*. It is not the remembered visual excitement of Enobarbus in his barge speech, but an actual visual presence in which the audience shares; not the one-sided rapt description of Iachimo as he watches the sleeping Imogen, but a rapt mutuality, where love and self-love merge, strangely anticipating both sentiment and imagery in a poem like Donne's "Good-Morrow" or his "Sun Rising." While the verbal imagery arises out of the visual situation, part of the wonder, as in a metaphysical poem, lies in the very ingenuity of the verbal conceits; for example, Elinor, losing herself in Edward's embrace, is like Narcissus drowning in his mirroring pool. But she dies, as the lovers die in "The Canonization," in two senses; and presumably "in England's armes" is a double image, too. Because the speech is set in a very public context, the raptness (as in Antony and Cleopatra's first dialogue) is tempered by self-consciousness; the tones of private love-making mingle with those of public demonstration. There is no description as such; every twist of the eulogistic argument, every new conceit, arises out of the stage situation of the newly crowned and glass-suited monarch and, in turn, modifies our apprehension of that situation – right through to the last line, which is both a touching climax to the imagery and a stage direction ("And I will stand on tiptoe for a kisse"). That line, with its concrete reference to the problems of kissing the tall King, also brings to rest the remarkable balancing in the speech, between homely Ned Longshanks and glorious "England," between Nell (the persona who, elsewhere in the play, like a true Mrs. Bagnet, will tuck up her skirts and follow her man to the wars) and brave Queen Elinor. Again, for a moment, Peele is capable of hinting at a range of ruler-lover relationships that looks forward to *Antony and Cleopatra*.

In talking about the visual situation, I am, of course, above all referring to the "sute of Glasse" which Edward is wearing. It seems to have been a precious piece of property of the Admiral's Men.[31] Elinor, in the first scene, builds up our expectations of the corona-tion scene mainly around this suit and the wonderful tableau it will create, again one in which majesty and love, adoration and narcissism, meet:

> My King like Phoebus bridegroom like shall marche
> With lovely Thetis to her glassie bed,
> And all the lookers on shall stand amazde,
> To see King Edward and his lovely Queene,
> Sit lovely in Englands stately throne. (ll. 263–7)

With all this pre-release publicity – and, if Hook is right in insert-ing the Quarto's three misplaced lines,

> And lovelie England to thy lovely Queene,
> Lovelie Queene Elinor, unto her turne thy eye,
> Whose honor cannot but love thee wel,

immediately before "Queene Elinors speeche," with a tremendous claim in the actual credit titles – the scene might easily have

---

31. It is generally accepted that this was the "longeshanckes sewte" which Henslowe records as "gone and loste" in an inventory taken on 10 March 1598, but which was found and listed in another inventory, three days later. (See ibid., p. 7.)

seemed anticlimactic. But, whatever the glass suit actually looked like, it is what we see of it through the language that matters: its power of many-faceted reflections. Edward is reflected in her eyes and she in every one of the crystal mirrors that make up the suit; and as we follow the breathless path of the conceits, the two become an image of majesty in love. She is in love with him *as* King, with the King's two bodies at once: "I die in honour and in Englands armes."

I make no claims for *Edward I* as a whole, merely for the raptness of occasional moments like this. Such raptness is much more prominent in *David and Bethsabe*. By the time he had written *Edward I*, Peele had, however fitfully, explored the wonder of monarchy, of evil and retribution, and of the king as lover. We do not know how he came to make the unusual choice of a biblical subject for his (presumably) next and last play. But it is an almost too neat conclusion to my quest that he should have chosen a king who was also both a lover and a penitent sinner, and a divine poet. I do not think Peele was aware of any such neat pattern to his career; but he must have been aware of writing a highly ambitious play. Wonder surrounds the hero and the subject by definition. It is articulated into a proto-Miltonic epic invocation by the Prologue, and it becomes the basic informing principle behind the verbal texture as well as the dramatic structure. In the language it comes out as a desire to load every rift with ore (except when, as in Nathan's parable, Peele follows the Bible almost verbatim), so that the heroic or amorous passages shine with celestial lights or sparkle with jewels, while the passages of sin and dejection are dark and horrid in the extreme. There is always a tendency for Peele's imagery to move between the two extremes of the entrails of the earth and the "lamp of heaven"; and here this tendency – contrasting the two extremes, or moving from one to the other – becomes in itself an organizing structural pattern.

But before we turn to the structure of *David and Bethsabe*, it is worth noting how much the play and its poetry are concerned with seeing. Characters are constantly telling us about the visual impressions they make upon each other, and usually they do so in an elaborate simile which, as it were, turns the interlocutor (whom we see on stage) into a wondrous picture. David exquisitely records how the eye and the desires of the beholder modify the beheld:

> Now comes my lover tripping like the Roe,
> And brings my longings tangled in her haire. (ll. 115–6)

Ammon addresses Absalon (who, ironically, is about to kill him) as "Thou faire young man, whose haires shine in mine eye/ Like golden wyers of Davids yvorie Lute" (ll. 747–8). And, in a famous set passage, Joab turns David's presence on stage into a pageant of the sun king:

> Beauteous and bright is he among the Tribes,
> As when the sunne attir'd in glist'ring robe,
> Comes dauncing from his orientall gate,
> And bridegroome-like hurles through the gloomy aire
> His radiant beames, *such doth King David shew*,
> Crownd with the honour of his enemies towne,
> Shining in riches like the firmament,
> The starrie vault that overhangs the earth,
> *So looketh David King of Israel.* (ll. 825–33; my italics)

There is a connection in the play between the characters' interest in how they see each other and the pervading sense that God sees them all. Characters repeatedly describe themselves as if in the sight of God. Absalon in his *hubris* sees his own beauty as a kind of election:

> Absalon, that in his face
> Carries the finall purpose of his God,
>
> .   .   .   .
>
> His thunder is intangled in my haire,
> And with my beautie is his lightning quencht,
> I am the man he made to glorie in. (ll. 1163–71)

David, on the other hand, sees his own sins as "printed in his browes." What God sees makes up the universe of the play, both in space and in time. Like Milton's God, he has "before [his] eyes" all human actions "From Adam to the end of Adams seed" (ll. 1740–1). And, like Milton's Adam, Peele's Solomon has to be warned against presumptuous attempts to see too much with merely human eyes:

> Wade not too farre my boy in waves too deepe.
> The feeble eyes of our aspiring thoughts
> Behold things present and record things past:

> But things to come, exceed our humane reach,
> And are not painted yet in angels eyes. (ll. 1726–9)

It is true that the last two examples come from a scene where Peele is engaged in wholesale borrowing from Du Bartas' *Les Artifices*; but, as I have tried to show elsewhere,[32] this scene is thematically very central in Peele's play. It is notable, too, that the evocative references to vision, human and superhuman, are Peele's own; Du Bartas "l'oeil de nostre pensée" becomes "the feeble eyes of our aspiring thoughts," and "not painted yet in angels eyes" is all Peele.

The sense that what we are watching on stage is happening in the eyes of God gives peculiar poignancy to the hero's moral progress. David knows that God "sees our hearts" (l. 993), and he discovers that, through contrition, it is possible to "find favour in his gratious eyes" (l. 1055). And the mark of God's grace is a new vision:

> vertue to mine eies,
> To tast the comforts, and behold the forme
> Of his faire arke, and holy tabernacle. (ll. 1058–60)

It cannot be fortuitous, then, that the play opens on a human vision and closes on a divine: that it moves from David "above" viewing Bethsabe to David below, imagining for his dead son the beatific moment when "Thou shalt behold thy soveraigne face to face" (l. 1914).

Some time ago now, I tried to analyse the structure of *David and Bethsabe* and to show how, though infinitely less articulate than *Paradise Lost*, Peele's play yet anticipates Milton's epic on the Fall and the Redemption.[33] In what I have just said, I am trying to suggest that Peele was using all the resources of the theatre to put across the wonder of falling and rising in the eyes of God. We see this more clearly, perhaps, if we notice how persistently the fall/rise structure of the play as a whole is repeated within the individual scenes, or within a pair of contiguous scenes. Sometimes the local pattern is of rise/fall, as when the virtual apotheosis of David victorious on the walls of Rabba is im-

32. "The House of David," p. 37. For Peele's borrowings from Du Bartas, see P. H. Cheffaud, *George Peele* (Paris, 1913), esp. p. 131; and H. D. Sykes, "Peele's Borrowings from Du Bartas," *NQ*, CXLVII (1924), 349–51, 368–9.
33. "The House of David," esp. p. 39.

Inga-Stina Ewbank   *152*

mediately followed by the announcement that all his sons are dead. Often one character rises as another falls. But in all these cases, the movement is pointed by the visual stage image as well as by the verbal imagery. As Absalon usurps David's throne, David's dejection –

> *Enter David . . . with others, David barefoot, with some lose covering over his head, and all mourning;* (1. 972 SD)

> *He lies downe and all the rest after him* (1. 991 SD)

– and the ritual scene of lamentation which translates it into words, are followed by the entry of

> *Absalon . . . with the concubines of David, and others in great state, Absalon crowned* (1. 1106 SD),

and by a speech from Absalon in which he contrasts his own sun-and-star-like glory with David "whose life is with his honour fast inclosd/Within the entrailes of a Jeatie cloud" (ll. 1107 ff.).

But the most significant fall/rise scenes conern David alone and take him from prostration to some form of celebration or, in moral terms, from sin to awareness of grace. The scene of Nathan's parable is perhaps the best example. David's speech of repentance –

> Nathan, have against the Lord, I have
> Sinned, O sinned grievously, and loe
> From heavens throne doth David throw himselfe,
> And grone and grovell to the gates of hell.
>   *He fals downe* (ll. 656-9 SD)

– is unmemorable as poetry but interesting as marking a truly emblematic stage situation. The speech explains what is seen, turning the stage itself into a moral map, a space between heaven and hell.[34] As the death of the child of sin is announced, the fact that this means, in David's morality, not only judgment but also absolution is brought home in visual language:

---

34. In later, more "realistic" drama, stage space can still be a moral measure: as when Isabella in *Women Beware Women*, having learnt that her uncle is after all her uncle, exclaims: "In that small distance from yon man to me/Lies sin enough to make a whole world perish" – the distance being both in blood and what the audience can see. (*Women Beware Women*, IV.ii. 131–2; ed. Roma Gill, London, 1968).

They bring in water, wine, and oyle. Musike, and a banquet.
They use all solemnities together, and sing, etc.

(ll. 712 SD and 716 SD)

David's words, on the other hand, are also taken up with the
symbolical import of his redemption:

> And decke faire Bersabe with ornaments,
> That she may bear to me another sonne. (ll. 708–9)

The last scene of the play is built on the same pattern. It begins
with David's prostration at the death of Absalon (he *"sits close"*
and Bethsabe *"kneeles downe"*) and leads to a reversal where
David *"riseth up"* and, in a speech of spiritual renewal, envisages
the beatitude of Absalon. But, instead of resorting to the external-
ized pattern of the scene just analysed, Peele is here trying to work
from inside David's experience, which means he has to rely almost
entirely on language. Absalon is to David here rather like Lycidas
(i.e. King) to Milton; it is not really the dead man's fate that
matters, but the spiritual state of the speaker. Absalon's rising to
heaven, where he will truly become that celestial light which both
he and David have constantly been compared to –

> Thy eyes now no more eyes but shining stars,
> Shall decke the flaming heavens with novell lampes (ll. 1908–9)

– marks David's redemption. And finally the wonder of a transfigured vision bursts upon us:

> and the curtaine drawne,
> Thou shalt behold thy soveraigne face to face,
> With wonder knit in triple unitie,
> Unitie infinite and innumerable. (ll. 1913–16)

Peele took the image which introduces the vision, "the curtaine
drawne," straight from Du Bartas ("la courtine tirée"), but I cannot believe that he was unaware how it echoed his opening stage
direction (*"He drawes a curtaine, and discovers Bethsabe . . ."*).
The play's last and greatest wonder is presented, within language,
as a theatrical "discovery."

Peele did not have the ability to realize characters and construct
a dramatic scene where, as in the final scene of *The Winter's Tale,*

silence carries the wonder of the impossible becoming possible. No more than Milton did he have a language for the mystic vision; and like Milton he tries to express the inexpressible through abstract nouns and negative adjectives: "Unitie infinite and innumerable." But if the play's climax, then, is a failure – a wonder talked about rather than realized – it is the kind of failure which demands respect, and to which attention must be paid. In its attempt to use biblical history to dramatize something of the wonder of sin and redemption, of death and renewal, *David and Bethsabe* is a link between the Mysteries and Shakespeare's last plays. And it is so because, throughout his career, Peele is ready to experiment with words, looks and wonders.

Part VII
Peele and *Titus Andronicus*

[20]

MUTIUS: AN OBSTACLE REMOVED IN
TITUS ANDRONICUS

BY BRIAN BOYD

Titus's killing of his son Mutius in scene i of *Titus Andronicus* has often been supposed both a textual afterthought and a demonstration of the hero's stiff Roman rectitude. Evidence of many kinds from many hands shows that *Titus* I. i is written by George Peele, although the structure of the play as a whole, as Gary Taylor notes, is clearly Shakespeare's. Peelean habits of immediate repetition add to the evidence of disrupted continuities that have led readers to identify the Mutius passage as an afterthought. The killing of Mutius by Titus also matches Peelean habits of symmetry and a Peelean preoccupation with the sacrifice of one's children. But the killing is inconsistent in detail and design with the Shakespearian part of the play. There, Titus implores mercy for two other sons even when he supposes they may be guilty of murder, and sacrifices his own hand to save them. This makes neither psychological nor dramatic sense if he has just killed Mutius without hesitation for a minor transgression. Remove the inconsistency caused by Peele's late addition, and *Titus Andronicus* loses what even advocates of the play admit is the received text's 'chief weakness'.

Titus's killing of his son Mutius in the opening scene of *Titus Andronicus* has often been seen as essential to the play's characterization of Titus as an unbendingly righteous Roman.[1] Yet the incident seems odd in both its immediate and its wider contexts. Titus kills his son abruptly, with a single line of dialogue in which to formulate and express his intent and without so much as a single word of subsequent regret. Indeed, he soon seems entirely to forget the killing for over forty lines (I. i. 299–341).[2] His fatal sword-thrust occasions a mere two lines of reproach apiece from his eldest son, Lucius, and his brother, Marcus, an astonishingly subdued reaction in a play focused on the deep suffering that all three are caused, and the revenge Titus in particular

---

1 'The apparently late addition of the Mutius material, for instance, contributes strongly to the structural patterning which critics have praised as characteristically Shakespearian': G. Taylor, 'The Canon and Chronology of Shakespeare's Plays', in S. Wells and G. Taylor with J. Jowett and W. Montgomery, *William Shakespeare: A Textual Companion* (Oxford, 1987), 115. For the 'apparently late addition', see below.

2 Within twenty lines of killing Mutius, and with his body still on stage, Titus winces at Saturninus's reproach (not for the killing, which Saturninus somehow has not seen, but for the abduction of Lavinia, effected by Bassianus with the help of Titus's brother and sons): 'O monstrous! What reproachful words are these? . . . These words are razors to my wounded heart' (I. i. 308, 314), then sulks that he has not been allowed to wait upon Tamora at her wedding ceremony and has been 'dishonoured thus' (I. i. 338–40)—all of this with no thought of the Mutius he has just killed. Citations are from *Titus Andronicus*, ed. E. Waith (Oxford, 1984).

TITUS: AN OBSTACLE REMOVED   197

is driven to, by the injuries inflicted on his remaining children. Over the fates of these children, Titus and Marcus and Lucius lament at often uncomfortable length in the remaining four acts, where the killing of Mutius is never once alluded to, just as if it had never happened.

I would like to propose an explanation: that for Shakespeare's Titus, Marcus, and Lucius, it never did happen.

Many have suggested that the killing of Mutius was an afterthought within the first scene.[3] I will adduce further evidence to show that this is so. But this is only part of the argument. Many have also suggested over the last century that at least some of *Titus Andronicus* was written by George Peele, and over the last eighty years evidence has been steadily accumulating and converging to show that in many different and often precisely quantifiable ways—in peculiarities of scenic construction, scenic content, staging, stage directions (phrasing and placement), speech construction, line construction, phrase construction, imagery, vocabulary (rare, favourite, common, and function words), verbal collocation, word length, word formation and inflection, alliteration, and metre—four scenes, the first three (I. i, II. i, and II. ii) and the first of the counter-action (IV. i),[4] together known as Part A—diverge radically from the Shakespearian norms evident in the remainder of the play (Part B) and fit norms unique to Peele.

Brian Vickers comprehensively and compellingly reviews the evidence in his *Shakespeare, Co-Author*.[5] Let me list just three examples:

1. In a play swarming with brothers (Saturninus and Bassianus, the two contending sons of the late emperor; Tamora's three sons, Alarbus, Chiron, and Demetrius; the general, Titus, and his brother, the tribune, Marcus; and Titus's twenty-five sons, brothers to the heroine Lavinia), the plural *brethren*, a form that Peele strongly prefers, occurs in Part A eight times more frequently than *brothers*, while in Part B the plural *brothers*, Shakespeare's overwhelming preference, occurs eight times as frequently as *brethren*.[6]

3 *Titus Andronicus*, ed. J. Dover Wilson (Cambridge, 1948), p. xxxvi; S. Wells, *Re-editing Shakespeare for the Modern Reader* (Oxford, 1984), 99–100; Gary Taylor, cited in *Titus Andronicus*, ed. Waith, 96 n.; *Titus Andronicus*, ed. J. Bate, Arden 3 (London, 1995), 104–7. M. Mincoff, *Shakespeare: The First Steps* (Sofia, 1976), 213, has argued—for him, very mildly—against construing Mutius as an afterthought.

4 As observed in Taylor, 'The Canon and Chronology of Shakespeare's Plays', 114.

5 *Shakespeare, Co-Author: A Historical Study of Five Collaborative Plays* (Oxford, 2002).

6 B. Boyd, 'Common Words in *Titus Andronicus*: The Presence of Peele', *Notes and Queries*, 240 (1995), 300–7; MacD. P. Jackson, 'Shakespeare's Brothers and Peele's Brethren: *Titus Andronicus* Again', *Notes and Queries*, 242 (1997), 494–5. Jackson searched the ninety-three 'Elizabethan' plays in the Chadwyck–Healey 'Literature Online' database, and found that no play but Peele's *The Battle of Alcazar* matched the high 'brethren' count of Part A of *Titus Andronicus*, apart from anonymous works such as *A Knack to Know a Knave* (9 *brethren*, 0 *brothers*) and *Selimus* (7 *brethren*; 0 *brothers*). He also notes that *Titus Andronicus* 'accounts for half the examples of *brethren* in the whole Shakespearian dramatic canon, and all but one of these are in the 'Peelian' Act I' (p. 495).

198 BRIAN BOYD

2. The word 'palliament' occurs in only one other Renaissance text, Peele's poem *The Honour of the Garter*, and has been shown to be Peele's own invention.[7]

3. Stage directions: 'and others as many as can be' at *Titus* I. i. 69 occurs in only one other known English play of the period, Peele's *Edward I*.[8]

Those who accept the evidence of Peele's participation in *Titus Andronicus* have also tended to accept that, since the structure of the whole play appears to be beyond the design skills of any other dramatist of the late 1580s or early 1590s, it must have been, as Gary Taylor suggests,[9] Shakespeare who drew up the author's plot of the play, from which Peele worked in writing the scenes he had been assigned. However, Vickers's recent investigations indicate that names and situations in Act I owe much to Peele's Latin education, to obscure episodes of Roman history with which Peele is elsewhere known to have been familiar and Shakespeare could not have been. Vickers aptly describes Act I as an 'overambitious display of imperfectly remembered classical learning'.[10] Nevertheless the coherence of the whole play, less marked though it is in the first act, confirms Shakespeare's key role in shaping its structure. He would seem to have sought help from Peele in establishing an initial situation, and to have repaid him by allowing him to write the opening of the play, from a plot he himself drew up from the materials Peele suggested.

I propose that the author's plot that Shakespeare drew up for the start of the play never included the killing of Mutius, that his own conception of Titus is quite at odds with his hero's killing a son casually and without regret, and that he composed his own part of the play unaware that Peele had added this incident. The addition of the Mutius passages, on the other hand, is perfectly in keeping with Peele's own habits of dramatic construction.

Taylor's suggestion that Shakespeare prepared the author's plot for *Titus Andronicus* disposes of the most confident argument against Peele's role in the play, Hereward Price's claim that even its most suspect part, the single long scene of Act I, is too highly structured to be the work of Peele or any other

---

7 H. T. Price, 'The Authorship of *Titus Andronicus*', *JEGP* 42 (1943), 55–81, and id., *Construction in Shakespeare*, University of Michigan Contributions in Modern Philology 17 (Michigan, 1951), argued that 'palliament' is wrongly used in *Titus*, and that the mistake must have Shakespeare's confused borrowing from Peele's poem; T. W. Baldwin, however, showed in 1959 that the word is not mistaken in its *Titus* context, and that Peele, 'as the inventor and only known purveyor of the word must remain grievously suspect' as co-author: 'The Work of Peele and Shakespere on *Titus Andronicus*', in *On the Literary Genetics of Shakspere's Plays, 1592–1594* (Urbana, Ill., 412); see also Vickers 2002.

8 MacD. P. Jackson, 'Stage Directions and Speech Headings in Act 1 of *Titus Andronicus* Q (1594): Shakespeare or Peele?', *Studies in Bibliography*, 49 (1996), 134–48, p. 136. Jackson adduces other decidedly un-Shakespearian and demonstrably Peelean features in the staging implications, the typographical format, and the wording of stage directions and speech headings.

9 'The Canon and Chronology of Shakespeare's Plays', 115.

10 *Shakespeare: Co-Author*, 192.

dramatist of the time but Shakespeare.[11] Since Price, others have analysed the achievement of the first act's structure in even more appreciative terms.[12] Nevertheless, one symmetry too many has been added to all the stately proportions and ceremonial architectonics of *Titus*'s opening scene. To match the sacrifice of Tamora's son, which Titus orders in the first half of Act I, Titus kills his own son Mutius in the second half.

As several editors have noted, the evidence of the text strongly suggests that the killing of Mutius was a later insertion into the original script, although apparently at the time of first composition.[13] I will try to show further that not only was the killing not Shakespeare's idea, but that when he wrote his own scenes he had no notion that Peele planned to add it to the play. Shakespeare seems to have composed his portion of the play either after reading a first version of Peele's contribution which still lacked the Mutius insert, or simply without waiting for Peele, in the expectation that his collaborator would faithfully flesh out the forelimb or two of the plot he had been apportioned.

Brian Vickers offers ample evidence to show that collaborative theatrical composition frequently resulted in inconsistencies, not only in the English drama of Shakespeare's time but a century later.[14] The killing of Mutius seems another instance of such unexpunged inconsistency. But if we return to Shakespeare's apparent intentions and purge Mutius from the text rather than leaving him for his father to eliminate, *Titus Andronicus* becomes a much less muddled play and Titus a much less incoherent hero.

Saturninus's rejection of Lavinia—'No, Titus, no, the Emperor needs her not' (I. i. 299)—seems so obviously an immediate response to Titus's 'Follow, my lord, and I'll soon bring her back' (I. i. 289) that it is hard to imagine him saving it up for the space of ten lines of verse within which there must also occur the onstage tussle that results in Mutius's death. As Mark Rose comments, moreover, 'surprisingly little is made of the killing at this point: Lucius, another son, offers a two-line protest and Titus a two-line reply, after which Mutius is ignored. When Saturninus enters to denounce Titus he does not mention Mutius, although presumably the corpse is lying in full view.'[15]

---

11 See n. 6 above; Vickers, *Shakespeare: Co-Author*, ch. 3, shows how Price repeatedly misrepresents the evidence and the argument of those who sought to show a hand other than Shakespeare's in the play.

12 See e.g. M. Rose, *Shakespearean Design* (Cambridge, Mass., 1972), 135: 'The opening scene . . . is a tour de force. . . . Dramatic effect is piled on dramatic effect with extraordinary profligacy, yet the artist's shaping hand is firmly in control. Nothing quite like this scene had been written for the Elizabethan stage before.' See also N. Brooke, *Shakespeare's Early Tragedies* (London, 1968), 27, and B. Boyd, 'Kind and Unkindness: Aaron in *Titus Andronicus*' in *Words that Count: Essays on Early Modern Authorship in Honor of MacDonald P. Jackson* (Wilmington, Del., 2004).

13 See n. 2 above.

14 See *Shakespeare: Co-Author*, ch. 1 ('*Sir Thomas More*') and ch. 7 *passim*.

15 Rose, *Shakespearean Design*, 137.

200   BRIAN BOYD

Similarly, Marcus's attempt to cheer up Titus

> My lord, to step out of these dreary dumps,
> How comes it that the subtle Queen of Goths
> Is of a sudden thus advanced in Rome?
>
> (I. i. 391–3)

seems so natural a response to Titus's lament, when Saturninus leaves to marry Tamora:

> I am not bid to wait upon this bride.
> Titus, when wert thou wont to walk alone,
> Dishonoured thus and challengèd of wrongs?
>
> (I. i. 338–40)

and so abrupt and insensitive a sequel to the farewell to the body of Mutius by Marcus and his nephews:

> No man shed tears for noble Mutius;
> He lives in fame, that died in virtue's cause
>
> (I. i. 389–90)

and to Titus's killing of his son three minutes earlier, that it seems best explained as a speech displaced from its original site by the later insertion of the passage (I. i. 341–90) in which the other Andronici plead with Titus to let Mutius be buried in the family vault.

This conclusion is also supported by the nature of Peele's repetitions in the rest of the scene. Though always inclined, through what one of his editors describes as 'intellectual laziness',[16] to slack repetition of the same vocabulary, Peele also tends to repeat himself quite pointedly, and in close proximity, when striving, as he is throughout this scene, for a note of elevation. Thus both Bassianus and Saturninus earlier agree to welcome Marcus's proposal to name Titus emperor. Bassianus begins, saying he so respects Marcus, Titus, and

> *Gracious* Lavinia, *Rome's* rich ornament,
> That I will here *dismiss* my *loving friends,*
> *And to* my fortunes and the people's *favour*
> *Commit my cause* in balance to be weighed.
>
> (I. i. 52–5)

Saturninus responds:

> *Friends* that have been thus forward in my right,
> I thank you all, and here *dismiss* you all,
> *And to* the *love* and *favour* of my country
> *Commit my*self, my person, and the *cause.*
> *Rome,* be as just and *gracious* unto me . . .
>
> (I. i. 56–60)

---

16 *The Life and Minor Works of George Peele*, ed. D. H. Horne (New Haven, 1952), 173.

Although, as the added italics indicate, verbal repetition is pervasive in the scene, echoes as dense as this occur only immediately;[17] twenty lines later, some of the same words may still be swimming in Peele's mind, but others will have jumped into the pool.

Now just after the lines that seem to add the killing of Mutius—so exactly where Peele would have needed to scrutinize his draft to see where he could insert a new passage—comes Saturninus's response to Titus (capitals indicate material repeated within the first two of the following passages, italics indicate material repeated between either of these and the third):

> *No, Titus, no*, the Emperor needs her not;
> *NOR HER, NOR THEE, NOR ANY* of thy stock.
> I'll trust by leisure him that mocks me once,
> Thee never, nor thy TRAITOROUS haughty sons,
> *Confederates* all thus to *DISHONOUR* ME.

> (I. i. 299–303)

Just before these lines, in the received text, comes this passage, the brief aftershock of the killing of Mutius:

> LUCIUS. My lord, you are unjust, and more than so,
> *In wrongful quarrel you have slain your son.*
> TITUS. *NOR THOU, NOR HE*, ARE ANY *sons of mine*;
> My sons would never so *DISHONOUR* ME.
> TRAITOR, restore Lavinia to the Emperor.
> LUCIUS. Dead, if you will, but not to be his wife,
> That is another's lawful promised love.

> (I. i. 292–8)

The capitalized echoes are of course compatible with composition in either order. But what is curious is that, almost forty lines later in the received text, comes another barrage of echoes of these two passages, exactly at the beginning of what looks like the next Mutius insert, the plea to bury him, which if the hypothesis is correct would presumably have been composed immediately after the second passage above, the end of the insert that records the killing itself:

> MARCUS. *O Titus*, see, *O* see what thou hast done!
> *In a bad quarrel slain a virtuous son.*
> TITUS. *No*, foolish tribune, *no; no son of mine*,
> *NOR THOU, NOR THESE, confederates* in the deed
> That hath *DISHONOURED* all our family.

> (I. i. 341–5)

---

17 For an even more striking example, see Peele's *Battle of Alcazar*, ll. 337–51: 'To *pay* thy *due and duties* thou dost owe, | *To heaven and earth, to Gods and Amurath.* | . . . *heaven and earth give ear* | *Give ear* and record *heaven and earth* . . . | . . . *hearken* and attend, | *Hear* . . . | . . . the true *succession* . . . | . . . to *succeed* . . . | . . . *Gods of heaven* . . . | That men *on earth* . . . | . . . my *due and duty* is done, I *pay* | *To heaven and earth, to Gods and Amurath.*' I have modernized the text in vol. ii of the Yale Peele (New Haven, 1961), in which *The Battle of Alcazar* is edited by John Yoklavich.

Only one of these echoes ('dishonoured') also echoes a line in its immediately preceding context (I. i. 340); the rest derive exclusively from a passage almost fifty lines earlier. In part this could be because the Mutius theme has been resumed, after a switch to the theme of Saturninus and Tamora, but that would not explain why an echo such as 'confederates . . . dishonour' should come from the beginning of the Saturninus section, when Saturninus is oblivious to the fact of Mutius's death. But later insertion of passages on Mutius's death and burial would have required Peele to dwell on precisely those lines of Saturninus, to assess where he could insert the lines on the death, and could readily have prompted that burst of echoes in the lines he then wrote to cover the burial.

These patterns of repetition strongly support the conclusion others have drawn from the two textual dislocations, Saturninus's delayed response to Titus at I. i. 299, and Marcus's abrupt question to Titus at I. i. 391: that the killing of Mutius is an insert.

If, then, Mutius was added later, is the addition likely to have been prompted by Shakespeare, who after all seems to have planned the rest of the act's plot, or by Peele? I will argue shortly the incompatibility of the killing of Mutius with the Shakespearian part of the play, in both detail and design, and with Shakespeare's other work of this (or indeed any other) period. But let me first show how closely the incident squares with Peele's habits elsewhere in the scene and in his other work.

The killing of Mutius reflects the system of exaggerated balances, stressed through patterns of Peelean verbal repetition, that runs through the whole of Act I, from the moment that Saturninus's opening speech ('Noble patricians, patrons of my right') is matched by Bassianus's reply ('Romans, friends, followers, favourers of my right'). This structural tic resembles nothing so much as the repetition of situations and parallel speeches that we find rife in Peele from the time of his first play, *The Arraignment of Paris*. Arthur Sampley, writing of *Edward I*, comments on 'the paralleling of one situation with another very similar, a trick which has been noted in the discussion of *The Arraignment*', where it is most prominent, but he notes it even in Peele's most successful play, *The Old Wives' Tale*.[18] Brian Vickers summarizes Werner Senn's demonstration that 'Peele regularly juxtaposed parallel situations but seldom in any dynamic way . . . "Peele's repetition of scenic situations and character-groupings remains somewhat mechanical and lifeless."'[19] In the killing of Titus's son, and especially the protracted appeal by his uncle and brothers to an initially unmoved Titus, Peele seems to have seen an opportunity to rework in his special way the sacrifice of Tamora's son, and the protracted appeal by his mother and brothers to a completely unmoved Titus.

18 'Plot Structure in Peele's Plays as a Test of Authorship', *PMLA* 51 (1936), 689–701: 694.

19 *Shakespeare: Co-Author*, ch. 7; Senn, *Studies in the Dramatic Construction of Robert Greene and George Peele* (Berne, 1973), 208, and cf. 92 ('the two main opponents in parallel situations', in *The Battle of Alcazar*), 104 ('repetition of a similar situation', in *David and Bethsabe*).

Peele, notorious for his repetitions of subject not only within plays but from work to work, translated one of Euripides' *Iphigenia* plays (probably *Iphigenia in Aulis*) while at Oxford,[20] and ever after, from his earliest extant work, *The Tale of Troy*, seemed predisposed to write of sacrifice, and even of the sacrifice of children by parents.

A date of about 1589 has often been proposed for both *Titus Andronicus* and *The Battle of Alcazar*, and the presence of a villainous Moor, and the marked links in vocabulary and verbal patterning between the opening scene of *Titus* and *The Battle of Alcazar*, especially *its* opening,[21] suggest that Peele turned to the latter soon after writing his part in the former.

One passage in *The Battle of Alcazar* remarkably fuses the sacrifice of Alarbus and the killing of Mutius. In arguing for Peele's authorship of *Titus Andronicus* I. i, Dover Wilson had cited the Prologue of *The Arraignment of Paris*:

> King Priam's palace waste with flaming fire,
> Whose thick and foggy smoke, piercing the sky,
> Must serve for messenger of sacrifice,
> T'appease the anger of the angry heavens
>
> (ll. 11–14)

He notes its similarity to the language surrounding the sacrifice of Alarbus, especially 'And entrails feed the *sacrificing fire*, | Whose *smoke* like incense doth perfume *the sky*' (I. i. 144–5).[22] A far more striking echo of these lines from *Titus* comes at the end of the following passage from *The Battle of Alcazar*. Rubin Archis, Abdelmunen's widow, declares to Calcepius Bassa:

> Rubin that breathes but for revenge,
> Bassa, by this commends her self to thee,
> Resigns the tokens of her thankfulness:
> To Amurath the God of earthly kings
> Doth Rubin give and *sacrifice* her son,
> Not with sweet *smoke* of *fire*, or sweet *perfume*,
> But with his father's sword, his mother's thanks
> Doth Rubin give her son to Amurath.
>
> (ll. 356–63)

These few lines uncannily blend the two deaths of sons in the first scene of *Titus Andronicus*: the death of Alarbus, in a mother's son offered for sacrifice, and the perfumed smoke of the sacrificing fire, and the death of Mutius, in a parent losing a child without complaint, and the verbal flash of the father's sword. But although the father's sword here seems to imply a mode of sacrifice to be employed in lieu of fire, it seems likely that Peele intends Rubin Archis

20 *Works of Peele*, ed. Horne, 42–4.

21 See Boyd, 'Common Words'.

22 *Titus*, ed. Dover Wilson, p. xxx.

merely to offer her son, alive and *armed* with his father's sword, into the service of Amurath. Not that he makes this easy to infer: the lines above constitute the whole of Rubin's only speech in this scene, and her last in the play, and it is only Bassa's response, more than ten lines later—that Amurath 'shall receive the imp of royal race, | With cheerful looks and gleams of princely grace'— that suggests a gentler fate for Rubin's son. The imagery of Rubin's speech reveals how closely the sacrifice of Alarbus and the killing of Mutius were linked in Peele's thoughts. Another passage shows again how carelessly Peele could suggest a parent killing his own offspring, although it was not what he meant. Introducing Act IV, the presenter refers to Muly Mahamet as 'this murtherer of his progeny' (l. 980). In fact the Moor has killed not his son but his brothers.[23]

If the killing of Mutius follows compositional habits and lines of least resistance in evidence throughout the first scene of *Titus Andronicus* and Peele's other work, his death accounts for nothing and actively contradicts much in the rest of the play. Peele may blunder into suggesting a parent killing a child, but Shakespeare does not.

Shakespeare's Titus, deploring the threatened execution of Martius and Quintus, avers: 'For two-and-twenty sons I never wept, | Because they died in honour's lofty bed' (III. i. 10–11). This has long seemed curious, since although he has buried twenty-two of his twenty-five sons, the whole point of the Mutius sections in Act I, scene i is that Titus feels his and his family's honour has been utterly besmirched by Mutius and the others who sided with Bassianus and against him ('To be dishonoured by my sons in Rome', I. i. 385). We would therefore expect Titus to think only twenty-one sons had died honourable deaths. But if Shakespeare never intended a Mutius to appear at all, if he composed his part of the play unaware that Mutius's death had been added, the lines make perfect sense as they stand.

The intricate planning of I. i prepares in complex ways for the play to follow. The killing of Mutius prepares for nothing. It has no consequences, it is never referred to later, it is even explicitly contradicted ('two-and-twenty sons'). Yet an event as significant as the hero killing his own child in the opening scene of a play would surely—*unless* it were a last-minute insert— have later repercussions. At the very least, it should offer a guide to his subsequent conduct and character. On the contrary, it stands at odds with the central features of Shakespeare's Titus.

In the Mutius passages, Titus flares with anger merely because Bassianus, with the support of Titus's sons, claims the woman to whom he has been betrothed, after Titus has agreed to Saturninus's request for Lavinia's hand.

23 Although 'progeny' can sometimes mean 'kin' or 'clan', it is used so only when it implies a descent from a common forebear. In referring to a specific individual's 'progeny', the word refers *only* to descendants. Peele's phrasing here is a typically lazy repetition of a line three speeches earlier, where the word has its normal sense, as Muly Mahamet's son asks what title has Abdelmelec—Muly Mahamet's brother—'To barre our father or his progenie?' (l. 946).

For no greater 'offence' than supporting a betrothed couple, he kills his son, with no regrets, but only a sense of outrage at the dishonour done to him and Rome in opposing the will of an emperor he has himself just placed in office. Yet in the first of the Shakespeare scenes, after two of his sons have been found in a pit with the murdered Bassianus, and after the discovery of a document designed to incriminate them, Titus does not deplore the dishonour they have brought on the family. Instead he immediately sues, in tears, for his sons to be freed until the trial. The next time we see Titus, he is again in tears, again for these sons still suspected of murdering the emperor's brother, and although he accepts the possibility of their guilt, he still thinks them inwardly uncorrupted:

> And for these bitter tears which now you see,
> Filling the agèd wrinkles in my cheeks,
> Be pitiful to my condemnèd sons,
> Whose souls is not corrupted as 'tis thought.
> For two-and-twenty sons I never wept,
> Because they died in honour's lofty bed;
>   [*Andronicus lieth down, and the Judges and others pass by him*
> For these, tribunes, in the dust I write
> My heart's deep languor and my soul's sad tears.

(III. i. 6–13)

Later in the same scene, when he, Marcus and Lucius are told they can redeem Martius and Quintus—although the young men are still charged with murder—if one of them chops off his hand, Titus promptly has his own lopped off. Is this the action of a father who could without a flicker of remorse kill a son guilty of the most minor offence?

It makes no sense for a dramatist to have his hero kill one of his children and barely notice. But Shakespeare does plan for his hero to kill his innocent child at the end of the play, when Titus stabs Lavinia after she has had the satisfaction of seeing revenge wrought upon Chiron, Demetrius, and Tamora. In this case, however, the killing is central to the play's design, and a measure of Lavinia's appalling plight, and it is carefully led up to and away from, through the parallels with Virginius and Virginia. Loving Lavinia though he does, her father thinks it kindest to release her from her pain and shame once she knows revenge has been exacted.[24]

The horror of a father driven to kill a child he loves as an act of mercy loses its point if this same father has killed another child without reason or compunction. In fact the whole play loses its point, as a revenge tragedy, if Titus feels compelled to wreak horrible vengeance on Tamora and her sons for what they have done to three of his children yet has casually killed another himself.

The slaying of Mutius is in stark contrast to the mutual concern of parent

---

24 See M. Charney, *Titus Andronicus* (London, 1990), 118: 'Titus's killing of his daughter . . . is completely within the value system of *The Rape of Lucrece*. The murder is shown as an act of love to which Lavinia gives her tacit consent.'

and child that runs throughout the three *Henry VI* plays from which *Titus Andronicus* derived so much impetus: the heroic case of Talbot, father and son, in *1 Henry VI*; Clifford and his son in *2 Henry VI*; York and his son, Margaret and her son, and the emblematic son–father and father–son pair in *3 Henry VI*—the last being the very scene that either prompted, or reflected the first inklings of, *Titus Andronicus*: 'and so obsequious will thy father be | . . . for the loss of thee, having no more, | As Priam was for all his valiant sons' (II. v. 118–20).[25] Titus, the tearful, pleading Titus of the first Shakespearian scenes in the play, already driven almost insane with grief and ready to sacrifice himself without hesitation for his children, has a direct connection with these parents in the *Henry VI* plays and a very tenuous link to the Titus who so briskly disposes of Mutius.

Critics unaware of Peele's authorship of the scene, and the possibility that Mutius is a late insert, have assumed that Shakespeare meant to display in Titus Roman ideals at their sternest and most repellent. But this simply does not fit with the Titus whose son Lucius can say to *his* son, at Titus's death:

> Come hither, boy, come, come, and learn of us
> To melt in showers; thy grandsire loved thee well;
> Many a time he danced thee on his knee,
> Sung thee asleep, his loving breast thy pillow;
> Many a story hath he told to thee,
> And bid thee bear his pretty tales in mind,
> And talk of them when he was dead and gone.
> [Marcus adds:]
> How many thousand times hath those poor lips,
> When they were living, warmed themselves on thine!
>
>   (V. iii. 159–67)

Shakespeare's Titus was a patriarch, all right, but not the stern tyrant who kills his son in the opening scene.

In short, I suggest that Peele added the Mutius passages (I. i. 287–8, 290–9, and 341–90)[26] without Shakespeare directing him to, and without Shakespeare being aware of the additions while he was writing *his* portion of the play.[27]

In the Shakespearian scenes of *Titus Andronicus* there is never any discord between Titus and his brother or sons. In the Mutius addition Peele made to the opening scene, on the other hand, Titus not only kills one son, but when

25 *The Third Part of King Henry VI*, ed. M. Hattaway (Cambridge, 1993).

26 If he added the killing of Mutius after reaching Bassianus's speech beginning at I. i. 411, he would also have had to insert the reference to the killing that now occupies I. i. 418, perhaps in a manner such as Wells suggests (*Re-editing Shakespeare*, 114).

27 There are other examples of loose co-ordination between the collaborators. Shakespeare, for instance, treats the Philomela story as a parallel to Lavinia's fate that is immediately explicit and obvious to the characters: to Aaron, when he apprises Tamora of the plan ('His Philomel must lose her tongue today', II. iii. 43), and to Marcus, when he sees its results ('A craftier Tereus, cousin, hast thou met, | And he hath cut those pretty fingers off, | That could have better sewed than Philomel', II. iv. 41–3). In the Peelean Act IV, scene i this parallel is one Lavinia can bring to

his brother and remaining sons implore him to bury Mutius answers 'no son of mine, | Nor thou, nor these, confederates in the deed | That hath dishonoured all our family, | Unworthy brother, and unworthy sons! . . . My foes I do repute you every one, | So trouble me no more, but get you gone' (I. i. 343–56, 366–7). Shakespeare did indeed wish to suggest a Titus of stiff Roman rectitude, but he could do that quite firmly enough in the plot he drew up for himself and Peele by having Titus renounce the offer of candidacy for the emperorship, and by having him endorse the 'right' of the eldest son of the late emperor. But judging by all the passionate plaints later in the play, it was never Shakespeare's intention to suggest, as the Mutius insertions do, that Titus could easily sever his sense of connection not merely with the one son Peele makes him kill but with *all* his remaining male relatives.

Apparently it was solely Peele's desire for balance—the two sons killed, the two family pleas that Titus resists—and his curious proclivity as a writer, ever since translating Euripides, to invoke parent–child sacrifice, that led him to insert the Mutius lines.

It may even have been that Shakespeare, after reading Peele's first version of the scene, requested him to dramatize, rather than merely to report, the sacrifice of Alarbus. Peele may then have scrapped the three lines of the report (I. i. 36–36b) often excised by editors as contradicting the subsequent onstage sacrifice, and added I. i. 96–149, the sacrifice of Alarbus; then, later in the scene, he may have inserted, of his own accord and in order to balance the killing of Alarbus and the pleas for his life, the killing of Mutius and the pleas for his burial. But although many have taken the Alarbus passage as also a later insert, some astute readers disagree, and for the moment the issue cannot be decided.[28]

the attention of Titus and Marcus—though Marcus has already noted it—only with the greatest of difficulty (IV. i. 41–59).

A second example: Peele's Marcus laments that Titus is 'yet so just that he will not revenge' (IV. i. 127), whereas Shakespeare's Titus two scenes earlier has asked 'which way shall I find Revenge's cave?' (III. i. 268) and has sworn to each member of his family, including Marcus, his dedication to revenge (III. i. 272–7).

A third example: in the Shakespearian part of the play, the tension between pity and pitilessness becomes thematically and verbally central, as in the final two lines of the play: 'Her life was beastly and devoid of pity, | And being dead, let birds on her take pity' (V. iii. 198–9). The word 'pity' occurs nowhere in the Peele scenes.

A fourth: apart from Aaron's being mentioned as 'the Moor' in stage directions, there is not a single reference in the dialogue of the Peele scenes to Aaron's race. Shakespeare makes everything of it, from his first scene ('What signifies my deadly-standing eye, | My silence, and my cloudy melancholy, | My fleece of woolly hair that now uncurls', II. iii. 32–4) to Aaron's determination throughout the later scenes to protect at all costs his son, the 'black slave' that 'smiles upon the father' (IV. ii. 120).

28 For the enactment of the sacrifice as an addition see *Titus*, ed. Dover Wilson, pp. xxxiv–xxxv; *Titus Andronicus*, ed. J. C. Maxwell (1953; 2nd edn. London, 1961), 5 n.; *Titus*, ed. Waith, 85 n., 88 n.; Wells, *Re-editing Shakespeare*, 99; *Titus*, ed. Alan Hughes (Cambridge, 1994), 146–7; and *Titus*, ed. Bate, 103–4, 134 n. Against: H. F. Brooks in *Titus*, ed. Maxwell (1961 edn.), 5 n.; Mincoff, *The First Steps*, 213; and MacD. P. Jackson, 'The Year's Contribution to Shakespearian Study, 3. Editions and Textual Studies', *Shakespeare Survey*, 38 (1985), 247–8.

The sacrifice of Alarbus is of course essential to the structure of the play, to the vengeful hostility Tamora and her family feel towards the Andronici. But in support of the argument that

The Mutius passages are another matter. Textual, structural, and contextual evidence all converge on the conclusion that the passage was written after the bulk of Act I, and was not part of Shakespeare's design as he wrote his share of the play.[29] Even if the killing of Mutius was accepted into the play in Elizabethan performance—and since it is included in the Folio text, which clearly derives in part from a theatrical manuscript, this seems to have been the case[30]—there seems ample justification for critics to treat the play as it appears to have been designed and written by Shakespeare, *without* the killing of Mutius, since such a version of *Titus Andronicus* offers coherence in place of the contradictions of the *textus receptus*.

Marco Mincoff, that eloquent champion of the early plays, overstates the case when he calls *Titus Andronicus* 'one of Shakespeare's most faultlessly plotted tragedies', but he also faces the play's limitations. He observes, largely on the strength of the killing of Mutius, that 'Titus's virtue not only leaves one

the onstage representation, rather than the mere reporting, of the sacrifice of one of Tamora's sons, is an insertion, I would make three additional points.

1. The grammatical shifts surrounding the first reference to sacrifice. I quote here from Q1, in *Shakespeare's Plays in Quarto*, ed. M. J. B. Allen and K. Muir (Berkeley, Calif., 1981): 'Hee by the Senate is accited home, | . . . | . . . Fiue times he hath returnd | Bleeding to Rome, bearing his valiant sonnes, | In Coffins from the field, and at this day, | To the Monument of that *Andronicy* | Done sacrifice of expiation, | And slaine the Noblest prisoner of the *Gothes*, | And now at last laden with honours spoiles, | Returnes the good *Andronicus* to Rome', A3ᵛ. These are not unlike the changes of tense and confusions of referent seen elsewhere in Peele, in, for instance, *The Battle of Alcazar*, ll. 6–12: 'And aide with Christian armes the barbarous Moore, | The Negro Muly Hamet that with-holds | The kingdome from his uncle Abdelmelec, | Whom proud Abdallas wrongd, | And in his throne instals his cruell sonne, | That now usurps upon this prince, | This brave Barbarian Lord Muly Molocco.' Here the subject of 'instals' is Abdallas; the time of 'instals' is as past as 'wronged', despite the present tense, while 'usurps' is genuinely present; 'This prince' refers both to Abdelmelec and Muly Molocco, two names for the same person, although the audience could not know that from the few lines so far. Despite its muddle, the *Titus* passage could indeed, *pace* Mincoff, have been intended by Peele to imply a sacrifice performed 'this day.'

2. Peele often relies on narrative where someone more naturally a dramatist would eschew it (in *David and Bethsabe* throughout, in *The Battle of Alcazar*, especially Stukley's bizarre deathbed autobiography, in *Edward I*, and in *The Old Wives' Tale*), and, as Arthur M. Sampley noted, Peele has 'not learned the secret of placing emphasis where it is due' ('Plot Structure in Peele's Plays', 696). In view of his practice elsewhere, therefore, Peele may well—again, *pace* Mincoff—at first have thought this merely narrated reference to the death of Tamora's eldest son sufficient.

3. Not only, as Ruth Nevo notes, are 'the bodies of Titus' sons, killed in the war . . . left suspended in mid-air awaiting the burial' that has been interrupted by the sacrifice of Alarbus ('Tragic Form in *Titus Andronicus*', in A. A. Mendilow (ed.), *Further Studies in English Language and Literature* (Jerusalem, 1973), 9), but after the sacrifice is over, and Titus blesses the bodies of his sons, he also dwells on the security of their state (I. i. 150–6) yet does not attribute it to the sacrifice which was supposed to guarantee that security, a lapse barely explicable if the sacrifice has just taken place.

29 In his tentative reconstruction of the first draft of Act I, scene i, Wells, *Re-editing Shakespeare*, 114–25, omits both the sacrifice of Alarbus and the killing of Mutius, but, since he assumes Shakespeare to be the author of the scene, he does not consider the likelihood that the Titus of the remainder of the play was constructed without Shakespeare having any inkling that his hero has killed his son.

30 Vickers suggests: 'perhaps we ought rather to conceive that Elizabethan theatrical companies accepted a certain amount of incoherence as inevitable, unlikely to be noticed in the excitement of performance' (*Shakespeare: Co-Author*, 439).

TITUS: AN OBSTACLE REMOVED   209

cold, but positively repels one, and it is there, apart from the actual writing, that the play's chief weakness seems to lie.'[31] The worst of the 'actual writing' is in Peele's Act I, as everyone agrees, whether or not they have heeded the evidence for Peele's participation. And the worst move in Act I, the killing of Mutius, the 'play's chief weakness', seems to have formed no part of Shakespeare's plans for his hero.

University of Auckland

31 Mincoff, *The First Steps*, 123, 118.

Name Index